MW00658204

145-202

263-263

263-356

357-381

567-580

MUHAMMAD'S PEOPLE

MUHAMMAD'S PEOPLE

An Anthology of Muslim Civilization

ERIC SCHROEDER

DOVER PUBLICATIONS, INC.
Mineola, New York

Published in the United Kingdom by David & Charles, Brunel House, Forde
Close, Newton Abbot, Devon TQ12 4PU.

Bibliographical Note

This Dover edition, first published in 2002, is an unabridged reprint of the work
originally published in 1955 by the Bond Wheelwright Company, Portland (Maine).

Library of Congress Cataloging-in-Publication Data

Schroeder, Eric, 1904–
    Muhammad's people : an anthology of Muslim civilization / Eric Schroeder.—
Dover ed.
        p. cm.
    Unabridged reprint of originally published: Portland, Me. : Bond Wheelwright,
1955.
    Includes bibliographical references and index.
    ISBN 0-486-42502-9 (pbk.)
        1. Civilization, Islamic. 2. Islamic Empire. I. Title.

D199.3 .S42 2002
909'.097671—dc21

                                                                    2002073493

Manufactured in the United States of America
Dover Publications, Inc., 31 East 2nd Street, Mineola, N.Y. 11501

Q UITTING A SEVEN YEARS' TASK and reckoning my debts, I would like to name with gratitude the scholarly predecessors in promulgation on whom I, as a very poor Arabist, have relied almost entirely for the sense of Arabic originals: Barbier de Meynard, Nicholson, Lane, Zotenberg, Lyall, Sachau, Klein, Guest, Margoliouth, Arberry, Palmer, Meyerhof, d'Herbelot, Payne, Campbell, de Slane, Mez, Browne, Jarrett, Pickthall, Massignon, Chenery, Steingass; to others my obligations are merely less bulky. For some of my own versions, despite incompetence, I reconsidered the Arabic texts; for most there seemed no need, and I did not, but reworked the older European translations throughout. This was not from want of respect in the case of English versions, but because too literal a reproduction of Arabic sentence-form would be intolerable in so long an English book, and because I aimed at an effect which a patchwork of manners would have destroyed. Many old felicities, where originality would be disadvantageous to the work in hand, were kept, as seems to be standard practice in the struggle of re-translation to do justice to the Koran.

The great Islamicist of our own generation, Gustave von Grunebaum, gave me criticism, much suggestion, and repeated encouragement during these years; and in his praise I have already had my reward. The first manuscript was submitted to him, to Langdon Warner, a true humanist, to my old teacher William Thomson of Harvard, to a devout Muslim friend, Khalil Ahmad Nasir, and to an eminent literary friend, I. A. Richards, with request for advice; and suggestions for its improvement were followed.

The book owes very much to the editorial care of Thea Wheelwright.

To the Foundation for the Study of Consciousness and Arthur Middleton Young I am obliged for a large contribution to the cost of publishing, and to my dear wife for long patience with preoccupation.

E. S.

9 Follen Street
Cambridge, Massachusetts

CONTENTS

INTRODUCTION   xiii

THE DESERT
    ARAB CHIVALRY OF THE IGNORANCE BEFORE MUHAMMAD   1

THE APOSTLE AND THE BOOK   23

THE FIGHT FOR LIFE   73

THE FIRST CALIPH   145

THE CALIPHATE OF CONQUEST   165

MISRULE   181

CIVIL WAR   193

THE WORLD AND THE FLESH   203

THE FIRST ABBASID CALIPHS
    AND THE BUILDING OF BAGHDAD   263

HARUN AL-RASHID   295

THE BROTHERS' WAR   343

INTELLIGENCE   357

RESTLESSNESS   381

VIOLENCE AND QUIETISM   397

MONEY, MONEY, MONEY
    THE LIFE AND DEATH OF A VIZIER   445

A SAINT AND HIS FATE   521

A GOVERNMENT JOB
    EPISODES FROM THE LIFE OF A PROVINCIAL STATE CLERK   555

The Passing of the Age of Reason   569

The Last Actual Caliphs   581

The Sophisticated   611

The Sword and the Pen
        Princes and Clerks   645

Despair   667

Comedies   679

Ornament
        The Tongue of Abu Zayd   691

The Man Who Never Laughed Again   705

The Mystic Path
        A Dervish Autobiography   713

The Abyss   759

The Public Road   769

Appendix
        Muslim Science: The Body and the Doctor   781

Chief Sources   817

Chronology by Caliphates   823

Index of Principal Persons   825

Index of Selected Topics   829

Index of Poems   834

Index of Selected Anecdotes   837

INTRODUCTION

AN IRAQ JUDGE, some thousand years my elder, having written down a collection of stories taken from other people, as I have done, was composing an Introduction, as I must do.

These times, said he, were filled with strange events: great wars, unforeseen revolutions, and weird coincidences; there were plenty of clever political schemes, many well-organized and lasting institutions. Of such things I have put a little into writing, and concisely, in such a way as to inform any intelligent person who would like to know something new of the consequences of benevolence and its opposite, and the ultimate results of action.

Trying to classify usually makes things dull; and this work has little value as tabulation. It was not intended analytically, nor was it meant to pigeonhole things. Probably it is on the whole not quite like anything else, and rather original. It will be not only more amusing for being a mixture: it will be more impressive.

I hope there may be some market for my anthology, and that the physical labor of writing all this down may not prove waste. At any rate it will be something if the work is an improvement on an equivalent amount of blank paper — please God, Whom I beseech to preserve me from both lies and mistakes. *HE SUFFICETH ME. THERE IS NO POWER NOR STRENGTH SAVE IN HIM,* said His Honor the Judge.

The use of history is like the use of dreams. We are larger really than we are actually; and there is some outlying reality of ourselves upon which history, like other arts, can play, supplying the needed images which today withholds. We move from interest to capital, from the dole to the treasury of time. *The sleeper whose sight is quenched,* said Heraclitus, *gets a light from the dead, and the waking man a light from the sleeper.*

To supply these strange congenialities it is necessary, in Croce's words, that the deed to be told vibrate in the soul of the historian, or, using professional jargon, that the documents be present and intelligible. Such vibration, the appearance in the mind of some personality long extinct as if alive, or of some past event in the concerning poignancy or importance of a present event, is in fact generally set up if at all by documents, by surviving fragments of the past. It is rarely helped by judgments or opinions, and never yielded by epitomes; and so, too often, the historian, who knows the documents but only divulges description and judgment, finds his subject much more exciting than his reader can.

That the documents be present and intelligible, or that the reader taste undiluted the content of the ancient bottle, I have tried to set forth Muslim civilization entirely in Muslim confession, and so to make a historian of the reader, who may think as he will of what is shown him. My reader was envisaged as a person very like myself, willing to be entertained, not wholly unwilling to ponder matter which might be worth remembering, more concerned with authentic character than with critical certification, serious but not prim, interested in spiritual matters (of course) without being indifferent to money and fun. A little research showed that my *camerado* was sufficiently uninformed about Islam to be a fair mark for the truth, if truth could be thrown at him.

A decisive exclusion of my own comment ensured some measure of the kind of truthfulness I desired. For liveliness in the matter, I kept as it were a finger on my pulse, observing what passages in the long tracts of document suddenly lived for me, and let that introspection dictate choice. Interest, not probability, was the touchstone for authenticity, and intimacy, wherever it could be had, the entitling qualification. The fragments I got were great and small; and the mass of them, worked with much shifting, splitting, and discarding into an approximate chronology, became a tale with expatiations where certain Muslim ghosts would walk, if they walked at all, wearing their own dress at least, speaking their own thought, described by those who knew them, and not by me, judged by men closer to them than I, and not by me. With the exception of the landscapes, quoted (with some Arabic terms translated) from Doughty's noble *Arabia Deserta,* which enclose the first chapter, there is nothing here which has not been reflected in a Muslim mind.

It is said that we can see into a generalization only so far as our knowledge of detail goes. If that is true, we know a man better through the right particular than by an equivalent amount of generalization, however just. A vivid act or utterance may imply the rest of an event or of a man, as branching away from that, the moment of historical authority which makes us *feel as if we knew* why things turned out so, or why a man had to do as he did. The right weaving of such right particulars could give a true history by anecdote, wherein life could neither be dissolved in generalization nor reduced to mere upshot. *For it is death to souls to become Water, and death to Water to become Earth,* said the Greek philosopher. And it is convenient that the Muslims themselves wrote history in this fashion, as I have essayed, so that the work has something of a Muslim form. The interspersed verse follows Muslim precedent: in spite of the disadvantages of verse-renderings I have employed them for the sake of ornament in the Muslim style, for the sharp occurrence of more orderly beat like a burst of music among the noises of the street, as verse is found in Muslim books.

Simplicity was hardly to be expected in the product: history is not tidy. No balance sheet is presented to sum up the operations of these bygone energies; and if at the end you do not know quite what to think, you are, so far as I can see, per-

fectly right. *Real knowing,* said a brilliant Sufi, *is continual
bewilderment.* The living mind of the most serious man is a flux
of faces and places, where scraps of Holy Writ linger among
the sums of bills, and the pretty thighs of certain dancers jostle
the monumental noses of certain comedians; and on the living
model there appear in this testimony of dead minds not only
the spiritual, the economic, the deliberate and effective, but the
indecent and involuntary, the mysteriously violent, the unex-
plained; much fact but some rumor also, invention and exagger-
ation.

Sympathy is a discovering how much of us is elsewhere;
and the feeling that a style of life so different from ours as the
Muslim springs from a humanity identical with our own discov-
ers how much of us was there before we were born. People, the
history-makers, seem to act largely from feeling; and the feeling
which still remains available as a constituent in historical documents is not accessible to *intelligence* directly. Any objectivity
here is secondary to a subjective experience, for the only way to
know a feeling is to feel it first. Not objectivity but a conscious
subjectivity is scientific here. From Muhammad's biography in
the second and third chapters, some little understanding of a
religious and social genius may certainly be obtained. But it will
not be a dispassionate understanding: its deepest reach will be a
Muhammadan bias, faint or lively as sympathy is a faint or
lively faculty. One might say that accuracy of response to any
adequate record of a heroic life will be proportionate to the
emotion stirred by its end, a passional perception that something
lovable, sufficient, and irreplaceable has been removed, as if
what's to come must be worse than what's gone. We can only
know Muhammad's death as historical fact inasmuch as we can
wonder, like his Companions, how we are to get along without
him. For the Caliphate, that massive fact in history, is the long
shadow of this feeling. And if we do not get the feeling, any
subsequent forming of notions about the Caliphate will be playing cat's cradle.

To fill the void of bereavement, then, the Caliphate arises.

Time goes on three hundred years, and the book a dozen chapters; and what in heaven's name has happened to the institution? The difference between the sublimity of the theoretical Caliphate and the brutality of the actual Caliphate appals. Not that there is any historical anomaly; the change illustrates in a normal way Acton's law: Power corrupts. But where is the human ideal, the social ideal, lodged now? In adjusting the book's form to historical form, I have inserted among the *brevia* larger biographical members: the Prophet, one Caliph, one Vizier, one Dervish. All these lives seem specially informative about their times, and their objectives mark distinguishable phases between the proposition of public religiousness and the conclusion of private religiousness in an age of public distintegration.

The wording shifts from somewhat archaic to plain English, to accompany changes in intellectual atmosphere which seem to correspond with parallel changes in the West between the seventeenth and twentieth centuries: iconoclastic puritanism, then grandeur, immorality, and rational enlightenment, then a revolt of intuition against the rational scheme, preoccupation with money or other abstractions, disappearance of the political establishment, and dismay or disillusion inaugurating what Spengler calls the second religiousness. This device allowed of the casting of Koranic passages into language not too far removed from that of our Scripture, so that solemn reversion in later times to Scriptural phrasing, as characteristic of them as of us, might sound right. Whether our next hundred years will produce our parallel through equally catastrophic wars, catastrophic corruption, and catastrophic incompetence remains to be seen. *This thing Time,* as the Man of Ma'arra puts it, *is a long poem of regular rhythm; but the Poet never uses the same rhyme twice.*

As prologue to Islam, an introductory chapter presents the heathendom of North Arabia. Here all will seem vague, a confused noise of swords and riding, voices bragging and muttering.

It is that relative chaos to which Muhammad and Islam gave religious and social form. Clansmen, equally passionate in tribal loyalties and enmities whether as wandering Arabs they bred camels and horses in the wilderness, or whether as settled men they farmed oasis villages or traded in little towns, these Arabians were in some septs converts to Judaism, a few Christian. Most of them paid a customary devotion to divinities in stones, pools, trees, and celestial bodies. Their nobility was championship; their glories were the feverish hours of vendetta, seduction, and reckless giving, and their deepest thought the beauty of kindred, and Time's hard dealing with the pleasant and the noble. Among these Muhammad was born. These were the bickerers whom his Revelation translated to conquest, the founding of cities and the cultivation of arts. And theirs too was the freedom to which the nostalgia of their sophisticated descendants looked back.

Your way lies before you. *Wa's-salaam.*

NOTE

Passages from the Koran are printed in italic capitals, *THUS.*

Arabic Names: Abu means *Father of. . .* Ibn means *Son of. . .*
A typical name, Abu Muhammad Amr ibn Zayd, consists of an honorific (Abu Muhammad), which would be used in polite address or reference, a personal name (Amr) and a patronymic (Ibn Zayd). Family names in later times take the patronymic form. A local name (e.g., Baghdadi — *of Baghdad*) and a reference to the profession (e.g., al-Hasib — *the Accountant*) may be added.

Money: A dirham is a silver coin of three grammes weight. A dinar is a gold coin of four and a quarter grammes weight. It is inaccurate, but will give some idea of the magnitudes involved, to think of a dirham as a dollar, and a dinar as ten dollars.

Dates: Time is reckoned from the Flight of the Prophet to Madina in 622 A.D. and the Muslim year is of twelve lunar months — about three per cent shorter than our solar year.

Pronunciation: *s* hard as in *sing.*
th hard as in *thing.*
kh as the Scotch *ch* in *loch.*
dh as *th* in *that.*
' as a guttural vowel or catch deep in the throat.
gh as a guttural roll, between *g* and French *r.*
q as a deeply guttural *k.*
ai as *y* in *cry.*
i when long as in *unique.*

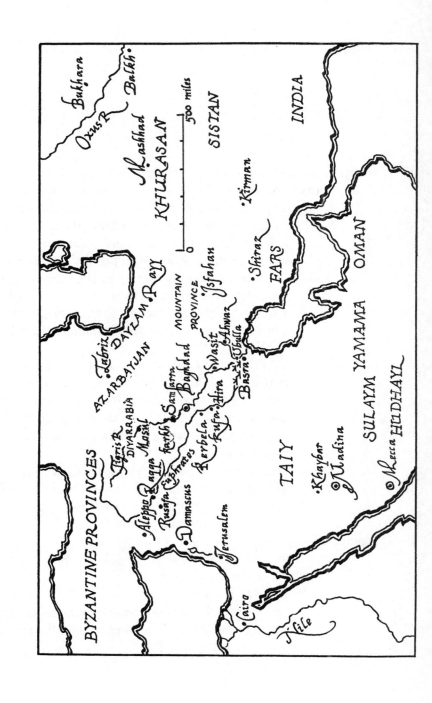

THE DESERT

ARAB CHIVALRY
OF THE IGNORANCE BEFORE MUHAMMAD

ALL ABOUT US IS an iron wilderness; a bare and black shining beach of heated volcanic stones. Few green stems of wormwood and southernwood, springing on the sharp lava shelves, give up a resinous sweetness under this withering broad sunshine. . . .

A vast bed and banks of rusty and basaltic bluish blocks . . . . stubborn heavy matter, as iron, and sounding like bell-metal: lying out eternally under the sand-driving desert wind, they are seen polished and shining in the sun. . . .

This Titanic desolation, seeming in our eyes as if it could not bear life, is good Beduin ground and heritage of the bold Moahib. Wholesome is that high attempered air, they have cattle enough, and those mountaineers are robust Beduin bodies of rude understanding. . . .

We rode in the further mountain way by ruins of dry-built walling; a kind of simple breast-works and small enclosures, such as the cotes which shepherds build to fold their lambs, (from the nightly wolf,) upon the mountains of Syria: besides these, there are some narrow cells that might be taken for graves laid above the ground. . . . There is another kind, which are round builded heaps and are perhaps barrows, the nomads say of them, "they are beacons, and mark the site of springs which were of yore, but the old knowledge is lost." If I asked any Beduin passenger of these things, he answered listless. . . . "Things of the former world, and before the True Believers."

* * *

Here halt, and weep, for one long-remembered love, for an old
Camp at the edge of the sands that stretch from the Brakes to
    Floodhead,
From Clearward to the Heights. The marks are not gone yet,
For all that's blown and blown back over them, northward,
    southward.
Look at the white-deer's droppings scattered in the old yards
And penfolds of the place, like black pepperseeds.

The two who ride with me rein closer to my side:
What! take thy death of grieving, man? Bear what's to bear!

I tell ye both, I'll be the better for these tears —
Where is the place among these crumbling walls to weep it out?

The same old tale ever — the same as with that other
Before her — the same again with her at the Whettingstead.
When women rose and stood, the scent of them was sweet
As the dawn breeze blowing through a clove-tree.
I suffered so for love, so fast the tears ran down
Over my breast, the sword-belt there was soaked with weeping.
And yet — the happy days I had of them, of women;
And that best day of days, the day at Neckbell Garth,
The day I got into her litter, into my cousin's litter.
Wretch! now I must walk! she said; and thanks to thee!
The girl talked on; the litter tilted and lurched with us —
Get down, Imrulqais! the camel will be galled!
And I: Go on — keep on — let go — slack that rein —
Thou'lt never drive me off; I'll taste that fruit again;
Give the beast his head; care not for him — we're together.
Come on, let's to the fruit! Lips are sweet as apples.
I have come by night to the like of thee, but pregnant, or nursing.
I have made such a woman forget her twelvemonth child
Till he cried out from behind her. She twisted to him with half
Her body; but half being under me lay still.

One day on a sandhill back she would not do my will,
And swore an oath, and swore she meant to keep her oath. . . .
Very eggs of white virginity, in tents forbidden, how many
Had I played with for my pleasure, and taken my time in the
　　　playing.
That night I passed the wardens who watched their tents, the
　　　men
Who would have welcomed me, for the glory of murdering me,
In an hour when Pleiades glittered in the night-heaven
Like a jewelled girdle, gem and pearl and gem;
In such an hour I came; she was all doffed for sleep
But for a shift; close by the screen of the tent she lay.
God's oath on me! she whispered, but thou hast no excuse!
And now I know that thou wilt be wild for ever.
Forth we went together; I led; she trailed behind us
A robe's embroidered hem, that tracks might tell no tales.
When we were past the fenced folkyards, then we made straight
For the heart of the waste, the waves and tumbled hillocks of
　　　sand.
I pulled her head to mine by the lovelocks, and she pressed
Against me, slender, but soft even at the ankle.
Thin-waisted she was, and white, sweetly moulded about the
　　　belly,
And the skin above her breasts shone like a polished mirror,
Or a pearl of the first water, whiteness a little gilded,
Fed of a pure pool unstirred by the feet of men.
Her very back was lovely, with wondrous hair — black, black,
Gloomy, thick as the clustering dates that droop a palm.
It curled, and seemed to creep upward toward the crown
Where braids were lost in the coiling and falling of many tresses;
Her little waist was supple as a twisted leading-rein;
Her calf pale as a palm-shaded reed at the water-girdle.

How many warned me from thee, with fierce hostility
Or tedious wisdom! I told both sorts to save their breath.
How many a night like a huge seawave falling stifled me

In thick veils, trying with ache upon ache my power to endure,
Till I have cried to Night, as his loins stretched out
Long as his thighs, and still his breast seemed never-coming:
O Night! Night! Long Night! Brighten to dawn,
Though comfortless as thou the drear coming of day.
What a night art thou! Thy unproceeding stars —
Are they fast and bound to some eternal crag?

And taking a water-skin from the house, I would strap it close
Over my shoulder — how often! — and meek to such a saddle
Crossing some hollow place like the flats of Starverib Waste
Have I heard the wolf, like a spendthrift who's gambled his dar-
     lings away,
Howl! He would howl. I would answer: It's a poor trade we
     follow
For profit, if thou hast kept as little as I have kept;
Whatever we get, thou and I, we bolt it; and it's gone.
A man will never be fat who thrives as we two thrive.

Enough! Look where I point: the lightning flickering yonder
Where the cloud's thick, like glancing hands that coil and pile
A crown of hair, or fire running up the chains
Of a lamp, slopped with oil by spilth of the hermit's hand.

There we sat between Staining and Littlemoss
And long we looked at it, and far away it seemed:
The right flank of the rain hung over the Nick,
The left over Shycover, and the Withers beyond.
Then down, down on Thicklet the pouring water swept,
And the huge trees there went chin-first to the ground.
Such a drift passed over Lowhill Crags
That whiteleg deer came down from every haunt and harbor;
And Tayma — not a palm still rose when it passed away,
Nor any tower, except it were laid in hard rock.
Hollowfell stood in the oncoming storm
Like a tall old man in a grey-stripe cloak.

At morrow's dawn, the peak of Trystinghill, wreathed round
With water and wrack, was no more than a wound-up distaff
      head.
Storm had scattered his wares over the Saddleflat
As a merchant new from Yaman throws down his loaded bales.

The little birds of daybreak in every upland ghyll
Sang away like drunkards mad with spicy wine.
But foul with earth, like roots of squills, the wild beasts drowned
That night lay in the daleheads where flood had turned to ebb.

* * *

If she lets thee love her, man, take a fill of pleasure;
But never choke a sob when then she turns and goes.
Dost find her sweet and soft? Think then, some other day
Some other man in luck shall find her as sweet, as soft.
Does she vow that parting cannot part sworn faith?
Fool! who ever saw faith with red-dyed fingertips?

Behold a man who never reckoned the pain of a labor!
A man of many ambitions, many ends, many ways!
Daylong in a Waste he goes; at evening enters another
Alone, riding Alarm bareback, and leading Death;
Outstripping Wind in the end, though Wind sweeps past him
      fast,
For the gust blows and sinks, while he fares on and on.
At last the needle of sleep sews up his eye; but he needs
No sentinel, for a ware man's courage will cry: Wake!
Soon as rise to sight the first of a following band
He stands; and draws a blade with edge bright from the whet-
      ting.
To see him shake it free from a breastbone is to look
To the backteeth into the roaring laughter of the Dooms.
Wilderness is his dear; he travels on
Where travels over his head the Mother of Starclusters.

A man like sun in winter, till
The Dogstar burned; then shade and cool.
Thin-flank, lean, but not from thrift:
A Giver, a Quick Heart, a Proud Man.
He journeyed with Wariness; where he halted,
Wariness lighted down beside him.
Long curls and lordly skirt at home,
But he fought his fight like a famished wolf.
Two tastes he had: of honey, of gall;
And all knew the bitter or the sweet of him.

THE DEATH OF THE KNIGHT RABIA,
CALLED BOY LONGLOCKS

Rabia espied far away the stir of dust. Ride on fast! said he to the womenfolk with him; this is no friendly troop that follows us, I fear. Keep straight to the road; I will wait here till the dust clear and I spy who they be. If I see cause to fear aught for you women, I'll fall on them in yonder covert of trees, and draw them away from the road. We'll meet again at the Pass of Ghazal, or Usfan in Kadid; or if I do not meet you there, at least you will have won to our own country.

He mounted his mare, and rode back toward the dust. He shewed himself to the pursuers riding forth from the trees, as they were searching the tracks of his company; and when they saw him, they came on against him in a body, taking it for sure the women were beyond him. Now Longlocks was a famous archer; and he began to ply his arrows, till he had slain and disabled a good few men. So having given them something to do, he spurred his mare after the fleeing women; and when he came up with them bade press on faster still. But the clansmen of Sulaym followed him up; so he turned a second time to encounter them. And so he continued, urging on the women and turning to face his enemies, until his arrows all were spent. They won to the country of Kadid even as the sun was sinking.

But the horses black with sweat followed fast behind, and the riders in hate and rage, feverish for revenge. Then he turned once more, with spear and sword, and did great slaugher among them. But here Nubaysha son of Habib bore down on him and thrust him through with his lance. That thrust stopped him.

I have slain him! Nubaysha cried.

Thy mouth lies, Nubaysha, said Rabia. But Nubaysha smelt at the blade of his lance, and said: Thou art the liar; I surely smell the smell of thy vitals!

At this Rabia turned his mare, and galloped in spite of his wound until he came up with the women, in the mouth of the Pass of Ghazal. He cried to his mother: Drink! Give me to drink!

O my son! she answered him; if I give thee any drink, thou'lt die straightway, even here in this place; and we shall be taken. Endure then — we may escape them yet.

So: Bind up my wound, then, he said. She bound it with her veil; and while she worked he spoke a verse:

Bind the binding on me fast!
Ye lose a knight like burning gold:
A hawk who drove a troop like birds,
And stooped, and struck forehand and back.

His mother answered:

We are of Malik's stock, and Tha'laba's,
We are the world's tale without end.
Our folk fall, man after man;
Our life is loss, day after day.

Now go; and while thy strength lasts, smite!

So he turned back to face them once again, at the head of the pass, while the women hurried on with all the speed they might. Longlocks sat upright on his mare, barring the road; and when he felt his death coming on him, he stayed himself upon his spear; so he stood in the twilight. When the men of Sulaym descried him there, still sitting his mare, they flinched from another onset, and halted a long while, thinking not but that he was still a living man. At last Nubaysha, watching him steadily, said: His head droops on his neck! Yon's a dead man, I swear!

He bade a clansman of Khuza'a who rode with them shoot an arrow at the mare. The man shot; and the mare shied. Right forward on his face Boy Longlocks fell. So they came up and spoiled his body. But they were afraid to follow the women any further; for by this time they must be safe home, near the dwellings of their own people. A man of Sulaym rode close.

Thou foughtest for thy women in life and death both! he said; and so saying thrust the heel of his lance into Rabia's eye.

A SISTER'S GRIEF

The rising sun reminds me: Him!
I remember him every setting sun.

* * *

In the cleft of the rocks below Sala lies
One slain. That dripping blood's avenged....

Many we were held on through noonheat;
Through nightfall still held on; at daybreak
Halted — keen-set as belted iron,
Blades once drawn that lightened like levin.
They were tasting sleep in sips, and nodding;
Down came Terror! and they were scattered.
We had our revenge: of the two kindreds
There got away what a pitiful few!

Though Clan Hudhayl broke his sword in the end,
How often he notched it on Hudhayl!
How many a dawn he fell on their camp,
And after good slaughter came plunder and spoil.

Hudhayl is burned! I burned them! I fearless!
I unwearied when they were weary —
Whose spear drank a deep first draught, and liked it,
And drank again, deep, of unfriendly blood.
I swore off wine till the deed should be done;
With no light labor I loosed that vow.
Reach me a cup at last, my cousin;
Fret for slain kin has wasted me.
We reached them a cup: the draught was Death;
The dregs Disgrace, Shame, and Dishonor!
Hyena laughs at slain Hudhayl!
Wolf grins at what's left of them;
Heavy-belly vultures flap their vans,
Trampling the dead, trying to fly,
Too full to fly!

Never shaykh of us died quiet in his bed.
Never unavenged was blood of us shed.
Others may say, and we can say No.
None can naysay when we say So!

LORD HARITH'S WOOING

Cousin, said Harith to me one day, dost think any man, if I asked him a daughter to wife, would deny me?

Ay, one man, said I.

Who so?

Aws of Taiy.

Ride with me, then said Harith. So we mounted one camel together, and rode till we came to Aws of Taiy in his own country; we found him at home. When he saw Harith, he said: Harith, I give thee greeting.

And I thee.

What brings thee hither, Harith? said Aws.

I am come a-wooing, he answered.

To the wrong place then, said Aws, and turned his back, and speaking not another word went in angry to his wife, a woman of Clan Abs. Who was that, she asked, who stopped at the door, with whom thou hadst speech so short?

That was Lord Harith, answered he.

How come thou didst not bid him alight? the woman asked.

He did like a fool, said Aws.

How?

He was come a-wooing.

Wouldst thou ever have thy daughters married? she demanded.

Ay.

And if thou wilt not give a girl to that Arab lord, to whom wilt thou wed her?

Nay, he answered, what's done is done.

Nay but, she said, see if thou canst mend the deed.

How? cried Aws. I do that? When it passed as it passed between me and him?

Say this to him, she answered: Thou foundest me angry, suddenly springing on me a matter unmentioned before; nor could I help but answer thee as I did; but now I pray thee turn again, and thou shalt have whatever thou wilt of me. Harith will surely come to thy bidding.

So Aws mounted and rode after the two of us. I was afoot, and happening to look round I saw him following. So I ran to catch up with Harith, who said not a word to me, being in bitter mood. Here comes Aws after us, said I.

And what have we to do with him? Come on! he said. When Aws saw that we did not wait for him, he cried out after us: Harith! Tarry! So we waited for him; and he spoke us the speech that his wife had made him; and Harith cheerfully turned to be his guest. Aws, as I heard, when he went in to his house, said to his wife: Call So-and-so to me (naming the eldest of his three daughters); and the girl came out to him, and he said to her: My daughter, this is the Arab lord Harith, Awf's son; he is come to beg a boon of me, that I should wed him to one of my girls; and I thought of wedding thee to him. What hast thou to say to that?

Do it not, she answered.

Why not? he asked.

I am foul of favor and temper both, she said. I am no cousin of his that he should respect me on that account, nor does thy country march with his, that awe of thee should stay him. And I fear lest one day he see in me something which shall displease him, and divorce me; and so I shall come to the fate of a divorced woman.

Rise, said Aws; and God bless thee! Call So-and-so to me (naming his second daughter). The girl called her sister in; and Aws spoke to her as he had spoken to her elder. She answered him after the same fashion: I am ignorant and awkward, and lack all skill of hand. I fear he will see in me what he will not like, and divorce me; and thou knowest what my lot would be. He is no cousin of mine to do me right, nor any neighbor of thine, to be afeared of thee.

Rise, and God bless thee! said Aws. Call Buhaysa to me (naming his youngest daughter); she was brought to him, and he spoke to her as he had spoken to her two sisters.

Be it as thou wilt, she answered.

I made this offer, said Aws, to both thy sisters, and they would not.

Nay but, she said, I am fair of face and cunning of hand, noble of temper, and honorable as thy daughter. Should he divorce me, God will bring him to no good end.

God bless thee! said Aws; and he came out to us and spoke: Harith, I give thee to wife Buhaysa daughter of Aws.

I accept her, said Harith. So Aws bade her mother get the girl ready and deck her for the bridal, and ordered a tent pitched for Harith, and lodged him in it. And when his daughter was decked out, he sent her in to her husband. But Harith only stayed inside with her a little while after she was brought, and then came out to me.

It went well? I asked.

Nay, said he.

How come?

He answered: When I put out my hand to take her, she said: No more of that! Wilt thou do it right before my father and my brothers? By God, no! that were unseemly.

So Harith got camels harnessed, and we started for home, taking her with us. For a time we travelled on; then Harith said to me: Go on ahead. And I went on, and he turned aside out of the road with the girl. But it was not long before he came up with me again.

It went well? I asked.

Nay, said he.

How come?

Harith replied: She said to me: Wilt thou treat me as a slave girl that has been hawked about for sale, or a captive woman taken in fight? By God, no! nothing until thou hast slaughtered camels and butchered sheep and called thine Arabs to the feast, and done all that should be done for the like of me.

I see, said I, that she is a woman of a high spirit and a wise mind; and this do I now hope, that thou shalt find her such a wife as shall bear thee noble sons, please God. So we went on until we came to our own country; and Harith there dressed camels and sheep and called a feast, and then went in to her. But after a little while only he came out again to me; and I asked him: It went well?

Nay, said he.

How come?

I went in to her, he answered, and said: Lo, I have dressed camels and sheep, as thou seest. And she answered me: They told me there was some nobility in thee, but I see it not. How so? said I; and she replied: Is thy heart light enough to marry women now, while Arab is killing Arab? What wilt thou have me do? I asked her; and she answered: Go out to those quarrelling kindreds of thine, and make peace between them; then come back to thy wife, and thou shalt not miss of thy desire.

By God! said I, there's a noble woman, and a wise one; and well spoken was that word!

Come on with me, said Harith then; and we set out and came to the clans of Abs and Dhubyan, and walked between them with peace. The peace was made on this condition: that the slain be reckoned up on both sides, and the price of the excess taken from the clan which had slain more than the other. And we two took upon ourselves the burden of the bloodwits; they came to three thousand camels all told, which were paid off in the space of three years. And so we came back home, with the fairest of fame.

And Harith lay with his wife at last; and she bore him sons and daughters.

*　　*　　*

Yet envy not even him of whom they say:
Ripeness and wisdom came with length of days.
Love life — live long — live safely — all the same
Long living leaves its furrow on thy face.

Time has taught me something; all other things have lied;
The wasting of the days lets things unguessed stand clear.
And I know this at last: how powerful men use power.
All powerful men get praise, whatever shame they earn.
This too I know: poverty wears great heart
Down, and the wearing's like the lick of a rawhide whip.
A poor man looks at glories he can never climb
And sits among the rest silent, silent, silent.

When a female child is announced to one such, his face darkens; he is consumed by wrath and hides from his own people, brooding: Shall he keep it to his disgrace, or bury it away beneath the dust?

The burial of daughters is a noble deed.

Umayma's gone, to stay where tall stones tell of the dead;
The waif is come to her quiet, and safe harbor underground;
And I sleep sound. Now Care never comes to wake me,
Nor Jealousy, since all I was jealous for is dead.
Death is no unfriend; I call not Death unkind.
Death gave me Peace, even if his greater gift was Pain.

Endure. For a man free-born only endurance is honor.
Time is fell; there's neither help nor heal of his hurt.
Even if it availed a man to obey his fear,
Or a man could parry trouble by any low consent,
Still to endure the full brunt, cut and thrust
Of Fate with a manly front, to endure's the only honor.

DURAYD THE ADDER'S SON

DURAYD WAS A victorious man, a lucky man in his plans.
He made near a hundred raids in his lifetime. A famous fight of
his was called the Day of the Sandhills. . . .

A sentinel posted on the sandhills cried: I see people coming — their hair is crisp and curly, and their shirts are saffron-
dyed.

Those will be of Clan Ashja, said Durayd; little care I for
them.

Now I see others, cried the sentinel. They look like boys.
They bear their lances lowered between the ears of their horses.

Those are of Fazara, said Durayd.

The sentinel called again: And now others come on, dark
men, swarthy-skinned, raising a black cloud of dust above them
mountain-high. How deep they score the ground with their
horses' feet! And these trail their lances behind them as they
gallop on.

These are of Abs, cried Durayd. Death rides with them! ...

After the fight was finished, Durayd, lying wounded by his brother's body, heard Zahdam of Abs say to his fellow Kardam: Methinks Durayd is not yet dead; I seemed to see his eyelid flutter. Get thee down and finish him.

Nay, he's dead enough, said Kardam.

Get thee down, I say, and see if he breathes.

So Kardam dismounted and went up to Durayd and examined him; and then remounted, saying: He's gone, for sure.

Afterwards, some clansmen of Abs and Fazara, on their way to Mecca in the Month of Truce, passed through Durayd's country; and being afraid they hid their faces in their kerchiefs so that only their eyes could be seen. But Durayd, seeing a party passing by, went out to meet them. What men are ye? he said.

One of the riders spoke: Is it of me thou wilt ask that question?

Durayd knew the voice of Kardam. Not of thee! he cried, nor of those who ride with thee! No need to ask who ye may be! And he embraced him, and gave him a horse and a sword and a lance. This is in requital of what thou didst for me the Day of the Sandhills, he said.

No grief for thy brother? my sister said...
Loss, sorrow: one grave filled, a fresh grave dug —
From this fever for revenge we can recover
Only by killing, or dying.

Durayd was the champion of his people, the Hawazin clans, and their captain in battle. He lived on into the time of Islam, but he never became a Believer; and he went out with his clan on the Day of Hunayn to help the party of the Unbelievers against the Prophet. They brought him into battle to have the good of his luck, and his wisdom in war. He was borne into

camp on a camel-litter, near a hundred years old, and almost
blind.

What valley's this? he asked.

Awtas, they told him.

A good place for a gallop, that, said he: not hard enough
to hurt a horse's foot nor yet so soft as to cumber his running.
But how comes it that I hear this roar of camels and braying of
asses, and the wailing of little children and bleating of sheep?

Malik brought down the children and women and herds
with the menfolk, they answered.

Bring Malik hither to me, said Durayd; and when Malik
came he spoke to him: Malik, thou art the captain of thy people
now, and on the turn of this Day hang for us all the days to
come. What means this noise of camels and asses and sheep, and
this wailing of children that I hear?

I thought to give each man his children and his goods to
keep that he might fight the stouter, Malik answered.

Ill bethought! said Durayd. A shepherd keeping sheep! O
the folly of it! Can anything turn Doom away? Hark ye, if this
Day is to be thine, nothing will help thee to it but men, men
with swords and spears; and if it goes against thee, thou hast set
women, babes, and wealth naked to shame and plunder.

After a little, he spoke again: What have the kindreds of
Ka'b and Kilab done?

There's not a man of those kindreds here, said Malik.

Then the blade lacks its edge and its luck both, said
Durayd. If this were to be a Day of glorious fortune Ka'b and
Kilab would not be absent — I would that ye had done as they.
Of the whole Clan Amir what's here?

The Children of Amr, the Children of Awf — no more.

Ay, the two striplings! They'll do no harm; but they'll do
no good. Malik, that surely was the deed of a fool to set the egg,
the precious egg of my people Hawazin to be trampled under
horses' feet. Send away these weaklings and these darlings up
into the high places of their country, those fastnesses of our
Clan; and then hurl men at thy foe, men on horseback. If the

Day fall to thee, all those behind thee are thine thereafter; and
if it go against thee, at least thou hast saved thy little ones and
flocks and herds, and thou wilt not be dishonored in the dishon-
oring of thy women.

But Malik cried: No, by God, never! Thou dotest! Thy
wit is feeble with old age! Either, ye men of Hawazin, ye obey
me now, or I run upon this sword of mine! For he grudged
Durayd the winning of any renown that day, that Durayd's
judgment should be exalted over his. And all that stood about
cried out: We'll obey thee — not Durayd!

And the Day was the Prophet's; and Malik fled with the
main part of the host, and got safe into Taif, leaving the families
and flocks of Hawazin to be a spoil. Some of the households
fled by way of the Nakhla road; the Prophet's horsemen followed
them up. And a young man of Sulaym named Rabia caught up
with the camel whereon Durayd was borne along in his litter.
Thinking it was some woman therein, he seized the leading rein
and made the beast kneel down; and lo! there in the litter was
a very aged man.

What's thy will? said Durayd.

Thou must die, the young man said.

Tell me thy name and lineage, Durayd demanded.

The youth told him, and then struck him a blow with his
sword. It failed to kill him.

That's a poor weapon thy mother gave thee! said the old
man. Take that sword of mine from the sword-case there behind
my saddle, and smite me with that — well above the shoulder
bones, and well below the round of the skull. That's how I would
smite my foe, in time long gone. And then go home to thy
mother and tell her thou hast slain Durayd the Adder's son;
for many's the day I have stood to defend the women of thy
people.

So the young Sulaymi struck at him again, with his own

sword. The head rolled out; and as the body sank over, Rabia
noticed the skin of his thighs, how it was as smooth and hard as
parchment, from constant riding of horses bareback. When he
got home, he told his mother of his deed.

O my son! she cried out, the man thou hast slain saved me
thy mother from captivity once, and thy father's mother too, and
my own besides.

Clan Amir's broken and gone. Nothing is left of her good
In the meadows of A'raf now — only ruined dwelling-places,
Ragged shadows of tents and penfold-walls and shelters,
Bough torn from bough, all spoiled by wind and weather.
All gone, the ancients gone, all her wise counsel gone,
None of us left but folk whose war-mares are only fillies.
Peace on Amir now; yet praise her and bless her still
Wheresoever on earth her way be, or her halting.

Beautiful he was whom ye left behind ye
There in Rakhman,
Thabit, Jabir's son, who killed his foe,
And poured for his friend.

*   *   *

AN HOUR BEFORE THE DAWN we heard shouted, THE REMOVE! The people rise in haste; the smouldering watch-fires are blown to a flame, and more sticks are cast on to give us light: there is a harsh hubbub of men labouring; and the ruckling and braying of a multitude of camels. Yet a minute or two, and all is up: riders are mounted; and they which remain afoot look busily about them on the dim earth, that nothing be left. — They drive forth; and a new day's march begins; to last through the long heat till evening. . . .

In our caravan were 170 camels, — bearing nearly 30 tons of butter — and seventy men, of whom forty rode on riding-camels — the rest were drivers. . . . There is an officer over such a great town caravan: he is one of the princely kin. . . . We were sorted in small companies; every master with his friends and hired servants. In each fellowship is carried a tent or awning, for a shelter over their heads at the noon stations, and to shadow the butter — that is molten in the goat-skins in the hot hours: the skin must be thickly smeared within with date syrup. Each skinful is suspended by a loop from the saddle-tree. . . .

After three hours journeying, in the desert plain . . . we are at the borders of the deep sand desert; and bye and bye the plain is harsh gravel under our feet: we reenter that granitic and basaltic middle region of Arabia which lasts from the mountains of Shammar to Mecca. . . . The caravans pass down

to Mecca by the Wady Laymun. Mecca is closed in by
mountains. . . .

At each midday halt the town camels are loosed out to
pasture. . . . The great brutes, that go fainting under their loads,
sweat greatly, and for thirst continue nearly without eating
till seventeen days be ended; when they are discharged at
Mecca. . . . The caravaners, after three days, were all beside
their short Semitic patience; they cry out upon their beasts
with the passionate voices of men in despair. The drivers beat
forward the lingering cattle, and go on goading them with
the heel of their spears, execrating, lamenting and yelling with
words of evil augury, Eigh! thou carrion for crows; Eigh!
butcher's meat. . . . The caravaners in the march are each day
of more waspish humour and fewer words; . . . And the drivers
whose mouths are bitter with thirst, will hardly answer each
other with other than crabbed or vaunting speech; as: Am I
the slave of thy father (that I should serve or obey thee)? . . .
How pleasant is the easy humour of all Beduins! in comparison
with the harsher temper of townsfolk. . . .

At length I saw this daylight almost spent. . . . We rode
on to a little bay and alighted. We were now in a civil
country — Meccan Arabia. . . . From hence to Mecca might
be twenty-two miles. The night fell dimly with warm and
misty air, and we knew, by the barking of dogs, that country
was full of nomads. . . .

We lay down here on the sand in our mantles; and
slumbered two hours: and then the trains of caravan camels,
slowly marching in the path, which is beaten hollow, came
by us again. . . . Riders mounted and set forward — we were
descending to Mecca! and some of the rude drivers say aloud
the devout cry of the pilgrims at the Arafat Hill there. . . .
But in the men of our caravan, a company of butter-chandlers,
that descend yearly with this merchandise, could be no fresh
transports of heart. They see but fatigues before them in the
Holy City. . . they are all day in the bazaars, to sell their wares;

and in the sultry nights they taste no refreshing. . . . At Mecca there is, nearly all months, a tropical heat. . . . The fellowships would lodge in hired chambers: those who were tradesmen in the City would go home. . . .

In the grey of the morning I could see that we were come to orchard walls; and in the growing light enclosures of vines, and fig trees. . . . And now we fell into a road — a road in Arabia! . . . We passed by a house or two built by the wayside. . . . From the next rising-ground I saw the town. I beheld also a black and cragged landscape beyond the town. We fell again into the road from the torrent-bed, and passed that lukewarm brook; which flows from yonder monsoon mountains. . . . The water-bearers went staggering up from the stream, under their huge burdens of full goat-skins; — there are some of their mighty shoulders that can wield a camel load! . . . The gate, where we entered, is called the Torrent Gate. The streets are rudely built, the better houses are daubed with plaster. The ways are unpaved. . . .

THE APOSTLE OF GOD
AND THE BOOK

It is said that when the heathen poet Zuhayr was over a hundred years old, he met Muhammad the Prophet of God; and the Prophet seeing him cried out: God! Keep me from the Daimon of this man!

Lo the Prophet! a Light lightening the world,
A naked sword out of the armory of GOD!

Muhammad Apostle of God

was born at Mecca in the Year of the Elephant (or in 570 A.D.), his mother being Amina of Clan Zuhra and his father Abdallah, of the Hashimite family of Clan Quraysh. His mother died while the Prophet was still at her breast, some say; but others, when he was two years old. His father had been dead four months when Muhammad was born. So he was given out to nurse to Halima, a Beduin woman of Clan Sa'd, till he was five years of age.

One day (Halima is said to have told) Muhammad and his foster-brother were with the cattle behind our camp when my son came running to us, crying: My brother! the Qurayshi! he says two men in white took him and laid him on his side and cleft his belly; and they were stirring their hands inside him! My husband and I ran out to him, and found him standing there with his face turned pale. What ails thee, child? we asked.

Two men in white garments came to me, he answered, and laid me on my side and cleft my belly open and groped for something — I know not what.

We brought him back to our tent. Halima, my husband said to me, the lad is stricken with a sickness, I fear; so take him home to his folk before it shows. So we took him back.

Thereafter his grandfather kept him, till he was eight years old, and then, dying, entrusted him to Abu Talib, Muhammad's uncle; and Abu Talib cared for him.

In his twenty-fifth year Muhammad married Khadija, a Qurayshi woman cousin to him, forty years of age. Her husband was dead, leaving her much wealth, with which she traded. Now Muhammad was known among the Quraysh as an honest man, and called the Trusty; so Khadija summoned him and said: Go, thou and my slave together, with my trading caravan to Syria this year. Some say she took him for hire, and others that she took him as partner. But when the caravan was back in Mecca, and the wares sold at a good profit, she sent for him and spoke to him thus: Thou knowest I am a woman well to pass in the world, and have no need of a husband. But, for my much goods, I would fain have an overseer; and I have cast my eyes on thee, finding thee faithful; thou shalt care for my wealth. Go seek thy uncle Abu Talib, and bid him ask me in marriage of my father for thee.

Fifteen years had Muhammad been husband to Khadija when, at the age of forty, he was called to be a prophet. She lived on some years after that; and in all those years Muhammad, out of love for her, took no other wife. He had by her three sons, four daughters; the boys died before his Call, but the four daughters lived.

Every year in the Month of Rajab it was custom for religious men to go up into Mount Hira and live there fasting. In this his fortieth year Muhammad, when he came down out of the Mountain, sought his wife and said: Khadija, I fear I shall go mad!

And why? she asked.

Because, said he, I see the signs of a madman in myself. When I walk in the road, from every rock and every hill I hear voices. And at night I see in dreams a huge Being, whose head toucheth heaven, whose feet touch earth. I know him not; but he looms nearer, nearer, as if he meant to seize me in his gripe.

Trouble thyself not, Muhammad, she said. Thou art an upright generous man, there can be nothing for thee to fear. But often now would Muhammad feel sick at heart; and even so often would he go again to Hira, and linger alone in the Mountain, and return home at evening with a darkened face.

It befell on a Monday, on a night of the Month Ramadan:

The Night of Destiny

The Spirit appeared to him, and bade him: *READ!* And he answered: I cannot read. Then the Spirit seized him with a mighty grasp and said again: *READ!* and he said again: I cannot. And the Spirit gripped him a second time, saying:

READ! IN THE NAME OF THY LORD WHO DID CREATE,
CREATE MAN FROM A CLOT.
READ! FOR THY LORD IS THE MOST BOUNTEOUS ONE,
WHO TEACHETH BY THE PEN,
TEACHETH MAN THAT WHICH HE KNEW NOT.

(This is of the Koran, the beginning of the Chapter of the Clot.) Then the Spirit left him. He came down out of the Mountain, overcome with a trembling, and returned to his house, repeating the Chapter. Chills came upon him; and he bowed his head and said: Cover me up! Cover me up! Khadija covered him with a cloak; and he fell asleep.

Then that Spirit returned, and cried to Muhammad with a great noise:

O THOU THAT ART CLOAKED,
ARISE! AND WARN!
THY LORD MAGNIFY!
THY RAIMENT PURIFY!
AND FROM INIQUITY GET THEE AWAY.

Thereat Muhammad threw off the cloak which covered him and stood up. His wife said: Wilt thou not sleep and take thy rest?

There is no more sleep nor rest for me, Muhammad said. He bids me call men to GOD. But whom shall I call? and who will believe me?

Call me the first, for I believe in thee, she said.

Now Muhammad had a familiar friend, one Abu Bakr, a man well-liked among the Quraysh, a man of authority, upright and rich, a merchant. It was custom when a man went into the Sanctuary at Mecca that he should walk the ritual circle round the Black Stone, and bow before one of the idols which were in the Holy House, and then, if he would, sit down in one of the companies that sat around the great men of the town. Muhammad was wont to sit in Abu Bakr's company, and tell him his affairs; so that when he received his Call, he bethought him of Abu Bakr.

In the morning he rose therefore, and went out to go to Abu Bakr; and lo! Abu Bakr was come forth to visit him, so that they met in the street. I was coming to take counsel with thee, Muhammad said.

And I of thee, said Abu Bakr; but do thou speak first, for my tale is long.

Then said Muhammad: Yesterday an angel appeared to me from God, and bade me call mankind to God, that they should believe in God, and believe that I am a messenger and apostle from God, and never worship these idols more. I was coming to ask thee whom I should call, to whom I should tell this thing.

Then let me be the first man to be called of thee, said Abu Bakr.

Overjoyed was the Prophet, and told him straightway the Formula of ISLAM (which word means *Submission to God*); and Abu Bakr pronounced that Profession of the Faith, namely:

There is no god but GOD;
Muhammad is the Apostle of GOD.

There is a Tradition handed down from the Companions
of the Prophet that he said: Of all the men to whom I ever
offered Islam there was never one who did not make some difficulty save Abu Bakr alone; he did not falter for one instant.

At the first Abu Bakr kept his Faith secret; but then
sometimes when he was in the Sanctuary talking with a man, he
would tell him of it and try to win him to Islam; and those who
accepted he took to the Prophet, and they uttered the Profession
of Faith. The first man that he converted was Othman; then
Abd al-Rahman son of Awf, then Zubayr, then Talha, then Sa'd
son of Abu Waqqas, and more, until they were thirty-nine Believers, keeping their Faith secret.

And God sent down Revelation:

THOU MUFFLED MAN!
KEEP WATCH THIS NIGHT, SAVE FOR A LITTLE,
A HALF, OR A LITTLE LESS
OR A LITTLE MORE, AND RECITE THIS KORAN IN
    MEASURE,
FOR WE SHALL CHARGE THEE WITH A WORD OF
    WEIGHT.
THE NIGHT WATCH IS WHEN FOOTING IS FIRMEST
    AND SPEECH SUREST:
THY DAY IS SPENT IN BUSINESS THAT HAS NO END.

CONSIDER THE PASSING HOUR:
TRULY MAN IS A LOST CREATURE,
SAVE ONLY THOSE WHO HAVE BELIEVED, AND
    DONE GOOD WORKS,
    AND EXHORTED ONE ANOTHER TO TRUTH,
    AND EXHORTED ONE ANOTHER TO PATIENCE.

NAY! I CALL ON THE DAY OF THE RISING OF THE
    DEAD!
NAY! I CALL ON THE ACCUSING SOUL!
DOTH MAN THINK WE SHALL NOT GATHER UP HIS
    BONES AGAIN?

YEA SURELY. WE HAVE THE POWER TO JOIN AGAIN
EVEN THE LITTLE BONES OF HIS FINGERS.
FAIN WOULD MAN DENY WHAT LIES BEFORE HIM,
ASKING: WHEN WILL IT BE, THAT DAY OF THE RIS-
ING OF THE DEAD?

BUT WHEN SIGHT IS CONFOUNDED,
AND THE MOON IS DARKENED,
AND SUN AND MOON ARE BLENT,
ON THAT DAY MAN SHALL CRY: WHITHER TO FLEE?
ALAS! THERE IS NOWHERE FOR ANY MAN TO FLEE!

THAT DAY SHALL CERTAIN FACES BE RESPLENDENT
LOOKING TOWARDS THEIR LORD;
THAT DAY SHALL OTHER FACES BE DESPONDENT,
KNOWING THAT CALAMITY IS UPON THEM.
NAY! WHEN THE LIFE COMETH UP INTO THE
THROAT,
AND THEY SAY: WHERE IS THE WIZARD THAT CAN
SAVE US?
KNOWING WELL THAT THIS IS THE PARTING
AS AGONY MELTETH IN AGONY,
THY LORD'S ON THAT DAY SHALL BE THE DRIVING!

* * *

Men, as they sat in their companies in the Sanctuary, began to talk: that Muhammad had founded a new faith, that he claimed to be God's Prophet and to have got from God a message; and that some believed in him, and were praying in secret. A certain Abu Jahl spoke up: If I find a man who hath believed in him, I'll crush his head as I would crush the head of a snake; and if I see Muhammad in this Sanctuary adore any other thing than my god Hubal, I will spill his brains with a stone. At least the slaying of a nephew will bring down the pride of Abu Talib.

God sent down the Chapter of the Dawn:
*SAY: I TAKE REFUGE IN THE LORD OF THE DAWN
FROM THE EVIL OF HIS CREATION,
FROM THE EVIL OF UTTER DARKNESS IF IT
COME ON,
FROM THE EVIL OF WITCHES WHO BLOW ON
KNOTS,
FROM THE EVIL OF THE ENVIOUS MAN IN HIS
ENVY.*

* * *

The Believers dared not go into the Sanctuary to pray, but prayed at home, or in Mount Hira. Abu Talib, hearing of the matter, made inquiry of Muhammad; and the Prophet told him, and would have converted him. But Abu Talib answered: I will not give up my old ways — they are my father's ways; but I will harbor thee.

Of the Unbelievers the Prophet's bitterest foe among his own kindred, the Children of Hashim, was his uncle Abu Lahab. It was revealed:
WARN THY TRIBE, THY NEAR KIN!
So Muhammad went to the Hill of Safa, and lifted up his voice; and the Hashimites came to his calling, and he said: Were I to warn you that some enemy was coming, would ye not believe me?

Ay, they answered.

Then I give you warning, said the Prophet, of punishment full dire:
*WHEN EARTH SHALL QUAKE WITH HER PREDES-
TINED QUAKING,
WHEN EARTH SHALL YIELD HER BURDENS UP,
AND MAN SHALL ASK: WHAT AILS HER?
ON THAT DAY SHE SHALL TELL HER TALE,
FOR THE BREATH OF THY LORD SHALL BE IN HER.
THAT DAY SHALL MEN COME OUT IN SCATTERED
COMPANIES, TO BE SHOWN WHAT THEY
HAVE DONE.*

THEN HE THAT HATH DONE ONE ATOM'S WEIGHT
 OF GOOD SHALL SEE IT,
AND HE THAT HATH DONE ONE ATOM'S WEIGHT
 OF EVIL SHALL SEE THAT.
ON THE DAY WHEN THE EARTH AND THE HILLS
 SHALL ROCK, AND THE HILLS BECOME A
 HEAP OF RUNNING SAND. . . .
HOW, IF YE DISBELIEVE, WILL YE SAVE YOURSELVES,
 ON A DAY WHICH WILL TURN CHILDREN
 GREY,
THE VERY HEAVEN BEING THEN RENT ASUNDER?

When the Apostle of God talked of the Day of Judgment, his cheeks blazed, his voice rose, his manner was fiery. He is a Prophet, he verily sees more than ye can see, said one. But his uncle Abu Lahab was in the crowd, and he stood up and said: Is it for this thou hast called us here, Muhammad? Perish thee! and perish thy religion! And he urged them all back to their homes, saying: Away with ye — Muhammad's mad.

Thereafter the Chapter of Fire was revealed:
PERISH THE HANDS OF ABU LAHAB! PERISH HIM-
 SELF!
HIS MONEY, HIS WEALTH SHALL NOT AVAIL HIM;
BUT HE SHALL BURN IN RAGING FIRE:
AND HIS WIFE SHALL CARRY THE FAGOTS,
WITH A PALM-FIBER ROPE ROUND HER NECK.

BY THE PEN AND BY THE WRIT!
THOU ART NOT, FOR THY LORD'S GRACE, THERE-
 FORE MAD.
THOU SHALT HAVE RECOMPENSE, IT WILL NOT
 FAIL;
THOU ART OF A TREMENDOUS MAKE
AND SHALT SEE, AS THEY TOO SHALL SEE,
WHICH OF YOU IS DEMENTED. . . .

HEARKEN NOT THEN TO REJECTORS
WHO WOULD HAVE THEE COMPROMISE, THINKING
    TO COMPROMISE THEMSELVES.
NEITHER HEARKEN TO EVERY MEAN OATH-MON-
    GER,
SLANDERER, SPREADER-ABROAD OF INFAMIES,
HINDERER OF GOOD, SINNER AND MALEFACTOR,
A GLUTTON TO BOOT, AND AN OUTSIDER,
BECAUSE HE HATH WEALTH AND CHILDREN,
A MAN WHO WHEN OUR REVELATIONS ARE RECITED
    UNTO HIM SAITH:
    MERE FABLES OF THE MEN OF OLD.
WE SHALL BRAND HIM ON THE NOSE.

           *   *   *

How many gods do ye worship? the Prophet asked a certain Qurayshi.

Seven on earth, one in heaven, said he.
SAY THOU: GOD IS ONE,
    GOD PERSISTS.
    HE NEVER BEGOT, HE WAS NOT BEGOTTEN,
    HE HAS HAD NO EQUAL, EVER.

           *   *   *

A QUESTIONER QUESTIONED CONCERNING THE
    DOOM WHICH IS TO COME
UPON THE UNBELIEVERS, WHICH NO MAN CAN
    TURN BACK,
FROM GOD THE LORD OF THOSE ASCENDING STAIR-
    WAYS
WHEREBY THE ANGELS AND THE SPIRIT ASCEND TO
    HIM IN A DAY
WHOSE SPAN IS FIFTY THOUSAND YEARS.

BE PATIENT, WITH COMELY PATIENCE,
FOR THEY SEE IT AS A DISTANT THING.

WE SEE IT AS A NEAR THING:
THAT DAY WHEN THE SKY SHALL BE AS MOLTEN
        COPPER,
AND THE HILLS AS TWISTS OF WOOL,
WHEN NO MAN SHALL QUESTION A FRIEND
THOUGH THEY STAND IN FULL VIEW ONE OF THE
        OTHER.

FAIN WOULD THE GUILTY REDEEM HIMSELF FROM
        THAT DAY'S PAIN AT THE PRICE OF HIS
        CHILDREN,
HIS WIFE, HIS BROTHER,
HIS KIN THAT HAVE HARBORED HIM,
AND ALL THAT LIE UNDERGROUND, IF THAT MIGHT
        DELIVER HIM.

NEVER! THIS IS THE FIRE OF HELL
HUNGERING TO ROAST;
SHOUTING FOR HIM WHO TURNED AND FLED
AND HOARDED AND KEPT HIS WEALTH CLOSE.

MAN IS A FRETFUL BEING,
IN MISFORTUNE AGGRIEVED
AND IN GOOD FORTUNE GRUDGING.
ONLY SUCH AS PRAY,
WHO CONTINUE IN PRAYER,
AND IN WHOSE WEALTH IS AN ACKNOWLEDGED
        SHARE
FOR THE BEGGAR AND THE DESTITUTE,
WHO ACCEPT THE REALITY OF THE DAY OF JUDG-
        MENT
AND FEAR THE DOOMING OF THEIR LORD
(FOR SURELY OF THE DOOMING OF HIS LORD NO
        MAN CAN FEEL SECURE),
WHO PRESERVE THEIR CHASTITY,
WHO KEEP TRUST AND COVENANT,

WHO BEAR FAITHFUL WITNESS,
WHO ARE CAREFUL IN PRAYER—
THESE SHALL DWELL IN GARDENS, HONORED.

BUT WHAT AILETH THE UNBELIEVERS
THAT THEY PRESS ROUND THEE STARING,
ON THE RIGHT, ON THE LEFT, IN HUDDLED COM-
    PANIES?
DO ALL THESE HOPE THAT THEY SHALL BE BIDDEN
    INTO THE GARDEN OF DELIGHT?
NEVER! WE CREATED THEM FROM WHAT THEY
    KNOW OF.
AND AGAIN, NO! I SWEAR BY THE LORD OF ALL RIS-
    INGS AND ALL SETTINGS THAT WE ARE
    WELL ABLE
TO BRING BETTER THAN THEM IN THEIR ROOM.
WE SHALL NOT BE OUTRUN.
THEN LET THEM CHATTER AND PLAY TILL THEY
    MEET THE DAY PROMISED THEM,
THE DAY THEY SHALL COME FORTH FROM THEIR
    GRAVES IN HASTE, LIKE MEN RUNNING A
    RACE,
BUT WITH FALLEN GAZE, AND ABASEMENT SLOW-
    ING THEM.

IT IS GOD WHO SENDETH THE WINDS. THEY RAISE
    A CLOUD, AND THEN WE DRIVE IT ON, UNTO
    A DEAD LAND, AND QUICKEN THEREWITH
    THE EARTH AFTER ITS DEATH.
SUCH IS THE QUICKENING OF THE DEAD.

AH! HOW CONVEY TO YE WHAT THE DAY OF JUDG-
    MENT IS?
AND AGAIN, HOW CONVEY TO YE WHAT THE DAY
    OF JUDGMENT IS?

IT IS A DAY WHEN NO SOUL HAS THE SLIGHTEST
POWER TO HELP ANY OTHER SOUL, BECAUSE
ALL POWER ON THAT DAY IS GOD'S ALONE.

WHEN THE SUN IS MUFFLED
AND WHEN THE STARS ARE DARKENED
AND WHEN THE HILLS ARE MOVED
AND WHEN CAMELS TEN MONTHS PREGNANT ARE
ABANDONED
AND WHEN WILD BEASTS GATHER ABROAD
AND WHEN THE SEAS SURGE UP
AND WHEN SOULS ARE ASSEMBLED
AND WHEN THE GIRL-CHILD THAT WAS BURIED
ALIVE IS ASKED
FOR WHAT CRIME SHE WAS PUT TO DEATH
AND WHEN THE WRIT IS ALL DISPLAYED
AND WHEN THE SKY IS TORN AWAY
AND WHEN HELL-FIRE IS LIT
AND WHEN THE GARDEN IS BROUGHT NEAR —
THEN SHALL EACH SOUL KNOW WHAT IT HAS PRE-
PARED.

NAY! I CALL TO MY WITNESS THE PLANETS
THAT SHIFT AND HIDE,
AND NIGHT AS IT CLOSETH,
AND MORNING AS IT BREATHES.
THIS IN TRUTH IS THE WORD OF AN HONORABLE
MESSENGER,
STRONG IN THE STRENGTH HE GOT FROM THE
LORD OF THE THRONE,
WHO MUST BE OBEYED, AND TRUSTED.
YOUR COMRADE IS NOT MAD:
HE SAW HIM, IN THE CLEAR MIDDLE AIR.
IT WAS NO HUNGER FOR THE UNSEEN,
NOR IS THIS THE UTTERANCE OF A DEVIL, TO BE
STONED.

WHITHER CAN YE TURN?
THIS IS NAUGHT BUT A REMINDER TO CREATION,
TO WHOMSOEVER AMONG YOU PLEASETH TO WALK
     A STRAIGHT PATH.
—NOR WILL YOU SO PLEASE, UNLESS GOD PLEASE,
     WHO IS CREATION'S LORD.

VERILY THE RIGHTEOUS SHALL DRINK OF A CUP
     WHEREOF THE MIXTURE IS OF CAMPHOR,
A SPRING WHEREFROM GOD'S SERVANTS DRINK:
     THEY MAKE IT FLOW ABUNDANTLY
WHEN THEY PERFORM THE VOW, DREADING A DAY
     WHOSE EVIL SHALL RUN FAR AND WIDE,
AND FEED THE POOR, AND THE ORPHAN, AND THE
     CAPTIVE, FOR HIS LOVE...
FOR WHICH GOD HATH KEPT THEM FROM THAT
     DAY'S EVIL, BRINGING THEM INTO BRIGHT-
     NESS AND JOY,
AND FOR ALL THEY SUFFERED HATH GIVEN THEM
     A GARDEN, AND SILK ATTIRE;
LYING ON COUCHES, THERE SHALL THEY FIND
     NEITHER SUN NOR BITTER COLD.
CLOSE OVERHEAD SHALL BE THE SHADE THEREOF,
     AND LOW SHALL HANG THE READY FRUIT.
GOBLETS OF SILVER SHALL CIRCLE AMONG THEM,
     AND BEAKERS OF GLASS,
SILVERY GLASS, IN MEASURE ACCORDING TO THEIR
     MEASURE;
THERE IS POURED THEM A CUP WHEREOF THE MIX-
     TURE IS OF GINGER,
FROM THE WATERS OF THE SPRING OF SALSABIL
     THEREIN;
AND ROUND ABOUT GO BOYS OF EVERLASTING
     YOUTH. WHEN THOU SEEST THEM THOU
     SHALT TAKE THEM FOR SCATTERED PEARLS;

*WHEN THOU COMEST TO THE SIGHT, THEN SHALT
     THOU SEE BLISS AND HIGH ESTATE.*
*THEIR RAIMENT SHALL BE FINE GREEN SILK, AND
     SILK WOVEN WITH GOLD; BRACELETS OF
     SILVER SHALL THEY WEAR; THEIR LORD
     WILL SLAKE THEIR THIRST WITH A PURE
     DRINK.*
AND LO! ALL THIS IS FOR YOU, IS YOUR REWARD.

*THERE ARE BEINGS THERE WITH WIDE AND LOVELY
     EYES,*
BEINGS LIKE HIDDEN PEARLS,
THE REWARD OF GOOD WORKS,
*IN WHOM WE HAVE PUT A POWER OF RENEWING
     GROWTH,*
OF VIRGINITY THAT RENEWS ITSELF.
*THEY ARE FOND OF PLEASURE, OF COMPANIONABLE
     AGE,*
THEY ARE FOR THOSE SET UPON OUR RIGHT HAND.

AND THOSE ON THE LEFT HAND —
WHAT OF THOSE ON THE LEFT HAND?
SCORCHING WIND AND SCALDING WATER
AND SHADOW OF BLACK SMOKE.

* * *

Look! it was said in the streets, there goes that fellow of
the kindred of Abd al-Muttalib who talks about Paradise!

THE WICKED USED TO LAUGH AT THE BELIEVERS
AND WINK AT ONE ANOTHER AS THEY PASSED,
AND GO HOME CHUCKLING,
*SAYING AS THEY SAW THEM: FAR ASTRAY, FOR
     SURE.*

SAY: I TAKE REFUGE IN MAN'S LORD,
    MAN'S KING,
    MAN'S GOD,
    FROM THE WHISPERING INSINUATOR'S EVIL
    WHO WHISPERS IN MAN'S BREAST.

BY THE PLEIADES AT THEIR SETTING!
YOUR COMRADE ERRETH NOT, HE DOTH NOT DE-
    VIATE,
NOR SPEAK FROM ANY DESIRE OF HIS OWN.
IT IS ALL INSPIRATION, A THING INSPIRED,
WHICH ONE OF DREAD POWER HATH TAUGHT
    HIM —
A STRONG BEING WHO APPEARED TO PLAIN SIGHT
EVEN ON THE HORIZON'S RIM,
AND THEN DREW NEAR, AND NEARER STILL
TILL HE WAS TWO BOW-LENGTHS OFF, OR LESS,
AND HE REVEALED UNTO HIS SLAVE WHAT HE RE-
    VEALED.
WHAT HE SAW WAS NO LIE OF HIS HEART;
WILL YE DISPUTE WITH HIM ABOUT WHAT HE SAW?
AY! AND A SECOND TIME HE SAW HIM, DESCENDING,
BY THE LOTE TREE AT THE WORLD'S END,
HARD BY THE GARDEN OF ABODE.
WHEN THAT WHICH COVERED IT DID COVER THE
    LOTE TREE,
THE EYE DID NEITHER FLINCH NOR FIX —
IN TRUTH HE BEHELD ONE OF THE GREATER REVE-
    LATIONS OF HIS LORD.

When Revelation came down upon the Prophet, anxiety oppressed him, his countenance was troubled, he fell to the ground like a drunken man, or a man overpowered by sleep. Even on a very cold day great drops of sweat would cover his brow.

Inspiration, he once said, comes in one of two ways: sometimes Gabriel communicates Revelation to me as one man to another, and that is easy; but at other times it is like the ringing of a bell, penetrating my very heart, tearing me; and that way hurts the most.

THE BLIND MAN AND THE SEER ARE NOT ALIKE,
NOR THE DARKNESS AND THE LIGHT,
NOR THE SHADOW AND THE BURNING SUN.
NEITHER ARE THE LIVING AND THE DEAD ALIKE.
  GOD CERTAINLY CAN REACH THE EAR OF WHOM HE PLEASETH; BUT THOU CANST NOT REACH THE EARS OF THOSE WHO ARE IN THEIR GRAVES;
THOU ART A WARNER ONLY:
WE HAVE SENT THEE WITH THE TRUTH, TO BRING GLAD TIDINGS AND WARNING BOTH; THERE IS NO NATION BUT A WARNER HAS GONE AMONG THEM.
IF THEY CALL THEE LIAR, SO ALSO DID THOSE BEFORE THEM CALL THEIR APOSTLES LIARS, THOUGH THEIR APOSTLES BROUGHT THEM CLEAR PROOFS—THE PSALMS, THE ILLUMINATING SCRIPTURE.
IN THOSE DAYS TOO I SEIZED THE UNBELIEVERS— AND WITH WHAT ABHORRENCE!

MAN PRAYETH FOR EVIL AS HE SHOULD PRAY FOR GOOD.

THAT MAN WHO LANGUISHES FROM REMEMBRANCE OF THE BENEFICENT, WE ASSIGN UNTO HIM A DEVIL TO BECOME HIS COMRADE.

HAST THOU SEEN WHO IT IS THAT BELIES THE FAITH?
IT IS THE MAN WHO SPURNETH THE ORPHAN,

WHO DOTH NOT URGE THE FEEDING OF THE POOR.
WOE UNTO THOSE WHO PRAY
UNMINDFUL OF THEIR PRAYERS:
WHO WANT PUBLICITY
AND ARE NIGGARD OF CHARITY.

(This is the Chapter of Almsgiving.)

THY LORD HATH DECREED THAT, WORSHIPPING NONE SAVE HIM, YE SHOW KINDNESS TO FATHER AND MOTHER. IF EITHER OR BOTH GROW OLD IN THY HOUSEHOLD, NEVER HUSH THEM RUDELY NOR CHIDE, BUT SPEAK TO THEM GRACIOUS WORDS,
AND FOLD THY WING IN SUBMISSION TO THEM, AND THINK: MY LORD! HAVE MERCY ON THESE TWAIN AS THEY DID CARE FOR ME WHEN I WAS LITTLE.
GIVE THE KINSMAN HIS DUE, AND THE NEEDY, AND THE WAYFARER. SQUANDER NOT WANTONLY;
SQUANDERERS ARE THE DEVIL'S BROTHERS, AND ALWAYS A DEVIL IS AN INGRATE TO HIS LORD.

STRAIN NOT THINE EYES (MUHAMMAD) AFTER THAT BLISS WE GIVE SOME WEDDED PAIRS AMONG MANKIND, NOR SIGH ON THAT ACCOUNT. BE IT THINE TO FOLD THY WING IN TENDERNESS OVER THE BELIEVERS.

GOD RECEIVETH ALL SOULS IN THE HOUR OF THEIR DEATH, AND THE SOUL WHOSE TERM IS NOT YET COME IN THE HOUR OF ITS SLEEP, KEEPING THAT FOR WHICH HE HATH ORDAINED DEATH, DISMISSING THE REST TILL AN APPOINTED TERM.

The Chapter of the Koran called Yasin is reverently recited in times of adversity and sickness, when fasting, or at the approach of death: —

ENTER PARADISE, THEY SAID;
 AND HE: WOULD THAT MY PEOPLE KNEW
NOW MY LORD HATH FORGIVEN ME, AND HATH SET
 ME AMONG THE HONORED. . . .
HAVE THEY NOT SEEN HOW MANY GENERATIONS
 WE DESTROYED BEFORE THEM, THAT SHALL
 NEVER COME BACK TO THEM AGAIN?
YET EVERY SINGLE ONE SHALL SURELY BE BROUGHT
 BEFORE US.
THE DEAD EARTH IS A TOKEN UNTO MEN: WE
 QUICKEN IT AGAIN, AND BRING FROM IT
 GRAIN FOR THEIR EATING,
PLANTING IN THE WILD GARDENS OF PALM AND
 VINE, SETTING THE WATER-SPRINGS TO
 GUSH, THAT THEY MAY EAT THE FRUIT
 THEREOF
FOR WHICH THEIR HANDS TOILED NOT. THEN
 SHALL THEY NOT GIVE THANKS?
GLORY TO HIM WHO DID CREATE ALL THINGS
 THAT MATE IN LOVE: PAIRS OF EARTH'S
 GROWING, PAIRS OF HUMAN KIND AND OF
 THINGS NOT KNOWN TO MAN!
NIGHT TOO IS A TOKEN UNTO MEN: WE STRIP IT OF
 THE DAY AND LO! ALL IS IN DARKNESS.
AND THE SUN RUNNETH ON TO HIS RESTING-PLACE
 — HE, THE MEASURE OF THE MIGHTY AND
 THE WISE!
AND FOR THE MOON WE HAVE APPOINTED MAN-
 SIONS TILL SHE RETURN AGAIN, THIN AS AN
 OLD AND WITHERED BRANCH OF PALM.
NEITHER MAY THE SUN OVERTAKE THE MOON NOR
 THE NIGHT OUTSTRIP THE DAY:
ALL FLOAT ON, EACH IN ITS SPHERE.

VERILY THOSE WHO HAVE WON PARADISE THIS
    DAY ARE HAPPILY EMPLOYED,
THEY AND THEIR LOVES, IN PLEASANT SHADE, RE-
    CLINING UPON THRONES:
ITS FRUITS ARE THEIRS; ALL THEY WOULD ASK IS
    THEIRS.
PEACE!
O WORD OF A MERCIFUL LORD!
EXTOLL HIM THEN, IN WHOSE HAND IS THE KING-
    DOM OF ALL THINGS:
TO HIM ARE YE BROUGHT BACK AGAIN.

MEN SAID: SHALL WE FORSAKE OUR GODS FOR A
    MAD POET?

THIS IS NOT POET'S UTTERANCE, O YE OF LITTLE
    FAITH,
NOR WIZARD'S UTTERANCE, O YE OF LITTLE MEM-
    ORY.
IT IS REVELATION FROM THE LORD OF BOTH THE
    WORLDS.

AS FOR POETS, THE MISLED FOLLOW THEM.
HAST THOU NOT SEEN THEM WANDERING IN EVERY
    VALLEY
TALKING OF DEEDS THEY NEVER DO?

WALK NOT IN VAINGLORY THROUGH THIS WORLD:
    FOR THOU COULDST NOT CLEAVE THE
    EARTH INTO VALLEYS, NOR STRETCH A
    THING HIGH AS THE HILLS ARE STRETCHED.

YET THEY SAY: NAY, THESE ARE ONLY MUDDLED
    DREAMS;
    AND: NAY, IT IS ONLY HIS FANCY;

AND: NAY, HE IS ONLY A POET. LET HIM SHOW US A MIRACLE.

MAN IS MADE OF HASTE.
  MY PORTENTS I SHALL SHOW YOU, BUT ASK ME NOT TO HASTEN.

ONE OF GOD'S PORTENTS THOU BEHOLDEST IN THE SUNKEN EARTH: AT THE SENDING DOWN OF WATER IT DOTH BEGIN TO THRILL AND SWELL:
HE WHO QUICKENETH THAT IS THE VERY QUICK-ENER OF THE DEAD; AND SURELY ABLE TO DO ALL THINGS.
ONE OF GOD'S PORTENTS IS THE SHIPS, LIKE BAN-NERS ON THE SEA:
IF HE WILL HE STILLS THE WIND, TILL THEY STAND MOTIONLESS ON OCEANBACK (A TOKEN SURELY FOR EVERY PATIENT, GRATEFUL HEART):
OR SINKS THEM, ON ACCOUNT OF SOMETHING THEY HAVE EARNED, MUCH AS HE FORGIVETH.

YET MEN SAY: WHAT AILETH THIS APOSTLE, THAT HE EATETH VICTUALS AND TRUDGETH ROUND THE MARKETS? HOW COME NO AN-GEL WAS SENT DOWN TO JOIN HIM IN HIS WARNINGS?
NO TREASURE DROPPED FOR HIM? NO PARADISE GIVEN HIM TO EAT FROM?

NEVER BEFORE THY TIME SENT WE ANY OF OUR APOSTLES BUT THEY LIVED ON VICTUALS AND WALKED THE MARKETS.

APOSTLES BEFORE THEE HAVE BEEN MOCKED.

*BUT WHAT THEY MOCKED ENCOMPASSED THE
     MOCKERS.*

*RECITE AS MUCH AS HATH BEEN REVEALED TO
     THEE OF THE SCRIPTURES OF THY LORD;
     AND ITS WORDS ARE TO BE ALTERED BY NO
     MAN,
A SCRIPTURE WHICH WE HAVE DIVIDED INTO POR-
     TIONS FOR THY RECITING TO MANKIND,
     FROM TIME TO TIME.
HAVE WE VOUCHSAFED THEM ANY SCRIPTURE TO
     HOLD FAST TO BEFORE THIS?
NAY! BUT THEY ONLY SAY: WE FOUND OUR FA-
     THERS FOLLOWING A RELIGION, WE FOL-
     LOW IN THEIR FOOTSTEPS.
IT WAS EVER SO—NEVER SENT WE A WARNER BE-
     FORE THY TIME, MUHAMMAD, INTO ANY
     CITY BUT ITS LUXURIOUS CITIZENS SAID:
     WE FOUND OUR FATHERS FOLLOWING A
     RELIGION, WE FOLLOW IN THEIR FOOTSTEPS.
AND WHEN HE SAID: WHAT! EVEN THOUGH I BRING
     YOU GUIDANCE BETTER THAN THAT
     WHEREIN YE FOUND YOUR FATHERS? THEY
     EVER ANSWERED: WE DO NOT BELIEVE IN
     WHAT YE BRING.
SO WE PAID THEM.
     AND SEE WHAT WAS THE END OF THE REJEC-
     TORS.*

*THEY SAY: THOU WITH THY REVELATION OF RE-
     MINDER, THOU CERTIFIED MADMAN,
WHY DOST THOU NOT BRING ANGELS TO US, IF
     THERE IS TRUTH IN THEE?
WE SEND NOT ANGELS DOWN SAVE WITH THE
     FACT; AND THEN IT IS TOO LATE FOR RES-
     PITE. . . .*

WE HURL THE TRUE AGAINST THE FALSE; IT SHAT-
TERS ITS HEAD;
AND LO! THE FALSE IS GONE.

WHEN WE WOULD DESTROY A CITY, WE SEND OUR
COMMAND TO ITS EASY-LIVING FOLK.
AND THEY CONTINUE IN THEIR SIN IN THAT
CITY.
AND SO THE WORD IS ESTABLISHED AGAINST
IT.
AND WE DESTROY IT WITH DESTRUCTION AB-
SOLUTE.
REMIND THEM OF THE BROTHER OF AD, OF HOW,
STANDING AMID THE HOLLOWED HILLS OF
SAND, HE WARNED HIS FOLK (AND HE WAS
NOT THE FIRST, NOR THE LAST), SAYING:
SERVE GOD AND NONE OTHER, FOR TRULY
I FEAR FOR YOU THE RETRIBUTION OF A
DREADFUL DAY.
ART THOU COME TO TURN US AWAY FROM OUR
GODS? THEY SAID. THEN BRING UPON US
THE MATTER OF THY THREATS, IF IT IS
TRUTH THOU TELLEST.
TO KNOW BELONGS TO GOD ALONE, HE ANSWERED
THEM; I DELIVER YOU THE MESSAGE I WAS
SENT WITH—YE WILL NOT LEARN, I SEE.
AND THEN, WHEN THEY SAW THE THING COMING
ON, AS IT WERE A DENSE CLOUD, TOWARD
THEIR VALLEYS, THEY SAID: HERE COMES A
CLOUD—WE SHALL HAVE RAIN.
NO CLOUD IS THAT: IT IS THE THING YE HURRIED
ON OF YOUR OWN WILLS—A STORM-BLAST
WITH BITTER TORMENT IN IT,
DESTROYING ALL THINGS BY THE COMMANDMENT
OF ITS LORD.

*MORNING CAME, AND NOTHING OF THEM WAS
SEEN — ONLY THE PLACES WHERE THEY
HAD DWELT.*

*   *   *

Muhammad's uncle Hamza was the strongest of that kindred, a mighty hunter and an archer. One day as he came back from hunting, he heard the sobbing of an old woman, a freedwoman of Abdallah's, and stopped to question her. O Hamza! she cried, 'tis for thy nephew Muhammad, whom Abu Jahl hath wounded.

Going into the Sanctuary, he saw Abu Jahl, went up to him, reviled him, and beat him with the grip of his bow about the head till the blood sprang. Then he went to Muhammad's house and said: Muhammad, I have avenged thee on Abu Jahl; I gave him a bloody crown with this bow of mine.

That is no revenge for me, mine uncle, said the Prophet. What then? demanded Hamza.

For you to say: There is no god but God! would be revenge, the Prophet said. And then and there Hamza uttered the Profession of Faith.

*   *   *

Abu Jahl and Omar son of Khattab — the Faith hath no enemies more bitter than those twain, the Apostle of God had said. Omar one day took his sword, saying: I will slay this Sabaean, this splitter of the Quraysh and blasphemer of their gods. But one stopped him, saying: Would that kindred let thee walk the earth after the slaying of Muhammad, think ye? Were it not better for thee to go back home and keep thine own household in the straight path?

Who of my household? Omar said.

Thy brother-in-law and cousin, Sa'id, Zayd's son. Thy sister Fatima. They are both turned Muslim, followers of Muhammad: look thou to them.

Omar turned back raging against them both. Now a certain Muslim, Khabab, was with them in the house. He had a leaf on which was written the Chapter Ta Ha of the Koran; and he was reading the Chapter aloud. When they heard the noise of Omar's coming, Khabab hid himself in a closet; and Fatima took the leaf and hid it under her thigh.

But Omar, as he came up to the house, had heard the sound of the reading; he said as he entered: What was that mumbling that I heard?

Nothing, they answered.

Ay, but I heard something, Omar said. And I have been told already — ye are become followers of Muhammad in that religion of his.

And he struck at his brother-in-law Sa'id. But Fatima sprang up to keep him off; the blow fell on her and drew blood. At that deed, they said to him: Ay, we are Muslims; we believe in God and His Apostle; so do thy will.

But when he saw the blood upon his sister, he was sorry for his deed. Give me that leaf, he said to her, from which I heard you reading even now, and let me see what it is, the thing Muhammad brought (for Omar could read and write).

We dare not trust thee with it, his sister answered him.

Fear not, said he, and swore by his gods that having read it he would give it back. Thereupon, hoping he might even be converted, she said: Brother, thou art unclean, coming from thine idolatry — and none may touch this writing save the purified. So Omar went out and washed himself; and she gave him the leaf; and he read the Chapter Ta Ha:

NOT TO THY CONFUSION DID WE REVEAL TO THEE THIS KORAN
BUT TO RECALL THE FEARFUL TO REMEM-BRANCE,
A REVELATION FROM HIM WHO DID CREATE THE EARTH AND THE HIGH HEAVENS,
THE MERCIFUL, WHO IS ESTABLISHED ON THE THRONE.

HIS IS WHATSOEVER IS IN THE HEAVENS, HIS
WHATSOEVER IS ON EARTH, HIS WHAT-
SOEVER GOES BETWEEN, HIS WHATSO-
EVER IS UNDERGROUND.
SAY ALOUD, AND HE KNOWETH THY HIDDEN
THOUGHT, AY, AND WHAT IS HIDDEN
DEEPER THAN THY THOUGHT.
GOD! THERE IS NO GOD BUT HE ALONE, AND
BEAUTIFUL BEYOND COMPARE ARE HIS
NAMES.
HATH THERE COME TO THEE THE STORY OF
MOSES?
and so to the end of the Chapter, where it is written:
ALL THINGS WAIT: DO YE TOO WAIT. YE SHALL
KNOW AT THE LAST WHO HATH FOL-
LOWED THE EVEN PATH, AND WHO
HATH HAD GOOD GUIDING.

How excellent are these words! cried Omar when he had
read to the end. No sooner did Khabab hear that than he came
out of hiding and said: Omar, it is my hope that God sent thee
hither in answer to the Apostle's prayer, for but yesterday I
heard him pray: God! strengthen Islam with Abu Jahl, or with
Omar!

Khabab, said Omar, take me to Muhammad, for I will go
to him and make my Submission to God and be a Muslim.

Now Omar was a man of whom the Prophet one time
said: If Satan were to see Omar in his road, he would climb a
hill to get out of Omar's way. And he said to the Prophet: We
have worshipped our idols Lat and Hubal in public; are we now
to worship God in hugger-mugger? It was soon after these days
that the Prophet went into the Sanctuary and recited the revealed verses:

VERILY YE AND THE IDOLS YE WORSHIP AS AGAINST
GOD ARE FUEL FOR HELL-FIRE.
FOR THE FIRE ARE YE BOUND.

HAD THESE THINGS BEEN GODS IT HAD BEEN
OTHERWISE; BUT THAT FIRE SHALL BE THE
DWELLING OF ALL,
AND THEIR PORTION THERE—SCREAMING AND
DEAFNESS. . . .
DO YE VERILY DISBELIEVE IN HIM WHO DID CREATE
THE EARTH, IN TWO DAYS? AND DO YE IM-
AGINE PEERS TO HIM? HE IS THE LORD OF
BOTH WORLDS!
HE SET THE HIGH HILLS OVER THE FACE OF EARTH,
AND BLESSED IT, AND TOLD OUT ITS SUSTE-
NANCE IN FOUR DAYS, FAIRLY, FOR ALL
WHO ASK.
THEN TURNED HE TO THE HEAVEN, WHICH THEN
WAS SMOKE, AND SAID TO IT AND TO THE
EARTH: FREELY OR P E R F O R C E, COME
HITHER!
WE COME FREELY, SAID HEAVEN AND EARTH.
SO, IN TWO DAYS, HE ORDAINED THEM, THE SEVEN
HEAVENS, AND INSPIRED IN EVERY HEAVEN
ITS WORK.
WE DECKED THE NETHER HEAVEN WITH LAMPS,
AND RENDERED IT INVIOLABLE:
AND THAT IS THE MEASURE OF THE MIGHTY, THE
KNOWER. . . .

IS HE WHO CREATETH LIKE UNTO HIM WHO DOTH
NOT CREATE?
YE MEN . . . HEARKEN! VERILY THOSE IDOLS YE IN-
VOKE BESIDES GOD COULD NEVER CREATE
SO MUCH AS A FLY, NOT THOUGH THEY
BANDED THEMSELVES TOGETHER TO DO IT.
EVEN IF A FLY FLY OFF WITH A PARTICLE
FROM THEM, THEY CANNOT SO MUCH AS
GET IT BACK—
SO PUNY ARE SEEKER AND SOUGHT ALIKE.

But men turned against Muhammad and drove him out
of the Sanctuary, and went in a band to Abu Talib, and said:
We'll hear no more.

Abu Talib therefore sent for Muhammad and said: Folk
are fair to thee, and thou unfair to them. They bid thee preach
and do as thou wilt, but only not insult their gods.

I'll not forsake this Cause, Muhammad answered, until
either God maketh it prevail or I perish in it — no, not though
they set the sun on my right hand and the moon on my left.
And he burst out weeping, and rose up to leave. But Abu Talib
called after him: Son of my brother, come back! He took Muhammad's head on his breast, and said: My son, go and say
whatever thou wilt; for I swear I will never deliver thee up.
And Muhammad did as he was Called to do, and recited of the
Koran, though none answered and none believed.

At the time of the Pilgrimage of the Arabs to the Holy
House at Mecca and the fair, Muhammad went out to Mount
Arafat to call the Arabs to God. Some of the wandering Arabs
became Believers. But the Unbelievers of Quraysh came against
them wherever they gathered, with mockings and insults, to
scatter them. A man afterward remembered the Prophet of God
preaching there, a pale man with long black hair, wearing a red
cloak; and the Unbeliever Abu Jahl stood near, heaving clods
at him, and calling to the Arabs not to give up their gods.

The Believers went no more to the Sanctuary now, but
shut themselves in their houses to pray, or went up into the
Mountain. . . . One day Sa'd son of Abu Waqqas went up to
Mount Hira to pray with the Believers, and a certain Qurayshi
was watching how he performed the prayer. When Sa'd prostrated himself, laying his forehead to the ground, the man
picked up a stone, and threw it at Sa'd's backside. Sa'd was patient. But when he prostrated himself again, the fellow took
another stone, and hit him a smarter blow than the first. When
Sa'd had done praying, he seized up a bone, from the skeleton

of a camel that lay by, and struck that Unbeliever on the head a blow that broke his crown. The man fled back bleeding to Mecca.

At first we knew not what words to say in our prayer, a certain Believer related long after; we used to salute God and Gabriel and Michael. But by and by the Prophet of God taught us another way of prayer to use.

Prayer

The Muslim prays thus:

ᢌFirst he performs the Ablution: washing the hands up to the wrists; then rinsing the mouth; then cleansing within the nostrils with water; then washing the face; then washing the right arm, and after that the left arm, to the elbows; then wiping the head with wet hands; then washing the feet up to the ankles, the right first and the left after.

ᢌThis Ablution finished, the Muslim, standing with his hands raised level with the ears, pronounces:

God is the Most Great.

ᢌThen, the hands folded on the breast:

Lo! I turn, being upright, to Him Who did originate the heavens and the earth, nor am I of those who associate aught with Him. And lo! my prayer, my sacrifice, my life, my death are all for God the Lord of both the worlds. He hath no associate in His Godhead: this am I commanded, and I am of those who submit. O God! Thou art King; there is none other god. Thou art my Lord; I am Thy servant. I have wronged my own soul; I do confess my faults. Do Thou protect me against all my faults; none can protect against fault but Thou. And guide me to the best of ways; none guideth to the best but Thou.

*And turn the ways of evil from me; none can turn evil ways
from me but Thou.*

> *IN THE NAME OF GOD THE MERCIFUL THE
> COMPASSIONATE.*
> *PRAISE BE TO GOD THE LORD OF THE
> WORLDS,*
> *THE MERCIFUL, THE COMPASSIONATE,*
> *THE MASTER OF DOOMSDAY.*
> *THEE WE WORSHIP,*
> *THINE THE HELP WE ASK.*
> *LEAD US IN THE STRAIGHT PATH,*
> *THE PATH WHERE GO THE CREATURES OF
> THY FAVOR,*
> *NOT THOSE OF THY DISPLEASURE,*
> *NOR THE ASTRAY.*
> *Amen.*

෫Some portion of the Koran is then recited; and, with the
words: *God is the Most Great,* the head is bent, and the hands
laid on the knees. So bowing, the worshipper pronounces thrice:
Glory to my Great Lord! and, again standing: *God will accept
who praiseth Him, and Thine is the praise, O our Lord.*

෫Then, prostrating himself so that the forehead touches the
ground, he speaks, at least three times, the words: *Glory to my
Lord the Most High!* and, raising his body, remains reverently
kneeling with hands on knees. A second prostration completes
the first Bow of prayer.

෫The worshipper rises, and, having performed a second Bow,
as from the beginning, remains kneeling to pray thus:

> *Praise, and prayer, and good works, are all
> for God. Peace on thee, O Prophet, and God's mercy, and His
> blessings. Peace be on us, and on all God's righteous servants. I
> testify that there is no god but God; and I testify that Muham-
> mad is His servant and His Apostle. O our God! prosper Mu-
> hammad and Muhammad's people, as Thou didst prosper Abra-
> ham and his people, Thou Who art to be praised and magnified.
> O our God! bless Muhammad and Muhammad's people, as Thou*

didst bless Abraham and his people, Thou Who art to be praised and magnified. Make me diligent in prayer, Lord, and my posterity. And accept the prayer. And, Lord, preserve me, and my father, and my mother, and all Believers, on the Day when the Reckoning will be taken.

ع‌Thus ends the prayer. Turning his head to the right, the Believer pronounces:

Peace be with you, and God's Mercy.

And turning his head to the left, he says again:

Peace be with you, and God's Mercy.

He rises, and it is finished.

* * *

It was revealed:

*ESTABLISH PRAYER AT THE TWO ENDS OF THE DAY,
AND IN THE FIRST HOURS OF NIGHT.
THE GOOD YE DO SHALL VOID THE EVIL THAT
YE DO. . . .
BE MODEST IN THY BEARING, AND SUBDUE THY
VOICE, FOR A HARSH VOICE IS THE BRAY OF
AN ASS.
A GOODLY SAYING IS AS A GOODLY TREE: ITS ROOT
STANDS FIRM, ITS BRANCHES ARE IN HEAV-
EN,
IT YIELDS ITS FRUIT IN EVERY SEASON, BY THE
GRACE OF ITS LORD.
GOD COINETH SIMILITUDES FOR MEN TO HEED:
YE MAY LEARN SOMETHING FROM THE CATTLE:
WE GIVE YOU TO DRINK OF THE CONTENT OF
THEIR BELLIES, FROM A PLACE BETWEEN
DUNG AND BLOOD FETCHING PURE MILK,
SWEET FOR ALL TO DRINK.
AND OF THE FRUITS OF PALM AND VINE YE GET
BOTH MADDENING DRINK AND NOURISH-
MENT. A MAN WHO WILL THINK WILL FIND
A MEANING THEREIN. . . .*

HE GIVETH ALL YE ASK OF HIM: IF YE WOULD
    COUNT GOD'S BOUNTIES YE WOULD NEVER
    MAKE THE TALE. HOW UNJUST IS MAN! AND
    HOW UNGRATEFUL! ...
GOD IS THE PARTER OF THE DAWN.
    HE HATH APPOINTED NIGHT TO SHOW HIS
    SILENCE, THE SUN AND MOON TO MARK HIS
    TIME, FOR THAT IS THE SET ORDER OF THE
    MIGHTY, WHO IS THE WISE.
AND HE IT IS WHO SET THE STARS FOR YOU, THAT
    YE MAY FOLLOW YOUR PATH BY THEM
    THROUGH DARKLING LAND AND SEA. ...
HE GIVETH LIFE. AFTER A WHILE HE GIVETH
    DEATH, SOME OF YOU BEING BROUGHT BACK
    TO LIFE'S FIRST, ABJECT STAGE, SO THAT
    AFTER HAVING HAD KNOWLEDGE A MAN
    AGAIN KNOWETH NOTHING.
    GOD IS THE ETERNAL KNOWER. ...
VISION COMPREHENDETH HIM NOT: HE COMPRE-
    HENDETH VISION.
    HE IS THE SUBTLE, THE AWARE. ...
ALL THINGS IN HEAVEN AND EARTH WILL FALL
    PROSTRATE BEFORE GOD AT LAST, WHETH-
    ER THEY WILL OR NO—PROSTRATE AS
    THEIR SHADOWS FALL AT MORNING, AND
    AT EVENING. ...
THERE IS NOT A LIVING BEAST BUT HE DOTH GRASP
    IT BY THE FORELOCK. ...

WE, GOD, BROUGHT YOU INTO BEING.
    THEN WE GAVE YOU SHAPE.
    AND THEN WE BADE ALL ANGELS: BOW DOWN
    BEFORE ADAM! AND THEY BOWED DOWN,
    ALL SAVE IBLIS (WHO IS SATAN). HE WOULD
    NOT BOW.

GOD SAID: WHAT HINDERED THEE, THAT THOU
DIDST NOT BOW DOWN WHEN I BADE THEE?
HE ANSWERED: I AM NOBLER THAN ADAM — THOU
HAST CREATED ME OF FIRE, AND HIM THOU
DIDST CREATE OF MUD.
GOD SAID: THEN GET THEE OUT! THIS IS NO PLACE
FOR THY VAINGLORY, SO BEGONE! THOU
ART DEGRADED.
GRANT ME REPRIEVE UNTIL THE DAY OF RESURREC-
TION, SATAN SAID.
GOD SAID: THOU ART REPRIEVED.
THEN, SAID SATAN, FORASMUCH AS THOU HAST
SENT ME FORTH TO BE A WANDERER, BE-
HOLD! I SHALL LIE IN WAIT FOR MEN AS
THEY WALK IN THE PATH OF THY RIGHT-
EOUSNESS;
I SHALL BESET MEN FROM BEFORE AND BE-
HIND, ON THEIR RIGHT HAND AND THEIR
LEFT: THE MOST OF THEM WILL THANK
THEE LITTLE, THOU WILT FIND.
AND GOD SAID: HENCE, THOU DEGRADED AND
BANISHED THING! I WILL FILL HELL WITH
YOU ALL, WHOEVER SHALL FOLLOW THEE.
ADAM! GOD SAID, DWELL THOU AND THY WIFE IN
THE GARDEN, AND EAT OF WHAT YE WILL.
BUT COME NOT NEAR THIS TREE, WHICH
WOULD BE TRESPASS.
THEN WHISPERED SATAN TO THEM, THAT HE
MIGHT MAKE UNSEEMLY TO THEM WHAT
OF THEIR BODIES HAD NOT APPEARED UN-
SEEMLY TO THEM YET, SAYING: ONLY LEST
YE SHOULD BECOME TWO ANGELS, OR PAR-
TAKE IN IMMORTALITY, HATH YOUR LORD
FORBIDDEN YOU THIS TREE.
SWEARING UNTO THEM: OF A TRUTH I MEAN YOU
GOOD.

SO HE BEGUILED THEM.
BUT WHEN THEY TASTED OF THE TREE, MANI-
FEST TO THEM WAS THEIR SHAME; FAIN
WOULD THEY COVER THEMSELVES WITH
GARDEN LEAVES,
WHEN CAME TO THEM THE CALLING OF THEIR
LORD: DID NOT I FORBID THAT TREE TO
YOU? AND TELL YOU THAT SATAN IS YOUR
DECLARED FOE?
THEY ANSWERED: O OUR LORD! WE HAVE DONE
WRONG AGAINST OURSELVES; AND EXCEPT
THOU FORGIVE US, EXCEPT THOU HAVE
MERCY ON US, WE ARE LOST INDEED.
AND GOD SAID: GO YE FORTH, EACH OF YOU THE
OTHER'S ENEMY.
ON EARTH YE SHALL HAVE HABITATION, AND
PROVISION FOR A WHILE.
GOD SAID: THERE SHALL YE LIVE
AND THERE TOO SHALL YE DIE
AND THENCE SHALL YE BE RAISED.

Pray to thy Lord, Muhammad, said the men of Mecca, that
He move back the mountains that hem us in, and widen the
good land for us, and thread it with rivers like the lands of
Syria and Iraq; or that He make our departed fathers rise from
the dead, best of all that He send old Qusay, Kilab's son, who
never told a lie, so that we may ask whether what thou tellest
us is true or false. If they declare thee true, we will believe in
thee.

DO THEY WAIT FOR NOTHING LESS THAN THAT
ANGELS VISIT THEM?
OR THY LORD COME? OR A MIRACLE FROM HIM?
IN THE DAY WHEN COMETH A MIRACLE FROM THY
LORD, FAITH AVAILS NOTHING TO A SOUL
THAT HAD NO FAITH BEFORE. . . .

AND MIRACLES REST WITH GOD ALONE — I AM ONLY A MAN, WARNING YOU.

NEVER THERE CAME A PROPHET BUT MEN MOCKED HIM.

WHEN WE SENT NOAH TO HIS PEOPLE, SAYING: I GIVE YOU PLAIN WARNING:

SERVE NONE BUT GOD; I FEAR FOR YOU THE RE-TRIBUTION OF A DAY OF PAIN,

THE UNBELIEVING GREAT MEN OF HIS PEOPLE SAID: WE SEE IN THEE ONLY A MAN LIKE OUR-SELVES; AND WE OBSERVE THAT NONE FOL-LOW THEE BUT THE MEANEST OF US, THE SILLY POOR.

WHEN NOAH BEGAN TO BUILD THE SHIP, THE GREAT MEN OF HIS PEOPLE MOCKED HIM AS THEY PASSED BY,

UNTIL OUR COMMAND WENT FORTH, AND THE WATERS BOILED FROM THEIR HOLLOW. . . .

WHEN WENT FORTH THE WORD: O EARTH! SWAL-LOW DOWN THY WATER, AND O CLOUDY HEAVEN! BE CLEAR!

AND THE QUELLED WATERS SANK, THE COMMAND-MENT BEING FULFILLED, AND THE SHIP CAME TO REST.

THEN IT WAS SAID: SO MUCH FOR SINNERS.

EVEN THUS IN EVERY CITY WE HAVE MADE ITS GREAT MEN TO BE ITS WICKED MEN, TO CONSPIRE IN EVIL.

YET IS IT AGAINST THEIR OWN SOULS THEY CONSPIRE, LITTLE AS THEY KNOW IT.

* * *

The Quraysh dared not attack the Prophet, on account of
Abu Talib, but they seized on the humbler and powerless among
the Believers, and beat them. As for the well-born on whom they
ventured no violence, these they insulted, called them liars and
laughed at them, spat in their faces when they met.

At last, certain Believers, coming to the Prophet, said:
We can bear this tribulation no more; and we fear lest we do
some deed or speak some word which shall offend God. Let us
depart, and go to some other land. The Prophet gave them leave.
Go into Abyssinia, he said, for its people are Christians and
Scripture folk — nearer like True Believers than idolaters are.

Some of the Prophet's company went accordingly into
Abyssinia. He and Abu Bakr, Omar, Ali and others stayed on in
Mecca. This exodus was called the First Flight; but the other,
the Flight to Madina after Abu Talib's death, which is called
the Great Flight of the Prophet, was for all the Believers. Those
who now fled were seventy persons, Ja'far son of Abu Talib, and
certain others, taking their wives with them.

When the Quraysh heard of it, they sent ambassadors to
demand of the Abyssinian ruler, the Negus, that he deliver up
all these people to be brought back to Mecca. And the Negus
sent to summon them to his presence.

What will ye say to the man when ye come before him?
said one to another.

We shall tell what we know, by God! and what our
Apostle hath enjoined on us, and tide what may!

To the audience the Negus had convened his bishops, and
the bishops had spread their books round about him. What is
this religion, he made inquiry of the Believers, for which ye
have forsaken your own folk, yet enter not for all that into my
religion, nor into the faith of any other church?

Ja'far son of Abu Talib made answer: O King! We were
once barbarians — worshipping idols, eating carrion, given to
lewdness, cutting the ties of kinship, wronging our neighbors,
the strong among us devouring the weak; and in this state did

we continue until God sent us an Apostle of our own, a man whose lineage we knew, and knew him truthful, faithful, chaste. God sent him to call us to Himself, that we should declare His Unity and worship Him, putting away the stones and idols we and our fathers used to worship along with Him. And our Apostle bade us be true, and faithful in trusts, to honor all ties of kinship and be good neighbors, to abstain from forbidden things and from blood. He forbade us lewdness and deceit, our devouring of orphans' wealth and our slandering of chaste women. He bade us worship God alone, setting naught else beside Him, and enjoined on us prayer, and alms, and fasting. So we trusted and believed in him, and accepted the revelation he brought from God; we gave up what was forbidden us; we enjoyed what was permitted us. It was for this that our people turned on us, to persecute and confine us and part us from our faith. Wherefore we came away to this thy land, preferring thee above all others to be our protector. And now, O King! we beseech that we may suffer no tyranny in thy presence.

Hast with thee aught of what thy Prophet brought from God? the Negus asked.

Ay! said Ja'far.

Let us hear it, said the Negus.

And Ja'far recited the Chapter of Mary:

*A MENTION OF THE MERCY OF THY LORD UPON HIS
    SERVANT ZACHARIAH. . . .
AND MAKE MENTION OF MARY IN THE SCIPTURE,
    WHEN SHE HAD WITHDRAWN FROM HER
    PEOPLE INTO A CHAMBER LOOKING TO-
    WARD THE EAST,
AND VEILED HERSELF FROM THEM.
    THEN SENT WE UNTO HER OUR SPIRIT: AND IT
    APPEARED TO HER IN THE LIKENESS OF A
    MAN OF HANDSOME FIGURE.
I SEEK REFUGE FROM THEE IN THE BENEFICENT,
    SAID MARY, IF THOU FEAREST GOD!*

*HE SAID: I AM ONLY A MESSENGER FROM THY LORD,
TO BRING THEE A GIFT, A FAULTLESS SON.
HOW SHOULD I HAVE A SON, SAID MARY, WHEN NO
MORTAL MAN HATH TOUCHED ME? I HAVE
NOT BEEN UNCHASTE.
BUT HE SAID: EVEN SO! THY LORD SAITH: THAT IS
EASY FOR ME AND IT IS EASY TO MAKE
HIM AS A SIGN AND MERCY UNTO MEN FROM
US. IT IS A THING ORDAINED.
AND SHE CONCEIVED A SON.
AND SHE WITHDREW WITH HIM TO A PLACE
REMOTE,
AND THE THROES OF CHILDBIRTH DROVE HER TO
THE TRUNK OF A PALM; AND SHE SAID: AH,
WOULD THAT I HAD DIED ERE THIS, AND
HAD BECOME A THING GONE AND FORGOT-
TEN.
THEN CRIED A VOICE UNTO HER FROM THE GROUND
BENEATH: GRIEVE NOT! FOR THY LORD
HATH SET A STREAM TO FLOW BENEATH
THEE;
SHAKE THE PALM-TREE STEM TOWARD THEE, RIPE
DATES SHALL DROP FOR THEE;
EAT, DRINK, AND BE COMFORTED. AND IF THOU
SEEST ANY MORTAL, SAY: I HAVE UNDER-
TAKEN A FAST TO THE BENEFICENT, AND
MAY NOT SPEAK TO ANY MAN THIS DAY.
AND SHE BROUGHT THE CHILD TO HER OWN PEO-
PLE, BEARING HIM IN HER ARMS.
THEY SAID: MARY! WHAT STRANGE THING
BRINGEST THOU?
O THOU SISTER OF AARON! THY FATHER WAS NO
EVIL-LIVING MAN, NOR THY MOTHER A
WHORE!
BUT MARY ONLY POINTED TO THE BABE.*

THEY SAID: HOW CAN WE TALK WITH A CHILD
IN THE CRADLE?
BUT THE CHILD SPAKE: BEHOLD GOD'S SERVANT!
AND GOD HATH GIVEN ME SCRIPTURE, AND
HATH APPOINTED ME TO BE A PROPHET,
AND BLESSED ME WHERESOEVER I MAY BE, AND
HATH ENJOINED ON ME TO PRAY AND GIVE
SO LONG AS I SHALL LIVE:
AND MADE ME DUTIFUL TO HER WHO BARE ME,
NOT ARROGANT AND UNBLEST.
PEACE BE ON ME THIS DAY OF MY BIRTH, AND ON
THE DAY OF MY DEATH, AND THE DAY I
SHALL BE RAISED ALIVE!
SUCH WAS JESUS, MARY'S SON.

Hearing Ja'far recite thus to them from the Koran, the Negus wept till his beard was wetted with his tears; and his bishops wept till the tears ran down upon their books. Verily! said the Negus to the Believers, this and what Moses brought emanate from one Lamp. Go in peace; I will not let them attack you, nor even dream of so doing.

Then from every tribe or kindred in Mecca were chosen two men; and these, assembling in the Sanctuary, composed an agreement: that they would neither speak to the followers of Muhammad, nor ask their women in marriage, nor give them women in marriage, nor buy of them nor sell to them. This writ they signed, taking all citizens of Mecca to witness.

When seven years had passed since Muhammad was called to be a prophet, Khadija his wife and Abu Talib his uncle died, both in the one year. Ali son of Abu Talib came to the Prophet.

Apostle of God, thine uncle is dead, and in Unbelief, he said.

Muhammad wept. O Ali! go, wash him, and bury him,

he said. But he said not a word of praying for him; nor did he
come to the shrouding, nor to the burial.

One day the Prophet went into the Sanctuary to pray. As
he bowed his face to earth, certain Unbelievers took filthy mud
and tossed it at his head. Muhammad wore his hair long to his
shoulders; and with his hair thus fouled, his head and face
were hardly to be known. He started up, and went to his house;
and one of his daughters wiped his head, weeping.

They would never have dared so while Abu Talib was
still alive, Muhammad said. And he departed from the city
three days' journey to Taif to seek harbor. Long after, a man
of Taif remembered him, standing on a high place, leaning like
a soothsayer on his staff, reciting to the men of Taif the Chapter
of the Comer by Night:

BY HEAVEN! AND BY WHAT COMETH TO THE DOOR
    BY NIGHT!
HOW MAY I TELL WHAT IT IS, THAT COMETH TO
    THE DOOR BY NIGHT?
THAT PIERCING STAR!
THERE IS NO HUMAN SOUL BUT HATH A KEEPER
    APPOINTED IT.
LET MAN CONSIDER OF WHAT HE IS CREATED:
OF A JET OF FLUID
COMING FROM A PLACE BETWEEN BACK AND RIBS.

AND GOD VERILY HATH POWER TO BRING MAN
    BACK TO LIVE AGAIN,
ON THAT DAY WHEN THE SECRET SHALL BE PUB-
    LISHED,
AND MAN SHALL HAVE NO MIGHT, NOR ANY TO
    HELP HIM.

BY HEAVEN, AND ITS WATER THAT COMETH AGAIN!
BY THE EARTH THAT GAPES FOR IT!

THIS WORD IS THE LAST,
AND NO LIGHT WORD.
 MANKIND CONSPIRES;
 I TOO CONSPIRE.

YET DEAL SLOWLY WITH SUCH AS BELIEVE NOT:
FOR A LITTLE SPACE LET THEM BE.

If thou art a prophet of God, demanded one of the shaykhs of Taif, how come thou needest protection of us?

Why did not God call one of the shaykhs of Mecca to be His prophet? inquired another.

And they called to their young men: Chase this madman of Quraysh out of town!

And weary as he was, so that he could go no farther, they drove him and stoned him beyond the bounds. The sun was burning hot; and Muhammad, coming to the gate of a vineyard which belonged to two kinsmen of his, went into the vineyard and sat him down on the edge of a built pool. The two his kinsmen, following, looked in and saw him sitting at the water's edge, covered with dust.

Thou seest the man yonder by the pool? said one of them to his slave who was with them. Wizard he may be, and possessed of a genie; yet is he our kinsman still — give him some grapes.

So the slave took Muhammad some grapes; and the Prophet ate, and went on his way. When he drew near to Mecca, he halted a mile outside the town and passed that night in prayer, and in reciting from the Koran.

BY THE EARLY MORNING
AND BY THE DARKENING NIGHT!
THY LORD HATH NOT FORSAKEN THEE, NOR DOTH
      HE HATE THEE.
THE LATTER PORTION SHALL BE BETTER FOR THEE
      THAN THE FORMER;

*AND SOON NOW SHALL THY LORD GIVE UNTO
THEE, AND THOU BE WELL PLEASED.*
*DID HE NOT FIND THEE AN ORPHAN, AND SHELTER
THEE?*
DID HE NOT FIND THEE ASTRAY, AND LEAD THEE?
*DID HE NOT FIND THEE POOR, AND MAKE THEE
RICH?*
THEN . . . .
TELL OF THE GOODNESS OF THY LORD.

It is related that Muhammad overheard the talk of genii
(who are elemental spirits) in that place:

*IT WAS REVEALED THAT A COMPANY OF GENII
WERE LISTENING. AND THEY SPOKE: MAR-
VELLOUS IS THIS KORAN WHICH WE DO
HEAR,*
*WHICH GUIDETH UNTO RIGHTEOUSNESS. THERE-
FORE WE DO BELIEVE IN IT, BELIEVING
HENCEFORTH THERE IS NONE OTHER GOD
BESIDE OUR LORD. . . .*
*WHEN LATE WE SOUGHT THE HEAVEN, WE FOUND
IT MANNED WITH WARDS OF FORCE, AND
METEORS;*
*ONCE WE MIGHT SIT IN CERTAIN SEATS THEREIN
AND LISTEN, BUT NOW A LISTENER FINDETH
A FLAME IN WAIT FOR HIM:*
*WHETHER HARM IS BODED TO THE DWELLERS
UPON EARTH WE KNOW NOT, OR WHETHER
THE LORD INTENDETH THEM SOME EVAN-
GEL. . . .*
*WE KNOW THAT WE CANNOT ESCAPE GOD IN THE
EARTH, NOR IN ANY FLIGHT;*
*AND HEARING THIS EVANGEL, WE HAVE BELIEVED,
FOR WHOSO BELIEVETH IN HIS LORD CAN
FEAR NO MORE, NEITHER LOSS NOR ARREST.*

* * *

When Pilgrimage time came round, Muhammad preached to the clans of Kinda, Kalb, and Hanifa.

One year, a man of Kinda later told, when I was a child, I went on the Pilgrimage to Mecca with my father. When we stopped for the fair at Mina, I saw a man with long hair and a beautiful face, standing before us shaykhly, uttering noble speech, that went to the hearts of men, offering his religion, calling us to God and bidding us turn from our idols. Behind him came a man long-bearded and black-haired, squint-eyed, with an Aden cloak over his shoulders, shouting: Keep away from this fellow! he is possessed of a genie! — he is a liar! — do not listen! — be faithful to your religion!

Who is that man? I asked my father.

That is the Qurayshi prophet Muhammad son of Abdallah son of Abd al-Muttalib, my father told me. He is calling the Arabs to his own religion.

Who is that other man? I asked then.

That is his uncle, Abu Lahab, my father answered; he is telling the Arabs that Muhammad is a cheat.

HELL LIES AHEAD FOR HIM!
  HE SHALL BE GIVEN TO DRINK A FESTER-
    ING WATER
  WHICH HE MUST SIP, BUT CAN HARDLY SWAL-
    LOW.
  FROM EVERY SIDE SHALL HE KNOW THE
    COMING-ON OF DEATH, WHILE YET HE
    CANNOT DIE —
A FIERCE DOOM LIES AHEAD FOR HIM!

On this Pilgrimage came six men of Clan Khazraj from Madina, a city of that country where dwelt the two clans of Aws and Khazraj. The villages round about it were inhabited by Jews. One time and another the clansmen of Aws and Khazraj had tried to seize these villages, and failed, the Jews having fortified them with towers. Now these Jews, by their reading in the Pentateuch, knew that a Prophet was to come; but they believed he would come out of the tribe of Israel, from Moses' kindred.

The Prophet visited the six men of Madina, and called them to Islam, and recited of the Koran to them:

HIS WORD IS TRUTH; AND HIS SHALL THE KING-DOM BE ON THE DAY WHEN THE TRUMPET IS BLOWN!

HE IS THE KNOWER OF THE SEEN AND THE UNSEEN, HE! THE WISE, THE ALL-AWARE.

TO ABRAHAM DID WE SHOW THE KINGDOMS OF HEAVEN AND EARTH, FOR HIS CONFIRMING.

NIGHT DARKENED OVER HIM; AND HE BEHELD A STAR, AND SAID: THIS STAR SHALL BE MY LORD.

BUT THE STAR SANK TO ITS SETTING, AND ABRA-HAM SAID: I CANNOT LOVE A THING WHICH SETTETH.

THEN HE BEHELD THE RISING MOON, AND SAID: THIS MOON SHALL BE MY LORD.

BUT THE MOON SANK TO ITS SETTING, AND ABRA-HAM SAID: LET MY LORD GUIDE ME, OR SURELY SHALL I BE ONE AMONG THE REST ASTRAY.

LAST HE BEHELD THE RISING SUN, AND CRIED: THIS SHALL BE MY LORD, FOR THIS IS GREATER THAN ALL OTHER THINGS.

BUT THE SUN ALSO SANK TO ITS SETTING. THEN ABRAHAM CRIED: O MY PEOPLE! NOW AM I FREED FROM PUTTING THINGS TO BE EQUAL WITH GOD, AS YE DO.

BEHOLD! I HAVE TURNED MY FACE TOWARD HIM WHO DID CREATE THESE HEAVENS AND THIS EARTH: NOW AM I OF SINGLE HEART, AND DELIVERED FROM MINE IDOLATRY. . . .

*WE BESTOWED ON HIM ISAAC AND JACOB; EACH
    DID WE GUIDE; AND NOAH DID WE GUIDE
    AFORETIME; AND OF HIS SEED DAVID AND
    SOLOMON, JOB, MOSES, AND AARON,*
*ZACHARIAH AND JOHN, JESUS AND ELIAS — GOOD
    WERE ALL THESE,
    AND ISHMAEL AND ELISHA AND JONAS AND
    LOT.
    EACH OF THESE DID WE PREFER OVER OUR
    OTHER CREATURES:*
THEY WERE OUR CHOSEN ONES. . . .
*WE INSPIRED IN THEM: FOLLOW ABRAHAM'S FAITH,
    THAT UPRIGHT MAN.*

*CONSIDER LOT! WHO SAID TO HIS PEOPLE: SURELY
    YE ARE GUILTY OF LEWDNESS THE LIKE OF
    WHICH NO NATION OF THE WORLD BEFORE
    YE DID,*
*COPULATING MALE WITH MALE, BESETTING THE
    HIGHWAY, ASSEMBLING FOR ABOMINATIONS.*
*AND NO REPLY THEY GAVE HIM, EXCEPT: BRING
    ON US GOD'S DOOM, THEN, IF THOU ART IN
    THE RIGHT.*
*WHEN OUR MESSENGERS CAME TO LOT, HE WAS
    TROUBLED FOR HIS HOUSEHOLD'S SAKE,
    HAVING NO POWER TO SAVE THEM. BUT
    THE ANGELS SAID: FEAR NOT, NOR GRIEVE;
    WE SHALL DELIVER THEE AND THY HOUSE,
    EXCEPT THY WIFE, WHO MUST BE AMONG
    THOSE WHO SHALL NOT LEAVE THIS PLACE:*
*WE ARE ABOUT TO BRING DOWN UPON THE PEOPLE
    OF THIS CITY A FURY FROM HEAVEN FOR
    THEIR TRANSGRESSIONS.*
*THEN, AT THE RISING OF THE SUN, A RUMBLING
    RAN UPON THEM; AND WE CONFOUNDED
    THEM WITH A RAIN OF FIERY CLAY.*

*AND OF THAT FURY LEFT WE A MONUMENT FOR
    UNDERSTANDING MEN —
IT STANDS UPON A HIGHWAY TRAVELLED TO THIS
    DAY.*

*HOW MANY A TOWN HAVE WE DESTROYED IN ITS
    SIN! WALLS FALLEN UPON FALLEN ROOFS —
A DESERTED WELL — A GAUNT TOWER!*

*THERE IS A DAY WHEN WE RAISE IN EVERY NATION
    A WITNESS AGAINST THEM FROM AMONG
    THEMSELVES.
AND THEE, MUHAMMAD, DO WE BRING TO WITNESS
    AGAINST THESE.
SAY: I SAY NOT UNTO YOU THAT I BRING GOD'S
    TREASURE WITH ME, NOR THAT I HAVE
    KNOWLEDGE OF THE UNSEEN; NOR SAY I
    UNTO YOU THAT I AM AN ANGEL. I ONLY
    FOLLOW WHAT IS INSPIRED IN ME.*

And the men of Madina believed, and made the Submission
to God, and were Muslims. Then Muhammad asked them if
they would give him harbor. Apostle of God, they answered, let
us go back to Madina, and tell our Clan of thee and thy religion;
and then another year thou shalt come home with us. It will be
more honorable to thee so.

They departed; and the Prophet stayed. In Madina they
told the clansmen of Aws and Khazraj of the religion of Islam,
repeating as much as they had learned of the Koran. This Muhammad, said the six who came from Pilgrimage, is that Prophet whose name is ever in the mouth of the Jews, for whom
they hope; and we counsel you to be beforehand with them, and
bring him here amongst yourselves.

The Faith, the Koran, and the Prophet's words seemed
good to the townsmen; and many were converted straightway.
At the time of Pilgrimage next year these gathered together,

and chose as envoys the same six men, joining to them other six; and these they instructed: Go, take an oath of loyalty to Muhammad, and bring him back with you; we are his men, our bodies and our goods.

When the twelve reached Mecca, they pitched their tents on the hill of Aqaba, near Mina; and Muhammad, coming there, took their oath: to worship God alone, to be modest, not to put to death their girl-children, not to lie, not to disobey God's Prophet but to guard him as their own bodies. Muhammad sent back with them to Madina one Mus'ab, who could recite all of the Koran as much as had yet been revealed, and knew the rites of Islam. In Madina, Mus'ab lodged in the house of a certain As'ad, who brought him every day to some fenced garden where men might come and hear him, and make the Submission.

Greatest among the fenced gardens of Madina was the close of the Children of Abd al-Ashhal, head of which house was Sa'd son of Mu'ad. This Sa'd one day seeing a great company of men gathered in his close, took a spear in his hand and went in, and found As'ad sitting beside Mus'ab in the middle of a great ring of people. At sight of Sa'd they stood up.

Get this fellow out of the close, and quietly, if thou hast a mind to turn death away from him and thee, said Sa'd to As'ad.

We will go, he answered. But what would it harm thee to listen to him a little?

Speak then, said Sa'd. So Mus'ab recited the Chapter: *HAVE WE NOT CAUSED THY BOSOM TO DILATE?*

Sa'd sat down. Speak it again! he said. So Mus'ab recited it a second time; and at the second hearing Sa'd believed. He turned about and called to all the kinsmen of Ashhal to gather near him, and thus spoke: Who am I, think ye?

A noble of our Clan, they answered; a well-considered man; a trusty man; our shaykh.

Hark ye then, said Sa'd: I have made up my mind to follow this religion, a thing I should surely not have done were it not the true religion. And with any man who will not follow this religion I will have no more to do.

And that very day the Children of Abd al-Ashhal became Believers, to the last man. Soon there was no kindred in Madina but what some kinsmen were Believers, save Aws; and of that clan men only believed after the Prophet's coming to Madina, after the battles of Badr and Uhud and the War of the Dyke.

At the year's end Mus'ab returned to Mecca to tell these things to the Prophet of God. Then Muhammad ordered his Companions to depart to Madina, one by one and two by two, and himself stayed on till the beginning of the month of First Rabi, waiting for the command of God. Abu Bakr and Ali only were left with him.

The Flight

Now THE QURAYSH held council at the Meeting House, and many spoke.

The man must die, said Abu Jahl at last. Choose we one from each kindred of Quraysh, and let them fall on and strike together. Then the Hashimites cannot take up blood-feud against any one kindred. Nor can they fight us all: they'll stoop perforce to take blood-money.

And this seemed good. The men were named; and when night darkened they took their posts about the Prophet's house and waited either for a chance of entry or for his coming out. Ali was in the house that night.

Muhammad had with him certain sums of money, lodged there by Unbelievers who trusted his honesty. Ali, said he, the time is come for me to go; but thou must stay. I charge thee with these moneys: return them to those who left them here. And now put on my cloak, and lie down on my bed. Fear not, none will harm thee.

So black was that night that the Prophet got away unseen. He stole to Abu Bakr's house. God bids me go now, he said, as soon as he was in.

May I come with thee, Prophet of God? said Abu Bakr.

Ay, thou shalt be with me, answered he.

Then Abu Bakr took five thousand pieces of silver, instructed his son Abdallah, his daughter Asma, and his freedman as to what they must do, and stole away, afoot and warily, with Muhammad.

The killers still watched the Prophet's house. Presently some man they knew not in the dark passed by.

Muhammad's away! said he, and was gone. They went up and peered through a crack in the house door. There, by a bed, a lamp was burning; and there lay the person of a man with a green mantle over him.

Nay, Muhammad's there, and sleeping still; we can wait till he comes out, they said.

Day dawned at last; the door was thrown open, and there was Ali, alone. They knew they had been tricked. When the chiefs of Quraysh were informed, they sent out spies to hunt the Prophet down, offering one hundred camels reward to any who should bring him back to Mecca, dead or alive. But the Prophet and Abu Bakr were lying hid in a cavern of the hills, three miles from town on the side that lay away from the Madina road. At nightfall, Abu Bakr's daughter Asma and his freedman stole to the Cave, and took them food, and told them of the doings of Quraysh. For three days, until the chase was given up, they waited in that cavern. Once the riders who hunted them passed by the mouth of it; but the way in was exceeding narrow, and lying in the mouth they saw a dove's nest with her eggs, and a spider's web stretched across; and so rode by.

Then Abu Bakr bade Asma bring up greater provision that night, and tell his man to lead up the camels for their riding, and the guide. So on the fourth night they issued from the Cave, and mounted their beasts, and set forward for Madina by an untravelled road.

And it was revealed from God: *SURELY HE WHO GAVE THEE THE KORAN TO BE THY LAW WILL BRING THEE HOME AGAIN.*

THE FIGHT FOR LIFE

LOSE TO MADINA the Prophet halted at Quba, and sat down in the shade upon a little hill. When the tidings ran that he was come, the townsmen went out to where he was; and on the Friday he spoke a sermon and led prayer, then mounted his camel. Every man reached for the Prophet's rein, crying: Come to my house! a house of plenty! defense enough and room enough!

Nay, leave the rein on the camel's neck; she knoweth where she is to halt, the Prophet said. And the camel went on till she came to the place where the Mosque stands at this day, and there knelt down, and the Prophet lighted off her. The piece of ground belonged to two orphans; and the Prophet bought the ground where the beast had knelt to build a yard for prayers (which was the first Mosque of Islam) in that place; and they built a hut for the Apostle of God at the side of the Mosque.

AISHA

At the time of the Prophet's coming to Madina, Aisha, daughter of Abu Bakr (whom he had married but not taken to live with him), was nine years old. He bade Abu Bakr send for his household to come to Madina; Abu Bakr sent his son Abdallah to fetch them. Aisha was brought to the Prophet's house.

When the Apostle of God married me, Aisha related after-wards, I was six; when he brought me to live with him I was nine, still playing with other little girls. He came to my room one day when I had been playing with my dolls and had set them on a cushion with a curtain drawn before them. The wind presently blowing aside the curtain, the Prophet saw them and asked me: What is that?

Those are my dolls, I said.

And what is that other thing I see amongst them?

A horse.

And what are those things on either side of it? he asked.

Its wings.

Do horses have wings then? the Prophet inquired.

Hast thou not heard? Solomon had winged horses! I said.

And the Prophet laughed so heartily that I could see all his back teeth.

I never felt jealous of any of the Prophet's other wives, only of Khadija, though she was dead even when I was first married; and I once exclaimed to him: It seems there is no woman in the world beside Khadija! Another time, Khadija's sister Hala knocked at our door, in a manner that reminded the Prophet of Khadija's knocking, and he said: That must be Hala by her knock.

The saying put me in such a fury of jealousy that I cried out: How thou rememberest an old woman, an old Qurayshi hag without a tooth in her head, a used-up thing, for all that God hath given thee a better in her place!

The Apostle of God was so angry that the hair bristled on his brow. By God! he said, the Most High hath never given me a better than she was: she believed in me when all the world were Unbelievers, and spoke for me when all denied, and helped me with her wealth when all the rest avoided me; and God gave me children by her.

Never again did I speak a mean word of Khadija.

Apostle of God, how dost thou love me? I asked him once. He answered: As the knot in the cord. I used to say at certain after times: How is the knot in the cord? and he would answer: As it always was.

Aisha, he said to me, if thou wouldst be like me, and wouldst be bound to me forever, then so live in this world that such provision as a journeying horseman taketh may suffice thee: never hoard up food for tomorrow, never call a dress old so long as it be unpatched; and handle money gingerly.

For this world is under curse, the Prophet said, and accursed are all things in the world save the remembrance of God, and such things as help us to that remembrance.

PRAYER KEEPETH A MAN FROM LEWDNESS AND INIQUITY: BUT THE CONSTANT REMEMBRANCE OF GOD IS SURELY BEST OF ALL.

THE EAST AND THE WEST BELONG TO GOD: AND WHITHERSOEVER YE TURN THERE IS GOD'S FACE.

GOD!

THERE IS NO GOD BUT HE, THE LIVING, THE PERSISTING.

NEITHER SLUMBER NOR SLEEP OVERTAKETH HIM.

WHATEVER IS IN THE HEAVENS, WHATEVER IS IN THE EARTH, IS HIS. AND WHO MAY INTERCEDE WITH HIM BUT BY HIS LEAVE?

HE KNOWETH WHAT IS IN MEN'S HANDS, AND WHAT LIETH BEHIND THEIR BACKS: WHILE THEY CANNOT COMPREHEND ANY PART OF WHAT HE KNOWETH SAVE BY HIS WILLING THEM TO COMPREHEND IT.

WIDE IS HIS THRONE OVER THE HEAVENS AND THE EARTH, NOR IS HE EVER WEARY OF PRESERVING THEM.

*FOR HE IS THE SUBLIME,
AND THE TREMENDOUS!*

*   *   *

In that year of the Flight of the Prophet, God revealed that it should be four Bows of prayer for the first and the second prayer, and for the prayer before sleep; and two Bows, as it had always been, for the morning prayer and the traveller's prayer.

When Abu Bakr prayed by night, he used to recite from the Koran in a low voice, but Omar in a loud strong voice. The Prophet asked Abu Bakr why he did as he did.

He unto Whom I speak will hear, said Abu Bakr.

And why, Omar, dost thou recite at the top of thy voice? To wake the drowsy up, and drive the devil away! said Omar.

* * *

WE HAVE BEHELD THE TURNING OF THY FACE TO-WARD HEAVEN.

AND NOW, LO! WE WILL TURN THEE TOWARD A QIBLA, A DIRECTION, WHICH IS DEAR TO THEE. SO TURN THY FACE TOWARD THE IN-VIOLABLE MOSQUE AT MECCA, AND YE, BE-LIEVERS, WHERESOEVER YE MAY BE, TURN YOUR FACES TOWARD THAT PLACE.

O YE WHO BELIEVE! WHEN THE CALL IS HEARD FOR PRAYER ON THE DAY OF CONGREGATION, HASTEN TO THE REMEMBRANCE OF GOD, AND LEAVE YOUR TRADING,

AND WHEN THE PRAYER IS ENDED, THEN DISPERSE, AND SEEK SOMETHING OF GOD'S BOUNTY.

AND KEEP GOD MUCH IN YOUR REMEMBRANCE, IF YE WOULD PROSPER.

MEN WHEN THEY SPY SOME CHANCE OF TRADE OR PASTIME BREAK AWAY FROM GOD'S REMEM-BRANCE TO THAT, AND LEAVE THEE, MU-HAMMAD, STANDING.

SAY TO THEM: WHAT GOD HATH IS BETTER THAN PASTIME, BETTER THAN ANY MER-CHANDISE.

One day a company of people sitting with the Prophet begged him to tell them a story.

Once upon a time, he said, there were three men, and these three men were wayfaring; and when the night came on they entered for shelter into a certain cavern. But while they lay asleep there came a boulder rolling down the mountainside, and closed fast the mouth of the cave. We shall never escape from this place, cried those men one to another, except we let our selfless deeds plead for us before God.

So the first man began: In time gone by, when I had a father and a mother, I had no worldly goods but only a single goat. Her milk I used to give to them; and every day I cut a bundle of firewood for sale, and with my winning bought food for the living of my parents and myself. One night it was late when I came home; and ere I could milk my goat, that I might steep the food in her milk, they fell asleep both. So I stood and waited, with the bowl of sop in my hand, though never a scrap had crossed my lips that day, till morning came, and they awoke. And then only, after they had eaten, did I sit down at last. And, O Lord! if this is truth I tell, send down deliverance to us; come to our help!

Thereupon, said the Prophet, the rock moved — a very little — and a tiny opening shone. Whereat the second man began: I knew a beautiful blind girl once; and deep in love with her was I. She would not listen to me. So I got together a hundred and twenty pieces of gold, and sent them to her, and promised her that she should keep all if she would lie with me one single night. She came to me. But God's fear seized on my heart; and I turned away my face, and bade her keep the money and depart. And O God! if this is truth I tell, send down deliverance to us; come to our help!

Then, said the Prophet, the rock moved again — a little farther — the chink was wider; but still they could not win out. So the third man began: I hired some laborers once to work for me; and when their work was done they took their wages and went, all save one man, who departed ere I might give him his

hire. With the money which he should have had I bought a ewe.
Next year she lambed, and there were two. The year after there
were four, till in few years I had a flock. When several years
were gone by, that laborer returned, and asked me for his former
hire. Go, take the sheep yonder, I told him, for all of them are
yours. He thought I mocked him; but I swore to him that it was
true, and so he drove away that whole flock. And O God! if this
is truth I tell, send down deliverance to us; come to our help!

Scarce had that third man finished his tale, the Prophet
said, than the rock moved clear away from the mouth of the cave,
and let those travellers three come forth.

THE READERS OF THE KORAN

In Madina men used to go at nightfall to the house of one
who could teach them, and pass the night in getting by heart
Chapters of the Koran. At dawn, the stronger ones would go
forth to gather firewood and draw water, and the richer ones
would sometimes buy a sheep and dress it and leave it hanging
ready in the Prophet's yard.

DISTRESS

But sometimes Muhammad would go to the room of one
or the other of his wives, Sawda, widow of the poor Believer
Sakran, whom he had married after Khadija's death, or Aisha,
and ask: Is there anything to eat? And the answer might be: No.

Then I fast today, he would say.

I am not like you, he said to his Companions once: I pass
the night with my Lord, and He giveth me food and drink.

We used to be as long as forty days on end and never lit
a fire, in those times, Aisha said afterwards.

What did ye live on? people asked.

Water and dates, she said.

For hunger the Prophet used to bind a stone tight over his stomach. I have seen the day, related the Companion Abu Hurayra long after, when I would be lying in a faint on the ground, halfway between the Prophet's pulpit and Aisha's door, and the people passing by setting their feet on my neck because they thought I was possessed of an evil spirit; and all the time it was plain hunger.

It was in the first year of the Flight that Muhammad gave his daughter Fatima in marriage to his cousin Ali son of Abu Talib. All the dowry he gave her was a bed woven of twisted palm leaves, a leathern pillow stuffed with palm fiber, an earthen pot, a waterskin, and a basket of raisins and dates.

One day, going to visit her, he found her dejected, and asked her why this was. It is three days now, she answered, that we have been without food in the house. And she fainted. O God! preserve her from famine! Muhammad cried.

And Muhammad sent out bands.

When the Apostle of God came to Madina, related the Companion Sa'd son of Abu Waqqas, the Juhayna clansmen (through whose country the Mecca trade road ran) came to him and said: Thou hast settled in our country, so give us a covenant that we may come to thee and take thee for our leader. Accordingly the Prophet gave them a covenant; and the Juhayna became Muslims.

Then in the Month of Rajab the Apostle of God sent us out from Madina, something under a hundred of us, and bade us fall upon a kindred of Kinana who dwelt hard by the Juhayna country. And so we did; but they were too many for us, and we took refuge with the Juhayna, and they gave us harbor. But they asked us: How come ye to fight in this the sacred Month of Truce?

We only fight in the sacred Month, we said, against them who did drive us out of our own.

Then we consulted. Some said: Let us go back to the Prophet of God and tell him how it fell out; and others said: Let us stay here where we are. But I, and some with me, said: Rather let us lie in wait for the caravan of the Mecca Quraysh, and cut it off.

But the first party went back to the Prophet and told him what had befallen. He rose up, his face red with anger, and said: What! did ye go from me as one company and come ye back divided? Division it is which did ruin them who were before ye. I will set one man over ye all, and not the best of ye, but one who can best brook hunger and thirst.

It was Abdallah son of Jahsh he set over us; that Abdallah was the first Prince or Commander in Islam.

And it was in the Month of Truce of the second year of the Flight that the Prophet called Abdallah and gave him the command. He put in his hand a sealed writing, and said: Take the road to Mecca; and on the third day from your setting out open these orders. As for those who are with thee, if any will not follow thee, compel them not.

When he was three days' journey from Madina, Abdallah opened the writing and read. There was a Meccan caravan on the way from Taif laden with fruit and grapes and other goods; and the caravan passed by not far from Abdallah's camp. And Abdallah and his men resolved to fall upon it. These are Unbelievers, they said: with them there is no need to keep the Truce. Abdallah and Waqid, who were cunning archers, shot at Amr, the leader of the train, and killed him. Of the rest, one fled, and got safe to Mecca; the other two rendered themselves prisoners, and Abdallah bound their hands fast. He took the train of camels and led away into the waste; then made for Madina.

Muhammad held the prisoners for ransom, and took the booty into his hand; but for the time he touched it not, waiting for the command of God. And it was revealed:

WAR IS YOUR ORDAINED LOT, HATEFUL TO YOU THOUGH IT BE.

*THEY QUESTION THEE ON THE POINT OF WARFARE
    IN THE SACRED MONTH.
SAY: WARFARE THEREIN IS A GRAVE MATTER. BUT
    TO TURN MEN FROM THE WAY OF GOD, TO
    DISBELIEVE IN HIM AND IN HIS SANCTUARY,
    TO EXPEL HIS PEOPLE THENCE, IS GRAVER IN
    GOD'S SIGHT. PERSECUTION IS WORSE THAN
    KILLING.*

*O BELIEVERS! IN THE MATTER OF MANSLAYINGS,
    WHAT IS ORDAINED FOR YE IS RETALIATION:
    A FREEMAN FOR A FREEMAN, A SLAVE FOR
    A SLAVE, A WOMAN FOR A WOMAN.
AND FOR HIM OF WHOM HIS BROTHER WILL NOT
    EXACT THE UTTERMOST, PROSECUTE HIM
    FOR THE BLOODWIT ACCORDING TO USAGE;
    LET PAYMENT BE MADE IN KINDNESS, AND
    THIS SHALL BE AN ALLEVIATION FROM
    YOUR LORD, AND A MERCY.*

God now gave the Prophet license to make warlike ex-
peditions; and it was revealed:
*SANCTION IS GIVEN TO THOSE WHO FIGHT BECAUSE
    THEY ARE OPPRESSED (AND GOD IS WELL
    ABLE TO GIVE THEM THE VICTORY IN
    FIGHT),
TO THOSE WHO HAVE BEEN WRONGFULLY DRIVEN
    FROM THEIR OWN HOMES ONLY BECAUSE
    THEY DO CONFESS: GOD IS OUR LORD.*

A man came to the Prophet and asked: What does it mean,
this fighting for God? We fight as all men fight: for anger, or
to keep our own.

The Prophet looked up at him (for he was standing) and
said: That man fighteth for God who fighteth that God's Word
may prevail over all.

*BELIEVERS SAY: IF ONLY A CHAPTER OF SCRIPTURE
HAD BEEN REVEALED.*

*BUT WHEN A CHAPTER ABSOLUTE IS REVEALED,
WHEREIN IS MENTION OF WAR, THOU SEEST
THEM WHOSE HEARTS ARE SICK LOOK AT
THEE WITH THE FACES OF MEN FAINTING
UNTO DEATH.*

WOE UNTO THEM FOR THAT!

*O YE WHO BELIEVE! WHEN YE FACE UNBELIEVERS
IN BATTLE, TURN NOT YOUR BACKS TO
THEM:*

*WHOSOEVER SO TURNETH HIS BACK, EXCEPT HE BE
TRYING FOR VANTAGE, OR MAKING HIS WAY
TO SOME TROOP OF HIS FELLOWS, THAT
MAN BY HIS ACT HATH INCURRED GOD'S
WRATH: HIS PLACE IS HELL, A DISASTROUS
JOURNEY'S END.*

*WHEN YE FACE UNBELIEVERS IN BATTLE, THEN LET
IT BE SMITING OF NECKS TILL YE HAVE
WORSTED THEM; THEN BIND THEM FAST.*

*AFTERWARD, EITHER GRACE OR RANSOM, TILL THE
WAR LAY DOWN ITS ARMS.*

THE DAY OF BADR

In the second year of the Flight, in the Month of Ramadan,
the Prophet had warning that a Mecca caravan, with the Qurayshi noble Abu Sufyan leading, was on the way from Syria.
He gathered his Companions and gave the order for march, and
they came to a place one day's journey from the Well of Badr.
The Believers were three hundred men or a few more.

Abu Sufyan had sent a man ahead with tidings to Mecca.
The Prophet's uncle Abu Jahl called out the townsmen; and
they marched out to meet the caravan, a thousand strong, and
among the rest Amir, brother of that Amr who had been slain

by Abdallah son of Jahsh. But Abu Sufyan meanwhile gave the
order for remove, and with his caravan turned out of the direct
road, setting his face to the seashore and leaving the Well of
Badr on his left; and so along the coast he fared by the longer
road to Mecca. When he came to the marches of the Mecca
country, he got tidings of the host, how it had passed that way
on the Madina road, and his own sons with the rest. So he sent
a man after them with a message: If ye went forth to save your
goods, they are already safe.

When the message was delivered, one in the host stood
forth and spoke: Ye men of Quraysh! naught will ye gain by
fighting Muhammad and them with him. If ye fall on him now,
for the rest of your lifedays each man of you will loathe to look
into the face of some other, who hath slain his uncle's son, or
I know not what other of his kindred.

But Amir the brother of the slain man Amr sprang up and
bared himself and cried: Woe and alas for Amr! Woe and alas
for Amr! And war was kindled, and all was marred, and they
held stubbornly on their evil course.

When the Apostle of God spied them far off trooping
down from the pass into the Valley of Badr, he cried: O God!
here come Quraysh with all their chivalry and pomp to fight
Thee and make a liar of Thine Apostle. O God! Thy help which
Thou didst promise! Bring them to the ground, O God! the
morning of this day!

He straightened the ranks of his Companions with an
arrow which he held in his hand. As he passed by Sawad son of
Ghazia, who was standing in front of the rest, he gave him a
little prick in the belly with his arrow and said: Stand in line,
Sawad.

Thou hast done me bodily harm, Apostle of God, the man
said; and since God sent thee to do right and justice, now give
me my revenge.

Take thy revenge, the Prophet said, and uncovered his
own body.

Then Sawad put his arms round him and kissed him on

the belly. What made thee do that, Sawad? Muhammad asked.

Apostle of God, thou seest what is before us, said he. This is the last time I shall ever be with thee, and I wanted my skin to know the touch of thine.

The Prophet prayed for him. And when he had straightened the ranks, he returned to a little shelter of boughs his Companions had made him, and entered it; and none was with him there but Abu Bakr. He continued in entreaty with his Lord for the help which He had promised, and fell thereafter into a light sleep; then he awoke, and said: Abu Bakr, be of good cheer; God's help is come to thee. Lo here Gabriel! holding a horse by the rein, leading it — I see the very dust on its front teeth!

He went forth again to his men and heartened them and said: By Him Who holdeth the soul of Muhammad in His Hand! there shall be no man slain this day as he goeth forward (not so if he retreat) but God shall bring him into the Garden.

One Umayr was eating some dates that he had in his hand. Hey! Hey! said he; is there naught betwixt me and Paradise but death by the hands of them yonder? And he flung his dates away, and gripped his sword, and fought till he was slain.

On the Qurayshi side, when the warriors went forward into battle, Abu Jahl cried: O God! bring woe this morning on the man who more than any of us hath cut the ties of kinship and done things that ought not to be done — 'twas he began all this!

Then the Apostle of God took up a handful of gravel stones and turning toward the Quraysh cried: Foul be those faces! And he hurled the stones toward them and ordered his Companions to charge. And the enemy were scattered: God slew many of their shaykhs and brought into captivity many of their nobles. While the Believers were laying hands on their prisoners, the Apostle saw displeasure in the face of a certain man who stood by the entry to the shelter, and said to him: By God! methinks thou likest not what our people are doing.

Even so, he answered. This is the first defeat, O Apostle

of God, which God hath let fall upon the Unbelievers; and I would liefer see them slaughtered than left alive.

When they brought the prisoners before the Prophet, among the rest was Uqba, of the kindred of Umayya, with a rope about his neck. Muhammad, said he, if thou slay me, who will care for my children after I am gone?

Hell-fire will care for them! Muhammad said.

Returning to Madina, the Prophet went to lodge in the hut of his elder wife Sawda. She had heard tidings already, how her father and her uncles, nobles of Quraysh, had been slain; and when Muhammad came into her room she began to weep and wail. The Prophet was vexed. Night was falling; he left her and went to Aisha's room, and passed the night there.

In the morning they brought the prisoners before Sawda's door, not knowing that the Apostle of God was with Aisha.

So ye held out your arms for your captors to bind, ye chits! Sawda cried. Could ye not fight? and be killed fighting, like my father and his brethren?

The Apostle of God had stepped forth, and he heard her. He went back in anger to Aisha's door; and they brought the prisoners to him there. Each prisoner he rendered to the man who took him, to keep till one should come from Mecca to ransom him. Among the captives was Abbas, the Prophet's uncle. Thou must pay ransom for thyself and thy nephews and thy confederates, Muhammad said to him.

But Abbas would not, and said that in his heart he had been a Believer, and that he had been in the battle against his will. Only God knoweth if that be true, Muhammad said. In outward act thou wast against us.

Thou hast already twenty ounces of silver of mine, that my captor took of me, Abbas said. Take them for my ransom.

Those are a bounty from my Lord to the Believers, the Prophet answered.

But I have no other money, said his uncle.

Then what is become of the money, Muhammad asked,

which, when thou didst quit Mecca, thou didst leave in secret with thy wife Umm Fadl, telling her how it should be shared among thy sons if thou shouldst not come back?

Who told thee of that, Muhammad? cried Abbas.

God told me that.

Thy God is certainly the Master of the Hidden! his uncle said. Stretch forth thy hand to me! I will declare that He is One, and thou His Prophet in very sooth. So Abbas pronounced the Profession of Faith, and undertook ransom for himself and three other men.

All that day Sawda wept, fearing divorce. She was a woman past the freshness of her youth; and she knew that the Prophet loved Aisha best. When the Prophet went to Aisha in the evening, she too went to that hut, and spoke to him face to face, and begged his pardon for the words she had uttered.

I forgive thee, he said.

O Apostle of God! she proceeded, I am growing old; and if now I beg thee to take me back to be thy wife again, it is not out of any desire to have of thee what women want of a husband. But my desire is that I may be counted on the Day of the Rising of the Dead among the number of thy wives, when they shall be called from their graves to come into the Garden. Take me back. And all the nights which thou shouldst spend with me in my turn, spend those nights with Aisha. Let her have a double portion of thee.

Aisha added her beseeching, until at last he took Sawda back to be his wife again.

* * *

It had been revealed:

TRUE BELIEVERS, AND ALL, JEW, CHRISTIAN, SA-
BAEAN, WHO BELIEVE IN GOD AND THE
LAST DAY, AND WHO DO RIGHT, THESE
SHALL HAVE THEIR REWARD FROM THEIR
LORD: NOR FEAR NOR GRIEF SHALL TOUCH
THEM.

Now, when God had visited the Quraysh on the Day
of Badr, so soon as Muhammad was home in Madina again he
called the Jews together in the Qaynuqa Market, and spoke to
them: Turn now, ye Jews, turn ye to Islam, ere God visit ye as
He hath visited Quraysh! God saith:

YE CHILDREN OF ISRAEL! REMEMBER NOW MY
    FAVOR WHEREWITH I FAVORED YE; AND
    NOW FULFILL YOUR COVENANT, SO WILL I
    FULFILL THE SAME.

FEAR YE ME!

AND BELIEVE IN WHAT I YET REVEAL CONFIRMING
    THAT PART OF SCRIPTURE WHICH YE POS-
    SESS ALREADY.

ESTABLISH WORSHIP; PAY THE POOR-DUE; AND BOW
    YE DOWN TO PRAY IN THE COMPANY OF
    THOSE WHO DO BOW DOWN.

But the Jews answered: We prefer to abide in the faith we
found our fathers in — they were better men than we, and more
learned.

SAY: YE PEOPLE OF SCRIPTURE! LET THERE BE A
    PACT BETWEEN US AND YOU: THAT WE
    WORSHIP GOD ALONE, THAT WE ASSOCIATE
    NONE OTHER WITH HIM, NONE OF US TAK-
    ING ANY OTHER LORD THAN GOD.

SHOULD THEY THEN TURN AWAY, THEN SAY: BEAR
    WITNESS, WE ARE THEY WHO HAVE MADE
    THE SUBMISSION, THE MUSLIMS.

(AS FOR THE CHRISTIANS) IT IS INCONCEIVABLE
    THAT ANY HUMAN CREATURE TO WHOM
    GOD HAD GIVEN GIFTS OF SCRIPTURE AND
    JUDGMENT AND PROPHECY SHOULD AFTER-
    WARD HAVE SAID: SERVE ME, RATHER
    THAN GOD.

ABRAHAM WAS NOT THEOLOGICALLY A JEW OR CHRISTIAN: HE WAS A RIGHTEOUS MAN, WHO HAD SUBMITTED HIMSELF TO GOD, A MUSLIM.

Muhammad spoke again with the Rabbis of the Jews and said: Fear God, ye Jews! and be Believers; for verily ye know from your own Scripture that the Revelation which I bring is true.

WHEN GOD MADE COVENANT WITH THE FORMER PROPHETS, HE SAID:

BEHOLD HOW MUCH OF SCRIPTURE AND OF JUDGMENT I HAVE GIVEN UNTO YOU. BUT AFTERWARD THERE SHALL COME UNTO YOU AN APOSTLE TO CONFIRM WHAT HATH BEEN GRANTED YOU; AND YE ARE TO BELIEVE IN HIM AND HELP HIM. DO YE CONSENT? AND WILL YE TAKE UP MY DOOM IN THIS?

THE PROPHETS ANSWERED: WE CONSENT. THEN UTTER YOUR WITNESS, GOD SAID, AND I WILL BEAR WITNESS WITH YOU.

Fear God, therefore, and be Believers, since ye know from your own Scripture that what I bring is true.

Nay, that is the very thing we do not know! the Rabbis answered; and they denied known truth, and held on in Unbelief.

THE LIKENESS OF THOSE WHO WERE CHARGED WITH THE MOSAIC LAW AND THEN OBSERVED IT NOT IS THE LIKENESS OF AN ASS CARRYING A LOAD OF BOOKS!

The Jews of Madina were wealthy men. Much bestial, much arms and armor they had, for they were skilled craftsmen. All the workshops in the city, the smith's craft, the shoemaker's craft, the jeweller's craft, were in their hands. There was only one wedding array in the whole city; the precious ornaments had to be hired from Jewish moneylenders.

Once Abu Bakr spoke to certain rich Jews on behalf of the Believers, and said: Which of ye will lend to God, a good loan? Doth God need ready cash? said Pinchas son of Azariah: He must be in sorely straitened circumstance!

GOD SURELY HEARD THAT SAYING WHEN THEY SAID: GOD NEEDETH CASH, IT SEEMS;WHILE WE HAVE PLENTY!

WE SHALL KEEP RECORD OF THAT SAYING, AY, AND OF THEIR FOUL MURDERS OF THE PRO-PHETS.

AND WE SHALL SAY: TASTE DOOM — BURNING!

THE JEWS WILL NOT ACCEPT THEE, NOR THE CHRISTIANS, EXCEPT THOU FOLLOW THEIR CREED.

BUT GOD'S OWN GUIDANCE SURELY IS THE VERY GUIDANCE. IF, AFTER ALL IT HATH BEEN GIVEN THEE TO KNOW, THOU WERT TO FOLLOW THEIR WILLS, THOU WOULDST HAVE NONE TO SAVE OR HELP THEE AGAINST GOD.

IS IT THUS? WHENEVER COMETH AN APOSTLE, BRINGING ANY MESSAGE OTHER THAN YOUR HEARTS' DESIRE, YE GROW INSOLENT. SOME YE CALL LIARS; OTHERS YE MURDER.

Whenever a Believer sits in company with a Jew, the Prophet once said, that Jew is considering how he may murder him.

O TRUE BELIEVERS! CHOOSE NOT AS INTIMATES OTHERS THAN YOUR OWN FOLK. NAUGHT WILL THEY SPARE TO RUIN YOU: THEY DE-LIGHT IN YOUR DISTRESS. ALREADY HAVE THEIR MOUTHS DECLARED THEIR LOATH-ING; YET WHAT IS HIDDEN IN THEIR BREASTS IS WORSE.

*YE ARE A PEOPLE TOO LOVING WITH THEM WHO
LOVE YOU NOT. YE BELIEVE IN THE BOOK,
IN THE WHOLE OF IT. THOSE OTHERS, WHILE
THEY ARE IN COMPANY WITH YOU, SAY: WE
BELIEVE. BUT WHEN THEY ARE ALONE
AGAIN, THEY GNAW THEIR VERY FINGERS
AT YOU FOR RAGE.
SAY: THEN DIE IN YOUR RAGE!*

* * *

*IT IS NOT FOR A PROPHET TO HOLD CAPTIVES TILL
HE HATH DEALT SLAUGHTER THROUGH
THE EARTH.*

In the next thirteen months the Prophet sent out seven
expeditions. The first was against the tribes of Sulaym and
Ghatafan: those Arabs fled, abandoning their cattle and their
tents and goods; and the Prophet bore all off. The second was
against the Jews of Qaynuqa: their strong place the Prophet
took. The men of Qaynuqa had leave to depart into Syria with
their wives and children, leaving their wealth behind them. The
Prophet took their goods, and levelled their strong place. And
it was revealed:

*KNOW THAT WHATEVER YE TAKE AS SPOILS OF
WAR, A FIFTH OF IT IS FOR GOD, FOR THE
APOSTLE AND FOR THE NEAR OF KIN, FOR
ORPHANS AND THE NEEDY AND THE WAY-
FARER, IF YE BELIEVE IN GOD AND IN WHAT
WE DID REVEAL UNTO OUR SLAVE ON THE
DAY OF DISCRIMINATION, THE DAY WHEN
THE TWO HOSTS MET.
FOR GOD'S POWER EXTENDETH OVER ALL
THINGS.*

That fifth was divided in the treasury into three parts: one third
of it for the Prophet, one third for his kindred, one third for
the poor and orphaned. And the Prophet held his part return-
able to his Companions.

Then noise came to Madina that the Qurayshi Abu
Sufyan was come himself to attack the town. That very day the
Prophet went out with two hundred horsemen; whereupon Abu
Sufyan fled in haste the same night, nor could the Prophet over-
take him. The fourth expedition was against a troop of Sulaym
and Ghatafan who had gathered to a head five days' march from
Madina. These too fled; and the Prophet found no man at their
trysting place.

In the same month Muhammad sent to kill Ka'b, Ashraf's
son, a Jew. He was a man mighty in speech, a poet; and when
the news of the Day of Badr was confirmed, he had gone to
Mecca and recited both elegies on the dead of Quraysh and
lampoons on the Prophet and his Companions and their wives.
When Ka'b came back to his place in the neighborhood of
Madina, the Prophet heard how he had made satirical poems
on him. Who will offer his life to God and rid the world of this
man? he said.

Seven of the Helpers (the Believing citizens of Madina)
agreed together to do the deed. They went to Ka'b's castle, and
lured him out to them, and took their swords and struck him
down. Then they came straight back to the town. It was the first
dawn; and they found the Prophet praying.

The Meccans had got ready a great caravan, with much
goods. Abu Sufyan and one of the sons of Umayya took the leading of it, and hired a guide; and the guide led them for safety
through the waste by trackless ways. But the Prophet got warning of it. He sent a band to cut it off, under command of Zayd,
Haritha's son. Zayd rode hither and thither through the wild, until at last he spied the caravan, lying encamped by night, hard by
a well; and there in the dawning of the day he fell on them. Abu
Sufyan and his fellows climbed to their camels' backs and fled;
but the guide was left in Zayd's hands, and Zayd brought him
back with the booty to Madina. The Prophet shared the spoil;
and as for the guide, he became a Believer.

The seventh expedition was the slaying of Abu Rafi,
shaykh of the Jews of Khaybar, a man of wealth and of clever

speech and a friend to Ka'b. Now the seven Helpers who had slain Ka'b were all clansmen of Aws; and the Helpers of Clan Khazraj meeting together and speaking of this, eight of them, young bold men, agreed to slay Abu Rafi. They went to Khaybar and climbed into the fortress by night; and going up to the room where Abu Rafi lay with his wife, they slew the man, and fled.

Fear fell on the Jews who dwelt about Madina; and they came to ask the Prophet for truce.

THE DAY OF UHUD

And now the Meccans gathered in a host, and gave the command to Abu Sufyan. He marched from Mecca bearing with him the idol Hubal from the Sanctuary, on a camel's back, and his wife Hind, and fifteen other women. They went by the Madina road, and coming near the town, halted, upon Mount Uhud.

Thereupon the men of Madina armed them. The Prophet ordered their prayer, and put his armor on, and marching to Mount Uhud arrayed the host over against the Quraysh, with their backs to the hill, that the enemy might not turn their flank. There was in that mountain a pass, by which the Un-believers might take the Believers in the rear; the Prophet there-fore sent into the mouth of that pass fifty archers, Helpers of Madina, ordering them: If the enemy turn against you to go by that pass, drive them back with arrowshot. Stand firm on that post, whether we conquer or whether we fail, until I come for you.

God's Apostle had two hauberks on his body, and girt at his side two swords, the one named Twinspine and the other Mottle. And now the two hosts went forward.

Abu Sufyan ordered a herald before his ranks, to cry: Ye men of Madina! Muhammad is of our folk, and we of his; and there is quarrel and blood between us. But with you we have no quarrel; you and we have the same blood in us. For-

sake this fellow and turn home in peace; leave us alone to deal
with Muhammad and the men from Mecca.

Thou foul dog! cried one for the Helpers, go tell Abu
Sufyan and Quraysh that till he shall have spilt the blood of
every man of us he shall not even see Muhammad's face!

A Qurayshi, who bore the standard of the Unbelievers,
came and stood opposite Ali son of Abu Talib. He brandished
his sword and called to him: Ali, ye say your dead go to Paradise,
and ours to Hell; come now and fight with me, and either thou
shalt help me to Hell with thy sword or I'll help thee to Paradise with mine.

I'll help thee to Hell, please God, said Ali. And they
began to fight. Ali hewed at the man with his sword; the blow
fell on his leg; and down he fell, and with him the standard.
But another, a man of his kindred, raised it up again. Thanks,
cousin! said the fallen man.

But Ali left him, saying: Unfit for Hell I deem thee. The
Prophet heard that word and smiled. Ali went back into the
ranks. Then the Prophet ordered his host to charge:

Ride, ye riders of GOD! *Lo* PARADISE *yonder before ye!*
And again:

PARADISE *lies in the shadow of swords!*
And the Believers rushed on the Quraysh. At the first shock
the Unbelievers were put to flight. Their womenfolk, who had
been placed behind the men, unmounted, unable to run, tucked
up their skirts and clambered up the hillside, to wait until the
slaughter should be over and men should come to make them
captives.

I saw Abu Sufyan's wife Hind scrambling uphill with her
skirts tucked up, said Omar afterward. Her legs were decked
with silver anklets — she's a swarthy woman.

But the Believers soon gave up the pursuit and began to
lay hands on the spoil. The band of fifty archers whom the
Prophet had posted in the mouth of the pass saw how it went,
and they broke into murmur: The enemy run! Ay, and the

Believers are getting at the booty! till at last thirty of them went off after pillage. Twenty stood fast.

But now came the Qurayshi Khalid son of Walid along the mountainside, and with him some two hundred men. They cut down the twenty where they stood, and so got through the pass to fall upon the rear of the Muslim host, charging with swords drawn. One horseman galloped after Abu Sufyan with the news; he rallied the Quraysh, and they turned to fight afresh. When the Believers saw the Qurayshi standard raised again, and Khalid slaughtering the Muslims behind them, they turned to flee.

To me! the Prophet cried to those who were near him. And he shouted to the men of the host. None hearkened. Abu Bakr and Omar were wounded; Othman fled. At last Ali won to the place where the Prophet stood with his Companions.

Apostle of God, my sword is broken, he said.

Take that, Ali, said the Prophet, and gave him the blade Twinspine. Ali took the sword, and hurled again into the mellay.

There's not a sword in the world like Twinspine, cried the Prophet, nor a champion like Ali!

For all that, the Unbelievers triumphed. And their women came down from the mountain, beating their tabors. Hind leaped and danced and sang:

We are the Daystar's daughters;
> *we are the pressers of cushions;*
Gay our throats with pearls;
> *and sweet our curls with musk;*
Fight, and be twined in our arms;
> *or fly, and of us be forsaken,*
And love no more, no more,
> *and love no more, no more.*

Now Hind, along the road to Uhud, had promised a certain Abyssinian slave, over and over again, that if he would slay

the Prophet's uncle Hamza she would give him all the ornaments of price she wore. And when the women came down
from the hillside, and the battle began again, Hind sought out
the man, and pulled off her body all her ornaments and heaped
them up and said: Lo here! I have kept my word: keep thine!
The slave took a javelin and went to look for Hamza, and found
him fighting with some Unbeliever. He threw his javelin, and
struck him low down in the belly. A few strides Hamza made,
and fell; the slave, coming up, recovered the javelin and struck
him again. That stroke killed him; and the Abyssinian returning to Hind received the jewels of her, and left the battle, and
went back to the baggage.

Then the Reader Mus'ab, standing near the Prophet, was
struck by an arrow and died. The standard fell, and grazed the
Prophet's head as it came down. A stone struck him in the
mouth: it broke two front teeth, and tore his lower lip so that
the blood ran dribbling from his beard. Another stone struck
him between the eyebrows; the blood ran over his eyes and
down his face. An Unbeliever smote him on the right flank
with a swordstroke; and though it pierced him not, yet the
Prophet fell from his horse. Nor might he get to his feet again,
for the weight of his hauberks and for weakness, so much blood
had he lost. The Unbeliever seized his horse's rein, and shouted
out: I have killed Muhammad!

When the Companions heard that cry, terror fell upon
them, and they scattered.

In a little while the Prophet managed to get upon his
knees. Ho Believers! Here am I, the Apostle of God! he cried
aloud. Sa'd son of Abu Waqqas heard his voice and came.
Muhammad was sitting up with his face all blood; only two
men were near. Sa'd kissed Muhammad's feet, he kissed his
hands.

O Sa'd! the Prophet said, can a folk who have bloodied
the face of God's Apostle ever prosper, thinkest thou? Stay near
me, Sa'd!

So Sa'd knelt down, emptying his quiver out upon the ground, and plied his arrows against the Unbelievers, while the Prophet handed the shafts to him one by one, saying each time: Shoot, Sa'd! and my sire and dam be ransom for thee! (which was a saying he never used to any other man). And so Sa'd kept the Unbelievers off.

At last Muhammad got to his feet, and saw the Believers flying. He and those with him gained a sandhill top, and Muhammad shouted: Comrades! here am I! God's Apostle is here! But those who fled rallied not; and the Prophet leaned his face against one of his Companions and burst out weeping. Presently he saw Omar and his own uncle Abbas — they were seeking for his body among the slain. He called to Omar, and they came up.

Mine uncle, give a shout! Muhammad said.

Abbas called aloud: Ho Muslims! Take heart! The Prophet liveth yet!

Some who had hidden came running back, and Ali, who was fighting still, heard and returned. He heaved the fallen standard up again and shook it out; and at last a hundred men were gathered round.

Abu Sufyan rode within earshot. A Day for a Day! he called to them, and rode away. The Unbelievers gave up fighting and drew off to their camp. Ali, climbing the mountain, saw them get on to their camels, leading their war-mares, and take the road to Mecca.

Muhammad ordered the burying of the dead and returned to Madina. As he went into the town, he heard a wailing from the gate of the Mosque, and asked what it might be.

Women, weeping for the dead who died at Uhud, they said.

He burst into tears. Hamza hath no woman to weep for him! he cried. So his Companions sent their womenfolk to his house to mourn for Hamza; and it is custom in Madina to this day at mournings to name Hamza first and weep for him.

It was revealed:

SAY: EVEN HAD YE STAYED PENT IN YOUR HOUSES, THOSE WHOSE DEATH WAS ORDAINED WOULD HAVE GONE FORTH TO THE PLACES WHERE THEY WERE TO LIE.
THERE SHALL NO SOUL DIE BUT WITH GOD'S LEAVE.
THE TERM IS FIXED.
EVERY SOUL SHALL TASTE OF DEATH.
AND ON THE DAY OF THE RISING OF THE DEAD YE SHALL BE PAID: WHAT YE HAVE EARNED.
WHOSOEVER ON THAT DAY IS TAKEN UP FAR AWAY FROM THE FIRE, AND MADE TO ENTER INTO THE GARDEN, HE IS THE TRUE VICTOR.
FOR THE LIFE OF THIS WORLD IS A COMFORT OF VANITIES ONLY.

WHAT THOUGH YE DIE OR BE SLAIN? I TELL YOU, YE ARE GATHERED UNTO GOD.
THINK NOT OF THOSE WHO ARE SLAIN IN THE WAY OF GOD AS DEAD.
NAY! THEY LIVE.
AND THEIR LORD IS THEIR PROVIDER.
IF GOD IS YOUR HELPER, NONE CAN PREVAIL AGAINST YOU.
BUT IF HE FORSAKE YOU, WHO CAN HELP YOU THEN?
HOLD FAST TO THE CABLE OF GOD, ALL OF YOU AS ONE: LET THERE BE NO DIVISION.
REMEMBER GOD'S FAVOR TO YOU: HOW YE WERE ENEMIES AND HE MADE PEACE BETWEEN YOUR HEARTS SO THAT YE BECAME BROTHERS BY HIS GRACE; HOW YE STOOD ON THE VERY BRINK OF AN ABYSS OF FIRE, AND HE PRESERVED YOU FROM IT.

*AND THERE MAY YET SPRING FROM YOU A NATION
WHICH SHALL ENTICE MANKIND INTO
GOODNESS, PERSUADING TO RIGHTEOUS-
NESS, FORBIDDING WRONG.*
TRIUMPH WILL BE THAT.

* * *

Then Muhammad sent to the Jews of the kindred of
Nadir, who dwelt in a fortified village hard by the gates of
Madina, and said: Take your goods, your wives and children,
and depart; and go where ye will; if ye will not go, make ready
for war.

*BECAUSE OF THE INIQUITY OF THE JEWS HAVE WE
DISALLOWED THEM THOSE EARTHLY GOODS
WHICH ONCE WERE LAWFUL TO THEM, AND
BECAUSE OF THEIR MUCH HINDERING FROM
GOD'S WAY,*
*AND BECAUSE OF THEIR TAKING USURY AFTER IT
WAS FORBIDDEN THEM, BECAUSE OF THEIR
DEVOURING THE WEALTH OF MEN BY GUILE.*
*WE HAVE PREPARED FOR UNBELIEVING JEWS AN
AGONIZING DOOM.*

The Prophet laid siege to them for eleven days, until they
rendered the place, on these conditions, to wit: that they should
depart out of the land and leave their goods behind, saving only
one camel load for every household. So they departed, some of
their chiefs to Khaybar, and the rest to Syria.

*THEY DEEMED THAT THEIR STRONGHOLDS WOULD
KEEP THEM FROM GOD!*
*BUT GOD CAME AT THEM, OUT OF AN AIRT
THEY RECKED NOT OF!*

LAWS

WAYS OF LIFE HAVE PASSED, BEFORE YOUR TIME.
    GO ABOUT THE EARTH, AND BEHOLD (IN RUINS) WHAT WAS THE END OF THOSE WHO REJECTED GOD.
WISE MEN REMEMBER GOD, WHETHER THEY STAND OR WHETHER THEY SIT OR WHETHER THEY LIE DOWN: THEY PONDER THE CREATION OF THE HEAVENS AND THE EARTH, TO THIS END: OUR LORD! THOU HAST NOT MADE ALL THIS FOR NOTHING.
AND IT IS GOD WHO HATH REVEALED TO THEE THIS BOOK, OF WHICH SOME VERSES (AND THESE ARE THE SUBSTANCE OF THE BOOK) ARE OF FIXED MEANING, AND OTHERS ARE AS PARABLES.
MEN WHOSE HEARTS INCLINE TO ERROR FASTEN ON THE PARABLES, BECAUSE THEY SEEK SUBTLETY AND INTERPRETATION.
NONE KNOWETH ITS INTERPRETATION BUT GOD. SOUNDLY INSTRUCTED MEN SAY ONLY: WE BELIEVE IN IT, THE WHOLE IS FROM OUR LORD.

PURITY

O TRUE BELIEVERS! COME NOT TO PRAYER, WHEN YE HAVE DRUNK, TILL YE KNOW WHAT IT IS YE SAY; NOR, WHEN ABLUTION IS DUE, TILL YE HAVE BATHED, UNLESS YE BE WAY-FARING.

*IF YE BE SICK, OR ON A JOURNEY, OR ONE OF
YOU COME FROM THE PRIVY, OR FROM THE
CLASP OF WOMEN, AND YE CAN FIND NO
WATER, THEN GO TO HIGH CLEAN GROUND
AND RUB YOUR FACES AND YOUR HANDS
THEREWITH. GOD IS BENIGN, HE IS FORGIV-
ING.*

PILGRIMAGE

*THE PRIMAL HOUSE OF SANCTUARY APPOINTED FOR
MANKIND WAS THAT AT MECCA, A BLESSED
PLACE, A BEACON TO THE RACES OF MEN,
WHEREIN ARE MEMORIALS NOT TO BE MISTAKEN:
EVEN THE PLACE WHERE ABRAHAM STOOD
TO PRAY.*
WHOSOEVER ENTERS THERE SHALL BE SECURE.
*AND PILGRIMAGE TO THAT HOUSE IS ONE OF MAN'S
DUTIES UNTO GOD, BINDING UPON EVERY
MAN WHO CAN MAKE HIS WAY TO THAT
PLACE.*

MANSLAUGHTER

*IT IS NOT FOR A BELIEVER TO KILL A BELIEVER,
EXCEPT BY MISTAKE.*
*WHOEVER KILLETH A BELIEVER BY MISTAKE
SHALL SET FREE SOME BELIEVING SLAVE
AND PAY THE BLOODWIT TO THE FAMILY
OF THE SLAIN, UNLESS FOR CHARITY'S SAKE
THEY REMIT IT.*
*IF THE SLAIN BE OF A HOSTILE FOLK, AND YET
A BELIEVER, THEN THE FREEING OF A BE-
LIEVING SLAVE SUFFICETH.*

IF HE BE OF A FOLK BOUND TO YOU BY COVE-
NANT, THEN THE BLOODWIT SHALL BE
PAID TO HIS FOLK AND A BELIEVING SLAVE
SET FREE.
WHOSOEVER HATH NOT THE WHEREWITHAL
MUST FAST TWO MONTHS RUNNING AS A
PENANCE ORDAINED OF GOD.
BUT WHOSOEVER SLAYETH A BELIEVER OF SET
PURPOSE, THAT MAN'S REWARD IS HELL FOR
EVER.
FOR THOSE WHO DISBELIEVE OUR REVELATIONS
WE SHALL BRING INTO THE FIRE. AS OFTEN
AS THEIR SKINS ARE CONSUMED, WE SHALL
CHANGE THEM TO FRESH, THAT THEY MAY
SAVOR THAT TORMENT.

PROPERTY AND INHERITANCE

MANKIND, BE CAREFUL OF YOUR DUTY TO YOUR
LORD, WHO DID CREATE YOU FIRST FROM A
SINGLE SOUL, OUT OF WHICH HE MADE A
MATE FOR IT; AND FROM THAT TWAIN
HATH SPREAD ABROAD ALL THE MULTI-
TUDE OF MEN AND WOMEN.
BE CAREFUL TOWARD GOD, IN WHOSE NAME YE
MAKE YOUR CLAIMS OF ONE ANOTHER, AND
BE CAREFUL TOWARD THE WOMBS THAT
BARE YOU.
GIVE ORPHANS THEIR PROPERTY.
IF YE FEAR YE CANNOT DEAL FAIRLY BY ORPHANS,
THEN MARRY OF SUCH WOMEN AS SEEM
GOOD TO YOU, TWO OR THREE OR FOUR;
IF YE FEAR YE CANNOT DEAL FAIRLY BY SO
MANY, THEN ONE ONLY, OR THE WOMEN
YE OWN.

*AND LET WOMEN HAVE THEIR DOWRIES; BUT IF
THEY FREELY REMIT YOU A PART THEREOF,
YE MAY ENJOY IT.*

*GIVE NOT OVER TO THE INCOMPETENT SUCH PROP-
ERTY AT YOUR DISPOSAL AS GOD HATH
GIVEN YOU FOR THEIR MAINTENANCE; BUT
FEED AND CLOTHE AND COUNSEL THEM.*

THIS IS GOD'S CHARGE CONCERNING CHILDREN:

*TO THE MALE HEIR THE EQUIVALENT OF THE
PORTION OF TWO FEMALES;*

*IF THE HEIRS BE WOMEN, TWO OR MORE, THEY
SHALL HAVE TWO THIRDS OF THE INHERI-
TANCE; IF THERE BE ONLY ONE, THEN THE
HALF;*

*TO THE PARENTS OF THE DECEASED A SIXTH
OF THE INHERITANCE IF HE HAVE A SON;*

*IF HE HAVE NO SON AND HIS PARENTS ARE
HIS HEIRS, THEN HIS MOTHER SHALL HAVE
A THIRD;*

*IF HE HAVE BRETHREN, THEN HIS MOTHER
SHALL HAVE A SIXTH;*

*ALL THIS AFTER THE DISCHARGE OF ANY
LEGACY HE MAY HAVE BEQUEATHED, OR
ANY DEBT.*

*AND YE SHALL TAKE A HALF OF WHAT YOUR WIVES
LEAVE IF THEY HAVE NO CHILD; BUT IF
THEY HAVE A CHILD THEN YE SHALL TAKE
A FOURTH OF WHAT THEY LEAVE, AFTER
THE DISCHARGE OF ANY LEGACY OR DEBT.*

*AND THEY SHALL TAKE A FOURTH OF WHAT YE
LEAVE IF YE HAVE NO CHILD; BUT IF YE
HAVE A CHILD, THEN AN EIGHTH OF WHAT
YE LEAVE, AFTER THE DISCHARGE OF ANY
LEGACY OR DEBT.*

*AND IF A MAN OR WOMAN LEAVE HERITABLE PROP-
ERTY, HAVING NEITHER PARENT NOR
CHILD, AND HAVE A BROTHER OR SISTER ON
THE MOTHER'S SIDE, EACH OF THEM SHALL
TAKE A SIXTH; IF THEY BE MORE THAN
TWO, THEN THEY SHALL BE SHARERS IN A
THIRD, AFTER THE DISCHARGE OF ANY
LEGACY OR DEBT NOT PREJUDICIAL TO THE
RIGHTS OF SUCH HEIRS.*

*THIS IS AN ORDINANCE OF GOD, AND GOD IS KNOW-
ING AND INDULGENT.*

*THESE LIMITS GOD HATH SET; AND WHOSOEVER
OBEYETH GOD AND HIS APOSTLE, HE WILL
BRING HIM INTO GARDENS WHEREUNDER
RIVERS FLOW, TO DWELL THEREIN FOR
EVER.*

THE COMMUNITY AND THE FAMILY

*THOSE BELIEVERS WHO GO NOT FORTH WITH THE
HOST, EXCEPT THEY BE DISABLED, ARE NOT
OF EQUAL RANK WITH THOSE WHO STAKE
THEIR GOODS AND LIVES IN THE WAY OF
GOD; GOD HATH GIVEN SUCH AS STAKE
GOODS AND LIFE A RANK ABOVE THE SED-
ENTARY.*

RANK IS FROM HIM.

*AND COVET NOT THOSE THINGS WHEREOF GOD
HATH GIVEN MORE UNTO SOME OF YOU
THAN UNTO OTHERS.*

*LET MEN HAVE THE BENEFIT OF THEIR EARNINGS;
LET WOMEN HAVE THE BENEFIT OF THEIR
EARNINGS.*

ASK GOD FOR BOUNTY: HE KNOWETH ALL.

MEN HAVE CHARGE OF WOMEN, BECAUSE GOD
HATH MADE THE ONE SUPERIOR TO THE
OTHER, AND BECAUSE MEN ARE AT EXPENSE
FOR THEM.
GOOD WOMEN ARE OBEDIENT; AND THEY GUARD
WHAT IS PRIVATE AS GOD HATH GUARDED.
AS FOR WOMEN FROM WHOM YE APPREHEND
DISOBEDIENCE, ADMONISH THEM, BANISH
THEM TO BEDS APART, USE THE WHIP ON
THEM.
IF THEN THEY SUBMIT TO YOU, TROUBLE THEM
NO MORE.
AS FOR THOSE OF YOUR WOMEN WHO ARE GUILTY
OF LEWDNESS, SUMMON FOUR OF YOUR-
SELVES TO TESTIFY AGAINST THEM; IF THEY
GIVE SUCH TESTIMONY, CONFINE THOSE
WOMEN TO THEIR HOUSES TILL DEATH RE-
MOVE THEM, OR TILL GOD OPEN SOME NEW
PATH TO THEM.
THE TWO WHO ARE GUILTY OF THE DEED, PUNISH
BOTH.
IF THEY REPENT AND AMEND, LET THEM BE.
FOR GOD IS RELENTING; HE IS MERCIFUL.
IT IS NOT IN YOUR POWER TO DEAL EQUALLY BE-
TWEEN WIVES, HOWEVER YE MAY WISH.
YET NEVER TURN WHOLLY AWAY FROM
ONE, LEAVING HER AS IN SUSPENSE. IF YE
MAKE UP THE QUARREL, IF YE BE CONSID-
ERATE, GOD IS FORGIVING AND MERCIFUL.
BUT IF MAN AND WIFE SEPARATE, GOD WILL COM-
PENSATE EACH OUT OF HIS ABUNDANCE,
FOR GOD IS ALL-EMBRACING, AND HE IS
WISE.

* * *

The True Believers agree in the names of eleven wives with whom the Prophet contracted and consummated marriage: first Khadija; second Sawda, widow of the poor Believer Sakran, whom he married after Khadija's death; third Aisha; fourth, Omar's daughter Hafsa, widow of Khunays who fell at the Day of Badr; fifth, Zaynab, called for her charity the Mother of the Poor, a woman twice widowed, having been wife to a Believer who fell at Badr, and afterwards to another who fell at Uhud; sixth, Umm Salama, widow of Muhammad's cousin Abu Salama who died of a hurt he got at Uhud; seventh, Zaynab daughter of Jahsh, who was divorced by Zayd. In later time he married, eighth, Juwayria, a woman from the spoil of Mustaliq whom he bought and freed; ninth, Umm Habiba, widow of a Believer who turned renegade in Abyssinia and died a Christian; tenth, the Jewess Safia of the spoil of Khaybar; and last, Maymuna, a woman twice widowed.

The Prophet had slave girls beside: Maria the Copt whom the ruler of Egypt sent him; the Jewess Rayhana of the spoils of Qurayza; another woman of the spoils of war; and a fourth whom Zaynab daughter of Jahsh gave him as a gift.

THE WAR OF THE DYKE

And now the Jewish chiefs rode hither and thither, calling for aid in war against the Prophet. The Meccan Quraysh consented and made a covenant with them and certain clans of wandering Arabs. When the Prophet got warning, by the counsel of Salman, a Persian in Madina, he ordered the digging of a dyke around the city, twenty cubits deep and twenty wide. He labored himself, and sang as he worked:

There's no true life but life in Paradise;
On Helpers and Refugees have mercy, Lord!

And the Believers sang in response:

Unto Muhammad have we plighted troth
To fight his foes and face them till we die.

In a month the dyke was finished. When the Unbelieving host came against Madina and beheld it so girt about, they were dumbfounded. Every day, since they might not cross, they mustered opposite the gates of the town; but no man sallied forth to fight. Twenty-six days they waited, without any battle; and suddenly God sent down a storm of wind at nightfall, which blew their tents about their ears. So Abu Sufyan resolved to raise the siege; and the Unbelievers departed that very night, leaving all that was cumbersome of their baggage behind them. And the wandering Arabs departed also.

* * *

In these days Gabriel descended to the Prophet and said: God bids thee not lay down thine arms till thou hast finished with the Jews of Clan Qurayza. So Muhammad besieged them in their village. After twenty-five days the Qurayza came out from their walls, saying: Be good to us and spare our lives.

I leave your doom to the dooming of Sa'd son of Mu'adh, the Prophet answered.

This Sa'd had been wounded in the hand by an arrow from the walls, and the blood would not stop flowing. Let all their throats be cut, said he, and their goods shared, and their women and children enslaved.

Thou hast doomed in accordance with the will of God, the Prophet said. And so it was done; and the Believers shared the spoil, the Prophet taking out his fifth and also a young girl named Rayhana. The rest he shared among his Companions, giving to every footsoldier one share and every horseman two shares.

Next he marched against Clan Lihyan; but those Arabs fled for refuge into the high hills of their country. So Muhammad went out against Clan Mustaliq. Much booty he took of them, and brought away their women and children to be slaves.

* * *

Salama son of Akwa tells this tale:

The Prophet's slave and I once took his camels out to pasture; and in the dead of night there came on us a raiding party, with Abd al-Rahman, Uyayna's son, their captain. He killed a herdsman and drove off the beasts, he and the riders with him. I bade the slave mount my led horse and go tell the Prophet his cattle were lifted. Myself I climbed a hill and turned my face toward Madina, and shouted: RAID! Three times I shouted, and then went after them.

I had my sword, and arrows to shoot at them and wound their horses. So it went. No fewer than thirty lances were aimed at me; and to lighten the load on their horses thirty cloaks were cast away. On every cloak as I passed by I threw a stone to keep it. At last, near midday of the day that followed, I saw some of the Prophet's horsemen coming up behind, and Akhram of Clan Asad ahead of the rest. At once the foe took to their heels. I ran down and seized Akhram's rein.

Have a care! said I; or they will cut thee off! And I counselled him to wait till the Prophet and the rest of his people should come up.

Salama, he replied, if thou believest in God and the Last Day, if thou knowest that the Garden is fact, and the Fire fact, then do not thou stand between me and martyrdom.

So I let go his rein, and he galloped after Abd al-Rahman. The man turned against him, and the two of them exchanged some thrusts with their swords, of which Akhram got his death and the other a disabled horse. I ran on ahead of our party, to drive the foe with arrowshot away from a well, where they had a mind to water their horses. Two of their beasts I caught; and led them back to the Apostle of God, who was come up now, and five hundred men with him.

The Prophet gave me a footsoldier's as well as a horseman's share of that spoil. Ay, and he made me mount his own camel behind him as we rode back to the city.

* * *

*CONSIDER THE UNBELIEVERS: THEIR DEEDS ARE
LIKE A MIRAGE IN THE WASTE, WHICH A
THIRSTY MAN DEEMETH TO BE WATER, UN-
TIL HE GETTETH TO THAT PLACE; AND
THEN HE FINDETH IT NOTHING, BUT, IN THE
PLACE THEREOF, GOD, WHO PAYETH HIM
WHAT HE HATH EARNED.
A SWIFT RECKONER IS GOD.*

THE TRUCE OF HUDAYBIA

Now the Prophet made up his mind to go to Mecca to fulfill the Pilgrimage. Seven hundred men of all sorts, every man armed, went with him; they led seventy camels for sacrifice. But the men of Mecca took their weapons and marched to encounter them. The Prophet halted at Hudaybia, a place near Mina in the Mecca country.

To him came Urwa, a nobleman of Mecca, and found him with his Companions sitting about him in a ring, and Mughira standing before him leaning upon a sword. Urwa was awed by what he saw; nevertheless he said: Muhammad, how long wilt thou make war against Quraysh? Man never heard tell of any king or shaykh who fought so long against his own folk, or slaughtered so many of them as thou. What dost thou hope from these outsiders? They will finish by betraying thee.

Thy tongue be torn out of thee! Abu Bakr cried, and thrown to thy god! Omar sprang up and dealt Urwa a blow with his fist; and the others laid hands on him and would have killed him, crying: Dost think, thou dog! we shall desert him as ye did? ye who called him cheat?

Urwa tried to speak; he stretched out his hand towards the Prophet; but at this Mughira drew his sword, saying: Who art thou, to brandish thy hands before God's Apostle? But the Prophet spoke: Leave me to deal with Arabs. So they let him go, and Muhammad conferred with him, and he returned to Mecca.

Ye know, he said to the men of Mecca, that one time and another I have seen various kings. Well, never did I see a king among his people obeyed as Muhammad is obeyed. I beheld his Companions, nobles of Quraysh and Arab shaykhs, sitting or standing before him, daring neither to cast a glance nor to speak a word as one man to another, hearkening in silence for whatever Muhammad might say. Let him spit, and they gather up his very spittle! ay, and the soiled water of his washing! His asking is that ye let him war against what Arabs he will, unopposed of you, and that ye let his people come on Pilgrimage.

The Quraysh therefore sent to treat with the Prophet; and the conditions were these: that as for this year he should turn back, not entering Mecca; but that next year at the same time the Meccans should leave the town empty for three days, and the Prophet and his Companions should go in, unarmed, and perform their ritual in the Sanctuary, and depart at the end of three days; that there should be a truce for ten years; that neither party should aid the other's enemies with men or with weapons; that for ten years every Meccan who should flee to Madina to become a Muslim should be sent back, and every Muslim who should flee to Mecca be sent back likewise.

These terms the Prophet accepted, but his Companions murmured. I know Muhammad is God's Apostle, said Omar, but I know not why he should swallow such a humbling from Unbelievers.

Our part is to obey; whatever he biddeth we must do, Abu Bakr answered.

Muhammad sent for some of the great men of Quraysh to come to a meeting, and bade Ali write down the terms. Ali began to write: *In the Name of God the Merciful, the Compassionate* . . . . But a certain Qurayshi arrested his hand. We reck not of any Merciful, said he, nor any Compassionate neither. Write as we are used to write.

Then Ali wrote: Muhammad the Apostle of God . . . .

whereat the Qurayshi stopped his hand again. If we believed
he was any Apostle, said he, we should not be keeping him
from our Sanctuary — write: Muhammad, Abdallah's son.

Never will I write so! cried Ali.

Ali! said Muhammad, cross those words out. I am both
God's Apostle and Abdallah's son. And he took the pen from
Ali's hand and asked: Which are the words *Apostle of God?*
With his own hand he struck them out, and then said: Now,
write Muhammad, Abdallah's son . . . . When the deed was
finished, Muhammad had the shaykhs of Quraysh who were
there attest it, and his Companions also.

Then he cut the throat of the camel for his own sacrifice,
and shaved his head; and the Companions, when they saw him
do it, shaved their heads and sacrificed the other victims likewise. This was in the sixth year of the Flight.

There never was a victory greater than this victory: for
when it was war, men did not meet; but when the Truce was
made, and war laid down its burdens, and men felt safe one with
another, then they met, they talked, they disputed. And no
man spoke of Islam, the Submission to God, to another but that
other espoused it, so that there entered Islam in the two years
between Hudaybia and the breaking of the Truce as many as
all those who had entered it before that time, or more.

*   *   *

A man once questioned the Prophet concerning the seeing
of God in bodily shape: Hast thou truly seen thy Lord?

Light? How could I see Light? the Prophet said.

THE VERSE OF LIGHT

*GOD IS THE LIGHT OF THE HEAVENS AND THE
     EARTH:
THE LIKENESS OF HIS LIGHT IS AS A NICHE
     WHEREIN IS SET A LAMP,*

*THE LAMP WITHIN A GLASS, AND THE GLASS
LIKE A SHINING STAR.*
*LIT IS THAT LIGHT OF A BLESSED TREE, AN
OLIVE NEITHER OF THE EAST NOR OF THE
WEST, OF WHICH THE OIL WOULD ALMOST
UTTER LIGHT THOUGH NO FIRE TOUCHED
IT.*
LIGHT UPON LIGHT!
*GOD LEADETH WHOM HE WILL INTO HIS
LIGHT,*
*HE SPEAKETH IN ALLEGORIES TO MEN, WHILST
HIMSELF IS KNOWER OF ALL THINGS.*

* * *

*BE NOT EXTRAVAGANT IN YOUR FAITH, YE PEO-
PLE OF SCRIPTURE, NOR SAY AUGHT OF GOD
BUT WHAT IS TRUE.*
*THE MESSIAH, JESUS, MARY'S SON, WAS AN APOSTLE
FROM GOD, HIS WORD WHICH HE CON-
VEYED TO MARY, AND A SPIRIT FROM HIM.*
BELIEVE RATHER IN GOD AND HIS APOSTLE.
*TALK NOT OF A TRINITY — IT WERE BETTER
YE WERE HUSHED.*
FOR GOD IS ONE SOLE GOD.
*FAR IS IT REMOVED FROM HIS TRANSCENDENT
MAJESTY THAT HE SHOULD HAVE A BE-
GOTTEN SON — HIS IS ALL THAT IS, IN THE
HEAVENS AND ON THE EARTH.*
*THE MESSIAH, THE SON OF MARY, WAS NO MORE
THAN AN APOSTLE; AND APOSTLES BEFORE
HIM CERTAINLY DIED.*
AND HIS MOTHER WAS A SAINTLY WOMAN.
BUT THEY BOTH HAD TO EAT FOOD TO LIVE.
*BOTH JEWS AND CHRISTIANS SAY: WE ARE GOD'S
CHILDREN AND HIS BEST-LOVED.*

SAY TO THEM: THEN WHY DOTH HE PUNISH
YOU FOR YOUR SINS?
O PEOPLE OF SCRIPTURE! NOW IS OUR APOSTLE
COME UNTO YOU, TO MAKE ALL THINGS
PLAIN.
THE MESSENGER OF GOOD TIDINGS AND OF
WARNING IS COME TO YOU.

In the sixth year of the Flight, the Prophet sent eight messengers to eight kings, to call them to God: one to the Governor of the Copts in Egypt, one to the Governor of Syria, one to the Prince of Yaman, one to the Prince of Oman, one to the ruler of Bahrayn, one to the Negus of Abyssinia, one to Heraclius King of Byzantium, and one to the Persian King. His letter to the Governor of the Copts in Egypt ran thus:

In the name of God the Merciful the Compassionate.

From the Apostle of God to the Muqawqis, chief of the Copts: Peace be upon him who followeth the guidance.

To proceed: I summon thee with the Call of Islam; make Submission to God as a Muslim and thou shalt live secure; and God shall double thy reward. But if thou wilt not, then on thy head will lie the guilt of all the Copts.

O ye people of Scripture, come to a fair covenant between us and you, that we serve God alone, associating no peer with Him, and no more take our fellow men as Lords beside God. But if ye will not, then bear witness: we are the ones who are the Muslims.

The Governor sent reply:

I am aware that there is a Prophet yet to arise; but I am of opinion that he is to appear in Syria. For the rest, thy envoy hath been received with due honor; and I send for thine acceptance two virgins such as are highly esteemed among the Copts, and a robe of honor and a riding mule.

Of the maidens one was called Maria; and by her the

Prophet had a son, Ibrahim, or Abraham, who died at the age
of two years. The Negus of Abyssinia let Ja'far son of Abu
Talib and the other Believers who were in his country depart,
and sent besides gifts of many kinds.

A REVELATION UPON A DOMESTIC MATTER

*WHEN THE PROPHET CONFIDED A FACT TO ONE
OF HIS WIVES, AND WHEN SHE AFTER-
WARDS DIVULGED IT, AND GOD APPRISED
HIM OF THE MATTER, IN PART, PASSING
OVER PART,
AND WHEN THE PROPHET SPOKE OF IT TO HER,
SHE SAID: WHO TOLD THEE THAT?
THE KNOWER, THE AWARE HATH TOLD ME,
SAID THE PROPHET.
IF NOW YE TWAIN TURN PENITENT TO GOD, 'TIS
A SIGN THAT YE HAD HEARTS GODWARD
DISPOSED.
BUT IF YE SIDE WITH ONE ANOTHER AGAINST
THE PROPHET, VERILY GOD HIMSELF IS HIS
PROTECTOR, AND GABRIEL, AND ALL THE
RIGHTEOUS AMONG THE BELIEVERS; AN-
GELS ARE HIS ALLIES, FURTHERMORE.
AND IT MAY WELL HAPPEN THAT HIS LORD, IF HE
DIVORCE YOU, WILL GIVE HIM IN YOUR
PLACE WIVES BETTER THAN YE ARE, TRUE
MUSLIMS, BELIEVING, OBEDIENT, PENITENT.
THE EXAMPLE SHOWN BY GOD TO SUCH AS LACK
BELIEF IS THIS: THE WIFE OF NOAH AND THE
WIFE OF LOT. BOTH BEING SET UNDER TWO
OF OUR RIGHTEOUS SLAVES DID YET BETRAY
THEM. NAUGHT MIGHT THEIR HUSBANDS
HELP THEM AGAINST GOD; AND IT WAS SAID
TO THEM; ENTER THE FIRE ALONG WITH THE
REST.*

*BETHINK YE OF MARY, IMRAN'S DAUGHTER: SHE
KEPT HER BODY CHASTE, WHEREFORE WE
BREATHED INTO IT SOMETHING OF OUR SPIRIT.
SHE PUT FAITH IN THE WORDS OF HER LORD,
AND HIS SCRIPTURES; SHE WAS OBEDIENT.*

Woman was made of a crooked rib, the Prophet used to
say, but if thou try to straighten it, 'twill snap. So treat thy
wives indulgently.

* * *

It had been revealed:

*SAY TO THOSE ARABS OF THE WILDERNESS WHO
FOUGHT NOT WITH US YET: SOON SHALL
YE BE CALLED TO FIGHT, AND AGAINST
MEN OF MIGHTY PROWESS, AND TO FIGHT
THEM TILL THEY BOW.
MUCH BOOTY GOD HATH PROMISED YOU.
AND YE SHALL HAVE IT.*

And now, in the seventh year of the Flight, Muhammad
undertook an expedition against Khaybar, a town belonging to
Jews, and the strongest of all their holds: seven castles, with
palm gardens planted about them.

Three of these castles Ali took, whereat the fourth and
fifth begged to surrender on such terms as had been granted to
the Jews of Nadir. These terms the Prophet granted them, and
they took their departure for Syria, leaving their wealth behind them. For three days more the siege was pressed; then
those who held out still in the two last castles begged to render
themselves on terms, desiring that the Prophet of God spare
their lives and take their goods, but that he let them live on in
that country to cultivate their orchards, and that every year at
harvest time he come and take of them the half of their harvest,
leaving them the other half. To these conditions the Prophet
gave assent, and he caused Ali to write down the terms of the
treaty. At the sharing of the spoil of Khaybar among the

Believers, he kept out for himself the woman Safia, whom he married.

When Khaybar fell, the Jews of the stronghold of Fadak, hard by, sent in haste, to surrender on like terms. The Prophet took the revenue of Fadak to himself, for his household, for alms, and for gift-giving. There was no sharing, because the host had not fought. But he marched against the great oasis in the Dale of Steads; and when the place surrendered he took the wealth and shared it.

* * *

It was in this same year that the Apostle of God had the pulpit made, and spoke his sermons to men from the top of it. In former days he had spoken standing, leaning his back against one of the palm-trunk columns of the colonnade which had been built along the side of the Mosque.

THE PILGRIMAGE FULFILLED

As the seventh year after his Flight drew to an end, the Apostle of God made ready to go to Mecca to fulfill the Pilgrimage to the Holy Places. His Believing Companions took the road with him, to the number of twelve hundred. The Quraysh had left the town; they gathered on the heights about or in the open places, to watch the march of the Believers.

Muhammad rode into Mecca on camel-back, with a poet holding his leading-rein and chanting as he walked:

Out of the way, ye Unbelievers! Out of the way before the Prophet!

My trust is in his Word, O Lord! In him I see the Truth of God!

Even as his visions bid, we strike; as God's Revealing bids, we strike —

Strokes that take heads from where they rest, and put an end to old acquaintance!

The Prophet made the customary circle round the Sanctuary running; and his Companions did as he did. Having so accomplished the visiting of the Holy House, they lay in camp three days, and on the third day slaughtered the camels they had brought for sacrifice, and ended the Pilgrimage. On the fourth day the Prophet departed.

GOD HATH BROUGHT THE DREAM OF HIS APOSTLE TO PASS, IN VERY TRUTH.

THOU SEEST MEN BOWING DOWN, PROSTRATING THEMSELVES, SEEKING GOD'S GOODNESS AND ACCEPTANCE: THE MARK IS ON THEIR BROWS, THE STAMP OF THEIR PROSTRATIONS.

EVEN SO WERE THEY FORESEEN IN THE SCRIPTURE OF JEW AND CHRISTIAN:

EVEN AS THE SOWN CORN, THRUSTING AND SWELLING ITS SHOOT,

RISING FIRM ON THE STALK, A DELIGHT UNTO THE SOWER,

AND A SIGHT FULL BITTER TO THEM WHO NOT BELIEVE.

THE FIRST BATTLE WITH BYZANTIUM

A certain chieftain, stipendiary ally of Byzantium, had murdered the envoy who bore the Prophet's letter to the Syrian Governor.

Now the Prophet chose three thousand men to make a raid on Syria, setting his adopted son Zayd as captain over them. And Khalid son of Walid, who had fought with the Unbelievers at Uhud, had come to Madina to be a Muslim since the fulfilling of the Pilgrimage; and he went with the host. The Believers rode on to the marches of Syria and camped at Ma'an, and thence came over against the enemy host near a township called Muta.

Zayd fought in the center of the battle till he fell; and then Ja'far son of Abu Talib reared the banner up again, and fought there in the center till he too was slain and the banner came down a second time, whereupon a certain man named Thabit snatched it up.

Not to be your captain I set hand to this, he cried, but as hating that the standard of the True Believers should fall to earth. Name ye now a man to take it, and the command with it.

Khalid, Walid's son, laid his hand upon the standard. And the Believers allowed him the command. They fought on till the closing of the dark, and then Khalid led back the host to their campground. Perceiving that the Muslims were too few to keep them from death if they fought to a finish, he gave the order for retreat. Of that the Prophet afterwards approved, and praised Khalid; for when the host came back to Madina, he rode out to meet them on horseback, with Ja'far's son, a child of five years, on the saddle before him; and when those who had come out of the city with him threw dust on the men and shouted: Runaways! he said: Nay! these are no runaways; these are they who shall turn again to battle, if God so please.

THE BREAKING OF THE TRUCE
AND THE TAKING OF MECCA

At the Truce of Hudaybia it had been laid down that neither the Prophet nor the Quraysh should aid the other's enemies. When the Truce was made, the Meccan clan of Khuza'a had declared themselves the Prophet's allies, and Clan Bakr had cut the bond of alliance with him.

A year or two the peace lasted; but in the end Khuza'a and Bakr took to their arms and began to fight again, and the Bakr clansmen asked aid of the Quraysh. The Quraysh lent them weapons. Some Qurayshis besides rode with the Bakr to raid Khuza'a and slew some men, whereupon Khuza'a sent a man to the Prophet to tell him how Quraysh had broken truce.

Breach truce → calm

The Apostle of God ordered his people to make ready to march against Unbelievers. No man knew against whom they were to go: some said Syria, some said Mecca, some said against the town of Taif, and some against Clan Thaqif. To every clan in the Madina country who had become Muslims he sent messengers to ask for men; and every able man in the city took his weapons and went out. At the end of the first day's march, the Prophet of God reviewed the host: there were ten thousand men. They went by the Mecca road, short stages, for seven days.

The Quraysh asked for tidings from Madina; but the Prophet had beset the roads, and men could not get through. At last Abu Sufyan offered to go himself; two other nobles joined with him, and they left Mecca on camel-back. It was night when they came to the place where the Prophet lay encamped, and they saw from afar off the campfires of the Muslim host.

The Prophet's uncle Abbas had left the tents that night, riding on the Prophet's own white mule, to make the rounds and visit the fires. He rode on a little way beyond the vanguard posts; and as he went on in the dark, he heard the voice of Abu Sufyan talking with his fellows. He knew the voice, and called out to him. They came near to one another, and Abbas asked Abu Sufyan what he did there.

I am come to gather tidings, the other answered.

The Apostle of God is here with ten thousand horsemen, said Abbas. Mount this mule behind me, and I will take thee to him. Thou must render thyself to him; thou wilt be slain otherwise, or taken by Omar's people — he hath the advance posts this night. Now between Omar and Abu Sufyan there was old enmity, because of Abu Sufyan's wife Hind: in the age of the Ignorance before Islam she was a loose woman, and had taken Omar for her lover in his youth, which was the beginning of a long feud between those two men.

So Abu Sufyan mounted behind Abbas. When they came within the light of Omar's fire, Omar saw Abu Sufyan and gave a shout: God be praised, Who sendeth thee without safe-conduct into Believing hands!

I gave him safe-conduct, Abbas said.

Omar ran off straight, to warn Muhammad. Abbas whipped up the mule; and so they reached the Prophet's tent together.

Apostle of God! cried Omar, here's Abu Sufyan, that God hath let fall into our hands without safe-conduct!

I gave him my safe-conduct, Apostle of God, said Abbas.

The Prophet was perplexed. Omar pushed close, to whisper in his ear; but Abbas drew the Prophet's head to his own breast. No whispering tonight! he said; if this man was of thy kindred thou wouldst not be so diligent to slay him.

Presently the Prophet said: I give him my safe-conduct too; keep him for tonight, and tomorrow bring him again to me. Next morning Abbas brought him before the Prophet; and Abu Sufyan made the Profession of Faith as a Muslim.

Then Abbas said: Thou knowest, Apostle of God, how Abu Sufyan is one of the chief men in Mecca; grant him now some favor that he may have authority of thee.

Then let all who shall take refuge in his house, at our coming, be spared, the Prophet answered. As they struck camp, he said to Abbas: Take Abu Sufyan to the place ahead where the road narrows, at the time the host is to pass by, that he may watch them filing past, and tell their number to the Meccans; and so those will not think of resisting us.

Accordingly the two of them, posted at the mouth of the valley, watched the troops pass out one after another; and Abbas named to him all the clans, Ghatafan, Sulaym, Juhayna, and the rest, to the number of five thousand men. Last came the Prophet of God riding in the midst of a troop of five thousand men of the Refugees and Helpers, all armed in helms and hauberks so that of their whole bodies a man could only see their eyes; they looked like men of iron.

By God! cried Abu Sufyan to Abbas. Great is the kingship of thy brother's son!

Foul fall thee for that! said Abbas. King is he not — he is a Prophet!

Then Abu Sufyan rode on hastily to Mecca. The Prophet too drew near. They told him: The Meccans have called in their confederate clans; they have mustered them with their own chief men of war on Arafat side; the rest are standing armed in the doorways of their shops and houses; but they have told their confederates that if Muhammad attack them not they will not fight.

The Prophet summoned Zubayr, who was captain of the vanguard, two thousand men, and said: Take thy troop and ride into the city; and plant thy standard on the hill by the east town gate. Khalid son of Walid was bidden to enter the city with two thousand men from the west side near Mount Safa where the confederate clans were arrayed, and halt there, not fighting unless he were attacked. Then with the rest the Prophet waited opposite the town, to see what would befall.

When he perceived that the Believers had occupied both the upper and the lower town, and planted their standards on the hills, he saw there was no resistance. Dividing the host into bands, he made his entry orderly and slowly, giving it out that all should be spared who went into the house of Abu Sufyan, or into the Sanctuary, or who kept within their own doors.

He rode into the town on a camel, wearing a black turban. Ali walked before him bearing his standard. Straight to the Sanctuary he rode, and at the gate got down from his beast, then walked into the court and made the ritual circling round the Holy House and the Black Stone. Meanwhile the Meccans came crowding from their houses to the Sanctuary. When Muhammad had accomplished his rounds, he bade open the door of the Holy House and take down all the idols from their places. And he commanded that they be smashed to pieces. The greatest, Hubal, which was massy stone, was thrown on the ground face down, at the Sanctuary gate, to serve for a threshold, that every man who went in or out henceforth might trample it under his feet.

As they did his bidding, the Prophet of God recited the words revealed:

THE REAL IS HERE; THE FALSE IS FLED.
THE FALSE IS FUGITIVE STILL.

And he went into the Holy House and prayed; then coming forth, he stood in the doorway and gazed into the court, full of the crowding people of Mecca. Grasping the ring of the door, and turning his face over the throng, he spoke, still standing on the doorsill: Now praise be to God, Who maketh His slave to triumph, Who doth fulfill the promise which He gave His slave!

Presently he spoke again: Ye men of Mecca! how think ye I shall deal with you?

Suhayl, Amr's son, who was still at that time an Unbeliever, stood up and said: As a gracious brother, as a gracious nephew of ours, for thou art of Quraysh. I think thou wilt pity these old and let these young live, that thou wilt spare these women and these little ones, and have grace for all, and forgive them, and leave them free.

At that word of Suhayl's the Prophet burst out weeping. After a while he spoke: I will say to you the words my brother Joseph spake unto his brethren, not blaming you as for this day: *MAY GOD HAVE MERCY ON YOU, AND HE IS THE MOST MERCIFUL OF ALL WHO KNOW WHAT MERCY IS.*

Then he shut the door of the Holy House behind him and came down; and mounting his camel went back to the place where the tent of dressed hide was pitched for him, on the hill by the banner Zubayr had planted. There he rested. Every band camped where it was.

And the Meccans came in companies to utter the Profession of Faith. Three days the Prophet remained, sitting at Mount Safa to take the oaths of the men of Mecca. Beneath him sat Omar, giving his hand on the Prophet's behalf to those who took the oath. On the fourth day the women of Mecca came to take oath and become Muslims.

It was revealed:

*O YE WHO BELIEVE! TAKE NOT YOUR FATHERS NOR
        YOUR BRETHREN FOR FRIENDS, IF THEY
        LOVE UNBELIEF BETTER THAN FAITH.
IT IS NOT FOR THE PROPHET, NOR IS IT FOR BE-
        LIEVERS, TO PRAY FOR THE FORGIVENESS
        OF IDOLATERS, EVEN THOUGH THEY BE
        NEAR KINSMEN, ONCE IT IS SURE THAT THEY
        ARE PEOPLE OF THE FIRE.*

> These to Heaven — all's one to me.
> And those to Hell — all's one to me.

* * *

After the taking of Mecca, Muhammad sent out companies
of True Believers to call certain clans with the summons to
Islam; and Khalid son of Walid was despatched to the wandering Arabs of Clan Jadhima. Riding to their country, he
halted near a well where his uncle and another had been pillaged and slain in the Ignorant time, as they came back from
trading in Syria once. Clan Jadhima accepted Islam, and laid
aside their weapons. Suddenly Khalid had them bound, as many
as he could get his hands on, and put them to death one after the
other.

When the Prophet was told of Khalid's deed, he was in
agony of mind; turning his face toward the Holy House, he
cried out: O God! I am guiltless of Khalid's deed! He called
Ali, and taking money from the treasury charged him to pay
the bloodwits to the kin of the dead and restore to them all of
which Khalid had despoiled them.

If all the Hill of Uhud were turned to gold, he said to
Khalid at his return, and thou the lord of it, and thou didst
lavish the whole on my Companions, thou couldst never now
lay up such treasure in Heaven as every man of them layeth up
in one single day!

* * *

All the clans of those parts made haste to turn Believers when Muhammad took Mecca, said a certain wandering Arab afterwards, and my father went on behalf of our folk to declare that we were converted. He brought back a message from the Prophet: that we must follow in our praying that one of us who knew the most of the Koran. Though at that time I was only six or seven years old, I happened to be that one, for when I was out herding cattle I had the chance to learn the manner of prayer from Believers as they passed by on their expeditions. So they set me to lead our prayers.

The shirt I wore was so short that when I made the prostration it used to ride up my back; and one of our women cried out: Could ye not cover your Reader's arse?

So they bought a piece of stuff for me and cut a frock of it. Never in life was I so glad of anything as I was of that shirt.

THE DAY OF HUNAYN

At Hunayn, two days' march from Mecca on the road to Taif, there had mustered a confederacy of wandering Arabs and of Thaqif, the chief clan of Taif; they were against the Prophet. Muhammad led out the ten thousand who had marched with him and two thousand Meccans newly become Believers, and joined battle with the confederates in the Valley of Hunayn. At the first shock the Believers were driven back; but they rallied, and charged again and again, till the Unbelievers turned and ran, leaving their women and children, and their flocks and goods, a spoil for the Believers. That day Durayd the Adder's son was slain, as was told before.

Without sharing the spoil the Prophet marched straight on to Taif, and besieged the place for twenty-five days. Then, perceiving that it was too strong for him, he bade lay waste the vineyards and gardens, and throw down the walls and uproot the trees; and so departing from Taif he marched to Ja'irana for the sharing of the booty of Hunayn.

A part of the spoil he used for gifts to certain great men of Mecca in whose hearts Belief was not rooted: there were ten, called the Hearts-to-be-wooed, who got a hundred camels each — of the House of Umayya, Abu Sufyan and his son Mu'awia and his uncle Safwan, Umayya's son; and seven men more. Others of Quraysh and certain poets got fifty camels each. One poet, a shaykh of Sulaym, refused his fifty, and composed a lampoon upon the Prophet of God, which hearing Muhammad said to Ali: Crop me that tongue which girdeth so at me! So Ali raised the poet's share to a hundred camels.

But though the Umayyad Abu Sufyan was now a Muslim, and though the Prophet gave him of the spoils of Hunayn a hundred camels to soften him and have his friendship, it was all in vain. The enmity went on between the House of Hashim and the House of Umayya, and none of the Umayyads save Othman alone, who had long been a Believer and was husband to the Prophet's daughter Ruqayya, sincerely loved the Prophet of God.

Here was the root of the jealousy that lay between Ali and Othman, and afterwards between Ali when he was Prince of the True Believers and Abu Sufyan's son Mu'awia. This was the cause of all that hereafter befell between them, of the seventeen battles they fought, of the death of forty thousand Believers slain at the battle of Siffin, and of the deeds which Mu'awia's son Yazid did in after time.

Not a single share of that spoil did the Prophet allow to the Helpers of Madina. They were ill-pleased, and went off to camp apart in a fenced garden. Muhammad, going to that garden, sat down. The Helpers gathered about him.

I trusted in your Faith, ye Helpers, said he, when I said in my heart that ye would not cast your eyes after this worldly gear which I would give to men whose Faith is weak. Even as I gave up my share I thought I might give up your shares also. Are ye not content, ye Helpers, that while every man of them driveth home camels and sheep ye shall go home from this expedition leading God's Apostle with you? I swear by God, if the whole world were to walk one way, and the Helpers walk another way, I should walk with the Helpers.

We are content! they cried with tears. We are all content!

The Prophet lifted up his hands, and turned his face to Heaven, and said: My Lord! look graciously upon all Helpers, and on their children after them!

Amen! they responded; and all were joyful again, and the Prophet went away.

KNOW YE THIS: THE LIFE OF THIS WORLD IS ONLY PLAY AND CHATTER, P A G E A N T R Y AND BOASTING AMONG YOURSELVES, THE COMPETITIVE GETTING OF WEALTH AND CHILDREN.

IT IS LIKE HERBAGE AFTER RAIN: THE GROWTH IS PLEASANT TO THE HUSBANDMAN'S EYE; BUT AFTER A LITTLE IT DOTH WITHER, AND THOU WILT SEE IT TURN YELLOW, TILL AT LAST IT IS NO MORE THAN TRAMPLED STRAW.

IN THE HEREAFTER IS GRIM DOOM: THE MERCY AND PLEASURE OF GOD.

BUT THE LIFE OF THIS WORLD IS ONLY THE GEAR OF ILLUSION.

What have I to do with this world? the Prophet one time said: I am like a horseman who halteth a little while in the shade of a tree, and after a little while departeth again.

A curse is on this world, and all things in the world, save the remembering of God, and such things as help us to remember.

He appointed a Governor over Mecca (this was the first Governor in Islam) and another man to teach the Meccans the Koran and the doctrine and the ritual of Islam; and so took the road home to Madina.

Next he led a host against Tabuk, a town of the Syrian marches, to avenge the defeat of Muta where Zayd and Ja'far were slain. John, its Prince, a Christian, came from the town to meet him and make peace, consenting to pay tribute. The Prophet then returned to Madina, and that was the last time he rode out to war himself.

HOW MANY RABBIS AND MONKS FALSELY DEVOUR THE PROPERTY OF MEN!
TO THEM WHO HOARD UP GOLD AND SILVER, NOT SPENDING IT IN THE WAY OF GOD, GIVE TIDINGS OF A DOOM OF PAIN:
ON THE DAY THEIR METAL SHALL BE HEATED IN HELL-FIRE, AND THEY BE BRANDED WITH IT — BROW, FLANK, AND BACK.
THIS DID YE HOARD UP: NOW TASTE OF YOUR HOARDING!

FIGHT SUCH PEOPLE OF SCRIPTURE AS DO NOT BELIEVE IN GOD, SUCH AS DO NOT FOLLOW THE TRUE FAITH, UNTIL THEY PAY TRIBUTE OUT OF HAND AND ARE HUMBLED.

THE PROPHET'S DEALING WITH
THE CHILDREN OF HATIM TAIY

Of all the wandering Arabs the most famous clan was Taiy, because of the generosity of their clansman Hatim. Many tales were told of Hatim Taiy, and this for one:

His mother being pregnant dreamed she was asked: Which wilt thou have? a generous son whose name shall be Hatim, or ten sons like others' sons? And that she answered: Hatim.

When the boy grew up, he would take his food out of the house, and if he found any to share it with would eat, but if not he threw it away. At the sight of that waste his father gave him a slave girl and a mare and foal, and sent him out to herd his camels. When he got to the pasture, he spied three men riding by and went to meet them.

Hast aught of entertainment, lad? they said.

Ye see these camels and yet ye ask? he answered. And he slaughtered three camels to feast them.

Nay, we wanted no more than milk! said one of them. If thou must needs be at charges, one camel's filly would have been enough!

I know that, Hatim said. But I saw you strange of face and fashion, and thought ye could not be of our country; and I wanted each man to have a tale to tell at home.

The three were poets, riding to the court of Hira; and they spoke verses in his honor, praising his generosity.

I wanted to show you some kindness, Hatim said; and now your bounty hath outdone mine. I swear I will hamstring every beast in this herd unless ye take and divide them unto yourselves.

The three poets did as he would have them, and went on their way; each man with ninety-nine camels to his share. When Hatim's father heard of it, he came out to look for him.

Where are the camels? he cried.

My father, Hatim answered, I used them to give thee ever-lasting fame: honor will be a part of thee as the ring is of the ringdove, for men will remember till the end of time some verse in praise of us.

Hatim Taiy was dead now, but his son Adi was shaykh. The Prophet sent Ali with a band against Adi, to summon him to Islam. Ali found the man fled, but took his sister captive and brought her to Madina; and they pitched a tent of dressed hide for her at the gate of the Mosque, out of respect for her father.

One day, as the Prophet was going into the Mosque, she stepped forth from the tent and stood before him, and spoke: Behold me, an old woman, the daughter of a famous man; thou too art spoken of as generous; it behoves thee to let me go free to my brother.

Thy brother is fugitive from God and His Apostle, said

the Prophet, and went on into the Mosque. But after three days
he spoke to her again: I grant thy wish. And he let her go with
gifts: a robe, a camel, and provision for her journey.

How did this fellow deal with thee? her brother asked
when she was home again.

I think it good for thee to go and see the man for thyself,
she answered.

So Adi mounted his camel and journeyed to Madina, and
found the Prophet sitting in the Mosque, with his Companions
around him. At a little distance Adi stood still, and greeted him.

Who art thou? Muhammad asked.

I am Adi son of Hatim Taiy.

The Prophet rose to his feet, a thing he never did for any
other Unbeliever, and took Adi by the hand, and led him to his
own hut, holding his hand all the way, and seated him on his
own straw-stuffed cushion, and himself sat down before him on
the ground.

Then he spoke to him, thus: In this world, Adi, God hath
given thee all thy need: lordship among thine own folk, and a
most famous name, that thy father left thee. Of these things what
couldst thou lose, if God were to give thee the Other World besides? And that World would be thine if thou wouldst take on
thee the Faith I speak of.

Adi kept silence.

By the God Who made me! Muhammad cried, this Faith
shall one day prevail from the rising to the setting sun!

In the end Adi became a Believer; and when he went back
to his clansmen they took the Faith likewise. Soon, as it was
noised about among the clans that Adi, Hatim's son, had been
treated with honor and was become a Muslim, men began to say:
This Muhammad is grown mighty.

So from the beginning of the ninth year of the Flight came
deputations from Arab clans of diverse parts of the wilderness
to make Submission as Muslims; and that year was called:—

THE YEAR OF DEPUTATIONS.

The first who came were some from Clan Tamim, seven great men. Dismounting at Madina, they walked into the Mosque, and seeing the court empty (for the Prophet was in one of the chambers beside), bellowed after their fashion: Ho there, Muhammad! till he came forth.

O Muhammad! said the Tamim, we are come to challenge thee to a vaunting-match; and if thou art the winner, we are thy men. (These vaunting-matches were a famous custom of the Arabs: two clans met, and, from each, two men declaimed poems and fine prose; that clan whose poem and prose were deemed the finer was counted winner.)

They sat down accordingly, the Tamim opposite the Prophet, and he with his Companions about him; and the orator of Tamim stood forth and vaunted at length the glories of his clan. When he had done, Muhammad charged his orator, Qais son of Thabit the Helper, to speak back, and Qais pronounced an oration which was counted the better. Then stood up the poet of Tamim, and after him the Prophet called on Hasan, Thabit's son, for a rhapsody; and Hasan vaunted the merit of Submission and the glory of God's Apostle. The beauty of his verse surpassed the beauty of the verses of Tamim; and the men of Tamim acknowledged the superiority of the Prophet and professed Submission to God. Muhammad gave each shaykh a dress of honor, and they departed to their own people, who turned forthwith to the True Faith.

WE BELIEVE! THE WANDERING ARABS SAY.
 SAY TO THEM: BELIEF YE HAVE NOT, SO RATHER SAY: WE SUBMIT!
 FOR FAITH IS NOT YET ENTERED INTO YOUR HEARTS.
 BUT IF YE ARE OBEDIENT TO GOD AND HIS APOSTLE, GOD WILL NOT STINT THE REWARD OF YOUR GOOD WORKS,
 FOR HE IS FORGIVING, AND MERCIFUL.

The clans must leave off this vaunting of their forefathers, the Prophet said. If they do not, verily they will be more abominable in God's sight than a dung-beetle pushing dung forward with its nose. God now will no more have you proud; there are only two kinds of men: righteous Believers, and sinners. Mankind are all Adam's sons; and Adam was made of mud.

That year the heathen Arabs came as they were wont on Pilgrimage to the Holy House of Mecca, that being still lawful to them on account of a covenant they had made aforetime with the Prophet. But now it was revealed:

A DISPENSATION FROM GOD AND HIS APOSTLE, FROM THE BINDING OF AGREEMENTS WITH THOSE IDOLATERS YE TREATED WITH A-FORETIME:

AND A PROCLAMATION FROM GOD AND HIS APOS-TLE TO MANKIND ON THE DAY OF THE GREATER PILGRIMAGE, THAT GOD IS FREE FROM ANY OBLIGATION TO IDOLATERS, AND HIS APOSTLE LIKEWISE,

EXCEPTING THOSE IDOLATERS BOUND BY TREATY WHO HAVE FAILED IN NOTHING OF THEIR OBLIGATIONS TO YOU, AND HAVE AIDED NONE AGAINST YOU; THEIR TREATY KEEP UNTIL THEIR TERM BE UP.

AND THEN, WHEN THE SACRED MONTHS HAVE PASSED, SLAY IDOLATERS WHERESOEVER YE FIND THEM, TAKE THEM CAPTIVE, BESIEGE AND BESET THEM WHEREVER AMBUSH MAY BE.

AND THEN, IF THEY REPENT, AND ESTABLISH PRAY-ERS, AND PAY THE POOR-DUE, LEAVE THEIR WAY FREE.

HE ONLY SHALL TEND THE MOSQUES OF GOD WHO BELIEVETH IN GOD AND IN THE LAST DAY, AND IS DILIGENT IN PRAYER, AND PAYETH POOR-DUE, AND FEARETH GOD ALONE.

God commanded the Prophet to publish this declaration
in Mecca on the day of Pilgrimage when Arabs from every clan
should be gathered together; he therefore bade Abu Bakr recite
it before men when they were gathered at Arafat, and make
known to them that henceforth no Unbeliever should be admitted
into the city. The Revelation was so proclaimed. And that was
the last time that Unbelievers ever came on Pilgrimage to Mecca.

*THE EARTH, VAST AS IT IS, WAS STRAITENED ABOUT
    THEM; THEIR OWN SOULS TOO WERE STRAIT-
    ENED THEM; AND THEN THEY KNEW FOR
    CERTAIN THAT THERE IS NO ESCAPE FROM
    GOD EXCEPT TOWARD HIM.
THEN TURNED HE UNTO THEM AGAIN RELENT-
    ING, THAT THEY MIGHT TURN AGAIN.*

Now came another deputation from Tamim, and one from
the clan of Sa'd ibn Bakr; and Khalid son of Walid, being sent
against Harith and against a town of Hamdan in Yaman, turned
them to Islam. Then came men from Clan Zubayd, then from
the Christian clan of Abd al-Qais, then from Hanifa, then from
the Christians of Najran, who made treaty, remaining Christians
but binding themselves to pay tribute. Then came a man from
three Himyar princes of Yaman; and the letter the Prophet wrote
them is known still:

*From Muhammad the Apostle of God, the Prophet, to
Harith and Nu'aym and Nu'man.*

*Now praise I unto you God, than Whom there is no
other god.*

*Further, your messenger came to us at Madina with
your message and told us how it was with you, declaring how
ye are now Muslims and have made slaughter of Idolaters.
Know that God hath led you aright if ye continue in well-
doing, obeying God and His Apostle, being steadfast in prayer,
giving the poor-due and bestowing out of your booty God's
fifth which is the Apostle's share.*

The poor-due enjoined on Believers is one tenth of the harvest from land watered by springs or rain, half a tenth from land watered by irrigation; of camels, from every forty one two-year-old female, from every thirty one two-year-old male; for every five camels one ewe, or for ten camels two ewes. And for every forty head of cattle one cow, for thirty a yearling calf, and for every forty sheep a weaned ewe.

This is the prescribed Alms which God ordained for all Believers; but if any man will give more, it is well for him. Whoso payeth, testifying that he is a Muslim, and helping Believers against Idolaters, that man is one of the Believers, having the same rights and the same duties as all others, and lying in the protection of God and his Apostle. And if any Jew or Christian become a Muslim, he too is one of the Believers, with the same rights and duties as they.

If a man cling to his Judaism or Christianity, he shall not be forced from it, but he shall pay the Tribute: a gold dinar of full weight for every grown man or woman, free or slave. . . . And Tribute-payers also are under the protection of God and His Apostle; but he that will not pay shall be their enemy.

Collect this Alms and Tribute from your countries and give it to them I have sent.

Muhammad testifieth that there is no god but God alone, and that he is His Slave. Let there be no more deceiving and betraying of one man by another, for God's Apostle now is patron of rich men and poor men alike. Know that this Alms-money is not to be touched by Muhammad nor his family: it is a charity to be given to poor Muslims, and to the beggar. Know further that I have sent unto you of the best of my Companions, pious and learned men; and I bid you treat them well, for our eyes are on them.

Now upon you Peace, and the Mercy of God, and His Blessings.

* * *

Next came a deputation from Clan Amir, and then one from that branch of Taiy whose shaykh was Zayd of the Horses. And the Prophet, seeing how all the clans were become Believers, sent out to every country a man charged to take the tax and send it to him. And at the end of the tenth year he made ready to go (and this was the last time) on Pilgrimage to Mecca.

THE FAREWELL PILGRIMAGE

Said Jabir, Abdallah's son: The Arabs flocked to Madina, every man fain to imitate God's Apostle and do as he did. 'Twas in the Month of Dhu'l-Qa'da he set forth, and we with him. And I looked out, and far as mine eye might reach were crowds of riders and folk afoot, going before the Prophet and following after him, to the right of him and to the left of him.

At Mecca, having accomplished the rites, he spoke to the people, forty thousand, at the Hill of Arafat, and taught them the rites of Pilgrimage, and finished the work of the Faith, saying:

Ye people! Hearken to my words; for I know not whether after this year I shall ever be amongst you here again.

FORBIDDEN YOU HENCEFORTH ARE CARRION AND BLOOD AND SWINE'S FLESH, AND MEAT ON WHICH ANY OTHER NAME THAN GOD'S HATH BEEN INVOKED, AND MEAT OF ANY BEAST STRANGLED OR CLUBBED OR KILLED BY FALL, EXCEPT YE KILL IT BY A DEATH-STROKE YOURSELVES;

FORBIDDEN TOO IS WHAT IS SACRIFICED ON STONES OF IDOLATRY, AND FORBIDDEN THE DIVIDING OF MEAT BY DRAWING ARROWS, WHICH IS AN ABOMINATION.

THIS DAY HAVE THE UNBELIEVERS DESPAIRED BE-FORE YOUR FAITH; SO FEAR THEM NOT: FEAR ME!

*THIS DAY HAVE I PERFECTED FOR YOU YOUR FAITH,
AND ACCOMPLISHED UNTO YOU MY GRACE,
CHOOSING FOR YOUR RELIGION THIS: ISLAM!
SUBMISSION!
AND IF YET ANY MAN BE DRIVEN INTO SIN BY AP-
PETITE, NOT BY WILL, GOD IS FORGIVING
STILL, STILL MERCIFUL.
THIS DAY ARE MADE LAWFUL UNTO YOU GOOD
THINGS: LAWFUL TO YOU IS SUCH FOOD AS
THE SCRIPTURE PEOPLE EAT, LAWFUL TO
THEM YOUR FOOD; LAWFUL TO YOU AS
WIVES ARE CHASTE WOMEN BOTH OF THE
BELIEVERS AND THE SCRIPTURE PEOPLE, IF
YE GIVE THEM DOWRIES AND LIVE WITH
THEM IN HONOR, NOT IN FORNICATION,
NOR TAKING THEM IN SECRET FOR YOUR
PARAMOURS.
WHOSO DENIETH THIS FAITH, ALL HIS WORK IS
VAIN; AND IN THE HEREAFTER HE SHALL
BE WITH THE LOSERS.*

Your lives and your property shall be sacred and inviolable for one another until the end of time.

The Lord hath ordained to every man his share of his inheritance: a testament to the prejudice of heirs is not lawful.

The child belongeth to the parent; and the violator of wedlock shall be stoned.

Ye have rights, ye men, demandable of your wives; and they have rights demandable of you. Treat your women well.

And your slaves, see that ye feed them with such food as ye eat yourselves, and clothe them with such stuff as ye wear yourselves. If they commit some fault ye are not willing to forgive, then sell them from you, for they too are the Lord's servants, and are not to be tormented.

Hearken to this speaking of mine, ye people, and understand it well; for know ye henceforth this: every Muslim is the brother of every other Muslim. All of ye are one Brotherhood.

Then he looked up to Heaven, and cried: My Lord! have I delivered aright the Message I was charged with, and fulfilled my Calling?

And the multitude answered shouting: Ay by God hast thou!

Be Thou my Witness to that, O God! the Prophet said, and lifted up his hands, and blessed them all.

WHEN THE HELP OF GOD IS COME, AND THE
*   VICTORY,*
AND THOU SEEST MANKIND ENTERING IN
*   TROOPS INTO THE FAITH OF GOD,*
THEN VOICE THE PRAISES OF THY LORD,
*   AND ASK HIS MERCY.*
*   HOW MANY HAVE HIS MERCIES BEEN!*

DEATH

Already at Pilgrimage time the Prophet was sick; and he continued so after he was at home in Madina. The malady increased upon him, and news of it was noised about in the world. He gave command to the Believers, notwithstanding, to make ready to march against Syria, and named Usama, Zayd's son, captain of the expedition. But soon thereafter he got warning that a man named Aswad had arisen in Yaman pretending to be a prophet, and that another, Tulayha, among wandering Arabs claimed the like, and that many had believed in these two and turned renegade to Islam. One Musaylima likewise prophesied, in Yamama. Muhammad's sickness grew worse, care settled upon him, and the marching of the host into Syria was put off. He sent letters to the princes of Yaman; and they gathered strength and fell on Aswad and slew him. When Muhammad heard of it, he gave thanks to God for Aswad's death, and said: The other two, Tulayha and Musaylima, will perish likewise;

for God will preserve my religion safe until the Day of the Rising of the Dead.

Then he called his wives together into Maymuna's chamber, and asked their consent to his staying in Aisha's room so long as his sickness should last. He went, leaning on his cousins Ali and the son of Abbas, to that room, and stretched himself on the pallet there. The fever so seized on him that he might not go out into the Mosque to pray; and at the hour of prayer he said to Aisha: The congregation are waiting for me and I cannot go to them — tell Abu Bakr to lead the prayer.

O Apostle of God! she answered, Abu Bakr hath too soft a heart. If he were to lead them in thy place, he could never pray for weeping. Choose some other man.

The Prophet bade her do as he told her, and yet again bade her do as he told her, she returning ever the same answer, till he said: Verily thou art of the breed of those women who tried to turn my brother Joseph out of the right path — tell Abu Bakr to lead the folk in prayer!

After that, Abu Bakr led prayer every day at the five hours. Then, in a few days, Muhammad, feeling himself a little stronger, and weary of being pent indoors, called for his freedman Abu Muwayhiba, and crooking his arm about his neck, passed slowly forth from the town to the burying-ground where the True Believers lay in their graves. And coming near to the graves, he said: Peace be with you, ye people of the graves! ye who are at rest from what cometh now on me. God have mercy on us, and on you. Ye are gone on before us; but we are following after.

Then he went back again to Aisha's room by the Mosque, and found her lying down, and complaining of a headache. Nay, Aisha, he said, it is for me to complain — not for thee.

I am sicker now than thou art, she answered.

If one creature loveth another, the Prophet said, that one is sorry to live on after that other. So what harm would there be, Aisha, for thee to die before me, if I buried thee, and prayed over thee, and laid thee myself in thy grave?

O ay! said she; thou hast a mind to come back from my
funeral to some fresh marriage!

The Prophet smiled, and lay down on the pallet; and fever
took hold of him anew, and never left him after that. In the
Month of First Rabi, the Apostle of God felt his death near. A
great crowd was gathered in the Mosque. With his brow bound
in a cloth, and leaning on his cousins Ali and Ibn Abbas, he went
out into the court. His face was smiling and very sweet. Being
too weak to climb the pulpit, or to stand upright, he sat down on
the ground and spoke a sermon to the people, praising God, and
greeting the prophets who had gone before him. Then he prayed
for all the True Believers slain at Badr and Uhud, at Khaybar
and Hunayn, and for all the men who had laid down their lives
for him. He urged on them diligence in Faith, and then added:
God hath a certain slave to whom He said: Which wilt thou now
— this world or the Other? and that slave chose the Other. God
was content with his choosing, and hath promised to call him
before His Face.

No man understood that it was of himself he spoke, except
Abu Bakr, who cried out with tears: O Apostle of God! let our
bodies and souls be ransom for thee!

Nay, never cry, Abu Bakr, Muhammad said; thou hast
been with me in this world, and shalt be with me in the Other.
Then he added: If I had ever taken any other beyond God into
my intimacy, it would have been Abu Bakr; I never had a companion more faithful than he hath been, nor hath any other man's
fortune availed me as his did.

There is after death, he presently said, a Day of Dooming
and Reparation; and there will be no more favor shown me on
that Day than any other man. Therefore if I have struck any
man among you an unrequited blow, let him strike me now. If I
have offended any, let him do as much now to me. If I have
taken any man's goods, let him now receive it again. Make me
clean of all guilt, that I may come before God guiltless to man.

Nay, God's Apostle, they cried weeping, all wrong of thine
is wiped clean out; and we are the guilty toward thee! Only one

man stood up and reminded Muhammad of three dirhams he had given at his bidding to some poor man.

Better to blush in this world than the Other! the Prophet said, and paid him what he owed. Then he got to his feet again, and went back into Aisha's hut, and that was the last time the people saw his body alive.

He lay down, with his head on his pillow.

O Apostle of God, who shall wash thee when thou art dead? some of his companions asked him.

My near kin, he said.

And who shall lay thee in the grave?

My near kin.

How shall we shroud thee?

In what I wear, or in a sheet of white Egyptian stuff, or in Yamani stuff.

Now he grew more sick; and the Companions went out of the room. He had a leathern jar, which he bade fill with water and set by him; and from time to time he would dip his hands in the water and wipe his brow and face, saying: Be with me, O my Lord! against the agony of death.

Abbas and Ali came in to see him. Mine uncle, Ali said, methinks the Prophet is a little better.

The Prophet is near his end, Abbas replied. I know the signs of death in men of Abd al-Muttalib's house; I read those signs now in his face. After a while he added: My son, go ask him what he would have in the matter of one to succeed him, to what family the authority should go. If he would have it stay with the Hashimites, the house of Abd al-Muttalib, we shall know it then, and not yield it up. And if he would have it go elsewhere, we will not claim it.

Mine uncle, Ali replied, we must not ask this. If now he saith the authority is to go to another house, never till Resurrection Day will the Arabs let us have it.

Abbas said nothing.

Next day when Abu Bakr finished prayer and had spoken the blessing, they told him that the Prophet had looked out from his doorway. Joyful, thinking Muhammad was to recover, he went hastily across to Aisha's room, where he found Muhammad cleaning his teeth with a stick of threadwood. Willing to make the Prophet merry, Abu Bakr said jesting to Aisha: The Prophet of God, now he is better, must lie tonight in another room!

He hath lain with me when he was sick, she cried; shall he lie with another now he is lusty?

The Prophet heard their talk and laughed; but he said nothing. Presently Abu Bakr went out, and announced that the Apostle of God was better.

For all that, Muhammad could no longer sit upright. Seeing his head fall back, Aisha sat down behind him, drew his body to her, and took his head on her breast. So he remained a little while, with Aisha holding his hand, and chanting: O God, Thou Hearer of men, remove this evil; Thou art the Healer; there is no other healing, only Thine, and Thy Cure is ruthless to sickness!

At one time the Prophet said: The most exalted Friend . . . . and thereafter no more.

Then, at a time betwixt Dawn Prayer and Noonday Prayer, sweat started on his brow, his mouth fell open, and shut again, a single drop of spittle dropped in the hollow between her breasts, and his soul departed. Aisha cried out.

It was a day in the Month of First Rabi, in the eleventh year of the Flight.

Ali went out weeping from the room. Omar, who was standing before the door, said to him: Ali, these fainthearts are saying the Prophet of God is dead! Ali answered him nothing. A man went to tell Abu Bakr, who, coming in haste, found Omar still at the door, with a crowd around him, crying: These fainthearts are saying the Prophet of God is dead — he is alive! and be those tongues torn out!

Abu Bakr, hearing, went into the hut. Aisha was wailing and tearing her face with her nails. Muhammad's body lay with his own mantle thrown over it. Abu Bakr uncovered the face, and bent down, till his brow well-nigh touched the brow of the

Prophet of God. Then he drew the mantle over the face again, and went out. Omar was still shouting to the crowd.

Gently, Omar! Abu Bakr said. Then he turned to the people and spoke: Lo! as for any who worshipped Muhammad, Muhammad is dead. But as for him who worshippeth God, God is the Living One and He dieth not. And he recited from the Koran the verse:

MUHAMMAD IS ONLY AN APOSTLE; APOSTLES BE-
FORE HIM HAVE PASSED AWAY. WHEN HE
COMETH TO DIE OR BE KILLED, WILL YE TURN
ON YOUR HEELS? THE MAN WHO SO TURNETH
WILL NOT HARM GOD, BUT GOD WILL REWARD
THOSE WHO ACKNOWLEDGE HIM.

It was as if the people had never known till then that such a verse had been revealed. When I heard Abu Bakr recite that verse, Omar used to say afterwards, my feet were cut from under me — ay, I fell on the ground; for then I knew that the Apostle of God, God's Prayer and Peace be on him! was dead.

PERSONAL RECOLLECTIONS

Ali and other Companions, questioned concerning the person of the Prophet, said at various times:

He was a man of middle height, of a fair ruddy complexion. His eyes were black, and his hair thick and bright, beautiful hair; his beard was of a good thickness, and he let it grow all round his face. He wore his hair long to his shoulders, loose sometimes, sometimes twisted in two plaits, sometimes in four. As to his body, his throat was white; and from his breast down to his navel ran a line of black hair, delicate as if it had been drawn with a pen. Other hair low on his body he had none. His head was roundish, and his back stout and sinewy. Between his shoulders he had a growth, big as a silver dirham, with hair growing round it. Such force of life was in his walk that a man might think him pulling his feet loose from stone; and yet so light it was that he

seemed to be stepping ever downhill. And he had such a sweetness in his face that when a man was in his company it was hard
to go away.

People used to ask Aisha how the Prophet lived at home.
Like an ordinary man, she answered. He would help sweep the
house, stitch his own clothes, mend his own sandals; water the
camels, milk the goats, help the servants at their work, and eat
his meals with them; and he would go to fetch a thing we needed
from the market.

He would go visit any sick; he would walk as a mourner
after any bier he met in the street; and if a slave bade him to dinner, he would go dine with him.

His grandson Husayn, Ali's son, said this: When I asked
my father how the Prophet used to be in his public life, he answered: He gave people their due always; he never neglected
good manners, but would greet his Companions duly and ask
after their health. If he came into a company he always sat down
in any place he found room. In his council, no one was allowed
to shout; if any present was guilty of a fault, he never exposed it,
but would try to cover it up. Nor did he ever interrupt another
man speaking. If he saw anything to disgust him in the person
of another, a change might come over his face, but he never remarked on it to the other person.

He ate kneeling, liking best to eat with a goodly number
at table, and used to say: The man who eats alone is the worst
of men. Meat was the food he liked best, and he would say: Meat
is good for the hearing! but what he mostly ate was dates. He
liked honey, and fresh butter; and he loved milk exceedingly; if
anyone gave him a drink of milk he used to say: God bless this
milk to us and grant us more of the same.

Ten years was I about the Prophet, his servant Anas said,
and he never said so much as Bah! to me.

On Pilgrimage once, Abu Bakr was angry with one who
had let a camel stray, and began to beat the man. The Prophet
did not command him to stop, but said, with half a smile, merely:
See what this Pilgrim is doing!

He loved fun. Many a jest, said Aisha, the Prophet made, and he always said God doth not punish a fair jest. The Companion Khawat son of Jabir told the following tale:

Once I was on a journey with the Apostle of God and his people; and we lighted down at a certain halt and pitched our tents. After a while, coming out of my tent, I spied a bevy of women, comely enough, opposite me, sitting talking. So I went in again, and put on my best raiment; then I walked over to the women and sat down in their company.

Suddenly the Apostle of God came out from his tent and saw me. Abu Abdallah, said he, what dost thou there, sitting with the women?

I was in awe of him, and answered hastily: Apostle of God, I have a balky drunken camel, and I came to ask these women to twist me a hobble-rope.

He passed on a few steps; then turned round on me, and said: Abu Abdallah, how, more exactly, was that drunken camel acting? When I replied not, he went on.

After we removed from that halting, whenever the Prophet saw me, he would, after greeting me, ask me that same question: How was that drunken camel acting? So when we got back to Madina, I kept away from the Mosque, out of fear that the Prophet would ask me there, to my confusion. I waited my opportunity to catch him alone in the Mosque; and when I saw it I went in, and began my prayer. Presently the Prophet came out of his own chamber, and performed a short prayer, two Bows, then sat down near me. I was afraid again, and prolonged my praying, in the hope that he, having finished first, might go indoors without asking me that question again; but when he saw what I was at, he said: Abu Abdallah, pray as long as thou wilt; I shall not go away till thou hast finished.

Now! thought I to myself, it behoves to find some excuse to appease the Prophet of God. So I brought my prayer to an end, and greeted him; and having returned my greeting, he asked me once again: Abu Abdallah, how was that drunken camel acting?

O Apostle of God! I answered, by Him Who made thee for a blessing to us, I swear that camel hath given up drinking since I became a True Believer!

Thereupon the Prophet said solemnly three times: God hath been merciful to thee! He never asked me that question again.

Every eye is an adulterer, the Prophet used to say; and again: Let a man answer to me for what waggeth between his jaws, and what between his legs, and I'll answer to him for Paradise.

These two are my posterity in the world, Muhammad used to say (meaning his grandsons Hasan and Husayn).

One day a certain man met him walking along, carrying his grandson Hasan pickaback, and said: 'Tis a great horse thou ridest there, lad!

'Tis a great horseman too, the Prophet said.

Of all his family (Abdallah, Zubayr's son, related) the one who most resembled him was Hasan. Once I saw Hasan come when the Prophet was prostrating himself at prayer and climb on to his back; the Prophet did not make him get off, till he got off of his own accord. And it is recorded from the saying of another that the Apostle of God used to put out his tongue at Hasan, and when the child saw how red it was he would laugh, and they would be merry together.

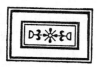

THE FIRST CALIPH

I wish I were that palm, Hasan overheard Abu Bakr say: to yield
men food, and when that was over, then be felled.

STRIFE BROKE OUT in Madina while the Prophet's body still lay unwashed in his house. The parts his Companions played in the time after he was dead, and Revelation finished, are dubious; only what they did in his lifetime is known for sure. The tale according to Omar's telling is this:

The Meccans who had fled with the Prophet, the Refugees, clustered about Abu Bakr, all except for Ali and Zubayr: those two stayed at home in Fatima's house.

Come with us, Abu Bakr, said I, to our brethren the Helpers. We set out accordingly in a body, until along the road we met two worthy men, who told us that the Helpers were gathered waiting in the porch of the kindred of Sa'ida.

And where are ye bound, ye Refugees? they asked.

To our Helper brethren, said I.

Have a care, they counselled us. Keep clear of them, and settle your own affairs.

By God! said I, but go to them we will! And we kept on our way, till we found them, in the Sa'ida porch. They were all assembled, and in their midst a man all muffled up in robes.

Who's that? I asked.

Sa'd, Ubada's son.

What's the matter with him?

Sick, sick, they said.

When we were seated, a spokesman for them stood up to speak. After glorifying God, he went on: And now, my word is this: that we are the Helpers of the Lord and the Host of Islam, whilst ye Refugees are a mere handful among us; and here ye come to uproot us, to keep us out of power.

When his speech was done, I wanted to speak. Indeed I had worked up a speech very much to my own mind, and intended to speak before Abu Bakr should; I feared he would not be trenchant enough, he being more placid and sedate than I. But Abu Bakr said: Softly, thou! And I, thinking better of his wisdom than of my own, would not cross him. And by God! when he spoke, he said every word I had in mind to say in my own set speech which I so fancied; and he spoke so much better as to leave me with nothing to say.

Now, he began, every word of praise ye gave the Helpers was their due, since, as ye surely know, God's Apostle once said this: If the whole world were to walk one way, and the Helpers walk another way, I should walk with the Helpers. But surely thou knowest also, Sa'd, Ubada's son, for thou wast sitting with us at the time, how God's Apostle said: The Quraysh are the rightful masters of authority over this people. The Arabs will never recognize this authority except in that same stock, in the Quraysh. I therefore recommend to you that ye choose one of these two men, whichever one ye please.

And he took hold of my hand, and the hand of Abu Ubayda, Jarrah's son.

I was pleased enough with all else he said; but by God! I should be easier in mind led out to have my head cut off, and that for a crime I never did, than I would be ruling a people if Abu Bakr were one of them I ruled.

But another from the Helpers was speaking now. I am a man, said he, as constantly consulted by people as a well-rubbed palm stem is consulted by camels itching with mange; and my counsel is this: one ruler from our people, and one ruler from yours, ye Quraysh.

Ay, said another, whenever God's Apostle appointed one

of you to any authority, he joined one of us with him; so let us
have two men, one from you, one from us.

The meeting fell into confusion, and voices began to be
raised so high that I feared a tumult. Give me thy hand, Abu
Bakr! I said. He put his hand in mine; and then and there I
swore fealty to him.

So much for Omar's tale. Omar then made a speech: Remember ye not, ye Helpers, how God's Apostle appointed Abu
Bakr to lead the people in prayer? Then doth any man here think
himself a better man than Abu Bakr?

God forbid! Nay, God forbid! they exclaimed; and presently one of them stood forth and said: Ye know, do ye not? that
God's Apostle was himself one of the Refugees; and we were the
Helpers of God's Apostle. By the same token are we now the
Helpers of his Caliph (which word means Successor), just as
we were his Helpers in his lifedays. And taking Abu Bakr's
hand, he said: Here is your master!

And all, Refugees and Helpers alike, now declared they
would be loyal to Abu Bakr.

When the morrow came, Abu Bakr sat down by the pulpit
in the Mosque, and Omar, standing before him, spoke to the
congregation of Muslims. After due praise and magnification of
God, he said: Surely the Lord hath centered your authority, ye
True Believers, on the best man of you all, that Companion of
His Apostle who is called in the Koran THE SECOND OF THE
TWO WHO LAY IN THE CAVE at the time of the Flight;
wherefore stand up and swear allegiance to him.

And the whole congregation swore a general allegiance to
Abu Bakr as Caliph of God's Apostle, his Successor and Vicar.

And now, ye people, Abu Bakr said, after due praise of
God, though I am by no means the best among you, yet have I
been given authority to rule you. Happy had I been had any
other man sufficed to this place in my stead. If ye expect of me
that I deal with you as God's Apostle dealt, I will not undertake
this task; for God's Apostle was a Servant of God whom He

honored with Revelation from Himself, and thereby preserved from error. But I am only a man, no better than any other. Watch me, therefore. If I do well, help me. If I go astray, then set me straight. And one thing ye had better know of me: I have a devil that possesses me sometimes; so when ye see me angered, keep away; for in that hour neither good counsel nor kind greeting can sway me.

Truth is a loyalty; falsehood a treachery. The weakest of you is strong in my sight, inasmuch as I must get him his right, if God will let me; and the strongest of you is weak in my sight, inasmuch as I shall take from him what he oweth, if God will let me.

I am a follower, not an innovator. Obey me so long as I obey God and His Apostle; but if I turn aside from God and His Apostle, then obedience to me shall no longer be any duty of yours. And now, stand up for prayers; and may the Lord have you in His Mercy.

Afterwards, Abu Bakr, looking about among the notables, missed Ali. He sent for him. When Ali came, the new Caliph said: Thou callest thyself uncle's son to God's Apostle, and his kinsman through his daughter too; dost thou wish to break the staff the Muslims must lean on?

It is not thy fault that things have turned out thus, Ali answered.

* * *

At the hour of Noonday Prayer they set about washing the Prophet's body for burial. Ali washed him, while the two sons of Abbas held him. Abbas himself and the Helper Aws looked on. After the washing, they wound the body in three shrouds: two white, and one of striped Yamani stuff, all seamless; and perfumed it.

I have heard the Apostle of God say that a prophet should be buried in that same place where he hath died, Abu Bakr said. So they dug a grave in the floor of Aisha's chamber, and laid the body on the brink; and all the people came, company after com-

pany, to pray over him. Thus passed the remainder of that day,
and half the night.

At midnight they buried the Prophet of God. His freed
slave Shuqran threw into the grave over him the coverlet on
which he ordinarily slept. No other shall sleep on this after thee!
he said.

* * *

Abu Bakr was a man of a very fair skin, slender, thin-
cheeked, and stooping; he could never keep up his lower garments from slipping over his loins. Deep-set were his eyes, under
a bossy brow. The backs of his hands were fleshless, and he dyed
his hair with henna.

Every man knoweth that my trading in cloth is enough to
provide for my family, Abu Bakr said to Aisha; but my hands
will be full now, wielding the affairs of the Believers. And soon
enough, while Abu Bakr toils for them, will his household devour
what's laid by.

Next morning, however, he arose, and was going out to the
market as of old, with some cloaks over his arm for sale, when
Omar met him.

Whither bound? said Omar.

To market, said the Caliph.

To market? cried Omar, when thou hast been given to rule
the Muslims?

But how will my household eat?

Come with me, Omar said. Abu Ubayda shall provide for
thee from the goods of the Believers. So they went together to
Abu Ubayda.

Caliph, said he, I'll set apart for thee one Refugee's pension
of the middling sort, neither a great man's nor a mean man's.
I'll allow thee besides a winter garment, and one for summer.
When a thing's outworn, bring it back to me, and take a fresh.
And thus assigning him a sheep's side a day for provender, he
gave him the wherewithal to keep his head and body covered.

THE QUELLING OF REVOLT

Usama, whom the Prophet had named captain against
Syria, sought out Abu Bakr in the Mosque. The Prophet of God
gave me orders, said he; but things were different then. Now I
fear that the clans will turn renegade; if they do so, 'tis against
them we should go.

Better be carrion for a bird's rifling, said Abu Bakr, than
take another matter in hand when some matter which God's
Apostle bade us do still waiteth our doing. And he gave Usama
orders to march. The troops departed.

But indeed certain clans no sooner heard how Muhammad
was dead than they fell away from the Faith, and said to the
collectors of the poor-rate: Pray we will, but pay this poor-rate we
will not.

The Companions came to the Caliph. Call back the host,
they counselled him; wilt thou send them against Romans far
away, in an hour when the clansmen of the Madina country itself
are falling from the Faith? But the Caliph's answer was: By Him
than Whom no other god exists! sooner let the dogs tug off the
Prophet's wives dead, by the leg, than I call back a host he sent, or
unbind from its staff any banner he hath bound!

Caliph, said Omar, then keep the clans thine, indulge them;
for they are on all fours with brute beasts.

I looked to have help of thee, the Caliph said, and here
thou comest on the other side! thou the haughty in the old Ignorance to be the craven in Islam! Why should I court them, with
lying poems and glozing words? Woe worth the day! for God's
Apostle is dead, and Revelation cometh down no more. But while
I can grip a sword in my fist I'll fight them, as long as they deny
me even so little as the price of a camel halter. And any who
maketh distinction between prayer and poor-rate, him will I
surely fight, for poor-rate is a duty of the Faith.

I saw, said Omar after, that there were no two ways about
it; but God had set Abu Bakr's heart hard to fight them; and I
knew that must be right.

Now the deputations who had come from certain clans to Madina, begging release from tax, saw well how few fighting men were left in the city; and when they went home they told their clansmen what they had seen. News got about, and revolt began to spread. The men of Abs and Dhubyan came to raid Madina itself, and spent the night not far from the town gate.

At the first glimmering of day, Abu Bakr made a sortie, and fell on the clansmen before they were aware of him. When the sun came up it showed so many dead that the Arabs fled, with the Believers after them slaughtering still, until they scattered into divers parts of the waste.

So Islam raised its head again. Three days later, the collectors whom the Prophet had appointed brought in the tax from three kindreds of Tamim. And after a while Usama returned from Syria, victorious, and laden with booty. The Caliph now took the field, with the whole host, Refugees and Helpers. They proceeded to the marches of Najd, and everywhere the clansmen and their households fled away before them. So the Refugees and Helpers said to Abu Bakr: Go home now to Madina to protect our children and our women we have left: thou mayest set some other man to command here.

Abu Bakr paid no heed; but when next morning he was got up on his camel for the day's march, Ali caught his rein and said: Whither now, Caliph of God's Apostle? I say to thee now the word which God's Apostle said to thee on the Day of Uhud: Thou must not make us anxious for thy person. Go back. If we lose thee, Islam will never be set in order.

Hearing that, the Caliph consented to return. He parted the host in eleven troops, distributed provision, and despatched them against different clans, under eleven commanders: Khalid son of Walid, Amr son of As, and others, each man with his orders written. And east and west they rode away into the wilderness.

KHALID AND THE SLAYING OF MALIK

Khalid was sent against the false prophet Tulayha. This man was head of the resistance; the others gathered to him; and Abu Bakr sent after the other ten captains, bidding them be ready to help Khalid. Khalid took reinforcement and marched on against Tulayha, scattering his allies of Fazara, so that he fled, and at last surrendered.

Then Khalid and his troop rode on. He slew those he slew, he took those he took. Against Hawazin he marched, and against Sulaym and Amir; and against Salma, a woman chief of Ghatafan whom he killed with his own hand, and the brigand Fuja'a, and against Malik, confederate of the false prophetess Saja of Mosul in the north.

Every clan submitted, and returned to Islam, and sent in the tax. To Malik's camp, however, Khalid sent fifty horsemen. 'Twas at the hour of Prayer they came to his tents; and they laid hands on the man and carried him off to Khalid.

Differing tales the riders told of what they had seen in Malik's camp. Some said they had heard no praying after the Believers' fashion; but others declared they had heard prayer.

Thou art an Unbeliever, and I know it! Khalid cried. 'Twas thou brought Saja down among us, to the shedding of Believing blood: thou art the root of the whole coil! Strike this dog! he said to a man of Asad who stood behind him with a drawn sword. The man struck, and took off Malik's head.

Now this Malik had a wife, a noblewoman of Tamim, a very beautiful woman. No sooner was her husband dead than Khalid took her for himself. But the slain man's brother came to Omar in Madina, and claimed justice for the murder of Malik. Omar took him before the Caliph to demand his right. My Brother was a Believer, and Khalid murdered him, he said. So Abu Bakr wrote to Khalid: *Leave thy men in camp and come hither alone, to answer a charge of murder.* Khalid saddled and set out.

The Prophet's freed slave Bilal was the Caliph's doorkeeper

now; and Khalid, knowing that Abu Bakr had been moved
against him by Omar, sent a messenger on to Bilal from the last
stage on the Madina road, to offer him two gold dinars, with this
request: that he let Khalid in alone to see the Caliph and not
admit Omar at that time. Bilal pocketed the dinars. Tell Khalid
to come tomorrow morning before sunup, he said to the man.
That was the first bribe in Islam.

On the morrow, Khalid rode into the town alone on camel-
back, in a cotton frock all blackened with the rubbing of his
hauberk, and wearing a red turban with two arrows stuck
through it after the fashion of famous warriors. Abu Bakr had
done praying and was gone into his house by the Mosque. Omar
was sitting with some others in the court. As Khalid made his
beast kneel at the gate and got off to go in, Omar, springing up,
ran at him in the gateway, and grasping him by the bosom of his
frock and his baldric, dragged him into the court. He snatched
the arrows out of Khalid's turban, broke them, and tossed them
outside. Enemy of God! he said. Thou didst murder a Believer
and take his wife; and I hope, by God! thou shalt be slain for
it this day!

Khalid said never a word. Before the faces of all who were
there Omar dragged him through the Mosque to Abu Bakr's
door. Wait! said Bilal: I will announce you to the Caliph of God's
Apostle. And he went in and said: Khalid is here at the door.
Of Omar he said nothing.

Call him in! the Caliph answered.

Bilal came out, and taking Khalid by the hand, said: Go
in to him.

When Omar would go in too, Bilal laid his hand on his
breast, saying: He only bade me let Khalid in. Omar, obeying,
stepped back; but as he sat down again he struck his hands
together and cried: Out on it! he'll beguile him with words.

Khalid, within, remained standing before the Caliph, who
presently spoke: Khalid, thou hast slain a Believer and taken his
wife.

Caliph of God's Apostle, I adjure thee in God's name, he

answered, to declare whether or no thou hast heard His Prophet say this: Khalid is the Sword of God on earth.

Ay surely; I have heard him say it, said Abu Bakr.

Well, God doth not strike with His Sword other than an Unbeliever's neck, or a hypocrite's, Khalid said.

'Tis sooth, the Caliph replied. Go back to thy post.

Omar was still sitting in the Mosque when Khalid came out. Khalid grasped his hilt and pulled his sword half out from its scabbard. Come on then, son of thy mother! he said to Omar; and went out and mounted his camel. Making no stay in the town even for an instant, he rode away towards his camp.

THE GARDEN OF DEATH
AND THE COLLECTING OF THE KORAN

When Khalid got back to camp, the Caliph sent him orders to attack the false prophet Musaylima in Yamama. This man, when God's Apostle died, proclaimed: Gabriel came and called me to be a prophet unto all the countries of the earth; and he gathered to a head in the stronghold of Yamama. After all his troops were mustered, Khalid arrayed the Refugees and the Helpers in separate bodies, and reviewed the clansmen who had come to his banner. There were thirty thousand men.

Then he set forward; and Musaylima the Liar came out against him, and a battle was fought till the Unbelievers were driven into a garden where the false prophet sat. But a certain Believer climbed the wall of that place, and ran to the gate and opened it; and there the Believers slaughtered seven thousand men, so that it was called ever after the Garden of Death.

So Musaylima the Liar — God curse him! — met his end: Wahshi the Abyssinian, who killed the Prophet's uncle Hamza on the Day of Uhud, was his slayer. Then those in the castle of Yamama opened their gates to the Believers; and Khalid took a fourth of their goods.

Among the Companions who fell at Yamama were Omar's brother Zayd, and Tufayl, and Maan, and Thabit, and others to the number of seventy. When the Prophet died, thousands of his Companions had no more than a smattering of the Koran; only six knew the whole of it by heart, and two of these were uncertain. Omar went to the Caliph Abu Bakr and said: I fear lest slaughter make fiery work among the Readers of the Koran on other battlefields than this, and much of the Book be lost; to my thinking it should be collected and written down, and that without delay. And the Koran was collected: from scraps of parchment and from thin white stones, and from palm leaves, and from the breasts of men.

THE BEGINNING OF TRADITION LORE

In those days, when two True Believers met, it was custom for the one to ask: What tidings? and for the other to tell him in answer some saying or tale from the mouth of God's Apostle, such as these:

I have heard God's Apostle — God's Prayer and Peace be on him! — pray: *Lord! keep me poor; let me die poor; and raise me from the dead again among the poor.*

Heaven's closer than your sandal-straps, and so is Hell, I have heard him say.

Love not this world, and God will love you; love not men's goods, and men will love you.

Envy wasteth good deeds as fire wasteth wood.

No father ever left his child a better inheritance than this, good manners.

Better than any other Holy War is war against self.

*No man ever drank a better draught than the anger he
swallowed down for God's sake.*

*Fear God in your dealings with beasts: ride them only
when they're fit to be ridden, and get off when they're tired.
Good done to beast hath its reward.*

*Your smiling in your brother's face is charity; your hearten-
ing a man to a good deed is charity; your forbidding the forbidden is charity; your showing a man his road in a country where
he is lost is charity; and your care for a blind man is charity.*

*Give your laborer his wages before his sweat hath dried on
him.*

*Three things above all gladden the eye of a man who seeth
them: green fields, running water, fair faces.*

The Prophet of God — God's Prayer and Peace be on him!
— once said: *I have loved three things much: prayer, and perfumes, and women.*

*   *   *

Of all men Abu Bakr was the most skilled in Tradition:
at divers times when the Companions consulted him (on a point
of right or wrong) he brought forward Sayings of God's Apostle
which no other man had heard. Among the Traditions narrated
by him are these:

*There shall not enter Paradise a body which hath been fed
on things forbidden.*

*Not a quarry is hunted to the death, nor any tree felled,
save it hath slackened in the praise of God.*

The thief must be put to death the fifth time he thieves.

The man who frees a slave inherits of him.

If a man came to Abu Bakr with a question of law, the
Caliph used to look first into the Book of God; if there he found
a decisive text, he decided according to that; if he found no text
and he knew a Tradition applying to such a case, he decided
according to that. But if he was at a loss, he used to go out into
the town and inquire of other Companions, saying: So-and-so
and So-and-so have come to me; do any of you know whether
God's Apostle ever decided a case of the kind? Sometimes a
number of men would gather round, each man relating some
decision of God's Apostle upon a like matter, and then the
Caliph would say: God be praised, Who hath made some of us
so mindful of Traditions!

But if he was hard put to it to find a Tradition which
seemed to fit the case, he would call together the chief Companions, the closer ones, and consult them; and if their opinions
concurred in a decision, he would decide accordingly. And Omar
used to do the same, after Abu Bakr's time.

Abu Bakr adjudged the damages for the cutting off of an
ear to be paid at only fifteen camels. Long hair and a turban, he
said, can cover the shame of that loss!

A man of Yaman once, whose right hand and foot had
been cut off for theft, came to Abu Bakr's house to complain that
the Governor in Yaman had done him wrong in the matter. He
stayed with Abu Bakr; and his diligence in night prayer caused
the Caliph to say: By thy father! thy night is not spent like a
thief's night!

But by and by an ornament belonging to Abu Bakr's
daughter Asma was missed. The Yamani went about the house
with the family looking for the thing, and crying out: O God!
Thine be the retribution upon him who robbed by night the folk
of this righteous household!

The ornament was found later, in the shop of a goldsmith;
and the goldsmith affirmed that he had got it of the mutilated
man. The latter having confessed, or the fact being proved, Abu
Bakr passed sentence on him; and his other hand was amputated.

To my mind, the Caliph said, his imprecation upon himself was a graver thing than his thieving.

* * *

Abu Bakr first established the public Treasury in the suburb where he used to live. He had no one guarding it; and when people said: Wilt thou not put a man to guard the place? he answered: Nay, the door is locked.

But when he removed into midtown, he transferred the Treasury to his house there. As the poor-rate came in, he used to distribute it amongst the poor. He also used to buy camels and horses and arms, and give them away for God's service in war. It was his wont to pay out the treasure as it came in, until the Treasury was empty.

ARABIA SUBDUED

Ala, one of the eleven captains, led his troop against the men of Bahrayn, who had turned renegade to the Faith. They returned to Islam, and gathering under Ala fell on the idolaters of Hajar; much booty they got, every footsoldier two thousand silver dirhams and every cavalier six thousand. The Caliph sent order for Ala to stay in Bahrayn as Governor, keeping his troop with him.

Through the coasts of Oman, through the coasts and isles and wastes of Mahra, an army of Believers marched. All submitted, and Ikrima, another of the eleven, stayed on as Governor in that country. Then into Yaman they marched from two sides; the people made no resistance, and Muhajir and Firuz the Persian were appointed to govern there. In Hadramawt, Ubayd was set to govern the people of Kinda, and Ziyad to collect the taxes; and the Caliph sent Omar to be Governor general over all those regions of farther Arabia, to be judge over them, and to teach men the rites and Law of Islam.

THE FIRST RAIDS ON PROVINCES
OF THE PERSIAN EMPIRE

In the twelfth year of the Flight, Abu Bakr heard by report
that the Persian Empire was grown weak, and its sway fallen into
womanish and childish hands. And he wrote to Khalid son of
Walid: *Leave Yamama now and go into Iraq: to Hira and Kufa;
then march on to their great city at Madain, and to Ubulla.* So
Khalid left his governorship, and rode into the Black Earth region of Iraq. The citizens came out of the nearer towns to ask
him for peace, consenting to pay tribute. Khalid had the terms
of peace and tribute set down in writing, and marched on till
he came to the gates of Hira.

Iyas of Taiy, who held the city for the Persian Kings, came
out to him. Choose now, Iyas, said Khalid, one of these three
courses: to take our Faith, or to pay tribute, or to fight; and these
my comrades love war and death as thou lovest pleasure and life.

Fight with thee we cannot, and forsake our faith we will
not; we will pay tribute, said Iyas. So the citizens collected two
hundred and ninety thousand dirhams of tribute.

Abu Bakr wrote, naming Khalid Governor of Iraq and
chief commander of all the armies, telling him what troops were
stationed in the wastes upon his border, and giving him leave to
call them to his own banner. So Khalid wrote, summoning the
four commanders nearest him, and having now eighteen thousand men, gave the order to march, first against the town
Ubulla, held by the Persian March-warden Hormuz with twenty
thousand men. The hosts met, Hormuz was slain, and the Persians fled.

On the morrow Khalid made his entry into Ubulla. They
took such a booty as Believers had never seen before. There was
a red tiara which Hormuz had been used to wear, set with jewels
worth a hundred thousand dirhams, the insignia, as they were
told, of the rank to which the Persian King had raised the man.

At the sharing of the spoil, Khalid sent this tiara, and an elephant taken in the fight, to Madina along with the Fifth.

And now Qaren, the Great King's viceroy in Ahwaz, marched against him with fifty thousand men; but at the meeting the Persians ran. Till dark came on, the Believers pursued and slew; and the count on the morrow was thirty thousand dead. Another army Khalid scattered; and he found himself master of the Black Earth of Iraq. He fixed his camp before the gates of Hira, and sent two agents into the towns of Iraq: one as collector to take the poor-rate from such as entered Islam, and the tenth and the poll tax from Unbelievers of the Scripture peoples, Jew, Christian, and Zoroastrian; the other as Governor, with troops at command, to hold the place. Next the Believers captured Anbar, a great and strong town over towards Madain, then Ain al-Tamr and Dumat al-Jandal to the west. Khalid's Governor of Hira took the Castle of Hasid; and Khalid himself surprised the Castle of Mudhayya.

In the castle at the time of its capture were found two men who had gone to Madina formerly to swear fealty to Abu Bakr as Muslims, and had got a writ from him to that effect. One of them, Abd al-Uzza, kept declaring that he was a Believer, and Khalid was told about it.

Strike them down, said he. If they were Believers, what were they doing here among Unbelievers? Both were killed, Abd al-Uzza even as he cried: Glory to God! Glory to Muhammad's Lord!

His son came to Madina to complain to Abu Bakr; and Omar spoke out against Khalid: Was not Malik's murder enough? For Malik was a Believer; but no — he must kill two Believers more!

What were they doing in such a place? said Abu Bakr. It was their own fault.

Nevertheless the Caliph paid the man his father's bloodwit out of the Treasury. Khalid killed your father by mistake, he said.

* * *

Abu Bakr went into a garden once, it is recorded, and saw a
ringdove there, in the shady leafage of a tree. He gave a sigh,
and said: How happy thou! to get thy eating of a tree, and thy
shelter underneath it, and never to be called to account — ah!
would to God Abu Bakr were so!

THE BYZANTINE PROVINCES INVADED

Much territory in Iraq, in this the thirteenth year of the
Flight, was now in Believers' hands, whilst as yet no part of
Roman Syria had fallen to them. The Caliph therefore called on
the Muslims to make ready for an expedition against that land.
He wrote to the people of Mecca, to Taif and Yaman, and to all
the clans of Najd and Hijaz, summoning them to Holy War,
whetting their appetite for fight, and for booty such as was to be
got of the Romans of Byzantium. To Khalid in Iraq he sent
order: Syria being still in Unbelievers' hands, I have sent an army
there. Thou too must march into that country, leaving in Iraq
what troops thou thinkest enough. I make thee commander of
the host which is in Syria, and send thee besides reinforcement
from Madina, that thou mayest give permission to any of thy
companions who will ask leave of thee to come home to the city.
Khalid accordingly marched into Syria.

A GRANT OF TERMS: DAMASCUS

*IN THE NAME OF GOD THE MERCIFUL THE
COMPASSIONATE:*
*These terms will Khalid grant the people of Damascus on
condition that he is admitted to their city: he promises to allow
them security for their lives and for their property and for
their churches. Their city wall shall not be rased. No Believer
shall be quartered on their houses.*
Thereunto we give them the covenant of God, and the pro-

tection of His Apostle and the Caliphs of His Apostle and the True Believers. Only good shall be theirs so long as they duly pay the poll tax (of one gold dinar and a measure of wheat a head).

* * *

In Ramadan of the eleventh year had died Fatima, daughter of the Apostle of God. There is disagreement upon the question of the time at which Ali (her husband) recognized the election of Abu Bakr as Caliph; some say it was ten days after Fatima's death. There are traditions recorded that one day Ali's son Hasan went up to Abu Bakr, who was on the Pulpit of God's Apostle at the time, and said: Come down off my father's seat!

I did not tell him to say that, I swear, said Ali.

I never thought it of thee, the Caliph answered.

* * *

Once in Abu Bakr's time, some folk from Yaman came to Madina. When they heard a Reader in the Mosque chanting the Koran, tears fell from their eyes.

We were like that once, the Caliph said; but our hearts have grown harder since.

And now Abu Bakr fell sick, of fever, and could no more come out to prayers. He sent for Othman son of Affan, husband to the Prophet's daughter Ruqayya.

Tell me thy opinion of Omar, he said.

Thou knowest him better than I, said Othman.

Even so . . . . the Caliph said.

Well, Othman answered, this I am sure of: that he is better than his manners. (The Prophet of God once said: God have mercy on Omar — he always speaketh truth, though it be bitter; and speaking truth hath left him without a friend.)

Some other men Abu Bakr consulted further, both Refugees and Helpers; then summoned Othman once more, and said: Write this down:

IN THE NAME OF GOD THE MERCIFUL THE COMPASSIONATE:

This is the testament of Abu Bakr son of Abu Quhafa, at his life's end in this world whence he is departing, at his life's beginning in the Other to which he goeth, a time when even the infidel believeth, and the sinner hath knowledge, and the liar speaketh truth.

I appoint Omar son of Khattab to be Caliph over you after me; hearken therefore to him, and obey. If he doth justice, that will accord with my expectation and knowledge of him; if he doth the contrary, then every deed hath its own wages. I intended good, but I know not the hidden. And now Peace be to you, and the Mercy of God and His Blessings.

Then Abu Bakr summoned Omar in private, and charged him with what he charged him withal; and Omar went away.

When he felt his death coming on him, he said to his daughter: Look, Aisha, the camel whose milk we drank, the platter we dished our food in, the clothes we wore — we have used all these while we swayed the affairs of the Muslims. When I am gone, give the things to Omar.

After his death, they dug a grave for him beside the Apostle of God, and laid him in it with his head level with the shoulder of God's Apostle.

FROM HIS ELEGY

Whoever endeavors in earnest to equal his lifedays' goodness,
Solitary will he be, and lonely upon earth.

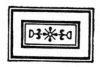

THE CALIPHATE
OF CONQUEST

Farewell, Syria, and for ever! said the Emperor as he embarked for Byzantium; and ah! that so fair a land should be my enemy's.

Weep too for the throne of the Sasanids, for the power and the glory, for the crown of so many kings!
Omar's age was come, and a faith unknown before: now stood the pulpit where the throne had been.

N THE MORROW, after Abu Bakr's burial, the Believers assembled in the Mosque, and Omar mounted the Prophet's Pulpit. It had three steps; and the Apostle of God had always stood on the uppermost. When Abu Bakr was Caliph, he had been used to stand on the second; but Omar on that day went no higher than the lowest step; he spoke thence to the congregation, gave thanks to God, and swore to do justice.

His first act after he came down from the Pulpit was to write a letter to Abu Ubayda appointing him chief commander of the host in Syria, and degrading Khalid son of Walid to a command under him.

Omar was the first Caliph to be called Prince of the True Believers. He was the first to use the scourge upon offenders, the first to establish dating from the Flight of the Prophet, and the first to establish Divans, or Public Registers.

I went into a yard once, says Anas, a former servant in Muhammad's house, and heard Omar talking to himself on the other side of a wall. Omar son of Khattab, Prince of the True Believers! he was saying: By God! that sounds good! But thou hadst better fear God, thou son of Khattab, or He will surely punish thee.

Once we were sitting at Omar's door, says Ibn Qays the Clubfoot, a great shaykh of Tamim, and a slave girl passed by in the street.

The Prince of the True Believers should take that woman to his bed, said somebody.

That woman is not for the Prince of True Believers' bed! Omar exclaimed. She is not lawful for him; she is the Lord's goods.

Why then, what is lawful to him? we asked.

Nothing of the Lord's goods is allowed to Omar beyond a garment for winter and one for summer, the Caliph answered, and enough for Pilgrimage and the rites, and eating for him and his household at the middling rate allowed a Qurayshi. Beyond that I have no more right than any other Muslim.

Many were the conquests of Omar's time. Emessa and Baalbek in Syria submitted, and Tiberias, and the whole of the Jordan country was conquered. Khalid was camped with his troops by the stream of Yarmuk which flows into Jordan, when news was brought that the Roman army of Byzantium was in the field, and making for that river. Khalid arrayed his host, assigning those who had fought at the Day of Badr a post apart. There were a hundred such with him.

As for you, he said to them, I ask you not to fight, but to bow down and pray that God come to our help this day.

The men of Badr began to pray, and to recite from the Koran; and the battle was joined.

And the Romans broke!

The Believers smote and slaughtered till the going-down of the sun; and then Khalid went up from the banks of the Yarmuk to occupy the Roman camp.

And the fear of the Arabs fell upon all kings.

A DEED OF SURRENDER ADDRESSED
TO OMAR BY SYRIAN CHRISTIANS

*IN THE NAME OF GOD THE MERCIFUL THE
COMPASSIONATE:*
*This is a document submitted to Omar son of Khattab, Prince
of the True Believers, by the Christians of the town of ———.*

*When you entered this land, we asked you to give us secur-
ity, for us and our families and property, and for our brothers
in faith.*

*You granted our prayer on the following conditions, to wit:
that we should not build new, either in our towns or in their
neighborhoods, any cloister, church, monastery, or hermitage,
nor restore or rebuild in the Believers' quarter of our town
any such that had decayed;*

*that we should not hinder True Believers from lodging in
our churches for three nights, and further that we should entertain them at our own costs for three nights; that we should
not harbor any spy nor receive any enemy of the True Believers
in our churches or our dwelling houses;*

that we should not teach our children to read Arabic;

*that we should not openly practice idolatry nor seduce peo-
ple into idolatrous practices; and further that we should not
dissuade any of our kin from making Submission to God as
True Believers if so minded;*

*that we should not wear caps or turbans similar to those
the True Believers wear, nor dress our hair in their fashion;
that we should not talk in their tongue nor assume their
names; nor use saddles for riding, nor wear swords, nor buy
weapons, nor carry weapons about us, nor have Arabic inscrip-
tions cut upon our signet rings, nor sell wine; that we should
shave our forelocks, and keep to our own style of dress, wearing belts about our waists in all places;*

*that we should not set up any cross on our churches; that
we should not hawk our books for sale in any street frequented
by True Believers, nor in their bazaars;*

that we should toll our church bells slowly; that in our praying we should not raise our voices too high; that in the public procession on Easter Day we should not carry palm leaves nor idols; that we should not raise our voices at funerals, nor carry any light with our funeral processions through any street or bazaar inhabited by True Believers;

that we should not buy slaves from the possession of True Believers, nor seek to discover their private affairs.

(To this document Omar added in his own hand):

that we should not strike True Believers; that we undertake to observe these terms for ourselves and our brothers in faith, in return for security of person and property. But should we violate any of the terms we have promised to keep, then that security may be taken from us; and you may do with us as you please.

* * *

We like your rule, said the people of the Syrian town of Hims; we like your justice, ye Muslims, far better than the cruelty and tyranny of the old times.

FALL OF THE PERSIAN EMPIRE

A certain Muthanna son of Haritha wrote to Omar advising him of troubles in Persia, and that on the throne now sat Yazdagird, a very young man. Omar sent for Sa'd son of Abu Waqqas and charged him as chief commander for Iraq. When Sa'd rode away with his troops, the Caliph went along with them for some hours' march, and spoke exhorting them, spurring them on to Holy War. Then he bade them farewell, and came back to Madina, while Sa'd went on. Between Hijaz and Kufa, Sa'd turned out of the road, into the wilderness, sending out spies to bring him reports, until he made up his mind to march on Qadisia, the gate of the Persian Empire.

From the inhabitants of Iraq messages were sent to beg Yazdagird for help. The Arabs have not yet forced us all to surrender, they said, but unless relief come quickly, we must give ourselves up to them. The great nobles likewise who owned estates along Euphrates bank spoke to the same effect, urging the King to send down his commander in chief, Rustam, into Iraq. Yazdagird sent for Rustam.

Your Majesty, said the general, I beg that you will allow me to prosecute my own plans. So long as you do not provoke a decisive battle, so long will fear of the Persians hold the Arabs in check. It is in this manner that I hope to preserve Your Majesty's house. God may be with us. And my counsel may be wise, for in war strategy sometimes avails more than any victory.

Yazdagird liked this counsel little. Can nothing else be done? he asked.

In military matters, Rustam replied, deliberation is always better than haste. And the present is an occasion for delay, for that will work to our advantage. It will waste the enemy to engage him piecemeal, rather than to inflict a single defeat on him.

But the King was alarmed by the appeals for help which constantly came in from the Iraqis. He threw caution aside, and ordered Rustam to march straight against the foe.

Envoys now began to go to and fro between Rustam and Saʻd. The Arab would be ushered to Rustam's presence to find him sitting on a gilt throne and leaning on gold-broidered cushions, in an open-ended hall spread with gold-broidered carpets, with his Persians wearing their diadems and gay with finery, and his elephants of war standing far to right and left. So the Believer would ride up, spear in hand, girt with his sword, and his bow across his shoulders, and picket his horse as close as he might ride to the place where Rustam sat. And though the Persians would cry out on him and try to intercept him, Rustam would command them to let him be; and the Arab would walk up close, leaning on his spear as he walked, thrusting it into carpet or cushion and ripping all with the spike of it, under the very eyes of the Persians.

I know that you are driven to these deeds of yours by nothing more than straitened living, by your poverty, said Rustam to one such.

But the Arab would answer him back boldly: the Persian continually heard shrewd words, and answers which startled him. Thus, for instance, Sa'd used to send a different envoy each time, and Rustam inquired of one so sent: Why do they not send us the man who was here yesterday?

Because there is no favoritism with our Prince, the Believer answered.

Another day, Rustam pointed to the Arab's slender spear, and asked disdainfully: What spindle is that thou hast in hand?

A burning coal is none the cooler, he retorted, for being small!

And to another Rustam said: What's wrong with thy sword? It looks so worn.

Shabby sheath, sharp edge! said he.

Sa'd's messengers were even brought to audience of the King of Kings. When they were gone back from that audience, Rustam dreamed a dream which he liked not. He felt foreboding of ill, and was loath to march out to encounter. But Yazdagird was insistent. Rustam therefore wrote to his brother and the great peers after this style:

From Rustam to Bindavan, Satrap at Court and Arrow of the Persian People, him whose hand, under God, scattereth hosts the mightiest and quelleth holds the strongest — to him and those about him:

Repair your castles, man them, and make ready. Under your very eyes the Arabs have thrust into your country, and left you no other way but to fight, if you would keep your lands and your children your own. My own advice was to block their way and wear them down by delay, till Fortune turned about again. But His Majesty would not hear my counsel.

The Fish has troubled the waters; the Ostrich Stars of Sagittarius are fair, and Venus is fair; but the Scales are even,

*and Mars is combust. I have no doubt but that our enemies
will be victorious.*

*Worst of all, His Majesty has announced that unless I
march against them he will take the field in person, in consideration of which I have no other course: I must take the offensive.*

Battle was joined, and fought for three days. On the last,
a little after noon, a storm of wind blew up, whirling dust against
the Persians; and one wild gust carried away the tilt over the
throne where Rustam sat, and hurled it into the Old Canal. It
was blowing from the west, and blinding the Persians with dust.
A few Believers got up on the throne itself; Rustam jumped down
and ran to where the baggage mules were stationed, laden with
his treasure. He hid among the bales with which they were laden.

A certain Arab, Hilal, gave a cut with his sword at the
strap of the bale behind which Rustam crouched; half the beast's
load fell on the Persian's back and staved in his ribs, though Hilal
had not seen him, and never suspected that he was there. The
Arab ran his blade into the sack — it breathed out a musky perfume. Rustam presently dragged himself as far as the Old Canal
and plunged into the water. But Hilal now caught sight of him;
he sprang in after him, and catching at his feet pulled him out
on to the bank, where he despatched him with a single blow of
his sword.

This done, he dragged the carcass by the legs and threw
it under the feet of the mules; then, climbing the steps of the
throne, he gave a shout: I have killed Rustam! By the Lord of
the Holy House I have! Here!

Warriors crowded towards him, but they could see neither
him nor the throne for dust. They answered with yells. The Unbelievers' hearts failed them at that cry; they took to flight.

Many came to their ends under the sword's edge, or in the
waters of the stream. Some sought the Tigris fords; but Sa'd
followed hard after, and crossing the fords after them did great
slaughter. And amongst the plunder of that day was taken captive a daughter of the King of Kings.

The Flag of Empire (an ancient banner of leather set with jewels) fell into the hands of an Arab named Dirar. It was accounted worth two million gold dinars, though some say Dirar let it go for thirty thousand. Sa'd put it afterwards with the treasures and jewels of Yazdagird when God gave them to the Believers, and sent it, with all the jewelled diadems and girdles and necklaces and other things, to the Caliph. Omar bade them take the Flag of Empire from its staff and cut it into small pieces, and so share it among the Muslims.

A certain Arab sold a woman from his share of the spoil of Iraq for only a thousand dirhams. But she was of high birth; and people laughed at the man for selling her so cheap.

But I never knew there was a number above ten hundred! cried the Arab.

There was in Madain, the Persian capital in Iraq, an audience hall where the King of Kings used to sit. Here was hung his crown, as big as a great barrel, made of gold and silver set with rubies and emeralds and pearls. The crown was suspended by a golden chain from the top of the vault in this hall, being too weighty for his neck to bear. Curtains were drawn before the throne until such time as the King of Kings had taken his seat and had introduced his head into the crown and settled himself in position; then the curtains were drawn back.

No man who had not seen that sight before could look upon the King thus but awe brought him to his knees.

But in the sixteenth year of the Flight, Madain was taken, and Sa'd son of Abu Waqqas led Friday Prayers in that same audience hall.

Yazdagird the King fled into Khurasan in the north; and his power was ever waning until he was slain there, in the thirty-first year of the Flight, he the last of the Persian Kings.

As he rode by the banks of the stream of Zark, Yazdagird descried in the gloom the shape of a mill, and dismounted, to find if here might be some shelter from the fury of his enemies. He went inside and sat him down on a bundle of hay.

At the coming-up of the sun the miller threw open the door of his mill; there stood he with a load of fodder on his shoulders, a man of mean birth, gazing at Yazdagird, a warrior with the eyes of a gazelle. He saw gilt boots upon his feet, and his tunic and sleeves broidered with gold and pearls, and said: Who art thou?

A Persian, and a fugitive, said the King.

If thou canst content thee with barley bread, and the poor cresses that grow by the banks of the brook, I offer it to thee freely, said the miller, for that is all I have.

Content, said he, but get me some holy barsom twigs for my ritual besides.

So the poor miller went out to borrow barsom. But those he met with took him before the traitor Mahwi, the King's enemy; and Mahwi said to the wretched drudge: For whom does the like of thee seek barsom? The miller told his tale; and Mahwi knew it must be Yazdagird. Go back, said he; and cut off his head straightway; if not, thine own shall fall.

The poor man heard the word; but little he knew the reach of the deed. It was night when he got home, and came into the presence of the King. Shame and fear in his heart, dry at the lips, he drew softly near, as he would whisper in his ear; then struck a dagger in his breast. And death was in the stroke. One sob the King gave; then his diademed head tumbled on the ground beside a barley loaf he had before him.

The world's soul is a mindless void; and witless is the turning Heaven. A mystery is its hatred, or its grace. 'Tis wisest not to care — to watch changes without anger, and without love.

Then came in two cruel-hearted serving men, and dragged out the King's body bleeding. They heaved it into the whirling eddies of the Zark; and there the corpse of Yazdagird drifted, face up for a while, and then face under.

THE FOUNDING OF THE DIVANS

Once on a burning summer's day, a freedman of Othman's related afterwards, I was sitting with Othman in Madina. Far off we saw a man driving two camel foals. Fierce was the heat; and we wondered much who would venture into such a sun. As the man came nearer, we saw, and to our great surprise, that it was Omar. Othman stood up and put his head out of the shade. But he soon drew it in again, so scorching was the air. When Omar presently came in to us, Othman asked for what reason he had gone out into that frightful heat.

Those two camel foals were sent in payment of taxes, Omar said; I wanted to drive them into the State pasturage myself. I feared they might stray.

In Omar's time there came to be in the State pasture as many as four hundred thousand camels and horses.

And once the Governor of Bahrayn, when he brought a half-year's revenue to Madina, told Omar that it amounted to a million dirhams. The Caliph laughed at him.

But he found out afterwards that it was true. When the people gathered in the Mosque for prayer, Omar spoke to them: I have got from Bahrayn a huge sum of money: will ye take your shares weighed out? Or must I count it over to you coin by coin?

In the fifteenth year (636 A.D.) the Caliph Omar, seeing how the conquests went on and on, and the treasures of the Persian Kings were taken as spoil, and load was heaped on load of gold and silver, of precious jewels and splendid raiment, resolved to make the Muslims rich by distributing all this wealth. But he could not tell how to manage the distribution.

There was at that time in Madina a certain Persian march-lord, who saw the perplexity of Omar, and spoke to him thus: O

Prince of the True Believers, the Persian Kings have a thing they call a Divan, in which is recorded the whole of their revenue and expenditure to the last farthing; and in the Divan those who are entitled to allowances are arranged in various ranks, that there may be no dispute.

Omar listened. He bade the marchlord speak more minutely of the matter. When he had grasped the working of it, he drew up the Muslim Registers, and assigned the allowances, appointing a stated amount for every Muslim, allotting fixed sums to the wives of the Apostle of God, and to his slave girls and near kin, until the money in hand was all paid out.

He would not let money accumulate in the Treasury. Once a man came to him and said: Prince of the True Believers, something it had been better to leave against times unforeseen.

The Devil put those words in thy mouth! the Caliph said; and may God preserve me from the mischief in them! That would be leading those who shall come after me into temptation. Come what may, the only provision I will make against the time to come shall be obedience to God and His Apostle, God's Prayer and Peace be on him! That obedience is provision enough for us, for that obedience got us all we have gotten.

At the time, in respect of the allowances, he thought it right that rank should be according to priority in Submission to God, and service rendered the Apostle of God on his battlefields. Kinship with the Prophet was taken into reckoning besides: By God! said Omar, we have not won the upper place in this world, nor do we hope for God's rewarding of our works in the Other, save only through Muhammad, God's Prayer and Peace be on him! He is our title of nobility; his near kin therefore are the noblest of all Arabs, and after them those are the nobler who are the nearer him in blood. For all that, if outlanders bring good works and we bring none, they will be nearer Muhammad on Resurrection Day, by God! than we shall. So let no man count on kinship; but let him work for what lieth in God's Hand to give. He that is hindered by his works will not be sped by his lineage.

The Caliph assigned annuities out of the State revenue:

to Aisha, Mother of the Believers, 12,000 silver dirhams;
to the other wives of the Apostle of God, 10,000 dirhams each;
to men of the kindred of Hashim and Abd al-Muttalib who fought at the Day of Badr, 10,000 dirhams;
to such Hashimites as became Believers after Badr, to the Helpers, to the Prophet's other blood-kindred, and to such Refugees as went out to the Day of Badr and their confederates and clients, 5,000 dirhams;
to Hasan and Husayn, 5,000 dirhams;
to those who Believed before the Flight, and those who fled to Abyssinia, 4,000 dirhams;
to the three Believing slaves who fought at Badr, 3,000 dirhams;
to those who Believed before the taking of Mecca, 3,000 dirhams;
to the sons of all who fought at Badr, to those who Believed after the taking of Mecca, and to the sons of all Helpers and Refugees, 2,000 dirhams;
to such Arabs of Yaman and Qays as had settled in Syria and Iraq, from 2,000 to 300 dirhams;
to such women as came to Madina after the Flight, from 3,000 to 1,000 dirhams;
to each weaned child of Believing parents, from 200 to 100 dirhams;
to all wives and children of Believing outlanders dead in Holy War or still fighting, 10 gold dinars.

THE CONQUEST OF THE WEST

Egypt was invaded in the twentieth year. Amr was commander of the western troop, and to him the Caliph wrote: *If this my letter, bidding thee turn back from Egypt, overtake thee be-*

*fore thou hast entered any part of that country, then turn back;
but if thou hast invaded the land before the coming of my letter,
then go on. And beg God for help.*

In the twenty-first year, Alexandria was taken by storm.
I have captured a city, Amr wrote to Omar, *from the description
of which I shall refrain. Suffice it to say that I have taken therein
four thousand villas, four thousand baths, forty thousand Jews
liable to poll tax, and four hundred pleasure-palaces fit for kings.*

Omar issued orders to the commanders of the armies to levy
poll tax only on full-grown men: forty-eight dirhams a head
where silver currency obtained, and four gold dinars where gold
was the standard.

The Iraqis had to supply thirty quarts of provisions and a
certain measure of fat monthly for every Believer, the Egyptians
an Egyptian great measure of wheat monthly, a quantity of honey
and fat, and linen besides, for the clothing of the troops; they
were bound to give free quarters to any Believer for three days.
The people of Syria and farther Mesopotamia had to give monthly
a great quart of wheat, three pints of oil and honey and fat. All
Unbelievers were given lead tokens to wear about their necks as
proof that they had paid poll tax duly.

A Land Tax was appointed also. In Iraq it was:

for every great acre of meadow, five bushels in kind and
five silver dirhams;

for every great acre planted with trees or palms or vines,
ten bushels in kind and ten dirhams;

for every great acre of sugar cane, six dirhams;

for every great acre of wheat field, four dirhams;

for every great acre of barley field, two dirhams;

for every great acre of other land, one bushel in kind and a
silver dirham.

* * *

Am I a king now? Or a Caliph? Omar once asked Salman
the Persian.

If thou tax the land of Believers in money, either little or much, and put the money to any use the Law doth not allow, then thou art a king, and no Caliph of God's Apostle.

By God! said Omar, I know not whether I am a Caliph or a king. And if I am a king, it is a fearful thing.

I went to a festival outside Madina once, said a Believer from Iraq, and saw Omar: tall and bald and grey; he walked barefoot, drawing a red-broidered cloth about his body with both hands; and he towered above the people as though he were on horseback.

Surely if I live, Omar said, I will, please God, spend a whole year in travel among my people. I know they have demands which are cut short before they come to my hearing: the Governors do not bring their needs before me, and the people themselves cannot get through to me. So I will go to Syria, and spend two months there, then to Iraq, and spend two months there, then to Egypt, then to Bahrayn, then to Kufa, then to Basra, two months in every place. It will be a year well spent, by God!

* * *

His daughter Hafsa, the Prophet's widow, his son Abdallah, and some others pleaded with the Caliph against his fasting. If thou wert to eat well, they said, thy eating would strengthen thee for the maintaining of the truth.

I understand your counsel, he replied; but it was in a certain path that I said good-bye to two Companions of mine; and if I turn out of the path where I walked with them, I shall never find them again at journey's end.

Omar would allow no captive over the age of puberty to stay in Madina. But a certain Mughira wrote to him from Kufa, saying that he was owner of a young man who was a cunning artificer, and asking permission for him to come to Madina, being

a master of many trades, a smith, a graver of metal, and a carpenter. Omar granted it; and Mughira tasked his slave with a
daily impost of four dirhams to be sent him out of his earnings.

The slave went to Omar and complained that the impost
was too much. But the Caliph judged that it was fair enough;
and the young man went away, saying bitterly: Omar's justice is
wide enough for all except me!

After some little time, the slave took a double-bladed dagger hafted in the middle, and hid, before daybreak, in a corner
of the shelter in the Mosque; and there he waited till Omar came
forth to call the people to Prayer. Even as the Caliph was crying:
Get ye into your ranks, before the saying of the Magnification!
he drew near the place of hiding; and the slave stabbed him,
three blows. Omar fell. A man of Iraq threw his cloak over the
slave, and the young man, still muffled in the folds of it, stabbed
himself to death.

They carried Omar to his own house. Since the sun was
now coming up, Abd al-Rahman, Awf's son, led prayers: the
Chapters he recited were the two shortest of the Book.

Ibn Abbas began to talk to Omar, praising his goodness;
but the Caliph said: Son of Abbas, if the fullness of the earth in
gold were mine, be assured I would give it all, to be ransomed
from the terror of Resurrection Day. And now I tell you this:
I appoint the Succession to be determined in consultation by Othman and Ali and Talha and Zubayr and Abd al-Rahman, Awf's
son, and Sa'd. And let my son Abdallah be present with them;
but he must have no part in the decision.

When he was dead, they carried his body slowly to Aisha's
chamber. His son Abdallah saluted her, and said: Omar desireth
permission.

Bring him in! said Aisha. And they bore him in, and laid
him there to rest beside his two Companions.

The luck of Islam was shrouded in Omar's winding-sheet,
it was said in aftertime.

MISRULE

When Omar was converted, Islam became even as a man advancing: every step takes him forward.

But when Omar was murdered, Islam became as a man retreating: every step takes him farther back.

If only the Apostle of God were still alive, the Caliph Othman would say in perplexity, there would have been Scripture revealed to settle this matter.

HEN OMAR WAS IN HIS GRAVE, the six of the council to choose a Caliph met. This seemeth good to me, said Abd al-Rahman, Awf's son: that we delegate authority to three of us only.

I will give my authority to Ali, said Zubayr.

I mine to Abd al-Rahman, said Sa'd.

And I give my authority to Othman, said Talha.

Then these three went apart; and Abd al-Rahman spoke: I do not want authority for myself — which now of you two will likewise give up his? and we will put it to the third, with God and all Islam as his Witness, to consider who in his judgment is the best man among all the Believers, doing his best for the welfare of the people.

But those two shaykhs, Ali and Othman, said never a word.

Give me the choice! said Abd al-Rahman then; and the Lord be my Witness as I shall not betray you, but shall name the better of you two.

Ali and Othman consented. Then Abd al-Rahman took Ali aside and said: Of you two thou wert the prior in Islam, and thou hast kinship with God's Apostle, as well thou knowest; now the Lord be thy Witness as thou shalt answer! If I give this authority to thee, wilt thou do justice? And if I set another over thee, wilt thou hearken to him and obey?

I will, said Ali.

Then Abd al-Rahman took Othman aside, and said the same to him; and so he got both their promises.

Next he called Zubayr to him. Supposing I were not to give allegiance to thee, whom dost thou recommend to me?

Either Ali or Othman, answered Zubayr.

Then Abd al-Rahman summoned Sa'd. Whom wouldst thou choose for this authority? he asked; for I and thou want it not for ourselves.

Othman, said Sa'd.

Then Abd al-Rahman sent for the people to swear allegiance. Standing up from his seat, he praised God and glorified Him, and thus proceeded: Now, Ali, I have considered all; and I see none so fit as Othman; so seek not to take the place ahead thyself. And he took Othman by the hand, and said: I swear allegiance to thee according to the Law of God, and the Law of His Apostle, and the Law of the two Caliphs after him.

Then Ali swore allegiance too, and all the Refugees, and all the Helpers.

Othman was the first Caliph to assign lands as fiefs to any large extent; and he was the first to appoint a Chief of Police.

He was Caliph twelve years in all. For six years he governed without reproach of the people, more beloved of the Quraysh than Omar had been, for Omar was severe with them, while Othman in his rule was easy, and supported their interest. But in his later time he began to appoint his own kinsmen of the Umayyad House to posts of authority. He gave Marwan a fifth of the whole revenue of Africa, and lavished the goods of Muhammad's people on his own kin. These things he justified as being the assistance to kindred which the Lord had enjoined in the Koran:

*SHOW KINDNESS UNTO PARENTS AND UNTO
    NEAR KINDRED*
and: *GIVE THE KINSMAN HIS DUE.*

Abu Bakr and Omar, he used to say, surely neglected their duty
in that respect.

But the people disapproved.

The sight of riches banisheth patience.

Patience is to faith as the head to the body: when patience dies, faith dies also.

Othman's officers in every great town were men allied by
blood to the Children of Umayya; and even if he took his office
from one such, he would set another of the same kindred in his
place. Also he appointed men who had never been Companions
of the Apostle of God, so that his Governors did things hateful
to the Companions.

The first matter in which he incurred reproach for preferring his own kinsmen to authority was his removal of Sa'd son of
Abu Waqqas, him who defended the Prophet at the Day of Uhud,
from the government of Kufa, and his appointment in Sa'd's
place of Walid son of Uqba, a man who had once spat in the
Prophet's face, but half-brother to Othman by their mother.

This Walid at Kufa on a certain occasion passed the whole
night long drinking with his boon companions and his singers.
On the morrow, at the first call of the muezzin, he sallied forth
into the Mosque with his dress in disorder, and staggered to the
mihrab niche to lead Prayer. Having prayed four Bows instead of
the ordained two, he glared round on the Believers and demanded: Do ye want me to go on?

Another account adds that, when he remained in the attitude of prostration for an extraordinarily prolonged time, men
listened and heard him mumbling: Drink — fill it up!

That's enough, and God never prosper thee more! cried
one of those close behind him in the front rank. And the congregation chased him out, pelting him with pebbles picked up in the
court of the Mosque. Walid got back to his palace muttering, like

a man offended, these verses from a heathen poet of the old Ignorance:

> *I lack no longer song-girls and wine,*
> *As once at Ayda;*
> *I wander no more an exile from pleasure,*
> *As once in the waste.*
> *Here at last I can steep my body*
> *In delicate drink,*
> *And walk the world in trailing robes*
> *Like a noble Lord!*

When at last Othman took the government of Kufa from
Walid and gave it to one Saʻid, the people of Kufa were still ill-
pleased, preferring even Walid, an easy man, to Saʻid, a gloomy
man affecting an austere virtue, who made a door to his palace
and kept aloof from the people.

In the twenty-seventh year of the Flight, Muʻawia, the son
of Abu Sufyan and Hind, Governor of Syria, led an expedition
against Cyprus; that was the first time that Believing troops
crossed the sea.

In the thirtieth year, Jur was taken, and many cities in the
land of Khurasan, far to the northeast — Nishapur, Tus, Sarakhs,
Merv, Bayhaq. When those vast lands were conquered, abun-
dant was the revenue, and wealth flowed in to Othman from every
side, so that he set up Privy Treasuries for his own use, and gave
huge bounties: he would order some kinsman a hundred thous-
and purses of four thousand dirhams each.

Early in the year thirty-four, Othman, hearing that Kufa
was in ferment, recalled the Governor, Saʻid, to Madina. But
after a while the Caliph sent him back to govern again. The men
of Kufa went out to meet him, crying: We'll have naught more
to do with thee! nor with Othman neither!

The people gathered in the Mosque at Madina, and sent the Companion Amir to speak to Othman.

The Believers are gathered in the Mosque, said he to the Caliph, blaming thee for this and that; and chiefly for that thou hast turned aside out of the True Way of the Prophet, God's Prayer and Peace be on him! and the two Caliphs who came after him. Then he added: Othman! fear God!

Who dares bid me fear God? said Othman. What knowest thou of God?

I know of God, answered Amir, and I know that all oppressors must one day stand before His Face! And he left the Caliph; and from that day on the Companions of God's Apostle planted their feet in Othman's house no more.

When the Governors came on Pilgrimage, Othman called them together, and said: Authority falleth now from me. Rebellion is lodged in every breast. What do ye counsel me to do?

If we were to blame, said some, they would blame us, not Othman.

Ay, said the Caliph, it is me they mean.

Do as Omar did! said Abdallah, Amir's son, Governor of Basra; he kept them ever busy on outland wars. Folk at peace are never content.

It is those townsfolk, the men they call the notables, who stir up the rest, said Sa'id, Governor of Kufa. Break them, and the rest will scatter.

Do as I do in Syria, began Mu'awia. But Amr spoke.

Othman, said he, or, if thou wilt, Prince of the True Believers, there's not a Companion in Madina whom thou hast not offended. Recall thine officers or give up this authority; then at least thou wilt bear the blame no longer. If on the other hand thou choosest to try force, then — IN THE NAME OF GOD!

Thou too! exclaimed the Caliph; art thou another malcontent?

Next day he ordered them to return to their governments,

recommending that they despatch those they governed to fight outland wars. When Mu'awia was busked and bound for the road, he went to see Othman once more.

Prince of the True Believers, said he, this is not over yet; and I fear to leave thee here. The Syrians are well tamed, as thou knowest; so come to Syria with me.

God forbid, cried Othman, that I should leave the city where the grave of God's Apostle is, and the House of the Flight!

So Mu'awia left him, and walked into the Mosque, dressed as he was for the road, with his sword-belt on his neck, and his bow strung. There stood Ali and Zubayr and Talha, talking. Mu'awia went up to them, and spoke long to them, saying at the last: And now, I leave this old man in your hands; have a care of him. It belongeth to your generosity to do it, and to your wisdom too, for if he is honored, ye will be honored in your own turn.

None of the three answered anything to that, and Mu'awia departed. But after a while, Ali spoke: It might be better to do as he said.

By God! said Zubayr, never lay a heavier load on thy heart nor on our hearts, than lieth this load of Othman's today.

A certain converted Jew, whom men called Ibn Saba, proclaimed the doctrine of the Second Coming of the Prophet; and many believed him, so that it stirred up rebellion against Othman's authority. Being banished from Basra, then from Kufa, then from Syria, Ibn Saba went on to Egypt, and taught his gospel there. The Christians, he said, believe that Jesus will come again. Yet True Believers have better cause to think Muhammad will come again, for God hath said in the Koran: *SURELY HE WHO GAVE THEE THE KORAN TO BE THY LAW WILL BRING THEE HOME AGAIN.* And he uttered another doctrine: God, said he, hath had four and twenty thousand prophets in this world, and every one of them had his vicegerent. Now the vicegerent of Muhammad was Ali; and Ali therefore ought to be his Successor, his Caliph; and therefore Othman got authority illegally, and his Caliphate is illegitimate.

So many began to call Othman an Unbeliever; but they kept their faith secret, and outwardly preached only righteousness of life.

The Egyptians complained of the government of Othman's foster-brother Abdallah son of Abu Sarh, and sought redress. They began to correspond with the Kufans and the people of Basra, plotting to march upon Madina. And in Rajab of the thirty-fifth year, the Egyptians set forward, giving out that they were on Pilgrimage, and riding straight to the Mosque at Madina gave voice to all their grievances against Abdallah, speaking to the Prophet's Companions as they sat in their customary places of prayer.

Thou Othman! fear God and repent!

Sit down, thou! the Caliph said; who art thou, to dare to call me to repentance?

But another man cried out: Othman, repent!

And wheresoever Othman turned to see who spoke, he heard the same words from another side; and they echoed from every corner of the Mosque; and every man called him Othman merely, and none gave him the title: Prince of the True Believers.

To the complaints of the Egyptians Othman answered at last: Then do ye choose a man yourselves, and I will set him over you in Abdallah's place.

Set Abu Bakr's son Muhammad over us, they answered.

So Othman wrote Muhammad ibn Abu Bakr his charge as Governor, and appointed him. And Muhammad and his company set forth.

But as they lay at the third day's halt from Madina, there

came up behind them a black slave on camel-back, lashing his beast like a man who pursues or a man who is pursued.

What's thy adventure? the company called to him. How come? for surely thou art in flight or in chase.

I am the Prince of the True Believers' slave! cried the man. Bound on an errand to the Governor of Egypt!

The Governor of Egypt's here! said one of the company.

Not the one I want, the slave replied, and rode on without staying. Muhammad sent a man after him; and he caught the slave and brought him back.

Slave, who art thou? demanded the son of Abu Bakr.

Slave to the Prince of True Believers, he began; but presently he said: I am the slave of Marwan (whose great-uncle Othman was). And so it went, till someone said he thought he knew the man to be one of Othman's slaves.

To whom wast thou sent? Muhammad asked.

To the Governor of Egypt.

With what?

A letter.

Hast thou the letter with thee?

No, said the slave.

They searched him, but found no letter on him. However, there was in his baggage a ewer, and in that ewer was something dry, which made a rustling sound. They shook it, trying to shake the thing out; but it would not come, and they therefore broke the ewer. Inside was a letter, addressed from Othman to Abdallah son of Abu Sarh. Muhammad called all his company to gather round, and opened the letter in their presence. And lo and behold! it ran thus:

When Muhammad, and So-and-so, and So-and-so arrive, arrange for them to die. Pay no heed to the charge I wrote him, but sit fast in thy government until thou hear further from me. Such as came to me seeking redress against thee I bid thee cast into prison; and thou shalt surely hear from me on that matter, if it please God.

Sore afeared and sore perplexed were they at the reading of that letter. They turned back to Madina, and sent for Ali, Talha, Zubayr, Sa'd, and the other Companions. The tale of the slave was told; and the letter read over.

Not a man but raged against Othman now.

When they brought it before the Caliph, he swore: By the Lord! I neither wrote this letter nor ordered it written, nor did I send the slave to Egypt!

On scrutinizing the letter more narrowly, some recognized the writing as the hand of Marwan, who served his kinsman as Secretary. So they demanded of Othman that he give Marwan up to them. The Caliph, fearing lest Marwan be slain, refused.

Then a party of the people laid siege to Othman's house, so that he could get no water. Ali and most of the Companions kept to their own houses. In the end Muhammad, Abu Bakr's son, with two companions climbed into the place from the house of one of the Helpers, unseen by Othman's men, who were on the roof. The Caliph was alone with his wife, reading the Koran.

Stay here, said Muhammad to the other two; his wife is with him! Let me go in first; and do ye come in when I lay hands on him. And then — have at him till ye make a dead man of him!

He went into the room, and seized the Caliph by the beard. O God! if thy father could see thee now, cried Othman, hateful to him would it be, to see thee do this to me! Muhammad's hand loosened its hold at the words; but the other two rushed in, and fell on Othman, killed him, and ran out of the house. His wife screamed; but her screaming went unheard in other noise, until she climbed up to the roof and cried from there: The Prince of True Believers is murdered!

Many went in, and found Othman lying dead; the news was quickly brought to Ali and Talha, Zubayr and Sa'd. The people hastened to Ali's house. We swear thee allegiance, they cried; so stretch out thy hand — some chief we needs must have.

That lieth not with me, said Ali: it lieth with the men of Badr! With whomsoever the men of Badr are content, that man shall be Caliph.

* * *

On the day when Othman was assassinated, his treasurer had in hand a hundred and fifty thousand gold dinars, and a million dirhams. His landed estates were accounted worth a hundred thousand dinars, not counting his herds of horses and camels. It was during his Caliphate that the Companions of God's Apostle acquired mansions and lands: Zubayr at his death left valuables worth fifty thousand dinars, and about a thousand horses, a thousand slaves of both sexes, and vast estates besides in Basra, Kufa, Fostat, and Alexandria. As for Talha, his lands in Iraq yielded a thousand gold dinars or better in rents every day, and his estate of Shirat even more. He built himself a town mansion in Madina of plaster-work, brick, and teakwood.

THE ELECTION OF THE CALIPH ALI

After five days the rebels called the men of Madina together and spoke to them: Five days now we have been without any Imam leading the Prayer, and things cannot go on thus. We know no fitter man to be Imam than Ali.

But Ali will not take up the burden of Imamate, answered some.

Press him home, till he consent, the rebels said.

So the Helpers went to Ali. But he put them off, still resisting, till certain men from Egypt said: If we go to our homes again without an Imam, such strife will stir as will never again be stilled.

At last Ali consented, on condition that Talha and Zubayr swore him allegiance; so those two came with others to him.

Small longing have I for this authority, said Ali; yet the Believers must have a chief; and right gladly will I swear allegiance to another — to Talha.

Nay, thou hast more right than I, said Talha.

One who stood by forced open Ali's palm, and bade Talha strike his hand thereto and take the oath. So Talha swore allegiance to Ali as Caliph. Zubayr did the like, and afterward, in the Mosque, the people took the oath.

Marwan and his son got away; and another man took Othman's shirt, all gory as it was, and rode off with it to Damascus.

CIVIL WAR

How was it, one of Ali's chiefs insolently inquired, that Abu
Bakr's Caliphate and Omar's Caliphate were both so peaceful,
and Othman's and thine so full of trouble and schism?

For a simple reason, Ali said: Abu Bakr and Omar had
Othman and me to help them in their time; but Othman and I
had only you and your like!

Ali WAS NOW ADVANCED IN YEARS, stout and bold, a very hairy man. He was of middle height or under, full-bellied, with a very large beard as white as cotton, which spread from shoulder to shoulder. He was of a tawny complexion.

They told Ali one day that Mu'awia had said that Ali and his house were distinguished for their valor, and Zubayr and his house for their splendor; but for his own part and that of the Umayyads, they pretended to no distinction except it might be for kindness of heart, and clemency.

A wily speech! said Ali. Mu'awia would spur Zubayr into riot, and me into hazard, that he might be free of us; and by proclaiming his own generosity he would curry favor with the crowd.

The new Caliph despatched a letter to Mu'awia demanding his allegiance. Its superscription ran: *From God's slave Ali, Prince of the True Believers, to Mu'awia son of Abu Sufyan.* Mu'awia kept the messenger waiting a month, and at last despatched to Ali a certain Qabisa, a Shaykh of Clan Abs, with a sealed letter thus addressed: *From Mu'awia to Ali.* When Ali took the letter from Qabisa's hand, he looked on the superscription, and exclaimed: There's no good matter herein. And opening it, he found only the words: *IN THE NAME OF GOD THE MERCIFUL THE COMPASSIONATE* — and no word more.

There is nothing in this letter, he said. If thou hast aught to say, say it — thou art safe.

Then Qabisa said: I have seen sixty thousand men in the Mosque at Damascus, weeping at the sight of Othman's bloodied shirt, and cursing his murderers.

Thou knowest, Lord! who did the deed on Othman! Ali cried; his blood is not on me.

* * *

Now both Talha and Zubayr had sworn allegiance to Ali reluctantly, and not of free accord. Soon after, they rode away to Mecca, where Aisha, Mother of the Believers, was; and taking her with them set out for Basra, proclaiming they would have vengeance for Othman's blood.

When Ali heard of it, he pursued them. They took a guide, however, and turned aside out of the road into trackless ways, and held on till they came to a place which went by the name of the Valley of Hawab, or the Valley of the Crime. Aisha's camel was in front of the rest, with the guide walking before her. As they drew near to a habitation of wandering Arabs in that hollow, dogs began to bark; and at the same time the guide called out: It's the Valley of Hawab, this place.

Aisha screamed out: Take me back! Now I remember the Prophet of God, how he was sitting with his wives once, and he said: I would I knew which one among you is the one at whom the dogs of Hawab will bark. Me! Me! I am the Woman of Hawab!

The guide's out of his reckoning, said Talha.

But Aisha only said: I want to go back.

So they halted there. At the first dawning of the day, they made Zubayr's son come running into camp crying: Ali's upon us! And Aisha was afraid, and bade them ride on, and make haste. And thus they went on toward Basra.

Ali and his army met their party near Basra. It was called the Battle of the Camel, because Aisha was brought on camel-back to it; and there the Companions Talha and Zubayr came by their deaths, and more, to the number of thirteen thousand. Fifteen nights Ali stayed in Basra, and then went on to Kufa, and governed as Caliph in that city.

Omar's son and the greater body of Companions inclined neither to Ali's side nor to that of the party who rallied round Aisha's camel. The People's Party, and those who thought as they did, maintained that neither Ali nor Talha and Zubayr were justified in fighting: only those who refused to fight did as they ought. But the People's Party continued to hold them all in veneration; and most of the people of Tradition concur in that.

REVOLT IN SYRIA

And now Mu'awia and his party in Syria revolted against Ali. When tidings came to the Caliph, he marched against them; and the armies met at Siffin in the thirty-seventh year of the Flight. For many days they skirmished, until at last the battle became general; and then victory inclined to Ali. Already the soldiers of the Syrian army began to cry: Think for your wives, ye Arabs! Your womenfolk! your daughters! For God's sake!

All's lost! said Mu'awia to Amr; think now for thy household; and thou mayest think too for the government of Egypt!

Amr counselled this: he bade all who had with them copies of the Koran fasten them on the tips of their spears. Many did as he said; and men heard them shouting above the noise of the medley: The Book of God between us and you!

We should obey! the Iraq Believers began to say one to another. And some who stood near Ali said: That's a fair offer — accept!

A murrain! said Ali; they display God's Book, but they mean neither to search it nor obey it! 'Tis a trap; 'tis guile! I know these men better than ye do.

But there was much dispute; and there were threats. Ali

bethought him of what had overtaken Othman. When at last someone offered to go and inquire Mu'awia's meaning, he answered: That's thine own affair — go to him if thou wilt.

To this man Mu'awia proposed: Let us all, both ye and ourselves, have recourse to what God hath commanded in His Book. Do ye choose a man as shall please you, and delegate your power to him; and we will choose another. Both shall be solemnly bound by oath to act in strict agreement with the Book of God, not to deviate from it; and both sides must submit to whatever decision those two may pronounce in accord with the rulings of the Book.

Most were glad enough at that, and declared they would accept. The Syrian party named Amr. Ali's people named Abu Musa, and said they would have no other. Do as ye will, said Ali. The meeting of the arbitrators was put off till Ramadan; and the armies separated, Mu'awia returning to Syria and Ali to Kufa.

THE ARBITRATION

In the year thirty-eight the two arbitrators met.

Thou knowest, O Amr, said Abu Musa after magnifying and blessing the name of God, and making mention of those things which had troubled Muhammad's people, that folk in Iraq will never love Mu'awia nor folk in Syria love Ali ever. Therefore let us depose them both, and name in place of them Abdallah son of Omar.

Will Ibn Omar take up the burden of vengeance for Othman? asked Amr.

Ay, said Abu Musa, if people push him to it.

Amr affected to think as Abu Musa did, yet named some other men. Abu Musa rejected all.

Then do thou, said Amr, stand up and speak to the people, deposing our two claimants together, and naming thereafter the man thou wouldst have Caliph.

Nay, do thou stand up first, answered Abu Musa, and speak; for the precedence is thy right.

Nay, replied the other, I will not take the precedence of thee. What we shall say will be the same; but do thou stand up first, as is proper.

Abu Musa accordingly stood forth, invoked and glorified God's Name; and then proceeded: Ye people, we have thought ripely on this matter; and we believe that the surest means of bringing peace again, of ending strife and the shedding of blood, and making all Believers of one mind, is to depose both Ali and Mu'awia. I therefore put aside Ali, as I put aside this turban. And raising his hands, Abu Musa put off his turban. We raise to the Caliphate, he went on, a man whose father was the Companion of God's Apostle, one who is himself a Companion: even Abdallah son of Omar. And he spoke praising Ibn Omar, and afterwards stood down.

Then stood up Amr. He invoked and blessed God's Name, and called Blessing on the Prophet of God, and then spoke thus: Ye people, Abu Musa Abdallah son of Qays hath just now deposed Ali, and stripped him of the authority which he claimed. I in my turn associate myself with Abu Musa in that; I too depose Ali; but in pursuance thereof I proclaim Mu'awia, and I declare that Mu'awia is the Caliph of God's Apostle, that he hath right to our obedience, and to our oath, on this condition: that he avenge the murder of Othman son of Affan!

A lie! cried out Abu Musa. We never named Mu'awia! We deposed him! and Ali too!

He is the liar, retorted Amr. He deposed Ali, but I never deposed Mu'awia.

One of Ali's party, Shurayh son of Hani, struck at Amr with his whip; but as for Abu Musa, he stole away as fast as he might, and got to horse and rode straight to Mecca. He never went back to Kufa, which was his home and the home of his children, and vowed that he would never come into Ali's presence again.

Amr returned to his own house; and Mu'awia, taking oath

of allegiance from the Syrian host, assumed the title of Caliph.

Let Mu'awia be accursed, O Lord, I beseech Thee, Ali prayed daily in the Mosque of Kufa; let Amr be accursed, and Habib, and Abd al-Rahman son of Khalid, and Dahhak son of Qays, and Walid! Be they accursed all!

THE SECEDERS

Now arose against Ali seceders from amongst his own companions and supporters, men whose cry was: Arbitration is God's alone! No government but God's! Ali, these Seceders declared, is the man intended in the Koran:

HE WHO SAITH: OUR LORD, GIVE UNTO US IN THIS WORLD. AND HE HATH NO PORTION IN THE HEREAFTER.

and:

HIM BEWILDERED, WHOM FIENDS HAVE ENTANGLED IN THE EARTH, WHILE HIS COMPANIONS CALL HIM TO TRUE GUIDANCE.

The Seceders went out and settled in camp near Kufa. Ali sent Ibn Abbas to plead with them; some he convinced, so that they returned to the city; but others in their obduracy marched away toward Nahrawan and lived in that country, by banditry, gathering strength till they numbered four thousand men. Then, coming to Madain, they cut the throat of Ali's Governor there.

They cry: No government! said Ali. But there must be a government — good or bad.

He marched against the Seceders, and killed thousands in battle.

ASSASSINATION

In the year forty, a company of Seceders met at Mecca. They talked of all their wars and tribulations; and a certain Ibn Muljam swore he would smite Ali. This man was in love with a woman of the Seceders' party, whose father and brother had been slain in fight against the Caliph; and he promised her three thousand dirhams and Ali's death for her dowry.

On the seventeenth night of Ramadan he went and sat down in the Mosque at Kufa opposite the door through which Ali used to come into the Mosque every morning at the muezzin's call to Dawn Prayer.

That morning, Ali woke, the muezzin came in and cried: To Prayers! and the Caliph went forth from his door calling: Ye people! to Prayers! to Prayers! Then Ibn Muljam started up before him, and hewed at him with a sword; the stroke, falling on his forehead, went through to the brain.

Friday and Saturday Ali lingered, and died on the Saturday night.

HASAN

Hasan son of Ali was grave, reserved, dignified, generous, a hater of strife and the sword, much given to marrying.

Abu Bakr once, in the days of his Caliphate, had noticed Hasan at play with other boys, and lifting him to his shoulders had said: Hasan, thou art very like the Prophet of God — not a whit like thy father Ali.

Ali had been used to say to people in Madina: Never marry any of your daughters to my son Hasan; he will taste them and then divorce them. And Hasan did habitually divorce his wives; yet he never put a woman away but she was in love with him all her life after. Ninety women he married in all; and it was seldom that any woman he married did not love him passionately.

He assumed the Caliphate after his father's assassination, and governed for six months odd.

Then Mu'awia took the field against him. Seeing that the issue lay in the Hand of God, Hasan sent to Mu'awia offering to resign the authority to him, on condition that he should not prosecute any man of Madina or Hijaz or Iraq for any act done during his father's lifetime, and that he should pay Hasan's debts in money. These proposals Mu'awia accepted; and so they made peace, and Hasan, putting himself down from the Caliphate, dwelt in Madina. When he fell again into straitened circumstances, an annuity of one hundred thousand dirhams was allowed him.

Thou shame of the Believers! his party would cry on him.

I would not have you butchered for a mere kingdom's sake, he replied.

When people reproached him for making peace with Mu'awia, and exhorted him to claim the Caliphate by force of arms, he set his face firm against it, on the ground that the Consensus of Believers was opposed to war. There is a Tradition recorded on the authority of Ibn Mas'ud that the Prophet of God once said: The Muslims have never consented in approval of a thing as good but it was good in the sight of God; nor have they ever judged a thing pernicious but it was pernicious in God's sight also.

Hasan wished to spare the blood of the men of Ali's Party, the sect of the Shi'a. And his brother Husayn agreed with this decision, saying: So long as Mu'awia is alive, let every man stay in his own house and draw his cloak over his head.

Hasan died by poisoning at Madina; it was his wife Ja'ada who gave him the poison. His brother tried to make him tell who had done it, but he would not. God's vengeance is terrible enough if it is the one I think, said he; and if it is some other, for God's sake, let no innocent die on my account!

Brother, he said to Husayn, our father cast his eyes after this authority, the Caliphate, but God turned it away from him, and Abu Bakr got it; afterward he raised his eyes to it again, but it was diverted from him to Omar; then again at the time of the six electors he was sure it would not slip him now, and yet it was diverted from him to Othman. When Othman was slain, they swore allegiance to Ali; but even then it was disputed, and to the drawing of swords; and it never rested quiet in his hands. And by God! truly I do not think the Lord will ever unite Prophethood and Caliphate in our House. Indeed, I know not what indignity the rabble of Kufa have shown thee already, to drive thee out as they did, before thy coming hither . . . .

Listen; I asked Aisha if I might be buried with the Apostle of God, and she consented; so when I am dead, ask her for that favor. But I expect nothing better of people than that they will try to stop thee; and if they do, have no argument with them.

When he was very near death, a horror of grief came on him, and Husayn said: What means this crying, brother? Lo! thou art going unto the Apostle of God and Ali, thy fathers, and Khadija and Fatima, thy mothers.

But Hasan answered: Brother, I am going into something of God's decreeing not like anything before — I seem to see a tribe of God's creatures not like anything I ever saw before!

When he was dead, Husayn went to ask Aisha for the burial, and she said: Yes, with all my heart. But Marwan, Mu-'awia's Governor in Madina, put a stop to things; and Hasan was buried in the Baqi cemetery by the side of his mother Fatima.

THE WORLD AND THE FLESH

God, Mu'awia, said the son of Abbas, gave to Muhammad His Apostle Companions who loved him better than life or goods, so that through them His Word did triumph. They were God's allies living; and now dead, are His friends. Guests of Futurity they were ere they came to it; it even seems as though they departed this world consequently on their own unworldliness.

Enough of that, Ibn Abbas, Mu'awia cut him short; let's talk of something different.

Architecture was what people talked about in Walid's time; in Sulayman's, it was cookery and women.

HIS IS THE ARAB CAESAR, Omar used to say when he saw Mu'awia. Mu'awia, the son of Abu Sufyan and Hind, was a tall man, fair-skinned and handsome, yet with something awesome in his look. He was proverbial for his forbearance. When a certain Arab said to him: By God! thou hadst better do right by us, Mu'awia, or we'll correct thee, be assured of that! the Caliph simply asked: How will you do that?

With a stick! said the man.

Very well, Mu'awia replied, I will do right.

When he became Caliph, he said to Abu Tufayl the Companion: Sign thy name with the rest, as a witness of Othman's murder.

I will not, said he; I was one of those who let the blow fall without lifting a hand to help him.

What hindered thee? demanded Mu'awia. It was thy duty to defend him.

The same thing as hindered thee — when Othman came to his end thou wast sitting fast in Syria.

But see, said the Caliph: I defend his cause in avenging his death.

Maybe, replied the Companion; but the pair of you put me in mind of that verse of the Hanafi poet:

Surpassing sorrow dost thou pay me dead
Who gavest not a crust to me alive!

* * *

Mere feeling kindles wars, Mu'awia once said; thus trivial matters eliminate things of weight.

So long as our hearts which hate thee are still in our breasts, said to him Adi, Hatim's son of Taiy, and so long as the swords we fought thee with hang still on our necks, so long, if thy cunning take half a span, shall our revenge take a span of thee. The peace of the sword, Mu'awia, lets not the sword sleep!

Those are words of a wise man — write them down, somebody! was all the Caliph said; and he pursued the conversation.

I do not use my sword when my whip will do, was one of his sayings; nor my whip when my tongue will do. Let a single hair still bind me to my people, and I'll not let it snap; when they slack, then I pull; but when they pull, then I slack.

What's approved today was reproved once, he said; even so things now abominated will someday be embraced.

Abu Bakr sought not the world, nor did it seek him. The world sought Omar, for all that he sought it not. But ourselves are sunk in it, to our middles.

I, said he, am the first King.

A CALIPH'S DAY

The Caliph's Palace at Damascus was paved throughout with green marble. In the middle of the court was a great fountain, flowing perpetually to water a garden of the fairest flowers, and all kinds of trees. Birds innumerable quickened and thrilled it.

It was Mu'awia's habit to give five audiences every day. After Dawn Prayer he received his Reporter and heard the reports; then they brought him his Koran, and he read a thirtieth Section of the Book. Then, returning to his private room, he did what was to do, and having said a prayer of four Bows, entered his audience-hall. First were admitted his personal officers, with whom he would chat a while, and then his ministers, who talked over any matter arising out of the previous day which they wanted to discuss. At this audience the Caliph's breakfast was served him, of the remains of the previous evening's supper, cold lamb or chicken, or some such dish. When matters had been discussed at length, Mu'awia used to withdraw to his own room to be at ease a little.

Page, set out the chair! he would call when he came out. Then he proceeded to the Mosque, where, after ablution, he would take his seat on the chair which had been set for him, leaning his back against the screen, with his bodyguards about him, and let approach who would: poor men, wandering Arabs from the desert, women, children, destitute folk, and so forth. Someone would complain of injustice — he would order redress; another of some encroachment — he would send guardsmen to put a stop to it; a third of some insult — he would order an inquiry. When no more suitors remained, he returned to the Palace, seated himself on his throne, and gave the order: Call the people in, in order of rank; and hinder no man from giving me good day. The usual form of greeting was: How is the Prince of True Believers this morning? God prolong his days! To which he would reply: By the Grace of God.

When his courtiers had taken their places, and all were seated, Mu'awia would address them, to this effect: Nobles! Men call you so, but not on account of any other nobility than that you are permitted to sit here; so it is for you to further the interests of those who are not so admitted to us. Then someone would rise, and speak of the death of So-and-so in Holy War against Unbelievers; and Mu'awia would order a pension to the man's children. Another might speak of the absence of So-and-so from his household; and the Caliph would urge that it be watched, its needs supplied, and service given.

His dinner was now served, at which time the Secretary would present himself, and place himself at the Caliph's elbow. If a petitioner was admitted, Mu'awia would invite him to sit down and help himself; and the man would take two or three mouthfuls while the Secretary read out his plea and executed Mu'awia's dictation upon the matter; which done, Mu'awia used to say: Servant of God, give place! and the petitioner rose. The next was called in, and so on until all petitioners had been seen. Sometimes he received as many as forty in a dinnertime. When the meal was cleared away, and all courtiers dismissed, the Caliph, retiring to his own room, admitted no man whomsoever to see him until the Call to Noonday Prayer, at which time he went into the Mosque and led the Prayers. After this, returning home, he prayed four Bows more.

He now received his personal officers again. If it was the winter season, he used to offer them what is called Pilgrim-cheer — pastries, biscuits, sugared curd-tarts, sweet porridge, buttered cakes, dried fruits, melon conserve. In summertime he gave them fresh fruit. His ministers now presented themselves again to receive any orders that were to be executed that day. This audience went on till midafternoon, when Mu'awia, having recited the midafternoon Prayer, retired, and for a while received nobody.

Appearing again at the end of the afternoon, he took his seat on the throne, summoned the courtiers to their places, and was served supper, which went on till the Call to Sunset Prayer, no petitioners being admitted to this meal. The dishes were cleared away, the Call to Prayer sounded, and the Caliph went in to lead in the Mosque. It was his wont on returning to say a further prayer of four Bows, reciting fifty verses of the Koran each Bow, alternately aloud and to himself. Then he withdrew once more, and saw nobody until he was called to Night Prayer, when he went again into the Mosque.

This Prayer accomplished, the personal officers, ministers and household officers were again summoned to audience. For the first part of the night the Caliph's ministers transacted necessary business with him; and then for a third of the night he listened to recitation, of the Arabs and their famous Days, of the outlanders and their kings and politics, the lives of ancient kings, their wars, their stratagems and institutions, and other matter out of the chronicle of past time.

After the literary colloquy, special delicacies would be brought to the Caliph from his women's apartments — halva and sweetmeats of that kind.

For the last third of the night, Mu'awia slept. When he woke (or if he could not sleep), he would sit up in bed and call for his books of royal biography, the histories and wars and secret stratagems of past kings. Special Pages, tasked with memorizing and repeating from these volumes, used to recite to him; and every night he would order some passages of history or biography, from annals or books of statecraft.

At the proper hour, he went to lead Dawn Prayer in the Mosque, and so entered again on the day's business as it has been described.

*   *   *

He was the first Caliph with whom his people ventured to indulge in familiar levity. Once, for example, a certain Khuraym came to audience with his lower garment tucked up. He was a man with very shapely legs.

Ah! said Mu'awia, if only those legs were on a woman!

The same for your buttocks, Prince of the True Believers! retorted Khuraym.

This Caliph was the first in Islam to employ post-messengers and he first established the Board of the Signet. The occasion was the following: he ordered a man a bounty of one hundred thousand dirhams, and the man opened the order and made it two hundred thousand. When the accounts were submitted to Mu'awia, he disavowed the order, and that very day he established the Board of the Signet. Abdallah of Ghassan was first appointed to it, and the Signet confided to him. On the stone of the seal was inscribed: *Every Work Hath Its Wages;* and the same legend continued in use to the last days of the Caliphate of the House of Abbas.

And this was the first Caliph to employ the service of eunuchs (in the women's apartments of his palace).

His wife Maysun, the mother of the prince Yazid, was a Beduin woman of Clan Kalb. Living in the Palace at Damascus she wrote:

> *A tent flapping in the desert air is dearer than this towering*
> *   house;*
> *Wind rustling over the sandy waste hath a sweeter sound*
> *   than all the king's trumpets;*
> *A crust in the nook of a wandering tent more relish than all*
> *   these delicate cates;*
> *And a noble clansman's more to my lust than the paunchy*
> *   longbeards about me here.*

When the Caliph heard of this poem, he sent her back to her clan; and it was with them that the prince Yazid was bred. Afterward, the children of the Caliphs of the Umayyad House used to be sent out to live in the desert, that they might learn to speak purer Arabic.

*   *   *

On one occasion Amr, still Governor of Egypt, came to Damascus to visit Mu'awia, who was now grown old and feeble. His freed slave Wardan was with him. The two old men fell into talk.

Prince of the True Believers, said Amr, what pleasures still keep their savor for thee nowadays?

Women? said the Caliph; no — I do not need women any more. To go fine? My skin's so used to stuffs the softest and richest, I cannot tell what's of the best any more. And eating — I have eaten delicate dishes so many that I can no longer tell what I like. No, I think I have no pleasure keener now than drinking cool in summer, and seeing my children and grandchildren go about me. And thou, Amr, what's thy last remaining pleasure?

A bit of cultivable land, said the conqueror of Egypt; enough to yield me some fruit, and a little profit over and above.

Then the Caliph turned to the freedman Wardan. Thou, Wardan, said he, what would be thy last enjoyment?

A noble generous deed! said he. Some deed that would live in the memory of all remembering men, and earn for me in Eternity.

The audience is concluded! cried Mu'awia; that's enough for today! This slave here, Amr, is a better man than thou or I.

Amr died, in Egypt, in the forty-third year of the Flight. When he felt his death coming on, he said this prayer: O my God! I have no immunity to claim, nor any power to defend myself: I have transgressed Thy commands and I have done things Thou didst forbid. And now, my God, in Thy Hands I lay my head. Presently he spoke again: Dig my ditch, make my earthy bed. Thereafter he kept his finger in his mouth till death came.

Seven years later died Sa'd son of Abu Waqqas, the conqueror of Persia. At the last he said to those about him: Now bring hither the frock I wore when I went forth to the Day of Badr, and put it on me: it was for this end I kept it laid up, from that day to this.

Sufficient for my Companions, the Prophet of God had said, *is the mention of their dying.*

* * *

Mu'awia first among Caliphs established his heir in the Caliphate during his own lifetime. Deputations from the Helpers came to him in the fifty-ninth year of the Flight; and in the company from Iraq was Ahnaf son of Qays. To this man's brother Dahhak ibn Qays Mu'awia spoke privately: Tomorrow at the general audience I purpose to make a speech, as God shall move me. When I have done, do thou speak; and speak for Yazid — 'tis part of thine allegiance. Win people to his election. I have already spoken to Abd al-Rahman of Thaqif, and to Abdallah Ash'ari and Thawr of Salm, to applaud thee and say something in thy support.

Next day Mu'awia, having taken his seat in audience, addressed the assembly, saying that he had considered the character and breeding of his son Yazid, and was moved to nominate him to be his heir in the Caliphate. Dahhak rose at once to second him, and called on the assembly to proclaim Yazid. Abd al-Rahman, Abdallah, and Thawr in their turn spoke in support of Dahhak and gave their votes.

But where is Ahnaf son of Qays? Mu'awia inquired.

Ahnaf stood up. People are too ready to contemn old rights, said he; and be seduced by present favors; and that is why Yazid seems acceptable. I bid thee reject the counsel of men who give advice and cannot give service, men too who talk out of little love for thee.

Dahhak sprang up in wrath. Rebels! Traitors! he shouted at the Iraqis. He would cram their words down their throats, he said; and Abd al-Rahman said the like.

But now a clansman of Azd turned to the Caliph. Thou art the Prince of the True Believers, he said; and when thou diest, the Prince of the True Believers shall be Yazid. And this for any who will say me nay! And he laid his hand on his hilt and drew his sword from the scabbard.

Sit down now, said Mu'awia; yet thou art the most eloquent speaker of them all.

In the course of the next year Mu'awia died, at the age, it is said, of seventy-seven years. He possessed a little of the hair of the Apostle of God and a paring of his nail; and he commanded as his last desire that these should be put into his dead mouth and eyes, adding: Do that, and then leave me alone with the Most Merciful of the merciful.

The new Caliph Yazid was passionately addicted to music; a lover of hawks and hounds, of apes and leopards; and fond of merry feasting. His appetite for revelry was shared by his courtiers and the men he set in power. It was in his reign that music appeared at Mecca and Madina. One of the fashionables of Quraysh took a house for the use of his friends as a club, and provided it with chess and dice and other means of pastime. People began to learn to play musical instruments, and to drink wine openly.

the slaying of hu sa yn

WHEN YAZID sent an envoy to the people of Madina to take the covenant of allegiance for him, both Ali's son Husayn and the son of Zubayr refused to acknowledge him. They quit the city by night, and escaped to Mecca.

Now the people of Kufa had written to Husayn in Mu-'awia's time, inviting him to come and head them. Husayn had refused then. But when Yazid was proclaimed, he reverted to what had been formerly meditated. Now it seemed good to go;

but again it seemed good to stay where he was. Presently envoys from Kufa came again with letters of invitation; and he made up his mind to start.

Do not go! was the advice of Ibn Omar: the Lord gave His Apostle his choice between this world and the Other, and he chose the Other; thou art a part of him — this world is not for thee. He fell on Husayn's neck, weeping, as he bade him farewell.

And Husayn started for Iraq, with eighteen of his own household and sixty others of Ali's Sect, of whom thirty were Companions of the Prophet of God.

Yazid wrote ordering the Governor of Iraq to oppose his entry; and the Governor despatched an army of four thousand men under Omar son of Sa'd the conqueror of Persia. And the people of Kufa left Husayn to his fate, as they had left Ali his father before him. When Husayn encountered Omar's cavalry, he fell back on Kerbela, having now about him a little troop of five hundred horse and a hundred foot.

At Kerbela BEFELL HIS SLAYING.

Too long would be the full tale of his death: for the heart cannot bear the telling of it. *VERILY GOD'S WE ARE, AND TO GOD IS OUR RETURNING.* Omar's host came on, and tried to force Husayn to surrender, surrounding his party so that they could get no water from the river Euphrates. Seven or eight days on that plain was he beset; in the end they fought. Thirty-two warriors found martyrdom there, of whom two were Husayn's sons, four his brothers, five his nephews, and five his cousins. Seeing all these fallen, Husayn mounted and galloped against his foes and smote, till he fell from his horse dying of thirst and seventy-two wounds. Only two of his sons were left alive: a babe in arms, and a lad lying sick in bed.

Short work! they told the Caliph. About time enough to butcher and dress a camel, or to take a little sleep.

It was an Arab of Clan Madhhij who gave Husayn the last blow. He hewed away the head and bore it off to the Governor at Kufa. Take it to Yazid, he said.

When the man came into the Presence, the Caliph had with him Abu Barza of Aslam. The Arab put the head into Yazid's hands. The Caliph struck Husayn's face on the mouth, bruising it with his ring.

That's enough with that ring! said Abu Barza. I have seen the mouth of God's Apostle touch that mouth, in a kiss — ah, how long ago!

See! see! the very earth is sick!
And the lands shudder at the slaying of Husayn.

When Husayn was murdered, the world stood still for seven days, and the sunlight on the walls glared yellow as saffron, and the stars struck one upon another.

The murder was on the tenth day of the Month Muharram, in the year of the Flight sixty-one. Men told that not a stone was turned in Jerusalem on that day but fresh blood was found beneath it.

ABD AL-MALIK

Tidings that authority had devolved on him reached Marwan's son Abd al-Malik at a time when he chanced to be sitting with the Koran in his lap. He closed the Book. This is our last time together, said he.

Abd al-Malik was the first mean Caliph. He was called *Sweat of a Stone* for that; and *Father of Flies* for his foul breath. He was the first Caliph who ever rebuked freedom of speech in his presence, and the first who told Believers they must not exhort the Caliph to righteousness. He changed the language of the Public Registers from Persian to Arabic, and was the first to have his own name struck on his coinage.

His only real intimate was Sha'bi; and to this man he said: Talk so long as I want to listen; and then, instead of flatteries (which I do not want), give me your own attention. Believe me, a talent for listening is much rarer than a talent for talking.

* * *

In the year after Abd al-Malik's accession, the Sect of Ali, or Shi'ites, struck with remorse that they had left Husayn to die, rose in revolt at Kufa, crying that they would never be cleansed of that guilt but by the slaying of his slayers, or the slaying of themselves.

The host of these Penitents crossed Euphrates, and the Syrian army marched to oppose them. Their encounter was by the Well of Warda. Breaking the scabbards of their swords, and tossing them away, the Penitents stood at bay, fighting off the Syrian host which gathered like night about them. Paradise! Paradise for Ali's Companions! they cried: Paradise! Paradise! for Ali's men!

And the Syrians, wondering at their courage and the brave stand of such a handful, themselves proposed an end to the fight, and truce. So the men of Iraq returned home alive.

And now the Seceders rebelled in Iraq, and made themselves masters of Basra. Muhallab of Azd had fought them before, and the Caliph was told: Muhallab is the only man for that business. When the Caliph sent to him, Muhallab said he would undertake it if he might keep the Land Tax from all the lands he cleared of rebels.

Wouldst thou share the kingdom with me? demanded Abd al-Malik.

Muhallab proposed two-thirds; this too the Caliph refused.

I will take a half, but I will go no lower, Muhallab offered;

and I must have besides what troops I need, nor will I answer the loss of them.

The troops Muhallab had were so scattered that the enemy marched through and mastered both banks of the Tigris.

A SECEDER SERMON

Know this, ye men: we did not leave our homes and goods out of a vain restlessness, nor in quest of pleasure, nor to claim old right, nor to win empire. But when we saw the lamps of justice all put out, then indeed *THE EARTH, VAST AS IT IS, WAS STRAITENED* upon us. We heard as it were a Herald call us to obedience unto the Merciful, and to the judgment of the Book of God.

We met your warriors. We called them to obey the Merciful and abide by the judgment of the Book; they called us to obey Satan and abide by the judgment of the children of Marwan. Then they came at us, galloping, clamoring, and riotous, for Satan laughed among them, and their blood seethed with his fires. And the wheel turned; and we went up and they went down, for such a smiting there befell as made the ungodly totter.

When Othman reigned, he walked six years in the ways of Abu Bakr and of Omar; and then worked Innovation in Islam. And the bond of unity was loosed; and every man wanted Caliphate for himself. Then reigned Ali, who wandered from the path of truth and proved himself no beacon for the guidance of men. Then reigned Mu'awia son of Abu Sufyan, that accursed son of an accursed father, whom God's Prophet himself did curse, who spilt innocent blood as it were water and made God's Servants his own slaves, a man who grasped the moneys of God into his own hands, a traitor to the Faith and a ravisher of women, who did the bidding of his lusts until he died.

And after him came his son Yazid, Yazid the drunkard, Yazid the huntsman, the tender of hawks and leopards and apes, who consulted not the Book but soothsayers, and followed his lusts to his death, God curse and punish him!

Then came Marwan, that excommunicate and accursed son of a father whom God's Prophet cursed, who drowned in the filth of his vices, God curse him and his fathers all! And then sat Marwan's sons upon the throne, children of that accursed House, who have devoured the moneys of God and mocked at His Religion and made His Servants their own slaves. And this wickedness has gone on and on. And O Muhammad's People, how have ye been unhappy and forsaken!

HAJJAJ

Muhallab wrote that he must have reinforcement. Who will go to Iraq? said the Caliph Abd al-Malik at his audience.

All sat silent, till Hajjaj ibn Yusuf rose and said: I am the man for that.

Sit down! said the Caliph. But when he had asked a third time, and all were silent still, Hajjaj stood up and said again: By God! I am the man for that, Prince of the True Believers.

Thou art the hornet for it! retorted Abd al-Malik. But he signed his commission, and Hajjaj set out.

On reaching Qadisia near Kufa, Hajjaj gave order that his troops should follow on behind him, marching all night; and then called for a fast camel loaded with waterskins. He mounted the beast bareback, with neither saddlecloth nor cushion, and rode away alone, his Koran in his hand, wearing a common travelling dress and turban.

And so he came to Kufa and entered the town alone, crying along the streets: To Prayers, all of you! In every quarter the men who should be with the army were sitting with their families and freedmen at home. Come on, let's stone this fellow! they said; and Muhammad ibn Umayr followed him into the Mosque, with

his freedmen at his heels. He saw Hajjaj sitting on the pulpit,
motionless and silent.

God damn the Children of Umayya! he cried, who give
Iraq to such a man as that! And he began to knock out bricks
from the Mosque to stone him, saying: By God! if they could
have found a worse they would have sent him! As he was about
to perform his purpose, one of his freedmen stayed him: Let him
be till we hear what he has to say. That fellow's only some
Beduin, surely, said others.

When the Mosque was full to crowding, Hajjaj pulled
back the kerchief that overhung his face, and stood up, unbinding
his turban from his head. Then without a word of the customary
Magnification or Benediction of the Prophet, he began to speak:

A famous man am I; my deeds increase my praise.
If I lay my turban by, well will ye know my face!

Take a look at me! Ha! I see straining eyes and starting necks —
heads ripe unto the harvest! Well, I am a master at that trade;
already methinks I see the glitter of blood between those turbans
and those beards.

The Prince of the True Believers hath emptied his quiver
out, and hath found in me his cruellest arrow, of sharpest steel,
of toughest wood. Ye Iraqis! rebels and traitors! Vile hearts! I
am not a man to be kneaded like a fig, ye whipping-slaves and
sons of slave mothers! I am Hajjaj ibn Yusuf, a man, I promise
you, who do not threaten but what I perform, nor shear but I flay.
No more gathering in crowds! No more meetings! No more
talk, talk! No more of: What's new? What's the news?

What business is that of yours, sons of bitches? Let every
man mind his own business. And woe to the man I get my hands
on! Walk straight ahead, and turn neither to right nor left. Follow your officers, take the oath, and cringe!

And remember this: I do not care to speak twice. I like
oratory for myself as little as I like cowardice in you, or treason,
such as yours. Let this sword once come out of its scabbard, and

it will not be sheathed, come winter, come summer, till the
Prince of the True Believers, with God's help, has straightened
every man of you that walks aside, and felled every man of you
that lifts his head.

Enough! the Prince of the True Believers has instructed
me to give you your pay, and to despatch you against the enemy,
under Muhallab's command. I give you those orders; and I
grant three days' grace. And may God hear this oath and call me
to account for it: every soldier of Muhallab's army whom I find
here at the expiry of that term shall lose his head, and his goods
shall be put to pillage. Page! read the letter from the Prince of
the True Believers.

The secretary began to read:
IN THE NAME OF GOD THE MERCIFUL THE
COMPASSIONATE:
*From God's slave Abd al-Malik Prince of the True Believers to
the True Believers and Muslims of Iraq: PEACE be unto you!
I praise unto you God THAN WHOM THERE IS NO OTHER
GOD.*

Stop there, man, said Hajjaj. Ye Iraqis! rebels and traitors!
vile hearts! ye men of schism and sin! shall the Prince of the
True Believers greet you with PEACE! and ye greet him not
with PEACE! again? If God leave me among you, I swear I'll
split and trim you like firewood, I'll teach you manners, in a new
school. Read the letter, Page!

When the man came to the greeting PEACE! everybody in
the Mosque returned: And PEACE and the Mercy and Blessing
of God on the Prince of the True Believers!

After the reading, Hajjaj came down from the pulpit, and
gave orders for the distribution of pay. Muhallab was at that
time fighting the Seceders of the Azrakite sect in the north.

On the third day Hajjaj himself took his seat to review
the army before the march. One of the notables of Kufa, Umayr
of Clan Tamim, addressed Hajjaj as he passed before him: God
save the Prince! Look at me — an old man, sick and broken down

with age; but I have sons. Let the Prince take the hardiest of them in my place, the best mounted, the best armed.

A young man will do as well as an old, said Hajjaj; and Umayr was making off, when two who were by said to Hajjaj: God save the Prince! do you know who that is?

No, he answered.

That's Umayr, Dabi's son, of Tamim — the same who sprang on the corpse of the Prince of True Believers Othman and smashed a rib in it!

Hajjaj called Umayr back. Old man! said he, was it thou didst spring on the body of Othman, the Prince of the True Believers, and break a rib?

Othman had put my father in prison, answered Umayr, and left him, old and sick, to die there.

Thy death, said Hajjaj, can be set against Othman's; we'll send men who can still fight against the Azrakites. Truly the death of thee, old man, will be a blessing to two towns, to Basra and Kufa both. And he looked him over from head to foot, whiles gnawing his beard and whiles letting it fall again. Then he came up close to the old man and said: Umayr, thou heardest what I said in the pulpit?

Ay!

A foul disgrace would it be, by God! for a man like me to make a liar of myself. Guards there! take this fellow and cut his throat.

It was done. Immediately after the killing, the troops rode away, nor did they loiter on the road till they joined Muhallab in camp.

Hajjaj, as Governor of all Iraq, put me in charge of agriculture and Land Tax (narrates Ubayd son of Abu Mukhariq); and I decided to inquire for some old Persian country gentleman to advise me. They told me Jamil, Suhayr's son, was the man for me; and I sent for him. He appeared — an ancient, his eyes hidden under enormous eyebrows.

I am a very old man, said he, that thou shouldst disturb me.

I need thy help and blessing, said I, and thy counsel in my office.

Brushing back his eyebrows with a piece of silk, he looked at me and said: What's thy will?

Hajjaj has put me in charge of agriculture, I replied; and he is a man inflexible to a grim degree. Give me advice.

Which of three things, said the old man, wouldst thou rather satisfy: Hajjaj, or the Treasury, or thy conscience?

All three if I could, I answered; but Hajjaj I dread — he is a fearsome master.

Well, said the ancient, keep these four rules: the first, leave thy gate open and keep no usher; in that way any man will know he can get to thee if he will, and thy deputies will be the more afeared of thee. Next, let thy underlings have long hearings with thee — a governor always gets a better name that way. Third, let thy decrees be fair, the same for the rich and the poor. Last, give no man's ambition the slightest hold on thee; never take a present from an underling, for the man who gives it will not be content till he has got twice as much again, let alone the unsavory tales that come of it.

Do these four things; and thou mayest flay thy sheep from the napes of their necks to their tails' ends, and they'll thank thee for it. And still Hajjaj can have nothing against thee.

On one occasion Hajjaj was in perplexity how he should settle a case of inheritance (says Sha'bi). He asked me my opinion on the proper division of an inheritance between a mother, a sister, and a grandfather.

Five Companions of God's Apostle, God's Prayer and Peace be on him! give five different opinions on that question, I replied: namely, Abdallah, Zayd, Ali, Othman, and Ibn Abbas.

What did Ibn Abbas say? he was a devout Muslim, said Hajjaj.

He considered the grandfather as being equivalent to a

father, leaving one third for the mother — nothing for the sister.

And what did Abdallah say?

He divided the property in six parts and gave the sister three sixths, the mother one sixth, and the grandfather two.

And Zayd?

Zayd made a ninefold division: three shares for the mother, two for the sister, four for the grandfather.

What did the Prince of True Believers Othman say?

He gave each heir an equal third, said I.

And what did Ali say?

Ali also divided the inheritance in six shares and gave the sister three of them; but he gave two to the mother and only one to the grandfather.

Hajjaj scratched his nose. The one thing is, he said, that we must not follow Ali's opinion. He subsequently ordered the Judge to decide according to the ruling of the Prince of True Believers Othman.

Once Hajjaj lay sick; it was told him that the men of Kufa were making ready to revolt. As best he might, he climbed the pulpit in the Mosque, and leaning on his crutches, thus spoke:

They said Hajjaj was dead? So much for that. Yet I look for no good this side the grave. God gave none of His creatures immortality save one, and that the vilest — Satan. I see every living thing a-dying, I see the withering of all that hath sap. Every man must be heaved to his dug grave. Earth shall gnaw away his flesh, earth swallow the fluid and the blood of him. And the two things he loved best shall begin to divide one another: his darling children and his darling money.

The only time when his court ever saw Hajjaj happy and genial was one day when Layla of Akhyal was brought before him, she of whom her cousin Tawba of Amir, now long dead, had once written:

If Layla of Akhyal should come and bid me Peace,
Though the earth covered me over, and heavy flags of
stone,
For joy I should bid her Peace again, or the owl of my ghost
Out of the grave should cry to her his mournful cry.

They tell me, said Hajjaj, that when thou wert passing near Tawba's grave thou didst not even turn out of the way to visit it. Thou hast been unfaithful to him: had he been in thy place, and thou in his, he would never have left thy grave behind him unvisited.

God save the Prince! I had excuse, said Layla.

What?

There were women with me, she said, who had heard that poem of his; I would not give them the chance to mock at him for not keeping his word.

Hajjaj liked this answer, and ordered her a generous bounty. They talked long together; nor did any man ever see him so gay as he was that day.

Hajjaj sent a certain Ghadban, a man of Clan Shayban, as a spy to bring report from Kirman in Persia of the doings of the Seceder Ibn Asha'th, who was in revolt. Ghadban presented himself before the Seceder chief.

What news from thy country? said the Seceder.

Bad news! said Ghadban. Thou hadst better dine on Hajjaj before he sups on thee!

Then, in the Mosque at Kirman, he mounted the pulpit, denounced Hajjaj for his deeds, pronounced him an excommunicate Unbeliever, and declared himself for the Seceders. But shortly after, the Seceder chief was taken prisoner, and Ghadban with him. For three years Ghadban lay in prison at Kufa.

When that time had gone by, Hajjaj chanced to receive a letter from the Caliph Abd al-Malik ordering thirty women for palace use: ten to be women of *najib* type, ten of *qu'd al-nikah* type, and ten of *dawat al-ahlam* type. Not understanding the meaning of these expressions, the Governor consulted his court at audience. Nobody knew.

However, one man spoke up: God save the Prince! the meaning of these terms can only be found out from some man who has lived as a wandering Arab and knows the desert people, a past master of raid and booty, and a man, moreover, who has been a wine-drinker, and is familiar with tippler's foul language.

Where is there such a man? inquired Hajjaj.

There's one in your prison now, was the answer.

Who is that?

Ghadban Shaybani, he was told.

So Hajjaj sent for Ghadban. Art thou not, he demanded, the man who said: Thou hadst better dine on Hajjaj before he sups on thee?

God save the Prince! replied Ghadban; that saying did little good to the man who said it, and little harm to the man it was said against.

Well, said the Governor, the Prince of the True Believers has written me a letter, the meaning of which is beyond me. See if thou canst fathom it.

Ghadban asked for it to be read to him; and, when it had been read, said: That is all plain enough.

What do those words mean? said Hajjaj.

The *najib* type of woman, answered Ghadban, is a woman with a proud head and a long throat, long in the neck above the shoulders, with a broad palm and a well-turned knee. If such a woman bear a child, 'tis a son like a grim lion.

The *qu'd al-nikah* type is a woman with well-creased buttocks and heavy breasts, full in flesh, every part of her body pressing some other part. And that is the woman to assuage the hunger and thirst of love in a man.

The *dawat al-ahlam* type is a woman of thirty-five or forty, to be used as one uses a she-camel whose milk comes smacking of hair and horn and sweat.

Well, said Hajjaj. And now, how much hast thou paid on account in our prison?

Three years, said Ghadban.

The Governor gave orders for him to be set at liberty.

* * *

A story is told of the court of Abd al-Malik. The Caliph had received a gift — some shields set with pearls and rubies — and was admiring them in the audience of his personal officers and intimates. He called on one of them, a man named Khalid, to take a shield and try it. Khalid rose, and maneuvered with the shield: but as he was brandishing it, he broke his wind with an audible sound.

What's a fart worth? said the Caliph, smiling.

A purse of four hundred dirhams and a length of velvet! cried somebody.

Abd al-Malik ordered purse and velvet given to Khalid as a bounty. At this, a courtier present extemporized:

> *He tried the targe and broke his wind*
> *And got a purse to calm his mind.*
> *O fart of farts, which filled his store!*
> *O fart of farts, which fed the poor!*
> *Why, any man who bears a bum*
> *Would do the same for half the sum!*
> *Now I know that wind is wealth,*
> *Let me too fart my Sovereign's health!*

Give that man four thousand dirhams! cried Abd al-Malik; but let him spare us his wind.

* * *

At last Abd al-Malik lay dying.

Among verses that he wrote is this:

> *All that delighted me is vanished*
> *Like lightning which hath flashed among eternal ruins.*

When his son Walid went in to see him, the Caliph quoted the verse:

> *How many a visitor haunts a sick man's place*
> *To see if he will die before his face.*

Walid burst into tears.

How's this, whining like a slave girl? said his father. When I am gone, thou must go forth in thy leopard-skin, with thy sword on thy shoulder, and if any man stand against thee, smite him on the neck. Let none but a submissive man die in his bed.

On the very day of his father's death, Walid was proclaimed at Damascus. He had been treated too softly by his parents, and grew up without breeding.

One day when I waited on Abd al-Malik, says one of that Caliph's courtiers, I found him deep in thought. I have been considering, said he, whom I may send as Governor to Arabia; and I can think of none.

Walid? said I.

His Arabic is not good enough, said the Caliph.

Walid heard of this. He bestirred himself, sent for grammarians, stayed at home with them about him for six months, and then made a fresh appearance — more ill-bred than ever!

We must not expect much of Walid, his father said.

On one occasion, Walid as Caliph misquoted from the pulpit the Koranic text as: *O THAT DEATH HAD MADE AN END OF I!*

His brother Sulayman was standing close below him. By God! he whispered to their cousin Omar son of Abd al-Aziz, I wish it had!

But this Caliph stirred up Holy Wars; and great were the conquests of his reign. In the year eighty-nine of the Flight the Isles of Majorca and Minorca were captured by the True Believers, and in the year ninety-one many fortresses beside the Caspian Sea. In ninety-two the whole of Spain was subdued, and Armail in Sind by the mouth of Indus; in ninety-three

Samarqand and the country of Soghd; in ninety-four Kabul, and Farghana, far beyond the Oxus River.

When he came to know Syria, so long a Christian land, Walid became familiar with the handsome churches, still Christian, of which the beauty was so seductive and the splendor so far renowned. He therefore made up his mind to build the Muslims such a Mosque at Damascus that they would have no eyes for those other monuments, a Mosque to be a peerless thing, one of the wonders of the world. He assembled master craftsmen for the building from Persia, India, the Western Provinces, and Byzantium, and appropriated seven years' yield of the Syria Land Tax to the cost.

And he wrote to his cousin Omar ibn Abd al-Aziz, who was his Governor at Madina, ordering him to demolish the old Mosque where the Prophet had lived, and to rebuild it, sending him for the purpose money, loads of mosaic, and marble, and eighty Christian artists from Syria and Egypt to work the embellishment.

He arranged for the circumcision of orphans, and appointed persons charged with their education. He assigned attendants to cripples and leaders to the blind; and besides what he did for the Mosque of the Prophet at Madina he settled a daily allowance on men learned in the Law there, and on the destitute and infirm of the city. He put all things in order by thoroughgoing regulation. Public begging was forbidden.

May the Lord have Mercy on Walid! said one, when he was gone; for where is the like of Walid, who conquered India and Spain and built the Damascus Mosque, and used to order me platters of silver to share among the Koran Readers of the Mosque at Jerusalem?

* * *

The first service Hajjaj had done the Umayyads was the conquest and slaying of Ibn Zubayr, who had revolted and held Madina as Caliph. He had had Ibn Zubayr's body gibbeted there, though his mother Asma, daughter of Abu Bakr, she who had brought food for her father and the Prophet of God when they hid in the Cavern at the time of the Flight, had begged Hajjaj for leave to bury her son.

Hajjaj came to visit Walid. He entered the Caliph's presence clad as he had journeyed, in his hauberk, with his quiver and bow slung at his back. Long they sat together; at last, as they still were talking, a slave girl came in, whispered something in the Caliph's ear, received his answer, and went away. Then she reappeared, again whispered something, again withdrew.

Abu Muhammad, said the Caliph, dost thou know what that was?

Surely no, said Hajjaj.

It was my wife, my cousin Umm al-Banin daughter of Abd al-Aziz, who sent that girl to me to say: What audience is this with an Arab in his war-harness, and thou in a plain robe? I told her the Arab was Hajjaj. And she was so frightened she sent again to say: I like not to see thee all alone with the Butcher of Creation.

Pay no heed to women's folly and chatter, Prince of the True Believers, cried Hajjaj. Women are to manage a fan, not manage affairs. Never let a woman know a secret, never let her know anything thou hast a mind to do, never let a woman grasp at anything beyond her reach, or dream beyond her dressing. And beware of women's advice: their counsel will make a coward of thee, and their wishes turn thee to a sluggard. Let their requests concern themselves. Sit with them little, and lie with them less, if thou wilt not have thy mind dulled and thy strength sapped.

With these words he rose and took his leave. Walid went straight in to Umm al-Banin and told her the whole. Prince of the True Believers, said she, I wish thou wouldst order him to come and pay his respects to me tomorrow.

Very well, said the Caliph; and on the morrow, when Hajjaj appeared at audience, he spoke to him: Abu Muhammad, go in and pay a visit to Umm al-Banin.

Let me be excused from that, Prince of the True Believers, said Hajjaj. But Walid insisted; and the Governor of Iraq betook himself to her apartments. A long time she kept him waiting in her anteroom; and even when she admitted him, did not invite him to take a seat, but kept him standing.

So thou art Hajjaj! she said at last: the man who would not let the Prince of True Believers be till Ibn Zubayr was dead. Had God not known thee to be the vilest thing He ever created, He would never have made thee guilty of the ruin of the Holy House, and the murder of the Woman with Two Girdles' son, Ibn Zubayr, the first-born of Islam. For long enough the wives of the Prince of True Believers have had to pluck the jewels from their hair and send them to market to feed thy soldiery. Without their aid, who would have thought thee worth the price of a sick sheep?

As to that counsel thou gavest the Prince, to stint his lawful pleasure with his wives, if such a loss were as much a blessing to them as the loss of thee would be a blessing to thy mother, he might well hearken; but to part them from a man like him — never will he lend ear to such advice! God's blessing on the poet who said of thee, the time thou didst run for thy life from Ghazala's spear:

A lion to me, but an ostrich in war.

Slaves there! turn him out!

How did it go, Abu Muhammad? inquired Walid when he got back to the audience.

She went on till I had rather be under the ground than on it, by God! said Hajjaj.

Walid laughed till his feet stamped on the floor. There, Abu Muhammad, he shouted, there's the true-begotten daughter of Abd al-Aziz for thee!

Hajjaj died in Iraq at the age of fifty-four, having been Governor for twenty years. His sickness came, it is said, through eating too much of the edible soil which they call Stamped Earth. A hundred and twenty thousand persons are said to have been executed by his orders. Harsh government may harm a few, he used to say; weak government harms all.

They tell that going one day in cavalcade to the Friday Prayer he heard a sound of groaning and lamentation, and asked what it was. The prisoners, he was told.

Hajjaj turned toward the sound. Rot in your places! he shouted; and be quiet!

He died that same week; that was his last ride. All he left at death was his Koran, his arms, and a few hundred dirhams.

* * *

A certain Meccan poet became the lover of Walid's wife when she was on Pilgrimage.

> *Good old Pilgrimage — what a stage!*
> *Good old Holy House — what a shrine!*
> *Good old girls — and how they nudge us*
> *At the time of kissing the Black Stone!*

He followed her to Damascus.

> *Rawda! thy lover's restless*
> *And heartsick, and cannot wait.*
> *Palace walls part us, said she.*
> *I'll find a way, said I.*
> *But think, God sees us, said she.*
> *God is Merciful, said I.*
> *My warning's wasted, said she;*
> *Then be ready when the watch drowse,*
> *And be here, unseen in your coming,*
> *Suddenly, like night-dew.*

Surprised by Walid, she hid the poet in a wardrobe chest. The Caliph requested a gift of her. She granted it. He pointed to the chest, and gave order for it to be carried to his own chamber. There a pit was dug, and the chest lowered into it.

Something came to my ears, the Caliph then said in a loud voice. If it be true, I bury what I am thinking of with this chest and it is gone forever. If it be false, then we only bury a wooden chest.

The earth was thrown in, and a carpet spread over the place.

Walid was the first Caliph to prohibit his being addressed by his personal name. Yet his signet ring bore this inscription: *Walid, thou must die.*

When I was helping put Walid's body in his grave, says his cousin Omar, he gave a kick within the shroud, as if he still stamped the earth.

*   *   *

His brother, the Caliph Sulayman, was a huge, an insatiable eater, a man who once ate at a sitting seventy pomegranates and a lamb, six chickens and a dozen pounds of currants. He loved luxurious stuffs, and above all a kind called *washi.* Everyone began to wear the material, for robes, cloaks, drawers, turbans, caps. The Caliph wore it for riding, at audience, and in the pulpit. No servant at the Palace presented himself wearing any other stuff: even the cook would not have dared to appear without an apron of it. And the Caliph gave order that his shroud must be made of the same.

Sulayman once looking in a mirror was struck with his own youth and beauty. Yes, he said, Muhammad was the Prophet, and Abu Bakr was called the Truthful, Omar was called the Discriminator and Othman the Modest, Mu'awia the Forbearing, Yazid the Patient, Abd al-Malik the Administrator, Walid the Oppressor. And I, I am Prince Charming!

> *He shakes his hips and claps his sides as if to say: Here I come! Recognize me!*
> *Ay, we recognize thee. And thou art hateful to God, hateful to all good men.*

PIETISM

Men took different paths in these days, and there came to be various styles of distinction. But the elect of mankind, with whom religion was still a passion, were known as Ascetics, and Devotees.

Tamim Dari, a Companion of the Prophet, who had been a Christian before he Submitted to God, used to pass the whole night long until daybreak in the repetition of this one verse of Scripture:

DO THOSE WHO WORK EVIL THINK WE SHALL LET THEM BE AS THOSE WHO BELIEVE AND DO GOOD, EQUAL IN LIFE AND DEATH? ILL DO THEY JUDGE.

DO THOSE WHO WORK EVIL THINK WE SHALL LET THEM BE AS THOSE WHO BELIEVE AND DO GOOD, EQUAL IN LIFE AND DEATH? ILL DO THEY JUDGE.

DO THOSE WHO WORK EVIL THINK WE SHALL LET THEM BE AS THOSE WHO BELIEVE AND DO GOOD, EQUAL IN LIFE AND DEATH? ILL DO THEY JUDGE . . . .

and so till the dawning of the day.

One man, when he had ended a sermon, used to tremble and weep. When people asked him why he did thus, he answered: I am about to enter on a grave matter now — to stand in the presence of the Most High to practice what I have just preached.

In these days lived Hasan of Basra, whose father had been the freed slave of a Helper woman in Madina. Subtle were the instructions Hasan gave in the science of practical religion:

You have two bad companions: the dinar and the dirham. Only when they leave you are they of any use to you.

God made fasting, as a training ground for His servants, that they many run to His obedience. Some win that race and get the prize; others fail, and go away disappointed. But by my life! if the lid were off, the well-doer would be too busy about his well-doing, as the evil-doer in his evil-doing, to get him a new garment or anoint his hair.

The wonder is not how the lost were lost, but how the saved were ever saved.

Fear must be stronger than hope. For where hope is stronger than fear, the heart will rot.

It seemed to him as though Hell-fire had been created for him alone. My asceticism, he said, is mere lust, and my patience cowardice. My patience in sorrow shows my terror of Hell-fire — that is cowardice; and all my asceticism in this world is lust for the Other, the quintessence of lust. But how excellent is a man whose patience is for God's sake, not for the sake of being delivered from Hell; and his asceticism for God's sake, not for the sake of getting into Heaven. One grain of true piety is better than a thousandfold weight of fasting and prayer.

Hasan of Basra and Shaqiq of Balkh visited the woman saint Rabi‘a, lying sick.

That person is not sound in faith, Hasan said, who does not patiently endure the Lord's chastening.

That person, said Shaqiq, is not sound in faith who does not find pleasure in the Lord's chastening.

But Rabi‘a answered: That person is not sound in faith who does not, contemplating the Lord, forget the chastening.

I ask forgiveness of God, Rabi‘a said, for the little faith I had in the time when I used to ask His forgiveness.

O God! if I worship Thee for fear of Hell, send me to Hell. Give to Thine enemies whatever Thou didst purpose to give me of this world's goods. And give Thy friends whatever Thou didst purpose to give me in the Hereafter. Thyself is enough for me.

My sorrow, said Rabiʻa, is not over things which make me grieve; rather my sorrow is over things for which I cannot grieve.

Dost thou hate the Devil?
No, said Rabiʻa.
Why not?
My love for God leaves me no time to hate him.

O Apostle of God, who is there that loves thee not? But love of God has so possessed every smallest part of my being that there is no room left me to love anyone else, or hate.

A Pietist Caliph

OMAR SON OF Abd al-Aziz had been born in Egypt when his father was Governor there. He memorized the whole of the Koran as a child; and his father sent him to Madina for his education. He used to sit at the feet of Ubaydallah, one of the seven great Doctors of the Law. Omar afterwards related Traditions on the authority of his father and others, including Anas the Prophet's servant.

Never after the Apostle of God was gone, said Anas, did I pray behind an Imam who was more like the Prophet in the way he prayed — he stayed a long time at his Bowing and Prostration, and cut short the Standing and Kneeling.

Walid as Caliph made Omar Governor in Madina; and he became Caliph by Sulayman's testament. When the will was read, and his name was there, Omar was stupefied. His piety and humility were extreme. He abolished the cursing of Ali from the pulpit, and used to recite, instead of that malediction, the verse: *FORGIVE US, LORD, AND OUR BRETHREN WHO WERE BEFORE US IN THE FAITH ALSO.*

Soon after his accession, his friend Salim went in to audience. Art thou glad or sorry to see me thus? Omar asked.

Glad for the Muslims' sake, sorry for thine, he replied.

I am afraid of being damned, the Caliph then said.

All will be well so long as you continue to fear, said Salim; what I fear is that your fear will come to an end.

Give me some counsel, Omar said.

This then, was the reply: Our father Adam was driven out of Paradise for one single sin!

Take for guidance what your predecessors approved; never go against them, for they were better and wiser than you are.

Strive eagerly to get Traditions, and get them from the men themselves, not from written records.

If the explanation of some passage in the Book of God presented difficulties, and if I heard of a man even as far away as the Pool of Jumad (in the farthest and wildest south) who could explain it to me, I would not grudge going.

A CONVERSATION IN THE MOSQUE AT KUFA

Is it even so, Abu Abdallah, that thou hast been with Muhammad? Didst thou see the Apostle of God plain? Wast thou familiar with him?

Even so, cousin.

Tell me something thou didst that had to do with him.

Once I was listening to a man reciting from the Koran. And I had heard the Prophet of God, God's Prayer and Peace be on him! recite that portion differently. So I took the man to the Prophet of God, and told him about it.

I could see in his face that he was displeased. Ye both read the Book aright! he said; so do not differ! Verily those who were before you differed. And they perished!

The Apostle of God, God's Prayer and Peace be on him! ordinarily took an ablution for every time he prayed. He cleaned his teeth with a stick of threadwood fiber, and rinsed his mouth; he always snuffed up water from his right hand, and blew his nose with his left. He washed his limbs twice or thrice, and wiped his head sometimes once, sometimes oftener, cleaning the inside of his ear with the prayer-finger and the outside with his thumb. He always cleaned his beard, and his fingers, and used to take off his ring for that. As he began the ablution, he used to say: In the Name of God! and when he had done he would say: I testify that there is no god but God, Who hath no peer; and I testify that Muhammad is His Slave and Apostle. Make me penitent and pure and a faithful servant to Thee. I ask Thy Pardon, and repent toward Thee! After ablution he never dried his limbs. When he washed his hands, he used to pour the water with the right upon the left.

For Prostration he always put his knees first to the ground, then his hands, and his brow and nose last. He used to plant his hands on the earth wide from his chest, and level with his shoulders, with his fingers close together. In kneeling for the Creed, he sat upon his left foot, with his right knee posted up; he laid his right hand on his right thigh and his left hand on his left thigh.

As to his fasting, he never began the Fast of Ramadan till he or some truthful Believer had seen the new moon of Ramadan, or till thirty days of the month before were past. On the festival of the breaking of the fast, before he went out to the Praying Place beyond the town he would break his fast by eating some dates; and it was always an odd number of them that he ate.

He used to fast voluntarily as well, very often on Mondays and Thursdays, less often on Saturdays and Sundays. And whenever he fasted of a Friday, he would fast the Thursday before or the Saturday after as well. In the third ten days of Ramadan the Month of Fast he used to go into retreat for Prayer and watching. He had little to do with people those days, but only recited the Koran, in a tent pitched within the Mosque.

Amongst his Companions the Apostle of God sat and rose up humbly. Often in company he sat bowed, drawing up his knees and putting his arms around his legs. Sometimes he would lean against something as he sat; sometimes he lay on his back; but if he lay so he used to cross one foot over the other.

He spoke slowly; and sometimes he would say a thing thrice over. He used to make gestures as he talked, on occasion putting his right palm to the thick of his left thumb. When he wondered at any thing, he used to turn the palms of his hands towards it; if he were angry, he turned them away. And it was another sign of anger if he fingered his beard. The whole range of his teeth could be seen when he laughed aloud.

When he swore, it was most often: By Him Who hath my soul in His Hand! or: By God!

In company he would not sit with his knees projecting beyond the knees of those who sat by him.

If he went to any man's house, he did not stand waiting for admission square before the door, but to the right or the left of it, asking permission to enter thus: Peace upon you! Peace upon you!

TRADITIONS OF THE PROPHET'S USAGE AT TABLE

Before eating, the Apostle of God used to say: In the Name of God. He bade his Companions, if they forgot this, to say at the meal's end: In the Name of God, for the first and the last.

He ordinarily ate kneeling, but sometimes sitting on his left foot with his right leg posted up, or, if he were famished, squatting with both legs posted up. He never ate from a table with legs, nor drank from a cup with a broken rim.

His food he took up with three fingers of his right hand, and he always took what lay just before him except when fresh dates and dried dates were served in one dish together, and except in the case of a certain stew, from which he would take the pieces he most liked wherever they lay in the dish. It is recorded that on occasion he made use of four fingers eating; but he never used two only. When he was done, he licked his fingers: first the middle finger, then the prayer-finger, and last the thumb. And he used to wash his hands both before and after meat, and then wipe his face and arms.

Very thin bread, bread with dried meat, lizards, spleen, kidneys, onions, garlic, and leeks he never ate; nor would he eat fish or sour things together with milk; or grilled with boiled meat; or dried meat with fresh; or meat with milk; or two binding with two relaxing dishes; or two heavy with two light dishes.

His bread was mostly barley bread of unsifted flour with all the bran left in. The meat he ate was of sheep, camels, wild asses, hares, bustards, and fish. He preferred foreleg and shoulder for the most part, but also praised the saddle. He also ate fried sheep-liver.

He cut his meat with his teeth, and used to say: Cutting meat with a knife is the Persian style. Yet it is recorded by sound Traditions that the Prophet himself used a knife on both roast shoulder and baked loin.

When he ate dates, he put out the stones on to the nails of his prayer-finger and middle finger, and threw them away; less often he collected the stones in his left hand. His manner of eating grapes was to put the berries into his mouth, press them with his teeth, and then put out the husks.

Water he drank in three draughts at a time, pronouncing before each: In the Name of God! and after the last: Glory to God! So long as the cup was at his lips he held his breath. Generally he drank sitting. When he had company, he gave them to drink first as a rule; but if on occasion he himself drank first, he passed the cup to the person sitting on his right hand.

There are Traditions that he said: When night sets in, say: In the Name of God! and cover the vessels ye keep your food and drink in, even if 'tis only with a chip of wood.

The Apostle of God never wore any other garment than these, to wit: a shirt, drawers, a kerchief, a cloak, a figured shawl, a plain shawl, a tunic, a fur, leather socks, easy sandals.

He mostly wore cotton stuff. He thought striped cloth a fine thing, but generally chose plain white for himself. He would not have his Companions wear plain red or plain yellow garments, but he approved the wearing of green, and himself wore clothes with a red pattern as well as things figured with green or black.

Donning a fresh garment, he put on the right side first; doffing it, he put off the left side first. Round his head he wound a white cloth as a turban, sometimes leaving the end to dangle down between his shoulders; on occasion also he wore a black turban. His shirt sleeves reached to his wrists or the roots of his fingers, and were cut somewhat wide. His sandals were of tanned oxhide, with two leather straps; but sometimes he went barefoot.

The Prophet wore a signet ring on the little finger of his right hand; other Companions remember him wearing it on the little finger of his left hand. Both usages are Lawful.

TRADITIONS OF THE PROPHET'S
USAGE IN PERSONAL MATTERS

The Apostle of God used to comb his hair and beard, but not every day as rich men do; and he anointed both. He clipped his mustache, and trimmed both that and his nails every Friday before he entered the Mosque. He used his right hand for ablution, for food, for the comb, and for cleaning his teeth and the like; but used his left hand in the privy. To take or give something he used the right also. Every night he put three spoonfuls of collyrium in his eyes. On a journey he always took with him a mirror, a comb, a bottle of ointment, a box of aromatics, a pair of scissors, and a bottle of oil; and at home he took these same things to the room of the wife he was to spend the night with. The Prophet dyed his hair with collyrium, though there is a Tradition that he used both collyrium and indigo, and another that he used *waras* and saffron. He used depilatory ointments, and had his wives apply them to him, though there is a Tradition that he used scissors and not depilatories. All Traditionists agree that he never entered a public bath.

If he sneezed, it was not very loudly, but covering his face with his sleeve and putting his other hand to his nostrils. Afterwards he would say: Glory to God! and he said: The man who hears should answer: God's Mercy on thee!

When night came on, he took an ablution, put off his day clothes, and put on his nightgown. Then he blew on his hands, recited a verse from the Koran, and rubbed his limbs. He lay down on his right side, putting the palm of his right hand under his right cheek, pronouncing: O God, in Thy Name do I die and live. Under his head he set a leather cushion stuffed with palm fiber. And when he rose from sleep, he used to say: Glory to God Who hath quickened us after we were dead; to Him we move and wake.

Fever he treated with cold water, headache with collyrium, inflamed eyes with rest, bellyache with purges, dropsy with milk and camel's urine, boils with Indian sweet reed. And he often used cupping.

When he had to go to the privy, he took off his signet ring; then he stepped into the privy with his left foot first, saying: O God, I take refuge with Thee from all uncleanness. He stepped out with the right foot, saying: Thy Pardon!

TRADITIONS OF THE PROPHET'S
USAGE WITH HIS WIVES

Toward his wives the Apostle of God was most open in affection. Sometimes when Aisha was drinking water he would take the cup from her hand and drink from the very place where she had drunk; and when she was eating meat from a bone, he would take the bone from her and do likewise. When it was with Aisha as it is monthly with women, he would lay his head on her breast, or lean over her and recite the Koran to her. If she lost her temper, he used to lay his hand on her shoulder and say: May God forgive her sins and calm her temper and deliver her from passion!

Every day, when afternoon prayer was done, he used to go into the room of each one of his wives and ask after her well-being; then, as evening closed in, he went to spend the night with her whose turn it was. In all matters of provision and distribution he was most careful to be just, and used to say: O God, this is my portion, things within my power; blame me not in matters beyond my power! by which he meant: Blame me not for injustice in the matters of love and sexual intercourse. Sometimes he would have intercourse with his wife at the beginning of the night, then bathe and sleep; otherwise he would only perform ablution after intercourse, then sleep, and bathe at the end of the night.

TRADITIONS OF THE PROPHET'S USAGE ON A JOURNEY

His day for setting out was Thursday ordinarily; but he also started on journeys upon Monday, Sunday, or Wednesday. After he was mounted he used to repeat thrice the Magnification: God is Most Great! and on the road he would say a Magnification as he breasted a rising ground, and a Doxology: Glory to God! as he went down a descent.

The Prophet disapproved men's travelling alone, and forbade women to travel unless a man, and by preference a near kinsman, went with them. And he said that good angels do not go along with wayfarers who have a dog or a bell with them.

Start at night, he recommended; that shortens the way. On

his return from a journey, he never entered the city at night, and forbade his Companions to do so. When he got home, he went first into the Mosque and said a prayer of two Bows.

* * *

I was at Palmyra once for the Friday Congregation, says Sha'bi; and I saw a vast crowd gathered; they were taking notes from the lecture of an old man with a flowing beard. Among other Traditions, he related a Tradition, on authority going back to the Prophet, that the Prophet once said: Two trumpets shall there be on Judgment Day — one laying all things low, without life and prone, the second summoning all things to another life.

Why, thou hast made two trumpets out of one! I cried out: *WHEN THE TRUMPET SHALL SOUND ONE BLAST,* says the Book, in the Chapter of the Reality.

Thou malefactor! the old man retorted: darest thou challenge what I have narrated on sound authority from the Prophet of God? And he snatched up his shoe, and cried to the crowd to fall on me. They took his side: they yelled that they would beat me, till I swore God created thirty trumpets!

In nothing do we see learned men more prone to untruth than in the fabrication of Traditions.

I heard from Sa'id, says a Traditionist, that Jabir son of Abdallah related to him the following:

At the time we were laboring with the Apostle of God, God's Prayer and Peace be on him! at the digging of the Dyke around Madina, I had a lamb, none too fat. We might dress that lamb for the Prophet of God, I thought to myself; so I told my wife to grind a little barley flour and bake some bread, whilst I butchered the lamb and dressed it for the Prophet.

In the evening when it was time to go home, I said to him: I have dressed one of our own lambs for thee, we have baked some barley bread to go with it, and happy shall I be if thou wilt come home with me. The Prophet consented to come; but he bade a crier cry to all: All follow the Apostle of God to the house of Jabir, Abdallah's son!

GOD'S WE ARE, thought I to myself, AND TO HIM IS OUR RETURNING!

Well, Muhammad was not long in coming, and all the people with him. He sat down; we set the food before him; he blessed it in the Name of God and ate. Then all the people, one company after another, ate in turn, till every single man who had been working at the Dyke went away filled!

Once when the Prophet was preaching, people stood up and interrupted: O Prophet of God, our crops are scorched and our cattle are dying — pray God to give us rain! Then the Prophet cried out twice: O God, send us rain!

It is added on the authority of the Companion Anas, the Prophet's servant: I swear by God that we could not see the veriest scrap of a cloud; but instantly a cloud gathered, and rain fell. The Prophet came down from the pulpit, recited Prayer, and went indoors. And it never stopped raining till the following Friday.

On that day, when the Prophet got up to preach, someone shouted: Our houses are falling in; our streets are impassable; pray God to remove the rain from us.

The Prophet smiled. Around us, O Lord — not on top of us! he cried. And instantly the sky cleared over Madina. Outside the town the rain continued to fall; but not a drop more fell in the city. I saw Madina at that time surrounded as it were by a glory.

Abd al-Rahman son of Awf narrates that his mother Shifa declared as follows:

I was midwife to the Prophet's mother Amina; and in the night when her labor pains seized her, and Muhammad Mustafa fell into my hands at his birth, a voice out of the Other World came to my ears, saying: Thy Lord show Mercy to thee! And from east to west the face of earth became so illuminated that I could see some of the palaces of Damascus by the light of it.

And it is reported that Amina declared: In that night a flight of birds turned in to my house, so many that the whole house was filled with them. Their beaks were of emerald, and their wings of ruby.

* * *

If death were mentioned in his presence, the Caliph Omar ibn Abd al-Aziz used to tremble in every limb. And every night he used to summon men who knew the Law, and converse with them of death, and of the Rising of the Dead.

Omar once expressing a longing for an apple, one of his household sent him one. How fragrant it is! he exclaimed; and how beautiful! Take it back, slave, and greet the man who sent it, and say: Thy gift has given us great pleasure.

The man is thine uncle's son, Prince of the True Believers, said one who was present; and I assure thee I have heard a Tradition that the Prophet of God used to eat things which were presented to him.

For shame! the Caliph replied; a present to the Prophet was a present — but to us in these days a present is a bribe.

The soul's salvation, said Malik the ascetic, lies in resisting the soul's desires. And on another occasion he said: They call Malik an ascetic; but the real ascetic is Omar ibn Abd al-Aziz, for the world came to him and he put it behind him.

I went in one day to get my meal from my mistress, says one of Omar's eunuch slaves, and she served a dish of lentils.

Lentils! Lentils every day! said I.

That's what thy master the Prince of the True Believers eats, my son, she replied.

When I first saw Omar, said one, the waistband of his drawers was not to be seen for the drooping fat of his belly. I saw him later as Caliph — and I could have counted his ribs by eye.

When he became Caliph, he began with his own kindred and confiscated their wealth to the Public Treasury, calling their possessions exactions. And when a certain man, nephew to Amr of Egypt, said at audience: Prince of the True Believers, the Caliphs before you used to bestow bounties, but you have forbidden such things; and since I have a family to keep, and some land, may I have leave to retire to my estate and improve it for their benefit? Omar replied: The man who spares me his keep is my favorite.

Think often of death, he presently added. If thou art too poor that will ease thy poverty; and if thy fortune is too easy that will tighten it.

The Marwanid branch of the Umayyad family came in a body to the Palace gate, and said to Omar's son: Tell thy father that the Caliphs before him used to make us grants and recognize our rank decently; thy father will not let us touch what he manages. The young man went in and delivered the message.

Tell them this, said Omar: My father says to you *I FEAR, IF I REBEL AGAINST MY LORD, THE RETRIBUTION OF A FEARFUL DAY.*

If we were to go in and see the Prince of True Believers, the Marwanids decided, we might soften him with a little good humor. So they went in. One of them began to talk, and told a jesting tale. Omar gave him a fixed look. Then another of them capped his cousin's story.

So this was the object of the meeting? said Omar: the lowest kind of talk.

A man who realizes, he once said, that his words are a component part of his actions will be sparing of his conversation.

When Omar appointed me Governor of Mosul, says Yahya of Ghassan, I found theft and housebreaking more common there than in most cities. Writing to give him an account of things, I therefore asked whether I should take men up on suspicion, and punish on mere accusation, or whether I was to arrest men only on clear proof, as the Law directed.

Only on clear proof, and in accord with the Law, he replied, and added: If justice will not make honest men of them, then may God not better them.

I did as he told me. Before I left Mosul, it was grown one of the most orderly of cities, and theft and burglary were rarer there than in most places.

A man once asked the Traditionist Taus: Is Omar the Mahdi (the Divinely Guided One who shall come at the End of Time)?

He is a Mahdi, replied Taus, but not *the* Mahdi.

Omar once asked me, says Mujahid: What do people say about me?

They say your mind is disordered, I said.

I can only compare Omar, says Iyas, with a master workman who has no tools to work with — by which I mean that he had no one to help him.

Once, passing with his companions by a cemetery, Omar bade them wait while he went to visit the tombs of some he had loved. And going in among the graves, he halted and spoke some words; then he came out again.

Does no one wonder what I said, he asked presently, and what answer I got?

What did you say, Prince of the True Believers? What was the answer?

I walked among the tombs of those I had loved, and greeted them; they returned no greeting to me again. I called to them; no one answered. And as I was calling so, the earth called to me; it said: Omar, dost thou know who I am? I am something which has changed the beauty of their faces, which has torn the ragged cerements from their skins and unstrung their hands and loosened their arms. As he said this, Omar wept almost to fainting.

It was not many days after that he too went to his grave.

Outside the abbey wall the diggers buried today
One who was the very beam of the scales for justice,
One who never in all his earthly days inclined
To a tempting eye, or a jewelled head, or galloping
coursers.

Omar the second Caliph, Othman, Ali, Marwan, and Omar son of Abd al-Aziz were all bald; and after that there were no more bald Caliphs.

THE CALIPHATE OF HISHAM
REVOLT OF THE HOUSE OF ALI
AND INTRIGUES OF THE HOUSE OF ABBAS

HISHAM, THE FOURTH OF Abd al-Malik's sons to be Caliph, was rough, churlish, and hard. He hoarded money, looked sharply to tillage, and bred horses. In the races he founded there ran together four thousand horses from his and others' stables, such a show as had never been seen either in the old Ignorance or in Islam. He encouraged weaving, improved arms and armor and the art of war, built castles on the frontiers, and dug underground canals and cisterns along the Mecca road. All men in his days walked in his footsteps and kept what they got: kindliness dwindled, charity ceased, and never were the ways of men so unkind as then.

In the sixteenth year of his Caliphate, Husayn's grandson Zayd revolted at Kufa, and marched against Hisham's Governor in Iraq, Yusuf of Thaqif. When night parted the hosts, Zayd was borne back wounded: an arrow had lodged in his forehead. By inquiry a village doctor was found to draw the arrowhead from the wound; he was not told who the wounded man was. But so soon as the steel was drawn, Zayd died.

They buried him in the bed of a water-hollow, and covering over the grave with earth and turf, turned a stream of water from a canal to flow over it. But the doctor marked the place, and on the morrow went straight to Yusuf, told him, and guided him to the spot. Yusuf had the body dug up and sent the head to Hisham. Then, having received orders from the Caliph, he fixed the carcass naked on a gibbet.

After some time, Hisham wrote ordering Yusuf to burn the corpse, and to cast the ashes on the wind.

The Zaydite sect were called by that name from this revolt with Zayd. A schism arose between them and the Imamite sect of Ali's party; and the Zaydites themselves were split in after-time into eight lesser sects, each one adding to the original beliefs of the body and developing different tenets. It was the same with the Imamites, who came to be split into thirty-three lesser sects. The whole Sect of Ali, the body of the Shi'ites, was divided at last in sixty-three sects, not counting lesser divisions within these founded upon minor differences of interpretation.

Many sects! Many doctrines! And many were the arguments for the coming of him who is foretold, the Divinely Guided Mahdi. On that point opinions varied between the Circle men, the Cypress men, the Light men, and other schools, all of whom were Imamites.

The Hashimite sect of Shi'ites maintained that every external thing has an esoteric aspect, every visible form a spirit, every Revelation a hidden meaning, every earthly symbol a corresponding reality in the Other World.

Ali, in their view, had in himself the knowledge of all mysteries. This knowledge Ali passed to a son of his by a certain Hanafite woman, and he to his son Abu Hashim, from whom they take their name. And it is the possessor of this universal knowledge who is, they say, the true religious head of Islam, the Imam.

The partisans of the House of Abbas (in the northeastern provinces of Khurasan and elsewhere) maintained that when the Prophet died the man most fit to be Imam was Abbas, as the Prophet's uncle and collateral heir. They rejected both Abu Bakr and Omar, and only accepted Ali because Ibn Abbas recognized Ali's Caliphate. According to them, Muhammad the son of Ali by the Hanafite woman was the true Imam after Ali, and this true Imam transmitted the Imamate to his son Abu Hashim, and Abu Hashim transmitted it to Ali the grandson of Abbas. This Imam Ali transmitted it to his son the Abbasid Imam Muhammad.

We Abbasids, Imam Muhammad used to say, have three opportunities: the death of the son of Abd al-Malik, the turn of the century, and the outbreak of rebellion which will surely come in Africa.

The African Muslims had in the main been an obedient and quiet people. But when in Hisham's time agents from Iraq began to go about among them, urging them to revolt, the Africans broke the bond of the Caliphate; and they have been separate ever since. This came about as follows.

To the first seditious whisperings they commonly answered: Nay, we cannot blame the Caliphs for the misdoings of their officers here. And if it was insisted: But what the man does here his master there has bid him do, they would reply: That we cannot believe without proof.

At last, in order to see for themselves, Maysara and some ten other men made the journey from Africa to the Caliph's court, and asked audience. This was not easy for them; and seeing how they were put off time after time, they told Hisham's Secretary their errand: Say to the Prince of True Believers that when the Prince his officer leads an expedition against the Unbelievers, he calls us out along with his own Arab troops. But at the sharing of the spoil he leaves us out. We have said: Content — our Holy

War wins us the more merit. When we go to storm a town, the Prince orders us forward and puts his Arabs in the rear; and we have cried to one another: Forward! we can fight for our brothers.

That is not all. They rip the bellies of our ewes and take the unborn lambs to make cloaks of white fur for the Prince of True Believers. They will kill a thousand ewes for skins fine enough to make one single cloak. We have said: For the Prince of True Believers all this is little enough. And we have let them do it.

But then they must needs have the fairest of our daughters from us. And then we say: Of this we find naught in the Book, nor in the Prophet's usage. We are Believers; and we must know whether the Prince of True Believers knows these wrongs are done or not.

I charge myself with this errand, said the Secretary.

But the men of Africa heard no more of the matter. When their money was almost spent, they wrote down their names on a paper, and gave it to one of the Caliph's counsellors. Here are our names, they said; if the Prince of the True Believers inquires for us, tell him who we were.

So they returned to Africa. And there they revolted, killed Hisham's Governor, and made themselves masters of the province.

THE ABBASID PROPAGANDA

In the hundred and first year of the Flight, the Shi'ite sectaries of Ali sent deputations to the Abbasid Imam Muhammad, who was then living in a village called Humayma near the Dead Sea. The first of these Shi'ite agents were Maysara, Abu Ikrima the saddler, Muhammad son of Khunays, and a druggist named Hayyan: these four came and offered to swear fealty to the Imam Muhammad.

Stretch forth thine hand, they said, to take our oath of fealty for an endeavor to get thee this sovereignty, that through thee God if He will may quicken justice and put an end to tyranny. For this is surely the time for it, the season foretold in very wise prophecies current among ourselves.

This is the season of our hopes and desires no less, replied the Imam Muhammad, by reason of the present fulfilling of a hundred calendar years from the Flight. For never does a century pass over a people but God manifests the truth of the champions of right, and confounds the vanity of those who countenance error, in accord with the Word of God (Mighty is His Name!): *GOD LET HIM DIE A HUNDRED YEARS, THEN RAISED HIM UP ALIVE.* Go therefore, issue a Call to the people, though in all caution and secrecy. And I pray God to accomplish your undertaking, and to make your Mission manifest to all. And there is no Power save in Him.

The missionaries therefore went about among the people inviting their allegiance to the Imam Muhammad, doing everything to heighten their disgust with Umayyad rule by dwelling on the scandalous lives and tyrannous administration of the princes of that House. Many of the inhabitants of Khurasan responded to the Call. But enough of their doings was known and talked about to reach the ears of the Governor of the province. He sent for them.

Who are you? he demanded when they were brought up before him.

We are merchants, was the reply.

Then what is all this that people are saying about you?

Why, what are they saying?

We have reports, said the Governor, that your real business is to spread propaganda on behalf of the Abbasids.

Prince, the missionaries answered, our selves and our business affairs keep us too occupied for any such activity as that.

The Governor therefore let them go. They kept away from Merv, the capital of the province, and began to travel about everywhere through the countryside and villages of Khurasan, apparently driving their trade but really calling men to the Imam

Muhammad. For two years they kept it up, and then returned to the Imam at Humayma, and informed him that they had planted in Khurasan such a tree as would bear fruit, they hoped, in due season.

Among those of note who died in Hisham's time was Abu Tufayl Amir son of Wathila, the last of all the Companions of the Prophet of God. The death of Hisham was the end of wise rule, for there were only three statesmen among the Umayyads: Mu'awia, Abd al-Malik, and himself.

His successor Walid was one of the comeliest of men, and one of the most violent. Walid's cynicism well appears in the verses he extemporized on the death of Hisham. When the messenger announced the event, and greeted him by the title of Caliph, he improvised:

> *I hear a weeping from Rusafa! 'Tis*
> *   Some ladies whom I know;*
> *And forth to pay a call of condolence*
> *   In trailing robe I go.*
> *The daughters of the late Hisham bewail*
> *   His death in bitter woe.*
> *Woeful indeed their fate is; well may they*
> *   Cry out they are undone;*
> *For call me impotent if I do not*
> *   Ravish them one by one!*

Walid was passionately fond of horses; and his horse Sindi was the best of his time. Once at a race run by his command for over a thousand four and five-year olds, a horse of his named Dazzler was in the lead; but not far from the finish the rider was thrown. Walid spurred his own mount to a gallop, came up with Dazzler, swung into the empty saddle, and came in first.

He was the first man who ever did that; and the sanction of his example put it within the rules.

One of his first acts as Caliph was to send to Mecca for the singer Ma'bad; and the musician was hurried to the Palace, without delay. They led him into a great hall, with a double basin of marble in the midst, holding a pool of water and a pool of wine. Beyond it hung a light transparent curtain right across the hall, and there behind the Caliph sat. Ma'bad was bidden sit down by the pool and sing. He began with a love song.

The song so moved Walid that he sprang up, dashed the curtain aside, and tearing off his perfumed coat plunged into the water-pool and drank deep. Slaves hurried off for fresh undergarments and perfumed them; and Walid, again seating himself, bade Ma'bad sing on. The musician took the lute and sang:

> *O empty walls! speak to my pain*
> *Who waver here, your pilgrim wan;*
> *And I will call the clouds of spring*
> *To pour their chilly showers*
> *Till I see your sad stones hid*
> *Close and deep in flowers.*

Bring a purse of fifteen thousand dinars! the Caliph called, when the song was done. As soon as it was handed him, he poured the coins into Ma'bad's bosom.

Say nothing of what you have seen here when you get back home! he warned him.

I once, says a courtier, heard Ibn Aisha sing Walid this song:

> *I saw Heaven's Maids too soon, at Sacrifice:*
> *Chastity could not look into those eyes,*
> *Fair as the stars which stand about night's rim*
> *Waiting to light the Moon when she shall rise.*
> *My Pilgrimage the merit of Works to win*
> *Ended tottering home with a load of Sin.*

O God, how beautiful, my Prince, as you are! Walid exclaimed. By the faith of Abd Shams (his Unbelieving ancestor), sing that again!

O by God and the faith of Umayya (another Unbeliever), once more! he cried when it was done. Over and over again he adjured him by one ancestor after another, to sing the same again, till he came to himself, and cried: By my own soul, once more!

At the end Walid ran from his throne and kneeling down before Ibn Aisha covered every part of his body with kisses. When he came to the sexual parts, the singer crossed his legs, not willing to be kissed in that place; but the Caliph, crying: There too, by God! I must! thrust down his face, exclaiming: O rapture! rapture! Then, tearing off his clothes, he heaped them on the musician, and stood naked till they brought him fresh things. Finally he ordered a thousand dinars and made the singer a present of his own riding-mule.

Bestride my saddle and begone! he said, for thou hast made me burn with a fire hotter than coals of tamarisk!

Walid was himself one of the most polished of poets; and this verse is of his composing:

Pour, and let me hear the chuckle of the flask;
Lutes have stolen from us the souls we thought our own,
So pour! my sins mount up like wine climbing the cup.
Nothing can now atone.

The people loathed him for his profligacy. At last they rebelled against him under his uncle Yazid the Retrencher; and Walid was slain. When his head was brought to Yazid, he had it set atop a spear.

Away with it! said Walid's own brother when he saw it; I testify that he was a winebibber, a debauched lecher who would have seduced me too to wickedness.

Beware of music, you Umayyads, said the Retrencher once: it lessens modesty and increases lust; and it saps virility. It is indeed like wine, and does what strong drink does. If you must needs have it, at least keep your women from it, song being such a spur to lechery.

THE FALL OF THE UMAYYADS

MARWAN THE ASS was the last Caliph of the House of Umayya. He got his nickname of Ass because he never wearied of fighting those who rebelled against him, but marched and marched, and patiently endured the hardships of war.

And now began the Blackshirts to rise in Khurasan and the eastern provinces, and to spread into the Persian Mountain Province and down towards Iraq. Noise of rebellion came from everywhere.

There never was a more wonderful story than the story of Abu Muslim. To a meanly-born poor villager God gave so much of power that he took in hand and carried to success one of the greatest enterprises ever planned. His origin is obscure, though some say that he came from a village in the Kufa district. First a steward, then promoted, he followed his destiny and joined himself to the party of the Abbasid Imam Muhammad, and Muhammad's son the Imam Ibrahim after him. Ibrahim sent him to his adherents in Khurasan, begging them to obey him and accept whatever he ordered or decided. Once firmly established, Abu Muslim took the color black as his badge: for dress, for flags, for banners. The war cry and password was: O Muhammad! O helped of God!

As Abu Muslim's cause went on from strength to strength, the cause of Marwan's Governor in Khurasan weakened. Much cunning, much guile did Abu Muslim use, inflaming the old feud between the southern and the northern clans among the Arab garrisons of the province. The Governor, Nasr, sent

despatch after despatch to warn Marwan how the cause of the
Abbasids grew from day to day. To one of his messages he added
the verses:

> *I see coals glowing among the embers, they want but
> little to burst into blaze.*
> *Fire springs from the rubbing of sticks, and warfare springs
> from the wagging of tongues.*
> *I cry in dismay: I wish I knew if the Umayyads are awake
> or asleep!*

But this letter found the Caliph fighting battles of his own
against the Seceders of Iraq and elsewhere, and busy with rebels
in Tiberias and Jordan and Syria. Among so many wars,
Marwan knew not what to do for Nasr, and only answered:
*The man who is on the spot sees what the man who is not there
cannot see; cut out the sore.*

The Governor, counting no longer on help from the
Caliph, wrote to the Governor of Iraq demanding support. But
he, busy with the revolt in his own province, left the letter
unanswered.

Now Abu Muslim openly raised the Black Standard, in a
village near Merv. It bore the legend: *SANCTION IS GIVEN
TO THOSE WHO FIGHT BECAUSE THEY ARE OP-
PRESSED.*

And men poured in from all sides to join him, from
Herat and Merv and Nishapur, from Balkh and Tukharistan and
Kash. They came all clothed in black, bearing clubs with black-
ened ends which they called Sticks for Unbelievers; on horseback,
on foot, and riding on asses, driving on their asses with yells of:
Git up, Marwan! on account of the Caliph's nickname.

Skirmishes and pitched battles ensued between Abu Muslim and Nasr; and the victory went always to the Blackshirts.
Consider now the Power of God (Exalted is He!) and how,
when He wills a thing, He prepares the means for it.

Wearied and helpless, Nasr retreated from Khurasan to Rayy, thence to Sava; and died at Sava of a broken heart. The Blackshirts now marched down into Iraq.

On the road to Rayy, Nasr had written informing the Caliph that he had left Khurasan; he added these verses to the despatch:

We lie where thou hast thrown us, like an ox brought to the slaughter.

When a stuff's worn to the warp, it mocks the mender's skill.

We tried to repair the rent, but it widened under our fingers.

The Caliph was actually reading this despatch when an officer of the Highway Police brought before him a courier whom he had intercepted on his way from Abu Muslim to the Abbasid Imam Ibrahim at Humayma. Marwan read the letter the man bore, and at once ordered his Governor in Damascus to instruct the local Governor of Balqa to go to Humayma and put Ibrahim under arrest.

This done, he ordered the Imam confined in the prison at Harran, along with several others of the Hashimite family and two of his own Umayyad cousins whom he suspected of disaffection.

A gang of Marwan's freedmen and bodyguards burst into the prison where we lay at Harran, and went into the cell where Ibrahim and the two Umayyads were, says one of their fellow prisoners. They stayed there some time, and put a padlock on the door when they came out. Next day we broke into that cell. We saw that they were dead by violence; but two young Pages who were lying half-dead by the bodies recognized us, and could answer questions. And this was what they said: The men put a cushion over each of the Umayyads and sat on it; they struggled a while — then they stopped. As for Ibrahim, they stuffed his head into a sack they had brought with them, it was full of quicklime, he struggled a while too — then he lay quiet.

Ibrahim's brothers and kinsmen got safe away from Humayma to Kufa.

We left home fourteen men, his uncle Isa used to say, seeking what we sought by the greatness of our resolve and the steadfastness of our hearts.

One of the Blackshirts, by name Abu Humayd of Tus, went on ahead of the army into Kufa. And there, in the Sweepers' Bazaar, he met a man he knew, one Sabiq, and asked for news of the Imam Ibrahim.

Marwan killed him in prison, said the other.

Who is heir to the Imamate now? inquired Abu Humayd.

His brother Abu Abbas.

And where is he?

Here in Kufa, like thyself — and his brother and uncles too, and some more of the House.

Why, when did they come?

Two months ago.

Then take me to them today! said Abu Humayd.

Nay, said Sabiq, meet me tomorrow in this same place.

So Abu Humayd hurried back to the Blackshirt camp outside the city, and told the news to some of the commanders of Khurasan. And next day the officers were taken to the house where Abu Abbas lay in hiding with his kinsmen. They hailed him Caliph, and took the oath of fealty. Then the army marched into the city, the ranks were arrayed, with the cavalry in the van, Abu Abbas and his companions mounted, and the cavalcade rode into the Governor's palace.

On the Friday, Abu Abbas went into the Great Mosque beside the palace. He preached standing, contrary to the usage of the Umayyads, who used to sit on the pulpit to preach. And the people shouted: Why, thou hast revived the True Way of the Prophet, O cousin of God's Apostle!

In his sermon, after due praise to God, Abu Abbas went on to rehearse the verses of the Koran which treat of what is due to kinship, citing them in favor of the House of Abbas. He wound up his discourse thus:

And when the Lord took His Prophet to Himself, various of his Companions stood up in authority until the kindred of Harb and Marwan (the Umayyads) usurped it, and ruled as tyrants, grasping all things to themselves. A while God bare with them, until they angered Him, wherefore He hath made our hands the instruments of His vengeance, and given us back our right again, that through us He may be bountiful to all outcast throughout the earth. And so He hath finished, with us, as He began. Yet have we of the Prophetic House no Grace except through God.

Ye men of Kufa, ye are the seat of our regard, the resting-place of our love. In this present action ye have not been slack; from this action the tyrant's cruelty hath not turned you; and to us ye are ever the most favored people of all, being of those who most honor us. Wherefore I announce to each one of you an increase of pension of one hundred dirhams.

Therefore be ready. For I am the impartial Spiller (of blood and of treasure alike), I am the destroying avenger.

Suddenly the chills of a fever fit seized him. But his uncle Dawud, who stood on the pulpit step below him, took up the burden of his speech. By God! he cried, between your time and the time of God's Apostle, God's Prayer and Peace be on him! ye have had no true Caliph but Ali, Peace be with him! and this Prince of the True Believers who stands behind me here.

Then they both came down from the pulpit; and Abu Abbas rode out to the Blackshirt camp.

The Caliph Marwan at this time was encamped on the Little Zab River, over which he had built a bridge. Abdallah, uncle to Abu Abbas the Spiller, marched against him with the Khurasan army and its officers.

He as general arrayed the Blackshirts on the day of battle. In the van came the Black Banners, borne by riders on Bactrian camels.

Look at their standards on those camels yonder, cried
Marwan to those about him, driving on like scraps of black storm
cloud! Even as he spoke, a flock of crows rose from a thicket
and flew thick about the foremost Black Flag, blending their
blackness with the blackness of the banners. Marwan saw, and
drew a gloomy augury.

Black mixed with black! do you see it? he said. The crows
were like black clouds.

The battle was joined. Marwan's force was routed, and a
huge number of his men slaughtered or drowned in the pursuit.
Three hundred of the kindred of Umayya died that day in the
waters of the Zab. Marwan himself fled to Mosul; but the
citizens closed their gates and hung out the Black Flag. So
Marwan crossed Euphrates and went on to the Jordan country.
While Abdallah was besieging Damascus, which he took, putting
many of its citizens to the sword, Marwan fled on to Egypt. And
there, at Busir in Egypt where he had pitched camp, a party of
Blackshirts caught up with him. They fell on his camp by night,
to the sound of rolling kettledrums and shouts of God is Most
Great! and Vengeance for Ibrahim! The tales of Marwan's death
in that night's fighting vary, but his slayer is said to have been
Amir ibn Isma'il. This man afterwards was trying to break into a
Christian chapel where Marwan's daughters and womenfolk had
taken refuge, when one of Marwan's eunuchs appeared, sword in
hand, to bar the way. The Blackshirts overpowered him, and put
questions to him.

Marwan bade me smite the necks of his daughters and
wives if he should be killed, said the eunuch. But spare me; for
if you slay me, by God, it's all over with the inheritance of God's
Apostle!

How's that? and be careful what thou sayest! they said.

You can kill me if I am lying, he answered; but come on,
follow me!

He led them outside the village to a sandy place, and then
said: Search here. The Blackshirts dug up the ground, and
there they found the Striped Cloak and the Finger-ring and the

Staff the Prophet used to hold as he preached. Marwan had had them buried in that spot to keep them from falling into the hands of the Abbasids. Amir sent the Relics to Abdallah, and he sent them on to Abu Abbas the Spiller; and so they passed into the succession of the Caliphs of the House of Abbas.

At the time of the Abbasid victory, Abu Jada, formerly Secretary and counsellor to Marwan, joined the Spiller, and became one of his personal officers and intimate companions. He was sitting in audience on the very day when Marwan's head was put into the hands of Abu Abbas, at the old house in Humayma.

Does anyone recognize this? said the Spiller, looking round.

I spoke up (says Abu Jada); I recognize it, I said. That is the head of Abu Abd al-Malik Marwan ibn Muhammad, who was our Caliph only yesterday; and may God accept of him!

The whole company glared scowlingly at me. But Abu Abbas only asked me: What year was he born?

In the year seventy-six, said I.

The Prince's countenance was altered, however; he rose, and the audience broke up. I went away thinking ruefully over what I had done. That mistake will never be forgiven, by God! thought I. He'll never forget that, no, not ever!

I spent the rest of that day making final arrangements, and wrote my will. When night came on, I performed my ablutions and betook myself to prayer; for if Abu Abbas was minded to do something he would send the doers of the deed at night. Thus I sat up waiting till dawn; and when the day broke, I mounted my mule and rode off racking my brain for someone to go to. I could not think of anyone better than Sulayman the Freedman, and finally sought him out.

Did the Prince of True Believers say anything about me yesterday? I inquired.

Yes, they were talking about you, he answered; and the

Prince said this: Abu Jada is our sister's son — if he is so faithful to his old master, his gratitude to ourselves will be the more real.

I thanked Sulayman and left him. When I presented myself again at Abu Abbas' audience as usual, he did not treat me otherwise than kindly.

EPILOGUE ON THE FLESH

I went with Abdallah, Ali's son, to spoil the tombs of the Children of Umayya in the Spiller's time (says Omar, Hani's son, of Taiy). We went to Hisham's grave first and pulled his body out, whole and sound still, except for the tip of his nose — that was gone. Abdallah gave him eighty licks of his whip before we burned him.

When we dug Sulayman up at Dabiq, there was only his spine and ribs left of him, and his skull. But we burned him too. We did the same for the rest of them, all the Umayyads who were buried at Qinnisrin and Rusafa.

When we got to Damascus and opened the tomb of Walid son of Abd al-Malik, we found nothing at all in the grave, neither little nor lot. As for Abd al-Malik himself, his skull was all we found of him.

Then we dug up Mu'awia's son Yazid, and there we found nothing but a single bone, and in the bottom of the sepulcher a little blackish dust, like a litter of ashes along the stone.

We dug them up like that all over the place, and burned all the bits of them we found.

THE FIRST ABBASID CALIPHS

AND THE BUILDING OF BAGHDAD

Lust wanes as power waxes, the Spiller said.

A treacherous, wily, faithless House the Abbasids were; intrigue and guile played a greater part than strength and force in the tale of that dynasty, especially during its latter days. Indeed the later Abbasid Caliphs lost all energetic and bold faculty, and relied on trickery and stratagem for everything.

There was, however, much good in that dynasty: they were a very generous House. With them the wares of Science found ready sale, and the merchandise of Culture commanded high prices; religious observances were respected, charitable foundations were profuse, and the world prospered; the Holy Shrines were well cared for and the frontiers bravely kept. Nor did these conditions change until their end drew on; but in that latter time violence became universal, government was unseated, and empire passed out of Abbasid hands.

O F ALL THE ABBASID CALIPHS ONLY THREE, the Spiller, and Mahdi, and Amin, were the sons of freeborn mothers. All the rest were born of slave women, Berbers, Persians, Abyssinians, Slavs, Turks, and Armenians.

And under this House the unity of Islam melted away. Arab names lapsed from the Public Registers. Turks were set in State office. Then Daylamites from North Persia came to wield power; and afterwards other Turks, who became masters of a mighty empire. In the end the dominions of the earth were parcelled out; and everywhere was some usurper, brutalizing his people and ruling as a tyrant.

At the beginning of his reign, the Spiller used to show himself to his courtiers; but a year or so later he began to sit withdrawn behind the Curtain, according to the usage of the old Persian Kings.

Abdallah, a descendant of Ali, came to the Spiller's court. Before a full audience of Hashimites and their clients, and other notables, the Alid, who had a Koran in his hand, cried: Give us our right, Prince of the True Believers, as God allowed us in this Book!

Your great-grandsire Ali was a better and juster man than I, the Spiller replied, and he was also Caliph. He gave something to your forbears Hasan and Husayn; and it would be only right for me to give you a similar sum. If I have given you so much, you have your due. If I have already given you more, this is hardly a proper return for my goodness.

The Alid, without a word, went out.

THE VIZIER

The first person to be called vizier was Abu Salama Hafs. The vizier is a man who acts as mediator between the sovereign and his subjects. His character must therefore have one side which accords with royal character, and another which accords with common human nature, so that his proceedings may be acceptable to the sovereign and popular with his subjects.

His capital consists in his trustworthiness and his integrity; for there are two proverbial sayings which apply to his position: *If the agent's faithless, the policy's useless;* and: *A known liar has lost his voice.* It is very important for him to be efficient and energetic, and absolutely necessary for him to have intelligence, and caution, cunning, and resolution. It is likewise desirable that he should be generous and hospitable, for with these qualities he will be willingly obeyed and gratefully spoken of. Further indispensable virtues in a vizier are blandness and long patience, dependability in practical matters, clemency, dignity, a grave mien, and the tone of authority in his address.

The functions of the vizierate were not defined, nor its procedures regulated, before Abbasid times. Instead, every sovereign had about him a number of courtiers and retainers; if any crisis arose, he consulted the wisest and shrewdest of these, each of whom acted in that sense as a vizier.

But when the Abbasids came to the throne, the vizierate was regulated, and the actual vizier, who had hitherto been called the secretary or counsellor, was now called the vizier.

Mansur, the Founder of Baghdad

Mansur, whose mother was a Berber concubine, was acknowledged Caliph by his brother the Spiller's testament. Of all the Abbasids he was foremost in majesty of demeanor, in bravery and caution both, in judgment and in haughtiness — a hoarder of his money, a hater of mere pastime, a man of cultivated mind and of most excellent conversation in scientific and literary matters. He had a natural bent for law.

His nickname among the common people was The Man for the Pennies.

One of his first acts was the murder of Abu Muslim of Khurasan, the author of the Abbasid propaganda˙ and the real founder of their dynasty. I would talk with you, he wrote to Abu Muslim, of matters which cannot be confided to a letter; come to me here — you will not be detained long.

At the first meeting, the Caliph received Abu Muslim kindly, and then gave him leave to retire to his private tent. Several times he rode to audience; and at last one day took his seat in the anteroom, being informed that the Caliph was performing his ablutions for prayer.

Mansur had given his orders to the captain and some others of his Guard: they were to post themselves behind the curtain by which Abu Muslim would sit, and not show themselves so long as they heard himself speaking; but so soon as he should clap his hands they were to run in and lay on with their swords, the man's head, his neck, or anywhere they could get at him.

The Caliph then seated himself. Abu Muslim was summoned to the inner room, went in, and saluted him. Mansur, returning his greeting, gave him leave to sit, and chatted with him a while; but presently began to abuse him for this and for that.

You may not use such language to me after all I did! said Abu Muslim.

Son of a whore! retorted Mansur, your deeds you achieved through our own high fortune and happy destiny — a black slave

girl could have done as much! Did you not put your name before
our own in your despatches? and demand the hand of our aunt
in marriage? and even pretend to be yourself a descendant of
Abbas our ancestor? Man of nought! you have climbed above
yourself.

Abu Muslim seized the Caliph's hand, and wrung it and
covered it with kisses, pouring out excuses.

Mansur now spoke the final word: God spare me not if I
spare thee! And he clapped his hands.

The guards rushed in. The captain struck first, but only
nicked him, his blade biting into the scabbard of Abu Muslim's
sword. Another man cut off a foot; then, striking thick and fast,
they hacked the body to pieces, Mansur exclaiming the while:
Lay on, God maim you all! lay on!

They rolled the body up in a mat. Presently Mansur's
general Ja'far son of Hanzala came in. What's your opinion of
Abu Muslim? the Caliph inquired.

If you have plucked so much as one hair from his head,
Prince of the True Believers, Ja'far answered, you must kill; and
then kill; and then kill again.

God blessed you with good judgment, said Mansur; do you
see what's in yonder mat?

Prince of the True Believers, said Ja'far as he looked on
the dead man, count this day the first day of your Caliphate.

Ay, said Mansur, and quoted the verse:
The traveller threw away his staff at last:
It was the road's end. He lay down to rest.

THE LOSS OF SPAIN

In the year 138 the fugitive Umayyad prince, Abd al-
Rahman, reached Spain and conquered it for himself. He had
the heads of Mansur's appointed Governor and his lieutenants
preserved in salt and camphor, and labels affixed to the ears.
These, with Mansur's diploma and the black gubernatorial ban-

ner, he had put in a sack, borne to Qayravan in Africa, and left
by night in the market place.

Thanks to God for putting the sea between me and such a
foe! Mansur exclaimed, when he heard of it; and one day thereafter he asked in audience this question: Who deserves to be
called the Falcon of Quraysh?

Yourself, surely, Prince of the True Believers.

No, the Falcon of Quraysh is Abd al-Rahman, who wandered alone through the deserts of Asia and Africa, and had the
great heart to seek his destiny, with no troop at his back, over the
sea in an unknown land.

Abd al-Rahman's reign was long; and Spain remained in
the hands of his posterity three hundred years.

THE FOUNDING OF BAGHDAD

Mansur rode through Iraq seeking the site for a new
capital. At the little village of Baghdad on the Tigris (where
Euphrates flows near) he was counselled: We think it best to
settle here, midway between these four agricultural districts of
Buq, Kalwadha, Qutrabbul, and Baduria. Thus you will have
palm plantations on every side of you and water near at hand;
if harvest fails or is late from one district, you can get relief
from another. You can get provisions by the Sarat Canal from
the Euphrates river traffic; Egyptian and Syrian caravans will
come here by the desert roads, and all kinds of China goods upriver from the sea, and Byzantine and Mosul produce down the
Tigris. And with rivers on both sides, no enemy can approach
except by ship or bridge.

The site is excellent for a military camp, Mansur said.
And here he built the city of Baghdad, called the Round City by
reason of its plan, and the City of Peace.

Exposition of doctrine was at first the special function of those who were called Readers, that is, of men able to read the Book of God. The Arabs were then generally illiterate; and anyone who could read the Book received a special title, the skill being so rare. Then, as Arab illiteracy passed away through increasing study of the Koran, the science of logical deduction from the text arose. And so Canon Law matured, both in practice and in theory. The title of Reader now gave way to those of Jurist and Doctor of the Law.

There were two main branches: that which supplemented the Prophetic corpus by private judgment and analogy was seated principally in Iraq; that of the Traditionists principally at the Holy Cities in Hijaz. The Iraqis, who were less devoted to Tradition, extended the scope and became experts in the method of analogy: the founder of the Iraq school as such was Abu Hanifa (after whom it was called the Hanafite School) and his associates. In Hijaz the leader was Malik ibn Anas of Madina (whence the Malikite School); later came Shafi'i (whence the Shafi'ite School). Certain Doctors, who eschewed analogy altogether, were called Zahirites: they regarded only the text of the Book and the Consensus of Believers as effective in determining right.

Malik was asked his opinion on the action of certain persons who, while on a raiding expedition, went ashore at Cyprus and proceeded to buy sheep, honey, and butter, paying Unbelievers for these provisions with dinars and dirhams (Muslim coins).

Malik disapproved of their action. I strongly object, he told us, to coins which bear the mention of God and words from His Book being given to a person who is unclean. I disapprove most strongly of such a practice.

I asked him whether we Believers might make purchases with dirhams and dinars from Unbelieving merchants who land-

ed on our own coasts, or from members of the tolerated cults
(that is, tribute-paying Jews, Christians, and Magians).

I disapprove of that, Malik replied.

He was asked whether money might be changed in Muslim
markets by money-changers who were members of these cults.

He replied that he disapproved.

* * *

It was about this time that learned Muslims began to com-
pose books — on Tradition, Law, and Koranic Interpretation.
Ibn Jurayj, the first man in Islam to write a book, was writing at
Mecca, Malik was writing at Madina, Awza'i in Syria, Ibn
Salama the Traditionist and others in Basra, Ibn Abi Urwa in
Yaman, and Thawri in Kufa. Ibn Ishaq was composing his
History of the Wars of Islam, and Abu Hanifa his treatises on
Jurisprudence and on the Theory of Private Judgment. And not
much after, Ibn Hisham wrote his, the first, Biography of the
Prophet of God.

Mansur was the first Caliph who had translations into
Arabic made from Outlanders' books, Syriac and Persian: among
others, Euclid, and the Fables of Kalila and Dimna.

This Book of Kalila and Dimna, writes the translator Ibn
Muqaffa, is one of those composed by Indian Sages, consisting of
Fables. In order to reap the full advantage of its study, it is
necessary to disengage the truths intended from their emblematic
expression, for reading without reflection will not be of solid
profit. Perusal of the book without penetration of its real scope
and purpose, which are deep, not obvious, yields no more nourishment than an uncracked nut. Its author certainly had four
objects before him: one, to please young readers (and these, at
first only captivated by the lively images, will find themselves at
a more advanced age possessed of an unsuspected fund of wisdom); second, to call the attention of Princes to the varying conduct of various creatures in varying circumstances; third, to make

his work survive by its power to amuse and intrigue; and fourth, to afford matter for thought to the philosophic mind.

A FABLE

Among the subjects of the Lion were two Jackals, named Kalila and Dimna, both cunning and sagacious in the highest degree. And one day Dimna said to Kalila: I wonder why the Lion keeps himself so close retired of late? I think I will solicit an audience; and if I find him in any indecision, I purpose to turn his embarrassment to my own advantage.

How can you, Dimna, who have none of the qualifications of a King's minister, hope to attract any favorable notice from the Lion? demanded Kalila. A King does not even necessarily choose the worthiest of his servants for the conduct of state affairs; to be near the royal person is often enough to make a favorite — the Vine clings to the nearest Tree, and that advantage you have never had.

My first endeavors, Dimna said, will be to prove by my own diligence and energy that I am fully qualified for the trust which others now enjoy; and to exhibit in the whole of my daily behavior that humility, that tolerance of unmerited calumny, that unruffled good breeding, which are the necessary qualities of a public man. Then, when once I arrive at being freely admitted to the Lion's familiar presence, my next step shall be a profound study of his temper and character; which when I have sounded to the bottom, I shall be careful to avoid any opposition to his mere whims or caprices; but if I see his mind already made up to any course from which I can anticipate advantage either to myself or to the State, I shall place it in the most favorable light, thus flattering his opinion of his own judgment. If, on the other hand, he issues some command mischievous or dishonorable to himself, I shall represent the possibility of evil consequence in the strongest terms; for it is the statesman's gift, as it is the painter's, to color objects with whatever complexion he pleases.

You will be playing a dangerous game, Kalila said; for there are three things which any man will be wise to avoid, owing to the impossibility of controlling the issues of them; one, incurring the confidence of a Prince; two, trusting a woman with a secret; and three, trying the effect of a poison on oneself.

If the chance of failure, Dimna replied, were sufficient reason for never trying, you would exclude from human endeavor all conduct of state affairs, all commercial enterprise, and all military achievement.

Well, I wish you luck, said Kalila; and Dimna betook himself to the Lion's court. . . .

Dimna, perceiving that the Bull was become the chosen intimate of the Lion, and partaker in all his pleasures, now absented himself from the Lion's audience for several days; and then took an opportunity of finding him alone.

What has kept you from us so long? the Lion demanded. Let us hope there is some good excuse. Has something unforeseen occurred?

Such indeed is the case, the Jackal answered; but I would not willingly enter upon a matter which must be as disagreeable to your Majesty as it is painful to myself. Most reluctantly should I be the bearer of information so unwelcome that even my known zeal in your Majesty's service would scarcely render it credible. Yet on the other hand, when I consider the duty which my station as your Majesty's creature imposes on me, it seems little better than treason to keep silence, even though I shall not be believed.

Let us hear what it is, said the Lion.

Your Majesty, said Dimna, a certain person with whom I am intimately acquainted, and whose veracity is beyond question, has informed me that the Bull Shanzaba has been holding private conversations with some of the principal persons of your Majesty's court, to whom he has observed that your Majesty begins to show those unmistakable signs of declining strength which

*foretell the term of your capacity for government. What can I
conclude from this but that Shanzaba, even if he does not
meditate engineering your Majesty's deposition by treachery
or violence, at the very least is preparing the way to be your
successor? What makes your Majesty's situation the more pre-
carious is that consummate subtlety and adroitness in the management of affairs of which the Bull is master.*

*We are not ignorant of that, the Lion said; but we hardly
think him capable of imposing on ourselves; or indeed, for that
matter, of intending treason. Why, we have made him a partaker
in all the comforts of our own state.*

*A person of low origin, replied the Jackal, may certainly
be faithful to his duty, a useful servant and a sincere counsellor,
so long as such virtues serve his own ambition. But once let him
attain that rank and power where he sees no superior, and this
same ambition, more highly advanced, will render him intolerant
even of an equal. Your Majesty, the Sovereign who spurns unpleasant counsel because its truth is disagreeable to his ear can
only be compared with a man desperately sick who throws away
his physic and will only swallow delicacies of his own choosing.
It is a Sovereign's duty to concern himself only for his people's
good and his own honor; that monarch is the feeblest of his kind
who occupies himself with the trifling affairs of today without
looking to what comes on tomorrow, for such a one will un-
failingly charge his ministers with incapacity when things at last
go wrong through his own easy and indifferent temper.*

*These are strong expressions, said the Lion, though a faith-
ful servant has certainly a right to our ear. But this Bull does
not possess the power to harm us; for it lies in our own power to
make a meal of him at any moment we will.*

*Let not your Majesty deceive himself! cried Dimna. What
the Bull could never accomplish by his own strength he will con-
trive through the aid of others. That indeed, from what we
know, appears to be Shanzaba's intention. It may not be appropriate for your Majesty to take open precautions against the Bull*

himself. But in that case, at least let me beg my Sovereign to be on his guard against what the Bull may instigate.

After some reflection, the Lion announced that he would summon Shanzaba, and appoint him a place removed from the royal person.

Dimna, well aware that if the Bull came to audience of the Lion his own behavior would be discovered for what it was, endeavored to dissuade the Lion from sending for Shanzaba, as a most imprudent step, since the Bull must certainly suspect from such a summons what was in the wind, and might then make his escape, with vengeance in his heart, and possessed of the power to represent himself as injured. Secret conspiracy, he concluded, is best countermined by secret measures.

But to punish a person on bare suspicion without positive proof of guilt is open tyranny! cried the Lion.

If these are the royal sentiments, said Dimna (seeing that the meeting could not well be avoided), let me hope at least that your Majesty will be on your guard with Shanzaba. I am confident that the King will not fail to penetrate the Bull's attempts at concealment, but will discover in his manner the evidences of his great design, of which the most unmistakable will be some marks of inner agitation, some discomposure of countenance at the sight of your Majesty, or some tossing of his head, a sure sign in a Bull that he means to use his horns.

With these words, Dimna begged permission to pay a visit to the Bull, with the object of reporting whatever he might see or hear which might avail the Lion at the coming interview; and, the Lion consenting, betook himself to Shanzaba's presence, displaying in his countenance the gloom of despair.

No man is safe, he darkly returned to the Bull's inquiries, whose life depends upon another's will, whose very existence lies at the mercy of one who cannot be trusted. You ask what brought me to this pass? 'Tis the decree of fate, think only that; for to fate's decision we must all submit. It is already Written in the Book that the great man cannot but be insolent, nor the fortunate other than improvident; and that no Prince's favorite may count his seeming safety real. The business, however, is none of mine.

Then whose? for whom are you so troubled? the Bull asked.

I will be frank, said Dimna. You cannot have forgotten the friendship I showed you when first we met, and I brought you to court. The same unaltered sentiments impel me now to reveal to you to what conclusion I am forced by my observation of the Lion and his behavior. I must warn you how perilous to yourself is your present situation at court. A certain person (and one of the highest character, a person absolutely incapable of falsehood) has told me that on a recent occasion the Lion said in the hearing of some of his attendants: This Bull's grown marvellously fat, and we need his services no longer; we might as well kill him — his meat will make a meal for some of those about our person. When I heard this, knowing as I do how irascible and how unpredictable the Lion's temper is, I determined to perform what our friendship demands, and put you on your guard.

But why, exclaimed Shanzaba, should the Lion be angry with me? I am sure I never did any wrong, either to him or any of his subjects! Surely the man who gives his friendship where it is not deserved sows his seed in a salt soil!

Waste none of your time in useless exclamation, Dimna warned him; but take measures for your own safety.

But how can I? cried Shanzaba, if the Lion has already determined on my death? I do believe the Lion is the best of sovereigns, and just in his actions; but O how easily might his favor to me be changed by malice and insinuation! For the effect of calumny repeated often enough, even on the most upright mind, is no less certain in the end than that of constant dripping water on the hard surface of a stone.

Well, what do you propose to do? asked the Jackal.

There's nothing for it, said the Bull, if I am to be forced to a trial of strength, but do all I can to come off the victor.

But it is the height of folly to thrust one's person into

danger, the Jackal cried, if there is any other means of escape. Never risk your life on the event of a battle.

I have no desire to fight a battle with the Lion, surely, confessed the Bull. I suppose I must stand on the fact that never, either in public or in private, have I given him any just cause for complaint, nor ever, up to this very moment, been wanting in respect.

This abject attitude was by no means what Dimna wanted, for he knew that if the Lion saw no signs of disaffection in the Bull's deportment, he himself would fall under suspicion. You had perhaps better go to the Lion, he therefore urged the Bull, and see for yourself. But let me tell you this: if you find him sitting erect, with his eyes flashing and his ears pricked, and his mouth open, it means that he is ready to spring.

Ay, said the Bull, if I find him like that, I shall know what to think.

When the Bull presented himself, it was indeed in just such a posture as Dimna had described that he beheld the monarch.

Ah, cried Shanzaba, surely a Prince's friend is like a man who warms a serpent in his bosom — he never knows when the bite will come!

Fearful was the glare the Lion fixed on him when he heard these words. No longer did he doubt Shanzaba's hostile intentions. And without further pause he sprang upon him.

The Lion will win, observed Kalila to Dimna; for a subject against a Prince is no more than one wave against the sea.

*   *   *

Ibn Muqaffa, the translator of Kalila and Dimna, was one of the most learned men of that age, a converted Magian from Persia, and suspected of being a Freethinker. He also wrote a treatise: On the Obedience due to Princes. Mansur's uncle, Isa son of Ali, employed him as Secretary.

Another uncle, Abdallah, revolted against Mansur; but

the revolt was crushed, and Abdallah went into hiding at the house of his brother Isa. Isa interceding for him with their nephew, Mansur consented to forgive him; and Isa instructed Ibn Muqaffa to draw up a letter of pardon in terms which should be absolutely binding on the Caliph. The Secretary therefore inserted in it the following clause:

If at any time the Prince of the True Believers break faith with his uncle Abdallah ibn Ali, then his wives shall be divorced, his horses confiscated to God's service in Holy War, his slaves freed, and all Muslims released from their allegiance.

When Mansur read this document before signing it, he inquired who had drawn it up, and was informed that it was his uncle's Secretary, Ibn Muqaffa.

Hatred is always to be feared, it is observed in the Book of Kalila and Dimna; but the hatred of a Prince is more terrible than any, for vengeance becomes a matter of conscience with a Prince.

Ibn Muqaffa had offended the Governor of Basra, where he lived, by jibes in time past. The Governor being a man with a very large nose, Ibn Muqaffa had greeted him with the inquiry: How are you both? (meaning him and his nose); and on one occasion when the Governor, quoting from the Book of Kalila and Dimna, had said: I have never regretted an occasion when I refrained from speech, Ibn Muqaffa had replied: Keeping his mouth shut is indeed particularly becoming to His Excellency.

The Caliph now sent a message to the Governor that he might put Ibn Muqaffa to death. He had the Secretary brought before him, and reminded him of these witticisms.

For God's sake, Prince, spare me! Ibn Muqaffa implored him.

Be my mother defiled if I do! the Governor cried, I mean to kill thee as never man was killed before. And he ordered

fire kindled in a great bread oven. Then, cutting joint after joint
from Ibn Muqaffa's members, he tossed them into the fire before
his own eyes; and at last had the man thrust bodily in and the
oven door closed on him. This is no crime, he said, you being
a Freethinker who undermined the people's Faith.

Where any desire of vengeance still exists, it is observed
in the Book of Kalila and Dimna, reconciliation is never other
than a means of advantage or precaution.

Mansur cast his uncle Abdallah into prison, where he lay
until his death was decided. When his warder, Abu Azhar, came
to carry out the sentence, he found the Prince in the company of
one of his young slave girls. He took the man first, strangled
him, and laid the body on the bed. As he was about to kill the
girl in the same way, she cried out: O not like that! Some other
death, Servant of God!
    That was the only time, Abu Azhar used to say, that I
ever felt pity when I went to execute a death sentence. I had to
look away when I gave the order. They strangled her, and laid
her on the bed at her lord's side. I twined their arms about one
another, like two lovers, and had the house pulled down on them,
so that they had the ruin for a tomb.

Not for this, said an Arab chief, not for bloodshed and
iniquity's sake did we give our loyal faith to the Prophet's House.

* * *

Mansur was the first Caliph who gave access to astrologers
and acted according to the indications of the stars. He was also
the first to employ slaves in State office, and to give slaves
precedence over Arabs.

ARAB COMPLAINTS

I knew you of old, ere Fortune did.
You sat in the Haymarket then.
A year went by; and in bright brocade
And samite I saw you again.

Your women used to sit in the sun
Moaning under the wheels
In tune with the moaning doves; but now
They trail silk at their heels,

Already quite forgetting how
They broke stone for our roads,
And how high they had to hoist their skirts
To receive their loads.

Concubines' sons are grown of late
So thick about the place,
Lead me, Lord, to another land
Where I shan't see a bastard's face!

O to have Umayyad tyranny back again!
And to Hell with Abbasid justice!

* * *

The ascetic Amr ibn Ubayd had been an intimate friend of
Mansur before his elevation. He once visited the Caliph.

Come near us and be seated, said Mansur; and let us have
some exhortation.

Amr spoke as follows: Thy power would never have been
thine if thy predecessors could have kept their hands on it. Then
be warned of that Night wherefrom a Day shall dawn after
which there will never be another night.

When Amr rose, the Caliph said: We have ordered you ten thousand dirhams bounty.

I do not need it, said the ascetic.

But by God you'll take it! exclaimed Mansur.

By God, I shall not.

What? cried Mansur's son Mahdi, who was present. The Prince of True Believers swear a thing shall be done and you swear the contrary?

Who is this young man? asked Ibn Ubayd.

My heir and successor, my son Mahdi.

Thou hast clothed him, the ascetic said, as the righteous are never clothed; thou hast given him a name (for Mahdi means the Divinely Guided who shall come) which is none of his, and smoothed a path for him wherein the more he prospers the more reckless he will be.

Have you any wish I can grant? asked Mansur.

Never send for me again, but wait till I come to thee, Amr replied.

Then we shall never meet again, the Caliph said.

That is my wish, said he; and went away. Mansur followed him with his eyes till he was gone. Then he turned him to his courtiers again, and said: All of you walk with stealthy steps; you are all beasts of prey, all—only Amr son of Ubayd is different.

Is there any left of the pleasures of this world that thou hast not yet enjoyed? someone asked Mansur.

One thing still, he answered: just to sit on a bench, with the Traditionists all about me, and the disciples writing from their dictation, and saying (when they miss a name): Whom didst thou name as authorities for that, God's Mercy on thee?

Next morning, his intimates and the members of the vizieral families duly appeared at the audience with their inkhorns and tablets as for a lecture; but Mansur said: You are not the ones. The ones I mean are men in travel-stained garments, the weary-footed, the unkempt, the couriers of the Earth, the real Transmitters of Tradition.

MAHDI

The calculation and sagacity of Mansur had been beyond praise. He had never shrunk from the most lavish generosity if it would pay returns; nor would he grant the smallest favor if it would not. There were six hundred million dirhams and forty million dinars in the Treasury when he died; and he had husbanded his money, going into detail that a common man would have neglected. As an example, he used to bargain with his cook that the cook might keep all heads, offal, and skins in return for furnishing stove-wood and seasonings without charging them to the kitchen account.

Mahdi distributed in alms every penny that Mansur had left, and all the revenues accrued to date.

You Beduin ass! he said to his remonstrating Treasurer, you think that money will not flow in whenever I want it? Extravagance is becoming in a gentleman.

In song and wine
Is my felicity,
And perfumed girls,
Music, and gaiety.

That verse is of Mahdi's composing.

And when somebody once mentioned Walid the Profligate Caliph in Mahdi's presence, and another of the company remarked that Walid was an atheist, Mahdi cried: Go to! the Caliphate is such a charge, it is so sublime an office, God would never have given it to an atheist.

Ten Traditionists, Ghiyath ibn Ibrahim among the rest, were summoned to an audience. Now Mahdi was very fond of pigeon-racing; and when Ghiyath was presented, and somebody said: Pray recite some Tradition to the Prince of the True

Believers, Ghiyath recited: So-and-so tells us that he had it of So-
and-so on the authority of Abu Hurayra that the Apostle of God
(God's Prayer and Peace be on him!) said: There must be no
betting save on a hoof or an arrow or a lance-head; and then
Ghiyath added: or on a wing.

Mahdi at once ordered him a bounty of ten thousand dirhams; but as Ghiyath rose bowing to thank him, he exclaimed:
By God, the nape of your neck looks like the nape of a liar's
neck — I'll swear you interpolated those last words! And he gave
order immediately that all his racing pigeons should be killed.

* * *

Tolerance is laudable, the Spiller had once said, except in
matters dangerous to religious belief, or to the Sovereign's dignity.

Mahdi persecuted Freethinkers, and executed them in large
numbers. He was the first Caliph to order the composition of
polemical works in refutation of Freethinkers and other heretics;
and for years he tried to exterminate them absolutely, hunting
them down throughout all provinces and putting accused persons
to death on mere suspicion.

Hast thou any doubt at all in thy mind, runs a catechism
of these times, that the Koran was brought down to the Prophet
of God by the faithful spirit Gabriel; that in that Book God has
declared what is lawful and what is unlawful, and ordained His
Rules, and established His Observances; and has expounded the
history of what has been and what is to be to the end of time?

I have no doubt, the catechumen shall reply.

Hast thou any doubt at all in thy mind that. . . .

I have no doubt.

Belief is a duty. Inquiry is heresy.

THE SECTS

ANYONE WHO WISHES to understand and distinguish the various religious sects must acquaint himself with the differences of opinion which have occurred within Islam, for since the Prophet's death many things have been occasions of disagreement. On the questions at issue, some have merely accused their opponents of error, but others have regarded those who disagree with them as excommunicate Unbelievers, so that people have split into factions and parties. And yet Islam embraces and includes them all.

The first dissension to arise among True Believers was disagreement, after the Prophet's death, on the question of the Imamate. The Helpers were going to invest Sa'd, but Abu Bakr quoted against them the Prophet's words: The Imamate belongs to the Quraysh. No other difference than disagreement concerning the Imamate arose during Abu Bakr's lifetime, or in Omar's time. But in the latter days of Othman certain persons disapproved of things that Othman did. In proceeding to public accusation of Othman these persons were guilty of sin — they departed from the strait and narrow path; for as a result of their action the things they disapproved of became a source of dissension among Believers which has continued up to the present day.

Then Othman was assassinated, and there was disagreement about that. The Followers of the True Way maintain that Othman was not to be condemned for what he did, and that his murderers did wrong and were unrighteous to slay him. But others still maintain the opposite; there has been dissension on that matter up to the present day.

Then Ali was proclaimed Caliph, and people disagreed as to his authority, some denying that he was the Imam, others refusing him active support, and others maintaining that he was rightfully both Imam and Caliph. On this point too there has been dissension up to the present day.

THE DOCTRINE OF THE IMAM

The word Imam means *Example,* or *Leader;* and in connection with ordinary Prayer it generally means the man who
leads the praying ranks. Philosophically it means a person who
comes from God as Successor (Caliph) and Representative of the
Prophet.

On the question of the appointment of the Imams, learned
men disagree. It may be asked whether any such appointment
was necessary, when the period of Prophetic Revelation came to
an end. If we say that it was necessary, do we mean that it was a
necessity for God Himself? The People of the True Way and
many Rationalists believe that the appointment depended simply
on the consent of mankind. And this in the face of various proofs
that the existence of the Imam was an *absolute* necessity.

First, we are bound to suppose that Lovingkindness is one
of God's Attributes. Obviously therefore God will do what is best
for His servants. And it is clear that Divine Lovingkindness
alone is sufficient warrant for the existence of the Imam, since
even human intelligence is sufficient to cause men in a state of
social organization to install someone who will keep them from
the corruption and violence of their fellows, restrain them from
various kinds of wrongdoing, and confirm them in faith, worship,
just dealing, and civilized habits. For that is the way in which
human behavior is regulated, advances toward the better, and
abandons the worse.

A second proof of the Imam's necessity is the necessity for
some guardian of the Apostolic Law. The verses of the Book are
succinct, but many of the implied commands are far from clear.
A divinely authorized Interpreter is therefore a necessity. This
is contrary to the opinion of Omar. For when the Prophet, then
on the point of death, asked for pen and ink for the writing
of a declaration to mankind which should preserve them from
error, Omar objected, with the words: He's wandering; surely
God's Book is enough for us. It is to be noted that this view is
that of Omar, the accursed Omar. Indeed, if God's Book *had*

been sufficient, then why should there have been and still be so much disagreement among those who rely on It?

The Imamate certainly rests on Divine and Apostolic authority. It cannot be determined by human consensus or election. First, since the Imam must be sinless, and sinlessness is a state which only God can recognize, it follows that the appointment must lie with God. Second, history shows that if a people do not have an authoritative ruler to restrain them, most men resort to force, and evil increases, which cannot be God's Pleasure. *GOD TAKETH NO PLEASURE IN EVIL;* and we may safely assume that He is disposed to remove and prevent it, which can only be accomplished by lodging governmental authority in the hands of one whose sole purpose is the advantage and salvation of the people. Third, both reason and Tradition establish the infinite Lovingkindness of God towards His servants, which is affirmed several times in the Book. One of the proofs of the infinite nature of this Favor is the plenitude of Traditional guidance in small matters such as the method of using depilatories, of trimming the beard, of using pumice stone, and so forth, little things expressly set forth for general understanding by Prophetic Usage and Sayings. But surely the appointment of an Apostolic representative as Guardian of the Law and Instructor in Faith is a more fundamental necessity than these trifles. If God did not deem these trifles insignificant, how can we possibly imagine that He could neglect what is, religiously speaking, a paramount need?

It follows that the appointment of a Prophetic Successor or Caliph was determined by God, and that God must have revealed to His Apostle the necessity and choice of an Imam. And all Believers agree on this point at least: that no Caliph was appointed by the Prophet unless it was the Prince of True Believers Ali, at the Pool of Khum.

There, at the Pool of Khum, the Prophet of God stood up to speak, and took Ali son of Abu Talib by the hand, and said: Am I not dearer to the Believers than their own lives?

Ay, Apostle of God! the Muslims cried.

And the Prophet then declared: If any man see his master in me, he will see his master in Ali. Then he said: Ye people, I am to go on before you now, but by the Fountain in Paradise we shall meet again. And there I shall ask how ye have dealt with the two Precious Things.

What Precious Things, Apostle of God? they asked.

And the Prophet answered: The more precious is God's Book, because It is from Himself, the gift of God's own Hand, as it were, given into your hands. But the other Precious Thing is my posterity, the People of the Household.

A fourth consideration is this: it was the Apostolic Usage to designate some person to exercise authority if the Prophet left Madina for a short time. He appointed Governors for towns and villages wherever there were Believers, and appointed Commanders over the army. These appointments were never left to popular choice: the Prophet sought Divine Command for his nominations. Is it conceivable that the infinitely important matter of a succession, involving laws and ordinances which would affect the welfare of the Muslim community till Doomsday, should have been neglected by the Apostle, or that he should have left that to popular choice?

For indeed, and fifthly, the people are incapable of judging what man is fit for an office so responsible. Their choice could only accord with the narrow understanding and unsteady purpose which are characteristically human. It could not possibly work for the common welfare, or be consonant with the Divine Wisdom, for every man would vote in accord with his own personal advantage, a procedure which, though it might have the sanction of force, could only prove a practical basis for a tyranny. It could never be a right way of determining the Imamate, or guiding a government based on Law. That the people *could* choose their Imams is an opinion as unreasonable as thinking them capable of choosing their Prophets — an obvious absurdity.

If Imamate were a matter of popular election, one of two consequences must follow. Either, first, the choice will be unsuitable, in which case God, Who knows by His Foreknowledge that the mistake will be made, is committing the religious direction of the Muslim community to an assembly which cannot but be wrong, and cannot but choose an unrighteous governor — an alternative we cannot consider for a moment, so inconsistent with the Wisdom of God would such proceeding be. Or, secondly, they might choose a good Imam. But in this case the task of making the Imam generally recognized and obeyed will present insuperable difficulties to men, though for God it would be easy. It follows that feeble mankind would have an exceedingly troublesome task forced upon them; and this is inconsistent with what we are told of the Most High, of Whom it is said: *GOD WILLETH YOUR COMFORT, NOT YOUR DISCOMFORT.*

* * *

I knew the learned Sufi Amr ibn Ubayd well by reputation (said the Imamite doctor Hisham). He was teaching in Basra; and since I did not like his arrogance, I decided to pay a visit to that city. It was a Friday when I arrived; and going straight to the Mosque, I saw a great crowd gathered around a man who wore a piece of coarse black woollen about his middle and another over his shoulders. It was Amr, and people were putting questions to him; so I pushed through the throng and sat down.

Learned sir, said I, I am a stranger here, and I have a question to ask, with your permission.

Very well, said he.

Do you have eyes? I inquired.

What kind of question is that, my son? he exclaimed.

My question, said I.

Ask as you will, then, said he, and as foolishly as you will.

Do you have eyes, then? I asked again.

Yes, said he.

What do you see with them?

Colors, people, said he.

Have you a nose? said I.

I have, said he.

What do you do with it?

Smell smells, said he.

Do you have a mouth? said I.

Yes.

And what do you do with it? said I.

Talk with it.

And you have ears?

Yes, said he.

What do you do with them?

Hear sounds with them.

Do you have hands?

I have, said he.

What do you do with them? said I.

Handle things.

And have you a mind? I inquired.

I have, he said.

And what do you do with that?

I apply my reason to what the senses yield me, he answered.

Why, said I, are the senses not enough by themselves? Surely they do not depend upon the mind?

No, said Amr, the senses themselves are not sufficient; nor, in however healthy a condition, are they independent of the mind. When the senses are uncertain, my son, as to the nature of something they have smelled or heard or tasted or touched, they refer it to the mind for assurance and clarification.

So God has made the mind like a governor for the body, I said, to banish the uncertainties of the senses?

Yes, said he.

Abu Marwan, I replied, it seems that the Lord of the Worlds has not left your bodily members and organs of sense without an Imam or guide to explain His Decrees and banish their uncertainties. Are we to suppose that He has left His whole creation confounded, that He has not given mankind an Imam to whom they may refer their uncertainties, Who may guide them towards Truth and relieve them of their anxieties?

To this Amr offered no reply. But he paid me the honor

of advancing towards me and inquiring: You are Hisham, I think?

No, said I.

Where do you come from?

From Kufa.

Of course you are Hisham! he cried. And seizing my hand, he led me forward and made me sit beside him. Nor did he speak again until I rose to depart.

Is the Imam necessarily sinless? was asked of the Shi'ite doctor Hisham ibn Hakam.

Yes, he answered.

How can you know that? they asked.

All sin, said Hisham, falls into one of four categories: greed, envy, carnal anger, and lust. The Imam cannot conceivably be capable of any of these. He cannot feel greed, for the whole world is submitted to his Signet, and he is trustee for the whole treasury of the Muslims. He cannot feel envy, the feeling of a man for his superior, since the Imam has no superior. He cannot feel carnal rage; he can only feel anger in God's service when called upon to punish, for mercy of course cannot be allowed to hinder the advancement of religion. He cannot feel lust, which is desire for worldly pleasure, since all his desire is for the Other World. Have you ever seen a man forsake a lovely face for an ugly one? or refuse delicious food for the sake of wormwood?

The Shi'ite Extremists elevate their Imams above the rank of created beings and regard them as Divine. These anthropomorphic tendencies are derived from Incarnationists, Transmigrationists, Jews, and Christians. For the Jews liken the Creator to the creature, and the Christians liken the creature to the Creator.

This anthropomorphism is primarily and characteristically

Shi'ite; only at a later period was it adopted by certain sects of
the Sunnites, or Followers of the True Way.

THE FIRST SUFIS

All these schismatic sects arose; disputes went on between
one sect and another, each maintaining that its own ascetics were
the true Saints. The elect of the Followers of the True Way (the
Sunnites), whose souls were still set on God, who kept their
hearts from the dilapidation of indifference, came to be known
as Sufis (the word means: Wearers of Woollen). It was a little
before the end of the second century of the Flight that this name
began to be applied to those great men.

* * *

We were on our way to Mecca by the Kufa road. One
overcast night, I heard a voice crying out from the womb of
darkness, and saying:

O my God! not by my own will have I transgressed by my
disobedience against Thee; my fault was one Thou didst fore-
ordain to me from all Eternity; pardon, pardon me my sin!

And then the same voice recited:

*O YE WHO BELIEVE! KEEP YOURSELVES AND
YOUR HOUSEHOLDS FROM THAT FIRE OF
WHICH THE FUEL IS MEN AND STONES!*

Then I heard a fall. But I knew not what it was, and
we passed on.

* * *

Ibrahim son of Adham, say the Sufis of a later time, was
of a princely family of Balkh. One day, he told, I was seated on
my seat of state, and a mirror was offered for my self-inspection.
I looked in it. I saw only a wayfarer toward the tomb, bound for
a place where there would be no friend to cheer me. I saw a long
journey stretching before me, for which I had made no provision.

I saw a Just Judge, and myself unprovided with any proof for my ordeal. My royalty became distasteful in that moment.

When he was out hunting one day, he followed so hard after an antelope that he left his train far behind him. And God gave the antelope voice. Wast thou created for this? it said to him; who bade thee do such things?

Ibrahim repented of his whole way of life. Abandoning everything, he entered the path of asceticism; and after this conversion never ate any food but what he earned by his own labor.

I came to the edge of a desert once, said he; and there an old man came up to me and said: Ibrahim, do you know what place this is? Do you know where you journey, thus unprovided and afoot?

I knew who the old man was. It was Satan. I pulled from my shirt-bosom what money I had — four coppers, the price of a basket I had sold in Kufa — and threw them away, and made a vow: that for every mile I travelled I would pray four hundred Bows. In that wilderness I lived four years. God gave me my eating without any toil of mine. Khidr the Green Ancient was my companion during that time — he taught me the Great Name of God.

Did you ever feel you had nothing more to wish for? was once asked of Ibrahim ibn Adham.

Yes, twice, he answered. The first time was on shipboard. Nobody knew who I was; I was wearing vulgar clothes; my hair was long and unkempt; I was a laughingstock to everyone on board. Among the other passengers was one man who liked to play the fool; this man was forever coming and tugging at my hair, even tearing it out by the roots, and plaguing me with all the impudence natural to his kind. At that time I felt absolutely satisfied, entirely happy to cut such a figure as I did; and this joy came to its highest pitch one day when the clown came over from his place and pissed on me.

The other occasion was once when I arrived at a village. It was raining heavily, the patched frock I wore was soaked through, and the cold of winter had quite overcome me. When I tried to go into a Mosque, I was refused admittance; then at three other Mosques where I sought shelter I was turned out. Grimmer and grimmer the cold crept over me; and in despair I turned in to a bathhouse and huddled my skirt against the stove. The belching smoke blackened my clothes and face all over. Then too I felt absolutely happy.

* * *

Three Veils must be drawn from before the Pilgrim's heart before the Door of Felicity will open to him. First, should the dominion of both worlds be offered him to be his for ever, he must feel no joy. Whoever feels joy in any created thing is still covetous; and *the covetous is shut outside*. The second Veil is this; should he possess dominion over both worlds, and should his dominion be taken from him, he must not grieve for his impoverishment. That would be resentment; and *the resentful is in torment*. The third is that he must not be seduced by any praise or mark of favor, for whoever yields to that pleasure is of mean spirit. A mean man is veiled. The Pilgrim must be of high mind.

* * *

Sufyan Thawri also wore the woollen frock. When he was dying, it is said, he purified himself sixty times for one prayer, saying: I will go out of this world clean at least.

If, said Thawri, you are better pleased when someone tells you you are a noble person than when you are called an impostor, then you may know for certain that you are still no good.

Glory be to God Who kills our children, God Who takes our living away, God Whom yet we love.

If a dervish frequents the rich, be sure of this: he is an impostor. If he goes to court, be sure of this: he is a thief.

I was in Mahdi's presence, says Ibn Hakim, when Sufyan Thawri the ascetic was brought in. He gave Mahdi only the common greeting, not the salutation it is proper to use to a Caliph, though the headsman Rabi stood towering behind the Sovereign, leaning on his sword and waiting for orders.

Well, Sufyan, said Mahdi, turning towards him with a smile, you escaped us once, eh? And again, eh? And now we have you. Are you afraid of what our doom may be?

Doom me, said Sufyan, and a King shall doom thee Who is powerful to sort true from false.

Prince of the True Believers! cried the headsman Rabi, shall such a clown affront the Prince like that? Let me give him one on the neck.

Silence, and be damned to thee! said Mahdi. This fellow and his like want nothing better than that we should kill them and go to Hell, while they are saved. No. Let his commission as Judge, at Kufa, be made out at once, and let it be expressly stated that no judgment of his shall be subject to revision.

The commission was made out, and handed to the ascetic. Sufyan Thawri took it. But no sooner was he out of the Palace than he threw it into the Tigris and took to his heels. Nor, though the police made search for him in all the towns, could he be found.

HADI

Hadi, the next Caliph, wanted to deprive his brother Harun al-Rashid of the succession appointed by their father Mahdi, and substitute his own son, Ja'far. But the Persian Secretary, Yahya son of Khalid the Barmecide, who was devoted to al-Rashid's interest, advised the Caliph against it. Prince of the True Believers, he said, should that thing happen which God

forbid and forfend, for may God prolong the life of the Prince of
True Believers! but should that thing come to pass, I say, would
the people ever consent that the Prince Ja'far, an infant, lead
them in Prayer? and on Pilgrimage? and to Holy War?

I suppose not, Hadi said.

Then is it not likely that one of the great princes of your
House would grasp the throne and power to himself, so that
authority would pass away to some collateral branch? The
Prince of the True Believers himself would have set an example
to his subjects of violating oaths and cheapening faith. But if on
the other hand you keep to your oath, and proclaim Ja'far heir in
succession to al-Rashid, you still stand firm. And afterwards,
when Ja'far is grown a man, you may ask al-Rashid to yield his
precedence freely to him.

I had never thought of that, by God! said Hadi.

But afterwards the Caliph determined to have al-Rashid's
renunciation willy-nilly, and even set spies on him. Yahya now
advised his patron to ask leave to go hunting, and made him
promise to stay away as long as he could. For the horoscope
cast at Hadi's birth indicated that he would shortly die.

Al-Rashid got permission, and rode away along Euphrates
side as far as the Anbar district, where he plunged into the desert.
Hadi wrote to recall him to court. When it was apparent that
Harun was inventing excuses to keep out of reach, the Caliph
broke into threats and abuse, and himself set out in pursuit. But
now he fell sick, and had to turn back. So terrible did his sickness grow that no man dared go near him; they sent in to tend
him some little eunuchs. The Caliph sent these for his mother;
and when his mother came, he took her hand, and laid it on his
heart.

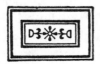

HARUN AL-RASHID

A city without peer in all the world was Baghdad then.

Al-Rashid had about him such a company as never met under any other man: he had the Barmecides for his Viziers and Abu Yusuf for his Judge, Marwan for his panegyrist and Fadl son of Rabi for his Chamberlain, Ibrahim of Mosul for his musician, and Zubayda for a wife.

Why should the Prince of the True Believers be so sad?

ARUN AL-RASHID SUCCEEDED, ACCORDING TO THEIR FATHER'S TESTAMENT, WHEN HIS BROTHER HADI DIED, ON THE NIGHT OF FRIDAY THE SIXTEENTH OF FIRST RABI IN THE YEAR ONE HUNDRED AND SEVENTY OF THE FLIGHT. IN THAT SAME NIGHT HIS SON MAMUN WAS BORN; AND IN THE WHOLE COURSE OF TIME THERE HAS NEVER BEEN ANOTHER NIGHT LIKE THAT, A NIGHT IN WHICH A CALIPH DIED AND A CALIPH SUCCEEDED AND A CALIPH WAS BORN.

Very fair and tall he was, exceedingly handsome, and captivating in manner as in person, both learned and well-bred. From the day he became Caliph to the day of his death he used to pray daily a hundred Bows, nor did he ever, unless for some extraordinary reason, neglect them. He used to give from his private purse a hundred dirhams every day in alms.

He once gave Ishaq of Mosul (Ibrahim's son) two hundred thousand dirhams; and he gave Marwan for a panegyric five thousand gold dinars and a dress of honor and a horse from the Royal Stud and ten Greek slaves.

He loved panegyric.

He used to weep over his own extravagance, and wept for his sins, especially when exhortation was addressed to him.

I never saw any shed more tears at Prayer, says Ibn Ammar, than these three: Fudayl (a converted highwayman), al-Rashid, and another man I knew. And Abu Mu'awia the Blind said: I related this Tradition to al-Rashid, that the Prophet of God said: *I would I might do battle for God's sake and be slain, and then be quickened again, and so slain again.* And Harun's tears fell until he sobbed aloud.

Al-Rashid regarded shrines with deep reverence, but hated religious disputation. When Bishr the Hanafite jurist's views upon the createdness of the Koran were described to al-Rashid, he exclaimed: I'll have his head off, if I get hold of him.

I was once relating a Tradition to al-Rashid, says Abu Mu'awia the Blind. Za'ida tells us, I related, that he had it of A'mash, who had it of Abu Salih, and he on the authority of Abu Hurayra, and he on the authority of the Prophet of God, God's Prayer and Peace be on him! that: Adam and Moses fell into a disputation; and Moses said: O Adam, thou art he whom God created with His Hand and breathed into thee of His Spirit; and yet thou hast betrayed mankind and lost them Paradise.

Thou art Moses whom God chose, Adam said; yet thou blamest me for a deed which God wrote down against my name before He did create the Heavens.

Adam bested Moses in that disputation, said the Prophet.

Sitting in the audience near the Caliph was an old gentleman of a Qurayshi family. May I ask, he sneered, where Adam could have met with Moses?

The Caliph swelled with anger. Bring the headsman's mat and the sword! he cried. Shall a Freethinker impugn a Tradition?

Prince of the True Believers, he did not mean what he said! I interposed; and I continued to pacify him, until at last he calmed down.

> *You hide with a Hell-raising tongue*
> *A decent Muslim heart:*
> *It's smart to be a Freethinker,*
> *And you're a would-be-smart.*

Most severely did al-Rashid reprove the court buffoon
Ibn Abi Miriam for permitting himself a joke at Prayers. The
Caliph was reciting the text:
*WHY SHOULD I NOT SERVE HIM WHO HATH
CREATED ME?*

Why not indeed? came the response from Ibn Abi
Miriam: I certainly don't know!

The Caliph could not help laughing. But he rounded on
the clown angrily: What? even at Prayer? Be careful, Ibn Abi
Miriam, of fooling with the Book and the Faith. Leave those
two alone; you can have the rest.

EXPIATION OF A SINFUL STEW

Al-Rashid came to dine with me at Raqqa once, says his
brother Ibrahim son of Mahdi. He always used to eat the hot
dishes first, and the cold side dishes afterward; and as the side
dishes were being served on this occasion, he noticed among
those set down near him a stew, which looked like a fish stew,
except that the pieces seemed to be cut too small.

Why has your cook cut up the fish so fine? he asked me.

Those are fishes' *tongues,* Prince of the True Believers,
said I.

Why, there must be a hundred tongues in that dish! cried
Harun.

More than one hundred and fifty, Prince of the True Believers! my servant Muraqib interposed.

What was the cost of such a stew? demanded the Caliph.
Muraqib explained that all the ingredients together came to

more than a thousand dirhams. Al-Rashid drew his hand back sharply from the dish. I'll not eat another mouthful, he exclaimed, until you have brought me a thousand dirhams.

When Muraqib brought him a thousand dirhams of my money, he ordered it given out in alms at once, explaining: I want to expiate the heathen folly of a thousand-dirham fish stew!

He then seized the plate itself. Take this plate out of my brother's house, he called to one of his own servants, and give it to the first beggar you meet.

Now that plate I had ordered specially for the occasion; and it had cost me two hundred and seventy dinars. So I signed to one of my servants to follow close at the heels of the other fellow and to buy back the plate from whosoever might get it. Al-Rashid, however, saw what I was at. He called back his own man. Page, said he, when you give that plate to the beggar, tell him this: that the Prince of the True Believers recommends him not to let it go for less than two hundred dinars, since it is certainly worth more.

Well, his servant gave away my plate. And by God, my servant could not get it back from the beggar who got it cheaper than two hundred gold dinars!

* * *

Harun al-Rashid was the first polo-playing Caliph.

He was also the first who memorized for delivery sermons which other men had composed for him. To this end he thus instructed Asma'i the grammarian and poet:

Never tell me anything in public; and even in private do not be too ready with advice. As a rule, wait for me to consult you, and content yourself with giving me a succinct answer to the question you are asked. Above all, beware of trying to monopolize me for the sake of your own credit and authority. Do not expatiate on the stories or Traditions you are to tell me unless I give you leave. If you see me judge amiss, lead me back gently to the right path. Never speak angrily to me. And never rebuke me.

Your chief function is to teach me what I ought to show
knowledge of when I speak in public, in the Mosques and elsewhere; and do not use obscure terms — I do not want high-flown
language.

THE VIZIER, YAHYA THE BARMECIDE

As soon as Harun al-Rashid was acknowledged Caliph, he
sent for Yahya. My father, he said to him, your fortune and your
counsel set me in this seat; and now I invest you with all my
power. And he sent Yahya his own signet.

Yahya's father Khalid son of the Barmak (hereditary High
Priest of the heathen temple at Balkh) had been a Secretary to
Mansur. In wisdom he had no peer, even among his own
posterity: not Yahya, for all his penetration, nor any of Yahya's
sons — the generous Fadl, the accomplished Ja'far, the noble Muhammad, the valiant Musa — none of these was Khalid's equal.

When, under al-Rashid, the Barmecides were raised to the
Vizierate, they drew the State revenues into their own hands so
entirely that in the end the Caliph had to apply to them even for
petty cash.

THREE FAMOUS SAYINGS OF THE VIZIER YAHYA

Promises are the nets of the generous; one can catch a good
man's good opinion with such a net.

No man has ever spoken to me but I have listened with
respect. By the time he had finished, either I respected him more,
or I respected him no more.

Power and wealth are loans: it must be enough for us to
have once had what we have no more; it must be our happiness
to leave behind us a monumental warning for some who will
come after.

At audience one day, Yahya being in presence, al-Rashid received the Intelligence Report from the Postmaster of Khurasan. It was intimated that the Vizier's son Fadl, then Governor in that province, was too preoccupied with his pleasures to attend to government.

When he had read through this despatch, the Caliph tossed it over to the Vizier. Read that, father, he said; and then do write something to him, something to pull him up.

Yahya having read borrowed the Caliph's inkhorn and wrote immediately on the back of the Postmaster's report: *God keep thee, my son, and God give me joy of thee. The Prince of the True Believers has learned with displeasure that your conscientiousness in hunting and revelry leaves you no leisure to govern your charge. Resume a more seemly style; for a man's contemporaries will base their opinions of him on his daily actions, good or bad, and on nothing else. And now farewell.*

Below, he added these verses:

> *I said daily: spend the day*
> *Getting honor — you can play*
> *When the dark draws curtains close*
> *Round the naughty and the gay.*
>
> *For delight there's the whole night:*
> *Shadows are the wise man's light.*
> *Only fools leave fun and sin*
> *Open to the eyes of spite.*

Perfect! cried al-Rashid, who had been following the writing word by word. As for Fadl, from the time he received this letter he spent the whole of every day administering his charge in the Mosque, until he laid down his office and returned from Khurasan to court.

THE RISE OF JUDGE ABU YUSUF

Abu Yusuf, Harun al-Rashid's famous Judge, had been a very poor man at the period when he sat under Abu Hanifa as a law student. Attendance at lectures kept him from earning a living; and at the day's end he used to go home to short rations in ill-kept quarters. Things went on in this way for a long time, his wife managing by hook and by crook to keep herself alive from one day to the next.

At last she could bear it no longer. One day, when her husband, having spent the whole day in the lecture-room, came home at night and asked for supper, she set a single covered dish before him; and when he removed the cover, he found beneath it nothing but a pile of notebooks.

What's the meaning of this? he asked.

You spend your whole day on it, so you can eat it at night! she cried.

Abu Yusuf was deeply affected. He went without food that evening, and next morning stayed away from lecture till he had earned enough money for his household eating, which done, he presented himself before Abu Hanifa.

How is it that you are so late? inquired his teacher. Abu Yusuf explained.

Why didn't you tell me, so that I could have helped you earlier? asked Abu Hanifa. But don't worry—if God lets you live, you will make enough money by the Law someday to feed on nothing cheaper than almond paste and shelled pistachios if you want.

Abu Yusuf himself used to say that long after, when he was in the Caliph's service and high in favor, a dish of almond paste and pistachios was served at the Imperial table. As I tasted it, he said, suddenly tears stung my eyes — I remembered Abu Hanifa.

Abu Hanifa was a very good man· Once an opponent, losing his temper, struck him.

I could repay that with another, said Abu Hanifa — but I shall not. I could complain of you to the Caliph — I shall not complain. I could mention this outrage you have done me to God in prayer — I shall beware of doing that. I could demand my vengeance from God Himself at Judgment Day — but if that Dreadful Day should break this instant, and my plea be heard, I should say only that I refused to enter Paradise without you.

* * *

The occasion of Abu Yusuf's entering the Caliph's service was as follows:

A certain General or military Prince who had forsworn himself wanted to consult a jurist. Abu Yusuf was fetched. After hearing all the details, he gave it as his opinion that the Prince was not technically guilty of perjury. This General not only gave him a sum of money by way of fee, but rented a house for him in his own neighborhood, and became his patron.

One day when the General presented himself at audience, he found the Caliph in a gloomy mood, and inquired what was the cause of his discomposure. It is a point of Law, said al-Rashid; fetch some jurist — we must ask. The Prince took this opportunity to introduce his own client Abu Yusuf, and sent for him to the Palace.

The rest of the tale is in Abu Yusuf's own words. As I entered the corridor which led from the Public to the Private Apartments, he said, I saw a handsome boy, obviously some member of the Imperial family, in one of the rooms which opened on that passage I was in. The boy was under guard. He made a signal to me with his finger, as if he was imploring my help; but before I could ascertain what he wanted, I was led on into the Presence. As soon as I came within sight of al-Rashid, I pronounced the proper Caliphal salutation and remained standing where I was. He inquired my name.

Ya'qub, God prosper the Prince of the True Believers, I replied.

What is your opinion, he asked without further preliminary,

of the case of a sovereign who himself sees a man committing a crime punishable by death? Is that sovereign obliged to inflict the penalty?

Not necessarily, I replied.

No sooner were these words out of my mouth than al-Rashid threw himself on the floor in prostration before God. It sprang into my mind that he must have seen one of his own sons committing that mortal offense (presumably adultery with a member of his father's harem), and that the person who had signalled to me for assistance was no other than the adulterous son. Presently al-Rashid raised his head.

What's your authority for that? he asked.

Because, I replied, the Prophet, God's Prayer and Peace be on him! has said: *Avert penalties by doubts;* and there is in this case a legal doubt which qualifies the necessity of penalty.

But what doubt could there be, he asked, when there is ocular evidence?

Ocular evidence, I replied, does not necessitate the penalty, any more than mere knowledge of the offense would necessitate it. The Law does not inflict penalties from mere knowledge.

Why not? he inquired.

Because, I answered, the penalty is a right of God. But it is the Sovereign to whom is committed the maintenance of this right; so that it becomes as it were his own right. Now no person may lawfully exact his own right merely on the grounds of his own personal knowledge; nor may he personally proceed to enforce that right lawfully in such a case. It is established by Consensus of Believers that either confession or evidence is required before a penalty may be enforced. There is no Consensus to the effect that knowledge alone is sufficient grounds for the enforcement of a penalty.

As I finished speaking, al-Rashid prostrated himself once more. He then ordered me a huge bounty, and a monthly allowance as an official Jurist, with instructions that I was to be attached to the Palace.

Before I was clear of the Palace Gate I had received one

bounty from the young man, another from his mother, and various others from his retainers — the makings of a fortune. I got the Caliphal allowance in addition to what I was already getting from the military Prince. And being officially attached to the Palace, I was often asked for a legal opinion by some Attendant, or for advice by some other Attendant. I always gave my opinion and my advice when they were asked for. I gained a degree of authority; I won respect. And I was constantly getting bounties. I went on from strength to strength.

Then came the day when the Caliph summoned me to a lengthy consultation upon a real emergency. What I had to say on that occasion was well received; and I continued to advance in his good graces until in the end he made me a Judge.

* * *

A wife of the late Caliph Hadi wrote asking Abu Yusuf for a legal opinion. His view was exactly what she wanted, and at the same time strictly legal and very learned. By way of acknowledgment, she sent a silver chest containing two smaller silver caskets of perfumes, a gold cup filled with silver coins and a silver cup filled with gold coins, several slaves, some pieces of rich furniture, an ass, and a mule.

A learned friend was sitting with Abu Yusuf when these gifts arrived. We have heard (he quoted from Tradition) that the Apostle of God, God's Prayer and Peace be on him! said: *A man who receives a gift should share it with the folk with him.*

But you are giving a Literalist interpretation to the text! cried Abu Yusuf. Our own Hanafite principle of Practical Adjustment would never allow of such an application as you propose. Presents in the Prophetic epoch consisted of dates and curds, whereas nowadays they are apt to be of gold and silver and other valuables. Let me remind you of what God says in His Book: *THAT IS THE GRACE OF GOD, WHICH HE BESTOW-ETH UPON WHOM HE WILL; AND GOD IS LORD VERILY OF MIGHTY GRACE.*

* * *

It is the Hanafite view that the Believer is still a Believer, and does not become an enemy of God, though he sin repeatedly; that sins do not constitute Unbelief; and that Grace is not incompatible with sin.

A Traditionist was seen drinking wine, at the house of a Christian.

What? they exclaimed. Drinking a forbidden drink? bought by a Christian's slave? and from a Jew?

We Traditionists, he replied, accept as sound authorities men of the stamp of Sufyan ibn Uyayna and Yazid ibn Harun. What, would you have us believe a thing sinful on the authority of a Christian, who had it of his slave, who had it of a Jew? By God! I only drank the stuff because its chain of authorities is so unsound!

Without our sins, O Lord, Your Mercy would be a dead letter.

> *Transgress His Law as often as you can,*
> *The Lord will yet relent, and all be well.*
> *When Doomsday comes, and you find all forgiven*
> *By that Most Mighty and Most Merciful,*
> *You'll gnaw your hands, to think of all the sport*
> *You might have had, and lost for fear of Hell.*

GABRIEL SON OF BAKHTISHU
THE CALIPH'S PHYSICIAN

Harun al-Rashid was once at Hira; and the Postmaster of that city appeared with a present: a dish of very rich fish, with a special sauce, for the Imperial table. But at dinner, just as al-Rashid was about to taste this dish, his Physician Gabriel ibn Bakhtishu forbade him to touch it, and signed to the Butler to lay it aside for himself. The Caliph observed the signal. When the meal and ablutions were done, the Physician took his leave.

Al-Rashid ordered me (relates the freed eunuch Sulayman) to follow Ibn Bakhtishu to his quarters and report what I should see. I obeyed, although I could see from Gabriel's manner that he suspected the task I had been assigned. However, he went to his quarters in the Postmaster's house, and asked for dinner. The meal duly appeared, and with it the selfsame fish.

Thereupon he called for three cups. In the first he put some of the fish, steeping it in wine of Tizanabadh. Having stirred it till it was thoroughly soaked, he observed: That's the way Gabriel eats it. Next, he put another piece of fish in the second cup, and poured over it extremely cold ice water, with the words: That's how the Caliph, God glorify him! would eat it if he did not qualify it with other things. In the third cup he put together a piece of the fish, various kinds of meat stew, some pieces of roast, sweet halva, hot sauce, relishes, and various scraps — one or two mouthfuls only — of all the dishes served. Then, pouring ice water on the whole, he remarked: That's how the Caliph eats if he mixes other things with his fish!

These three cups he committed to the Butler, with instructions that they should be set aside until the hour when the Caliph should rise from his rest; which done, he himself assailed the fish and ate till he could eat no more, washing it down with unmixed wine. Then he lay down to rest, and I departed.

When al-Rashid awoke, he asked me what was the news, whether or not Gabriel had eaten of the famous fish. I told him what had passed. He called for the cups to be brought him at once. In the first, which Gabriel had called his own, and had filled up with unmixed wine, the fish was reduced to shreds, and liquefied as if by seething. In the second cup, which he had regarded as the Caliph's, the bit of fish had swollen to twice its former size. But in the third, which Gabriel called the Caliph's mixed meal, the viands had already putrefied: they gave out a stench so foul that al-Rashid was seized with nausea as soon as it was near him.

He bade me take the Physician a bounty of five thousand dinars. Who can blame me for loving the man who rules me so well? he said, as I went off with the money.

BARMECIDE GENEROSITY

Says the singer Ishaq, son of Ibrahim of Mosul:

I owned a very beautiful girl, whom I had brought up, and myself trained with such care that she was at last exceptionally accomplished. I decided to offer her as a present to Yahya's son Fadl the Barmecide.

Ishaq, said Fadl when I mentioned the matter, keep the girl by you for the moment. An envoy from the Governor of Egypt has just been here to ask me a very special favor. I will tell him when he next calls that I have taken a great fancy to this girl of yours, and he will know that if he would have my ear he had better buy her for me. But mind! when he asks the price, don't let her go for less than fifty thousand dinars.

So I went home. It was not long before the Governor's envoy came to pay a call on me. He made inquiries about the girl; I brought her out. He made an offer of ten thousand dinars for her. I refused. He went by degrees as high as twenty thousand, and then to thirty thousand! At the sound of that price I could hold in no longer — Done! I cried. I made her over to him, and took the money.

Next morning I went to call on Fadl, and told him how the transaction had passed off. He smiled.

Now for the Byzantine Ambassador! said he. The Ambassador also needs my good offices; and I will make the same price for him. Take your girl home again; wait for the Ambassador. But be sure you do not let her go cheaper than fifty thousand this time.

With the Byzantine Ambassador, however, it went the same way again. Again the sound of thirty thousand dinars was too much for me, and I let the girl go at that price. When I

visited Fadl next day he returned her to me once more. I will
be sending the agent of the Governor of Khurasan tomorrow,
he said.

This time I screwed up my courage. I demanded and got
forty thousand dinars. And when on the following day I paid
my respects to Fadl, and he inquired how I had done, I replied:
I sold the girl for forty thousand dinars; and by God, I nearly
went out of my mind at the sound of the figure! My soul your
ransom! that girl has brought me one hundred thousand dinars.
There's nothing more for me to wish for in this world — I can
only say: May God reward you!

But Fadl the Barmecide ordered the girl brought out to
us. He made me a present of her, and told me to take her home
with me and keep her.

That girl, I reflected, is fraught with the blessing of God
beyond any other earthly thing. And I decided to free her; and
married her. She is the mother of my children.

Men used to say the days of the Barmecides were one long
wedding day, and an everlasting feast.

AN APOCRYPHAL TALE

One day the Caliph Harun al-Rashid went riding into the
desert, and Abu Yusuf with him, and Ja'far the Barmecide, and
the poet Abu Nuwas; and by and by as they rode, they came upon
an ancient man, leaning on a donkey. The Caliph bade Ja'far
ask him where he was from; so Ja'far said: Where are you from?

From Basra, said the Beduin.

And where are you bound?

For Baghdad.

And what are you going to do in Baghdad?

I'm going to get some medicine for my eye, replied the
ancient.

Ja'far, said the Caliph, we must have some fun with this fellow.

If I make fun of this fellow, answered Ja'far, I shall hear more than I care to hear.

I give you my command as Caliph, al-Rashid insisted. Make fun of the man!

So Ja'far addressed the Beduin again: If I give you a prescription for your eye which does it good, what will you give me back again?

God (Whose Name be exalted!) shall requite thee for me, the old man said, with better than I can give thee.

Listen then, and pay good heed, said Ja'far; and I'll give you a prescription I have never given any other man.

What is it?

Take three ounces, said Ja'far, of light airs, and similar quantities of sunbeams, moonshine, and lamplight; mix thoroughly, and leave to stand in a well-ventilated place three months. Then, bray for three months in a bottomless mortar, pour into a broken saucer, and set in a well-ventilated place to stand three months more. When ready, apply three drachms every night while asleep. And please God, you will be cured.

The Beduin heard this through. He laid himself out flat along his donkey's back and let fly a terrible great fart.

Pay thyself out of that for thy cure! said he; and after I've used the stuff, if God doth cure me thereby, I'll give thee a gift: a slave girl — who shall serve thee alive such a service as God shall shorten thy term withal; and when thou diest, and God doth hurry thy soul to the Fire, shall shit on thy face for sorrow, and blubber, and beat her nether cheeks and howl aloud: O nincompoop, how nincom was thy poop!

And the Caliph laughed till he fell over his horse's tail.

* * *

They tell a story that Ja'far the Barmecide was drinking one night with al-Rashid, and the Caliph said to him; Ja'far, I hear you bought that girl So-and-so, whom I have been negotiating for so long. She is a girl I want very much; do sell her to me.

But, Prince of the True Believers, I do not want to sell her, Ja'far answered.

Give her to me then, said the Caliph.

I am not willing to give her either, retorted Ja'far.

Zubayda be triply divorced but you'll either sell her or give her to me! exclaimed al-Rashid. (This is an absolutely binding form of oath.)

And my wife be triply divorced if I do either! shouted Ja'far.

Soon enough they came from their drunken tempers to themselves. They were in a grave dilemma, as both well knew; and neither knew how to get out of it.

The only man to help us out of this pass, the Caliph said at last, is Abu Yusuf.

So the Judge was sent for. It was midnight before the Palace messenger reached his house; and Abu Yusuf rose from bed in alarm. There must be some dire crisis in Islam, or they would not send for me at this hour! he exclaimed as he hurried out to mount his mule. Bring the mule's nose bag along with you, he added to the groom; she has not finished her feed, I think; when we get to the Palace, put the bag on her again — she can eat the rest of her fodder while I am with the Caliph.

Hear and obey, said the groom. And so the Judge rode away to the Palace. He was shown to the Presence at once; and al-Rashid made him sit on the divan beside himself, where no man was seated as a rule.

We have sent for you, late as it is, he began, to give us your advice on a serious business, which we cannot cope with. And he explained the dilemma of the two binding but contradictory oaths.

Prince of the True Believers, said Abu Yusuf, this is a very simple business. Ja'far, he went on, turning to the latter, you must sell half the girl to the Prince of the True Believers, and then give him the other half — you will both be quit of your oaths in that way.

The Caliph was greatly relieved; and the company carried out the forms of the transaction.

Let her be brought to the Palace straightway, said al-Rashid; I am impatient to call her mine. So the girl was sent for, and shown in.

I should like to sleep with her tonight, said the Caliph to the Judge. I cannot wait, and keep away from her, for the full period of legal purification. Can this be managed?

Bring me, Prince of the True Believers, one of your male slaves, replied the Judge: not a freedman — a slave; and authorize me to marry her to him. Then he has only to divorce her before consummation to make it perfectly lawful for you to sleep with her; for a Believer may cohabit with a woman divorced before consummation without waiting for the expiry of purification.

This further ingenuity was even more pleasing to the Caliph. Bring a slave! he cried; and as soon as the man was brought in, he said to the Judge: I authorize thee to marry this woman to this man. So Abu Yusuf proposed the marriage to the slave, and the slave accepted the proposal, and Abu Yusuf performed the necessary ceremony. When it was done, he said to the slave: Now, you pronounce her divorced — you shall have a hundred dinars for this night's work.

But alas! the slave refused to pronounce the formula. The Judge raised his offer. The slave still refused, until at last the Judge had bid him a thousand dinars. When he heard this offer, the slave asked: Has it absolutely got to be me who must divorce her? Could you do it? Has the Prince of the True Believers power to do it?

No, you must do it, Abu Yusuf replied.

Then by God, said the man, I'll never do it!

Al-Rashid rounded in a fury on the Judge: What now?

Be calm, Prince of the True Believers; all is perfectly simple, Abu Yusuf said. You must now make this slave the property of the girl.

Very well, I give him to her, said al-Rashid.

Now, you say: I accept, the Judge instructed the girl.

I accept, said she.

I now pronounce this man and this woman divorced, declared Abu Yusuf; for the man having become his spouse's servile property, the marriage is by that fact annulled.

Harun al-Rashid sprang to his feet. So long as I am alive, 'tis the like of you shall be Judge! he cried; and calling for some trays of gold, he poured them out before the lawyer.

Have you got anything to put this in? he suddenly asked. The Judge bethought him of his mule's nose bag, and sent for it. And he took that nose bag home full of gold.

There is no easier or shorter road to the good things of this world and of the Next, he observed to the visitors at his Divan next day, than the path of learning — see what I got for answering two or three questions.

Mark this incident well, polite reader, for it contains more than one point of beauty: consider the complaisance of Ja'far; consider the Caliph's magnanimity; and consider the more than common erudition of the Judge — may God the Most High have Mercy on all their souls! As to the expiation of the oaths, Abu Yusuf's ruling would hardly be confirmed by jurists of the Shafi'ite School; Abu Yusuf treated it in accord with the views of his own, the Hanafite School. But God (be He exalted!) knows best which view is right. And only He.

TWO GOVERNORS OF EGYPT

When al-Rashid appointed his cousin Abd al-Malik Governor of Egypt, he gave him the following instructions:

Regard yourself in your charge as a broker, who must someday account to God for some slaves of His; a sensible merchant will not go on putting stock up for sale if he sees prices too low.

As military commander, keep these rules: no plundering till your own position is absolutely secure; and always worry more over your own plans than over your enemies' plans.

In the year 178 Abd al-Malik was accused of treason by his Secretary.

I was with al-Rashid (says the poet Asma'i) when Abd al-Malik, who had been recalled, was brought into the Presence. He was in chains.

Aha! said al-Rashid, glaring at him. It's as if I saw it all now, Abd al-Malik, that rain of blood, and the lightning crackling in the cloud! and when the storm goes by, the wristless hands, the trunkless heads upon the ground! Have a care, you Hashimites, have a care! I have smoothed the rough for you; I have cleared the muddy; you think the reins of the world are in your hands. But have a care — there's trouble coming; and it will trample you with all four feet.

Prince of the True Believers, said Abd al-Malik, shall I use my first shot? or my last?

Thy last!

Then fear God, said Abd al-Malik, for all thou rulest, Prince of the True Believers; and tremble before Him for what is trusted to thee. For thee too the rough ground is smoothed — the very hearts of men beat with the fear of thee and the hope of thee. For all that, thou art where the Kilabi poet said:

> Fast in a narrow pass
> Where counsel and cunning and force
> Are useless. . . .

Now the Vizier Yahya the Barmecide was anxious to discredit the Hashimite Prince with al-Rashid. Abd al-Malik, he interposed, you have the reputation of a man implacable in hatred, we know.

God save the Vizier! answered Abd al-Malik, if hatred be the memory of kindness done me, and of wrong; true enough, in my heart these things are eternal.

Write that down, Asma'i, said al-Rashid, turning to me;

I have never heard Abd al-Malik's definition of hatred from any
other man. Then he ordered the accused Governor back to
prison.

I looked at his neck more than once, by God, and thought
of the sword, said the Caliph, turning to me again; but one thing
prevented me — the precedent it would set in my family.

* * *

Why should the Prince of the True Believers be so sad?
said the poet Abu Nuwas. By God, I never saw a man so unfair
to himself as the Prince of the True Believers is. The pleasures of
this world and the Other are in your hand: why not enjoy them
both? The pleasures of the World to come are yours for the sake
of your charity to the poor and the orphan, your performance of
Pilgrimage, your repairing of Mosques and founding of schools
and improving of land: for all these things THERE IS IM-
MENSE REWARD.

As for the pleasures of this world, what are they but these:
delicious food, delicious drinks, delicious girls? Think of them —
the tall girls, and then the girls who are neither too tall nor too
short, and then the fine-made small girls; gentle fair-haired girls
and voluptuous dark ones; girls of Madina; girls of Hijaz; girls
from Byzantium and girls from our own Iraq — with bodies
straight and proud as Samhari lances, witty as they are lovely:
what glancing speech! and O what speaking glances!

> *Four sweets*
> *For cark and care!*
> *Four that sway*
> *Body and soul*
> *And eye to joy:*
> *Flowing water,*
> *Brimming bowl,*
> *Gardens gay,*
> *And faces fair.*

While Abd al-Malik was still under restraint, his brother
Isma'il, who was with him, was sent for to come to the Palace.

They only want you to get drunk with them, said Abd al-
Malik, and sing for them. You're no brother of mine if you
do. . . .

When I got to the Palace (says Isma'il), al-Rashid made
me dine with him. After dinner the Physician Ibn Bakhtishu prescribed wine.

I'll not drink unless Isma'il will drink with me, said al-
Rashid.

I am under oath not to do anything like that, Prince of
the True Believers, I cried.

But al-Rashid insisted. We drank three glasses each. Then
the Curtain was drawn, and girls came in to sing and dance. The
Caliph listened, toying with a rosary of jewels, but presently
took a lute from one of the girls, and throwing the strung jewels
over the neck of it planted both lute and rosary in my lap. Come
on, he said, sing us something — you can expiate that oath of
yours out of the price of that bauble.

So I sang:

> *My hand to sin was never taught,*
> *My feet to fault have never led;*
> *Till now, nor ear nor eye have brought*
> *One wicked thought into my head.*
> *If now some fated sin I must deplore,*
> *My lot's the human lot: I must endure*
> *What O so many others bore before!*

Al-Rashid was highly delighted. He called for a lance, and
then and there bound on a Banner of Government for Egypt, and
handed it to me.

I was Governor of Egypt for two years. I loaded the
province with justice, and came back to the capital five hundred
thousand dinars richer than I had left it.

* * *

When the Abbasid Prince Muhammad, first cousin to the Caliph Mansur, died at Basra, al-Rashid confiscated his whole property there and elsewhere: goods and money amounted to more than fifty million dirhams, without reckoning his landed estates and houses, and other real property. The Prince's daily income was said to have been about a hundred thousand dirhams.

This Muhammad was riding through the streets of Basra one day in the marriage cavalcade of one of his female cousins, with Sawar the Judge riding at his side, when a man sprang out before his horse. It was a clown, known to the whole town by the name of Muttonhead.

Muhammad! he cried, is it just for thee to get a hundred thousand dirhams a day, while I have to beg for my half-dirham a day, and then go without it as often as not?

And he turned to the Judge. If this is what you call justice, said he, I don't believe in it.

* * *

Once when I went on Pilgrimage to Mecca with al-Rashid (says the Chamberlain Fadl ibn Rabi), and all the Rites were over, he asked me: Is there any man of God in the city here whom I could visit?

Yes, there's San'ani, I replied. So we went round to his house and talked with him for a while. As we were leaving, al-Rashid told me to ask if he had any debts. He said Yes; so the Caliph gave orders that they should be paid.

Fadl, said he when we were out in the street again, I still feel the longing to see someone, some greater man than that. So I took him to call on Sufyan son of Uyayna. That visit passed off in the same manner, with al-Rashid giving an order to pay his debts as he left.

I remember now, he then said: Fudayl is here — let's go and see him. Fudayl proved to be in an upper room; we could hear him repeating a Verse of the Koran. We knocked on the door. Who's there? he shouted down.

The Prince of the True Believers, I called.

And what have I to do with the Prince of the True Believers? Fudayl answered.

I thought, said I, there was an Apostolic Tradition that
a man must not make himself too mean even in his devotion to
God.

There is, he answered; but Delight in His Will is glory
to a quietist — you may see me as mean, but I see myself as highly
exalted. However, he came down and unbarred the door. He
had blown out his lamp, and he withdrew into the far corner of
the room; the Caliph, when he went in, had to grope his way
towards him. Their hands touched.

Fudayl gave an exclamation as if of pain. Never have I
felt a softer hand! he said. Very strange will it be if that hand
escape the Divine Torment!

At once al-Rashid broke down, in tears so bitter, sobs so
deep-fetched that he swooned. O Fudayl! he said when he was
himself again, give me some word to hold by.

Fudayl spoke: When thy ancestor who was uncle to God's
Chosen One asked if he might rule men, Prince of True Believers,
this was what the Prophet answered him: *I will give thee a greater
gift than that, mine uncle — for one moment thou shalt rule thyself.* And this is what he meant: for thee to be utterly obedient to
God for one moment's duration is more bliss than a thousand years
of being obeyed by others. When the Dead Rise, what was power
is remorse.

Go on, said al-Rashid.

When Omar son of Abd al-Aziz became Caliph, Fudayl
went on, he sent for three he knew and said: What am I to do in
this my tribulation? for such I believe it to be. One of the three
answered: If thou wouldst live thy tomorrow free of the Pains of
God, see in every old Muslim thy actual father, in every young
Muslim thy actual brother, in every child thy actual child. For
thy father — rise up and visit him. For thy brother — give (not
take) honor. For thy children — love.

After a while, Fudayl spoke again: Prince of the True Believers, I am afraid for thee! that handsome face of thine will go

down into the Fire at last, I think. Thou must dread God, do what thou owest Him to do. And better than heretofore.

Harun asked him whether he had any debts.

Yes, there is what I owe God — obedience to Him. And woe is me if He should call it in now!

I am speaking of debts to men, Fudayl, said Harun.

God be praised! He is very good to me, and I have no cause to complain to Him of His servants, Fudayl replied.

Well, use this for some purpose of your own, said the Caliph, pressing a purse of a thousand dinars on him.

All I said has done you no good! cried Fudayl. Already you do the wrong thing again.

How? How wrong? exclaimed Harun.

I would have you be in Heaven; you would have me be in Hell. You cannot see what is wrong with that?

It was over. We took our leave of him. The tears stood in Harun al-Rashid's eyes, and in mine. O Fadl, the Caliph said as we came away, there is a King indeed.

When afterwards Ibn Uyayna (who had accepted the Caliph's bounty) reproached Fudayl for refusing it, Fudayl seized the divine by the beard.

Thou, a great Doctor of the Law, to be so wrong! he cried. If these people, these Abbasids had got their money lawfully it would have been another matter — I could lawfully have accepted it.

COURTIERS

At one of al-Rashid's audiences (says Ishaq) I recited a poem I had composed, celebrating the virtue of munificence, which ended with the lines:

> *No true poet can be poor,*
> *Nor a poet's heart know fear,*
> *When the Prince of True Believers*
> *Has himself a poet's ear.*

No, certainly no poet shall be poor (please God!); how indeed should he? cried al-Rashid. Fadl! give Ishaq a hundred thousand dirhams. And let us ascribe to God the beauty of this verse he brings us: no less perfect in point than it is exquisite in arrangement.

Why, Prince of the True Believers! I said. Your criticism is better literature than my verse!

Fadl, said he to the Chamberlain, give him another hundred thousand.

In that moment (wrote Asma'i afterwards) I realized that Ishaq had an even keener nose for money than I had.

I certainly wish, said Abu Atahia to Abu Nuwas, that I had got that verse in first — the one in which you praised al-Rashid:

I feared thee once. That fearful time is o'er;
I see thou fearest God. I fear no more.

Ja'far the Barmecide one day ordered his horse. Bring a purse of a thousand dinars along with you, he said to one of his train; I am going to Asma'i's. If you see me laugh at some witticism of his, give him the money, but not otherwise.

The call was paid. Asma'i was witty and amusing; but Ja'far, after listening with a grave unsmiling face for a while, took his departure.

You surprised me very much just now, said one of his cavalcade to him. You intend to give Asma'i a thousand dinars; the man exhausts himself in efforts to amuse you; and you leave him without so much as a smile. It is not like you to put money back in your pocket once you have pulled it out.

My dear fellow, said Ja'far, Asma'i has already had a hundred thousand dirhams of my money, and yet I still see a houseful of decrepit rubbish: his coat was shabby, his cushion was filthy — everything about him was squalid. Some sign of prosperity would say more than all his conversation; the sight of some result from my generosity would flatter me more than any panegyric he could

write. What is the use of giving him presents if he has not gratitude enough to look the better for them?

WHAT IS LOVE?

The Vizier Yahya, who was a learned and enlightened
man, fond of discussion and inquiry, used to gather about him
controversialists not only of the orthodox schools but of the Freethinkers, and leading lights of the various sects.

We have heard here on past occasions, he said at one of
these assemblies, a good deal of discussion of the theory of Occultation and Manifestation, of the Uncreate and the Created, Time
and Eternity, Force and Inertia, the Unity or Multiplicity of Divine Substance, the nature of Reality and its opposite, the philosophy of bodies and their accidents. We have examined the grounds
for approving or doubting Traditionary authority. We have asked
whether the Divine Attributes are real or impossible. Potentiality
and Actuality, Substance and Quality, Modality and Relation,
Life itself and the Annihilation of it, we have speculated upon all
these. We have debated whether the Imamate is a Divine or an
elective institution, and disputed the lawfulness of the legal Roots
and of deduction from them.

But today I should like you to speak of Love. And this time
let us not have controversy, but let each man say what Love is, in
few words, and frankly.

The Shi'ite theologian Ali ibn Haytham spoke up first.
Love comes, said he, not only because kind will after kind, but in
order that two spirits may become one. The Beauty of God, which
is the pure subtle principle of substances, is the ultimate origin of
Love.

I say, said the Rationalist shaykh of the Basra School, that
Love is a seal for the eyes and a brand for the heart, a poison that
runs through the body, through every alley of the bowels, irration-
alizing reason and maddening intelligence. Love sullies and be-
trays and is unlucky. It is one drop from the great Ocean of Des-

truction, the first sip from the Pool of Death. And yet its force is
a natural force, the attractiveness of a creature's pretty shape.

Nay, Vizier, said an Imamite dialectician, Love is itself the
proof that the principle of sympathy or attraction is immaterial.

Twelve Believers spoke in all. At last a Magian, or Zoroastrian divine, gave his view: O Vizier, we know Love as a fire or
heat, first kindling in the pericardium, then spreading and burning
in the region between ribs and heart. But Love inheres not only
in living things; the same fire is celestial. It is a spiritual fire in a
prior sense, and material only in causal process. Love's the flower-
ing of young life, Love's the Garden of Giving, Love in the soul
is the Magic and the Bliss of being ensouled. Love the quickening
of the elements! Love lit in the stars! Love blowing in the wind!
Love the pattern of the mystery! Beauty, the Intelligence to perceive it, Sensation, organic Life — Love needs all these: both the
opposites and what unites the opposites. Being heavenly first,
Love moves in the spheres above us; and the passion of sublunary
creatures moved by Love answers to those motions in the greater
spheres.

* * *

A large number of divines signed a petition which was to
be presented to al-Rashid. It ran thus:

*Prince of the True Believers! how wilt thou answer on the Day
of Resurrection? and how justify thyself in the Presence of the
Most High, for having given Yahya ibn Khalid and his sons
and his kinsmen such unlimited lordship over True Believers,
and for having entrusted the government of the Muslim Community to them, being as they are in secret Unbelievers and
Freethinkers?*

Harun al-Rashid passed this document on to Yahya. The
divine who wrote it was thrown promptly into prison.

* * *

In the year 175 al-Rashid had decided that his successor
should be his son Muhammad, to whom at that time he gave the

surname of Amin. The child was then only five years old; but his mother Zubayda was determined that he should be the heir.

I presented myself at the night audience once (says Asma'i), and I discovered al-Rashid in a state of great agitation, now sitting up, now lying down, and from time to time shedding tears. He kept muttering the verse:

Commit the weal of the Slaves of God to a man of single mind;
Nor let thyself be led astray by words from a shallow head.

And I felt sure that some important decision was weighing on his mind. It was not long before he bade the eunuch Masrur go fetch the Vizier.

When presently Yahya appeared, the Caliph said to him: Abu Fadl, the Apostle of God, God's Prayer and Peace be on him! died intestate; Islam was young then, and Faith was fresh; and yet the Arabs made no bones about deserting Abu Bakr — you know what happened. I want to appoint my successor, in my own lifetime. I want to appoint the one in whom I see good habits and respectable powers of action, the one whom I know capable of governing well. And that one is my son Abdallah. But my Hashimite kinsmen are all in favor of Muhammad (Amin), despite his being what he is, a mere slave to his own lusts and fancies, a spendthrift, the sharer of his thought with slaves — even with women. Yet, if I prefer Abdallah, I make the whole Hashimite house our foes. Tell me what you think, for your devices always have blessing on them, thank God for it!

The only mistake which cannot be corrected, Prince of the True Believers, said Yahya, is precisely a mistake in this very matter of the succession — error there is disastrous and irremediable. But looking into this affair demands some other place, and other company.

Al-Rashid, understanding that the Vizier wanted private speech with him, bade me go aside. I accordingly rose from my place and withdrew as far as the corner of the audience hall, where I sat down. However, from my corner I could gather what they were saying. They talked on and on. In fact, the discussion lasted the whole night; nor did the Caliph and the Vizier separate before it was settled that the succession should pass from Muhammad Amin not to any son of his but to Harun's son Abdallah.

Harun al-Rashid now gave Abdallah the surname Mamun, and appointed him Governor over all the northeastern provinces.

The Barmecide Tragedy

COURTIERS ARE LIKE travellers climbing a mountain height, who fall — the higher they get, the more certain to be fatal is the fall.

It was not till the year 187 of the Flight that al-Rashid brought the Barmecides to ruin. Various explanations have been given, accounting for their fall, the obvious grounds being their monopoly of the revenues and their ordering the release of a certain Alid (suspect of malignancy) whose confinement was entrusted to them; but the innermost reasons have never been known. Men say all kinds of things; only God really knows.

Certainly the Caliph at one time loved Ja'far so dearly that he ordered a robe cut with two collar-openings, so that they might both wear it together.

Ja'far, he said to him one day, in all the world there's not a creature dearer to me than thou, nor one whose company I more enjoy. Only my sister Abbasa sits so close to my heart. When I consider how I love you both, I find that I can no more do without thee than do without my sister. For when I am with her, I feel the lack of thee; and when I am with thee, I feel the lack of her. But now I have devised how I may have the joy of both your loves together.

God prosper the Prince of True Believers and direct his thought in all his counsels! responded Ja'far.

I intend to marry her to thee! announced the Caliph. Such a marriage will allow thee to be present when I spend an evening with her, to see her unveiled and be in her intimate company when I am also of the company. That must be all — there can be nothing more between you.

Ja'far accordingly renounced any real conjugal rights; and the marriage was arranged. But . . .

Men most deceive themselves, not one another.
Who can be ever utterly thy brother?

In the presence of the Caliph's eunuchs and some favorite freedmen, Ja'far had to swear before God, and bind himself with terrible oaths, never to visit his wife, never to be alone with her, never to be in the same house with her unless al-Rashid was also there. So sworn, he considered himself bound and contented himself: when they were in company, he avoided his wife's eye and kept his glance cast down for the Caliph's sake.

It was otherwise with Abbasa when she discovered how things were. She wrote to her husband. He drove away her messenger with abuse and threats; when she tried again, he did the same. Understanding at last that she was never to have what she wanted of him, she began to work on Ja'far's mother, a vain and stupid woman. She won her goodwill with sumptuous presents — jewels, huge sums of money, and the rest — until she was certain that she had made a slave of her, as devoted and as doting as a mother. Only then did she discover to the woman something of

her designs, representing the consequences to herself — the glory
of having a son bound to the Caliph by ties of blood — and persuading her that if her purpose came to pass, her own security and
Ja'far's were sure, nor need they ever after fear disgrace or loss
of favor.

Ja'far's mother believed it all. She promised to devise some
effective means, and leave nothing undone till they were brought
together.

One day she went to Ja'far's apartment. My son, she said,
I have heard of a girl in one of the palaces here who has been
brought up as if she were a princess: perfect breeding, perfect
education, perfect grace and charm. What's more, she is a most
lovely creature. Such a figure — such qualities — no one has ever
seen the like. I am going to buy her for thee; it is all settled between myself and the owner, or nearly settled.

Ja'far listened eagerly. He thought about the girl till he
thought of nothing else, while his mother, to whet his appetite,
kept him waiting. At last, when she felt sure, from his insistent
reminders that she keep her promise, that Ja'far was frantic with
impatience, she said: I have arranged to have her brought to thee
on such and such a night. And she sent to Abbasa to let her know.
The princess prepared herself duly, and went, on the evening
named, to the palace of Ja'far's mother.

That night Ja'far was drunk when he came away from al-
Rashid's Audience and repaired to his mother's house for the
meeting. As soon as he got there he asked for the girl; they told
him she had arrived. When Abbasa went to his room, he, far too
drunk to recognize her, mounted, and lay with her.

Is the lust of princesses to thy liking? she asked, when he
had had his fill.

What princesses? he answered.

I am thy mistress Abbasa daughter of Mahdi, she said.

Ja'far started up in horror, sober that instant. Going straight
to his mother, You've sold me cheap! he said. You've pushed me
to the brink of an abyss; and see for yourself how this will end!

Abbasa was pregnant when she left. She gave birth to a

boy, whom she committed to one of her eunuchs, with a waiting woman to be his nurse. Presently, afraid the affair would be known, she sent them both, with the child, to Mecca. And time passed by.

* * *

A copy of anonymous verses was brought and shown to al-Rashid. It ran:

Go to the trusted Slave of God
Whose dreadful power it is
To loose and bind here upon earth,
Go, and tell him this:

The royalty of Yahya's sons
With thine own compares.
They may question thy command;
None may question theirs!

Ja'far builds his hall as built
No foreigner before —
Amber and aloes for the roof,
Ruby and pearl for floor.

We think he'll have thy realm when thou
Art stowed safe in a grave,
Though he who vies with thee his lord
Is what? A puffed-up slave!

Out hunting one day with al-Rashid (says his cousin Isma'il), I was riding at his side; and the way led for a long while through some estate of Ja'far the Barmecide's. Ja'far and his own cavalcade had ridden ahead without waiting for us.

Look at these Barmecides! al-Rashid said suddenly; to make them rich we have made our own children poor.

By God, something's wrong! I thought to myself.

When I waited on the Caliph next day, I found him sitting

overlooking the Tigris bank, and gazing across the water towards
Ja'far's palace on the western side.

Do you see that? said al-Rashid. That crowd of troops and
slaves? all those cavalcades pressing round Ja'far's gate? And not
one waits at mine!

God save the Prince of True Believers! I cried; do not
think such thoughts. Ja'far is nothing but your servant and slave,
your Vizier and the commander of your troops. If soldiers are not
to stand at Ja'far's gate, at whose gate should they stand?

A little later Ja'far came over to wait on the Caliph. When
he went away, al-Rashid presented him with two of his own
private Attendants.

Three days later, I went to call on Ja'far. One of the two
slaves al-Rashid had given was standing in attendance, so I was
careful. Now the Caliph had recently appointed Ja'far Governor
of Khurasan, and had ordered him his banner and troops, and
very splendid insignia.

Ja'far, said I, the province you are going to is a very
prosperous and rich one. If I were you, I would make over one of
my estates here to some son of the Prince of the True Believers.

Your cousin the Caliph, Isma'il, he replied, lives on what I
give him. It is through us that his dynasty exists. Can he not be
satisfied that I have left him nothing to care or trouble about,
either for himself or his children, his attendance or his subjects?
that I have filled his Treasury and heaped up money for him?
Must he cast his eyes after what I have reserved for my son and
his posterity when I am gone? Why should I give way to the
envy and arrogance of the Hashimites, and have to worry about
money now?

For God's sake do not think like that! said I. The Caliph
has never said a word to me of any such matter.

Then what do you mean by talking like that? cried Ja'far.
Let him ask for any of these things and by God it will be the
worse for him!

After this, I kept away from Ja'far and al-Rashid both.
One is the Caliph and the other is a Vizier, I thought: why

should I meddle in the matter? But the Barmecides have had their day, I think.

The slave, I heard afterwards, repeated every word Ja'far had said to the Caliph.

One night in al-Rashid's saloon, relates the musician Ibrahim of Mosul (some say the story is his son Ishaq's), a song I sang was well received; and the Caliph bade me sing on. So on I sang, until he fell asleep, and then I stopped, laid aside my lute, and withdrew to sit in my usual place.

Suddenly a young man appeared, singularly handsome and well-made. He was dressed in a robe of light painted silk, and was extremely elegant. This youth came into the saloon, greeted me, and sat down. His arrival unannounced at such an hour, and in such a place, greatly puzzled me. It must be one of al-Rashid's sons, I thought; but it is one I never saw till now.

The young man fingered my lute for a few moments; then taking it up from where I had left it, laid it in his lap and tuned it, as accurately as any mere creature of God could tune it, but in a mode I did not recognize. Then, after a prelude more beautiful than any other prelude I ever heard, he sang a song, beginning:

Let's drain a cup or two together
Ere we go where we must. . . .

When the song was done, he threw aside the lute. Sing like that, bastard, if you must sing! he said; and with these words he left the room. I ran after him.

Who was that young man who went out just now? I demanded of the Chamberlain.

No one went either in or out, he answered.

But yes, I said, just now a man was here with me. And I described his appearance.

No, as God hears me, no one went either in or out, said the Chamberlain.

I was dumbfounded. When I went back to my seat, al-

Rashid was awake. What happened to you? he asked. So I told him my story; and he was exceedingly surprised.

I think you must have had a visit from the Devil himself, he said. Can you sing the air you heard?

I repeated the song. He seemed pleased with it, and ordered me a bounty before I left.

The Vizier Yahya, who acted as overseer of the Caliph's harem, had forbidden the Caliph's wives to choose particular favorites among the eunuchs for their service. He now ordered the harem doors locked at night, and the keys brought to himself.

This was the last straw to Zubayda, Harun al-Rashid's cousin and principal wife. She went straight to the Caliph.

Prince of the True Believers! she cried, what does Yahya mean by not letting my people do their service, and treating me in a manner degrading to my rank?

No one may complain of Yahya to me, said al-Rashid.

You and your Barmecides! exclaimed Zubayda; you are like a drunken man drowning in deep waters! If you were not so fuddled and waterlogged as you are, I could tell you a tale about Ja'far, not so pleasant in the hearing as other tales you may have heard. But if you are still besotted with your Barmecides, I will leave you alone.

What is it? he demanded.

Zubayda told him what Abbasa had done with Ja'far. Al-Rashid was speechless.

Hast thou proof of this? he said at last. Or any witness?

What proof clearer than the child? she retorted.

Where is the child?

He was here for a time, but she began to be afraid that all would come out, Zubayda said; so she sent him away to Mecca.

Does a single person besides thyself know about this? asked the Caliph.

There's not a woman in thy Palace but knows it! she said.

Al-Rashid said nothing more on the subject, and for some time dissembled his rage.

I was in attendance before al-Rashid one day (says the Attendant Ahmad), with no one else by. Perfumes were burning; and the air was thick with the sweet smoke. The Caliph had lain down, covering his head with the skirt of his cloak to keep his eyes from smarting, when Ja'far the Barmecide appeared. He told his business, got a favorable answer, and retired.

When he was gone, al-Rashid lifted his head; and from his lips these words came: O God, I pray Thee, either so favor Ja'far that he kill me, or grant me such sudden power over him that I may have his head from his body; for this anger and this jealousy are destroying me.

He was speaking to himself; but the words reached me. I began to shake all over. If he knows I heard, he will never leave me alive, I thought.

Suddenly lifting his head clear of the covering, he demanded: Didst hear?

I heard nothing, I said.

There's no one else about; but as sure as that censer's in thy hand, thou hast heard every word. If thou hast any regard for thy life, keep this secret.

God prolong the Prince of True Believers' days! I did not hear a word! I protested.

With this he seemed satisfied.

Vengeance becomes a matter of conscience with a Prince.

The Caliph announced that he intended to make the Pilgrimage that year, and bidding Ja'far attend him, took his departure for Mecca. Abbasa wrote at once to her eunuch and the nurse to take the child to Yaman. But at the Holy City al-Rashid set confidential agents to inquire about the child and the two servants. He discovered that the story was true.

Back from Pilgrimage, the Caliph spent only a little time in Baghdad, and then went over to Anbar on the Euphrates. On the day determined, he sent for one of his confidential agents and instructed him to go to Baghdad and make an inventory of the property of all the Barmecides, of all their Clerks, of all their children, and of all their relatives. He enjoined the strictest secrecy.

That day he himself passed with Ja'far in feasting and various pleasures, in the quarter of Anbar which is called the Convent. When Ja'far took leave, al-Rashid actually rose to walk out with him, and saw him mounted. Then he returned, seated himself on his throne, bade his people clear away what remains of the feast still lay about, and sent for the black eunuch Masrur.

Go to Ja'far son of Yahya at once, he said, and bring him here; tell him a despatch is just come from Khurasan. When he is inside the outer gate, post the guard there; and put slaves to keep the door to the Inner Apartments. Do not let any of his people in with him, but bring him in alone, and lead him aside to that Turkish tent I bade thee set up yesterday; when he is inside, take off his head and bring it to me here. And do not breathe a word of this order to a single creature. No questions! if there is any disobedience I will have thy head brought me along with his. That's all — begone! And make haste, before he hears anything from any other quarter.

So Masrur went off, and asked to be admitted to Ja'far, who was by this time undressed and had lain down to sleep.

The Prince of the True Believers sent me to summon thee to the Presence, said Masrur as he was ushered in. He was so insistent and imperious that I dared not but obey.

But I have only just left him, said Ja'far. What's the matter?

There are letters come from Khurasan which thou must read, answered Masrur.

So Ja'far dressed and put on his sword, and went back with him. As he passed the outer gate, he noticed the posting of the guard. Then he saw the slaves standing by the door to the

Inner Apartments. He turned round. None of his own people were behind; and his heart misgave him. But Masrur led him on to the tent, and told him to go inside and sit down. The tent, Ja'far saw, was empty.

Masrur! he whispered, my brother! What's the matter?

Ay, I'm thy brother, said the eunuch; and I'm thy guest to boot. But if thou ask me what's the matter — thou knowest well enough: thy time's come. The Prince of True Believers has told me to take him thy head, and without any delaying.

O my brother! O Masrur! cried Ja'far, weeping, and falling to kissing the eunuch's hands and feet; thou knowest how good I have ever been to thee, beyond any other Page, beyond any other man in the whole Household — I did thy asking always, day or night. Thou knowest how I stand with the Prince of True Believers, how he trusts me. Someone has told him lies about me. Here, I have two hundred thousand dinars: I give them to thee now. Only let me get away from this place!

I cannot do it, returned Masrur.

Then take me to him, set me before his face.

I cannot do it, said Masrur again. I dare not face him a second time before it's done. I know there's no chance for thee, not any chance at all.

Then just take a little time! Ja'far cried. Only go to him now and say: I have done thy bidding. See what he will say. Do as thou wilt after that. Only do that! and I take God to witness, and His Angels, I'll give thee the half of all I have. I'll make thee Commander in Chief of the Army. I'll give thee all I have!

So he went on, weeping and imploring, until at last Masrur said: Well, that might be managed. And taking Ja'far's sword and belt away from him, he called forty black slaves to watch the tent, and went to the Caliph.

Al-Rashid was sitting down, streaming with sweat. He was clutching a walking cane, and digging it into the ground. At the sight of Masrur he burst out: Be thy dam bereaved of thee! What hast thou done with Ja'far?

I have done thy bidding, Masrur said.

Then where's his head?

I left it in the tent.

Bring it here to me this instant.

Masrur went back to the tent. Ja'far was on his knees at prayer now. The eunuch made no delay, but drew his sword, and struck off Ja'far's head. Then, picking it up by the beard, he bore it off and threw it on the ground before the Caliph. The blood continued to drip out of it.

Al-Rashid gave a fearful sob, and burst into tears. Gnashing his teeth on the cane, he presently began to shout at the head, as it lay there, digging the cane into the ground with every word: O Ja'far! did I not make thee mine own peer? And O Ja'far! what requital did I get? Wrong! and a broken word! Ungrateful, insensate fool! Reckless of what must come when thy luck must turn, in the turning of time! Ja'far the traitor in my house! Ja'far my shame! O the sorrow thou hast brought on me, Ja'far! and on thyself! O Ja'far! Ja'far! Ja'far!

* * *

At a late hour that night (relates the poet and grammarian Asma'i), I received a summons to the presence of al-Rashid. When I entered, he said: Asma'i, I have composed a poem; I want you to hear it.

Pray let me hear it, Prince of the True Believers, I responded. He accordingly declaimed:

> *Had Ja'far feared death, a bridled steed*
> *Had borne him far.*
> *His hour was come: no wizard could have charmed*
> *His evil star.*

When I took leave and was on my way home from the Presence, the news of Ja'far's slaying was already in every mouth.

Immediately after Ja'far's death, his father the Vizier Yahya and his brother Fadl son of Yahya were arrested and closely confined. Of this time Fadl spoke in a famous verse:

Out of the World we went, still we were of the World,
Neither dead to the World nor living in the World;
And when our warder brings us what we must have to live,
We look on him in wonder, and think: He's one of the
World!

Khalil ibn Haytham, the warder in charge of the Barmecides, relates:

One day Masrur the Eunuch came to me. He had several slaves with him, one carrying a folded napkin; and I thought at first that al-Rashid had relented, and was sending them some present. Masrur told me to send for Fadl. When he arrived, Masrur said: The Prince of the True Believers bid me say this to thee: I called on thee for a full account of the property of thy family, and thou tellest me the whole is accounted for; but I am satisfied that there are large sums held back. Masrur has orders, if thou wilt not give him precise information on this head, to give thee two hundred lashes.

Now, Abu Abbas, Masrur went on, take my advice: don't set thy money above thy life.

Fadl lifted his head high. Abu Hashim, he replied, I have never told the Caliph a lie. The Prince of the True Believers knows as well as thou dost, that our family have always maintained reputation at the expense of wealth; how then today should we keep back our wealth at the expense of our lives? Execute thine orders, if thou hast any.

Unwrap! said Masrur. Out of the napkin fell a whip with a knotted lash. So fiercely did the slaves lay it on that Fadl looked as if he were dead when it was done. We gave him up for dead anyway.

Yahya ibn Khalid ibn Barmak died in prison in the year 189 of the Flight; and Fadl ibn Yahya died three years later.

Ja'far's head was gibbeted on the Bridge at Bagdad, and the Caliph proclaimed that any who wept for the Barmecides, or wrote elegies on them, should be gibbeted likewise.

*   *   *

I had business one day at the Treasury Office; and as my eye ran over one of the ledgers that lay open, I noticed the entry:

One Dress of Honor and Gubernatorial Insignia
           (Ja'far ibn Yahya) dinars 400,000.

It did not seem so very long after that I was in the Office again, and saw this item entered on the current page of the same ledger:

Naphtha and wood-shavings for burning body
           (Ja'far ibn Yahya) kirats 10.

*   *   *

The world's soft to the touch. So is the adder, so sudden in venom.

One day a man of the City Police, passing a deserted palace, saw a man standing there, with a paper in his hand. It was an elegy over the fall of the Barmecides; he was reciting it, and with tears. The policeman arrested him and took him to the Palace.

Al-Rashid allowed him to speak. He had been one of Yahya's Clerks, and told a tale of his patron's generosity which so moved the Caliph that he let the man go. Afterwards he granted a general permission to poets to write elegies on the Barmecides; and if anyone spoke ill of them in his presence, he would say: Enough of that, unless you can fill the void they left.

Presently he removed from Baghdad to Raqqa on Euphrates.

The accomplishment of an egoistic purpose is the key which opens a door into Hell.

Musalla's dreary now; I go to the Dunes no more;
Mirbadan's dull, and Labab,
And the Mosque where chivalry sat by piety;
Dull those great courts; and dull the gardens I haunted
I and the few gay friends — the flush of youth
And the elegance of high breeding.
The dolorous stroke of Time is fallen: they are departed
*   like Sheba's people,*
Scattered into far-away lands.
And the world will not renew them, for it cannot.
When I knew they were gone, that never again,
So long as I lived, would anyone return,
I kept a stiff lip in a style of my own: various pleasures
*   shared and devoured me.*
For the pain of loss ends all with me: it is over then
*   between me and my brother.*

* * *

A letter came to al-Rashid from the Roman Emperor, breaking off the truce which had been established between the Muslims and the Empress Irene. It was thus worded:

> *From Nicephorus the Roman Emperor to Harun Sovereign of the Arabs.*
>
> *Our Imperial Predecessor ranked thee as a rook and herself as a pawn, and therefore sent in tribute to thee load after load of her wealth. But that was the weakness of a woman and the folly of a woman.*
>
> *On receipt of this Our letter, thou art to return every penny of her wealth thou hast received; otherwise the sword shall make a settlement between Us and thee.*

As al-Rashid read through this letter, he grew so inflamed with rage that no one present dared so much as glance at his face, much less speak to him. His courtiers shrank away, his speechless Viziers ventured not one word of counsel.

An inkhorn! he cried; and instantly wrote on the back of the Emperor's missive:

> *IN THE NAME OF GOD THE MERCIFUL THE COMPASSIONATE:*
>
> *From Harun, Prince of the True Believers, to Nicephorus the Roman dog.*
>
> *I have read thy letter, thou son of an Unbelieving mother. Thou shalt see, not hear, my answer.*
>
> *Farewell.*

And he took the field that very day. Nor did he call a halt until he was at Heraclea where the famous battle was fought. It was a victory for the Believers so decisive that Nicephorus, imploring peace, engaged to pay tribute annually. The offer was accepted. But when al-Rashid was got back to Raqqa, the dog, fancying the Caliph's return that winter impossible, violated his engagement. No one dared tell the Caliph of the violation until

Abu Atahia wrote some verses on the subject; and these were
shown him.

Hath he really done that? exclaimed al-Rashid, and marching immediately back, he did not spare for hardship but held on
until he made his camel kneel down for dismounting in the
Emperor's very court. He took no rest until his purpose was
attained, and his Holy Warfare accomplished. In the year 190 he
took Heraclea; and his troops spread far and wide over the
Roman territories.

* * *

When the Vizier Yahya died in prison, a paper was found
on his body, written: *The plaintiff is gone on, but the accused
will not be far behind, for the Judgment of that Just Judge Who
erreth not, Who needeth no witness.*

This paper was brought and shown to the Caliph.

THE FEARFUL DREAM

Once when I waited on al-Rashid at Raqqa (says Gabriel
the Physician), finding him much distempered, scarce able to
open his eyes, or to move his limbs, I inquired the cause.

I have had a dream, said al-Rashid: I fancied that an arm
with a hand (I knew it, but I could not remember whose it was)
thrust out from under my bed, and showed me in the open palm
a little red earth. Then a voice, the voice of somebody I could not
see, spoke: This is the soil of the place thou art to be buried.
I asked: What place is that? The voice answered: Tus. Then
it was gone, and I awoke.

I assured him that this dream only arose from a disordered
stomach, and from overmuch worry concerning that rebellion
which had broken out in the eastern provinces. I prescribed
rest and recreation; and before long I supposed the matter forgotten.

THE LAST JOURNEY

That revolt, the rebellion of Rafi son of Layth in Khurasan, spread over all the region of Transoxiana; and at last al-Rashid himself took the field.

When al-Rashid marched for Khurasan (says Sabah Tabari), I rode with him as far as Nahravan, and had occasional conversation with him by the way.

Sabah, he said to me one day, I do not think that after this thou wilt ever see me again.

Nay, the Lord bring the Prince of True Believers safe again! I responded.

I do not think thou knowest how it is with me, he insisted.

No, certainly, I answered.

Come where I can show thee, said al-Rashid; and he turned out of the road, signing to the Attendants to keep back. God's Faithfulness bind thee to keep my secret, Sabah, he said; and then uncovered his stomach. Bound tight about his stomach was a silken bandage.

I have not told a soul I am sick, said he; for each one of my sons hath a spy set upon me. Masrur is Mamun's secret agent; Gabriel the Physician is Amin's; I do not know who the other is. There's not one of my children but counts my breathings and reckons the days I still have to run, and feels I have lived too long already. Wilt thou see the proof? I will call for a horse presently, and thou wilt see: they'll bring me some rawboned nag whose gaits will make my sickness worse.

And he ordered a fresh horse. They brought him just such a beast as he had described. He gave me one look; then mounted, and bade me farewell, and took the road for the North.

On the way his malady grew worse. The physicians paid little attention to it. At last the Caliph sent to the next town for a Persian practitioner. That town was Tus. Several samples of urine, including that of the Caliph, were taken to the man for examination; and on examining al-Rashid's he said: Tell the man whose water this is that it is all over with him, and he should make his will — there is no cure for him. When they told the Caliph of this prognostication, he broke down and wept, tossing his body to and fro.

A rumor that he was dead actually got about, and he heard of it. At once he called for a riding-ass and tried to mount. But his legs hung down slack, and he could not hold up in the saddle.

Help me down, he muttered; those who thought the worst were right.

His camp lay in a garden in one of the villages which surrounded Tus. One day he suddenly staggered to his feet, apparently in great distress; but he was too weak to stand, and fell to the ground again. As his wives and Attendants crowded round him, his eye sought out Gabriel ibn Bakhtishu.

Remember? he said; that dream I dreamed at Raqqa, the dream about Tus?

Then raising his head a little, he looked for Masrur. Bring me some of the soil of this garden, he said.

Masrur returned with a little of the garden soil in his open palm, and held it out to al-Rashid.

That's the hand! that's the arm! he shrieked out; the dream! this is the red earth!

And he utterly broke down, weeping and sobbing like a little child.

He commanded that several shrouds be brought and shown him, and chose one for himself. Then he bade dig a grave for him. When it was ready he went out to see it; and as he looked into it recited: *MY WEALTH HATH NOT AVAILED ME; MY POWER IS GONE FROM ME.*

But before he died, the brother of Rafi, the rebel against whom he was marching, was brought captive into camp. The Caliph sent for him.

'Tis thou hast driven me and brought me down to this, he said; and by God I will slay thee with such a slaying as never man was slain withal!

And he had the man's members hacked off one by one.

At the last he called for a thick blanket, and ordered it spread over his body-servant Sahl. Presently he had a paroxysm of pain. Sahl jumped up.

Lie down again, Sahl, said al-Rashid; I do not want thy tendance. But after a while he called out: Sahl! Where are you?

Here, lying down, his servant answered, but my heart won't let me rest for all that.

Al-Rashid gave a laugh. Sahl, said he, in a time like this a man must remember what the poet said:

> *Come as I am of a proud race.*
> *I can show Fate a stony face.*

And that was the last thing said by Harun al-Rashid.

*   *   *

Get sons — for Death! Build high — for Ruination!
March on — this road goes to Annihilation!

THE BROTHERS' WAR

When al-Rashid went on Pilgrimage in 186, he had taken his sons Amin and Mamun with him, and had the Act of Succession naming them and appointing Mamun to succeed Amin engrossed and posted on the Holy House.

I was on Pilgrimage that year (says a man of Basra); and people talked a great deal about the Proclamation, and the Oath of Loyalty taken before the Holy House. On my way home, I overtook a clansman of Hudhayl. As he led his camel along, he was singing this:

> *That loyalty will dwindle with days;*
> *That jealousy will kindle to a blaze!*

What's that? I cried.

That? said he. That means swords will be drawn, and the realm torn.

How so?

Look at the beast! said he. He stands idle while two men argue. And look yonder — two crows wallowing in blood! The end can be strife and sorrow only.

The Caliph's thrown that among his sons which will work them woe, and that among his people which will work them havoc.

L-RASHID BEING DEAD, and his son Mamun at Merv in Khurasan as Governor, the Prince Salih sent one of Amin's freed eunuchs to give Amin the news. The eunuch took the Insignia — the Prophet's Cloak and Staff and Ring — and rode post to Baghdad, which he reached in twelve days.

Amin's first act as Caliph was to order the levelling of a piece of ground near the old Palace of Mansur for a polo field.

The Treasury balance at al-Rashid's death showed one hundred million gold dinars, and furniture, jewelry, bullion, and livestock to the value of a hundred and twenty-five thousand dinars.

Amin bought eunuchs — wherever he could get them. He kept them about him day and night: at table, at drinking parties, even when transacting State business; and he would have nothing to do with women in matters of pleasure, either free or slave. He used to call his white eunuchs his grasshoppers, and his black ones his ravens.

When Zubayda saw how passionate was Amin's addiction to these Pages, and how absolute a hold they had over him, she selected a number of young girls, in face and figure unusually seductive. Then, putting on them turbans of the brocade used for the royal liveries, curling their hair and binding it in a hairnet behind, as the Page-boys wore their curls, and fitting them with close-girt tight tunics which made the most of their curves, she sent them as a gift to her son.

As they filed before Amin, their charms prevailed, and from that day on he took pleasure in the embraces of women.

In his second year, he removed his brother Qasim from the Government of Iraq, to which al-Rashid had appointed him. When Mamun heard of this deposition, he cut off all communication with the Caliph, omitted his name from the border-inscriptions of official Dresses of Honor, and dropped his title from the coinage minted in Khurasan.

FADL

A typical border-inscription,
from an official Dress of Honor:
IN THE NAME OF GOD. God's Blessing on God's Slave al-Amin Muhammad, Prince of the True Believers, whom may God long preserve. This is of his ordering from the State Factory of Dresses of Honor in Egypt, by agency of Fadl son of Rabi, Freedman Client of the Prince of the True Believers.

Fadl son of Rabi was now Vizier; it was he who according to report suggested to Amin that he annul the succession of Mamun, and name his own infant son Musa his successor. It was not long after Qasim's removal that Amin sent to Mamun desiring him to yield the succession to Musa, on whom, he stated, he had bestowed the title Proclaimer of the Truth.

The following verse by a Baghdad wit went round:

The Caliph's goings-on are queer,
And queerer those of the Vizier;
Queerer than either ours! We swear
Allegiance to a little dear
Who's not yet left his nurse's lap,
And can't yet wipe his little rear!

Mamun rejected Amin's demand; whereupon Amin sent for the Act of Succession which al-Rashid had deposited in the Holy House and tore the document to pieces.

Mamun was now assured that his right of succession was set aside. He promptly assumed the title of Prince of the True Believers himself, and was accordingly addressed by those about him. Against Amin's general he despatched his own officer Tahir, who defeated and killed his adversary and sent his head to Mamun.

When the news reached Baghdad, the populace raised a great tumult, and all the Amirs (or military Princes) sent the troops they commanded to claim arrears of pay from the Caliph.

THE SIEGE OF THE CAPITAL

TAHIR, MARCHING ON, encamped first at Hulwan, five days' march from Baghdad. Here he scattered the force Amin sent against him; and the Caliph soon found himself surrounded by enemy troops, both east and west of the City, Mamun's officer Harthama lying encamped on the Nahravan side near the Khurasan Gate and the Three Gates while Tahir beset the western suburbs from Yasiria to the Gate of Unlading and the City Dump. Two of the military Princes Amin sent against Harthama went over to the enemy, with their whole forces.

I went one day to visit Amin (relates his uncle Ibrahim, son of Mahdi by a negress, and one of the most famous musicians of his time). It was when the blockade had closed round him. At first the Attendants refused me admittance, and I had to take a high tone to force my way in. Amin I found staring through the grill at the river — in the Palace there was a large pool fed from the Tigris through a conduit fitted with an iron grill. I saluted him. But he went on staring at the river; his Attendants and Pages were groping about in the pool. I thought he must be out of his mind. When I bowed and greeted him a second time, he only replied: Didn't you know, Uncle? my Collar-Fish has got out of the pool into the river! (He gave the name of his Collar-Fish to a fish which had been caught young and which he had had decked with a double bangle of gold, with great rubies set in it.)

I walked straight out, and gave him up for lost. If he ever were going to get over his imbecility (I thought), surely he would have grown up at a time like this!

Amin now took half a million dirhams from the Treasury and distributed it. But he only gave to his newly-appointed officers, to each of whom he also presented by way of compliment a vial of precious perfume; to his veteran officers he gave nothing.

Tahir's spies informed him of this. He at once entered into correspondence with the offended parties. By threat and promise, by inciting subalterns against their superiors, he managed to fan resentment into active mutiny. When the mutiny broke out, a poet said:

Tell the Vicar of God, as he calls himself,
That some bottles of scent have scattered his host!

Tahir immediately moved in from Yasiria to the Anbar Gate and pressed the siege. The fighting went on day and night. Great buildings and monuments were ruined. Food became outrageously dear. Brother fought brother, son struck at father, as one or another backed Amin or Mamun. Houses came crashing down; palaces went up in flames; property became a thing of memory.

One of her attendant eunuchs relates how Amin's mother
Zubayda went to her son in tears. He shouted at her: Stop it!
Women's howling and women's horrors won't save a throne! A
breast for suckling babies won't shelter the Caliphate — it's a government! Get out! Get out!

Harthama now sent a force to occupy the Kalwadha neighborhood. He began to levy tithes on all merchandise coming up
to Baghdad by boat from Basra and Wasit, and proceeded to
place his engines for the bombardment of the City. The sufferings he caused the inhabitants were such that sorties were sent out
against him recruited from vagabonds and prisoners taken out of
the gaols.

These fellows fought almost naked, a man having no more
than short breeches and a girdle, a helmet of palm fiber, a palm-
leaf buckler, and a club of matted rushes, tarred, and stuffed with
gravel and sand. The nude officers were mounted pickaback on
other nudes.

Crowds of inquisitive people came out to watch the naked
fellows do battle, against well-mounted foes equipped with cui-
rass and hauberks, brassarts and lances, and shields of Tibetan
hide. At first the Nudes had the best of it, but when Harthama
sent reinforcements they were thrown into disorder: the human
steeds tossed off their riders, and the whole mob of Nudes was
driven in. The sword took its toll not only of them but also of
the spectators who had come out merely to watch them fight.

Amin, desperate for money, had his gold and silver plate
melted down and coined; and he doled out pay from that source.
Tahir was now master of Harbia and the other suburbs adjoining
the Anbar, Harb, and Qutrabbul Gates. The fight raged in the
very heart of the West Side; and engines of war made havoc of
the quarters occupied by both parties. The City of Peace (so it
had been called) was now a scene of conflagration and ruin; the
glories of Baghdad were a thing of the past. Its inhabitants, fleeing in desperation from the streets and lanes where they had

dwelt, roamed homeless from one place to another; and panic was general. For fourteen months the struggle went on. The citizens had houses no longer, the Mosques were deserted and the public prayers abandoned.

What the high would not defend, the fists of the low struck fiercely down.

God's Justice bursts on His creatures, the Reckoning for their sins,
And man destroys himself: there are only the bitter losers, the cruel winners.
Every great man fights for himself; every bad man would be great.
The wolves have tasted blood, and they come on. It is too late for fear.

At a great battle in the Slave-Barrack district on the West Side, the slaughter was so enormous that every road and street and alley and lane was choked with corpses. Still they set on, yelling: Hi! for Mamun! and Hi! for the Deposed! Every house in the neighborhood was pillaged and fired.

I spoke to one who lay deadly wounded and dying:
Alas for thee! who art thou, poor fighter for Amin?
I for Amin? said he: I fought for nothing — not kin
Nor country nor opinion, I fought not for my faith,
Not even for cash in hand. I fought, but it was for nothing.

Amongst all these horrors, any man or woman, young or old, who got away alive to Tahir's camp with anything that could be saved, counted himself blest beyond compare. Of the troops defending Amin there now remained none but the naked rapscallions with their palm-leaf and rush-mat armor. Tahir, pressing his advantage, occupied one street after another; and as each passed into his hands, its inhabitants declared for the victorious party. Meanwhile his engines poured destruction on the quarters which still held out. Trenches were dug among the ruins of the houses and inns and palaces. As Tahir's men piled ruin on ruin, Amin's partisans found shelter under remnants of lumber and canvas and such scraps of wreckage, until their resolution, amidst collapse and conflagration and slaughter, prompted Tahir to cut off entirely all supplies from Basra and Wasit, and to block all the roads. As a result, while a silver dirham would buy twenty pounds of bread in a street occupied by Mamunis, in Amin's district a dirham would buy only a single pound.

Amin began to feel the pinch himself. He sent for one of his officers and charged him: Take levy of anyone at all who has any money or any valuables, whether they're citizens or whether they're foreigners; arrest anyone even if you only know by hearsay that they have anything. He attached another fellow to assist the man, and the pair of them fell upon the citizens. Mere suspicion was grounds enough; and they actually collected a good deal of money. But people, especially those of the propertied classes, now deserted the City in crowds, passing out on pretext of making the Pilgrimage.

So brutally were even women of the most respectable families treated by the Caliph's officers that a meeting of the merchant associations was held in the Karkh quarter for the purpose of sending a written message to Tahir to explain that only force kept the citizenry in Baghdad.

One of those present, however, pointed out that any correspondence with Tahir would only give Amin pretext for further brutality. There is no way out, he ended; there is only God.

When Tahir moved his camp into the garden by the Anbar

Gate, the plight of Amin became absolutely desperate: he held nothing now beyond the walls of the old Round City of Mansur.

The Caliph called a consultation to consider means of escape. Every man urged some plan of his own.

Write to Tahir, said one; give him suitable assurances and promise to put your kingdom and authority in his hands (as Vizier). He might accept.

Bereave thy dam! what a fool I was to ask thee! exclaimed Amin. He is incapable of treason, I know that: he cares for nothing but doing things which will make him famous.

However, he sent a message to Harthama, the other general, with protestations of personal regard; and Harthama promised him protection against any attempt on his life. When Tahir heard of this, he was highly indignant; nor did his anger abate until Harthama promised to turn Amin over prisoner to Tahir on his arrival. The deposed Caliph was to be brought by boat from a quay by the Khurasan Gate.

On the night which Amin had chosen for his escape, a band of his adherents presented themselves before him.

Prince of the True Believers, they said, among your intimates you have not one loyal man; but here are we, seven thousand of us, soldiers, and you have seven thousand horses in your stables. Let every man take a horse; and this very night let us open one of the Gates and get away from the City. They cannot stop us in the dark; and by tomorrow morning we shall be in Upper Iraq. Once there, you collect money and men, you march through Syria, you get safe to Egypt. In Egypt you call in more troops, more money; and you head a cause again.

By God, there's a plan! cried Amin.

And he made up his mind to try it. But among the Pages were some in Tahir's pay who sent him hourly reports of what went on in the Palace. So Tahir got wind of the plan at once. He was alarmed, for he knew that such an attempt might well succeed. He immediately sent this message to three of the courtiers: Unless you put a stop to this plan, I demolish your houses, ravage all your estates, confiscate your fortunes, and take your lives. The three courtiers hurried to the Caliph without loss of time, and succeeded in persuading him to give up the whole enterprise.

Harthama now appeared at the quay nearest the Khurasan Gate; he was in a skiff. Amin ordered his mare, a black with white socks and blaze, called Zuhayri, and sent for his two sons, Musa and Abdallah. He clasped them in his arms and held their faces to his own. God guard you for me! he said, weeping; I don't know if I shall ever be with you again.

Then he rode away, with a torchbearer walking before him. He was wearing a white dress, and a black hood pulled over his head. When he reached the quay, there was the skiff waiting for him. He dismounted, and slashed the hocks of his mare. Harthama, coming forward to meet him, kissed him between the eyes.

Meanwhile, Tahir, who had got word of the Caliph's flight, had sent several barges full of men to row out on the stream beyond. Harthama had only a few of his people with him. As soon as the skiff put off from shore, Tahir's men stripped, dived under it, and capsized it, tipping everyone in the skiff into the river. It was all Harthama could do to save his own life by catching at one of the barges and clambering aboard. He was put ashore and returned to his camp on the eastern bank.

As for Amin, he tore off his clothes and swam away till he was near the Sarat Canal, then came ashore. One of Tahir's equerries had his quarters here; and a groom, noticing that the fugitive smelt of musk and perfumes, laid hands on him and brought him before his superior. The equerry sent to Tahir for further orders.

Amin's freedman Ahmad had been with him in the skiff when it upset. He saved himself by swimming, but was captured and hauled aboard by one of Tahir's men, who would have killed him had he not bought his captor off by promising him ten thousand dirhams in the morning if he were spared.

They took me (says this Ahmad) into a very dark room. It was not long before someone else came in — a man half-naked, with no garment but his underdrawers, a turban pulled over his face, and some ragged scrap about his shoulders. The people of the house were told to keep a good watch over us, and we were left alone. Presently the other man pulled away the turban from his face: it was the Caliph, Muhammad Amin! The tears came into my eyes. *VERILY GOD'S WE ARE AND TO GOD IS OUR RETURNING!* I exclaimed.

He looked at me. Are you one of them? he asked.

I am your freedman, my lord, said I.

Which one?

Ahmad son of Sallam.

I know you; I saw you before; you were in the boat, said the Caliph.

Yes, said I.

After a few moments, Here, Ahmad! he cried.

Here I am, my lord, I said.

Come closer; put your arms round me — I feel horribly frightened.

So I took him in my arms — I could feel the pounding of his heart. After a while he spoke again: Tell me — my brother Mamun: is he still alive?

How could all this fighting be if he were not? I answered.

God punish them! they told me he was dead, said the Caliph.

Ay, God punish those Viziers of yours, said I; it was they brought you down to this.

No more of that, Ahmad! he returned. Speak well of my Viziers. I am not the first who took on more than he could manage.

Wrap yourself in my shawl, I begged him; take off those rags.

No, Ahmad, he answered. These things are good enough for a man in my place.

There was an interval; then he spoke again: They must take me before my brother Mamun — I feel sure of that; will my brother order my death, do you think?

Surely not! I cried. He'll surely spare his own flesh and blood!

He sighed. They say Royalty hath neither bairn nor bowels, he murmured.

Harthama promised safe-conduct, and your brother will surely give you safe-conduct, I said. Then I urged him to recite the Prayer of Recollection and the Prayer for Pardon. While we were praying together, the door opened, and an armed man came in. He looked into the Caliph's face, a long hard look; and having made sure of knowing him, went out again, locking the door behind him. It was the Tahirid Muhammad; and I knew then that the man with me was as good as dead. All I could think of was to recite the Late Night-Prayer; and thinking I might not have time to finish before they killed me too, I stood up to begin.

Ahmad! Amin called out, don't go away from me — say your prayers close by me; I feel horribly afraid again!

So I came closer. A few moments later we heard the tramp of horses. There was a knocking on the door. Then it was thrown open, and there stood a gang of Persians with drawn swords. At the sight, Amin stood up.

The murderers hesitated on the doorsill, telling one another to go on, and pushing one another forward. Amin was grasping a cushion in his hand.

I'm the cousin of God's Apostle! he screamed; I'm the son of al-Rashid! I'm Mamun's brother! O my God! God will require my blood of you!

One of them, a freedman of Tahir's, advanced on him and aimed a blow with his sword at the top of the Caliph's head. Amin, dashing the cushion in his face, sprang on him, and snatched for the sword.

He's killing me! He's killing me! yelled the man, in Persian. His fellows ran up, and one of them thrust his sword into Amin's side. Then they threw him face down, cut his throat from behind, and hacked away the head, which they bore off to present to Tahir.

One of Amin's eunuch concubines, Kawthar, was caught later that night: he had with him the Ring of the Prophet, the Cloak, the Sword, and the Staff. Next morning the Caliph's head, by order of Tahir, was displayed over the Iron Gates in East Baghdad. The carcass was buried in a garden hard by.

Afterwards the head, wrapped in stuff soaked with resin, was sent to Mamun in Khurasan. When it was shown him, he shuddered and burst into tears.

Prince of the True Believers! cried Fadl son of Sahl to him, Glory be to God for this exceeding favor! Surely the Apostle of God, God's Prayer and Peace on him! would be well pleased if he could see thee now, set as it has pleased God to set thee!

Mamun had the head impaled on a stake and set up in his courtyard. Then he mustered his troops for a distribution of bounty. Each man, as he took his money, was ordered to curse the head: all obeyed the order.

When one man, a Persian, who had stepped forward to be paid, was told: Curse the head! he cried out: God curse him! and may He curse his sire and his dam and all their brood to boot! and may He stuff them up their mothers' - - - -s!

There was an outcry: Thou hast cursed the Prince of the True Believers along with the rest!

But Mamun merely smiled, as if he thought nothing of it. However, he had the head removed, and forbade any mention of the deposed Caliph. The head, embalmed, and packed in a basket, was sent back to Iraq and buried with the carcass.

On the death of Amin, a poet wrote:

Why should I weep you? Because you were silly?
And giddy? and infinitely vain?
Because you forgot the five hours of Prayer
In a lust of thirst for the drink forbidden?
Why should we mourn you? For leaving us naked
To engines of war and to pillage?

But afterwards in the day of dispute and persecution on the doctrinal question of the Createdness or the Eternity of the Koran, the great Doctor of the Law Ahmad ibn Hanbal said:

I am confident that the Lord will be Merciful unto Amin for the sake of his repudiation of Isma'il son of Ulayya when he was brought before him; for the Caliph said: Is it thou, thou son of a whore, that sayest that the Koran's created, and not uncreate out of all Eternity?

INTELLIGENCE

I would rather win an argument than win a battle, said Mamun. There is no pleasure keener than observing the workings of the human mind; and those discussions are best which afford insight into men.

How unpleasant is ambition in a prince! but worse than that is strong feeling in a judge who has not yet mastered a case; and even worse is the merely superficial religiousness of jurists. Worst of all are money-mindedness in the rich, frivolity in the old, laziness in the young, and cowardice in the military.

A fellow will bring me some wooden thing, Mamun said once: perhaps only a stick — it is never anything worth more than a dirham. He tells me: The Apostle of God held this in his hand; or: Out of this the Prophet one time drank; or: He once touched this. And without any guarantee or proof of authenticity, out of sheer love and reverence, I accept the thing. And I give the fellow a thousand dinars or so. Afterwards I will lay it to my face or eye, hoping to be cured of some illness or other. And yet it is nothing but a bit of wood, quite incapable of doing any good, without the slightest virtue except the Prophet's touch — alleged.

 WAS MAMUN'S TUTOR WHEN
HE WAS A CHILD (says Yazidi).
One day when I went to him, he was
in privacy; so I told an Attendant to
inform him I was come. He kept me
waiting. I sent in again. He still kept
me waiting. I sent in again; and still he
kept me waiting.

This young man is very much addicted to frivolity, I observed to the company.

That he is, said they; and what's more, he is always in a
bad temper when his lesson is over, and his Attendants have to
suffer. You should correct him.

When Mamun appeared at last, I ordered him brought
before me, and administered seven strokes of the whip. He was
still rubbing the tears into his eyes when the Attendants called out
announcing: Ja'far ibn Yahya! The boy took a kerchief and dried
his eyes, then gathered up his skirts, went to his own carpet, and
sat down cross-legged. After a few moments, he said: Let him
come in.

Ja'far the Barmecide entered. I expected Mamun to complain about me, and sat down apart from the company. Ja'far
walked up to him, and talked with him a while, until at last he
made him laugh. Then he took leave. I came forward again.

I was expecting you to complain of me to Ja'far, said I.
Why, Abu Muhammad, I would not tell my father al-

Rashid about it, he replied; why should I tell Ja'far? Indeed, I need correction.

Even in youth Mamun applied himself to learning. He summoned jurists from all quarters, and became an expert jurist himself. In his maturer years he went deeply into philosophy, and into all the sciences of the ancients.

Philosopher is a Greek word, meaning: *lover of wisdom.* Mamun as Caliph sent envoys to the Emperor of Byzantium with the object of having all the Greek scientific works translated into Arabic. From that time on, such Muslims as concerned themselves with speculative knowledge applied themselves to the study of those Greek sciences. Of all philosophers, the most profound and the most celebrated was Aristotle, called the Prime Instructor; but the Muslims carried their investigations so far as to be able to refute a number of his opinions.

Many applied themselves to mathematics and its dependent sciences, such as astrology. The first Greek geometrical treatise, the Elements of Euclid, had already been translated in Mansur's reign. Aristotle's work on Physics, the science of bodies, of motion and rest, was translated in Mamun's time. Galen's writings on Medicine served as manual to all subsequent physicians. Magic and the science of talismans had been studied among the Assyrians and Chaldeans, and among the Egyptian Copts.

Muhammad ibn Musa and his brothers also attracted translators even from distant countries by the offer of liberal bounty; and they too brought the marvels of science into Muslim knowledge. Geometry, engineering, the action of the heavenly bodies, music, and astronomy were the principal subjects to which they gave attention; but these were only a few of their acquirements.

In these days the Clerk Abdallah Nashi, for example, the author of many beautiful poems, including that which begins:

Old homes of all we loved, have ye voice to soothe sore longing?

Not a sound returns. But the silence speaks — how complete an answer!

wrote a single ode of four thousand verses all ending in the same rhyme — *na* — in which he reviewed the various philosophic and religious systems, the different sects and their tenets. He also composed other voluminous works in verse upon the various sciences.

It was such studies which ultimately led Mamun to promulgate the doctrine of the createdness of the Koran (of which more hereafter).

Of all the Abbasid House, no more intelligent man was ever Caliph.

Mamun loved chess. This whets the mind! he used to say; and he was the originator of certain plays.

Don't let me hear you say: Let's have a game! It must be: Let's have a fight! he would say. But for all that he was no champion player, and often exclaimed: I have to manage the world, and I am equal to the task; but managing two spans square is too much for me!

THE SECT OF ALI

A year after his accession, a powerful faction rose in Iraq supporting the claim to the Caliphate of the Alid Muhammad ibn Ibrahim; another Alid, Muhammad ibn Sulayman, broke into rebellion at Madina; at Basra two others, Ali ibn Muhammad and Zayd ibn Musa, made themselves masters of the city. That same year another Alid raised Yaman against the government; and next year Mecca and Hijaz revolted under the Alid Muhammad ibn Ja'far, nicknamed Beau Brocade for his beauty and graceful accomplishments. This last proclaimed himself the Imam and assumed the title of Prince of the True Believers.

One should postpone the use of force as long as possible, was one of the maxims of Mamun. The Caliph was notoriously sympathetic with the Sect of Ali.

In that year, the two-hundredth from the Flight, he sent

envoys to Ali Riza, great-great-great-grandson of Husayn, to escort him in honor to the court at Merv, for Mamun had not moved the seat of government to Iraq. The Caliph gave him an affectionate welcome and proceeded to call the chief men of the State to council.

He had, he informed the council, held a census and review of all living descendants of Abbas and of Ali. Among all those members of the Prophetic House then alive he had found none more fit for authority over the Muslims than Ali Riza. In pursuance, he declared Ali Riza his heir in the Caliphate. Mamun now had gold and silver coinage struck in Ali Riza's name, gave his daughter in marriage to Ali Riza's son, abolished black as the official color for robes and banners, and established green as the Caliphal livery instead.

When news of all this reached Iraq, the Abbasids were infuriated to see themselves thus excluded from power. There were counted in the census thirty-three thousand lineal descendants of the Prophet's uncle, male and female; and every man of Abbasid descent, with his freedmen and retainers, now pronounced Mamun deposed, and took the oath of allegiance to Ibrahim son of Mahdi, whom they proclaimed Caliph.

In the year 203, however, Ali Riza died — of eating poisoned grapes, it is said. Mamun himself recited the Funeral Prayer over him.

IBRAHIM SON OF MAHDI IN BAGHDAD

In Baghdad there was a period of wild disorder. The mob, the criminal classes, and the soldiery fell upon peaceful citizens and travellers, robbed them of their goods, and sold the booty openly in the markets. Magistrates being powerless either to restrain the outrage or give redress, the pious and propertied united to put a stop to it. An ascetic or Dervish named Khalid who appeared calling on all True Believers to re-establish order had a great following, and fought, beat, and punished the banditry. Shortly afterwards, one Sahl, a member of a Helper family, appeared with a Koran hung at his neck, summoning people to put an end to violence and act according to the Book of God and the True Way of the Prophet. Hashimites of all ranks supported him; he made his headquarters in the Tahir Palace, set up recruiting offices, and patrolled the City, forbidding the citizens to pay blackmail for protection.

When on one occasion Khalid the Dervish observed to him that he in no wise blamed the Sovereign for what had happened, Sahl replied: As for me, I'll fight any man who goes against the Book and the True way, be he Sovereign or any other.

Ibrahim ibn Mahdi's soldiers finally captured him; and he barely got off with his life.

One cannot make God's cause triumph without God's help.

* * *

When at last Mamun marched on Baghdad, Ibrahim went into hiding. He lay low in the Ghalib Market quarter. The Caliph gave orders for his arrest; and one night, four years later, a negro policeman arrested him in Long Street, disguised in a woman's dress and attended by two maids.

Mamun spared his life, but ordered that the female habiliments in which he had been arrested should be left on him, and that the prisoner should be exhibited to the public gaze in that dress at the guardroom by the Palace Gate. After a few days of such exposure, the Prince was taken back into the Caliph's good graces.

One of the pleasant stories told of Ibrahim during the time that he was roaming the City incognito is the tale of his adventure with the barber. Not only were Mamun's agents out after him, but a large reward had been offered for any information as to his place of retreat.

About noon one summer day (says Ibrahim), I left my hiding-place, and wandered aimlessly on till presently I found myself in a blind alley. Seeing a man, a negro, standing before one of the doors of the adjacent houses, I went up to him and asked if he would let me shelter from the heat a while in some corner of his place.

Certainly, said he; and threw open the door. I went in. The negro showed me into a room with carpets and cushions, very pleasant and clean. He then excused himself, shut the door on me, and went away. A suspicion darted through me: this fellow had heard of the price on my life and was gone to sell me. But while I was still pondering uneasily, he returned, followed by a porter bearing an ample supply of bread and meat, a new chafing-dish, and some crockery.

I am, my life your ransom, a barber-surgeon, said he; and I know how unsavory you must think my trade. So pray make use of these things: I have not touched anything of them.

I was feeling very hungry; so I rose and cooked myself something; and I never ate food that tasted better.

And now, said he when I had done, what is your feeling in the matter of date-wine?

I have no objections! said I.

Thereupon he did as he had done with the food, and set before me a brand-new drinking service, which he had never used.

And now, he continued, do you permit, my life your ransom, that I sit in your presence, and drink your health? I will fetch myself some more wine.

Pray be seated, said I. When he had drunk three cups, he went to a closet and produced a lute.

My lord, said he, it is not for one of my condition to ask you to sing. But I may appeal to you as a client to a patron: if you could be pleased to sing something, your slave would be ennobled by your condescension.

How do you know I am such a singer? I demanded.

God and His Praise! he exclaimed: you are far too famous to be unknown to me — you are Ibrahim son of Mahdi, for whose whereabouts Mamun has offered a hundred thousand dirhams reward!

At that, I took up the lute and tuned it. As I was about to sing, he interposed: My lord, would you be good enough to sing something of my choosing?

I assented. He promptly named three pieces in the execution of which I was unrivalled.

Know me by all means! I cried; but how do you come to have heard of those particular songs?

I used to be in the service of Ishaq son of Ibrahim of Mosul, he replied. Many's the time I've heard him talk about the great masters of music and their personal repertoires. But who could have guessed that I should ever hear one of those songs, and sung by you, my lord, and in my own house?

So I sang to him. I took a great liking to the man, and stayed with him till night came on and it was time to go. As I was leaving (I had a purse of dinars with me), I said: Take that, and reimburse yourself for your expense. We shall have more for you someday, please God.

That would be too fantastic, he objected. I had thought of offering you what I have myself, by God, and of begging you to grace me by accepting it; but I felt that it would be presumptuous. Nor would the man take a thing from me. But he went out to set me on my way, and then said good-bye. I have never seen him since.

* * *

I so enjoy forgiving people, Mamun used to say, that I am afraid I may not get any reward for it in the Hereafter. If people knew how I love to pardon them, they would commit crimes as a preliminary to coming to see me.

I once (says Judge Ibn Abi Duwad) heard Mamun say to a man: You may be a traitor, you may be faithful — I shall not hold you responsible for either. You may continue to do wrong — I shall continue to do right. You will go on committing evil and I will go on pardoning until at last forgiveness itself shall make you a better man.

Mamun was indeed so forbearing that he used to irritate us (says Ibn Bawwab). On one occasion we were standing in the Presence; the Caliph, who happened to be cleaning his teeth at the time, sat concealed by a curtain in a place overlooking the Tigris.

We heard a boatman passing by on the stream say: That Mamun? You suppose I think anything of him? a man who killed his own brother?

The Caliph simply smiled and said to us: Can any of you think of some scheme by which I might obtain merit in the eyes of that excellent man?

I have never looked into the causes of any rebellion against me, said Mamun, without discovering that oppression by my Governors was at the bottom of it. Nor was I ever so embarrassed by anything as I was by the answer of a certain Kufan, whom the citizens of Kufa had sent up as a deputy to complain to me of their Governor.

You are lying, for the Governor of Kufa is a just-dealing man, was my reply to his complaint.

The Prince of the True Believers is undoubtedly telling the truth, the deputy answered; and I am undoubtedly lying; and this being so, surely when you appointed this just man Governor of Kufa it was to the prejudice of all other cities. Pray appoint him to some different city now, that he may overwhelm them with his justice as he has overwhelmed us.

Be off with you, I'll remove him, said I.

PURITANS

A political faction calling itself the Sufi party appeared at Alexandria, which enjoined on its members the performance only of acts pleasing unto God (according to its own view), but which did not believe in Government.

Mamun used to hold a salon every Tuesday for the dis-

cussion of questions in Theology and Law. The jurists and
scholars who presented themselves at the Palace on these occasions
were first ushered into a room spread with carpets and invited to
remove their shoes and be seated. Then refreshments were served,
and all urged to help themselves. After they had washed, anyone
who found his headgear uncomfortable was at liberty to lay it
aside; and the meal being now over, censers were brought in, the
guests inhaled and perfumed themselves, and everybody left the
room to be ushered to the Presence. The Caliph, having welcomed the company, used to conduct the discussion, with entire
impartiality, without arrogance or pedantry; and the talk went
on till sunset, at which hour a second repast was served, and
everybody took leave.

On one of these occasions (says Yahya ibn Aktham, formerly Judge at Basra), Mamun was engaged in discussion when his
Chamberlain Ali came in and said: Prince of the True Believers,
there is a man at the gate. He is wearing a coarse white frock
tucked up to his knees, but he asks if he may take part in the
discussion.

I knew it must be some Sufi or other, and was going to
make a sign that he should not be admitted. But Mamun un-
hesitatingly said: Show him in. And in came the man, clothed as
the Chamberlain had described him, with his shoes in his hand.
He halted at the edge of the carpet and called out: Peace be unto
you! and the Mercy of God, and His Blessings!

And Peace to thee! returned the Caliph.

Have I leave to approach? said the man.

Approach! said the Caliph, and be seated. So the fellow
sat down.

Have I leave to speak? he inquired.

Speak, said Mamun, so long as thou art assured thy speech
will be acceptable unto God.

This throne here, the stranger began, on which thou sit-
test — dost thou sit thereon by the common agreement and consent of the body of the True Believers, or by abuse of power and
the violent forcing of thy sovereignty upon them?

I sit on this throne, replied Mamun, neither by their common consent nor by my own violence. Before my time there was a Sovereign (Harun al-Rashid) who swayed the affairs of the True Believers and whom they bore with, perhaps willingly, perhaps unwillingly; and he appointed me and another (Amin) to succeed him in this authority, calling on such True Believers as were there present to witness his act. Then he took an oath of allegiance from all the Pilgrims to God's Holy House at Mecca, to me and to that other. They gave their oaths, perhaps willingly, perhaps unwillingly. The man who was associated with me in the succession went the way he went. When I succeeded to this authority, I knew that I needed the common consent of the Muslims, of all, east and west. I therefore pondered the matter. It seemed plain to me that if I simply left the affairs of the Muslims to their own guidance, the bond of Islam would be slacked, covenants would fail and the State be torn asunder; that all would be disorder, woe and war; that God's ordinances would be kept no more, that none would go on Pilgrimage nor go out to Holy War; that there would be none to lead the people; that the roads would be beset by highwaymen and the weak oppressed by the strong. I therefore took on this authority in order to protect the True Believers, to fight their foes, to guard their roads, to lead them, until such time as they unite in consent to the elevation of some man they shall all approve. To that man I purpose to resign my authority. I shall become his subject like any other Muslim. Take this message from me to the Muslim people! Tell them: the moment they have agreed upon a chief I abdicate my authority.

Peace be unto you! and the Mercy of God and His Blessings! said the Sufi, rising to his feet. And he stalked away.

Follow that man; see where he goes! said Mamun to the Chamberlain.

Ali went out to see the order executed. When he came in again, he gave the following report:

I sent some of my people to shadow the man, Prince of the True Believers. He went on till he came to a Mosque; and there were fifteen men waiting for him, of like mien and dress with himself.

Well, they said, didst thou see the man?

I did, said he.

And what did he say to thee?

Not a word but of good! said the deputy. He told me that he had taken the affairs of the Muslims in hand so that he might guard the roads, and maintain Pilgrimage and Holy War, and defend the oppressed, and see to it that God's Law doth not become a dead letter; but so soon as the Muslims agree upon a chief, he is ready to abdicate, and hand over his authority to the man of their choosing.

Well, the others said, that seems all right. Then they all went away in different directions.

Mamun turned to me when he had heard this report. You see, Abu Muhammad, said he, it was not too difficult to satisfy these worthy people.

Glory be to God Who hath inspired thee with so sure and right a judgment, Prince of True Believers, was my reply: a judgment as accurate in words as it is in deeds.

* * *

This same Judge Yahya wrote several treatises in the field of jurisprudence dealing with the legal Root-principles (the Book, the Traditional True Way, Consensus, and Analogy), and with their deducible consequences. His most famous work was a book under the title of *The Notice,* in refutation of the Iraqi School of jurisprudence; and he engaged in various controversies with the great Judge Ibn Abi Duwad.

One day (says Yahya) Mamun said to me: Yahya, I would like to relate some Traditions.

Who could do so more appropriately than the Prince of True Believers? I replied.

Then have a pulpit set for me, said the Caliph. The pulpit was set, and he mounted it; and the first Tradition he gave us was one through Hushaym with a chain of authorities from the Companion Abu Hurayra that the Prophet said: *Imrulqais is the leader of the poets into Hell-fire.* He went on to relate about thirty other Traditions, and then stepped down.

What did you think of our lecture, Yahya? he asked me.

A splendid lecture, Prince of the True Believers! I told him. You have afforded instruction to us all, high and low alike.

Nonsense! said the Caliph. I could see that you didn't enjoy it in the slightest. A lecture really needs a different kind of audience — shabby men with inkhorns for taking notes.

* * *

I saw the Devil passing in the distance (says a certain Sufi), and called out to him: What do you want here?

What can I do with you? he answered; you have freed yourself from what I used to tempt you with.

What's that? said I.

The world, said he, and went on his way.

But then he turned and looked at me. I have still one lure for you — the love of young boys.

And when the Almighty pleases to bring some servant of His into contempt, He drives him to this same sink.

At the time when Yahya ibn Aktham was Judge at Basra, the citizens sent a deputation to Mamun to complain of his homosexuality, and of his corruption of the young men of the city. Mamun at first only replied that he would have listened to any complaint against the actual judgments of Yahya. But after hearing a poem by the Judge, in which Yahya classified sodomite's minions according to their physical characteristics, he recalled him from his office to the capital.

As it fell out, Yahya came to be an intimate of the Caliph's. He was so little ashamed of his pervert tastes that on one occasion when Mamun ordered him to muster a troop for the execution of some mission, the Judge enrolled four hundred beardless boys,

chosen for their beauty alone. It was of this that a poet wrote the
lampoon:

> *Come and see the wonder, friends: the rarest ever seen!*
> *A troop where all the troopers are boys of beauteous mien;*
> *Their chief a Judge, whose shaft, well-straightened, deals*
>   *dread strokes,*
> *Whose strategy leads to battles of bliss, not battles of knocks.*
> *When a trooper sees action, he bows to the ground on his*
>   *hands and face*
> *While the shaykh bends over him, wielding a more than*
>   *knee-length mace,*
> *Till he leaves him laid low, and pierced in a truly vital*
>   *place.*

*   *   *

Never since Islam was first preached did even a Sovereign
lavish such bounties as did Mamun's Finance Minister Hasan ibn
Sahl when the Caliph descended the Tigris to marry his daughter
Buran. To every Hashimite gentleman or military Prince, every
Clerk or other notable present at the occasion he gave a ball of
musk, each ball enclosing a note on which was written the name
of some estate, some slave, some blood-horse or other valuable object. Each guest broke open his ball and read the note, then visited the steward in charge and made his claim. Gold and silver
coins, bottles of musk, and eggs of ambergris were scattered
among the crowds of common people.

When Mamun was preparing to return upriver to Baghdad,
he said to Hasan: Name your request, Abu Muhammad.

Yes, Prince of the True Believers, I will, said Hasan. I beg
this: that you think of me as you always have. That is something
only you can do.

The Caliph granted him the whole revenues from Fars
and Susiana for one year.

Among the poems celebrating the occasion was the couplet:

> *God's Blessing on the union of Mamun with Buran!*
> *Thou hast her, son of Harun, that daughter of O what a*
>   *man!*

A somewhat ambiguous line, was Mamun's comment.

THE CRITICAL SPIRIT

In religious matters Mamun favored the Rationalist sect, those who call themselves the maintainers of the Divine Unity and the Divine Justice.

The Rationalists explain those Koranic passages in which expressions are used implying material attributes in God by asserting that such expressions are used figuratively. They deny that *WILLING, HEARING,* and *SEEING* can subsist distinctly in the Divine Being; and for them this denial is the assertion of Divine Unity.

They believe, in pursuance of this dogmatic view of Unity, that God is not comparable with objects, is not Himself a body nor a quality nor a substance nor an element nor a thing, but is the Creator of all such, not perceptible to the senses either in this world or the Other. He alone exists in Eternity; all which is not He exists in time.

The second Rationalist dogma, on the subject of Free Will, is that God does not love evil. He is not, they maintain, the author of human actions, but ordains what pleases Him and forbids what displeases Him. Every good deed is of Him; but He has no part nor lot in wickedness such as He has forbidden. He could, had He so willed it, have compelled men to His obedience; but He has not willed that, willing rather that men be subject to trial. The Rationalists are unanimous in regarding man as the determiner and creator of his own acts, good and bad. No moral evil or iniquity, no Unbelieving or disobedient act can be referred to God, since if He had caused unrighteousness to be He would be Himself unrighteous. The All-Wise does only what is beneficial and good; and a wise regard to the well-being of His servants is incumbent on Him. This is the Rationalist doctrine of His Justice.

On the subject of Uncertain Status (as Believer or Unbeliever) their dogma is that a transgressor guilty of deadly sin is not to be classified either as Believer or Unbeliever, but simply as transgressor, liable to the eternal damnation pronounced against transgressors as such.

Their opponents who call themselves maintainers of the True Way (Sunnites) hold that God does whatsoever He pleases; and this is their notion of Divine Justice, whereas according to the Rationalists only what accords with reason and wisdom is Justice, only the doing of acts which tend to good and well-being.

In the view of the Followers in the True Way, all that is obligatory on man may only be known by hearsay (of Revelation and Tradition). Only secular knowledge, they believe, is attainable by reason; and reason, according to them, cannot tell us what is good or what is bad, or prescribe what is obligatory on man.

The Rationalists say on the contrary that *all* knowledge comes through reason, and that even without Revelation man is capable of recognizing the Creator, and of distinguishing between virtue and vice, by process of reflection.

THE ATTEMPT TO MAKE
PEOPLE REASONABLE BY LAW

IN THE YEAR 212 Mamun promulgated the Rationalist dogma of the Createdness of the Koran, conjoined with a proclamation of the superiority of Ali over Abu Bakr and Omar.

The common people shrank from the doctrine with such horror that the country came near to rebellion. Mamun was nicknamed the Prince of Unbelievers. The attempt having failed, Mamun desisted from his object until the year 218.

THE INQUISITION

Upon the question of doing good and hindering evil the Rationalist dogma is fast: it is obligatory on all Believers, and may be enforced, even with the sword. And in the year 218 the Caliph (who used to say: I would rather win an argument than win a battle) set up an Inquisition to enforce the dogma of the Createdness of the Koran, addressing this directive to the Governor of Baghdad:

The Prince of the True Believers is aware that the common herd of such unwise and ignorant persons as seek no enlightenment from reason and its evidences fail of any realizing sense of the Transcendence of GOD, and of any faculty to distinguish HIM from His creature, inasmuch as they have embraced the heretical opinion that His Koranic Revelation was in the Beginning, and was not created by HIM in time, whereas the Most High has said: VERILY WE HAVE MADE THE SAME A KORAN IN ARABIC; and whatever HE has made HE has created. Such persons further pretend that they are the true maintainers of Tradition, that they represent the True Way and the orthodoxy of the Faith.

It is proper that the integrity of any person holding such opinions be held suspect, and his testimony as a legal Witness be considered invalid.

You are therefore to assemble all Judges in your district, and read them this directive, and proceed to question them as to their belief in regard to the Createdness of the Koran. All such Judges as confess the Createdness of the Book are to question any Witnesses appearing before them as to their belief in this matter, and are to disallow as invalid the testimony of all Witnesses not confessing the Createdness of the Book. You are further to submit a copy of all reports upon Judges in your district. Orders will be issued accordingly.

* * *

The Judge and his friends drink on far into the small hours of the morning, as they diligently search the question: Was the Koran Created?

We have heard, from Abu Nu'aym, who had it of Sulay-

man ibn Isa, who had it of Sufyan Thawri, who said: Hammad
said to me: Go tell that Abu Hanifa that I repudiate him as a
polytheist. Sufyan went on to say, said Sulayman: Because he is
in the habit of saying that the Koran is Created.

But: —

The Most High has said: *VERILY WE HAVE MADE
THE SAME A KORAN IN ARABIC.* Now whatever He has
MADE He has created. The Koran is to be understood literally.
It is not for us to understand it in any other way, except under
compulsion of proof. In every other case it is to be understood
literally.

And: —

God has also said: *WE TELL THEE OF THE HISTO-
RIES OF THE APOSTLES;* which means: of something which
had previously occurred. This implies that He is telling of events
subsequent to the occurrence of which He produced the Koran.

But: —

The Traditions related on the authority of the Alid Ja'far
ibn Muhammad that the Koran is neither Creator nor Created are
sound Traditions, for he related them on the authority of his pa-
ternal uncle Zayd ibn Ali, who had them of his grandfather Ali
ibn Husayn, who was the great-grandson of the Prophet of God.

But: —

There can be no possible doubt that God's words *WE
SENT NOAH TO HIS PEOPLE,* if existing (eternally) at a
time when there was no Noah and no people, would be a report
of something which did not exist — a lie, in short. And similarly
His words *TAKE OFF THY SHOES,* if addressed (in Eternity)
to Moses when Moses did not exist, would be speech with the
nonexistent; and how could a nonentity be addressed? It follows
that all commands in narratives in the Koran must be speech
originating at the time the person spoken to was spoken to. The
speech therefore must be in time (and not in Eternity).

But: —

Muhammad ibn Husayn tells us on the authority of Amr
ibn Qays, who had it of Abu Qays of Mala, who had it of Atiyya,

and he on the authority of Abu Sa'id Khudri, that the Apostle of God, God's Prayer and Peace be on him! said: *The Word of God is as superior to other words as God is superior to His creation.*

This implies not only that the Koran is the Word of God; it implies also a distinction between the Word of God and the creation of God.

But: —

God has said: *WHEN DEATH COMETH...THEN ARE THEY RESTORED TO GOD THEIR LORD THE TRUE.* And that proves that He is not in His creation, and His creation is not in Him!

The Judge and his friends drink on. . . .

* * *

A further letter from the Caliph instructed the Governor of Baghdad to send seven individuals to him at Raqqa for interrogation. They were accordingly sent, and questioned, and on confessing the Createdness of the Koran sent back to Baghdad. The Governor was now ordered to inform all jurists, shaykhs, and Traditionists of what the seven had admitted. Some jurists now gave way; others still refused.

I went with Abbas ibn Abd al-Azim (says a certain Abu Bakr) to visit Abu Abdallah ibn Hanbal (the great fundamentalist Doctor of the Law); Abbas had some questions to put to Ibn Hanbal.

Some people here have recently set up to say that the Koran is neither created nor uncreate, Abbas began. I consider such people more of a public danger even than the Jahmites who strip God of His Attributes. Woe to you: if you say the Book is not uncreate you should surely admit that It is created.

Yes, those people are a bad lot, agreed Ibn Hanbal.

What do you yourself believe on the point, Abu Abdallah? Abbas inquired.

Ibn Hanbal seemed greatly surprised that there could be any doubt on such a matter. Is there any uncertainty? he exclaimed, when God has said: *ARE NOT CREATION AND COMMAND HIS?* and He has said elsewhere: *THE MERCI-FUL HATH TAUGHT THE KORAN AND HATH CREAT-ED MAN?*

He called attention to the distinction drawn between *MAN* and *THE KORAN,* and the use of the words *TAUGHT* and *CREATED* as consequent upon the distinction. *TAUGHT — CREATED* — he kept on repeating, insisting on the difference between them. The Koran, he said, is of God's Knowledge; and it contains His Names (or Attributes). What do these people believe? Don't they believe that His Attributes are uncreate, that God is *eternally* Powerful, Knowing, Strong, Wise, Hearing, Seeing? As for ourselves, we have never doubted that God's Attributes are uncreate, that His Knowledge is uncreate. And since the Koran is part of God's Knowledge, and contains His Names, therefore we do not doubt that the Book too is uncreate. It is God's Word — by It He discourses eternally.

Why, what Unbelief could be worse than that? he cried — thinking that the Koran is created? Such people must necessarily think that the Names of God and His Knowledge are created likewise. People take this question only too lightly: they say it is only the Koran they consider created; they even treat the matter jestingly, as if it were a joke. Little do they realize how serious it is. For it is Unbelief. I do not like to say all that is in my mind — people make inquiries, but I prefer not even to discuss the question. I am called close-lipped as a result, I hear.

Then, I put in, anyone who maintains that the Koran is created, even if he does not hold that God's Attributes or Knowledge are created, but goes no further into the matter — am I to call such a man an Unbeliever?

He is one, said Ibn Hanbal, according to us. On the matter of the Koran, he went on, we should not entertain the slightest doubt. We hold that It contains God's Names and is part of

God's Knowledge; and in our view anyone who says that It is created is an Unbeliever.

I was beginning to argue against his position, when Abbas, who had listened attentively to what had been said, interposed. Haven't you heard enough? he said.

Indeed this is enough! said Ibn Hanbal.

Mamun then wrote to the Governor instructing him to summon all recusants for interrogation. When the assembled recusant jurists had the Caliph's letter read to them, they hesitated under question, and gave ambiguous answers, avoiding direct admission and denial both.

What do you say? demanded the Governor of Bishr ibn Walid. Is the Koran created or not?

I have expressed my opinion to the Prince of True Believers himself, on more than one occasion, Bishr replied.

Well, what is it now? This is a new order, said the Governor.

My opinion is: that the Koran is the Word of God.

That is not the question, the Governor said. I am asking you if it is created.

I cannot give any better answer than I gave before, answered Bishr; and what is more, I have special permission from the Prince of True Believers excusing me from discussing the question.

And what have you to say? inquired the Governor, turning to Ibn Abi Muqatil.

The Koran is the Word of God, he answered. But if the Prince of True Believers has any orders for us, to hear is to obey.

Ziyadi gave a similar reply.

The Governor then addressed himself to Ibn Hanbal: What do you say?

It is the Word of God.

Is It created? the Governor insisted.

It is the Word of God, repeated Ibn Hanbal. I shall say nothing further than that.

The rest were all questioned, and their answers recorded. Ibn Baka's reply was: I declare that the Koran was made, and brought into existence, on the authority of the revealed text to that effect.

And what is made, pursued the Governor, is created.

Yes, said he.

Therefore, said the Governor, the Koran is created.

I do not say that It is created, replied Ibn Baka.

The report of all these answers having been sent to Mamun, a rescript was received, acknowledging receipt of the report, and proceeding:

> You are to suspend the exercise of judicial powers and the license to relate Traditions of every person not admitting that the Koran is created. As regards Bishr's statement, he is a liar: he has no special exemption from the Prince of True Believers beyond the fact that the Prince of True Believers has had reports of his sincere profession that the Koran is created. Summon him for further interrogation: if he recants, publish his recantation broadcast; but if he persists in his Unbelief by heretically denying the Createdness of the Book, take off his head and send it to me. The same for Ibrahim ibn Mahdi: question him; and if he assents, well and good; if not, take off his head. As for Ibn Abi Muqatil, remind him that it was he who once said to the Prince of True Believers: Certainly thou hast power to loose and to bind. As for Ibn Hanbal, tell him that the Prince of True Believers is familiar with the data on which he bases his arguments, and draws from them only one inference — that Ibn Hanbal is an ignoramus and a liar. As for Ibn Ghanim, tell him that the Prince of True Believers knows how he spent his time in Egypt, and how much money he made in a single year out of his office as Judge. . . . All obstinate recusants whose names follow those of Bishr and Ibrahim ibn Mahdi in your list are to be sent here as prisoners for interrogation, and, in case of persistent recusancy, execution.

On hearing this rescript, all gave way except Ibn Hanbal and three others. These, put in fetters by the Governor's order, were on their way to interrogation by the Caliph himself when the news of his death met them. And thus was the Lord Merciful to them.

* * *

Mamun sat with his head sunk on his breast. Thoughtful and sad he looked; and I was afraid to approach him in such a mood. But he glanced up at me, and with a gesture of his hand motioned me to come nearer. I obeyed, but his head only drooped again. And so he stayed a while.

Presently he looked up once more, and said: Isma'il, weariness is the soul's essential circumstance, weariness and the longing for some change. And the soul takes as much delight in loneliness as ever it takes in companionship.

Human devices, said Mamun, cannot turn a thing back if the thing is coming on, nor can they advance something itself retrograde.

Belief is the all-heal for human pain. Scepticism only conjures up the crowding cares.

Mamun died leading an expedition against the Byzantines. He was encamped at Badandun in the Roman territory when a fever seized him. His Attendants covered him with blankets; but still he shivered and cried out: O the cold! the cold! Rallying after a while, he asked what the name of that place Badandun signified in Greek.

It means: Stretch your feet out, they told him.

This struck the Caliph as an evil omen, and he asked what the name of the district was.

Raqqa, was the reply.

Now it had been foretold, from the horoscope erected at

his birth, that he would die at Raqqa; and for this reason he had always avoided making any long stay in the Muslim city of Raqqa on Euphrates. When he heard this reply from the Romans, he realized, and gave up hope.

O Thou Whose Kingdom never passeth away, he said, have Mercy now on one whose kingdom is gone from him.

When his brother Mu'tasim saw that he was sinking, he bade one of those who stood near to recite the Profession of the Faith in Mamun's ear; and the man did so, raising his voice in the hope that the Caliph might be able to repeat the words after him.

No use shouting, said the physician Ibn Masawayh. At this moment he could not tell the difference between his God and Mani!

Mamun's eyes opened, startlingly large, and glittering with an extraordinary light. His hands clutched towards the doctor, and he tried hard to speak. But no words came. His eyes turned towards heaven, and filled with tears.

RESTLESSNESS

The blame is God's. Great heart, great fame, great will
Are useless in our time.

AMUN WAS SUCCEEDED BY HIS BROTHER MU'TASIM, who was brave, strong, high-spirited, and without education. Mu'tasim used to hold his arm out (says Judge Ibn Abi Duwad) and say to me: Bite my arm, as hard as you can. I would decline, and he would insist: It won't hurt me. So I would try. But lanceheads would have made no impression on that arm — much less teeth.

THE TURKISH GUARDS

Mu'tasim was a passionate collector of Turkish slaves. He commissioned his freedmen to buy them up, until he had a troop of four thousand Turkish Guards. They wore brocade liveries, and gilt belts and ornaments, to distinguish them from ordinary soldiers. He had also a regiment of guards, called the Westerners, recruited from Egypt and Yaman; and Khurasani troops, of which the Ferghana Guards were the most notable.

These Turks soon amounted to a large army, and one very burdensome to the people of Baghdad. They would, for instance, gallop their horses through the bazaars quite reckless of the safety of feeble passengers or children. More than once the citizens took their revenge; and more than one guardsman was killed for riding down a woman or an old man, or some child or blind person. Mu'tasim therefore decided to remove from the capital.

THE NEW CAPITAL AT SAMARRA

The Caliph made various journeys of exploration through the regions on or near Tigris, and came by and by to the Samarra country. An ancient Christian monastery stood here, among wide plains, and in a healthy air. Mu'tasim noticed, after three days of hunting in the neighborhood, that his appetite was unusually good. So he sent for the monks, bought their estates, at a price of four thousand dinars, chose a situation for his Palace, and laid its foundations.

Architects, laborers, and master-craftsmen were brought in from every province of the Empire. Seeds and plants from every region were set out. To his Turks the Caliph gave separate grants of land, a master plan for the city was drawn up with the bounds of the various fiefs and quarters, roads were marked out, and special bazaars for every craft and trade. People began to build their houses. Walls rose on every side; and soon caravanserais and castles stood finished, the country was covered with plantations, and threaded with canals drawn from the Tigris and its affluent streams.

When the common people heard descriptions of the new capital, they migrated in hordes, bringing their merchandise and all the variety of things men and beasts use, until life at Samarra was prosperous and pleasant.

BABAK

WHAT ROUSED THEE to revolt?

Misery, Prince of True Believers, who art the shadow of God on earth.

It had been in the year when Ibrahim son of Mahdi went into hiding after the Baghdad revolution that a famine prevailed in the eastern provinces. There was plague in Khurasan and elsewhere; and in the same year Babak's revolt broke out in the Badh country, the mountains through which Araxes flows.

There were in those mountains and their foothills in Persia two men, Persian outlanders, both members of the Khurramite sect, both powerful chiefs. These two disputed the leadership of the Khurramites in those hills. One of them was named Jawidan; and Babak was his steward. The other was called Abu Imran.

Abu Imran on one occasion came down out of his own fells to harry Jawidan. A battle was fought, and Abu Imran routed and slain. But Jawidan got home to his stronghold with a troublesome wound. Three days he lay in his house, and then died.

Now his wife had conceived a passion for Babak; and the steward had already given himself to her lust. No sooner was Jawidan dead than the woman came to Babak and said: Listen. Thou dost not lack for strength and cunning. Jawidan is dead. I have not told his followers yet. Be ready tomorrow: I will summon them here to thee.

As he listened to her words, Babak's ambition awoke. In the morning she sent out a summons, and Jawidan's warriors came in. Why did he not send the summons himself, they asked, if he had commands for us?

Ye were scattered in your homes in many villages, she said; and had Jawidan sent out the summons as he was wont, the rumor would have run abroad; and so this time he laid his commands on me, for fear of Arab malice. And his commands I convey to you, if ye will accept them, and act.

Say on, they answered; we have never thwarted bidding of his yet, nor will we now.

Then this is what he told me, said the woman. He said: I shall die this night. And my spirit will go forth from my body and enter into the body of this lad my servant; for him do I purpose to set in authority over my people. Verily Babak will bring to pass for himself and for you what none hath ever brought to pass nor shall ever bring to pass hereafter; for he shall possess the whole earth and slay all tyrants and restore the religion Mazdak brought to men (a communism of wealth and women). By him shall the lowest of you become mighty, and the meanest exalted. Therefore, after I am gone, tell this to my people; and say that in any man who thwarts me or maketh up his own mind contrary there is no true religion.

We accept his testament, Jawidan's men replied.

Then the woman called to bring a cow, and commanded that it should be butchered and flayed, and its skin spread out. On the skin she set a bowl of wine, and broke bread into it, and laid more bread round about it. Calling them up man by man, she bade each of them tread the skin with his foot, take a piece of bread, dip it in the wine, and eat it, saying: I believe in thee, Spirit of Babak, as I believe in the Spirit of Jawidan. She told each man to take Babak's hand, make obeisance to it, and kiss it. They obeyed.

Then she offered them food and wine, and seating Babak on her bed, seated herself beside him in the face of all the company. When every man had drunk three cups, she took a sprig of basil and offered it to Babak; he accepted it; and this was their marriage.

Babak used to tell those he would convert that he was God. He introduced among the Khurramites such murdering and rapine, such wars and tortures as they had never used before; and in the course of twenty years they slaughtered 255,500 persons, at the lowest computation. During Mamun's reign, Babak's peasant troops occupied all the surrounding lands, killing or driving out the regular garrisons.

At last the Caliph Mu'tasim despatched fresh forces against him, under the Persian general Afshin, Prince of Surushna on Jaxartes. Babak was beaten back in many a bloody fray to his own borders. His armies melted away; his great warriors were dead; and he drew back into the mountains of Badh where he was born, the region called Babak's country long after he was gone. Seeing the straits he was in, he turned fugitive, taking with him only his brother, his women, and a few he trusted, disguised as travellers and merchants and caravan leaders. So he came to the marches of Armenia, and the lands of Sahl, one of the Patricians of that kingdom.

Sahl first brought him into his castle and feasted him. Then suddenly he had him seized and loaded with heavy chains.

Is this treachery, Sahl? said Babak.

Son of a whore! said the Patrician; thou, a cowherd or a shepherd, it was no business of thine to rule a kingdom and make laws and command armies!

And ordering his people to fetter all Babak's company, he sent immediately to Afshin to tell him his enemy was taken. Afshin sent four thousand men to bring them to his camp, and welcomed Sahl with high marks of distinction, giving him a robe of honor and a diadem, and with his own hand leading to him a horse of honor. He also granted the Patrician exemption from tribute. A despatch was straightway sent to the Caliph by carrier pigeon.

Everywhere, as the news flew about, men burst out glorifying God. The joy was universal, and letters were sent to all provincial capitals informing the citizenry that the rebel who had defeated the armies of the Sovereign was now a captive.

When Afshin finally drew near to Samarra with his prisoners, the Caliph's son, the Princes, and the notables of the State rode out to meet him at his last stage. A gray elephant, the gift of some Indian King to Mamun in time past, a colossal beast in trappings of red and green brocade and parti-colored silk, was sent out to the camp, together with a Bactrian camel taller than ordinary, richly decked likewise. There were sent also a coat of red brocade with jewelled embroidery over the breast, another rich robe, and a tall Persian cap of which the parti-colored border was set with all sorts of pearls and precious stones.

They put the richer robe on Babak, and the other on his brother. They set the Persian caps on their heads; then they led forward the elephant for Babak to ride, and the camel for his fellow.

What is this monster? Babak asked.

Now the army was drawn up in two files, cavalry and infantry in full armor, with flags and banners displayed, stretching in continuous line from Afshin's camp for five hours' march as far as the Palace at Samarra; and Babak, followed by his brother on the Bactrian camel, moved on between the two ranks of troops, swaying to the tread of his elephant. To right and left he looked on all those troops and all that military pomp, wistfully, as if sorry that he had not spilt their blood, but not daunted.

It was a Thursday, the second of Safar in the year 223; and the people had never seen such a glorious day nor such parade.

The Caliph Mu'tasim greeted Afshin with unusual courtesy, and called him up to a place of high honor at the Audience. Then Babak was brought in; and his warders were ordered to walk him up and down.

Are you really Babak? said the Caliph presently.

There was no reply. Mu'tasim repeated his question, and more than once; but Babak said not a word.

Woe to thee! hissed Afshin, leaning towards him; shall the Prince of True Believers deign to address thee and thou keep thy mouth shut?

I am Babak! said the man at last.

Mu'tasim prostrated himself in prayer. When he rose, he ordered Babak stripped; and the Attendants pulled off the sumptuous robes. The headsman struck off Babak's right hand, and buffeted his face with it; then the same with his left hand. Then they lopped off his feet. He twisted and kicked in his blood on the headsman's leather carpet, jabbering fast, offering untold wealth for mercy, until he saw that no one would hearken; and then he began to beat on his face with what was left of his wrists.

Run your sword in between two of his ribs, said Mu'tasim

to the headsman. Keep well below the heart, keep it going a bit longer.

The headsman obeyed. At last the Caliph bade him strike off Babak's head.

The members were then fastened to the trunk again, and the headless carcass set up on a gibbet. The head itself was first sent to Baghdad and exposed to public view on the Bridge; afterwards it was sent into Khurasan and paraded through the towns and rural districts before the eyes of the people, who still remembered Babak's great days, and thought of him as one who might level the kingdom, and overturn and reform the ranks of society.

The body continued to hang on a tall gibbet among the outermost houses of Samarra; and that place kept the name of Babak's Gibbet long after the town of Samarra was empty and desert.

The day of Babak's death, Ibrahim ibn Mahdi, the Caliph's uncle, recited from the pulpit, in place of the sermon:
Prince of the True Believers, Glory, Glory to God!
Thy warfare is accomplished; God is thy Warrior.
Let God's good slave Afshin take luck for his reward;
The blow he struck has fastened a radiance on his face.

On Afshin were bestowed a jewelled crown, a diadem set with no stone meaner than emerald and ruby in gold, and two pearled and jewelled girdles. To his son Hasan, Mu'tasim gave the hand of Utruja daughter of Ashnas, a Prince of the Turkish Guards. The girl was famous for her beauty and accomplishments; and the Caliph himself sang at their wedding verses of his own composing.

Babak's brother was sent to Baghdad to suffer. When on the way he was lodged in Baradan Castle, three leagues above the City, he asked his warder: Who art thou?

I am a son of Sharwin Prince of Tabaristan.

Praise to God! said the prisoner, that He hath granted me a Persian gentleman of the old stock to see me die.

No, said Ibn Sharwin, pointing to the headsman, the same who had executed Babak. It's only he who is to manage thy business.

Then thou art the man for me, said the prisoner, turning to the headsman; and this other fellow here is a mere outlander. Tell me now: wast thou bidden give me aught to eat, or not?

Tell me what you would like, the headsman replied.

Make me some sweet wheaten porridge, said Babak's brother. He ate heartily, and said, at the end of the meal: To-morrow, please God, thou shalt see how a Persian gentleman can die. Then he asked for date-wine, and drank, very slowly, till dawn was near and it was time to go on to Baghdad.

There, on Tigris Bridge, his hands and feet were cut off; and his body was gibbeted on the East Bank.

* * *

About a year later, a Mazyar or chieftain of Tabaristan, who had been in rebellion against the government, was captured and brought to Samarra. He declared that it was Afshin who had instigated him to revolt, on behalf of their common religion; for both, he said, held fast to the old Magian faith.

Afshin had also, in the course of a campaign against the Emperor of Byzantium, neglected an opportunity of capturing the Emperor. He is a King, said he: Kings ought to look after one another.

Already, on the day before the Mazyar's arrival at Samarra, Afshin had been put under arrest, as a result of information given by his Secretary.

TRIAL FOR TREASON

Afshin's examination was conducted by Ibn Abi Duwad, Ishaq son of Ibrahim, and Ibn Zayyat. The Mazyar, a Magian

High Priest, a Marchlord from Sughd, and two other men from Sughd in tattered clothes were present as witnesses.

These last were the first called to give evidence. They bared their backs, which were seen to be raw from scourging.

Do you know these men? Ibn Zayyat asked the prisoner. I do, replied Afshin. This man is a muezzin and the other is an Imam. They made a Mosque at Surushna, my capital, for which I punished each of them with a thousand stripes. My reason was this: I had made a covenant with the other princes of Sughd that I would leave the people of the province unmolested in the religions they professed. And these two men broke into a temple containing images worshipped by some of the Surushna people, threw the idols out, and converted the place into a Mosque. For this deed I punished each of them with a thousand stripes, as being guilty of aggression, and of interference with people's worship.

Well, said Ibn Zayyat. But what about that book which is in your possession, that book which you have had embellished with gold and jewels and brocade, and which contains blasphemies against God?

That book, replied Afshin, I inherited from my father. It is a compilation of the wisdom-literature of the old Persians. As for its alleged blasphemies, I profit by the literary merit of the work and ignore the rest. It was richly illuminated and bound, as it is now, when I inherited it. I saw no need of stripping off the ornament; I kept it as it was. After all, you do the same: you admit the *Book of Kalila and Dimna* and the *Book of Mazdak* in your own houses. I did not feel it incompatible with my profession of Islam.

The Magian Priest gave his evidence next. The prisoner, he deposed, was in the habit of eating the flesh of animals killed by strangulation, and he used to urge me to eat such meat, pretending that it was tenderer than the meat of animals butchered with a knife as the Law prescribes. Moreover, every Wednesday he used to sacrifice a black sheep, divide it with his sword, and pass between the two halves of the carcass, and then eat of the flesh. And one day he said to me: I have become one of these Arabs in everything I detest, I have gone as far as eating their oil and riding their camels and wearing their sandals; but so far I have not lost so much as a hair! meaning that he had never used depilatories as the Muslims use, nor submitted to circumcision.

Tell me this, cried Afshin to the Judges: do you consider the man who is telling you all this a valid Witness in Law?

No, we do not, the Judges admitted (for the man was a Magian who did not become a Believer till Mutawakkil's time).

Then what do you mean, said Afshin, by admitting the testimony of a man you cannot believe? Was there, he went on, turning to the Priest, some door or window looking into my house from yours, that let you spy on me?

No, replied the Priest.

Was I not wont, pursued Afshin, to invite you to my house as my guest, and communicate my private affairs, and talk over things Persian with you, and speak of my love for Persian ways and Persian folk?

Yes, he answered.

Then you are neither a True Believer, said Afshin, nor a true friend, bringing up against me in public things I said to you in confidence.

The Judges now called forward the Marchlord of Sughd.

Do you know this man? they asked Afshin.

No, said he.

Do you, the Judges asked the Marchlord, know this man?

I surely do, he replied. Then turning to the prisoner he went on: How long, trickster, wilt thou keep up this parrying, and try to cover the truth?

What's thy meaning, longbeard? retorted Afshin.

How do thy people write to thee? asked the Marchlord.

By the same titles as they wrote to my father before me, and my grandfather before him.

Tell us how they address thee, the Marchlord insisted.

I will not, said Afshin.

Do they not head their letters to thee So-and-so-and-so

(he spoke some words in the Surushna dialect) and does not that mean in Arabic: To the God of gods from his servant So-and-so?

They do that, Afshin admitted.

What? cried Ibn Zayyat. Do True Believers suffer themselves to be addressed like that? Why, what's left for Pharaoh when HE GATHERED AND SUMMONED AND PROCLAIMED: I AM YOUR LORD THE SUPREME?

All this was old custom, said Afshin: the way the people addressed my father and my grandfather, and myself in the days before I became a Muslim. I did not want to lower myself in their eyes, for fear of weakening the allegiance they owed me.

For shame, Afshin! exclaimed Ishaq ibn Ibrahim. How can you swear to us by the Name of God? How can we believe you then? How can we accept your oath and treat you as a True Believer while you are making such pretensions as Pharaoh made?

Abu Husayn, Afshin replied, it was Ujayf who cited that Text, and against Ali ibn Hisham. And now you cite it against me. See who will cite it against you tomorrow!

But now the Mazyar was called forward.

Do you know this man? they asked Afshin.

No.

Do you know this man? the Mazyar was asked.

Yes, said the Mazyar.

This is the Mazyar, they said to Afshin.

Ah yes, the prisoner said, I recognize him now.

Have you ever had any correspondence with him?

Never, Afshin declared.

Has he ever written to you? they asked the Mazyar.

Yes, he answered. His brother Khash wrote to my brother a letter which said: The only men who could have made this Most Radiant Faith prevail on earth are myself, yourself, and Babak. Babak came by his death through his own folly. I would have saved him, but he was too infatuate to be helped. As things stand, if you will revolt, these Arabs must needs send me to fight

you, and all my chivalry with me. Then when I am despatched
against you (and we join forces), we shall only have to deal with
the Arabs, the Western Guards, and the Turks. An Arab is like a
dog — you can throw him a crust and then smash his head with
a mace. Those Western gnats are a poor few; and as for that
devil's spawn of Turks, their bolts are soon shot, and then one
charge of our knights will finish them. So will Religion return
to what it was in the old Persian days.

This man is merely bringing charges against his own
brother and against my brother, pleaded Afshin. They have
nothing to do with me. Even if I myself had written this letter,
and to him, with the object of winning his confidence so that I
might advance on him without his knowing my purpose, there
would be nothing wrong. As a man who has served the Prince
of True Believers with my hands, I have the better right to
serve him with my wits, using any means to take his foes unawares and bring them to him captive, and so win honor in my
master's eyes, even as Abdallah the Tahirid won honor.

Judge Ibn Abi Duwad now put in a question. How comes
it, he inquired, that you, if you really are a Muslim, have never
undergone the rite of circumcision, wherein resides the whole of
Islam and of legal purity?

I feared harm to my health from the operation, said Afshin.

You? a soldier?

Abu Abdallah, cried Afshin, I know you are a Judge who
would as soon condemn a multitude of men to death as set your
hood straight!

Ibn Abi Duwad turned round to the other two. It is evident
enough, he said, what sort of a man this is. Away with him! he
said to Bugha the Turk.

Bugha seized Afshin by the girdle.

This is exactly what I expected from the lot of you! shouted
Afshin. But Bugha pulled up the skirt of his robe over his head,
and dragged him back to his prison half-throttled.

Afshin died by starvation in his cell. His corpse was gibbeted at the Empire Gate, with the idols he had worshipped strewn
about the foot of the gibbet. Afterwards they made a bonfire of
the whole, and all were annihilated together.

But the Mazyar received no pardon. After being paraded
about the town, he was flogged to death, and his corpse gibbeted
beside that of Babak. The Mazyar's gibbet gradually settled side-
ways, so that the two carcasses came close together.

My pulse settled down when those two settled as quiet neighbors:
Babak, and Mazyar.
In stooping stance, as drawing aside to hide some secret they
know
From inquisitive passers-by,
Black-liveried as though the hands of the hot wind out of the
waste
Had woven them vests of pitch.
Morning and evening they ride the gaunt steeds led for their
mounting
From the carpenter's grim stable;
And yet they never stir; and yet as up I stare
The fancy comes into mind
That they fare onward, somewhere,
For ever.

*   *   *

Mu'tasim had ordered Ibn Hanbal scourged — thirty-eight
stripes — in the hope of forcing him to acknowledge the Createdness of the Koran. Later, a little while before Ibn Hanbal died,
some who had come to visit him asked him what he had to say
about the men who had him flogged.

What should I have to say? he answered. They flogged me
for God's sake. They thought that I was wrong and they were
right.

*   *   *

Following his father Mu'tasim's example, the next Caliph, Wathiq ordered the Governor of Basra to interrogate all Imams and muezzins as to their opinion on the Createdness of the Koran. At the same time he sent to Baghdad for Ahmad ibn Nasr Khuzai the Traditionist. Ahmad was brought in fetters to Samarra and questioned as to his opinion on the Koran.

It is not created! he declared.

And what is your opinion as regards God's visibility to bodily sight at Doomsday?

God has said, Ahmad answered: *ON DOOMSDAY YE SHALL BEHOLD YOUR LORD EVEN AS NOW YE BEHOLD THE MOON.* And he added a Tradition confirming his view.

You liar! said Wathiq.

Nay, thou art the liar, Ahmad retorted.

What? cried the Caliph; will He be seen, as a limited physical shape, spatially circumscribed, comprehended by a physical eye? I deny a God with such Attributes! What do you say? he added, turning to some of the Rationalist doctors who were present.

Such a man may lawfully be put to death, they answered.

A sword! said Wathiq. Now, when I stand up to kill him, you keep your places. I put the burden of all my sins on this Unbeliever, who worships a god I do not worship, a god I do not recognize as God, with attributes like that. Headsman! the mat! Ahmad, in his fetters, was placed on the mat; and the Caliph, walking up, struck off his head.

The body was gibbeted at Samarra, and the head impaled at Baghdad, with a notice attached to the ear: *This is the head of Ahmad ibn Nasr ibn Malik. God's Slave the Imam Harun (Wathiq) invited him to confess the Createdness of the Koran, and to deny the similitude of God to human form; but he remained obstinately recusant, for which may God hurry his descent into Hell-fire.*

A man was posted to guard the head, and armed with a spear to turn it if it should settle or blow round to face the Direction of Mecca. One night (this man afterwards related) I saw the head turn round, and face towards Mecca; and then it recited the Chapter Yasin, fluently.

* * *

Men are so corrupt nowadays that if they see anyone of sound faith, they call him a heretic.

VIOLENCE AND QUIETISM

A Caliph dies — not one man weeps, or cares.
Another takes his room — not one is glad.

The Turk as Sovereign Lord behaves,
And all earth's children else like slaves.

Delight in Fate, said Muhasibi.

HEN WATHIQ DIED, EVERYONE WAS IN SUCH A HURRY to go and swear allegiance to his successor Mutawakkil that the Caliph's corpse was left unattended. A lizard came and pulled out his eyes and ate them.

* * *

No sooner was Mutawakkil Caliph than he issued an order prohibiting research and philosophic discussion, and all those things which had been the rage from Mamun's days to Wathiq's. He enjoined orthodoxy and authoritarianism, and insisted that Traditionists confine themselves to Tradition and the True Way.

Never in any age, it is said, was so much money spent. On the Haruni Palace and the Kiosque of Ja'far he was supposed to have spent more than a hundred million dirhams. On freedman clients, guardsmen, and Attendants he showered bounties, over and above their lavish monthly salaries and bonuses; and according to report he had four thousand concubines, and slept with every one of them.

Yet the Treasury still contained four million dinars and seven million dirhams at the time of his death. No man got to the top of his profession in Mutawakkil's days without getting rich also, whether his profession was a serious or a frivolous one.

* * *

However, Mutawakkil must be reckoned among the most excellent of the Caliphs, because he made it a legal crime to believe that the Koran is created.

In the year of Mutawakkil's accession, Judge Ibn Abi Duwad suffered a paralytic stroke, which left him helpless as a fallen stone, God stint his reward!

* * *

Mutawakkil sent me to Madina (says Yahya ibn Harthama, Captain in the Guard) with orders to bring Abu Hasan Ali ibn Muhammad, whom the Shi'ites regarded as the true Imam, to Samarra for questioning. Accusations of disloyalty had been laid against him.

Such a weeping and wailing I never heard as when I went to fetch him; but I tried to quiet the household, and told them I had no orders to do him any harm. My search of the house discovered nothing but a Koran and prayer books and things like that. So, though I had to take him off, I treated him with the greatest respect.

On the way one day — the sun was rising in a clear sky — Ali put on a cloak and knotted his horse's tail before mounting. At the time I could not imagine why; but shortly afterwards it clouded over, and there was a torrent of rain.

Ali turned to me. You were puzzled when I did as I did, said he: I know you were. And now you are thinking I had some supernatural knowledge of what has come on. But it is not as you think; only that I was bred in the desert and know the winds that blow before rain. This morning the wind that can only mean one thing was blowing. I smelled rain and got ready for it.

When we reached Baghdad, we stayed first with Ishaq ibn Ibrahim, who was Governor of the City at that time. Ishaq took occasion to say to me: Abu Yahya, this person has the Prophet's blood in his veins. You have some influence with Mutawakkil; but if you use it to urge this man's execution, remember that God's Apostle himself will be an enemy of yours.

But I have seen no harm in him! I protested. His conduct leaves nothing to be desired so far as I have observed it.

From there we went on to Samarra. In the town I met Wasif the Turk, an officer I knew intimately. As God hears me, said Wasif, if a single hair of his head falls, I shall want satisfaction for it — personally!

Rather taken aback by this attitude, I told Mutawakkil how highly regarded Abu Hasan Ali was. And the Caliph at first gave him a handsome bounty and conferred all kinds of honors.

However, an information was lodged that the Imam had not only books but also weapons for the use of the Sectaries hidden in his house. One night therefore Mutawakkil sent some Turkish Guardsmen to break in on him when he least expected it. They found the Imam all alone in his own room, with the door locked. He was clad in a hair shirt and a woollen turban, facing the Direction of Mecca, and chanting from the Koran, with no softer mat than gravel laid between himself and the floor.

It was the dead of night; but they bore him off, clad as he was, to Mutawakkil. The Caliph was engaged in drinking; but he received Ali respectfully, and being at once informed that nothing suspicious had been discovered in the house, made him sit at his own side, and offered him the cup he held in his hand.

Prince of the True Believers, said Ali, such liquor as that was never infused in flesh or blood of mine yet. Let me be excused.

You are excused, said Mutawakkil. But let us hear a few pleasant verses then.

I know very little poetry, said Ali.

Nay. Let us hear something, insisted Mutawakkil.

So Ali began to recite:

They revelled out the night on high,
Bravely warded round;
Then down from power perforce they stooped
To graveward underground.

The Tomb had taken each one in
When a voice cried in air:
Where are they now? the throne and crown,
The purple and the vair?

Where are the faces hidden now
Which were so delicate,
Secure from sun and common eyes
Behind the Screen of State?

The question ceased. The Tomb returned
Its all-sufficient terms:
Those faces, said the sepulchre,
Fat the feasting worms:

Late they sat, and deep did drink,
And heartily did eat.
Turn about! the time is come
For them to play the meat.

The company, appalled, gave Ali up for a dead man. But when they ventured to look at the Caliph, they saw him in an agony of weeping. The tears were trickling from his beard.

Take the wine away! he said presently. And turning to Ali, he asked: Tell me, Abu Hasan, are you in debt?

Yes, I owe four thousand dinars.

Let that be paid, said Mutawakkil; and he ordered that Ali be conducted respectfully home.

Nevertheless, Abu Hasan Ali ibn Muhammad was confined at Samarra by the Caliph's orders, and there remained a prisoner for twenty years. He died mysteriously in the year 254, in the time of the Caliph Mu'tazz. The Caliph summoned his own brother to pronounce the Funeral Prayer; but so huge a crowd gathered for it, so loud was the tumult and the wailing, that the

bier was taken back from the Mosque to his house, and the Imam
buried there in the courtyard.

*   *   *

Two years after his accession, Mutawakkil issued an order
forbidding the Sectaries to visit the shrine of Husayn at Kerbela,
or Ali's Tomb near Kufa. At the same time he instructed one
Zayrij to see to the demolition of the tomb of Husayn son of Ali,
to rase it to the ground and root out every trace of it.

Though Zayrij offered a reward to the first man who
should lay his hand to the work, not one would lift a finger, for
fear of God's Vengeance, till Zayrij himself took a pick and attacked the upper part of the Tomb. Then the masons fell to.
They dug down to the grave-pit, and reached the niche where the
coffin lay.

But within the casket they found neither the vestige of a
bone nor anything else.

The surrounding buildings were likewise levelled, and the
site ordered to cultivation. The place remained waste, however;
and people at Baghdad wrote on street-walls and in Mosques re-
viling Mutawakkil. Satirical poems were written, among others
this:

> *The Umayyads foully murdered him,*
> *The son of the Prophet's daughter.*
> *Now the uncle's brood, who came too late*
> *To bear a hand in the slaughter,*
> *Go for his grave, and tear at the stones,*
> *So deep they hate his rotting bones.*

TWO OFFICIALS

The accomplished Ishaq ibn Ibrahim had been Governor of
Shirvan at the time when Suli, a well-known Clerk and poet,
passed through that country on his way to Khurasan, where Mamun had just proclaimed the Alid, Ali Riza, his successor. In

honor of the occasion Suli had composed a poem vaunting the superiority of the Alid House, and asserting their prior right to the Caliphate.

I told Suli that I thought his verses magnificent (says Ishaq), and asked him to leave me a copy. He made the copy; and in return I gave him a thousand dirhams bounty and a riding-animal for the remainder of his journey.

Later, in Mutawakkil's time, the turn of luck set Suli at the head of the Board of Fiefs, as successor to my old patron Musa ibn Abd al-Malik. Suli wanted to hold an inquiry into Musa's conduct in office; so he ordered the Clerks to prepare an indictment. A list of charges was drawn up, and there was a good deal involving me in it. I had to attend the inquiry. However, I was able to produce unexceptionable evidence to clear myself. But Suli refused to admit it, nor would he pay any attention to the Clerks who ventured to speak on my behalf. He used the most insulting expressions. On one item of the charges involving me he put me on oath, and proposed to me the Clerical Oath, saying: The State Oath won't be binding on you, since you are a heretic, a Sectary of Ali!

Allow me a few words in private, I said immediately.

He consented, and we drew aside. I cannot, said I, suffer a charge which endangers my life to pass: if you report to Mutawakkil using such language as I have heard from you just now, it is all up with me. I am willing to let every charge but that of heresy stand. But the real heretic is the man who maintains that Ali son of Abu Talib is more meritorious than Abbas, and that the Alids have a better right to the Caliphate than the Abbasids.

Whom do you mean by that? said Suli.

I mean you! said I. I have a written document to that effect in your own handwriting. And I reminded him about the poem.

At once he showed signs of alarm. Give me my manuscript back! he exclaimed.

Not so fast! I replied. As God hears me, you shan't have it until you guarantee, and in such terms as I can trust, that you will not prosecute me for a single thing that I did during my administration, that you will tear up this present list of charges, and that you will have no examination of my accounts made.

Suli gave me acceptable guarantees, and then and there tore up the indictment. I handed him back his manuscript — he stuffed it into one of his boots. And so I went on my way; nor was I ever troubled with any prosecution.

*   *   *

A fancy once took Mutawakkil that he would give a drinking party, and that everything in sight should be yellow. Accordingly a dome-chamber of sandalwood was erected, and covered and hung with yellow satin. Before the Caliph's seat were arranged yellow melons, yellow oranges, and yellow wine in a gold service. Only slave girls of yellow complexion, clad in yellow brocade, attended; and orders were given that the conduits feeding the tiled pool over which the dome had been built should be supplied with enough saffron to keep the water yellow as it flowed through.

But the party went on and on; and the saffron gave out. Safflower was used as a substitute, and the Attendants concerned felt confident that the Caliph would be dead drunk before the safflower was finished. But the party went on, and the supply of safflower too began to run low; and when it was almost gone, the Caliph had to be told, for there was no time to get more from the market.

Mutawakkil stormed at them: They should have laid in enough; his whole day would be spoiled if the yellow water stopped flowing. He told them to take brocades with yellow-dyed underlay for the gold thread, and leave them soaking in the conduits. This order was executed, and all the brocades of that sort in the Treasury were exhausted before Mutawakkil drank himself unconscious at last.

The estimated cost of the yellow streams, in saffron, safflower, and ruined stuffs, came to fifty thousand dinars.

MUTINY

I was in attendance at Mutawakkil's tent when we were encamped near Damascus (says one Sa'id ibn Nakis) at the time of the mutiny. The men had crowded into a mob, clamoring and yelling for their arrears of pay. Swords were out, and then arrows began to fly — I stepped outside and saw them flying directly above the Caliph's tent. Mutawakkil called to me: Fetch Rija here!

I went to fetch Rija. Rija, said the Caliph, what's behind this demonstration? and what do you think we can do?

Prince of the True Believers, said Rija, when we started on this expedition, I thought something like this would happen. I gave you the advice I gave you; and you were pleased to ignore it.

What's done is done! said the Caliph, leaning angrily towards him. Tell me what you think we can do here and now!

Order a distribution of pay, Prince of the True Believers.

That's what they are demanding, said Mutawakkil; but I cannot see what has made them so mutinous.

Prince of the True Believers, give the order for payment at once, Rija urged. After that, let us see.

So the Caliph gave the order for distribution. When the coin had been brought, and was being told out, Rija came back into the tent and said: Now, Prince of the True Believers, have the drums beaten, and give orders for the march back home to Iraq — the men won't even touch their money.

Orders were given accordingly. The men left their pay, in such a hurry to get home that the paymasters could be seen clinging to them, trying to hand them money which the soldiers would not stay to take.

INTRIGUES

Of his sons, Mutawakkil first appointed Muntasir his successor, with reversion to Mu'tazz, and then to Muayyad after

Mu'tazz. But later, out of love for the mother of Mu'tazz, he wanted to give him precedence, and asked Muntasir to renounce the prior succession. Muntasir refused. The Caliph immediately summoned him to Public Audience, and degraded him from his position, with threats and insults.

Muntasir, using a former Turkish Page of Wathiq's as go-between, made overtures to the officers of the Turkish Guards. His successes roused the hatred of his father; and the Vizier, Fath son of Khaqan, who was avoiding all contact with Muntasir and pressing the claims of Mu'tazz, did everything he could to embitter the Caliph's resentment. But one by one Muntasir succeeded in winning the Turks from their allegiance to Mutawakkil.

One of the Turks, a man named Bugha the Younger, had some grudge of his own; and he determined on the Caliph's death. Sending for a fellow countryman and creature of his, a certain Baghir, fierce and fearless enough, he began to sound him: Baghir, you know what I think of you, and how I have promoted you over others' heads. I have some right to your obedience; and I have some orders — what do you say?

You know what I say, Baghir replied. Tell me what it is, so that I can do it.

It is my own son Faris! said Bugha. He does all he can against me; and I have proof positive he has sworn he'll have my blood.

Well, what are my orders? said Baghir.

This. Faris comes to see me tomorrow. Do you attend; and this shall be our signal: I will lay my cap on the ground. The instant you see that, strike to kill.

I'll do it, Baghir said. But yet I fear you'll repent, and hate me after for the deed.

Nay, God keep you from that! said Bugha. . . .

Next day, when Faris came, Baghir stood ready to strike, watching for Bugha to put his hat on the ground. But Bugha did nothing, until Baghir, thinking he had forgotten, signalled with a glance. No! said Bugha aloud. Later, when Faris was gone, he explained: I thought how young he was, and he my son, and I felt I must let him go.

Hear and obey! You know best, was Baghir's reply.

What would you feel about undertaking a more serious business than that? Bugha inquired.

What you want: tell me, and I'll do it! said the other.

It's this, then, Bugha told him. The Caliph's son Muntasir, to my certain knowledge, is plotting against me and others of us. He means my death; so I want his. What do you say to that?

Baghir thought it over for some while, with his head sunk on his chest, then said: It's no good!

Why not?

Kill the son and leave the father alive? The father will kill you all for it.

Well, what do you think?

Begin with the father, said Baghir. The son's business will be easier when he's out of the way.

Be damned! can it be done? cried Bugha. Who could do that?

I'll do it — I'll walk right in on him, and he'll be a dead man when I come out.

Bugha pretended to hesitate. There's no other way, Baghir urged him; and you, if you will, can come in behind me. Either I kill him or I miss my stroke; and if I miss my stroke, you can kill me — you can run me through and say I was going to murder my lord.

Now at last Bugha felt sure of his man, and he confided to Baghir all the preparations for the murder of the Caliph Mutawakkil.

THE ASSASSINATION

Mutawakkil was murdered at the third hour of the night, on the third of Shawwal in the year 247 of the Flight. The tale of the murder is told by the court-poet Buhturi, who witnessed it.

One night (says Buhturi) a company of us, including several of the Caliph's Table Companions, were at Mutawakkil's late Audience. We were talking about swords; and somebody present said: I hear, Prince of the True Believers, that there is a man at Basra who owns an Indian sword, a sword without a peer, such a blade as never man saw the like. And he gave details. When he had heard him through, Mutawakkil ordered a letter to the Governor of Basra instructing him to buy the thing, at any price. The despatch went by State Post, and it was not long before a reply came from the Governor: the sword in question had been sold to a Yamani.

So Mutawakkil decided to have agents make inquiries in Yaman for the weapon and buy it; and orders were despatched to that effect. We were again in Presence when Ubaydallah ibn Yahya arrived with the sword, reporting that its former owner in Yaman had parted with it for ten thousand dirhams.

Mutawakkil was in high feather — he shouted out a Glorification that his wish had been granted, drew the blade from the scabbard, and fell to marvelling at the beauty of it. Everyone of us had something suitable to say about the thing; and then the Caliph sheathed it and put it away under the rug he was sitting on.

Next day, he said to the Vizier Fath ibn Khaqan: Find me one of the Pages, some man of known strength and courage; I want to entrust him with this sword, and have him stand behind me with it through all the audiences in the day.

As he was speaking, the Turk Baghir came into sight. There goes Baghir the Turk, Prince of the True Believers, said Fath. I have heard great things about his courage and resolution — he is the man the Prince of True Believers is looking for.

So Mutawakkil called him up, entrusted the sword to him, and gave him his instructions, promoting him and doubling his allowance by way of preliminary. And by God! that sword was never used, nor did it once leave the scabbard from the moment Mutawakkil handed it to Baghir until the night when Baghir struck that same blade into him.

I saw Mutawakkil do an uncanny thing that night of his assassination. The talk at the Audience had turned on Pride; we were telling stories of the haughty ways of kings, and had become rather serious. Mutawakkil was saying that arrogance disgusted him, when suddenly he turned in the Direction, prostrated himself in Prayer, and fairly ground his forehead on the floor. Then he scooped up some dust from the place, and sprinkled it on his beard and head. I am only one of God's slaves, bound for the dust, he said; it is only right for such a thing to bow down, and not be proud.

I felt curiously depressed by this incident — I found myself wishing that he had not sprinkled his head and beard with dust like that. However, he soon called for wine. When it had gone to his head, one of the musicians present sang. Mutawakkil was very appreciative; but then, turning to the Vizier, he exclaimed: O Fath! there's not one left of all who heard Mukhariq sing that song — only me and you! and he burst into tears.

Again, I had the same dismal foreboding. That's the second, I said to myself.

At that moment, a servant of his wife Qabiha's made his entry, carrying a bundle — a Dress of Honor, wrapped up. Prince of the True Believers, said the messenger, Qabiha sends to you to say: I ordered this Dress of Honor for the Prince of True Believers; and now, thinking it beautiful, I offer it for his wearing.

The parcel contained an incomparable cutaway coat, red, and a cloak of red silk as fine as Dabiqi stuff. Mutawakkil tried on the coat, and wrapped the cloak about him. I myself was on the lookout for an opportunity of improvising some compliment, some verse which might have got me that coat as a bounty, when suddenly Mutawakkil gave a violent start, pulled off the cloak, and tore it from end to end. Then, bundling it up, he handed it back to Qabiha's servant, saying: Tell her: Keep this cloak; it will do for my shroud after I am dead.

GOD'S WE ARE, I whispered, *AND TO HIM IS OUR RETURNING.* By God! his hour is come!

Mutawakkil was now very drunk; on such occasions it was

usual for the Attendants who stood at his back to set him straight again on his throne every time he lost his balance.

As we were sitting there — it was about the third hour of the night — all at once Baghir and some other Turks came in. They had their faces muffled up, but they had their swords in their hands, glittering in the lights. They rushed forward and made straight for the Caliph; Baghir and another Turk clambered up on to the throne.

That's your lord, you villains! cried Fath. Every Attendant, every courtier, every Table Companion ran for his life — of all the company I saw not one left but Fath, who had grappled with some Turks and was trying to keep them off single-handed. I heard Mutawakkil screaming. Baghir had struck him with the sword he had trusted him with, a blow on the right side that laid his flank open. Then he gave him a like wound in the left flank. Fath came at him to defend his master, but someone thrust his sword into the Vizier's body, so hard that it came out at his back. Fath took it without dodging or trying to parry — I never saw his like for courage or unselfishness — then threw his body on Mutawakkil; and they died together.

The two bodies were rolled up in the carpet on which they had been killed, and pushed into a corner. No one did anything about them that night, or most of next day. It was Muntasir in the end who, after he had been acknowledged Caliph, gave orders for them to be buried together.

MUNTASIR AND THE SHI'ITES

MUNTASIR HAD LITTLE of the tyrant in him. He was a generous benefactor of the Alids, who had been so bitterly persecuted that the very survival of Abu Talib's house had been endangered.

A very zealous Sunnite (or Follower in the True Way) had been appointed Governor of the Shi'ite town of Qumm. It was a Qumm passionist of Ali's Sect who said:

Whenever a man sees the heavens red, like fresh blood — whenever a man sees the sun glow red upon the wall, like a mantle dyed with red — every time let him remember the slaying of Husayn.

Such was the hatred felt in Qumm for the Companions who had preceded Ali in the Caliphate that there was not one person named Abu Bakr or Omar, the Governor was told, to be found in the city.

The Sunnite called the citizens before him.

As God Almighty hears me, he said to their chief man, unless you can show me a man called Abu Bakr or Omar, a man of Qumm, I will take harsh measures against you.

The citizens asked for three days' grace. They fairly ransacked the town; and leaving no stone unturned, they found at last a creature who bore the name of Abu Bakr — a poor barefoot wretch, naked and squinting, the most hideous thing God ever made. His father was a man from elsewhere who had settled at Qumm; that was how an Abu Bakr came to exist there. The citizens presented themselves, and this creature, before the Governor. He broke out in violent language.

What? he shouted, you bring me the most hideous thing God ever made? Would you make a fool of me? And he ordered a flogging then and there for the deputation.

The Prince must do his pleasure, said a humorous citizen; but the Qumm climate will not grow Abu Bakrs bigger or better than this.

The Governor could not help laughing; and he let them go.

When Muntasir became Caliph, he put an end to the persecution of the Alids. He forbade anyone to molest their Shi'ite Sectaries, and allowed all freely to visit Husayn's shrine at Kerbela and Ali's shrine near Kufa, pilgrimages which Mutawakkil had forbidden.

* * *

PRAYER USED AT THE SHRINE OF ALI

❧Peace be to thee, O Friend of God.
  Peace be to thee, O Proof of God.
  Peace be to thee, O Caliph of God.
  Peace be to thee, O Stay of the Faith.
  Peace be to thee, O Heir of all the Prophets.
  Peace be to thee, O Warder of the Fire and the Garden.
  Peace be to thee, O Master of Rod and Brand.
  Peace be to thee, O Prince of the True Believers.
I testify that thou art the First of the Oppressed, first of all them
bereaved of right by might; and therefore I will bear all things
and hope all things. God curse them who did oppress thee and
supplant thee and resist thee, with such a mighty curse as all
graced kings and all prophets who bear Divine Behest and all
true worshippers of God may curse them withal. And God's
Grace on thee, O Prince of the True Believers, on thy spirit and
on thy body.

AT KERBELA

❧God accept of my prayer for peace on the souls illuminate of
the two valiant Imams, the Two Martyrs whom God hath loved,
Abu Muhammad Hasan and Abu Abdallah Husayn, and of all
Imams, and of the two and seventy Martyrs of Kerbela Plain.

* * *

They say that someone asked the Imam Ali ibn Muhammad: O descendant of the Prophet of God! teach me that good
and perfect word which I may repeat whenever I visit the tomb
of any of the Imams. And this is what the Imam replied:
❧It is requisite that a pilgrim should have bathed. When you
enter the court and see the Tomb of the Imam, stand still, and
thirty times pronounce: God is Great!

❧Then advance, and halt again, and again pronounce thirty times: God is Great!

❧Then you may go close to the Tomb, and repeat: God is Great! forty times, which will complete one hundred Magnifications.

❧Then pray thus: Peace upon you, O Ye of the Household of the Prophet and of the Place of the Prophet, the place where angels congregate and Revelation was granted, where the Mercy of God was shown, where knowledge is preserved and wisdom is fulfilled, where guidance comes to men and forgiveness is made perfect.

Ye are the Lords of all Bounty, Elements of all Goodness, Pillars of all Virtue, Governors of all God's Servants, Supports of all Cities and Gates of all Faith, the Trusted of God and Elect of all God hath sent.

Peace upon the True Imams, who are the Lights in our darkness, who summon men to goodness, who are the Proofs of God on earth at the first as at the last.

I testify that there is no god but God Who hath no peer, and that Muhammad is the Chosen Servant, the Apostle with whom He is well pleased. And I testify that ye indeed are the very Imams who guide to the True Way, Sinless, Noble, Near to God, Pious, Upright, Elect, Obedient, to whom God hath given His own Light, whom He hath designated His Caliphs here on earth, to be Guardians of His Mysteries and Trustees of His Wisdom and Interpreters of His Revelation. Ye gave your lives to please Him; ye bore all ye suffered for His sake.

❧And when the pilgrim has prayed at all the appointed places, he should pray thus at the last:

Peace upon thee now, the peace of this farewell, the peace of a friend who will not forsake thee nor ever change toward thee. God grant this visitation be not my last to thee, nor my last pilgrimage to this place of thy martyrdom and burial. May God reckon me thine, and bring me to that Pool of Plenty in Paradise where I may be named among thy people. Through thee may God be pleased with me; and grant me a place in thy bounty.

Let me live at the time of thy Coming Again; let me bear my part when thou dost rule. Accept of my striving in thy behalf, and be my sins forgiven through thine intercession.

Guide me into the Love of God; and grant that forgiven and favored I may come to those Best Things which are the end attained by such pilgrims as love thee, the faithful of thy Sect. God grant I make this pilgrimage again, and grant me to enter again into Life Eternal by the sincerity of my purpose in faith and discipline and humility. And God grant me daily bread: enough, permitted, not unclean. O God, keep me in the remembrance of the Imams; and let me rejoice in that Mercy, the mastery of all my lusts, salvation, faith, and grace, which Thou hast reserved for such as love them, and go as eager pilgrims to these their tombs, and who are near to Thee and near to them.

My father, my mother, my life, and all I have I dedicate to thee. Forget me not; but speak my name in the Presence of Him Who doth preserve thee.

O God, give Thy Blessing to Muhammad and his House; and cause this my greeting to reach their spirits and their bodies. Peace now on him who lieth here, and on all the Imams; and the Mercy of God on the Prophet and all people of his House, Peace and great Mercy.

Verily God is enough, and how greatly enough.

* * *

If a man hankers after a martyr's crown nowadays (it was said), he need only go as far as the shrine of Ali at Kufa and cry: May God have Mercy on Othman son of Affan!

It is related on sound authority back to Umm Salma that the Apostle of God said: *Whosoever hath loved Ali, verily that man hath loved me; and whosoever hath hated Ali, verily that man hath hated me; and whosoever hath hated me, verily that man hath hated God!*

And a Tradition is related on authority tracing to Ibn Abbas that he said: The Lord never revealed the words: YE

TRUE BELIEVERS but that Ali was understood to be the chief
of them. And there is a Tradition through Ibn Asakir that the
Apostle of God said: *Looking upon Ali is worship.*

(In nothing do we see learned men more prone to falsehood than in the fabrication of Traditions.)

In the year 226 died the military Prince Abu Dulaf, a
famous poet and general, and a fanatical Shi'ite.

My brother Dulaf (says Isa son of Abu Dulaf) loathed and
despised Ali ibn Abi Talib and all his Sect. Once when I was
sitting at home with him, in our father's absence, Dulaf said to
me: You know these Shi'ites tell a Tradition that a man who
hates Ali must be a bastard: well, you know how jealous the
Prince our father is, and how little he would tolerate a trespass
on his harem — but I detest Ali!

At that moment Abu Dulaf came into the hall. We started
to our feet.

I heard what Dulaf said, the Prince declared; the Tradition he was making fun of is incontestable, and its authority
sound. And I swear that Dulaf was actually born of an illegal
union. I will tell you: once when I was ill, my sister sent a
message to me by a slave girl. With this girl I was in love; and
although she was in her monthly period at the time, my desires
were too much for me. On her then I begot this son. Later, when
her pregnancy showed plain, my sister gave her to me.

Abu Dulaf's Shi'ism and love for Ali aroused such hatred
in Dulaf that he even cursed his father. He is said to have told
the following story:

When my father died, I had a dream: some man whom I
did not recognize appeared before me and said: The Prince wants
you. So I rose and followed him. He led me along to a
deserted horrible looking house, and in and up a flight of steps;
and then into a tall room, with its walls all blackened with smoke.
The floor was littered with ashes. A man was crouching there,
stark naked, his head sunk on his knees.

Is that Dulaf? he said.

Dulaf! said I.

Presently he spoke again:

> *If only when we died we were forgotten,*
> *All living things would find their rest in death.*
> *But not so — when we die, we come to Judgment*
> *Where we must answer every act we did.*

You understand? he asked.

Yes, said I. Then I awoke.

THE TURKISH GUARDS

After he was Caliph, Muntasir turned against the Turks. Caliph-killers, he called them. But they went cunningly to work, and finally sent a bribe of thirty thousand dinars to Muntasir's Physician. This man, prescribing a bloodletting for the Caliph, bled him with a poisoned lancet, of which he died, being only twenty-six years of age, and having been Caliph less than six months.

The Turkish officers presently held a council. If now you set up any son of Mutawakkil's, said a spokesman, not one of us will be left alive; there is nothing for it but to make the son of Mu'tasim Caliph. Accordingly the Turks swore allegiance to Musta'in, the son of Mu'tasim.

But two of their own number, Bugha and Wasif, had Mutawakkil's assassin Baghir put to death; and the other Turks turning against them, these two fled to Baghdad, taking the Caliph Musta'in with them. On their arrival, they installed him in the palace of Muhammad the Tahirid, Military Commandant of Baghdad, and, stripping him of all real authority, reigned themselves as absolute rulers. A rhyme was current in those days:

> *Our Caliph now is in a cage,*
> *A Turk on either hand;*
> *Like a parrot he repeats*
> *Whatever they command.*

Musta'in had put his cousin Mu'tazz son of Mutawakkil in confinement. But the Caliphal Freedmen at Samarra now agreed to fetch Mu'tazz from his prison, proclaim him Caliph and swear allegiance, and then march against Musta'in and his party at Baghdad. The fighting went against Musta'in; and the Commandant of Baghdad agreed to his deposition. He was removed to Wasit, and thence under strong guard towards Samarra. On the road, a large body of horsemen appeared ahead. Sa'id the Chamberlain commanded them. He rode straight up, lashed at Musta'in's face with his whip, and then, having him thrown on the ground, squatted on his chest and cut off his head. Remounting, he rode away with the head to the Caliph Mu'tazz; the body was left lying in the road until some common people took the trouble to bury it. Bugha and Wasif returned to Samarra.

So long as Bugha was alive, the Caliph Mu'tazz never slept easy. Nor did he ever go unarmed, by day or night, so great was his terror of that man. I am in perpetual fear, he sometimes said, that Bugha will fall on me out of the sky, or start up from the earth before my feet.

A year after his accession, the Ferghana Guards murdered Wasif the Turk; but Bugha escaped for the time. But next year, when Bugha had decided to leave Samarra for Mosul, the Freedmen broke into his palace and looted it. Bugha's own troop scattered; and though he got away alive in disguise to a boat on the river, some troopers of the Western Guard fell on him at Samarra Bridge and killed him.

When the Turks saw that their chiefs were not safe from the Caliph, and that Mu'tazz favored the Western and Ferghana troops, they went in a mob to the Palace, savagely taxed Mu'tazz with what he had done, and demanded money. Wasif's son was at their head. Mu'tazz stoutly denied that he had any money to give them. The Treasuries were empty.

A number of the Turks set on him. They dragged him by the foot, beat him with clubs, and forced him to stand in the sun, in the fierce heat of the day. Abdicate! they shouted, slapping him in the face. Then, sending for Judge Ibn Abi Shawarib and a group of Witnesses, the Turks declared Mu'tazz deposed.

Their next measure was to send to Baghdad for Wathiq's son Muhtadi, who had been banished to prison there. After a day and a night on the road, Muhtadi reached Samarra. The Princes rode out to meet him, and he was installed in the Jawsaq Palace.

Mu'tazz offered to abdicate in return for security for his life, womenfolk, children, and property. But until he should have seen Mu'tazz, and heard his abdication from his own mouth, Muhtadi refused to take his seat on the throne or to receive the popular oath of allegiance. So Mu'tazz was fetched to him; he was clad in a dirty shirt, and had a kerchief bound round his head. At the sight, his uncle Muhtadi ran to meet him. Kissing him, he made Mu'tazz sit beside himself on the throne.

Ah! what sort of a thing is this authority? Muhtadi said.

It is something I am not equal to, the Caliph replied. I was not made for it.

Muhtadi offered to act as intermediary towards a reconciliation between his nephew and the Turks; but Mu'tazz only answered: No, I don't want it. And anyway the Turks would never agree.

Then am I released from my oath of allegiance?

You are absolved, said Mu'tazz.

At once Muhtadi turned away his face. The deposed Caliph was taken back to prison; and six days later he was murdered there. He was exceedingly beautiful; and Ali ibn Harb, who taught Tradition to his son Ibn Mu'tazz (the poet), said: Of all the Caliphs I saw he had the fairest face.

ATTEMPTS AT REFORM

The Caliph Muhtadi set himself to lead a life of virtue and religion. He called learned men to court, and appointed divines to state office. You Hashimites, he used to say, let me walk in the footsteps of Omar son of Abd al-Aziz, so that among you I may be what Omar was among the Umayyads. He cut down all expense for luxuries, ordered the gold and silver plate in the Treasury broken up and coined, and had the painted figural decoration effaced from the walls and ceilings of the Palace. The butting rams and fighting cocks which had made sport for the Caliphs before him he had slaughtered, together with all the wild beasts in the Royal Menagerie. Brocade carpets and every sort of rug not expressly sanctioned by Law were declared illegal.

To one of the Turks he wrote a letter, suggesting that he assassinate, or at least arrest, the son of Bugha, and himself assume the command of the Turkish troops. But the recipient of this letter showed it to Ibn Bugha, saying: I don't like this; and this is everybody's business.

The Caliph is said to have made a similar proposal, *vice versa,* to the son of Bugha himself; and the two chiefs saw that he was trying to pit them against one another. They agreed that Muhtadi must be killed; and drew their troops round Samarra.

One evening shortly before Muhtadi was killed, between Sunset Prayer and the breaking of his fast, an intimate of the Caliph's heard him pray: O God! it is a true Saying of Thine Apostle, God's Prayer and Peace be on him! that Thou wilt never turn away the supplication of a just Imam — and I have been scrupulously just to my people; or of one who is wronged — and I am being wronged; or of one who has not broken fast — and I am still fasting.

And with this exordium, he proceeded to call down vengeance on his enemies.

The Prophets' men were other-worldly men, whose thoughts were of Futurity — men like Abu Bakr and Omar and Ali. But you — your men are Turks and Ferghanis, Westerners and Outlanders, whose only appetite is for the goods of this world. How could you lead aright, as you set up to do?

The Western Guards and Ferghana Guards fought for Muhtadi; but at last he fled the field and rode into the city, crying for aid to the citizens. In vain he galloped through street after street, calling: To the rescue! with members of the Helper families riding before him.

He hid; but he was soon pulled out of his retreat and taken before one of the Turkish officers. It is generally thought that he was stabbed to death with daggers; but some say he was killed by crushing of the testicles, and others that he was pressed to death between great planks, or strangled, or suffocated under rugs and cushions.

At the time of his assassination, his cousin Mu'tamid was lying prisoner in one of the rooms of the Kiosque Palace. The Turks fetched him out and swore allegiance to him.

Mu'tamid, son of Mutawakkil, proceeded to appoint his brother Muwaffaq Governor General of the Eastern Provinces, and his son Governor of Egypt and the West. Then the Caliph turned his whole attention to amusements and sensual pleasures, and took no further thought for his subjects. After some time had passed thus, Muwaffaq as Regent kept the Caliph secluded and a prisoner.

Mu'tamid was the last Caliph who dwelt at Samarra.

The Mahdi

THERE DIED IN MU'TAMID's reign Hasan, called al-Askari, considered by the Shi'ites to be the Eleventh Imam, and descendant in the ninth generation from Ali son of Abu Talib. The Twelver Shi'ites regard him as the father of the Divinely Guided Mahdi, the Twelfth Imam who is Occulted or withdrawn from sight, the Lord of the Age whose Second Coming is expected.

The Occultation

The disappearance of the Twelfth Imam took place in his own house at Samarra which he had inherited from his father the Imam Hasan, in an underground chamber to which a flight of steps led down. At the time of his vanishing he was either six or seven or nine years of age: the records differ.

To suppose that he died during his father's lifetime is wrong. It is necessary for us to believe that he was born and that he is still alive, though withdrawn from human sight, and to believe that by the Will of God he is to appear again at the End of Time.

It is recorded that the Imam Ali the Younger (son of Imam Husayn son of Ali son of Abu Talib) said: We are the Leaders of Muhammad's People, and the Proofs of God among mankind. Through us when Doomsday comes the men of Ali's Sect will draw near the Garden with faces, hands, and feet white as if they had been washed in Light. As long as the stars shall be the wardens of the sky, so long shall the angels feel no fear of the coming of Judgment. And as long as we shall be on earth, Judgment and its pains shall be put off. If there were no Imam of our House in the world, the very earth would crumble, with all who dwell thereon.

When this Imam was asked: Could men get any good from a Proof of God who was withdrawn from their sight? he answered: Such good as they get from the sun behind a cloud.

This explains how even during his Occultation the grace and blessedness of the Imam permeate this world. When simple people fall into error, his guidance will come to them. They will see that they have had guidance, though they will not know that it was he who guided them.

In many ways this Withdrawal is a blessing to the majority

of mankind. For God knows that if the Withdrawn Imam should appear from his Occultation, most men would not recognize him. And if his person were present, severer duties, such as Holy War against all enemies of religion, would be obligatory. Many princes and great men believe in the Imam now during his Occultation; but when his Second Coming actually occurs, and he reduces the noble and the humble to one level, as he will, many will find that intolerable, and will fall into Unbelief.

In fact, when the Eleventh Imam died, the body of the Shi'ites fell into disagreement as to whom of the Prophet's descendants they expected; and they ultimately split into as many as twenty minor sects on this point.

In the year 270 there was inaugurated in Yaman the mission of him who called himself the Mahdi, ancestor of the heretic Caliphs of Egypt, the Fatimids. For eight years more this man secretly prosecuted his design, and then, going in the guise of a Pilgrim to Mecca, disclosed his mission to certain clansmen of Qutama who were there on Pilgrimage. They believed his pretensions and took him with them on their return home westward through Egypt. He became convinced of their fanatical devotion and their courage, and went on with them to Mauritania. It was there that the Mahdi's rise to power began. When, in 280, his agents had reached Cyrene, and his purpose was talked of far and wide, the Governor of Africa sent troops to scotch the disaffection, and a battle was fought. But in vain — the Mahdi's authority grew apace.

A certain Husayn of Ahwaz was sent as Fatimid missionary into Iraq. On the way he fell in with a Qarmatian sectary, one Hamdan. It was in the neighborhood of Kufa, and Hamdan was driving a laden ox towards the city. When they had tramped along side by side for an hour or so, Hamdan said to Husayn: You have come a long way, I see; you look like a weary man; take a ride on the ox.

Nay, I have no orders to do that, answered Husayn.

You only do as you are ordered? Hamdan inquired.

Yes.

Who tells you what you may do and what you may not do? Hamdan asked.

My King and thine, said Husayn, to Whom belong this world and the Other.

Hamdan, taken aback, said nothing for a while. God alone, he rejoined at last, is King of this world and that Other.

True enough, said Husayn, but *GOD GIVETH HIS KINGDOM UNTO WHOM HE WILL*. And he began to unfold the doctrine of the Mahdi.

By the time they reached the city, Hamdan was enough impressed with his message and its urgency to take the man to stay in his own house, where his fervor in devotion was such, fasting all day and passing his night in watch and prayer, that the neighbors envied him the privilege of being host to such a man. Husayn took the oath of allegiance to the Mahdi from such as he converted, earning his living meanwhile as a tailor. Both his society and the wearing of the clothes he made were believed to bring a blessing.

THE COMMON HERD

A group of us used to discuss Abu Bakr and Omar, Ali and Mu'awia, as educated men are in the habit of doing. The Mosque crowd passed to and fro, and sometimes people would stand awhile to listen to our conversation. One day, one of our auditors, an intelligent-looking man with a long beard, interrupted us with the question: How long is all this talk going on about Ali and Mu'awia and this that and the other fellow?

Why, what is your own opinion of these men? said I.

Of whom?

Well, what do you think of Ali, for instance?

Wasn't he Fatima's father? said the man.

And who was Fatima?

The wife of the Prophet, God's Prayer and Peace on him! he answered. Aisha's daughter she was, and sister to Mu'awia.

And when I asked him further: What do you know of Ali's history? the fellow replied: Ali was killed at Khaybar, along with the Prophet of God, God's Prayer and Peace on him!

Street preachers have many tricks. This is one. If they find a densely crowded street, one preacher will take his stand at one end of it, and proceed to quote Traditions testifying to the excellence of Ali. We have heard, he will declare, from Muhammad ibn Ibrahim Fuzari, on the authority of Abdallah ibn Bakhr Huwari, and he on the authority of Abu Hasan Ali ibn Amr, and he on the authority of Hasan ibn Muhammad ibn Juhur, and he on the authority of Ali ibn Bilal, who had it of the Imam Ali Riza, Peace be to him! who had it from Musa ibn Ja'far, and he from Ja'far ibn Muhammad, and he from Muhammad ibn Ali, and he from Ali ibn Husayn, and he from Husayn ibn Ali, and he from his father Ali son of Abu Talib, Peace be to him and to them all! who had it from the Prophet of God, God's Grace on him and his Household! who had it from the angel Gabriel, and he from Michael, and he from Israfil, and he from the Eternal Tablet and the Eternal Pen, that God Most High hath said: Verily the friendship of Ali is My Stronghold, and whoso entereth into My Stronghold shall rest secure from My Punishment.

At the same time, his accomplice stands at the other end of the street glorifying Abu Bakr with exceeding glorification. We have heard (he cries) on authority tracing to Anas that the Apostle of God, God's Prayer and Peace be on him! said: Surely the love of Abu Bakr and gratitude towards him is obligatory upon every single one of my people. And we have the same from the Tradition of Sahl ibn Sa'd. And Abdallah ibn Ahmad tells us from Omar that he said: Verily the fragrance of Abu Bakr is more savory than the fragrance of musk!

In this way they get both the dirham of the most reactionary Follower in the True Way and the dirham of the Shi'ite. Afterwards, they divide the proceeds.

The two great rarities of our time are a divine whose practice accords with his knowledge and a mystic whose language proceeds from any actuality of experience.

QUIETISM

SUFISM CANNOT BE UNDERSTOOD without combining its theory with its practice; and learning the doctrine is much easier than putting it into practice. The gnosis or Knowledge which is its final stage cannot be reached by instruction, but only by ecstasy and the transformation of the moral being. To describe health is quite another thing from being healthy; and similarly the difference between knowing what renunciation is and actual renunciation is vast. Sufism consists in experience — not in definitions.

When I probed the real motives behind my career as a religious teacher, I found that my teaching, instead of being consecrated to God, was actuated by a vain thirst for reputation. I perceived that I stood on the edge of an abyss. A while I remained thus torn asunder between the opposite forces of worldly passion and religious aspiration; then I went away, and remained for years absorbed in solitary meditation and devotion, using the Sufi forms.

During my successive periods of meditation, there were revealed to me things I cannot possibly put into words. All I can say for the reader's benefit is this: I have learned from a source which is sure that the Sufis are the true pioneers on the path of God, that nothing is more beautiful than their life, nothing more admirable than their Rule, nothing purer than their morality. A Sufi's rest or activity, either outward or inward, is lit with the light which streams from the Central Radiance — Revelation.

The first step is cathartic, purging the heart of all that is not God's; and its indispensable part is the drawing-up of the heart by prayer. The last stage is being lost in God. I say the last stage, but I mean by that the furthest stage which may be reached in the exercise of the will. To tell the truth, that final stage is only the first stage in the true contemplative life, the porch by which the initiate goes in.

From then on, revelations begin. Human language cannot reach the heights they come to who go by that way. Even an attempt to suggest inevitably leads into great errors. Those who come there should say no more than the lover's lines:

> *I shall not try to say what there befell;*
> *Call me happy; ask no more — I cannot tell.*

*   *   *

Sahl of Tustar's method of bringing his disciples to perfection in mortification was this: he told the would-be Sufi: Try to say God! God! God! continuously for the whole day; and the same the next day, and the same again, until at last the disciple became habituated. Then Sahl ordered him to repeat the words through the night also, until the utterance became so inveterate that it continued even in sleep. At this point, the shaykh said: Now stop saying the word God altogether; and bend all your faculties to keeping the thought of God continuously in mind. This exercise the disciple continued until he became at last lost in the thought.

Two of Sahl's sayings are these:

To love is to extend obedience.

Only saints possess the divine right to say: I.

SAINTS

Saints act as subordinates to the Prophets, whose Missions they merely confirm. The saints are seekers, pilgrims. But the Prophets have arrived and found; and they come back with God's

Command to preach. The very body of an Apostle is as pure and near to God as the heart and spirit of a saint.

Orthodox Believers and Sufis agree that the Prophets and such saints as are kept from sin are superior to angels. Rationalists hold the opposite view, maintaining that angels, as beings of a higher sphere, more subtly compounded and more obedient to God, are superior even to the Prophets. The refutation of the Rationalist view is this fact: God commanded the angels to worship the Prophet Adam.

Angels feel no lust, covet not, are void of guile, and obey God by instinct. But men are prone to sin — Satan runs in the very blood within their veins. If such a creature turns from sin to follow devotion and mortify his lower soul, he is in reality superior to the angel, who is not the battlefield of lust and needs no recourse to means.

* * *

At one period in my life (says the Sufi shaykh Junayd), I felt a longing to see in vision what Satan was like. And as I stood in the Mosque one day, an old man came through the gateway. His face turned towards me; and at the sight of it my heart clenched with horror. He came nearer, and I cried out: Who are you? the look of you — the mere thought of you — I cannot bear it!

I am him you wanted to see.

The Accursed One! I exclaimed. Then answer now my question: why would you not bow down to Adam, for which God cursed you?

Junayd, said he, how could you imagine that I should bow down to any except God?

This answer startled me. But then a secret voice inside me whispered: Say to him: You're lying — if you had been an obedient servant you would not have disobeyed His Command.

And as if he heard the whisper in my heart, the old man cried out: O God! You've burnt me!

And suddenly he vanished.

A man once asked the mystic Bayazid: Who is the true Prince?

The man who cannot choose, said Bayazid: the man for whom God's choice is the only possible choice.

Bayazid of Bistam (in North Persia) is the greatest of all Sufi shaykhs, and is reckoned one of the ten great Imams of Sufism. From the very beginning his life was founded on mortification of self and on devotion; and he was always a lover of Theology. For thirty years, he used to say, I was strenuous in mortification; and I found no mortification more severe than the learning of divinity and the acting on its precepts. Without the ratiocinations of Theology all my struggles would have ended in utter failure.

There is truth in that saying. The bridge of the Sacred Law is narrower and more perilous than the Bridge of Dread.

God said: I was a Hidden Treasure, and My Desire was to be found; therefore I created Creation—that I might be known.

Whosoever knoweth himself, knoweth his Lord.

The vestiges of the knower, said Bayazid, are effaced; his essence is noughted by the Essence of Another, his track lost in the Track of Another. Thirty years God was my mirror. But now I am my own mirror; that which used to be I, I am no more. To say I and God denies the Unity of God. I say I am my own mirror, but it is God that speaks with my tongue — I have vanished. I glided out of my Bayazidhood as a snake glides from a cast skin. And then I looked. And what I saw was this: lover and Beloved and Love are One. Glory to Me!

A WOMAN SUFI

Ahmad of Balkh took the Contemptuary path in Sufism, and always dressed as a soldier. Hide the glory of your poverty, he used to say, meaning that a man should never let people know that he is a dervish.

His wife Fatima, who was daughter of a Prince of Balkh, was a famous Sufi; and when Ahmad went to visit Bayazid at Bistam she accompanied him. When she saw Bayazid, she removed her veil, and talked with so little shyness that her husband became jealous.

How is it you are so free with Bayazid? he asked her.

Because, though you are my natural consort, he is my religious one, she replied. Through you I come to my desire; but through Bayazid I come to God. The test of the difference is that he does not need me — you need me.

And she continued to behave as frankly with Bayazid until one day, noticing that her fingers were rouged with henna, he asked her why.

O Bayazid! she answered. So long as you never noticed my hand or its henna I was at ease with you. But now you have looked at me. We cannot lawfully be companions any more now.

* * *

Sincerity is God's earthly sword: it cuts everything it touches.

* * *

A high-minded man's Unbelief is nobler than a covetous man's Islam, said Bayazid. And Murta'ish said these things about the true dervish:

The Sufi is a man whose thought keeps pace with his foot (that is, he is entirely *present,* his soul always where his body is, and his body always where his soul is).

* * *

Sufism is beauty of nature. Sufism is deadly earnest.

* * *

The great Sufi Nuri was so called (the name means: the Man of Light) because when he spoke, even though the room was dark, it seemed to his auditors that the whole place was illuminated by his spirituality. By that same light he was able to read the inmost thoughts of his disciples, to such a degree that Junayd used to call him the Spy of Hearts.

He held that Companionship (rather than Retirement) is an obligatory part of the dervish Rule, to be practiced by always preferring the companion's well-being to any claim of one's own. He did not believe in solitude, and used to say: Beware of Retirement — it's all interwoven with Satan.

There is a Tradition that the Prophet said: *Ye will not enter Paradise until ye have faith, nor will ye perfect your faith until ye love one another.*

Nuri's Companion was Junayd. Nuri never flattered or indulged, and once he said: Coming to see Junayd, and finding him seated in the professorial chair, I said to him: Abu Qasim, when you conceal the truth from people, they put you in the place of honor; when I tell them the truth, they pelt me with stones.

He was assiduous in mortification. Once for three days and nights he stood in his chamber, never moving, and never ceasing to wail aloud. Junayd went to visit him.

Abu Hasan, said Junayd, if you have found howling aloud to God of any use, tell me, so that I too may howl aloud. But if you have discovered that wailing is of no avail, then give yourself to acquiescent delight in God's Will, that you may be happy.

Nuri stopped his wailing. Abu Qasim, he said, you teach me a good lesson.

Abu Hafs of Nishapur had come to Baghdad and was talking with the Sufi shaykhs in the Shunizia Mosque.

How would you define generosity? someone asked him.

One of you must speak first, said Abu Hafs.

Junayd began. In my opinion, he said, generosity consists in never being aware of generosity in oneself, or thinking of it as one's own.

How well the shaykh has spoken! Abu Hafs replied. But yet I think that I should say that generosity consists in doing justice and never expecting justice.

Stand up! cried Junayd to his disciples: Abu Hafs has spoken better than Adam or any man of his get since!

There is a Tradition that the Prophet said: *Patience and generosity — that is Faith.*

Sufism is the patient endurance of command and prohibition.

A man is veiled by his will from the Will of God.

DELIGHT IN FATE

Muhammad ibn Isma'il the Sufi, afterwards nicknamed Khayr, left Samarra, his native town, to go on Pilgrimage. His road lay through Kufa, and at the gate of that city a certain silk-weaver laid hands on him. You're my runaway slave! he cried, your name's Khayr!

Believing this dispensation to be from God, the Sufi offered no opposition to the weaver, but lived on patiently in Kufa many years in his employment, answering: At your service! whenever his master called him. In the end, the weaver felt remorse for what he had done.

I made a mistake, he said to Khayr. You are not my slave.

So Muhammad ibn Isma'il departed, and reached Mecca at last. He always preferred to be called Khayr. It would not be right, he used to say, to alter a name that a Believer gave me.

Khayr is the best of us all, Junayd often said.

Man only takes what God has given, or leaves what God has taken away.

SHIBLI

Originally Shibli was a Chamberlain at Court. But he was once sitting among other auditors listening to Khayr, and had the experience of conversion. As a result, he became Junayd's disciple and made the acquaintance of many of the Sufi shaykhs.

When he first came to Junayd, the great Sufi said to him: Your head is full of conceit, Abu Bakr, grounded on your position at Court. No good will come of you until you have transferred yourself to the market streets, and begged from every man you see there until you discover your actual value.

For three years Shibli obediently begged his way through the bazaars. He got steadily less and less; and at last one day he begged through the whole market without receiving a penny. To Junayd he went therefore, and told him what had happened.

You see now, Abu Bakr, said Junayd, that your actual value to mankind is nil. So you had better put them out of your mind. That begging I ordered you was not intended as your livelihood — it was for the sake of your learning something.

One day Shibli came in a rapturous ecstasy to Junayd. But he saw that his master was depressed. What is wrong? he asked.

Never mind, Junayd replied: the seeker must find at last.

No, no! cried Shibli. It is the finder who must seek!

Shibli is an intoxicated mystic, was the judgment of Junayd. If he were to sober down, he would be an Imam, from whom people could derive much good.

Among Shibli's sayings are these:

Poverty is a sea of troubles, and all those troubles are glory.

Gold wherever we go,
Pearls wherever we turn,
Silver in the wilderness!

For a long time I used to think that I was happy in the Love of God, and intimate with Him in contemplation. But now I know that intimacy is impossible except with one of one's own kind.

But, Lord, I will never turn back from Thee, not though Thou put heaven as a yoke on my neck and earth a fetter on my foot, not though Thou make the whole universe thirsty for my blood.

Real Knowledge is the realization of one's inability to arrive at Knowledge. Knowledge is bewilderment without end. O Thou Who dost guide the bewildered! make me more bewildered than I am.

When he was walking through the Karkh Quarter once, he heard some religious charlatan discoursing, and saying: Silence is better than speech.

True enough in your case, said Shibli. For your speech is vanity; and at least your silence would be no worse than a pointless joke.

Shibli was seen tossing money, four hundred dinars of it, into the Tigris. What are you doing? people asked him.

The proper place for pebbles is the bottom of a river, said Shibli.

Why not give that money to the poor?

Glory to God! he cried: There would be no piety in wishing them worse off than myself!

One day, as he went into the bazaar, the crowd called after him: There goes Crazy!

Shibli turned and answered: You think of me as crazy; and I think of you as sensible people. And I hope God will make me crazier than I am. And I hope too that He will make you more sensible than you are.

He was at last adjudged insane, and committed to the Asylum in Baghdad. Some visitors came to see him.

Who are you? he said.

Friends of yours, they answered.

Shibli pelted them with stones, and his visitors took to their heels. If you really had been friends of mine, he called after them, you would not have run away from what I did to annoy you!

* * *

TESTS

There was in those days a Traditionist and ascetic calling himself Ghulam Khalil, who by an ostentation of piety and mysticism had introduced himself to the notice of the Caliph and various courtiers.

If a dervish frequents the rich, you may be certain that he is a bad man. Whenever anyone prefers associating with the rich to sitting among the poor God punishes him with spiritual death. This hypocrite slandered the Sufi shaykhs and their disciples, with the object of getting them banished. Now the Sufi Sumnun, who has left many sublime and subtle observations on the real nature of love, had become a great popular figure in Baghdad at that time, and a certain woman had fallen in love with him. She made propositions to him which he refused; and then she went to Junayd, and begged him to advise Sumnun to marry her. When Junayd sent her away, she visited Ghulam Khalil, and accused Sumnun of having attempted her virtue. He listened eagerly, and repeating these slanders to the Caliph, induced him to order Sumnun's execution.

But as the Caliph was about to give the order to the headsman, his tongue stuck in his throat. Sumnun escaped for the moment. And that same night, the Caliph dreamed that his reign would last no longer than Sumnun's life. So next day he sent for the Sufi, asked his pardon, and installed him in favor.

* * *

It is well known that as a result of Ghulam's persecution Nuri, Raqqam, and another were arrested and conveyed to imprisonment in the Palace. Ghulam pressed their execution as heretics until the Caliph yielded and ordered their death.

When the headsman approached Raqqam to execute the sentence, Nuri rose to his feet, and with a cheerful and humble mien offered himself in Raqqam's place.

Young man, said the headsman, people are not usually so eager to greet the sword. It is not your turn yet.

Yes, it is, said Nuri, for my doctrine requires such preference of my Companion's well-being to my own.

A messenger went to tell the Caliph of this loving tenderness of Nuri's. He was so puzzled that he sent a reprieve, and charged the Chief Justice to inquire into the accusation of heresy. The Judge took them to his own house for interrogation. But he found them under question perfect in all the ordinances of the Law, and began to feel ashamed of his own previous indifference to their fate.

Judge, said Nuri, you have asked very many questions; but you have not yet asked a searching one. Know this: God has servants who only eat through Him, drink through Him, sit through Him, live through Him. They only rest in contemplation of Him; and if they were cut off from that contemplation, they would cry out in anguish.

The Judge was taken aback. In his report to the Caliph, he said: If these Sufis are heretics, whom can I call a real believer in God's Unity? The Caliph therefore sent for them to his own presence and bade them ask some boon.

The only favor we ask is that you ignore us.

The Caliph found his eyes full of tears.

MU'TADID

WHEN THE REGENT DIED, his son Mu'tadid took over the management of the State, declaring the Caliph's son destitute of any right to the succession. But once he was himself well settled in the Caliphate, the real ruler was his freedman Badr. Every face in the Empire was turned towards this man.

Tell the official Lords of Mighty Grace
Through whom alone a wish for work comes true:
Give me a job — and that is my career.
Give not — and my career is to smear you!

* * *

The moneyed man may say whate'er he will,
Rapt ears attest his oratoric skill.
When Money talks, he may talk through his hat,
But all will murmur: There's much truth in that.

My noble and exalted friend! — How long
His generosity has thrilled my song!
But somehow mounting debts do not decrease,
And dwindling means never, it seems, increase;
When I proclaimed the man's munificence
Was I, I wonder, absolutely wrong?

* * *

I brought my poem and you criticized
The prosody. 'Twas my mistake — you bring
That proverb to my mind:
The man who kissed the arse got his reward —
Wind!

* * *

We bow and scrape before that ape
In hope of some share in his malversation;
But all our attitudes earn for us
Is the ignominy of prostration.

ON THE VIZIER'S MEANNESS

His Highness' mother must have peddled the pickles she
made!
And his father must surely have followed the same respect-
able trade!

* * *

The Vizier in gaol? How nice to think
Of those satins changed for tatters!
How haircloth pants will fret his skin!
How grand he'll look in fetters!

STREET SCENE

One of the military Princes in Baghdad had run up an enormous account with a leading tradesman, and would not pay.

I had made up my mind, says this merchant, to appeal to Mu'tadid himself. Whenever I went in person to see the Prince, he had his gate shut and let his slaves insult me; I had also tried intermediaries, and that had been useless. I had even appealed to the Vizier, and he too was no effective help.

But when I decided to go to the Caliph, a friend of mine said: I'll recover your money for you without that — come along now.

So I rose, and we went out together. He took me to the shop of a tailor in Tuesday Street — an aged man, sitting there sewing away, and reciting from the Koran as he worked. My friend explained the situation and asked him to come and see me righted. And the Prince's house being quite near his shop, the old gentleman set off with us. But as we walked along, I lagged behind a little, detaining my friend.

You're exposing this very old man to nasty treatment, I whispered, and yourself and me too. All he'll get at the gate of my client will be cuffs, and you and I with him; for the Prince took no notice of So-and-so and So-and-so when they expostulated with him — not even of the Vizier. Is he likely to pay any attention to our friend here?

My companion laughed. Don't worry, he said; just come along, and keep your mouth shut.

Well, we arrived at the Prince's gate. No sooner did the slaves catch sight of the tailor than they came running up to kiss his hand; the old man would not allow that, however.

What brings you this way, sir? said the porter. The master's out riding, but if it's anything we can do, just tell us, and we'll do it straight away. If not, please to come in and take a seat till he gets back.

This was rather encouraging. We went in and sat down to

wait; it was not long before the Prince was back. He too was all deference at the sight of the old tailor.

You must give me your commands before I change, he cried.

The tailor spoke of my business.

I swear I have no more than five thousand dirhams in the house, said the Prince; but please take those, and please take all my gold and silver harness in pledge for the balance: I'll pay within the month.

To this of course I was delighted to assent. I accepted the money on account and the harness in pledge, and made the tailor and my friend attest the arrangement: if the balance of account were not paid within the month I was at liberty to sell the pledges. After the attestation we all left; but when we got back to the tailor's shop I threw down the money before him.

Sir, said I, God restored this to me through you; and if you will accept a quarter, a half, or a third of it, I shall be most pleased, and I offer it with all my heart.

You are in a great hurry to return evil for good, friend, answered he. Get away with your money, and God's Blessing on you!

But I have a further favor to beg of you, said I.

Tell me what it is.

Tell me why the Prince gave way to you, when he had disregarded some of the most important people in the Empire?

Sir, said the tailor, you have got what you wanted; please do not take up any more of my time: I have my living to earn.

But I insisted, and at last he told me this story:

For forty years now I have been leading Prayer and teaching the Koran in the Mosque hereby, though I earn my living by tailoring — the only trade I know. I was on my way home from Sunset Prayer one evening a long while back, and I passed a Turkish soldier, who used to live in that house there. At the same time there was a woman passing by, with a very lovely face; and I saw this Turk, who was drunk, catch hold of her and try to drag her into the house. She struggled, and called for help. But she got no help; no one had the courage to come forward to her rescue, for all her crying. As she pleaded, she kept saying, among other things, that her husband had sworn he would divorce her if ever she spent a night away from home; and the Turk if he kept her by force for a night would bring ruin on her home, as well as guilt on himself and disgrace on her. I went up to the Turk.

Stop! said I. Let her go!

He merely aimed a blow at my head with a club he had in hand. It hurt me badly. Then he forced the woman into the house.

I went home and washed off the blood and bandaged my wound. The pain eased by the time I had to go to Evening Prayer; and when Prayer was over, I addressed the congregation: Who'll go with me to argue with that godless Turk? We must not come away till he lets the woman go.

They all fell in with me, and we went and made a great noise at the Turk's gate. It was not long before he came out, with a crowd of slaves at his back, who gave us a drubbing; the Turk himself made straight at me, and dealt me a blow which nearly finished me. My neighbors carried me home like a dying man; and there my family treated my wounds. I dozed a little; the pain was too much for deep sleep. But about midnight I was wide awake again, quite unable to sleep for worrying.

At last a thought came: That fellow has surely been drinking all evening, I said to myself; he will have no idea what time it is. If I cry the Call to Prayer now, he'll think that dawn is breaking, and will let her go, so that she can get to her own house before it's light. And so she'll escape at least one evil — the ruin of her home — on top of what she's suffered already.

So I left the house, and stumbled as best I might to the Mosque, and climbed the minaret, and gave the Call to Prayer. Then I sat down, and looked over into the street, hoping to see the woman come out. If she did not appear, I would begin to recite Prayer. Then the Turk would be sure morning was come, and he might let her go.

A little time went by. There was no sign of the woman. But of a sudden the street was full of Guardsmen, horse and foot and torches.

Who was that who Called to Prayer? they cried. Where's the man who was sounding the Call at this hour?

At first I was too frightened to speak; but then it occurred to me that I might get some help for the woman now, so I shouted from the minaret: I was the one.

Come down here to answer to the Prince of the True Believers! they called.

Help's at hand, I said to myself; and down I went. It was a troop of Guards under Badr the Freedman himself. He took me straight before Mu'tadid. My limbs shook at the sight of the Caliph; but he told me not to be afraid, and then asked what had possessed me to alarm the True Believers with a Call out of time? so that people would go too soon to their work, and people who were intending to fast would go without their meal at the very hour when the Law allowed them to take some sustenance.

If the Prince of the True Believers will grant me security, I can explain, said I.

Your life's safe, said Mu'tadid.

So I told him about the Turkish trooper and showed him my injuries.

Bring that soldier here at once, and the woman, said the Caliph to Badr.

I was taken into a room aside. It was not long before the soldier and the woman were led in. Mu'tadid questioned her; and she described the affair as I had done. Having listened to her story, the Caliph instructed Badr to send her home under trustworthy escort — the escort must go in with her and explain the whole affair to the husband, giving him this message: that the Caliph requested him not to send her away, but to treat her with all kindness. Then I was brought in again, and Mu'tadid turned to the soldier.

How much is your allowance, fellow? he demanded.

The Turk gave the amount.

And your pay?

So much.

And your perquisites?

So much.

And you have had these bounties too! Mu'tadid went over a string of gratuities, amounting to a huge sum. The Turk admitted it.

How many slave girls have you?

The man gave the number.

Were not these women and this fortune enough? said Mu'tadid then; but you must needs violate the commands of God and injure the majesty of your Sovereign? and not only do this wicked deed but assault the man who tried to make you do right?

The guilty Turk said nothing.

A sack! said Mu'tadid; and he ordered besides some of the pestles used for grinding cement, and bonds and fetters. The Turk was bound and chained, and thrust into the sack; then Attendants, at the Caliph's bidding, began to pound him with the great pestles.

I stood looking on. The man's screaming went on for some time. Then it stopped — he was dead. Mu'tadid ordered the body thrown into Tigris, and all the contents of his house seized.

When all was over, the Caliph turned to me. Sir, said he, whenever you see a wrong done, however great, however small a wrong, order it righted, and rebuke the doer, even if *he*'s the culprit (and he pointed to Badr). If anything goes amiss, and you are not heeded, then sound the Call to Prayer at this same untimely hour — that will be a signal between you and me. I shall hear, and shall send for you — and to any man who ignores or hurts you I will do what I did tonight.

I invoked a Blessing and went away. But the tale got about; and I have never asked anyone to right another man, or to stop what he was doing wrong, but he has obeyed, and satisfied me, for fear of Mu'tadid. I have never had to sound the Call out of season from that day to this.

* * *

Mu'tadid's two great passions were women and architecture. The Pleiades Palace cost him four hundred thousand dinars, and covered three leagues. As to women, he ruined his constitution by sensual excess.

There is a wild fawn harbors in my heart,
That inmost wilderness past vale and hill.
I know it for a fawn, its neck so curves,
And it is shy and has a wild thing's will.

I strain her in my arms — and still my soul is sick for her.
What can there be more intimate than that spasm?
I fasten on her mouth to ease the torture,
And kissing only maddens me the more.
Nothing the lips can suck will cool this fever,
Nought slake my dry heart, but our very spirits
Obliterate, blent!

She runs away, O you who grow old!
She flies her hunter.
Chase her, you'll never get your game —
For you, you are her game!

Mu'tadid was pitiless, energetic, and bloody: he delighted in torture. If any Prince or Attendant incurred his anger, the Caliph had a hole dug in his presence, the victim was thrust in head downward, and the earth thrown in so that his lower body was left exposed. The soil was stamped down until the man's soul took leave through his anus. Another of his tortures was this: the sufferer was fast bound and fettered, and his ears, nostrils, and mouth stuffed with cotton. A bellows was thrust up the anus, and worked until the body was swollen to enormous size. At last an incision was made in both temple arteries, which by this time stood out like thick cords; and out came the life. Or the victim might be set up naked and pinioned at the far end of the Palace court, and shot to death with arrows. Mu'tadid had dungeons built and equipped with engines for torture, under the charge of a Chief Torturer.

A GHOST IN THE PLEIADES PALACE

In the year 284 the Caliph saw in the Palace an apparition. It came in various guises: now as a white-bearded ascetic garbed like a Christian; now as a handsome young man with a black beard; then again as an old white-bearded man, but dressed like a merchant. Sometimes the apparition had a drawn sword in its hand, and struck and killed some Attendant who might be with the Caliph. Even through shut and barred doors it would appear — wherever the Caliph was: in a room, in a court, anywhere. He saw it once on the roof.

There was a great deal of talk; and the story got about amongst high and low. Outgoing caravans carried it abroad. As to the nature of the ghost, everyone had his own theory. Some thought the Caliph was haunted and tormented by a malignant demon; others maintained that it was a Believing Genie, who saw Mu'tadid set on a course of crime and bloodshed, and haunted him with the object of deterring him by terror. According to others, the apparition was only a Palace servant who was carrying on an intrigue with one of the Caliph's slave girls, and by the aid of natural philosophy had compounded some peculiar drug which rendered him invisible when held in the mouth. But all this was guesswork. What is certain is that Mu'tadid sent for exorcists, and fell a prey to agitation and horror so extreme that in his frantic state he ordered decapitations and drownings, floggings and imprisonment, for numerous Palace servants, both male and female.

Five years later he fell deathly sick, and died within the month. Those in attendance not being sure whether he were dead or not, the physician went up to him and felt for his pulse. Suddenly Mu'tadid opened his eyes, and gave the doctor a kick which sent him staggering several paces away, and mortally injured him. Immediately afterwards, the Caliph expired.

> *The loss of youth is the full taste of death;*
> *In death at last the death-taste disappears.*

* * *

His successor Muktafi let himself be ruled by one of his freedmen and the Vizier Qasim ibn Ubaydallah, then, when Qasim died, by the Vizier Abbas ibn Hasan. Muktafi's Caliphate lasted five years. When he fell sick of the disease which killed him, he made inquiries about Prince Ja'far, his father's son by a Greek woman. The Prince, he was informed, had reached the age of puberty. So Muktafi declared the boy his heir. Ja'far was then thirteen years old. No one so young had ever wielded the Caliphate.

MONEY, MONEY, MONEY.
THE LIFE AND DEATH OF A VIZIER

Fundamentally, said Ibn Furat, government is a game of chance, or rather a conjuring-trick. Being good at it is called statesmanship.

Do you want to be obeyed? Then don't order the impossible.

A T THE TIME IT BECAME APPAR-
ENT THAT THE CALIPH MUK-
TAFI'S ILLNESS WAS SERIOUS, his
Vizier Abbas ibn Hasan began to wonder whom he ought to nominate to succeed him. He could not make up his
mind.

It was customary for one of his
four Chiefs of Bureau (namely Ibn Jarrah, Ibn Abdun, Ibn Furat,
and Ali ibn Isa) to ride along with him on his way from his own
palace to that of the Sovereign. The first to be consulted on the
question which was exercising the Vizier's mind was Ibn Jarrah:
he suggested Prince Ibn Mu'tazz, and spoke highly of his character.

Next day it was Ibn Furat's turn to ride with the Vizier,
and his opinion was now asked. This was a matter, he replied,
in which he had no experience; and he therefore begged to be
excused; he was accustomed to being consulted about official
appointments only.

That is simply hedging! said Abbas, with visible annoyance. Your judgment is perfectly good!

So, since the Vizier insisted, Ibn Furat gave this answer:
If the Vizier's choice has fixed upon a certain individual, then
let the Vizier ask God's Blessing and proceed with the appropriate measures.

He knew well enough (said Ibn Furat afterwards) that I

was referring to Prince Ibn Mu'tazz: rumors were going round about the Vizier's favoring him. But he continued to press me: I want only one thing of you — your candid opinion.

If that, I replied, is what the Vizier requires, then my opinion is this: for God's sake do not nominate for the position of Caliph a person who knows all about this man's house and that man's money, this man's gardens and that man's slave girl, this man's estates and that man's horses. Do not nominate somebody who has been in society and has practical experience, who knows how things go in this world and has too shrewd ideas as to who is the real owner of what.

Say that again, said Abbas; and he asked me to repeat it more than once. Whom do you suggest then? he inquired at last.

Mu'tadid's son Ja'far, I replied.

What? said he: Ja'far is only a child!

True enough, said I. But he is Mu'tadid's son. Why bring in a man who will really govern? a man who knows how much property we Clerks own, who will take the administration into his own hands and regard himself as independent of us? Why not deliver the Empire to a person who will leave *you* to administer it?

On the third day Ali ibn Isa's advice was asked; and the Vizier tried hard to make him suggest a name. Ali absolutely declined. I shall suggest no one, he said; only let God be feared, and let religious considerations weigh with you.

Abbas himself inclined to agree with Ibn Furat. And the Caliph's own testament naming Ja'far his successor coincided. So as soon as Muktafi died, late in the day on Saturday, the twelfth of Dhu'l-Qa'da, the Vizier Abbas went, though with many misgivings on account of his youth, to salute Ja'far as Caliph.

Ja'far took as Caliph the name Muqtadir (the Powerful through God), and told Abbas to do whatever he thought proper. The Vizier accordingly gave out the Accession Bounty to the troops.

THE CONSPIRACY IN FAVOR OF IBN MUʿTAZZ

A plot was afoot, however, to set Ibn Muʿtazz on the throne; the Prince had given his consent on condition that no blood be shed. But one of the conspirators waylaid the Vizier Abbas in the street as he was riding out to a garden of his beyond the city, and struck him a blow with his sword which killed him. The result was uproar and confusion, through which this same conspirator galloped off to the Racecourse, where he counted on finding Muqtadir playing polo. But Muqtadir had heard the shouting, and hurried back into his Palace. And the Palace gates were locked.

So all concerned in the plot gathered at the Vizieral Palace in Mukharrim, and sent asking Ibn Muʿtazz to join them there; all had gone well, they assured him. Officers, troops, the principal Clerks from the Bureaus (even Ali ibn Isa and Ibn Abdun), the Judges and everybody else of any importance except for Ibn Furat and the people personally connected with Muqtadir, all were assembled; and all swore allegiance to Ibn Muʿtazz as Caliph. The latter sent a message to Muqtadir ordering him to remove to the Tahirid Palace, so that he himself might occupy the Royal Palace.

Muqtadir himself returned a submissive reply. But his personal Retainers, and notably the Eunuch Munis, the Privy Treasurer, and the Queen-Mother's brother, took counsel: Are we going to give up as easily as this? They distributed arms to their men, and sailed upriver toward the Vizieral Palace in Mukharrim.

Ibn Muʿtazz took to his heels at once, with his newly appointed Vizier and Chief Justice and Chamberlain. But they were all captured; and Ibn Muʿtazz conveyed a prisoner to the Palace. A few days later it was announced that he had died; and his remains were given to his family, wrapped in horsecloths.

Ibn Muʿtazz had been a cultivated man, an excellent

speaker, and a first-rate poet, distinguished for clarity, felicity, and inventiveness. These are lines of his:

> *A star is gone — as if I'd lost a friend,*
> *Or someone near and dear to me had died.*
> *A falling star glides on along the dark;*
> *The falling tears along my lashes slide.*

And these:

> *Her eyes are all seduction,*
> *Her heart is all of stone;*
> *Her look implores forgiveness*
> *For the damage it has done.*

And these:

> *Season for folly — gone. Naughty time — fled.*
> *Plain is the black lie on my whitening head,*
> *My withered body hideous to see.*
> *How could she, with that smooth round throat, love me?*

Ibn Furat's First Vizierate

When Muqtadir was settled in the Caliphate after the extinction of the conspiracy, he handed the Government over to Ibn Furat, who proceeded to administer it as if he were Caliph himself. Muqtadir devoted his whole time to his amusements, avoided male company — even that of professional singers — and had only women about him. Various women and slaves came to be of the greatest political importance.

Ibn Furat continued to expend the money that was in the Caliph's Privy Treasury, not stinting until he had exhausted the whole. He had pointed out to Muqtadir that if he were to punish all who had joined the conspiracy of Ibn Mu'tazz, the result would simply be disaffection: there would be more traitors about, persons in fear of their lives whose only hope of safety would lie in revolution. So he advised burning the lists containing the names of Ibn Mu'tazz' partisans. And this Muqtadir allowed.

But one of the conspirators, Judge Abu Omar, was lying imprisoned at the Palace, in the charge of the Privy Treasurer. The Judge was under sentence of death. His father, a very old man, and one of Ibn Furat's party, used to beg with tears for his son's deliverance from execution whenever he was in the Vizier's company. The only means by which he could compass the Judge's escape, said Ibn Furat, was to hold out to Muqtadir hopes of a vast sum of money, to be paid to him personally.

In return for his son's life, the old man offered to beggar both his son and himself; so Ibn Furat preferred a request for the pardon, in consideration of the whole property of the Judge and his father being made over to the Caliph.

Muqtadir, consenting, said that for the purpose of getting the money he left Abu Omar in the Vizier's hands. Ibn Furat imposed a fine of one hundred thousand dinars, and confined Abu Omar in the Treasury Office until the money should have been paid. When the Judge had raised ninety thousand, Ibn Furat permitted him to go home, excusing him the remainder, but informing him that he was to stay in his house and pay no visits.

PROVINCIAL APPOINTMENTS

To the Government of Armenia and Azarbayjan the Vizier appointed Ibn Abi Saj, allowing him to retain the provincial revenues in return for an annual payment of one hundred and twenty thousand dinars to the Public Treasury in the capital.

The then Governor of Fars had got his province pretty much into his own hands; and his Secretary came to Baghdad to arrange for his master to continue in his Government, on condition of remitting a fixed sum to the Treasury in lieu of the actual revenue from Fars. But the Governor's mind was poisoned against this Secretary in his absence by one of his officers. He degraded him, and appointed a new man to the place. The new Secretary urged him to revolt, pointing out that the Imperial troops were at some distance and could not get quickly to Fars, so that he might well keep back the customary payment to the Sovereign, set his affairs in order, conciliate his provincial troops to himself, and then wait and see.

The degraded Secretary managed to get a letter to Ibn Furat, informing him of what was going on; and the Vizier wrote at once to the Eunuch Munis, who was at Wasit with an Imperial force. Munis marched to the frontier of Fars.

To him the Governor made overtures: he requested that he transmit an offer to the Sovereign: if he were granted the Government of both Fars and Kirman he would pay considerably more than his predecessor had paid for the same fiefs in Muktafi's time, that sum having been four million dirhams.

Munis consented to this proposal, and transmitted to the Vizier on the Governor's behalf an offer of seven million dirhams. Ibn Furat declined it. Munis gradually raised the Governor's bid to nine million without deduction for delivery, declaring as he made this offer that the Governor would really need the balance of the money he could raise, for the pay of the Fars and Kirman troops. They were also expensive provinces to run, he pointed out.

But Ibn Furat would be satisfied with nothing less than thirteen million. Munis advised the Governor to meet the wishes of the Sovereign and the Vizier. But in vain: the Governor declined to go any higher than ten million. This obstinacy annoyed Ibn Furat; he suspected Munis of having been unduly tender with his opponent.

A DEPENDENT CLERK

There is a story of those days which Ibn Muqla, the famous calligrapher and later Vizier, used to tell:

I was a Clerk in the service of Abu Hasan ibn Furat before he ever became Vizier. When he was appointed for his first term, and had been invested with the Robes, he sent for me.

Collect So-and-so and the other dealers who buy from Government, said he, and offer them thirty thousand *kurr* (one hundred and eighty thousand camel loads) of this year's produce from Agricultural Iraq. You can arrange the price with them. But demand two dinars pre-emption fee on each *kurr;* and insist on immediate payment of that pre-emption fee. When you have got the money, let me know.

I called the dealers who bought from Government to a meeting, arranged the price, and stated my stipulation — immediate payment of the pre-emption money. They said they could furnish the sum within three days, and I communicated this offer to the Vizier. He accepted it, and told me, as soon as I had the money in hand, to write the dealers a memorandum to the Bureau of the province, ordering the grain to be delivered and the agreed price to be received. On the third day they duly brought the pre-emption money; and I wrote the order for delivery.

But various supervening affairs kept me too busy to see the Vizier; and it was only after two days had elapsed that I told him I had the pre-emption money, and had had it for a day or two. I asked for instructions as to its disposal.

Good heavens! he exclaimed, were you thinking that I meant the money for myself? That shows what a low opinion you have of me. No, no! with that sum I meant to put your own affairs on a sound basis. I want to lay you under an obligation, which will serve as a little memento of our association, and at the same time will give you financial security.

I kissed his hand in gratitude. When I got home, I simply could not contain myself for joy. And when I realized that I was now a man of property, I began to dream about being Vizier myself someday. I made up my mind both to fit myself for the office and to leave no stone unturned to get it. From that time on, the idea was never out of my mind, until at last my dream came true.

END OF THE FIRST TERM

After three years, eight months, and thirteen days of office, Ibn Furat was placed under arrest, and his palace under surveillance, the bailiffs violating the privacy of his women's apartments in a disgraceful manner. His own residence and those of his Clerks and other dependents were actually looted.

The newly appointed Vizier was Abu Ali Khaqani. He proceeded to name the various heads of departments, and assigned them their official ratings. He appointed Ibn Thawaba to the Board of Confiscations, to the Bureau of Abbasi Estates, and a new special Bureau for the administration of the confiscated Furat Estates. Ibn Thawaba was also entrusted with the inquisition upon Ibn Furat and his dependents and Clerks.

These Ibn Thawaba treated far too badly, with various modes of torture. Ibn Furat himself was repeatedly brought up for question, and sometimes grossly insulted and abused. Umm Musa, the Stewardess of the Palace, was present on these occasions. When the ex-Vizier paid him back in the same coin, calling him all that was bad, Ibn Thawaba wrote to Muqtadir giving it as his opinion that Ibn Furat would never have dared to behave in such a manner were he not relying upon undeclared financial resources as extravagant as his impudence. He therefore begged leave to proceed to physical means of pressure.

The Caliph told him to do whatever he thought fit. So Ibn Thawaba put chains and fetters on Ibn Furat, clothed him in a hair shirt, and left him exposed to the sun for hours at a stretch. He nearly died under this treatment. When Muqtadir heard about it, he ordered Ibn Furat to be removed to one of the Private Apartments and put in the charge of the Stewardess Zaydan. Here he was well treated and comforted, but only after he had sworn a solemn oath that there remained no money, real estate, or valuables beyond what he had acknowledged under question.

This oath was accepted by Muqtadir, who called off Ibn Thawaba, and even took to consulting Ibn Furat in his confinement about affairs of State, showing him the despatches of the viziers to himself, and ordering his rescripts in accordance with Ibn Furat's advice.

KHAQANI'S INCOMPETENCE

COMPLAINTS AGAINST THE Vizier Abu Ali Khaqani began to come in thick and fast. The new Vizier found his time so fully occupied with paying court to the Sovereign and taking care of his own personal enemies that he had no time to read despatches, either incoming or outgoing. He therefore relied on his son, who was supposed to bring important despatches to the Caliph's attention, and to act as his father's deputy in general administration.

This son was an alcoholic. He did pay some attention to the affairs of the military officers and stipendiary troops, and made appointments to Governorships; but he neglected all else. Although he had appointed one Clerk to Incoming Despatches and another to Outgoing Despatches, and summaries were duly made for Abu Ali and his son, neither of them read these until the affairs they treated were past and done with. The memoranda of remittances, even the checks, remained unopened in their files; and of the contents of the files they had not the slightest idea.

In this way, under the administration of Abu Ali Khaqani and his son, things got into an appalling mess. In one week he would appoint more than one Governor to the same district — as many as seven, it is said, to Mah al-Kufa in the course of twenty days, who all happened to meet at a hotel in Hulwan! The reasons of course were the fees which his sons and Clerks took from the appointees. There are all sorts of stories about him, some in writing, some in memory.

Khaqani tried to endear himself to the hearts of both notables and commoners, the former by telling Imperial and military officers not to use servile expressions at the head of their letters to him, and the latter by praying among the common people in street Mosques. His conduct degraded and disgraced the

Vizieral office. If anyone asked him a favor, he used to beat his breast and say: With all my heart! People used to refer to him as Old Beat-the-Breast.

But money began to run short, and he found himself unable to provide payment in full for the stipendiary troops, the military Princes, and others. In consequence, the soldiers mutinied, and went out to the Oratory, taking most of their officers with them. The affair began to look serious, and the Vizier was threatened with violence. Muqtadir told him the stipends must be paid. Abu Ali made excuses, emphasizing the deficiency of supplies, and the fall in revenue. And he took occasion to observe that the moneys extracted from Ibn Furat and his dependents had gone into the Caliph's Privy Treasury, out of which the Privy Treasurer declined to make any contribution to Government expenses. Accordingly, Muqtadir ordered half a million dinars paid out of the Privy Treasury, the sum to be devoted to satisfying the demands of the mutineers.

The Caliph now realized the extent of the current disorder and mismanagement. He consulted the Eunuch Munis. Present conditions, said Muqtadir, indicated the need of having Ibn Furat back in the Vizierate.

Munis, however, was still offended with Ibn Furat, because of the latter's refusing the settlement of affairs in Fars which he, Munis, had recommended. He therefore told Muqtadir that it would be bad for prestige if provincial Governors were to hear that the Sovereign had degraded a Vizier and had then, after a few months of dismissal, been compelled to recall him to office: the Sovereign's action would be interpreted simply as greed to get his hands on the Vizier's property. Among universally competent Clerks since Mu'tadid's time, people who had managed things and been Chiefs of Bureaus, he went on to say, one should reckon the two Furats, one of whom was now dead and the other in disgrace, and Ibn Dawud, and Ibn Abdun, both of whom had been killed at the time of the conspiracy. The only other universally competent man was Abu Hasan Ali ibn Isa: there was no one else capable of running the Empire. Ali, said Munis, was a reliable Clerk, loyal, pious, single-minded, a safe and competent person.

So the Caliph ordered Munis to send his freedman Yalbaq to fetch Ali from his retirement at Mecca. On his arrival at Baghdad, Ali ibn Isa assumed the office of Vizier.

The Administration of Ali ibn Isa

Munis, and the brother of the Queen-Mother, and various other Caliphal officers and Retainers rode in the cavalcade which escorted Ali home from the Palace after the ceremony of his investiture with the Robes. The persons of Khaqani and his sons and dependents were put in his hands on the same day. Ali imposed moderate fines, and insisted on these being paid in full. He then allowed Khaqani to return to his own house, under custody, but with elaborate precautions for preserving his womenfolk from insult.

Ali at once set on foot an investigation into the state of the various departments of Government, to be conducted in the official Vizieral Palace in the Mukharrim quarter. Thither he himself went every morning, and there he worked up to the last moment at which late Evening Prayer is said.

To every provincial Governor he sent the usual notification of the bestowal of the Robes and his appointment to the managing of the Bureaus and the Empire. For the time being he confirmed them all in their several posts, bidding them use their best efforts to secure the prosperity of their provinces. His despatch ended as follows:

> It is now the commencement of the fiscal year and the beginning of a new season; a period during which Land Tax should yield considerable sums. I know of no special questions which I need to ask, nor of any special matter of which I should remind you. I will only instruct you to remit a substantial portion of the proceeds of this tax without delay, and to send in advice of the remittance together with your acknowledgment

of this despatch as soon as you have received it and noted its contents. You are then to write me a report on the state of your province, including a statement of account which will be readily intelligible here, and showing both how you have discharged your official duties and what additional measures you have taken to render the resources of your province large and productive.

The appropriation of revenues and other funds to particular expenditures may be postponed until you are in receipt of further despatches and instructions from me. This postponement is in order that I may have time to form an opinion as to the soundness of the principles on which you are proceeding. Make up your mind to the fact that I shall tolerate no laxity nor intromission with what is due to the Prince of the True Believers; nor shall I leave a single dirham of his money unaccounted for; nor shall I put up with any negligence of the interests of Government, whether the offending party be a stranger to me or a member of my own family. You should be less concerned to earn my favor by personal considerations than to deal justly and equitably with the subjects under your charge, and to ease them of every improper burden, light or grave. On these heads I shall hold you no less responsible than I hold you answerable for the honest administration of the Sovereign's revenues and the due protection of his property. Advise me at regular intervals without fail of your various proceedings, so that I may know what you are doing. All if God so please.

After the investigation was completed, Ali appointed various persons to the Bureaus, and dismissed others. He then set inquiries on foot to discover which provincial officers were in the habit of misappropriating Government revenue and living in grand style on the proceeds, or neglecting the development of their provinces and devoting their energies to other pursuits. All such he dismissed. He put the frontiers into a state of defense, had the hospitals repaired and the salaries of their overseers paid up to date, ordered supplies for the patients and their attendants, and ordered repairs to the public Mosques. The necessary instructions for these measures were issued to all provincial Governors, together with a supplementary order concerning Appeals, as follows:

> IN THE NAME OF GOD THE MERCIFUL THE COMPASSIONATE: *Whenever before the term of New Year's Day an Appeal is filed setting forth that some portion of the appealing party's harvest has been ruined by unforeseen mishap, only your most reliable and specially competent assistants shall be assigned to the inquiry into the facts. Assessments shall be reduced whenever the results of the investigation admit of it. But after the expiry of the aforesaid term, you will proceed to exact the Land Tax in full, without favor to the strong or injustice to the weak. Court publicity in every aspect of your charge. All if God so please.*

RESULTS AT THE LOCAL OFFICE

We had been working (says an Inspector in the Nahrawan Province) on the harvest assessments. And one of the peasants, without saying anything to us, went to the gate of the Vizier Ali ibn Isa to complain of an overassessment on one of his fields.

Out of a blue sky we received a visitation — an officer with a whole troop of surveyors from the Baduria office, and with them an escort of cavalry and infantry! We gave ourselves up for cashiered. However, my colleague begged me to go and wait on the officer at his camp outside town, and find out what it was all about. I did so; and then I was told about the complaint.

Do you remember what the assessment was on that land? my colleague asked me when I got back.

No, said I.

Better go and make an accurate survey, said he. So I took our local survey staff; and by taking the most minute care we got the exact dimensions of the field. In the previous survey it appeared that we had made it twenty-two great acres; but this time it came to twenty-one and a fifth.

I argued in excuse that the previous measurement had been made when the corn was standing, whereas this time it was measured after reaping: there was nothing surprising about a variation of this amount found between two surveys made under such different conditions. With this the officer went off.

Presently there arrived a terribly menacing letter from Ali ibn Isa, breathing fire and slaughter if he should discover that a single other person had been the victim of unfair treatment either at the hands of the Survey or any other branch. In consequence, we did not venture to make our demands very strict that year. When next year came around, the revenue was up thirty per cent: everyone was talking about the reign of justice and telling everyone else that this was the end of robbery and extortion. It certainly encouraged people to get more out of their land.

Ali ordered the abolition of the Supplementary Tax (on trees) in Fars, abolished the Mecca Customs, and the Marine Market Duties in Ahwaz, and the Wine Tax in Diyarrabi'a. So masterly was his management of Vizierate, Bureaus, and Empire affairs in general, in such a prosperous condition did he put the country, that he both increased the revenue and was hailed as a blessing by the world in general.

CONSIDERATIONS OF POPULARITY

At the time Abu Ali Khaqani was dismissed, a lot of documents had been forged in his name. And a number of what purported to be orders of his embodying grants (of money, lands, and so forth) were brought to Ali ibn Isa. He felt doubtful about their authenticity; so he collected them and sent them round to Khaqani, requesting him to examine the papers and report to him which were genuine and which were spurious.

It so happened that Khaqani was at prayers when the messenger was shown in. So the man laid down the papers before
Khaqani's son, and delivered his message to him. The young
man had begun to sort the genuine orders from the forgeries,
when his father made a sign to him to stop.

As soon as he had done praying, Khaqani took up the
papers and glanced through them. Then, shuffling them together
again, he returned the whole lot to the Vizier's envoy, saying:
My compliments to the Vizier, and please inform him that all
these deeds are genuine. I ordered these grants. The Vizier of
course will use his discretion about ratifying them.

Do you want, he demanded of his son when the messenger
had retired, to make me gratuitously unpopular? and yourself be
a cat's-paw for the Vizier? We are out of office now. Why should
we not make a little political capital, by letting all these forged
orders be ratified? If they are ratified, we get the credit and he
has to find the money. If he nullifies them, we get the grateful
feelings and he gets the hard feelings.

People liked Khaqani for his behavior in this matter.

Ali had ordered that a memorandum be drawn up showing
the total revenues of the Empire and a complete list of expenses
which had to be met. The total for expenditure was considerably
larger than that for revenue.

He therefore proceeded to abolish the increases of appropriation which Khaqani during his Vizierate had granted to the
Army Board and the Board of Fiefs. Now this extra money had
been shared by all ranks of the Army from Princes downward,
by court servants and Attendants, and moreover by every Clerk
and other employee in the two Bureaus. The sum was a vast one;
and by withdrawing it the Vizier made innumerable enemies.
Mean; miserly; starving the Army: that was what people said.
But he had no alternative: the Sovereign's expenses he had found
to be greatly in excess of his revenues — a condition which if con-

tinued could only end in the ruination of the Treasuries, and as a result of expenditures which were not really useful.

Ali had also made himself unpopular with courtiers, with many inhabitants of the capital, and with the Retainers, by cutting certain additional funds which the persons who had shared in them had come to regard as their rights and perquisites. People began to find his tenure of office very tiresome.

Endeavors were made to smear him, and to poison Muqtadir's mind against him; and certain persons began an intrigue to get Ibn Furat in again.

INTRIGUE

A Clerk of Ibn Furat's, by name Ibn Farajawayhi, had contrived to escape at the time of his patron's arrest. He remained in hiding during Khaqani's Vizierate, and when Ali ibn Isa came in. After Ali had been in office about a year, this Clerk began to correspond with Ibn Furat (in his confinement in the Palace), using the Court Physician as go-between.

In his letters to Ibn Farajawayhi, the ex-Vizier sent drafts of statements which the Clerk was to submit as his own to Muqtadir, statements containing criticisms of Ali ibn Isa and his Clerks and deputies, pointing out how the Vizier never fined any official whom he had himself employed, as if any man whom he had once trusted was not to be treated as untrustworthy. Ibn Farajawayhi was, further, to call attention to delays in the payment of stipends to the royal children, members of the harem, and Attendants, Ali having reduced the pay-year of princes and harem to eight months and that of dependents and servants to six, and cut the one hundred and fifty thousand dinars monthly budgeted to Household Cavalry stipends by two thirds.

When he received these letters, Muqtadir used to show them to Ibn Furat in his confinement. The former Vizier assured the Caliph that Ibn Farajawayhi knew what he was talking about, and could be believed.

Finally the Clerk wrote assuring the Caliph that if Ali ibn Isa were dismissed and Ibn Furat installed, the latter would restore the allowances of the princes, harem, Attendants, and the reduced Household Cavalry to their former figure, the money to be paid regularly and in full. Further, he would undertake to provide the Caliph with forty-five thousand dinars every lunar month from the following sources: fines to be levied on discharged officials, forced refunding by officials of undeclared profits of office, and fees for continuance in provincial office. When Muqtadir showed this missive to Ibn Furat, he declared these promises to be absolutely dependable, and even signed a document personally guaranteeing the whole series of undertakings.

Ali gradually became aware than an intrigue was afoot to restore Ibn Furat to the Vizierate. He offered to resign the post; but Muqtadir would not accept his resignation, and had it given out in the Palace that Ibn Furat was gravely ill.

It chanced that a captive rebel who was then lying prisoner in the Palace died at this juncture. Now it is the practice to conceal the death of any captive rebel to whom his associates give the title of Imam, since they never proclaim a successor so long as their Imam remains alive, but always appoint a new one when the Imam's death is known. So it was given out in the Palace that Ibn Furat had died: the dead rebel's remains were laid out and his obsequies performed as if for the late Vizier. The Funeral Prayer was pronounced by Ali ibn Isa himself, who returned home from the ceremony in great distress, declaring sorrowfully that the art of despatch writing had passed away that day.

But as time went by, Ali learned through various channels that Ibn Furat was still alive, and that the intrigue in his favor was going ahead. A man should not accept all he hears, observed Ali to his friends.

In the year 303 the Hujari Infantry mutinied and set fire to the stables of the Vizier. They demanded an increase of pay.

And an increase was granted: three dinars a month to those of Retainer rank, three quarters of a dinar to each infantryman. The mutineers then returned to duty.

At times Ali was so disgusted by the corruption of the courtiers and their outrageous greed that he would request Muqtadir's permission to resign his office. Muqtadir always scolded him for making such a request, until one day of the following spring.

On that day Umm Musa, Stewardess of the Palace, went to call on the Vizier, wishing to make arrangements about the money to be distributed among the harem and Attendants at the approaching Sacrifice Day festivities. Ali ibn Isa having left word at his gate that he was not receiving visitors, his chamberlain did not venture to announce her, but turned her politely away.

Umm Musa was furious. As soon as Ali heard that she had called and been turned away, he sent someone after her to make his excuses, in the hope that she might come back. But she refused, and going straight to Muqtadir and the Queen-Mother told them such a string of slanderous lies about Ali that seven days later, as he rode to the Palace, he was informed that he was dismissed and under arrest by the Caliph's order. His property and estates, however, and those of his dependents, were not touched for the moment.

Ibn Furat's Second Vizierate

On that same day Ibn Furat was invested. The Clerk who composed the text of his Despatch of Notification to the provinces in Muqtadir's name was actually Ibn Thawaba, his former examiner. An admired passage ran as follows:

Inasmuch as the Prince of the True Believers has found him indispensable to himself and imperatively requisite to the Empire, and inasmuch as the Clerks of the several Bureaus, in their various branches and ranks, all recognized in him their

master and confessed his universal competence, referring to
his judgment all their differences of opinion and seeing real-
ized in him the ideal to which themselves aspired, convinced
that he alone is that sagacious statesman, that he alone is that
experienced administrator who knows how the milk of reve-
nue is to be extracted and its sources tapped:

Therefore, the Prince of the True Believers has once
more drawn him from the sheath in which he lay; and lo! his
blade has its old edge; so that he has begun to steer the State
as though he had never left the helm, and to manage the busi-
ness of Government as though he had never for one instant
quitted it.

And furthermore, the Prince of the True Believers has
seen fit to omit the paying of no form of honor which he had
ever been granted, and the bestowing upon him anew of all
those various rewards and guerdons which had been for a time
withdrawn from him;

In pursuance of which, he has deigned to address him
by his honorific of Abu Hasan, etcetera, etcetera. . . .

It was not long before Ibn Furat proceeded to arrest Ali's
dependents, his brothers, his Clerks, and his deputies in the Bureaus of Iraq, of the East, and of the West. He imposed fines on
all except two, whom he confirmed in their appointments, at
Isfahan and Basra respectively, as being protégés of Umm Musa
the Stewardess. Besides fining all discharged officials, he insisted
on their itemizing and refunding their undeclared profits of
office; and, since he had undertaken to pay the Caliph and his
mother fifteen hundred dinars a day from this source, he even
went so far as to set up a regular Undeclared Profits of Office
Bureau!

For the moment he found himself well supplied with ready
money, owing to his predecessor's having collected some of the
Land Tax in advance of the beginning of the new fiscal year,
besides the vast amount which had been realized from fines and
guarantees (sums which individuals undertook to extort from
degraded officials and others if these were put in their power),

and from various letters of credit which had arrived enclosed with invoices from Fars, Isfahan, and other eastern provinces on the supposition that they would come into the (honest) hands of Ali ibn Isa.

The whole was expended, on Cavalry stipends, on the Attendants and Pages, and for other pressing purposes.

* * *

At Ibn Furat's table there sat down daily nine Clerks of his party, four of them Christians. He invited them to sit both opposite and beside him. As a first course, a plate of the various fruits then in season, arranged with the most delicate art, was set before each guest, and a huge dish of similar fruits placed in the center for purely decorative purposes. With each plate was laid a knife for slicing and peeling quinces, pears, and peaches; and a glass dish for skins and so forth was set beside every place. After the fruit, the plates were removed, and ewers and finger bowls brought in.

Next came a great leather tray with a cover of woven cane-work, spread with Egyptian linen; and fresh napkins were laid round it. The cover was removed, and the meal proper began. Ibn Furat used to keep up continual conversation; and he hospitably pressed his guests to eat more, as one dish followed another, for two solid hours. When they had done, the guests withdrew to a side room to wash, servants pouring water for them while the house-eunuchs stood ready with towels of Egyptian linen for drying their hands, and sprinklers of rose water for scenting their faces.

The daily consumption of meat in Ibn Furat's kitchen, and of ice in his saloons, was such as was never equalled in any private man's establishment either before or since. And the same went for sherbets — drinks were offered to all visitors whomsoever — and for wax for his candles, and for paper also, used in the Bureaus. Every time he was called to the Vizierate the prices of wax and ice went up; and the price of paper went especially high. And these prices fell every time he was turned out of office.

TROUBLE WITH A GOVERNOR

Ibn Abi Saj, who held the two provinces of Azarbayjan
and Armenia as fiefs, in consideration of an annual payment
to the Treasury of Baghdad, had paid his dues regularly during
Ibn Furat's first Vizierate. But during the successive ministries of
Khaqani and Ali ibn Isa he had delayed payment of the bulk
of these dues, and by now he had amassed enough to make him
think he was sufficiently powerful to revolt. He marched suddenly into the neighboring province of Rayy.

Munis was commissioned with the military operations
against him, and marched at once, sending orders to all Princes
on his line of march to join him. When he got tidings of this, Ibn
Abi Saj sent a series of letters, professing to desire an amicable
settlement with the Government and offering seven hundred
thousand dinars annually for the farming of the Land Tax and
Public Estates in the Rayy Province. Muqtadir would not assent
to this proposal; so he next wrote begging leave to stay in Rayy
in charge of Public Security and the Army Office only, keeping
open the Offices of Prayer, Land Tax, Estates, Justice, Post, Intelligence, Despatches, and Poor-rate for officials to be appointed by
the Sovereign. But Muqtadir replied that not for a single day
should he be allowed to stay in the Government of Rayy after
having dared to enter the province without orders.

Ibn Abi Saj was now very ready to get out of his situation
with reinvestment in his former Governments. Ibn Furat recommended that his proposal to this effect be accepted, even guaranteeing a satisfactory sum which he would force Ibn Abi Saj to pay
into the Treasury.

But the Court Chamberlain Nasr, and a certain courtier
named Ibn Hawari, opposed this plan, insisting that Ibn Abi Saj
ought not to be confirmed till he had come up to the capital and
set foot as subject on the Carpet of the Sovereign. They told the
Caliph that Ibn Furat had a secret understanding with the rebel.
So Muqtadir ordered the military plans prosecuted.

When Ibn Furat found himself accused of encouraging a rebel by Nasr and Ibn Hawari, he realized that in those two persons he had two enemies. He resolved on retaliation; and when either the Chamberlain or his ally Shafi Lului, Postmaster of Baghdad, had a favor to ask, he generally refused it.

IBN MUQLA ON THE MAKE

Some time before this, Ibn Furat had got his Clerk Ibn Muqla the job of Secretary to Nasr the Chamberlain. It was not long before Ibn Muqla took offense at one of the Vizier's appointments. So he divulged to Nasr that Ibn Furat had recovered, from deposits which he had managed to keep secret and intact, no less than half a million dinars, and this after he had sworn, at the time of his fall, that his assets included no further unacknowledged deposits. Nasr repeated this to Muqtadir, with the object of poisoning his mind against the Vizier; and both Nasr and Ibn Hawari dangled the prospect of being Vizier himself before Ibn Muqla, in the hope that he would tell more tales, calculated to envenom the Caliph still further.

But presently the story of Ibn Muqla's treachery leaked out. Even the public got to know; and Ibn Furat's nephew at last told the Vizier himself what was now common talk.

I might as well doubt my own children, replied Ibn Furat, or you, as doubt Abu Ali ibn Muqla, a man whom I have raised and befriended.

But afterwards he could not help being convinced that it was all true. In the hope of diverting Ibn Muqla from the course he was pursuing, he mentioned to him a few things he had heard repeated as having been said by Ibn Muqla, and professed his surprise that such absurd rumors could ever get started. But he only succeeded in alarming his old dependent. The latter redoubled his efforts to ruin his former patron, and transferred his loyalty entirely to his new one, Nasr the Chamberlain.

FORMAL RECEPTION OF AN EMBASSY

Baghdad in June of the year '5 was visited by two envoys from the Byzantine Emperor. They came by the Euphrates route, bearing splendid presents and other expressions of friendship, with the object of soliciting a truce.

On their arrival they were lodged in the palace built by Mu'tadid's Vizier Ibn Makhlad. By Ibn Furat's order it was specially furnished and fitted out for them, with all the utensils and other things they could possibly need, and liberal provision of supplies, including animals for butchering and sweetmeats for the ambassadors and their whole retinue.

When they asked if they could have an audience of Muq-tadir for the purpose of delivering their missive, they were told that an actual audience would be an extremely difficult matter, and only possible after an interview with the Caliph's Vizier, at which they would have to explain their objects, get his approval of the arrangements, and beg his good offices in securing the grant of an audience and in advising the Caliph to accord their petition. Judge Abu Omar, who had escorted them from the frontier and acted as their interpreter, accordingly bore to Ibn Furat their request for permission to visit him; and the latter promised them an interview on an appointed day.

The Vizier gave orders that on that day the streets all the way from the ambassadors' palace to the Vizieral Palace in Muk-harrim should be lined with soldiers, and that his official Retainers and Guard and the Vice-Chamberlains stationed in the Vizieral Palace should form a solid line from the gate to the reception-room — a vast saloon with a gilded ceiling, gorgeously furnished and hung with curtains so rich that they almost looked like carpets. Thirty thousand dinars had been spent on new furniture, carpets, and hangings; and nothing that could adorn the palace or add to the magnificence of the occasion was neglected. The Vizier himself took his seat upon a superb prayer-carpet, with a lofty throne at his back, Attendants in front and behind, to right and left, and a throng of civil and military officials filling the saloon.

By the time the two envoys were ushered in, they had seen all along their route such troops of soldiers and such crowds of citizenry as might well fill them with awe. When they had entered the Public Section of the Vizieral Palace, they had been told to be seated for a while in an open vault of the Great Court, which was full of troops. Presently, they had been conducted down a long corridor leading from the back of this vault into the Garden Court, out of which they turned into the room where the Vizier was seated.

Saloon, furniture, and the crowding company, all so sumptuous, were a dazzling spectacle. The ambassadors, who were accompanied by Judge Abu Omar and attended by the Prefect of Police and his whole force, were led up to stand before the Vizier, their salutation to whom was interpreted by the Judge. Ibn Furat pronounced a reply, which was relaid to them; and they then preferred their request for an exchange of prisoners of war, and solicited the Vizier's good offices in obtaining Muqtadir's assent to this proposal.

On this subject, he informed them, he must interview the Caliph, and would be obliged to act in conformity with what orders he might then receive. They begged that he would arrange for their introduction to the Caliph; and this he promised to procure.

The ambassadors were then given leave to depart, and led out by the same way as they had entered. All the way back to the Palace of Ibn Makhlad troops were still drawn up along the roads, in full dress uniform and complete armor, their surcoats being of royal satin, with peaked satin hoods over their helms.

Ibn Furat presently applied to Muqtadir for leave to introduce the envoys, and instructed the Caliph in the answer he was to pronounce. For the occasion he ordered all officials, civil and military both, and all ranks of the army, to ride out in the direction of the Royal Palace, and to station themselves on horseback lining the streets all the way from the Palace of Ibn Makhlad.

Conformably to these orders the Cavalry took up their positions in full dress and complete armor; and every court, vault, and corridor of the Palace was dense with men-at-arms. Rich furniture was set out through the whole building. When he had finished his preparations and seen that every slightest detail was complete, the Vizier sent word to the envoys that they should now present themselves.

As they rode towards the Palace, they were awe-struck by what they saw — the troops, so many, such gorgeous uniforms, such perfect equipment. On their arrival, they were conducted along a passage leading into one of the many courts, thence into another passage opening upon a court vaster than the first, and so on and on, the Chamberlains marshalling them along corridor after corridor, across court after court, until they were wearied-out with tramping, and in a state of complete bewilderment. Every corridor, every court, was thronged with armed Retainers and Attendants.

At last they drew near to the saloon in which Muqtadir was to be reached. There stood the high officers of State, ranged according to their different ranks, there sat Muqtadir on the Imperial Throne, with the Vizier Abu Hasan ibn Furat standing close by him, and Munis and the other Princes of immediately subordinate rank stationed to right and left.

When they were ushered in, the ambassadors kissed the Carpet, and took their stand no nearer than a place indicated to them by Nasr the Chamberlain. They delivered the Emperor's missive, in which the redemption of prisoners was proposed, and begged that the proposal might be graciously considered.

The Vizier thereupon pronounced the reply for the Caliph. Moved, he declared, by his compassion for these True Believers, and out of his zeal to obey God, Who enjoins on His People the liberation of Believers, he accepted the proposal. He would send Munis to supervise the exchange.

When the envoys quitted the Presence, cloaks and turbans of gold poplin were conferred on them; and on their interpreter Abu Omar. He rode home with them; and the formalities of the ransoming, for which Munis had made arrangements, were immediately settled. The Byzantine prisoners whose redemption was the object of the embassy were to be ransomed as paid for, at the convenience of the envoys; and Munis and the officers who were to travel with him to Byzantine territory were issued one hundred and seventy thousand dinars from the Public Treasury for their undertaking. To all Governors of the provinces through which they were to pass Munis wrote ordering supplies, each envoy received a personal present of twenty thousand dirhams, and then, accompanied by Munis and Abu Omar, the embassy left Baghdad.

Under Munis' supervision, the exchange and redemption of prisoners was completed before the end of the year.

IBN FURAT MAKES AN ENEMY

During Ali's Vizierate, one of Ibn Furat's dependent Clerks, by name Ibn Jubayr, had thought it prudent to retire to Wasit. The revenue for the Wasit district had been farmed for years by a certain Hamid ibn Abbas; and during the course of his residence in the city Ibn Jubayr made it his business to find out what the total collections amounted to, and thus how much went into Hamid's pocket over and above the guaranteed sum he paid in to the Public Treasury.

When he returned to the capital to resume his old place under Ibn Furat as Chairman of the Primary Committee in the Bureau of Agricultural Iraq, Ibn Jubayr told the Vizier what he had found out. He was even able to list the various sources of Hamid's surplus; and Ibn Furat was a good deal impressed.

Some time later, the Clerk asked the Vizier for permission to write to Hamid bringing up some of the facts pertinent to his revenue contract. Ibn Furat hesitated, but in the end granted leave, and Ibn Jubayr wrote officially to Hamid as from his Committee (one of the functions of which was to determine the taxation in gross). Hamid sent in a reply, and correspondence on the subject went on for some time. When the matter was not dropped, Hamid's deputy wrote to Ibn Jubayr personally, remonstrating with him for having brought the matter up in his Committee in the first place.

But Hamid himself, who suspected that the attitude taken by Ibn Jubayr in the correspondence was assumed by arrangement with the Vizier, and in full knowledge of the latter's intentions as concerned himself, took alarm. So he sent an agent to the capital to try to arrange for his being appointed Vizier himself, instructing the man to obtain the good offices of Nasr the Chamberlain towards that end. The agent set about his business. He dilated to Nasr on Hamid's high-mindedness, and at the same time undertook to extort vast sums from Ibn Furat and his dependents. Messages of similar purport were also conveyed to the Queen-Mother.

SHORTAGE OF MONEY: THE VIZIER ARRESTED

Ibn Furat had found himself obliged to postpone payment on the Cavalry stipends. In excuse, he talked about the financial stringency, due to the expenses of military operations against Ibn Abi Saj, and to the reduction of revenue resulting from this rebel's seizure of the funds due from Rayy. It was all in vain: at the beginning of the year 306 the Cavalry mutinied and marched out to the Oratory.

Ibn Furat wrote requesting Muqtadir to advance two hundred thousand dinars from the Privy Treasury, and offering to contribute another two hundred thousand personally towards the Cavalry arrears. The Caliph was highly incensed by this demand; his rescript reminded the Vizier that he had undertaken not only to meet all public expenses as he had done in his first ministry, but in addition to furnish a stated sum to the Caliph personally. He could not have imagined, he said, that Ibn Furat was capable of preferring so impudent a request. In his reply, the Vizier pleaded the excuses given above; but Muqtadir was by no means placated.

Against him Ibn Furat had now not only the enmity and fear of the Chamberlain, but also the fiscal shortage which had compelled him to apply to the Caliph for an advance. Thus various circumstances aided the intrigues and reinforced the offers of Hamid's agent, playing directly into his patron's hands.

A message was sent to Hamid from the Palace, ordering him to leave Wasit and proceed to the capital, giving notice of his departure by carrier pigeon. As soon as Muqtadir got this notice, he sent one of his freedmen with Nasr the Chamberlain to arrest Ibn Furat, his son Muhassin, Ibn Jubayr, and a number of other dependents. All the prisoners were brought to the Palace, where Ibn Furat was confined by himself under the care of Zaydan the Stewardess as before, the rest being put in Nasr's charge.

HAMID AND ALI IBN ISA

HAMID SOON ARRIVED IN Baghdad. The Chamberlain put him up for the night in his apartment at the Palace. Ibn Furat's old enemy the courtier Ibn Hawari paid a call on the new arrival in order to curry favor with him; and the Guards officers and courtiers dropped in one by one.

Hamid sat there talking. Two things were soon apparent: that Hamid had a very nasty temper, and that he had not any conception of the duties of a Vizier. Muqtadir was told.

He sent for Ibn Hawari at once, and scolded him for supporting the nomination of such a man. Ibn Hawari replied by dwelling on the newcomer's vast wealth, the huge fines he had guaranteed to extract, the way his own officials respected him, his good moral character, and the impressive number of armed Retainers he supported. In the course of his reply, the courtier suggested a solution: set Ali ibn Isa at liberty again and make him President of all the Bureaus; in that capacity he could act as Hamid's general deputy.

This solution, unless at Hamid's own request, the Caliph declined to consider. So Ibn Hawari had to go back to Hamid, to advise him to beg this favor of Muqtadir when he had his audience. He expatiated on the heavy volume of business that had to be got through in the Bureaus, on the greed of the Attendants about court and the brutal manner in which, he warned him, they would press their claims. Venturing to hint that even if Hamid did not of his own free will do what was suggested, it would be done anyway, and in his teeth, he ended by assuring him that this advice was offered in the spirit of sincere friendship.

Accordingly, when Hamid had his audience and was invested, he kissed the ground at the Caliph's feet and requested that Ali ibn Isa be set at liberty, and that the Vizier be granted permission to appoint him his deputy-general over the Bureaus and the provinces.

I don't suppose, said Muqtadir, that Ali ibn Isa will consider this proposal, or be satisfied with second place after having held the first.

Why on earth not? exclaimed Hamid. A State Clerk is no better than a tailor; and a tailor, even if he stitches at a thousand-dinar coat one day, has to stitch at a ten-dinar coat another day.

This outburst at a formal audience provoked some hardly suppressed mirth.

THE FURATS UNDER EXAMINATION

Three days later, Hamid and Ali went by boat to the Palace, and appeared in the Presence as soon as permission was granted. They introduced an ex-official named Madharai, with whom they proposed to confront Ibn Furat at the examination of the latter's conduct in office which was to be held in the Palace.

When at the hearing itself this person was brought face to face with Ibn Furat, he testified that he had himself transmitted to Ibn Furat, during his first Vizierate, four hundred thousand dinars of undeclared profit from the Syria Army Offices; and he testified further that two Governors of Egypt, Ibn Bistam and his son, had likewise transmitted eight hundred thousand dinars by way of commission and undeclared profit from the Egypt districts, at the rate of two hundred thousand a year.

There was a full showing of Judges and Clerks at the examination; and Muqtadir himself was seated where he could hear the proceedings without being seen.

Ibn Furat's method of defending himself against this charge was the following: This official, he said, was employed in Egypt and Syria during the Vizierate of Ali ibn Isa. And he has just confessed that it was part of his office to levy such sums as he mentions, for he asserts that in his capacity as administrator of the Syria Army Offices he transmitted some of them to me, and that the Bistams likewise transmitted stated amounts. Now Ali ibn Isa has also been Vizier — for four years. Either then similar sums were transmitted to Ali ibn Isa, in which case he is liable to the Sovereign for them; or they were not transmitted, in which case this official is himself liable for them. We have his own acknowledgment that in the time of my first Vizierate he collected the sum which he names — four hundred thousand dinars; but we have only his assertion that he ever transmitted it to me. So that as part of a charge against me he confesses his own guilt. As to the charge against me, I declare that it is false. The ruling of God, His Prophet, and the Jurists in such cases is familiar to you all.

At this point Hamid broke out into violent abuse, and uttered a very coarse insult to Ibn Furat.

I bid you remember, Ibn Furat retorted, that you are on the Sovereign's Carpet, and within the precincts of the Imperial Palace, and not in the kind of place to which you are accustomed — some granary from which you want your cut! Nor am I a peasant for you to bully, nor a Collector for you to whip. Be kind enough, he continued, turning to Shafi Lului, to send to our lord the Sovereign the following statement in writing: Hamid aspired to the Vizierate, an office for which he is wholly unfit, for one reason only — because I was holding him liable for more than a

million dinars excess of collections beyond remittances, due upon
the Wasit districts, which he farmed. I was insisting, and in no
uncertain terms, that he refund this sum to Government; and he
imagined that one way of keeping it in his own pocket, and piling
up fresh profits, would be to become Vizier. As Vizier of the
Prince of True Believers, the proper thing for him to do would
be to resign the farming of the Wasit districts, and have them
audited, so that it would appear whether he was making money
for himself or not; and the proper person now to investigate and
administer the department is Ali ibn Isa — no one is in any doubt
as to the difference between him and Hamid in technical knowledge of fiscal and economic matters. The mere fact that Hamid,
while actually Vizier, is keeping the farming of these districts in
his own hands foreshadows a future of treachery and embezzle-
ment!

Pluck out his beard! shouted Hamid.

Since nobody had the audacity to obey this order, he himself sprang on the ex-Vizier and began to pull at Ibn Furat's
beard with his own hand.

The tension at the hearing had been such that Madharai,
at a previous point, and before Hamid's display of bad language
and attempt on Ibn Furat's beard, had been heard offering to
sign a guarantee then and there for half a million dinars if Ibn
Furat were put in his power. Ali ibn Isa, unlike the vituperating
Hamid, had gone no further than interjecting some observations,
perfectly courteous, to Ibn Furat at certain points in his defense.
As to Ibn Hawari, he was trying to make Ibn Furat see him in
the role of a peacemaker between himself and Hamid, though
it was apparent from his drift that he intended to damage Ibn
Furat's case as much as he could.

When Muqtadir heard Hamid's foul language, and then
saw him lay hand to his enemy's beard, he sent a servant to withdraw Ibn Furat from the hearing and take him back to the room
where he was confined. Both Ali and Ibn Hawari thereupon
told Hamid that the way he had behaved to Ibn Furat had
merely damaged their own position; and Madharai, opponent

to Ibn Furat as he had shown himself, said to him as he was led away: If you are fined as a result of this hearing, I will contribute fifty thousand dinars.

As soon as Ibn Furat was gone, Nasr the Chamberlain, Ali, and Ibn Hawari all rounded on Madharai at once. You came here, they protested, to cross-examine the man. And before you are well through, there you are offering him a bribe and trying to make friends with him.

The man you pitted me against was one you all warned me to be wary of, retorted Madharai. You said, as I came in: Don't forget whom you'll be talking to! And as for you, you said: Be careful what you're about now! And your words were: Don't forget this: you are risking your life by giving this testimony. When I heard his manner of defending himself, I simply did what I thought was the most prudent thing to do!

Another official, Ibn Hammad of Mosul, was now brought forward; he examined Ibn Furat in the presence of Shafi Lului.

The Vizier and the President, he opened his attack by saying, both warn you to keep your own interest in mind. Now, you have been getting in rents and produce an annual income of twelve hundred thousand dinars, and from undeclared profits of office a similar sum. That is a great deal of money. So you had better, before any settlement of your case is considered, and merely as a present means of preserving your life, give your bond for a million dinars, to be paid at once. Otherwise you are going to be handed over to those who will treat you as traitors ought to be treated who conspire against the Empire. For the Sovereign knows all about your correspondence with Ibn Abi Saj, and your encouraging his rebellion.

I would have thought, answered Ibn Furat, that saving your own neck, and getting out of the very unpleasant situation you are in, would have kept you busy enough, without running to and fro with messages of this sort. For four years you were in the employ of Ali ibn Isa. During those four years you embezzled a vast amount of property. When I undertook the administration, you went into hiding. The person who replaced you wrote me a statement notifying various falsifications in your books of account, and itemizing the undeclared profits you had made. Those records are on file now in the Imperial Archives.

You're no match for Ibn Furat! said Shafi to Ibn Hammad. You had better go and examine his son Muhassin.

So Ibn Hammad took himself off. He managed to get Muhassin's bond for three hundred thousand dinars.

Hamid's next proceeding was to have Muhassin up before himself. He demanded money. Muhassin replied that he could not now furnish more than twenty thousand dinars.

Beat him up! Hamid ordered.

Some blows were administered. Then Hamid observed that the young man had a thick growth of hair on his head; and supposing that this deadened the pain of the beating, he called for a barber to be fetched. Muhassin was removed, shaved, and brought in again, and then beaten about the head till he was nearly killed. There were a lot of people looking on.

Ali ibn Isa now interceded, requesting that the Vizier be content with fifty thousand dinars. But Hamid swore that he would not take less than seventy thousand. Muhassin at last signed a bond for that amount. In spite of this, Hamid ordered him a hair shirt and various other tortures. After begging contributions from people, Muhassin paid sixty thousand. Ali ibn Isa contributed ten thousand dirhams. It took Muhassin a long time to raise the sums for which he had given his bond; but many people interceded for him, and in the end Hamid allowed him to return home.

It was Ibn Furat himself that Hamid most wanted to get his hands on. Muqtadir was not unwilling, but he insisted that one of the Attendants must be responsible for Ibn Furat's life.

If Ibn Furat knew, pleaded Hamid, that he was not going to be tortured to the limit, he would hold out.

Muqtadir then suggested handing him over to Ali ibn Isa, or to Shafi Lului, both of whom he trusted. He could not make

up his mind about Ibn Furat: at times the craving to get hold
of his money came uppermost, and at other times he could not
bear the thought of the old Vizier dying under Hamid's hands.

Zaydan the Stewardess came to know what the Caliph was
thinking. She told Ibn Furat. He wrote to the two Bankers
(Joseph Bar-Phineas and Aaron Bar-Amram) an order to pay
to the Caliph's Palace the sums deposited with them, amounting
to seven hundred thousand dinars. He made out another draft on
Ibn Qaraba the middleman and another on Ibn Idris the Carrier,
and sent them all by Zaydan to the Caliph.

Muqtadir transmitted them to Hamid and Ali ibn Isa for
collection. They saw with chagrin that they were not going to
get possession of Ibn Furat's person; both Ali and Ibn Hawari
asked Hamid what he thought was the real meaning of Ibn
Furat's action.

Just like the Caliph's luck! was all Hamid said.

Doubtless the Vizier is right, said Ali. Only I am sure that
Ibn Furat would never have parted with this immense sum for
nothing, since far less would have been enough, were it not that
he is pursuing a further plan — to get us and our property into
his power.

That must be it, Hamid said.

I think so too, said Ibn Hawari.

FRICTION

For two months Ali ibn Isa presented himself at Hamid's
residence twice every day; then his attendance gradually dropped
until he was visiting only once a week. Then, at the beginning of
the year '7, Hamid lost all credit with the Caliph, so that Ali was
really the sole administrator. The Vizier found his functions
limited to wearing his black robe and appearing on horseback at
the Palace when there was a Court. When he presented himself
at Audience, Muqtadir addressed his whole conversation to Ali
ibn Isa.

The Vizier now thought of undertaking to farm the Land Tax and the Estates, Public, Royal, and Additional, and the confiscated Abbasi and Furati Estates, for Agricultural Iraq, Ahwaz, and Isfahan. He wanted to have at any rate some say in Baghdad affairs. And he hoped to show a sufficient surplus on these undertakings to eclipse Ali's reputation with Muqtadir for competence and honesty.

Accordingly, on one occasion when they were together in the Presence, he thus assailed Ali: You have got your fingers on the whole administration, so that I am left out in the cold: you never think of even consulting me about anything nowadays. But it is time the Prince of True Believers knew the facts. You have allowed four hundred thousand dinars to go to waste every year in Agricultural Iraq, Ahwaz, and Isfahan. Here and now I guarantee to farm the revenue for those provinces for four years, budgeting for remittances to the capital and for appropriations the same figures as you authorized when you were Vizier; and beyond that I guarantee to provide a surplus of four hundred thousand dinars every year.

I cannot approve of Hamid farming these revenues, said Ali. He has a reputation for cruel exploitation, for imposing new duties, and for anticipating collections. A person who acted on such principles might show a surplus for a year or two, no doubt; but he would ruin what might take many years to repair. He would have dried up the revenue at its source, and given Government a bad name.

There was a long argument. Muqtadir brought it to an end by saying: Hamid here is offering to increase the revenue, and a proposal like that can't be turned down; but if you, Ali, are prepared to farm these provinces on the terms Hamid offers, I would rather let you have them.

I am a Clerk, not a revenue officer, Ali replied. It is much more in Hamid's line; and it is his idea. But the fact that he is able to offer such terms, Prince of theTrue Believers, is due to my having made these territories prosperous, by my tenderness with the inhabitants. Cultivation for the year '7 is now at an end —

he cannot pretend that putting more land under cultivation is the object of his revenue-farming; the time for that was over long ago.

Muqtadir, however, promptly ordered the right to farm such and such revenues assigned to Hamid, and took his bond for the sum mentioned; and the two officials left the Palace together.

Orders were issued by Ali ibn Isa to the Bureau chiefs to send in the Budget figures from their various offices for recent years, since these years had been unusually productive. So a Budget was issued, with figures for the amounts to be remitted to the Treasury, for special appropriations, and allocations to permanent expenses, corresponding to the average figures for the three years '3, '4, and '5. The totals were:

for Agricultural Iraq and Ahwaz:	33,000,000 dirhams
for the Public, Royal, and Additional Estates, and the sequestered Abbasi and Furati Estates:	8,800,000 dirhams
for Isfahan:	6,300,000 dirhams
Total:	48,100,000 dirhams
Surplus guaranteed by Hamid, 400,000 dinars, valued at:	5,800,000 dirhams
Grand total:	53,900,000 dirhams

In the year '8 Hamid was in arrears. He requested Muqtadir to order a number of Clerks to be placed at his disposal for the clerical work of his revenue-farming office. Ali ibn Isa was insisting that he produce the money for which he had made himself responsible; and Hamid found that he would have to

get leave to go to Ahwaz in search of funds. A good deal of
friction ensued between Hamid's Clerks and Ali's.

It was not long before first the common people and then
the court were disturbed by a sharp rise in the cost of living.
There was a series of riots. At a public meeting attended by some
leading commoners complaints were made of the rising prices;
Ali was hooted as he rode in the streets; and soon afterwards the
mob, after looting the establishments of numerous Baghdad corn-
chandlers, gathered at the Palace gate and made an uproar.
Hamid was recalled to the capital; but the day after his arrival,
the Household Troops began to clamor about the rise in prices,
the mob rioted in the public Mosques, smashed the pulpits,
stopped Prayer, stripped people of their clothes, and flung brickbats about. A number of persons, including a Judge, were hurt.
Some wit said:

> When people felt pinched by the rising prices,
> They thought it might help to heave some bricks
> At a Judge. Don't people have strange devices?

The crowds attacked Hamid's house, and on the Saturday
morning fired the bridges, opened the prisons, and looted the
houses of the Chief of Police and others. Meanwhile the Palace
was disturbed by an outcry from the regular infantry stationed
there, yelling about the rising cost of living.

So Muqtadir ordered the shops and warehouses owned by
Hamid and the Queen-Mother and the royal princes and the
chief officers of State to be opened up, and the wheat they contained sold, at a reduction of four dinars the *kurr*, barley being
proportionately lowered. Orders were issued to all wholesalers
and retailers to sell their stocks at these reduced figures. The
crowds calmed down; and the prices of food fell.

As a result of these disorders, however, a rescript was received from the Caliph cancelling Hamid's contract for revenue-
farming. And a general Proclamation was issued to be read in all
bazaars, highways, and pulpits, forbidding all ministers of State
and officers of the Army and Guards to undertake the farming
of revenue in any province whatsoever. Hamid had to write

dismissing his agents and instructing them to hand over their functions to Ali's men, to his very great chagrin.

MUNIS HONORED

Soon after these tumults had died away, alarming reports came in from Egypt: the Fatimid ruler of the West was moving towards that province. Munis, who had at last defeated Ibn Abi Saj and brought him a prisoner to the capital, was commissioned to Egypt for operations against the Fatimid.

Despatches came in after the turn of the year announcing the complete defeat of the Western ruler and the pillaging of his camp. These despatches were read from the pulpits, the title al-Muzaffar — the Victor — was conferred on Munis, and letters of notification in the Caliph's name sent to all provinces. Munis was also given the Governments of Egypt and Syria.

Ibn Abi Saj was released in the course of the following year, at the Victor's request, and granted an Audience, being even permitted to ride in black to the Palace. He kissed the Carpet and the Caliph's hand, a Robe of reconciliation was thrown over him, and he was mounted on a gilt-saddle State horse. Then, a few days later, Muqtadir held a Court in the Hall of Public Audience at which he appointed Ibn Abi Saj Minister of Prayer, Public Security, Finance, and Estates for the Rayy, Qazvin, Abhar, Zanjan, and Azarbayjan districts. The provinces named were converted into personal fiefs, on condition of an annual remittance to the capital of five hundred thousand dinars over and above the defraying of all regular expenditures and costs of the military establishments in those regions.

When he left the Palace, there rode home with him Munis, Nasr the Chamberlain, Shafi Lului, and indeed all the Army and Guards officers in the capital at the time, so that his house was fairly choked with soldiers and arms — it was a brilliant occasion.

In the year '11 Muqtadir invited the Victor Munis to drink in the Presence and invested him with the Robes of a Table Com-

panion to the Caliph. The Robes ordered for this particular ceremony were stiff with gold.

HAMID AND ALI DISMISSED

After five years of office, Hamid was dismissed from the
Vizierate, and Ali ibn Isa from the Bureaus. There were more
reasons than one for the change.

For one thing, rumors had reached Hamid that Muqtadir,
influenced by the howl which all kinds of court dependents were
raising against Ali ibn Isa, was thinking of reappointing Ibn
Furat. Ali had got into arrears with court stipends and those of
the harem and royal princes; he had cut down the salaries of
Attendants, Palace servants, and Household Cavalry, taken two
months' pay off the stipends of ministers, and four months' off
those of Paymasters, Secret Service men, Postmasters, and Judges,
so that general feeling against him was beginning to run very
high.

It occurred to Hamid that he might guarantee to extort a
sum of money from Ali ibn Isa if he were put in his hands. He
made this offer to the Caliph, and went on to profess his readi-
ness to farm the Government as a whole. Muqtadir told him to
write a personal memorandum stating his guarantees and offers,
and naming his proposed appointees. Hamid wrote the memorandum and sent it in; and Muqtadir went round to Ibn Furat's
apartment to show it him.

Even if Hamid had every past master of administration
now alive at his back, said the prisoner, he would still be incapable of governing the Empire, even of managing the Bureaus.
Ali ibn Isa, with all his ups and downs, is a far better man than
Hamid. Why! I myself could guarantee five times as much as
this.

I'll give you the chance, said Muqtadir.

Another factor was this: rumors were going round about
one of the royal princes, a grandson of Mutawakkil's, who was

enormously rich, and very sumptuous in his style and dress, his horses and conveyances. This prince was a close friend of Ali ibn Isa's: so much so that Ali was supposed to be bringing him along for the Caliphate. Ibn Hawari was also believed to be helping to engineer the business.

One of Ibn Furat's partisans had smuggled into Muqtadir's Private Apartments a paper on which was written the verse:

> *Greetings! Greetings!*
> *Cock of the Caliph's roost!*

It went no further; but this couplet is the least offensive of a well-known and very improper poem. The man took care that the paper should be dropped where the Caliph would see it on his way to one of the Private Apartments; and Muqtadir picked it up. It threw him into a state of violent suspicion, directed upon Ibn Hawari; and he determined that Ibn Hawari must die.

Then Ibn Furat's son Muhassin addressed a note to Muqtadir, undertaking to extract seven million dinars if Hamid, Ali, Nasr, Shafi, Ibn Hawari, Umm Musa the Stewardess and her brother, and the two Madharais were put in his power.

One thing added to another finally made up Muqtadir's mind; he would restore the Vizierate to Ibn Furat. So Ali ibn Isa was arrested when he came downriver to the Palace on the 9th of Second Rabi in the year 311. He was given in charge to the Stewardess Zaydan, who put him in the very apartment where Ibn Furat had been lodged, and from which that person was now removed to be invested afresh with the Vizierate.

IBN FURAT VIZIER: THE THIRD TERM

IBN FURAT ORDERED HIS CHAMBERLAIN to arrest Ibn Hawari and all his dependents. He assigned the courtier a spacious apartment, cleanly furnished, in his own palace, and then sent to negotiate with him on the subject of his fine. After much haggling, the amount was fixed at seven hundred thousand dinars for him personally, exclusive of his clerks and dependents.

The Vizier proceeded to order raids on various places where such dependents might be lying low; he ferreted them out one by one. His son Muhassin went beyond all limit in the tortures he inflicted on those he got his hands on. From Ibn Hammad (who had examined *him* in time gone by) he obtained a bond for two hundred thousand dinars; and when he had the document in his possession, he handed Ibn Hammad over to his exactor, who gave him a savage beating. It was not savage enough for Muhassin, however. He had his prisoner brought into his own presence, and gave him such a buffet on the head that the blood spurted from his nose and mouth, and he died on the spot.

Muhassin, anticipating Muqtadir's displeasure, was now in great alarm. But the Caliph, far from raising any objection, sent him the official Robes of a Table Companion a few days later, and increased his stipend by two thousand dinars a month in addition to his salary as President of the Bureaus.

The royal singing-girls sang a chorus in the Presence to the burden:

Well done, Muhassin! well done!

THE CASE AGAINST HAMID

Having got Hamid into his possession, the new Vizier sent to demand a statement of his assets. He admitted the possession of two hundred thousand dinars.

Ibn Furat's next move was to bring him up before the Jurists, Judges, and State Clerks, and submit him to prolonged examination. The defendant made a good case until Ibn Furat produced a document which he had found in the files of a certain retainer of Hamid's, a man employed in the sale of the crops from an estate he farmed. With this paper the Vizier confronted Hamid, introducing the retainer himself to testify that it was genuine. The man admitted it. He had filed it by mistake; for it was Hamid's custom every year to collect all his bills and throw them in the Tigris. But when Fate was leading him to his ruin, he forgot to ask his assistant for this particular document, which chanced to have been written haphazard on the back of some paper or other and was filed with a bundle of similar papers.

According to this note, the proceeds for the sale of crops for a certain year was five hundred and forty thousand odd dinars, exclusive of barley which had been transmitted as fodder to Baghdad. So it appeared that the surplus pocketed by the revenue-farmer was more than double the sum for which he had contracted! And prices in that year (the second of the contract) had been low; prices in all subsequent years had been higher.

This disclosure did Hamid a great deal of harm. Ibn Furat seeing this asked the Judges and State Clerks to put in writing and sign their opinions: that so far the case had gone against the ex-Vizier. He had conducted his examination with civility, using no harsh or offensive expressions, but merely putting the case against Hamid, and giving him every chance to put up a defense.

Far otherwise Muhassin, who insulted Hamid in the vilest terms, and said that the only way to get money out of him would be to use the same tortures on him as he had used on others. He undertook, if Hamid were put in his power, to get a million dinars out of him on the spot. The Vizier tried to check his son; but Muhassin would not be repressed.

Your son, said Hamid at last, has been most offensive; and I have put up with it, not out of any regard for him certainly, but out of respect for the Vizier's court. Where I stand now, I have nothing more to fear but death; and only my feeling that I must treat the Vizier's court with respect holds me from paying him back in the same coin.

Ibn Furat turned to Muhassin. I swear, said he, that if you insult him again, I will request the Caliph to excuse me from continuing the examination. This threat was effective, and Muhassin relapsed into silence.

Hamid's final statement, although the examination was repeatedly resumed, was always the same: that he had no more money than he had declared, and having already sold his estates and commercial interests, his house and furniture, he had no further means of raising any.

This attack seemed to be ineffective, therefore; so Ibn Furat arranged for a private interview with Hamid in an apartment where there would be no other person present listening. Addressing the prisoner in courteous terms, he swore to him that if he would tell the truth about his property and treasures, he should not be delivered to Muhassin, nor removed from the Vizieral Palace where he now was: his life would be safe, and he might either remain in the palace an honored guest, as long as suited him, or retire to Fars as Governor, or indeed anywhere he might choose. And he might take one of the Sovereign's servants with him to ensure his safety.

You will remember, Ibn Furat went on, after confirming these offers with the most solemn assurances, that you guaranteed to the Prince of True Believers to obtain a certain sum of money from me if I were put in your power; and you will remember that at that time I redeemed myself by paying seven hundred thousand dinars, declared voluntarily. In that way I kept myself out of your hands, for you seemed to have forgotten the many kindnesses which I and my brother showed you in times past. The Caliph now is bent on handing you over to Muhassin — and Muhassin is a young man who has a reckoning against you for tortures, such tortures as had never before been used on a Vizier or a member of a Vizieral family, but which were inflicted on him by your orders. My advice to you is to ransom yourself with your money (as I did). That is the only way to save yourself from being handed over to Muhassin.

To this advice, thus backed, Hamid at last, when Ibn Furat had bound himself by solemn oaths, inclined. He divulged to the Vizier the whereabouts of sundry hoards he had buried, in pits dug with his own hands, wherein he had himself deposited treasure amounting to half a million dinars. Further, he confessed to having deposited with various highly-placed persons and members of the Witness class sums to the amount of approximately three hundred thousand dinars, and to being the owner of costly apparel and perfumes to a considerable value, now on deposit in Wasit.

For all this Ibn Furat took his bond; and then rode off hastily to the Palace, without saying a word to his son Muhassin.

Muqtadir was delighted. He offered to put anyone on whom Ibn Furat would guarantee a payment in his power. He suggested Nasr the Chamberlain, Shafi Lului, and various others. But Ibn Furat advised that Shafi be sent without delay to secure Hamid's Wasit deposits. So Shafi went, dug up the buried treasures, drew the deposits, and brought everything back to the Caliph.

THE END OF HAMID

For a while Hamid stayed on in safety at the Vizier's Palace. But one day when Muhassin had gone with his father to Audience at the Royal Palace, the young man spoke to the Caliph, under the Vizier's very nose. A vast part of Hamid's fine, he said, still stood against him; but if Hamid were put into his power, he would guarantee another half-million dinars out of him.

Muqtadir promptly told Ibn Furat to hand the ex-Vizier over to his son.

Ibn Furat ventured to object: he had given his word to Hamid, he said, that he would not commit him to Muhassin.

But the young man refused to drop his proposal, and urged it until the Caliph repeated his command in a tone which the Vizier dared not resist.

So Hamid was surrendered to Muhassin, who had him conveyed to his own residence. There he demanded the sum he had guaranteed, and applied some torture. Hamid only repeated that he possessed no more wealth of any sort or kind. Muhassin gave orders, and he was buffeted about the head until he fell down unconscious. Then more blows were laid on his body, until at last he came to a little.

What do you want of me? he asked.

The money, said Muhassin.

There's nothing left, Hamid said; there's only my private estate.

Then make out a power of attorney for the sale of that, answered Muhassin.

Hamid did as he was bidden; and the deed was attested by a Judge who was present. Muhassin, after treating him with mortifying insults, sent him, under guard, downriver to Wasit for the sale of his lands and goods.

According to the story current in Baghdad, Hamid asked, on the night he left, for some eggs. Some were brought him, and he ate some raw for his breakfast next morning. Muhassin's eunuch had poisoned these eggs somehow; and soon after swallowing them Hamid began to cry out with pain, and was seized with violent diarrhoea. By the time he reached Wasit he was prostrate. The eunuch left him at the house of a certain Bazawfari, with whom Hamid had left deposits, and got away as fast he could.

Hamid's malady continued, though he took no food but barley porridge; and Bazawfari, in order to secure himself from suspicion, sent for the town Judge and Witnesses and wrote out the following affidavit:

Hamid was suffering from diarrhoea when he reached Wasit. It had come on during his journey, between Baghdad and Wasit; and he was in the condition mentioned when Bazawfari received him. If the complaint should prove fatal, his death will therefore have been due to natural causes, and in no wise attributable to Bazawfari.

This affidavit he sent to Hamid, who pretended that he was willing to sign it; so the Judge and Witnesses went to his room. When he saw that they were all present, Hamid made the following declaration: That Unbeliever and criminal Ibn Furat, who makes no secret of his rejection of the rights of the Abbasids (and preference of the Alids), gave me his word of honor, and swore to me by his oath of allegiance and with forfeit of divorcing his wives that if I made a true statement of all my possessions he would not deliver me to his son Muhassin, and would secure me from all forms of torture, allowing me to go to my home and appointing me to some honorable office. In consequence I made a true statement of all I possessed. And now he *has* delivered me to Muhassin, who has tortured me in most exquisite ways and treacherously gave me poisoned eggs, from eating which I got this malady. Bazawfari had no hand in this murder. But he has done this, among other things: he has taken money and valuables of mine and stuffed them into tattered old brocade cushions, which are being offered for public sale at five dirhams apiece. Those cushions have three thousand dinars' worth of valuables in them; and he is buying them in himself. That is my declaration. I call on you to attest it.

Bazawfari realized that he had been tricked. The Secret Service agent for Wasit sent Ibn Furat a complete report of Hamid's statement. Shortly after, Hamid died.

IBN FURAT'S TILT WITH ALI

When Muqtadir had ordered Ali ibn Isa's arrest, he had sent him a message demanding a true statement of his assets; and Ali had replied in writing that three thousand dinars was all he could produce.

Just at this time it happened that news arrived of a raid upon Basra by Abu Tahir the Qarmatian chief. The Qarmatians (a secret society, esoteric in doctrine and equalitarian in propaganda) were a heretical sect whose opinions had spread far and wide among the uneducated classes. Their first insurrection had been in the Wasit district in Mu'tamid's time. In the year 293 their chief had appeared in Bahrayn, and since then his power had increased. He had raided Basra and its districts, and had defeated Government troops in several engagements. In Muktafi's time the Qarmatians had broken out in Syria, destroying and ravaging. Where Truth is revealed, Law is abrogated, they believe. Their chief had proclaimed himself the Mahdi and had been prayed for as such from the pulpits. And now the Qarmatians had massacred the men of Basra, and after occupying the city seventeen days had loaded their camels with all the goods and women and children they could carry, and retired to their own territory.

Ibn Furat immediately dispatched a force. His general captured a number of prisoners, and sent them up to Baghdad. These men stated under question that the Basra raid had been prompted by Ali ibn Isa, and they averred that on more than one occasion Ali had sent the Qarmatians presents and arms.

When Muqtadir was shown the general's despatch in which this information was given, he told Ibn Furat to examine Ali, and to confront him with these Qarmatians as witnesses. The Vizier gave orders for Ali to be brought up for examination.

At the hearing, Ali objected. When a man is in a situation like mine at this moment, under the Sovereign's frown, people will bring false charges against him to his face, especially if the Vizier himself is unfriendly and has a grudge against him, he said.

So Ibn Furat took up another question: Ali's administration of the provinces. And among other matters he brought up the affair of the two Madharais, Husayn and Muhammad.

When I served my second term as Vizier, said Ibn Furat, one of my provincial Governors obtained a bond from the Madharais for two million three hundred thousand dinars. It was a compromise settlement on what was due from them to Government on two counts: Land Tax on the Egypt and Syria Estates, which they had been farming, and undeclared profits of office, made when they held offices under you during your first Vizierate. Of this sum they paid only half a million dinars in my time. You, no sooner had you become President of the Bureaus than you dismissed my Governor and reappointed these two Madharais — these barefaced embezzlers of the Sovereign's property. And you composed a letter in the name of the Prince of the True Believers (whose life God long preserve!), addressed to these two, in which they were excused the whole of the balance due! You pretend that you did this by order of the Prince of the True Believers; but when I brought the matter to his notice, he assured me that he had given no such order and could not believe that anyone would have had the audacity to do such a thing.

I was no more than Hamid's Clerk and deputy at that time, said Ali: the Prince of True Believers had instructed me to take orders from him. Hamid told me that the Prince of True Believers had commanded that the sum should be excused these two officials, and he wrote an order to that effect; I merely countersigned Hamid's order, with a note that it was to be engrossed and go through, in the usual way when a Vizier's deputy gets an order from his chief.

But you were always fighting with Hamid! and arguing about every trifle! retorted Ibn Furat. You even scrutinized his assessments for the Estates he farmed himself! How was it that you failed to solicit the Prince of the True Believers' approval when this enormous sum was at stake?

For the first seven months I was merely Hamid's Clerk, Ali replied. Later, the Prince of True Believers saw fit to rely principally on me; but this business of the two Madharais took place in the early days of Hamid's administration.

Then why, pursued Ibn Furat, did you fail, when the Prince of True Believers placed his reliance upon you, to tell him the facts about this malversation of Hamid's? Why did you take no steps to correct it?

I let it go, said Ali, because at an earlier date I had had Husayn Madharai up before the Caliph and at that very Audience had obtained his bond for a million dinars annually, to be remitted to the Treasury net, without deduction of a single dirham, in return for a contract then assigned him, according to the terms of which he was to farm the Land Tax and Estates in Egypt and Syria, and to pay all permanent expenses and army stipends in those regions. An itemized specification of expenditures under these heads was made out for each district. And for moneys due on account of delay or withholding in the resultant transactions

I held him responsible — to the tune of one hundred and thirty thousand dinars. That was the utmost I could do. His bond is in the files now, in the Bureau of the West.

You have been employed in the Bureaus since you were a child, said the Vizier; for many years you were President of the Bureau of the West; you have been Vizier; and for quite a long period since you have been managing the Empire. Have you ever heard of one single instance of an official remitting a debt currently due in consideration of a sum to fall due at some future date? and dependent on the proceeds of revenue-farming? But grant that you, to use your own expression, *let it go* for practical reasons: well then, during the five years of your management I suppose you did get the money this revenue-farmer had guaranteed?

Some of the money was transmitted in the first year, Ali replied; but then came the invasion of the African Alid (the Mahdi) who occupied most of the Egyptian districts. Munis the Victor was commissioned to repel the aggressor, and most of that money was diverted to army pay and military expenses. The balance due had to be cancelled, because the invader had levied such exactions on the districts in Egypt that it simply could not be raised.

The Alid was routed in the month of Safar of the year '9, said Ibn Furat. So the revenue-farmer is liable for the two whole years which have elapsed since his defeat — have you obtained the two million dinars from him?

What reply Ali ibn Isa put up to this is missing from the record. When he had done, Ibn Furat said to him: I am under present orders from the Prince of True Believers to compel you to refund the moneys you have improperly amassed at his expense. If you are wise, you will reveal them voluntarily, and so save yourself from being subjected to torture.

I am not a rich man, Ali answered: the utmost I can produce is three thousand dinars.

The Vizier then turned to the subject of the court allowances. You, he said, in the five years of your administration, reduced the allowances of the harem, of the royal princes, of the Attendants, and of the Household Cavalry, allowances which I, during both my first and my second Vizierates, had managed to pay regularly. You cut them down by forty-five thousand dinars a month, and you also reserved the proceeds of the Private Estates, making a yearly total of five hundred and forty thousand dinars, or a grand total for the whole period (including the proceeds of the Private Estates) of six millions. That money is somewhere — either embezzled by you or wasted by you.

The revenue I obtained from these Estates, Ali returned, and which I saved out of the allowances of persons who did not need so much, I used — to cover the deficit and balance the budget. And the Caliph's Privy Treasury I did not touch. As for your practice — allowing to go to court expenses forty-five thousand dinars which you had got out of undeclared profits — I do not approve of your methods of raising money, nor do I permit officials to make undeclared profits. I forbade and abolished such practices instead of exploiting them, because they only lead to waste of the Sovereign's property, the vexation of his subjects, and the devastation of his lands. Your method of making ends meet was simply to transfer funds from the Privy Treasury to the Public Treasury. The court was delighted — but the Treasury was emptied.

Along these lines the wrangle went on for some time. At a later hearing Ibn Furat brought up the subject of the presents and arms sent by Ali to the Qarmatians, and the correspondence and other amenities which had passed between him and them.

My purpose, Ali explained, was to bring them back to their allegiance; my method was conciliation. It was effective: it twice restrained them from attacking the Holy Pilgrimage during my Vizierate, and from raiding the Kufa and Basra districts. It also led to the liberation of True Believers whom they had taken prisoners.

And what could be worse, demanded Ibn Furat, than your recognizing Abu Sa'id and his Qarmatian gang as True Believers at all, being as they are men who deny the Koran and the

Prophet's Mission, men who plundered Oman and led away captive such of its inhabitants as they did not murder? What could be worse than maintaining correspondence with such people, while you let the pay of the Basra garrison fall into arrears so that the men deserted their posts and let the Qarmatians in, to murder the citizens?

Ali put up a long defense; but at last Nasr the Chamberlain and Muhassin asked the Vizier to allow them a word in private with Ali ibn Isa. Ibn Furat gave leave; and the two told him he had better submit to a fine. Ali gave way. They fixed his fine at three hundred thousand dinars, one third of which was to be paid within a month from the date at which he should leave the Palace, for some place where personal security and liberty to receive visits would be assured him. Ibn Furat took his bond, and sent the document to be countersigned by Muqtadir.

Ali requested the Vizier to leave him the income from his private estates for the current year, so that he might pay it as part of his fine.

That would be fifty thousand dinars, observed Ibn Furat.

I should be glad enough if it came to twenty thousand, said Ali; it does not yield as much as that.

(In point of fact, when Ali was later banished to Mecca, and the estates were sequestered, they were found to yield about fifty thousand annually. There is a story told by Humani of Wasit: I once heard Ali ibn Isa upbraiding Baridi, who farmed the revenue for Ahwaz and Wasit, and asking him whether he was not afraid of God's Vengeance when he swore at a hearing in the Palace that his family estate in Wasit yielded only ten thousand dinars income, since it was plain from his books of account that it yielded thirty thousand.

I was only, Baridi replied, following the example of your Excellency, God support you! when Ibn Furat asked you about your income. So pious a person as your Excellency would never, I felt sure, have perjured himself unless he believed like a good

Shi'ite that suppression of the truth was permissible in the presence of one from whom injury was to be apprehended!

And the expression on Ali's face was that of a man who has been obliged to swallow a stone.)

There was difficulty in raising the money for Ali's fine. The Caliph, on one side, refused to let him go till he got some money; Ali, on the other, insisted that he could not raise the money till he was released from the Palace. Muhassin had him up twice and pressed him for payment. The first interview was conducted gently; but the ex-Vizier paid no more than the price of a house he had sold. So Muhassin at the next had him put in fetters.

At the sight, Nasr the Chamberlain left the room. To Muhassin's now repeated demands Ali only returned: If I could raise the money here, I should not now be in these fetters.

Muhassin ordered a hair shirt put on him. He held his ground. Muhassin ordered that he be given some cuffs. Nazuk, the Baghdad Chief of Police, who was present, also now rose to go.

Where are you going? said Muhassin.

I will not stay to see this old gentleman tortured, said Nazuk; I have kissed his hand for ten years.

So Ali was sent back to his apartment.

Ibn Furat was greatly disturbed when he heard how Muhassin had treated Ali: he told his son that he had seriously compromised them both by doing as he had done — he should never have gone further than the fetters. And he wrote at once to the Caliph to intercede for Ali: He had been more grieved, he wrote, to hear of what had happened than by anything that he could remember — he had been unable to touch a mouthful of food since he heard the news; for Abu Hasan Ali ibn Isa was one of the most distinguished members of the Clerkly profession, he had served the Prince of the True Believers, he was then an inmate of the Palace, which circumstance alone should have rendered his person sacred. Such a man might make mistakes, he went on, but it would be worthy of the Prince of the True Believers to forgive. In conclusion, he begged that the fetters and the hair shirt might be removed from his person.

Ali ibn Isa deserved many times what he had got, was Muqtadir's reply: Muhassin's treatment was the right one. Still, he would accept Ibn Furat's intercession for him, and was giving the appropriate orders. Ali ibn Isa would be delivered to the Vizier.

So Ali was sent to the Vizier's Palace. Ibn Furat did not want to keep him there, since Ali was an old man and might fall sick, and any malady would be ascribed to the Vizier's ministrations. He sent for Shafi Lului to take him to his own house.

While they were waiting for Shafi, Ibn Furat had some reproaches for Ali. He criticized his handling of certain trust funds or Pious Foundations established by Ibn Furat, part of the income of which was devoted to religious uses and part to his children and retainers (a regular legal device at this time for saving property from the Government). These trusts the Caliph had ordered to be returned to Ibn Furat (after their confiscation), and Ali's management of them had been, said the Vizier, indefensible, either from the point of view of religion or in common decency (the trusts had apparently been returned much deteriorated in value).

I confess, said Ali, that I was negligent in that matter, and can only beg the Vizier to excuse me.

Muhassin, who was sitting with them, broke in, abusively and at great length. Ali gave him the same reply, but with additions, in the course of which he used the expression: Really, you make me laugh!

The phrase exasperated Muhassin, and even annoyed his father. The young man retorted in coarse language, and Ibn Furat, after trying to quiet him, turned to Ali and said: Abu Ahmad Muhassin is Clerk to the Caliph, you should remember, and high in the Sovereign's favor. So Ali apologized for using such an expression.

As they sat there, Hasan, a son of Ibn Furat's by his concubine Dawla, came into the room. Ali rose from his place and kissed the boy on his head and eyes. This gesture of respect was going rather too far, thought Ibn Furat.

Abu Hasan, you should not do that, he said. But I suppose Hasan is the son of Abu Hasan! And opening his pen-box, he then and there wrote an order on his collection agent to pay Abu Hasan Ali ibn Isa, without deduction for commission, the sum of two thousand dinars, to be credited against his fine. He then told Muhassin to give an order of the same sort, and the young man made one out for a thousand dinars.

Ali then rose, expressing his gratitude, and departed in company with Shafi Lului, who had by this time arrived, and who, giving him the seat of honor in his launch, took him to his own house.

There was not one man who had served as Clerk under Ali ibn Isa but offered and indeed actually sent contributions to the fine, according to his means. Ali declined to accept any aid except from Ibn Farajawayhi and from two of Ibn Furat's sons, from each of whom he accepted five hundred dinars. When he had paid the greater part of his fine, the Vizier asked Muqtadir's permission to remove him to Mecca. This was granted, and Ibn Furat assigned him seven thousand dirhams for travelling and other expenses.

From Ali's dependents, Clerks, and agents Ibn Furat proceeded to exact huge sums by means of torture; he gave his son Muhassin a free hand. People could hardly recognize him as the man whose generosity was so famous. Ibn Hawari was repeatedly beaten and scourged, and at last put to death by Muhassin's agent in Ahwaz, whither he had been sent for the collection of his fine.

Orders were sent for both the Madharais to be conveyed to the capital. There Husayn Madharai was examined before the Judges and Bureau chiefs, and obliged to give his bond for two million four hundred thousand dinars. Presently Ibn Furat decided that this was too high, reduced the sum to one million seven hundred thousand dinars, took Husayn's bond for that amount, and got the Caliph's approval of the change.

He now treated Husayn with the utmost kindness, expressed admiration for his ability, and spoke most flatteringly of his intellectual powers. He had never talked, he said, to a more intelligent official, nor a more courageous one. Would he be willing to make a statement in Ali ibn Isa's presence that the latter had received undeclared profits from him, during his Presidency of the Bureau of the West, and during his Vizierate?

Husayn Madharai begged to be excused.

Why, inquired the Vizier, do you prefer not to do in Ali ibn Isa's case what you did in my case?

I am by no means proud of what I did on that occasion, said Husayn. It won me no golden opinions, in spite of the excuse I might plead in the unfriendliness the Vizier had shown me during his second term, leaving me to the mercies of Ibn Bistam, giving that official power over me. How could anybody think well of my doing the same thing again, and to Ali ibn Isa, who has been a faithful friend to me in the old days, and recently?

Ibn Furat did not insist.

The other brother, Muhammad Madharai, was then brought to hearing. He defended himself on various points.

You are not, said Ibn Furat, a more brilliant man than your brother Husayn, and Husayn tried to put up a more elaborate defense than this — but it broke down.

Torture and menace were unnecessary: he got Muhammad's bond for one million seven hundred thousand dinars and handed him over to Muhassin. He was perfectly safe at Muhassin's house, but only stayed there one day. The young man, though he treated his prisoner with open contempt when they met, let him go because Muhammad had brought round for him a huge quantity of money, fine clothes, valuable jewelry, and beautiful slaves.

An incident which had taken place in one of Ibn Furat's Vizierates was recalled by Judge Abdallah ibn Ahmad:

A certain man who had been unemployed for a long time (says he) at last forged a letter of introduction in the name of Ibn Furat to the Governor of Egypt, made the journey to that province, and presented the letter. The Governor suspected that it was not what it purported to be — the language was too emphatic, the number of blessings was not appropriate to the bearer's rank, and the style did not seem quite right. So, giving the man only a small bounty and ordering him an allowance till he should have considered the matter further, he enclosed the paper with a note of explanation in his private bag to the Vizier.

Ibn Furat was in company with friends when the packet was brought him. He opened it, and read the spurious letter, which stated that the bearer had by services in time past laid Ibn Furat under grave obligations. The whole affair was communicated to the astonished company.

What ought to be done to the man? asked Ibn Furat.

He ought to lose his hand for forging the Vizier's writing! said one.

Amputating his thumb; flogging and imprisonment, were suggested. Another of the Vizier's friends said: Tell the Governor to banish the man — to have taken all that trouble for nothing will be punishment enough.

How very mean and disagreeable you all are! said Ibn Furat. Here is a man whose ambition it is to conjure with our name. He faces the long journey to Egypt. Not having the *entrée* here, perhaps, or any claim upon us, he relieves us of the trouble of writing him a letter by writing for himself what he hopes will do the trick for him, and sallies forth, counting on us to pry him loose a bit of luck. And the kindest fate wished on him by the most good-natured of the lot of you is what? Just disappointment!

He dipped his pen in his ink-box, turned the forged paper over, and wrote in his own hand: *This letter is mine; I do not know why you suspected that it was not. And are you personally acquainted with every man who helped us in our time of advers-*

*ity? This excellent man is one such; and his claim on us is
greater than this letter acknowledges. Give him a liberal bounty,
look after him, and let him have as good an appointment as he is
qualified for.* This rescript went off at once.

Long afterwards, Ibn Furat had a visitor, a fine-looking
man, well dressed and attended. When he was admitted, he
began to call blessings on the Vizier, and broke down in tears.

God bless you, sir! cried Ibn Furat, who had never seen
the man before. What is the matter with you?

I am the forger, said his visitor, who wrote that letter,
which the Vizier in his charity, and God reward him for it!
acknowledged for his own.

Ibn Furat laughed. How much did he give you? he asked.

From his own funds, and a treasury allowance, and as
salary in a post he gave me, I have had twenty thousand dinars.

God be praised! said Ibn Furat. But if you care to stay
with me, I will see that you get many times as much. He found
by trying him that the man was a qualified Clerk, took him into
his service, and helped him to such a fortune as made him a
devoted dependent.

Once during his third Vizierate the talk in Ibn Furat's
reception room turned upon the life of students of literature and
Tradition; and someone said: As like as not, one of these scholars
will have to stint himself of food for lack of the few pennies he
has to spend on paper and ink.

Ibn Furat was a man of wide sympathies and warm heart.
He had been a generous supporter of poets; and when the miserable life of these poor students was described to him, he exclaimed at once: They need help in their careers? Then I am
theirs!

He gave orders for twenty thousand dirhams to be spent
providing free paper and ink for poor students.

DIMNA WARNS THE LION AGAINST THE BULL

Consider, polite reader, the tale told on page 271.

Munis the Victor was now back in Baghdad, after a brilliant victory over the Byzantines. It was soon common talk that he did not like all this torturing, or the death of Hamid either. And the men of the Household Cavalry who had lost their jobs in the various retrenchments were doing all they could to get enrolled among Munis' regulars, in the hope of earning some pay.

Ibn Furat was not pleased to have Munis in Baghdad. After about a week had passed, he confided to Muqtadir at a private Audience that Munis was scheming to attach the troops to himself.

If he succeeds, said he, Munis will be a Prince of Princes, he will be the real ruler of the whole Empire. Your officers, and even your Retainers, are perfectly ready to take their orders from him *now*.

He harped on the peril to such effect that shortly after, when Munis was at Audience, the Vizier also being present, Muqtadir said to him: There is nothing I should like better than to have you stay on here — it is not only that I like being with you and always feel that things are well when I see you, but I feel the advantage of having you at hand for transacting Empire business. The only thing is this: the disbanded Household Cavalry people are demanding pay, an enormous amount, which simply cannot be found, not half of it. If I were to give orders that they should go to posts in Syria or Egypt, they would not obey them, on the excuse that they could not afford to. As you know, Rayy and the neighboring provinces are closed to us — there's a rebel in power there; and Armenia and Azarbayjan are closed provinces made over to Ibn Abi Saj. It is unfortunate that if you stay on in Baghdad these troops will insist on being enrolled in your army; for if I forbid it, they will mutiny and there will be trouble; and if I allow it, we can't properly use either the Diyarrabi'a or Diyarmudar or Syria revenues for their pay. And the revenue from Agricultural Iraq, Ahwaz, and Fars simply can't be

stretched to cover the expenses here and your army as well. So
it seems as if it would be best for you to go on to Raqqa. There
you will be in the heart of your own province; you can send out
your agents for revenue and collect all that money the Madharais
gave bond for. And what is more, the ministers of Public Security
and Land Tax in both Egypt and Syria will stand in awe of you
if you reside in your province. It will really guarantee the prosperity of the Empire.

Munis understood well enough that this was a plot of Ibn
Furat's. The Vizier, he saw, was his enemy. However, he merely
begged and obtained permission to remain in Baghdad for the
rest of Ramadan and keep the Feast there.

After the Feast, he went to take official leave of Ibn Furat.
The Vizier, in spite of Munis' remonstrances, rose from his seat
to his full height to receive him, and tried to insist on the Victor's
taking a seat beside himself on the same carpet. But this Munis
declined. He preferred a number of requests, all of which were
granted. When he was about to take leave, Ibn Furat was going
to rise again in his honor, but Munis adjured him by the Caliph's
head not to move.

The Victor then paid his farewell visit to the Caliph and
went out to his camp. It was a stormy day that day.

DANGER

Suddenly news reached Ibn Furat at Baghdad that young
Abu Tahir the Qarmatian had fallen upon the Pilgrim Caravan
of the year '11 on its way back. He had routed the guards,
butchered crowds of Pilgrims, taken prisoner various members
of the Sovereign's household, women as well as men; then, with
the camels from the whole Pilgrimage, and such men, women,
and children as he liked the looks of, prisoners, he had withdrawn
to Hajar, leaving the rest of the Pilgrims stranded without food or
camels, so that most of them had died of thirst and exhaustion.

Where go they now, the litters tossed on camel-back,
The caravan? They float in the quivering heat. They're
    gone.
They will toil across the skirt of Redstone Fell;
One train, as if some quick whim took it, will turn sharp
For Syria, and another bear toward Iraq.
I am left here alone. From my fell captor, Pain,
No one ever will come to redeem me. My quest lay
Toward a journey's end that I shall never see.

On both sides of the river the streets were in a ferment
when the news got about. Women ran out of their houses barefoot, tearing down their hair, beating on their faces till they were
bruised black, shrieking about the streets. And out too ran the
womenfolk of the ruined officials — the men Ibn Furat had
ruined. It was a spectacle hideous beyond example.

To control the public commotion, the Vizier ordered
Nazuk, the Chief of Police, to patrol the public Mosques on both
sides of the river; and by deploying all his men, cavalry, infantry,
and flame-throwers, he succeeded in quelling the mob.

The first survivors from the Pilgrimage soon arrived. They
told their story to the Vizier; and late that same day he rode,
though with a sinking heart, to Muqtadir to recount the tale. The
Caliph called in Nasr the Chamberlain to the conference.

Now was Nasr's chance to attack Ibn Furat in the Caliph's
presence; and he burst out fiercely: Yes! now you ask What is to
be done? you, who shook the very columns of the Empire to the
risk of ruin when you took Munis away who was its champion.
Who's to rescue the Throne now? Who but you betrayed the
Sovereign's troops and these men and women of his House to the
Qarmatians?

To Muqtadir he said that he should write recalling Munis
to the capital without an instant's delay; and the Caliph agreed.
The despatch went off at once.

Ibn Furat was assaulted by a mob who hurled brickbats at
his barge, and Muhassin was also stoned as he rode down from

his house to his own boat. The streets were crowded with people yelling that Ibn Furat was the Arch-Qarmatian, the one who would never rest till Muhammad's people were destroyed to the last man.

Muqtadir tried to patch up a reconciliation between the Chamberlain and the Vizier. Everyone must stand shoulder to shoulder in support of the Empire, he said; all must unite to resist the Hajar brigand.

When Munis reached Baghdad, the citizens streamed out to meet him; it seemed that everyone was there. Even Ibn Furat sailed to pay his respects, contrary to his own custom and all Vizieral precedent. When the Victor's chamberlain announced that Ibn Furat was come to visit him, he came out to the water-gate of his house and begged the Vizier to condescend no further. But Ibn Furat insisted, and came up from his barge to congratulate Munis on his happy return. When he took his leave, the Victor escorted him up to the very moment when he stepped into his vessel.

Now Muhassin began to be uneasy about the officials he had broken. He had pocketed large deductions from their fines, and he dreaded a disclosure of all the undeclared profits he had made. He therefore sent a number of them to an associate of his in Basra, ostensibly to exact the arrears of their fines. But when this man had them in his hands, he slaughtered them like so many sheep.

Rumors began to circulate that Ibn Furat's fall was impending. Sons and Clerks of his went into hiding. The whispers grew more persistent, until Muqtadir, wishing to silence them, wrote the Vizier a letter stating, with solemn asseverations, that his feelings towards both Ibn Furat and Muhassin, and his confidence in them, remained what they always had been. He assured them that they might rely on his determination to be their friend. In closing, he ordered them to publish this letter in Baghdad, and to have copies sent to all provincial ministers of War and Finance.

THE FALL OF IBN FURAT

Shortly after this, in the year '12, the Vizier and his son had gone by water to the Palace, had their audience, and were on the point of leaving, when Nasr the Chamberlain requested them to be seated.

What had happened was this: the Retainers of the Hujari regiment had petitioned Muqtadir for their arrest. Muflih the Negro had delivered the petition. But he advised the Caliph to go slowly, on the ground that it was dangerous, and bad policy, to dismiss a Vizier at the demand of his enemies, and was simply inviting the Retainers to interfere in State affairs.

Muqtadir presently decided that Muflih should tell Nasr to let the Furats go; but at the same time he ordered Muflih to assure the Retainers that the wishes expressed in their petition would be respected. Muflih came into the room where the Vizier was and delivered his message, and Nasr gave them permission to leave. Ibn Furat sprang up and took to his heels; through corridor after corridor he raced until he reached his barge, with Muhassin after him.

When they got back to the Vizieral Palace, they had a long private conversation, which finished, Muhassin went home to his own house, where he stayed only long enough to give a few orders. Then he departed and went into hiding.

His father, with unruffled mien, took his seat in the Vizieral Office, called up the chief Clerks, and attended to business as usual. By the time the Clerks left at the end of the day, they had begun to feel doubtful about the accuracy of the rumors which had come to their ears, so gay and nonchalant had the Vizier seemed, talking and joking just as usual, and giving or refusing orders in his customary style.

One of his Clerks tells the story of the following day. The Vizier (says he) came into the Office and sat down to business next morning. During the morning a sealed note was delivered to him — a thin one, as I observed; and he opened and read it. I didn't know at the time who the sender was, but I heard afterwards that it was Muflih. Some time later, a second note arrived, from some soldier or other in Palace service, I heard; and when Ibn Furat had read this second message, he seemed uncertain what to do for a moment. Then he sent for his steward, and whispered something in his ear; and the steward went out again. The Vizier thereupon dismissed the Clerks for the day, telling us that he would be in the Office early on the morrow. Then he rose from his seat and went out in the direction of his private apartments.

The Clerks went their several ways. But I, just as I got to the doorway, remembered a job the Vizier had given me. It was not done; so I went back to my place and sat down to finish it.

Suddenly I looked up. Nazuk the Police Chief had entered the room. He had his sword on, and was holding a dagger in his hand; and Munis' chamberlain was behind him. Neither of them looked his usual cheerful self, and each had about fifteen armed Retainers with him. When they saw that the Vizier was not in the Office, they went on into the private apartments. Through the same door Ibn Furat was soon led out. They had not even let him stay to put on his turban. He was forced into a barge and rowed away to Nazuk's house. At the same time two of his sons, and such Clerks of his as were still about, were put under arrest.

YOUNG KHAQANI

THE YOUNGER KHAQANI had spent Ibn Furat's third Vizierate in hiding. His father, the former Vizier, was now senile, an invalid, and an imbecile. But when Ibn Furat's position was imperilled by the Pilgrimage disaster, the younger Khaqani set on foot an intrigue against him and Muhassin, submitting to Muqtadir an estimate of what he thought he could make them disgorge. Nasr the Chamberlain, Munis, the Caliph's cousin Harun, one of the Stewardesses, and various others spoke in his favor; so Muqtadir, calling him to a private audience, offered him the Vizierate and the Presidency of the Bureaus. The Robes were conferred, and both Munis and Harun were among those who rode home with him from the ceremony.

What! cried Ibn Furat when he was told that Khaqani was Vizier: this is not my downfall — it's the Empire's!

ATTEMPTS TO GET AT IBN FURAT'S MONEY

Public criers were sent out to proclaim that Muhassin and certain other named individuals must appear before the authorities, and to announce that any person in whose house any one of the aforesaid might be found was thereby liable to the plunder and destruction by fire of his property, and an additional penalty of one thousand stripes.

A certain Ibn Ba'ud Sharr was appointed to examine Ibn Furat. At first this person tried to get him to remember and reveal his deposits by mild persuasion only. This gentle treatment encouraged him to admit that he had lodged sums amounting to one hundred and fifty thousand dinars with various dealers, whose names he gave. When these funds had been recovered and transmitted to the Privy Treasury, Ibn Ba'ud Sharr made fresh demands. The ex-Vizier replied that he had no money left.

The examiner now tried a little mild torture. But Ibn Furat was not the man to yield to torture: he firmly refused to pay a penny.

Muqtadir's cousin Harun therefore went to see the Caliph. Khaqani had done the Sovereign a disservice, he urged, in handing Ibn Furat over to a man like Ibn Ba'ud Sharr —he should have dealt kindly and flatteringly with him, for he was not a person who would yield to violence. So Muqtadir sent Khaqani word that Harun must be present at future examinations, and that Ibn Furat must be gently treated.

In the matter of food and drink the examiner had been stinting Ibn Furat, sending in bran bread, cucumbers, and rain water. But now Khaqani sent a profusion of good cheer, with plenty of ice and fruit, and a message to apologize for past short-comings. He had been entirely unaware, he said, of the treatment Ibn Furat had received.

This was followed by a courteously worded and coaxing message, requesting him to make a true and full statement of his assets, and not defy the Sovereign — such an attitude it was impossible to condone.

Tell the Vizier from me, was Ibn Furat's reply, that I am not a greenhorn, whose examination can be conducted by cajolery. I do not say that I cannot provide the money. But I am not going to pay ransom for my life until I am sure of it; and I am not going to feel sure of it until the Prince of True Believers personally writes me a pardon, and it has been attested by the signatures of the Vizier and the Judges, and, further, until I have a similar pardon in the handwriting of the Vizier. Furthermore, he must put me in charge of one of the following two persons: either Munis the Victor, enemy of mine though he is, or Shafi Lului. Unless these conditions are complied with, I am perfectly ready to be killed.

Khaqani sent his answer. If it were in my power, he said, to obtain such a guarantee for you, I should certainly do it; but the mere suggestion on my part would make the most important people in the Empire my enemies, on your account; and in any case you would not gain anything along these lines, since the Caliph has already referred your case to his cousin Harun.

A meeting was now arranged in Khaqani's house. Ibn Furat was brought in, and at first questioned by Ibn Ba'ud Sharr. He was immovable; and the examiner began to use insulting language. Harun, who was present, rebuked him.

Do you hope to obtain money from Abu Hasan ibn Furat, he inquired, by methods like that? And turning to the ex-Vizier, and using the most courteous terms, he took up the examination himself.

You, Abu Hasan, have a greater knowledge of affairs, he said, than all of us who are here examining you put together.

And among other things you certainly know that a Vizier must not defy a Caliph when the Caliph is incensed against him.

Prince, replied Ibn Furat, give me your advice. For when a man is in a plight like mine, his wits desert him. And as a result of Harun's gentle conduct of the interview, Ibn Furat at last gave his bond for a fine of two million dinars, of which one quarter was to be paid at once. But that quarter was to include what he had already paid and any sums which might since have been recovered from deposits which he had not revealed. He stipulated that he be allowed to conduct the sale of his properties himself, and that he be transferred to the house of Shafi or some other person in the Sovereign's confidence. He was further to be allowed materials for correspondence with anyone he chose to write to. Harun made him put his name to all this, and took the document off to Muqtadir.

THE CAPTURE OF MUHASSIN

Muhassin meanwhile had been lying low in Karkh, using his mother-in-law Hinzaba's house as headquarters. Every morning she used to escort him, disguised as a woman, to some cemetery (a usual promenade for women in Muslim towns); and every evening she would bring him to some place where he could spend the night in safety.

One day she had taken him, dressed as usual in female attire, to the Qurayshi Cemetery on the far north side of the city. When evening drew on, it seemed a dreadfully long way to go back to Karkh. One of the women in her company suggested a place belonging to a very reliable lady she knew, a widow, who had no man in the house.

Thither Hinzaba went, with her women and .her son-in-law. To the mistress of the house she explained that she had an unmarried woman with her who had just come from a mourning-party which had made her feel very low in spirits; could she possibly let this lady have a room where she could be quiet?

The widow showed them along a corridor and into a room, and then left them, closing the door behind her. There they sat, Muhassin and the women. Presently a colored slave girl came along the corridor to set a lamp. Hinzaba had left the room to fetch Muhassin some sugar-porridge which they had been offered; and as she re-entered, the girl peeped into the room. Muhassin had by this time thrown back some of his attire; and the girl saw that he was a man.

She went and told her mistress. Late at night the lady entered the room, looked at her guests asleep, and recognized Muhassin.

It was his bad luck, and it shows that God had now forsaken him, that the woman happened to be the widow of one of Ali ibn Isa's bailiffs. This man, being brought for examination to Muhassin's office, had died suddenly of shock, at the mere sight of the tortures he saw being administered, and before Muhassin had said a word to him.

The widow went straight to the Palace, and being admitted to Nasr the Chamberlain, told her story. He told Muqtadir. The Caliph had an order sent to Nazuk to ride out and arrest Muhassin; and the Prefect lost not an instant in executing it. Though it was midnight, the arrest was notified by the beating of drums through the city, to the great alarm of the citizens, who thought the Qarmatians must have seized the capital itself.

They carried Muhassin to the Vizier's Palace in Mukharrim, where he was taken in charge by Ibn Ba'ud Sharr. The latter immediately had him so violently tortured that he gave a bond for three million dinars. Harun afterwards went round to the Palace to question Muhassin, and encouraged him to recollect and divulge where his deposits were. But although torture was applied for two consecutive days, Muhassin would not reveal the whereabouts of a dirham. He was not going to lose both his life and his money, he said.

So Harun decided to have a hearing. He sent for Shafi Lului and the Clerks to be present, as well as Muhassin and Ibn Ba'ud Sharr, and began by administering severe torture.

If we grant, he then said, that you cannot pay the whole sum for which your bond has been taken, can you not at least produce a hundred thousand dinars?

I can do that, Muhassin answered, if you just give me a little time, and if only the torture stops.

We'll give you time, said Harun. Write your bond for a hundred thousand.

Muhassin wrote out a bond undertaking to pay within thirty days, and signed it. Harun read it over.

Do you think you are going to be alive thirty days from now? he exclaimed.

Humbly Muhassin replied that he would do whatever the prince commanded.

Write that you will pay within seven days, said Harun.

The young man asked to have the paper returned to him, so that he might write another in its place. When he got hold of it, he immediately chewed it up and swallowed it. He declined to write another. Though they put fetters and collar on him, and a hair shirt, and knocked him about the head with clubs, even to make him write a bond on the same terms as he had written before, he still refused. They sent him back to prison and applied exquisite tortures; but not one dirham would he yield.

THE LAST HEARING

There was now a hearing in the office of the Vizier Khaqani, at which Munis, Nasr the Chamberlain, the Judges and a full showing of Clerks assisted. When Ibn Furat had been brought in, the Vizier himself began to conduct the examination. But Khaqani was no match for Ibn Furat, who more or less made a meatball of him. For example, when Khaqani said: You have had a million dinars of income from your estates in the last eleven months! Ibn Furat replied: These same estates, when they were sequestered, were managed by Ali ibn Isa for ten years, during his Vizierate and Hamid's; and he never got more than

four hundred thousand out of them — you are claiming that I
work miracles. Or again, when Khaqani accused him of attach-
ing collections from the Sovereign's Estates to those from his own,
the ex-Vizier answered: The Bureau files are open: you had better
look up the record of revenue from the Imperial Estates for the
time I managed them, and for Ali ibn Isa's time, and Hamid's,
and also for your father's Vizierate, when *you* were managing
them: you will soon see whether during my administration revenue from the Imperial lands went up or whether it went down.

By and by the examination turned to the subject of the
killing of the broken officials in Basra, responsibility for which
was laid to Ibn Furat.

It is either the one or the other of two alternatives, he
replied: either it is alleged that I killed them myself — in which
case, since I have not been away from the capital and these deaths
with which I am charged took place at a distance, I cannot be
held guilty. Or else it is alleged that I wrote ordering these executions — in which case I simply refer myself to the officials who
would be involved, the local ministers of Public Security, the
Sovereign's confidential advisers, the people in the Finance or
Government offices, for evidence that I sent any such orders.

Your son was the killer, somebody said.

I am not my son, replied Ibn Furat; and it is me you are
examining.

If your son killed them, you killed them! broke in Ibn
Ba'ud Sharr.

That, said Ibn Furat, is contrary to the ruling of God and
His Apostle. God says: *NOR SHALL ANY BEARER BEAR
ANOTHER'S BURDEN.* And: The Prophet of God, God's
Prayer and Peace be on him, said: *Is this your son?* Yes, he said.
Then the Prophet said: *You will not be responsible for him nor
he for you.* In any case, you have got Muhassin; so you can ask
him. If he is liable to retaliation on a charge of murder committed at a distance from where he was, but where another person is alleged to have acted as his agent, the law in such cases
is well known.

This reply nonplussed everybody. However, the President of the Army Board whispered to Nasr the Chamberlain: If the Chamberlain think fit, he may put the following question: When you used to say to people you were pressing for money: Either you pay or I hand you over to Muhassin! did you intend that Muhassin should feast them on sugar-porridge, or that he should torture them? Now, anyone who condones torture condones slaughter, for a man will sometimes die of a single stroke of the lash, let alone severer treatment.

Nasr repeated the question to Ibn Furat.

The Caliph, whose life God long preserve, was Muhassin's patron, he answered. At the time you refer to I was in confinement, though Muhassin was at large. Muhassin guaranteed what he thought fit; but everything he proposed to do was passed on by Muflih, and other confidential advisers of the Sovereign who acted as intermediaries. At a later date, when I became Vizier, I tried to deal gently with people; but under mild treatment they declined to pay what it was right for them to pay. Obstinate cases I handed over to the official whom the Sovereign had appointed, the man to whom I had been ordered to commit them.

You are trying to throw the responsibility for these deaths on the Caliph, said Munis. But we have the Caliph's own word that he ordered none of them, except in the case of Ibn Hawari.

I have here, Nasr then said, a message sent to you by the Sovereign. I want you to listen to it; and I want to hear what you have to say about it.

What is it? inquired Ibn Furat.

This is it, said Nasr: *I put certain persons in your power,* the Sovereign writes, *because you had guaranteed me certain moneys, and I insist on having either one thing or the other: either pay me the money or return me the persons.*

As to the moneys, replied the ex-Vizier, sums were duly paid into the Treasury. As to the people, I never guaranteed them any long lives: they died when their terms were come.

You seem to have an answer and an excuse for everything, put in Munis the Victor. But what excuse can you pretend for

banishing me to Raqqa, as if I were some fined official or a
traitor to the Caliph's House?

I banish you? cried Ibn Furat.

Then who did? demanded Munis.

Our master gave the order that you were to be sent away,
said he.

Our master ordered that? Never!

I have a document in his own handwriting, said Ibn Furat.
He wrote me a letter; and that letter, as being an autograph, I
have carefully kept. In it he complains of the way you have
behaved at various times, and of the enormous amount of money
it cost for you to conquer countries which you proceeded to un-
conquer by your mismanagement and misconduct.

Where is this document? cried the Victor.

You have it. It is along with other documents which I
ordered kept in the bamboo case, the case with a label on it in
my writing to say that it is to be used for keeping important
papers. Among other things there you will find the order that
you are to be sent to Raqqa, and to be under surveillance until
you start.

Fetch the bamboo case, said Khaqani. There it was, sealed
with Ibn Furat's seal; and there was the actual order, along with
other autographed letters from Muqtadir such as Ibn Furat had
referred to. Khaqani took possession of the others. But Munis
took the order, and demanding immediate audience of Muqtadir,
requested him to read that paper.

The Caliph was in a fury. He ordered Harun to scourge
Ibn Furat, who was accordingly placed in the pillory. But after
he had received no more than five strokes, Harun said to him:
Now, my friend, pay up your money. Ibn Furat gave him a bond
for twenty thousand dinars, saying: There's my money. Immediately afterwards, Harun had Muhassin out of prison and scourged
almost to death. In vain: he refused to pay anything at all.

At this, Harun went to beg the Caliph to excuse him from
further examination of the Furats. These people, said he, just

do not intend to pay — they have made up their minds to be killed.

Finally Nazuk was put in charge of them. The Chief of Police tortured them mercilessly, inflicting such a variety of torments on Muhassin that his body putrefied, and there was nothing left of him that could still feel pain. His father, thrice scourged with strong cords, still would not yield a dirham.

THE CONCERT OF ENEMIES

Now Muqtadir lost all patience with Khaqani. He had not seen any of the money yet, he complained, which the Vizier had promised to extract from the Furats.

That, replied the Vizier, is because the case was not left to diplomacy. When Ibn Furat was withdrawn from examination by men of his own profession and handed over to the military, he realized that nothing would save his life; so he thought he might as well save his money. The son simply followed his example.

I went to the limit as far as torture goes, on both of them, pleaded Nazuk; so much so that Muhassin's body — the body of that fastidious Muhassin — is putrefying. All the same, he stood unheard-of tortures. It's days now since he tasted food — he just drinks water. Most of the time he's unconscious.

If that's how it is, said Muqtadir, both of them had better be brought here to my Palace.

That is the right course! declared Munis and the rest of them. Khaqani even assured the Caliph that God Himself was guiding him.

Thus they left the Presence. But while they were still in the Palace precincts, and before they separated, Khaqani whispered to the others: If Ibn Furat is brought here, his dependents will offer to pay for his life, and Muhassin's. And once he gets the Caliph's ear, as he will do when he's settled in the Palace, he will tell where his money is, in return for security, his own

and his son's. Once sure of his life, he'll guarantee every man of
us! It won't be hard to get Muqtadir to put us in his power. The
prospect of saving our stipends and getting our fiefs and estates,
the huge sum he can get together — all for the Caliph! The thing
to do is for all the military officers to swear an oath as one man
that if they hear of Ibn Furat and his son being brought to the
Palace, they will throw off their allegiance!

Life won't be worth living otherwise, said Munis.

The execution of the scheme was undertaken by Harun and
Nazuk. They assembled the officers of the Hujari Regiment,
and Munis' chamberlain Yalbaq administered the oath to them.
This done, they presented themselves in a body before Munis and
Nasr, and declared their intentions. The Victor suggested that
the officers should demand the removal of both Furats to his,
Munis', palace. And he proposed that if Muhassin were to die,
his father should be spared.

If Muhassin dies, objected Harun, it will not be safe to let
his father live: how could he ever be trusted after the killing of
his son?

The officers then went to Muqtadir and told him frankly
that unless Ibn Furat and his son were put to death, every officer
in his service would mutiny. And Harun urged the executions
in an even more urgent tone, saying that otherwise he would not
answer for the officials not conspiring to proclaim some other
member of the Hashimite family Caliph; and then the mischief
would be beyond cure.

They called on Khaqani to add his persuasions. But the
Vizier protested that he would have no part in the shedding of
blood. I should regard their execution as a grave mistake, he
said: execution should never be made easy or recommended to a
king. If it is, a king thinks little of killing his ministers, and will
put them to death for the slightest error or misdemeanor.

DEATH

On the Sunday following, when Ibn Furat's food was brought to him in his lodging at the Vizieral Palace, he told them to take it away again — he was keeping fast. And that evening, as the hour for breaking fast drew on, he said he would not break his fast that night. They urged him to change his mind.

Tomorrow I am to be put to death, he said; it is quite settled.

Nay, God forbid! was the rejoinder.

No, he replied; yesterday I saw my brother Abu Abbas in a dream, and he said to me: *The Monday after tomorrow you shall break fast with us.* He never told me anything in my sleep but it came true. Monday is tomorrow. It is the day the blessed Husayn son of Ali was slain.

The morrow came; and the conspirators went downriver to the Palace. They were not admitted. So returning to the Vizieral Palace, they penned a letter demanding that Ibn Furat and his son be put to death. Muqtadir in reply asked time to think the matter over. They wrote back again to say that if the execution were delayed beyond that day, something would happen to the Empire which could not afterwards be undone.

At this, Muqtadir wrote back to the Chief of Police ordering him to behead them both, and to bring their heads to the Palace. Nazuk replied that this was a very serious matter, in which he could not act upon a mere rescript. So the Caliph told the Chief Eunuchs and Eunuchs to convey to him officially the order of the Caliph that he was to carry out his instructions as written. Still Nazuk replied that he would not act upon a message — he must have a command from the Caliph's own lips.

Ibn Furat from his room was keeping in touch with what was going on. When he was told that the officials had all left the Vizieral Palace, and that Nazuk had gone home, he seemed somewhat relieved. But learning presently that Nazuk had not gone home, but had gone again to the Royal Palace, he was gravely perturbed.

That afternoon the Chief of Police returned to the Vizieral Palace, and entering the apartment where Ibn Furat was confined, sat down. He had sent his eunuch with some negroes to decapitate Muhassin; and soon enough the head was brought in.

Put it in front of him! said Nazuk.

Horror came over Ibn Furat: he knew the sword was to be his end. Is it the sword for me, Abu Mansur? he cried to Nazuk; plead for me with the Prince of True Believers — tell him how much money I have still! plenty of deposits left — and wonderful jewels!

It's too late for that now, replied Nazuk, and gave the order for his head to be taken off.

He took both heads to show to the Caliph. Muqtadir ordered that they be thrown in the water. So the heads were thrown into Euphrates, and the trunks into Tigris, from the Tabbanin Bridge at Baghdad. On the day of his death Ibn Furat was seventy-one years and some months old.

May God have Mercy on him.

A SAINT AND HIS FATE

Hallaj and I believe the same thing, said Shibli; but my madness saved my life, and his intelligence led him to his death.

The utmost the ordinary religious man can think of, said Hallaj, is still concerned with his own lot and his own soul, for the creature is slave to bias. But real Reality, in the realizing of it, is simply this — sanctity.

USAYN son of Mansur, called HALLAJ, or the Carder, was born a Persian. At first a disciple in Sufism to Sahl of Tustar, he left him without asking his master's permission, in order to attach himself to Makki. Makki too he left, and again without asking permission; and tried to become one of Junayd's circle. But Junayd would have nothing to do with him. I do not admit madmen, he said.

Hallaj wrote brilliantly, both allegories and theological and juridical formulations. All his mystical utterances are like the first visions of novices, though some are more powerful, some feebler, some more acceptable, some more improper than others. When God grants a man a Vision, and he tries afterward to put into words what he saw in the height of ecstatic power, and helped by Divine Grace, his words are apt to be obscure, and the more so if he expresses himself hastily, and under the influence of self-admiration.

People will call such utterances: Sublime! whether they believe them or not. But whether they accept or reject them, they will equally fail to get anything of the reality intended by the words. Some orthodox theologians reject Hallaj altogether, on the ground that his sayings are pantheistic. But the offense lies solely in the expression, not in the meaning.

Hallaj was an ecstatic. He never was *confirmed;* and what a man says can only be considered authoritative after he has become confirmed. So, much as I love the man, I still do not know what I think of him. Yet, when my own visions began, he was of great help to me.

It is absurd to call him a wizard. All intelligent Followers in the True Way agree that no Believer can be a wizard, for contraries are incompatible. And piety was Husayn ibn Mansur's garb as long as he lived: prayer and praise and continual fasting. If what he did had been sorcery, he could not have brought forth these good fruits. So that some of the things he did, not being sorcery, must have been miracle. And miracles are vouchsafed only to a saint.

I happened to be walking down one of the lanes of our town behind Husayn ibn Mansur (says Musa of Bayda), when the shadow of some person standing on a roof fell across him. Lifting his head to see who it was, he found himself gazing at a very beautiful woman.

He turned sharp round. You shall see, he said to me, though you may wait long to see it, that the wrong my eyes have done will come home to roost someday.

On the day, long after, when he was gibbeted, I was there in the crowd, weeping; and he noticed me from the scaffold. Musa, he said, the man who raised his head to the thing you saw, the man who raised himself to what was forbidden him, has to be raised above the heads of a crowd now, even as you see. And he pointed to the gibbet.

HE COMES TO BAGHDAD

We were sitting in the circle of the Sufi Shaykh Junayd one day (says Ali Hadrami) when a youth with a beautiful face, wearing two frocks, came up, greeted us, and took a place. For a while he remained sitting; then Junayd, noticing him, said: Have you any question you would like to ask?

How may we know the difference, said the young man, between mere character and the substance of ourselves?

That question sounds to me like silly inquisitiveness, said Junayd. Why not ask me about something which is really going on in your mind — your longing to be superior to your contemporaries, for instance? And he said nothing more for a moment, then signed to Abu Muhammad Jurayri to rise. We all got up.

Junayd beckoned the young man nearer and spoke to him. His last words I heard; they were: . . . the gibbet your blood will stain!

The boy burst into tears, and then got up and left. Jurayri followed him as he went away; he betook himself to the cemetery and sat down. And this is what Jurayri told me:

This fellow (I thought) is at the beginning of his adolescence; it is shyness which has made him run away. Perhaps he's very poor. So I sent a friend to buy me some bread and sweetmeats, and a toothstick and some soap. Then I went in search of the boy and sat down near him. His head was sunk between his knees, but he raised it, and at sight of me gave evident signs of distress. While I was waiting for my friend's arrival, I tried to comfort him, then, when the food came, said: Please, help yourself. He helped himself and ate a little.

Where are you from? I inquired presently. Where were you born?

Bayda, he said; but I was brought up in Khuzistan and at Basra.

And what's your name?

Husayn ibn Mansur.

I rose then and said good-bye. It was forty-five years after that day when I heard the news that he had been crucified.

From Baghdad Husayn went to Mecca. A whole year he remained in the courtyard of the Mosque without stirring from his place except for ablution and the ritual circling of the Black Stone, caring neither for sun nor rain.

We begged him (says a certain Sufi) to let us have his frock. We got all the lice out of it and weighed them: they weighed twenty grains. His mortifications were as extreme as that.

One of his companions relates this:
Even if, I said to him, some intimation, some mysterious sign comes into your consciousness, nay, even if such moments become a steady mystical condition, you should not think you have been enabled to know the Hidden. Nonsense! I know the Prophets disapprove of that, as you will find out tomorrow, at Lecture.

But my friend, said Husayn, it is the Master Himself Who comes to teach me the very things the Traditionist repeats to us! I can only rely on Tradition so far as these inspirations make me perceive things directly, and see the harmony of Tradition with my own intuition.

One day as I was walking with Husayn ibn Mansur (says his master Makki) in a narrow street at Mecca, I happened to be reciting from the Koran as we went along. He heard me.
I could utter such things as that myself, said he.
From that day on, I saw him no more.

So he returned to Junayd. Why have you come back here? Junayd demanded.
To live as a member of your circle, shaykh.
I do not take madmen as Companions, replied Junayd. Companionship demands sanity. Sobriety is the mark of sound spiritual state; intoxication is the mark of too much longing.

UTTERANCES OF HALLAJ

When in my thirst I stooped my face to wine,
Dark in the cup I saw a shadow. THINE!

THE ECHO

My heart became an eye; and my Lord shone in view.
I whispered: Who are you? and echo answered: You!

Ah!
Was that me? or Thee?
Two Gods!
Far be it, far be it from me to say there are two Gods!
Yet between me and Thee lies this torment of 'Tis me.
Take my 'Tis me from between Us with Thy 'Tis Thyself.

Change speech, forsake the phantom-world. Use neither
measure nor harmony with God! Let passion speak; be lost and
follow your love. Follow upward, fly between mount and hill,
all mounts of thought and hills of certainty, till at last you are
enabled to contemplate What you see. And that will be the
Night of Plenty which ends the Fast.

THE ECSTASY

Make me one, my Only One, in such true God-is-One
As no way reaches of the beaten ways of the world . . .
I am Reality! 'Tis only to Itself Reality is real!
Robed in Itself! It cannot leave Itself!
O blaze of darting lights! O glittering flashes of lightnings!

Into the Light flutters the moth, and is gone, and is Flame.
Still art Thou with me, here between Heart and heartflesh!
Thou art these tears — wilt flow from my lids away from
*   me?*

Again he came before Junayd. Reality is Myself! he cried.
Not so, said Junayd. It is *through* Reality that you exist. I
see your blood staining the gibbet.

PHRASES

The recall, then the silence, then the speechlessness;
And the study, then the discovery, then the committal.
The clay, then the firing, then the glowing,
And the grey cold, then the shadow, then the sun.
The stony ground, then the meadow, then the desert;
And the river, then the sea, then the shore.
The drunkenness, then the sobering, then the craving;
And the approach, then the meeting, then the intimacy.
The grasp, then the hold, then the crushing;
And the separateness, then the joining, then the combustion.
The clutching, then the thrusting, then the tension;
And the figuration, then the apparition, then the adhesion.
— Phrases for any to whom this is a penny world;
Voices behind the door (but if one goes in, the voices hush).

* * *

Hallaj returned to Tustar, where he remained for nearly two years, discarding the Sufi frock and wearing the sleeved coat of a soldier. He became so popular that the Sufis of the time were jealous of him.

Husayn ibn Mansur never used a cushion for his elbow (says one who was his servant twenty years); nor did he ever lie down on his side to sleep. He would remain standing all the night. When his eyes closed for weariness, he used to crouch down, with his sides resting on his knees, and doze a little.

You should treat yourself friendly, someone said to him once.

My body is a friend I never had great pleasure with, he answered.

To be one of God's own, says Husayn ibn Mansur, is to be a man without master or disciple, preferring nothing, distinguishing nothing, neither distracted nor recollected, one who has nothing of or for himself, nothing at all. In him is only What is;

and It is in him without his containing it, as the Desert is in any desert tract.

What others say corresponds with his thought, their thought corresponds with his wishes. His wish looks afar; his rule is severe; his wisdom is his ignorance, and his ignorance is his sole reality, even as his sin lets him trust. His name is his rule, his mark this: that he burns as with fire. All that may be said of him is that he longs.

Keeping the Law is his style, sins are his training ground and souls his court, Satan his instructor, any companionable thing his pet, humanity his secret, dilapidation his pomp, humiliation his theme, Paradise his garden, and ruins his palace here.

His surroundings are sterility, his avenues ashes, his doctrine the keystone of his actual state, and his state mere impotence, for any other state would provoke God's Wrath.

Such is the adequate man.

For five years then Husayn travelled: into Khurasan, Sistan, Kirman; thence to Fars, where he began to preach and to hold gatherings, calling people to God. He wrote various works for his followers in Fars; then, departing, came to Ahwaz and preached there. So deeply did he search the consciences of his hearers, and reveal to them what lurked hid in their hearts, that they used to call him Hallaj al-Asrar, the Carder of Consciences. The short form Hallaj clung to him the rest of his life. From Ahwaz he went down to Basra; but he stayed there no long time.

At one time (says Judge Muhammad ibn Ubayd) I sat as a pupil with Hallaj. He was practicing devotion in the Mosque at Basra in those days as a Koran-teacher; it was before he made his absurd claims and got into trouble. One day my uncle was talking to him; I sat by listening. And Hallaj said: I shall leave Basra.

Why so? my uncle inquired.

People here talk about me too much; I am tired of it.

What are they saying? my uncle asked.

They see me do something, said Hallaj; and without staying to make any inquiry, which would have disabused them, they go about proclaiming that Hallaj gets answers to prayer, even that he performs evidentiary miracles. Who am I, that such things should be granted to me? I will give you an example: a few days ago a man brought me some dirhams and told me to spend them for the poor. There were no poor about at the moment, so I put them under one of the Mosque mats, by a pillar, and marked the pillar. So long as I waited, no one came by; so I went home for the night. Next morning I took my place by that pillar and began to pray; and some dervishes, poor Sufis, gathered about me. So I stopped my prayer, lifted up the mat, and gave them the money. And they have set the rumor flying that I had only to touch dust for it to turn to silver!

He told various similar stories, until my uncle rose and said good-bye to him. He never went to see Hallaj again. There's something of the deceiver about that man, he said to me. We shall hear more of him someday.

Continuing in the devotional life, Hallaj went on from stage to stage of it, believing that a man who purified his body through ascetic discipline, occupied himself entirely with good works, and abstained from all desires, would rise from one degree of purity to another, till in the end his nature would be rid of all carnality. And when nothing carnal was left, the Divine Spirit, out of which Jesus came, would settle in him, so that all he did or commanded would be acts or behests of God.

THE DIVINE CALLING

Belief calls a man to the Straight Path.

The Submission calls him to self-giving, and Favor calls to contemplation.

Understanding calls him to further vision. Reason calls to experience. Knowledge calls to listening. Wisdom calls to unbending and peace.

Man's soul calls him to God's service. The abandonment of all to God calls to trust. Fear calls to awe. Hope calls to calm.

Love calls man to longing, and longing to ravishment; and that ravishment calls him into God.

Know this, that a man who keeps himself fully and wholly obedient to the Law follows a Path which will not lead him astray, as far as the Stations of the realization of the Unity of God. But once he has come to those Stations, consideration of the Law drops from his sight, and gleams from the Abyss of Truth work upon him. And when those lights and flashes become a steady beam, declaring God's Unity becomes an impiety, and the Law an extravagance. If he pronounces the formula HE, GOD, IS ONE, it is only by a forcing of himself.

> *There is a selfhood in my nothingness —*
> *THINE — which must be so long as I shall be;*
> *An All between myself and all things else,*
> *And all things doubled in that mystery.*

> *I am my Love; my Love is I;*
> *Two ghosts this body occupy.*
> *If you see me, He's What you see;*
> *When you see HIM, you will see ME!*

Govern your breathings, and your minutes, and your hours; govern that you remember and this you do.

He who knows whence he comes knows whither he is to go.

He who knows what he does knows what will be done with him. He who knows what is to be done with him knows what is asked of him. He who knows what is asked of him knows what he should have. He who knows what he should have knows what he should give. And he who knows what he should give knows his own.

But the man who knows not whence he comes, nor whose he is, nor where he is, nor how he is, nor of what he is, nor what he is, nor for what he is, that man is one of those who let life pass away, moment after moment, unused.

I saw a bird, a winged bird, who denied my glory, and flew by, and asked as he flew where peace should be found.

Clip your wings — the shears are self-noughting, said I; or you will never be able to follow me to that place.

But with these wings I fly towards my Beloved, said the bird.

Unhappy creature, said I, *NONE IS LIKE UNTO HIM, WHO IS THE HEARER AND THE SEER.*

And the bird fell into the ocean of thought; and there he drowned.

> *Who, hungering for God, lets Reason lead him*
> *Goes where his own perplexity must feed him;*
> *There shall he frolic, charmed by each suspicion*
> *That springs from his own wavering condition,*
> *Until, grown old, he bleats at last:*
> *Is God a fancy, like the rest?*

As we were walking once with Hallaj down a lane in Baghdad, we heard the playing of a flute, so lovely that tears came to our eyes.

What is that? said someone.

That? said Hallaj: Satan weeping for the loss of the world.

God, as all-prior in eternity, God in Himself, was Alone.

There was no Other. He in His Pre-eternity, the only Knower
of all Knowledge, Power, Love, Desire, Wisdom, Majesty, Beauty,
Glory, was in contemplation. Then emerged one idea out of a
totality of ideas, out of Himself; God discoursed, out of a totality
of discourse; God spoke from a totality of Word. He uttered
praise out of a totality of acclaim. He worked an artifice from
the totality of His artifice, compounding a strife, out of a totality
of strife, with a delight out of a totality of delight.

In this communion with Himself, Essence speaking to
Essence, the Idea in which out of all possible ideas He contem-
plated Himself, that Idea was Love, His Love in His Solitude;
His Self-contemplation was through Love, for in the Essence of
God Love is the Essence of His Essence.

God spoke, saying that He would declare the attributes of
this Love in Solitude. And looking into pre-eternity He created
a Form or Image, the Image of His own Essence. Now, when
God looks upon a thing, He creates His own Image there for all
eternity. And God, for one moment out of His infinite time,
looked upon this Image, greeted it, hailed it, spoke to it, blessed
it for a moment out of His infinite time, then raised it into life.
Thus was the Image, which was the form of Adam and of man,
granted access to what God knows, which, before that moment
of Divine greeting, it could not know. And in that moment God
became the Creator of humanity.

SATAN

When God commanded Satan: Bow down before Adam,
Satan answered: I will not bow before any other than Thee. Of
all the dwellers in Heaven there was no champion of God's Unity
so strict as Satan.

Moses met Satan on the side of Sinai, and asked of him:
Satan, why wouldst thou not bow down?

Because I believed that only One is to be adored, said Satan.
Disregarding God's Command?

That was trial, Satan said, and not Command.

Was it not sin? thy face has faded since.

Wisdom lasts, said Satan, although the wise man's face may wither for it.

Dost thou still remember Him?

O Moses, Satan answered, pure thought needs no memory; and thought is His memorial with me, as it is mine with Him. I serve him now with a purer service, in a present emptier of self-purpose, and remembering to His greater glory. In Heaven I served Him for my own well-being, but now I serve for the sake of His. Because of my zeal for Him alone He made me lonely. Because my eyes dazzled He blasted me. Because He had made me what I was to be in His Foreknowledge He stripped me. Because He had established my desire for decay He made me unlike the rest. Nor, by His Truth, have I failed His Decree in aught, nor murmured against Destiny; nor have I cared for my lost beauty. Through these Dooms I walk upright. Let Him torment me in His Fire for ever and ever, I shall not bow down before any other; for I know He has nor peer nor Son, and my love for Him is pure love.

* * *

As to Satan, the most eloquent of mystics have remained dumb. Satan is closer bound than they to his adoration; Satan is nearer to Being than they; to his zeal Satan sacrificed more than they, he kept his word better than they, and he is closer than they are to Him Who is adored.

His disaster overtook him when trust ended, in the moment when he said: I am nobler than Adam. From that instant he remained shut out beyond the Veil, not knowing what the Form of Adam hid. He fell, to sprawl in dust, and twined himself for ever and for ever with damnation.

For the *O* of Satan's final *No* is *GOD WHO IS THE LIVING GOD.*

* * *

For those who obey, sin, once they know Whom it is they offend, is death.

If a man would taste of Graces, let him reduce his soul to one of these three states: as when he was in his mother's womb, disposed without power to interfere and fed without even knowing he is fed; or quiet as he shall be in the tomb; or helpless as he shall be at Judgment.

* * *

From Basra Hallaj went a second time on Pilgrimage; thence returned to Basra, and to Ahwaz; and then, taking his wife and child and some of his more important Ahwaz disciples with him, he went up to Baghdad. There he stayed a year; and then, committing his son to one of the disciples, departed again.

To India first he went, thence into Khurasan and Turkistan as far as the marches of China, calling people to God, and writing books for them. After his return, the letters which came to him at Baghdad from India were addressed to him under the title of the Intercessor, those from China and Turkistan under that of the Provider. Khurasan letters addressed him as the Seer, those from Fars as Abu Abdallah the Ascetic, those from Khuzistan as the Shaykh who is the Carder of Consciences. Some people at Baghdad called him the Ecstatic, and others, at Basra, the Dazzled Man. And strange stories began to be told of him after he came back from these travels.

Then a third time he went on Pilgrimage, and spent two years in the Holy Cities. From this Pilgrimage (says his son) he came back greatly changed from what he had been before. But he bought a piece of land at Baghdad, and built himself a house.

Hallaj wished to convert a certain Ibn Harun, a man who used to hold salons where the better-known Baghdad shaykhs engaged in discussion. When all the guests were seated on one of these occasions, Hallaj opened the conversation with this riddle:

Have you no time to recognize me?
Then recognize my verity!
My first is softer than my fourth,
My fifth is longer than my third,
My second commonest of all
The thrice three threes. What is the word?
Divine; and you shall see me stand upright
Where Moses stood, on Sinai, wrapped in light.
Everyone was baffled.

It happened that Ibn Harun's little son was sick at that time, and sinking fast. And the host presently said to Hallaj: My boy is sick; I wish you would pray for him.

He is already healed, said Hallaj; don't worry any more.

It was only a few minutes later that the child was brought in, looking as if he had never been ill. Everyone present was dumbfounded; Ibn Harun pulled out a sealed purse and offered it to Hallaj.

Shaykh, said he, use this as you will.

Now the saloon where they were sitting opened on the Tigris bank. Hallaj, taking the purse, which contained three thousand dinars, threw it into the river.

You had some questions to ask me, I think, he said, addressing the company of shaykhs; but what questions could *you* ask of *me?* for I see only too well how right you are, and how wrong I am.

And with these words he went away.

Next day, Ibn Harun paid visits to the various shaykhs who had been present with Hallaj, and showed them the very purse which Hallaj had tossed into the stream. Yesterday, said he, I could not stop thinking about that present I had offered him; and I began to wish he had not thrown it into the river. Scarcely an hour after that thought came into mind, a poor disciple of his came to my gate to say: The shaykh greets you and bids me say to you: Make an end of regret and take this purse; to one who obeys Him God gives power, even over earth and water. And he put my own purse in my hand.

Knowledge of Me as I am is both too vast for the sight and too subtle, minute, and dense for the understanding of a fleshly creature. I am I — without attribute. I am I — without qualification. Actually *My Attributes have become humanity;* and this My Humanity is the cancellation of pure spirituality. I have only one quality: Deity.

By My own Decree a Veil screens Me from Myself; and for Me this Veil is the prelude to Vision. When the moment of Vision comes, then all attributes of My qualification — Deity — disappear.

Only thus am I parted from Myself. I am the *subject* of *I am;* I am not Myself. I am Metaphor (man for God) and not *ķin* to man. I am Apparition, and not an infusion into a material vehicle. My Rising is not a recoil into Eternity, but simply a Reality beyond the range either of the senses or of analogy.

Angels and men both have some knowledge of that Metaphor, that Apparition. Not that they know the real nature of this sole qualification: they know only according to the instruction they have received, and every man according to his capacity. *EACH TRIBE KNEW AT WHAT SPRING IT WAS TO DRINK.* For one man it may be a drug; it will be pure water for another. One sees only some human shape. Another sees only the Peerlessness of God; and his eye is therefore darkened by that qualification of Deity. One man wanders in the waterless valleys of research, another drowns in the oceans of thought — all are wide of Reality, for *all choose some goal* and therefore follow some wrong path.

God's intimates are those who ask Him for the Path only. They count themselves as nothing, and He devises glory for them; they make themselves nothing, and He makes their glory actual; they abase themselves, and He displays them as great marks.

Such men go to seek for wanderers. They set their glory low. And these are they whom He seizes from their human attributes by His own qualification — Deity.

Hallaj converted many people to his system, and some important men among the rest. It was the Reactionaries he most hoped to win over, for he thought of their belief as a good preliminary to his own; and he sent an emissary to Ibn Nawbakht, a member of that sect.

Ibn Nawbakht was a cautious, intelligent man. Your master's miracles, he said to the disciple, may well be conjuring-tricks. I am, he went on, what I may call a martyr to love: I enjoy the society of the ladies more than any other thing on earth. Unfortunately, however, I suffer from baldness. I have to let what hair I have grow long, and pull it over my forehead, and hold it there with my turban. And I have to disguise my grizzled beard with dye. Now, if Hallaj will give me a head of hair and a black beard, I will believe in whatever system he preaches; I will call him the Prophetic Vicar or the Sovereign if he likes; nay, I'll call him a Prophet, or even the Almighty.

When Hallaj heard this reply, he gave up hope of Ibn Nawbakht, and left him alone.

The man who would reveal God's secret to His creatures, the man too who wishes that the moment of his ecstasy may last, feels a suffering beyond human power to endure. Suffering lost its bitterness for Job when God blazed into his mind. For this my suffering and tribulation, he said, I have no more reward to hope; pain is become my native land, and pain my only bliss.

Happiness is His gift. But Suffering is Himself.

* * *

One night — it was bright moonlight — I went out to pray (says Ibn Fatik) at the grave where Ibn Hanbal lies in the corner of the Qurayshi Cemetery. And there I saw in the distance a man standing, facing the Direction. He did not notice me as I drew near; but I made out that it was Hallaj, weeping aloud.

I heard him say: O Thou Who hast made me so drunken with Thy Love and Who dwellest alone in Thine eternal solitude!

Thy Presence is a mere knowing Thee, without Thy coming; Thy Absence the Veil of names, though Thou departest not. I pray Thee by that holy closeness Thou dost send down on me at times, and by those higher degrees I ask of Thee, I pray Thee not to give me back to my selfhood when Thou hast seized me from it! Do not let me see my soul again, now Thou hast once hidden me from myself! Multiply those in Thy cities who hate me; multiply against me those of Thy faithful ones who demand my death!

Suddenly he saw me, and turned, and came smiling towards me. Abu Husayn, said he, I have got no further than the novice's first degree.

How? cried I. First degree? What state could be more exalted than what I have just seen?

No, said he, I was lying. 'Twas scarcely the first step of a simple Believer. It is the first State of Unbelief!

And he cried out, three times, and fell. I saw blood on his lips; but he gestured with his hand that I was to go away. So I left him.

Next morning I saw him in the Mosque of Mansur. He took my hand, and stooped and said: Don't tell people what you saw of me last night.

I saw Hallaj in the Qati'a Market once. He was weeping bitterly and crying: Hide me from God, you people! Hide me from God! hide me from God! He took me from myself and has not given me back; and I cannot perform the service I should do in His Presence for my fear of His leaving me alone again. He will leave me deserted, abandoned! and woe for the man who knows himself outcast after that Presence!

People were weeping to hear him. Then Hallaj stopped, by the gate that leads into the Attab Mosque, and began to speak — words some part of which we understood, but part was obscure.

Surely, said he in the clearer part, if He create creature of

His, it must be in pure goodwill towards it. And if then He blazes upon it sometimes, and sometimes hides Himself from it behind a Veil, it is still always that the creature may go onward. If that Light never came, men would deny the very existence of God. If It was never veiled, all would be spellbound. That is why He will let neither state last for ever. For me in this moment there is no Veil, not so much as a wink, between me and Him — a time for quiet, that my humanity die into His Deity while my body burns in the fire of His Power; that there be an end to trace and relic, face and word.

And then he said something which we could not understand: What you have to learn is this: that ordinary material things subsist atom by atom in His Godhead; that particular decrees are performed by Him as man.

Then he recited these verses:

Prophecy is the Lamp of the world's light;
But ecstasy in the same Niche has room.
The Spirit's is the breath which sighs through me;
And mine the thought which blows the Trump of Doom.
Vision said it. In my eye
Moses stood, on Sinai.

THE WARNING

Have no truck with Us! Look at Our Finger
Prettily tinted with Our lovers' blood!

* * *

I entered unannounced into Hallaj's room one day (says Ibn Fatik); someone had been in before me. Hallaj was in prayer, and his brow pressed to the ground. He was saying: O Thou Whose Closeness girds my very skin, Whose Mystery spurns me far away as lie all things in time from the Eternal, Thou shinest so before me that I think Thou art all these things; and then Thou dost deny Thyself in me, till I declare Thou art nothing

here. And this can neither be Thy Distance, for that would fort-
ify my selfhood, nor Thy Closeness, for that would help me;
neither Thy War, for that would destroy me, nor Thy Peace, for
that would comfort me.

Then, noticing my presence, he raised himself. Come in,
you do not disturb me, said he.

So I went farther in and sat down in front of him. His
eyes glowed like burning coals, and they were bloodshot.

My dear son, he said, I hear people are going about saying
I am a saint, and others saying that I am impious. I prefer those
who call me impious; and so does God.

How so, master? I said.

They call me a saint because they respect me; but the others call me impious out of zeal for their religion. A man who is
zealous for his religion is dearer to me, and dearer to God also,
than a man who venerates a creature. What will you say yourself,
Ibrahim, on the day when you see me hanging on the gibbet, and
killed, and burned? Yet that will be the happiest day of all my
life.

Well, don't stay here, he said presently. Go, and into the
Grace of God.

When the giving of Love is entire,
And What Love cries to is bygone in the stress of its crying,
Then a man verifies
What passion testifies:
Prayer is Unbelief,
Once one knows.

Ay, go. Tell them I sailed for the deep Sea,
*   And that my ship has foundered, far offshore.*
By Holy Cross I must go on to death;
*   To Holy Cities I can go no more.*

I have renounced the Faith of God.
  Obligatory on me
It was to do what for Belief
  Would be iniquity.

Hallaj went one day into the Mosque of Mansur and cried: Gather round, and listen to what I have to tell.

And a great crowd assembled: lovers and followers of his, and haters and critics too.

You ought to know this, said Hallaj: God has made me your outlaw. Kill me.

People in the crowd began to weep; but Abd al-Wudud the Sufi pressed nearer to him and said: Shaykh, how could we kill a man who prays and fasts and recites the Word?

Shaykh, said Hallaj, the motive that really stays you from shedding my blood has nothing to do with Prayer or fasting or reciting the Word. So why not kill me? You will have your reward for it, and I shall come to my peace. For you it will be your Holy War; for me it will be my Martyrdom.

When Hallaj left the Mosque (says Abd al-Wudud) I followed him home and questioned him: Shaykh, what you have said troubles us. What did you mean?

Dear son, said he, no task is more urgent for the Muslims at this moment than my execution. Realize this, that my death will preserve the sanctions of the Law; he who has offended *must* undergo them.

His preaching went on. At last the Jurist Ibn Dawud gave this opinion: If what the Prophet — God's Prayer and Peace on him — brought us from God is true, then what Hallaj says is false. He concluded a violent attack with the words: He may lawfully be put to death.

Ibn Furat gave order for the arrest; but Hallaj left Baghdad with one of his disciples. This was in the year 297.

In the year 301 Hallaj was arrested at Susa and sent up to the capital. Evidence was collected in both Ahwaz and Baghdad that he had claimed divinity; he was also accused of asserting that the Deity took up His abode in members of the Alid House. For the time being he was committed to imprisonment in the Royal Palace.

In the euphoria of passion, said Hallaj, I have been exuberant. And the punishment for exuberance has overtaken me.

*　*　*

It was not till the year '9 that the affair came to a head, and to an end in his death and burning. All this time he was lodged in the Palace, well treated and allowed to receive visitors. His fraudulent pretensions made a complete dupe of Nasr the Chamberlain, who had charge of him; and Hamid ibn Abbas, then Vizier, heard tales that Hallaj had gained an ascendancy over various Attendants and other people about court by pretending that he could raise the dead and perform at pleasure any of the miracles attributed to the Prophets. Certain State Clerks, and even a member of the Hashimite family, were reported to be acting as his apostles and declaring that he, Hallaj, was God (the blasphemy of it!).

These persons were arrested, and confessed under cross-examination by Hamid that they were acting as the man's missionaries, and were convinced that he was a god, with power to raise the dead. But when they repeated these statements in the presence of Hallaj himself, he repudiated them: God forbid, said he, that I should pretend to divinity, or to Prophecy — I am merely a man who worships God and practices prayer and fasting and good works; that is all.

Hamid sent for Judge Abu Omar, who followed the Malikite school of Law, Judge Ibn Buhlul, who was a Hanafite, and a number of eminent Jurists and Witnesses. He asked them to give an opinion on the case. The Jurists refused to sanction his execution without evidence of a capital crime, nor would they accept evidence on such a charge without some proof, or confession of guilt. The Caliph Muqtadir ordered Hallaj sent to Ali ibn Isa, then President under Hamid. But Ali shrank from the task of examining him, and begged to be excused; and the prisoner was conveyed to Hamid's palace.

At this point, a woman was sent to Hamid to give testimony. She was daughter to Hallaj's disciple Samarri. When questioned by Hamid as to what she knew of Hallaj, she declared that her father had taken her to see him, and on that first occasion Hallaj had given her sundry presents. The woman spoke well and pleasantly, and made a favorable impression. Among other things she related how Hallaj had said to her: I am going to give you in marriage to my dearest son Sulayman, who lives at Nishapur. A man and his wife, you know, are apt to get into arguments; or she may dislike something her husband does. You will be going to him very soon, and I have commended you to his love; but if he does anything you do not like, you do this: fast for a whole day. Then at the end of the day, go up on to your roof, strew cinders and coarse salt, and take your stand on that, and break your fast in that position; then turn your face to the quarter where I am, and tell me what it is he does that you don't like. I shall hear you, and see you.

One morning, she went on, I was going downstairs from the roof into the house. Hallaj's daughter was with me, and he himself was below. When we were got down far enough to see him, and he us, his daughter told me to bow down to him.

Why, ought we to bow down to any but God? I said.

Hallaj heard us. Yes, he said: God is in Heaven, but He is also on earth. Then he called me to him, and put his hand in his sleeve, and brought it out full of musk. He gave it me, and many handfuls more. Put this with your perfumes, he told me: a woman needs plenty of perfume when she presents herself before her husband.

Another time, he was sitting in a room which was spread with matting; and he called me in, and pointed to one of the corners, and told me to lift up the mat and take as much as I wanted from underneath. So I went over to the place; and when

I turned up the mat, there was a regular floor of gold dinars all over the room, a most extraordinary thing.

This ended the woman's examination; but she was detained in Hamid's house until after the execution. Hamid now set spies to hunt down Hallaj's disciples. In their houses were found a great number of documents, written on Chinese paper, some of them in gold ink. Some were mounted on satin or silk, and bound in fine leather. Among other papers were curious files of letters from his provincial missionaries, and his instructions to them as to what they should teach, how they should lead people on from stage to stage, how different classes of people should be approached according to their level of intelligence and degree of receptiveness.

A PHENOMENON

My father and I (says the State Clerk Ibn Zanji) had been visiting Hamid one day, and the Vizier left the room for a moment. So we went out to the Public Saloon and sat down on the bench. Harun the Collector presently came in. He greeted my father, and they had just fallen into conversation when Hamid's slave who had charge of Hallaj appeared at the door and beckoned Harun outside. Harun, not knowing what was the matter, hurried out. But it was not long before he came back, looking very pale.

My father was alarmed by his appearance. What has happened? he cried.

That was the slave in charge of Hallaj who signalled to me, said Harun. He told me outside there that he had been going to take in Hallaj's daily tray when he saw that Hallaj was filling the whole room with his person, stretching all the way from roof to floor, and from wall to wall — there was no room left. This apparition frightened him so that he dropped his tray and fled. The slave's in a fever now, he added; he's shuddering and trembling.

Before we had recovered from our astonishment, Hamid sent out to us inviting us into his private room again; so we went in and began to tell him about the slave. Hamid sent for the man. He really was feverish. The Vizier demanded what had happened. He repeated the story as we had heard it.

You're lying! said Hamid, with some words of abuse. You've been scared with Hallaj's conjuring-tricks or something, damn you — get out!

The slave got out. But it was a long time before he got over his feverish condition.

Afterward, Nasr the Chamberlain got the Caliph's permission to build Hallaj a separate place of confinement (says Hallaj's son Hamd), and a small house adjacent to the prison wall was furnished. Its outer door was walled up, a courtyard wall built round it, and a door opening into the prison pierced. For a year he was allowed to receive visitors. Then this was forbidden; and for five months no one came near him, except that once I saw the disciple Ibn Ata, who was smuggled in somehow, and on another occasion a man named Abu Abdallah ibn Khafif. I used to spend the nights outside at my mother's house, and my days inside with my father at that time.

ABU ABDALLAH IBN KHAFIF'S STORY

As I passed through Baghdad on my way home from Pilgrimage that year I felt great curiosity to see Hallaj. At that time he was no longer allowed to receive visits; so I went and pleaded with an army man of my acquaintance, who said a word to the Keeper.

The man admitted me to the prison unobserved, along with a group of high officials who arrived on horseback at the same time; once inside, he led me along to where there was a door newly opened in the wall. He pointed to it and said: Go through there.

I went through. There was a comfortable pavilion (built, I was told, at the expense of Nasr the Chamberlain, one of Hallaj's rich followers) with a pleasant saloon, spread with carpets and hung with gold-broidered curtains as rich as I had ever seen. A young man and another older man who looked like a servant were sitting there; they rose and greeted me, and invited me to sit down.

It's a long time since we saw anyone but the Keeper here, they said.

Where is the shaykh? I inquired.

He is busy.

Why, what does he have to do here?

You see that door there? said the servant. That leads to the prison where the tramps and highwaymen and beggars lie; he goes to visit them, and makes them turn their thoughts to God: they do penance under his direction.

As we sat there talking, Hallaj came in and walked toward us. I took a good look at him. He had a charming face, and was wearing a clean tunic and a white woollen cloak. On his feet were folded slippers in the Yamani style. Sitting down at one end of the long seat, he greeted me and asked of what country I was.

Of Fars.

And which town?

Shiraz.

He asked me various questions about the Shiraz shaykhs, which I answered as I could.

And whence do you come now? he then asked.

From Mecca.

Concerning the Mecca shaykhs he also made inquiries, and then asked: Have you seen any of the Baghdad shaykhs?

Yes.

How is Abu Abbas ibn Ata?

He is very well.

If you see him again, said Hallaj, pray give him this message: that he is to keep those manuscripts in a safe place. But how did you succeed in getting in to see me?

Thanks to an army friend of mine, said I, a man I used to know at Shiraz.

Our conversation was interrupted by the sudden appearance of the Keeper of the prison. He was trembling with fright, and came and kissed the ground before Hallaj.

Why, what's wrong? said the shaykh.

I have to answer an accusation — they've laid an information against me! said the Keeper. They told the Caliph that I've taken a bribe and let a Prince escape and put a commoner in his place. My life's at stake.

Go to him now; you will have no trouble. God will preserve you, said Hallaj.

The man went off.

Then Hallaj rose, stepped into the middle of the room, kneeled down, lifting his hands with the first finger pointed directly upward, and said: Lord! Then he bowed forward till his cheek rested on the ground. The tears flowed from his eyes till the place was wet with them; and then he lay still, as if he had fainted. He was still lying there when the Keeper reappeared.

Tell me what happened, he said then.

I'm pardoned! said the Keeper.

At that, Hallaj, rising from where he lay, went back to his former place. What did the Caliph say? he asked.

He said: I sent for you just now to have your head off; however, I decide to pardon you; but don't let this happen again. What they said against me is lies, I told him. He ordered me a Dress of Honor then, and some gifts in kind and a bounty in money, the Keeper concluded.

Hallaj at this moment was reclining at one end of the divan seat. This seat was about fifteen cubits long — perhaps a little longer; and at the *other* end of it a small napkin was lying. And now I saw Hallaj stretch out his hand toward this napkin and simply pick it up! Whether it was his arm which extended to that length, or whether it was the napkin which moved toward him, I cannot make up my mind; but when I saw it happen, the thought darted through me: Yes, that's exactly what they accuse him of — magic!

He wiped the sweat from his face. I stayed no longer, but took my leave.

Afterward I went round to see Ibn Ata and told him what had happened, and gave him the message.

If you see him again, said Ibn Ata, tell him: Yes, though they send me where he is gone, I will keep those papers in a safe place.

By and by Hamid turned up a letter written by Hallaj which contained the following passage:

If a man would go on Pilgrimage and cannot, let him set apart in his house some square construction, to be touched by no unclean thing, and let no one have access to it. When the day of the Pilgrimage rites comes, let him make his circuit round it, and perform all the same ceremonies as he would perform at Mecca. Then let him gather together thirty orphans, for whom he has prepared the most exquisite feast he can get; let him bring them to his house and serve them that feast; and after waiting on them himself, and washing their hands as a servant himself, let him present each of them with a new frock, and give them each seven dirhams. This will be a substitute for Pilgrimage.

My father (says Ibn Zanji) was reading this letter in evidence at a hearing; and as he finished this passage, Judge Abu Omar turned to Hallaj.

Where did you get that doctrine? he asked.

From Hasan of Basra's *Book of Devotion,* Hallaj replied.

That is false, said the Judge. Outlaw! we ourselves heard Hasan of Basra's *Devotion* when we were studying at Mecca, and there is nothing like that in it.

When Abu Omar used the term *Outlaw,* Hamid broke in, ordering him to put it in writing. The Judge went on trying to give his attention to Hallaj; in his opinion this doctrine was Atheism, and as such punishable with immediate death, for the

atheist is given no chance of repentance. But Judge Ibn Buhlul
gave his opinion that this in itself did not constitute a capital
crime, unless Hallaj were to confess that he not only recorded
this doctrine but also believed it — men sometimes record heretical doctrines without holding them. If Hallaj will declare, he
went on, that he merely reports this doctrine, but does not himself
believe it, then he should be summoned to recant; and if he re-
cants there will be no case against him. If he refuses, then indeed
he will deserve death.

But Hamid would not allow the examination to continue;
he kept insisting — and finally in a tone which there was no gain-
saying — that Abu Omar put in writing his opinion that Hallaj
was an Outlaw. The Judge obeyed and signed; and the others
present at the trial began to follow suit.

When Hallaj saw what was going on, he cried out: My
blood must not be shed like this. You have no right to outlaw me
by a quibble. My religion is Islam, my sect the True Way — there
are books of mine maintaining the True Way in the bookstores
at this moment. I adjure you in the Name of God, *do not shed
my blood.*

During the whole time the people present at the hearing
were putting their names to Abu Omar's opinion, he kept this up.
When the signatures of all present were on the paper, Hamid sent
it off to the Caliph Muqtadir.

Nasr the Chamberlain went to warn the Queen-Mother.
I am afraid, he told her, that God's Vengeance will come on your
son for the death of this devout teacher. So she went to Muqtadir and begged him to spare Hallaj. It was no use: the Caliph,
ignoring her request, sent to Hamid the following rescript:
*Inasmuch as the judicial sentence is as you have transmitted it to
us, have him taken to the Police Office and scourged with a
thousand stripes; if he is not then dead, order his hands and feet
amputated and his head then struck off; set his head on a stake
and burn his body.*

But that same day Muqtadir fell sick of a fever. This
coincidence served to inflame the fancies of Nasr and the Queen-

Mother; even Muqtadir felt uneasy, and sent Hamid a hurried order to put off the execution. So it was delayed for some days, until the Caliph recovered and his fears abated.

Hamid now urged that the prisoner be put to death without further delay. Muqtadir tried to put the question aside as unimportant.

Prince of the True Believers, said the Vizier, if this man is left to live, he will corrupt the Law and make apostates of your subjects. That will be the end of your dynasty. Let me carry out the sentence. If any trouble comes of it, you may order me to death myself.

Permission was granted. It was agreed that the Chief of Police should come after dark, for fear of a rescue, and bring a company of slaves and men mounted on mules, dressed as grooms, so that Hallaj might be set on one of the mules and huddled along in the middle of the crowd. Nazuk carried these instructions out, and conveyed Hallaj away that night, Hamid's retainers riding with them as far as the Bridge. The Chief of Police himself passed the night with his men, who lay picketed round the Session House building.

On the night before his delivery to execution (says his son Hamd), Hallaj stood up and performed the ordinary Prayer of two Bows. After that, he fell to repeating the word *Illusion, illusion, illusion. . .* to himself, and so continued till the night was more than half spent. Then for a long while he remained silent. Suddenly he gave a cry: *Truth! Truth!* and sprang to his feet. He bound on his turban, donned his cloak, stretched out his arms, and facing the Direction, fell into an ecstasy and talked with God.

Ibrahim ibn Fatik his servant and I, who were with him, both remembered some parts of what he then said: these: —

See, he said, we are ready to be called as Thy witnesses, and come for refuge into Thy Grace; into the splendor of Thy Glory, into the Brightness, for Thy declaring of whatever Thou pleasest. *IN HEAVEN — GOD. ON EARTH — GOD.* O Setter of the Cycles and Shaper of Forms, O by Whose Decree these bodies are compounded! Thou wilt come shining to sight, when Thou wilt, on whom Thou wilt, and as Thou wilt, even as Thou didst blazon Thy Decree in the image of that *FAIREST FORM* of Adam, that Form which shall blazon forth the Word, the sole form gifted with knowledge and speech, and free power and proof.

Thou it was didst assign this Thy witness here his part to speak as Thyself. How then is it come to this? For Thou it was didst will my beginning, Thou Who didst seize my being to use it for Thy symbol, Thou Who didst proclaim it, at my last and highest, as My Divine Being, Who didst display the Reality of my knowledge, and those miracles I wrought. Thou it was didst raise me up at my ascensions to those thrones of my own pre-eternity, and didst cause me to speak the BE! of my own creation.

How is it come to this? that now I go to die, to suffer a felon's death, to hang on a gibbet, my body to be burned, my ashes given to the winds and streams for keeping? Ah!

Surely, surely the least portion of this flesh which has been Thine incense is promise for the body of my Rising, promise of reality more sure than the mightiest hills are real!

Then he began to speak in verse:

For souls whose witness now departs, to go beyond Until,
* into the Witness of Eternity,*
                              Hear my sorrow, Thou!
For those miracles whose dialectic shut the mouth of argu-
* ment,*
                              Hear my sorrow, Thou!
In the name of Thy Love! for all the valiancy of that saintly
* chivalry, who rode themselves as steeds,*
                              Hear my sorrow, Thou!
For them to be lost and gone, like unheeding Ad, or the
* long-lost Worldly Garden!*
And then, the abandoned herd, wandering, stumbling,
Blinder than beasts, blinder than flocking sheep.

He fell silent again. After a while, his servant Ibrahim said: Master, give me some word for a keepsake.

Your self! he answered. Unless you enslave it, it will enslave you.

When the morning dawned, they came to fetch him out into the Square. As I watched him go, he was dancing in his chains.

HIS PASSION

A crowd beyond counting was assembled.

I was there (says Abu Hasan of Hulwan) the day they executed Hallaj. They brought him from his cell bound and chained; but he was laughing.

Master, said I, why are you like this?

He answered only with a verse:

> *My Host, with His own ruthless courtesy,*
> *Passed me His Cup, and bade me drink. I drank.*
> *Round went the wine; sudden I heard Him cry:*
> *Headsman! the Mat and Sword! This is the end*
> *Of drink with Liodragon in July.*

When they had brought him as far as the gibbet, and he saw the scaffold and the nails, he laughed till the tears ran from his eyes. Presently, turning to look at the crowd assembled, he saw Shibli among the rest.

Abu Bakr, said he, have you your prayer carpet with you?

Yes, said Shibli.

Will you lay it for me?

Shibli laid out his carpet. Hallaj performed a Prayer of two Bows, reciting the passage *WE SHALL TRY YOU* with the first and the passage *ALL SOULS TASTE DEATH* with the second. When his Prayer was finished, he spoke; I can only remember some of his words, the following:

O our God! Who dost glow in all places and art not in any place, I beseech Thee by the truth of Thy Word which declares that I am, by the truth of this my word which declares that Thou art, I beseech Thee, my Master, give me grace to be grateful for this happiness of Thy giving, that Thou didst hide from others what was unveiled to me, the raging fires of Thy Face, and forbid them to look, as I was permitted to look, into things hidden in the Mystery of Thee.

And these Thy servants who are gathered to slay me, in zeal for Thy Religion, longing to win Thy Favor, forgive them, Lord. Have mercy on them. Surely, if Thou hadst shown them what Thou hast shown me, they would never have done what they have done; and hadst Thou kept from me what Thou hast kept from them, I should not have suffered this tribulation. Whatsoever Thou wilt do, I praise Thee! Whatsoever Thou dost will, I praise Thee!

Then he was silent. The headsman stepped up to him and dealt him a smashing blow between the eyes; the blood poured from his nostrils. Shibli cried out, and rent his dress, and fell fainting.

The headsman was ordered to administer one thousand strokes with a scourge. It was done. Hallaj uttered no cry, nor did he plead for pardon.

Only according to one witness, when he had endured the six-hundredth blow, he cried out to the Chief of Police: Send for me! and I'll tell you what will more profit the Caliph than the storming of Constantinople!

They told me to expect some such offer, answered Nazuk, or a bigger one. It won't get you out of your stripes — nothing will.

After that Hallaj said nothing more until the thousandth blow came at last. His hand was then amputated, then his foot; and he was fastened on the gibbet.

There he hung till nightfall, when an order arrived from the Caliph Muqtadir giving permission for his beheading. However, the officer in charge said: It is late now — leave him till to-morrow.

When morning came, he was taken down, and dragged forward for decapitation. It was at this time that he spoke his last words: All who have known ecstasy long for this . . . the loneliness of the Only One . . . alone with the Alone.

He was set a little way in front of the gibbet, and his head struck off. The trunk was rolled up in a strip of reed-matting, and soaked in naphtha, then burned.

I was there (says the Clerk Ibn Zanji). I was standing up as tall as I could on the back of my mule — I had not been able to get into the Square. The trunk twisted on the coals as the flames burned it. When there was nothing left but ashes, they were collected and thrown from the Minaret over the Tigris. The head was set up on the Bridge for two days, and then sent to Khurasan to be exhibited in the various districts.

All booksellers were summoned to appear and obliged to take an oath that they would neither sell nor buy any work by Hallaj.

His disciples asserted that the person who had endured the scourging was not he, but some enemy of his on whom his likeness had been cast. Some of them even claimed to have seen him afterward, and to have heard something from him to that effect, along with more nonsense not worth the trouble of transcribing.

God threw a man into the Sea, with his arms tied behind
    his back,
And said to him: Careful! careful! or you will get wet in
    the water!

A GOVERNMENT JOB

EPISODES FROM THE LIFE OF A PROVINCIAL
STATE CLERK

*Be cruel to none, though cruel power lie to thy hand —
In the shadow of vengeance the sad oppressor walks.
Thou must needs sleep; the broken, sleepless, cries
His curse on thee to One Whom sleep not overtakes.*

THERE USED TO BE BAD FEELING (my great-uncle Abu Qasim ibn Abi Allan of Ahwaz, State Clerk, told me) between a man called Ibn Qudayda and myself. This Ibn Qudayda happened to be agent, at a time when I was out of Government service, for certain estates belonging to the Queen-Mother; and some of these lands lay adjoining my own. In matters of irrigation and labor he caused me great annoyance — he meant to ruin my estate and humiliate myself.

For a time I put up with it all; but then one day he arrested one of my farm laborers and beat him savagely about the face. So I sent one of the Clerks on my estate over to complain, to insist that Ibn Qudayda alter his behavior, and to bring my laborer back. But Ibn Qudayda received my messenger with very harsh language; and when the Clerk got back, he told me the man meant mischief and advised me to try another course.

Why, what happened? I asked.

My Clerk described his reception. I began to think. I could see no way of defending myself against what he could do to me; and I could see no way of taking the offensive except offering to farm the Queen-Mother's estates myself, a measure which would put his person in my power and enable me to demand his accounts, and so get him into trouble. So I wrote to the Queen-Mother's Secretary, soliciting the right to farm her estates. Over a three-year period I offered an increase of thirty thousand dinars on the revenues contracted for by Ibn Qudayda, on condition that Ibn Qudayda be put in my hands, to be compelled to give an account and to pay whatever the scrutiny showed due from him, which sum was to be paid to Baghdad over and above the increase of revenue previously proposed.

I sent the letter off by special courier. But no sooner was the man gone than I began to wish the letter unwritten. I had no idea of the actual yield of those estates: I should never have made such an offer: it would have been less trouble to endure the fellow's malice. Worrying like this, I threw myself on my bed. While I lay in that state halfway between asleep and awake, I seemed to see an old man come into my room. He had white hair and beard, and was dressed like a Judge, in a blue hood, a tall Persian hat, and boots of red leather. He spoke; and these were his words: What troubles you about this business? In the first year of your farming you will make ten thousand more than the increase you promised; in the second you will lose ten thousand; and the third year you will come out even. The reward for your trouble will be vengeance on your enemy.

Startled by these words, I became wide awake; and I asked at once whether any visitor had been admitted. Nobody, I was told. The incident encouraged me somewhat.

Twenty-two days later, a courier arrived from Baghdad with letters for me: my proposal had been accepted. One of the letters was addressed to a resident agent of theirs at Tib, who was superintendent of all their agents in the Ahwaz district: it was an order for him to proceed to Ahwaz and place Ibn Qudayda in my charge. To this agent I sent a cheque for a thousand dinars by way of compliment, adding a note to request a visit from him, and enclosing the letters I had received.

A few days later, as I was sitting with the Governor of Ahwaz in his palace on the bank of the Little Tigris, we saw a great retinue approaching along the Mamunia road. The Governor, imagining that someone was come to remove him from office, was in a great fright, and sent a man to make inquiries. He was soon back, with the intelligence that it was the Queen-Mother's agent. So the Governor, taking me with him in his boat, crossed the river to pay the functionary the compliment of meeting.

When we met, the resident agent informed the Governor that he wanted to see Ibn Abi Allan.

That was my name, said I (we had not known each other by sight before).

The agent bade me rise from my place, and set me above everybody present. Now, said he, I want Ibn Qudayda.

A messenger was sent to summon the man. When he appeared, the agent had him put in fetters, and then said to me: Abu Qasim, he is in your charge!

What is all this about? cried the Governor; and the company were beginning to make unpleasant remarks, until I explained how the fellow had forced me to take this course.

And so, with Ibn Qudayda in my custody, I went off to my own house. To the Queen-Mother's agent, who went with me, I paid sufficient attentions, and gave sufficient gratuities and presents, to make sure of a friendly attitude on his part; and he gave me a contract for the farming, to come into effect next day. On the third day, with another tip of a thousand dinars from me, he departed; and I, in my own house, with some reluctance put Ibn Qudayda to the torture.

By violent means, I got out of him money for the Queen-Mother, for her Secretary, for her agent, and even for myself enough to reimburse me for the agent's entertainment and tips. After the lapse of a few months I released him and let him go home, now heavily in debt. He had to sell part of his personal estate, and was thoroughly humiliated and wretched.

I attended to my farming, and at the year's end found myself ten thousand dinars to the good. What the old man of my dream had told me had come true so far, I noticed; so instead of entering the sum on my balance sheet, I deposited it with my banker. Prices fell next year; and I lost a similar amount. So I used what I had kept from the year before to cover my losses. In the third year I came out exactly even, made nothing, lost nothing. Accordingly I brought my accounts up to date and wrote asking to be excused from further farming of the estates — Ibn Qudayda, I knew, had had a fall quite heavy enough, and was in no position to undertake the business again. Indeed, he had not the substance to be trusted with it.

But the Queen-Mother's Secretary was by no means willing to let me retire. He insisted that I renew the contract, and at the increased rate. Ibn Qudayda also had agents at work egging him on to put unfair pressure on me; and finally the Secretary sent one of the highest officials in the Queen-Mother's service to fetch me up to the capital.

This personage arrived by boat, with an escort of alarming appearance. I was horrified at the idea of going off with him: I saw myself under arrest and put to torture without any means of escape. So I offered him the hospitality of my house and gave him presents and tips, including five thousand dirhams in cash which seemed to make a great impression on him. Having got him installed as my guest, I suggested that since my establishment was a large one, and I wished to put everything in order, I be allowed a week's respite during which I might stay quietly at home making the necessary arrangements: After which, said I, I will come with you. He gave me permission; I immediately told my brothers, my brothers-in-law, and my Clerks to invite him on a round of visits, to spend a day with each, slaves, retinue, and all. They were to keep the visitors from hearing of my movements, to occupy them entirely with drinking parties and chess and singing-girls. All did as I asked.

I got away under cover of night, in patched clothes, riding on an ass, and taking only two slaves and a guide. Bills for five thousand dinars I had with me, but no other money. While I pursued my road, the time of the Queen-Mother's official was taken up with his round of parties; and I had reached Wasit before he heard that I was gone.

When at last he heard, he was in a terrible state, and went off downriver to Ubulla instead of returning to his post. I meanwhile was getting near Baghdad; and soon after, I sneaked into the City and threw myself on the mercy of Abu Mundhir Nu'-man ibn Abdallah, who had been a friend and companion of mine in the days when he was Governor at Ahwaz; I had worked in the same office with him. Abu Mundhir introduced me to Ali ibn Isa, who was Vizier at that time, and explained my position to him. He had long been anxious to meet me, said the Vizier: he had heard so much of my clerkly skill. And he handed me a few documents to draft. I composed the texts then and there, in the Vizier's presence; and my performance won his praise, even his admiration. At Ali ibn Isa's house I lay for some days, during which my whereabouts were concealed from the Queen-Mother's Secretary. I then spoke to the Vizier; and the Queen-Mother herself was approached. But she would not hear of my business being settled without my personal appearance at her office.

You had better do it, said the Vizier; I am behind you, so don't be afraid.

As soon as I presented myself at the office, I was put under arrest. I let my friends know; and Abu Mundhir himself came to the office to mediate. He arranged a compromise settlement by which I was to pay three thousand dinars (or thereabouts; I am not quite sure what figure my great-uncle named), for which he wrote a guarantee on my behalf. He took me home with him; and out of the bills I had brought I paid him the sum guaranteed.

Ali ibn Isa wanted me to go into his own office afterward; but I explained to him that I had really abandoned Government service, and had only undertaken the farming because I was forced to. And I told him the whole story. So he excused me, and I returned home to Ahwaz.

Years passed. The old enmity between Ibn Qudayda and myself was still there — the only difference was that he was now underdog. Then one day an order arrived at Ahwaz from the Sovereign offering his Private Estates in the district for sale.

(What had happened in the capital is told by Judge Ibn Buhlul the Younger:

One Court day [says the Judge] I attended at the Palace, and was sitting waiting in my barge at the water-steps, with the other Judges, the Princes and Clerks all sitting waiting for admission in their own boats, when a summons came down for me — and for no other Judge. When I en-

tered Muqtadir's presence, Ibn Muqla, who was Vizier at
the time, was standing before him.

Your father, said the Caliph to me, was a real support, and
thank God you are with us to fill his place. Look how these
slaves pester and plague me for money! If they were to lose
me, they would be wanting me back on the throne again
soon enough! I have decided to sell my Nimrod Estates at
Ahwaz; do you write to your deputy there and tell him to
make arrangements with Baridi for the sale. Have Baridi
help him. [Baridi was then farming the Ahwaz revenue.]
If the matter is of importance to the Prince of True Believers, whose life God long preserve, I replied, I will go down
to Ahwaz myself to arrange the matter.

I won't give you so much trouble, Muqtadir answered; I
just want you to write to your deputy about it. So when I
left the Palace, I wrote to Ali Tanukhi, who was my deputy
Judge for the district, and told him about it.)

In Ahwaz (continues Ibn Abi Allan) people began to buy
in the Estates, for as little as half the value of a year's produce,
or even less. I bought as much as I wanted, at a fantastic bargain.
Abu Abdallah Baridi bought an enormous amount for himself,
though under the names of various other persons, and I advised
him, made the selection, and looked after the job of concealing
the arrangements. For myself, I was comparatively short of funds
at that time. Ibn Qudayda was also a buyer. We all took possession of our lots.

Presently fresh orders arrived from the Sovereign demanding a very large additional payment — I think it was a hundred
thousand dinars.

(In Baghdad, says Judge Ibn Buhlul, the days passed by;
and Ibn Muqla was in course of time dismissed, and
replaced by the Vizier Sulayman. Sulayman appointed
his friend Ibn Harith to replace Baridi at Ahwaz; and
this Ibn Harith demanded from the purchasers of the
Estates a vast additional sum of money above what they

had already paid. But he wrote also to the deputy Judge informing him that a large amount of the sum realized was not to be remitted to the Treasury, but to be reserved for his, Ibn Harith's, private account.)

Baridi (continues Ibn Abi Allan) consulted me: how was this increase to be provided?

The buyers will never undertake to pay it for your sake, I told him; for the deeds of sale were perfectly definite in their terms. But Baridi, ignoring my advice, called the purchasers together for a talk. They declined to pay; and all he got for his trouble was that they looked on him as an enemy, and he had offended me. After a while, he told me that he knew no one else for the business: there was only myself, and I simply must manage it for him. He pressed me so urgently that at last I said I would raise the money, on condition that he gave me a free hand; and this he promised to do.

So I sat down with one of my slaves; and we proceeded to distribute the payment as a rate on the local purchasers, omitting myself and Baridi, on whom we imposed nothing, reducing the assessment in the cases of our friends, and increasing it correspondingly in other cases. I had made up my mind to assess Ibn Qudayda at twice the rate which was proportionately due from him, and he was put down for that amount. The people concerned were then summoned to discuss the imposition.

All declared they would not pay this rate, and asked on what principle it was imposed. After the wrangling and discussing had gone on for some time, I spoke, to the effect that whoever thought fit to pay the rate should pay it; but if anyone objected, he had only to give me an account of all produce he had obtained from the Estate he had bought, and I would return to him any balance that remained of the price he had paid, after subtracting the value of the produce, and take over the land myself, undertaking to pay the additional rate myself.

At the sound of this, however, it soon appeared that every man had bought land which had been farmed by his dependents or his local community, or land which had been worked by himself and his fathers before him for a hundred years, or else land which he and his fathers before him had always wanted, and had been on the lookout to buy for a hundred years, or else land which, though admittedly he had bought it cheap, he had since greatly improved. The idea of my becoming the owner caused general consternation; and one and all undertook to pay the rate as I had assessed it, without further question.

(Now for some time, as Judge Ibn Buhlul's account goes on, I had had a grudge against Ibn Harith, although I had done nothing about it. One day when there was a Court I had gone downriver as usual, and we were sitting waiting in our boats, when the deputy Chamberlains came out to summon me by myself to the Presence, the other Judges being again left outside. So I went up and presented myself before Muqtadir. The Vizier Sulayman and Ali ibn Isa were there; and he was talking business, arranging grants, introducing and considering various matters.

We are perfectly satisfied, said Muqtadir to me, with the way your deputy Judge in Ahwaz handled the business of our orders about the Nimrod Estates; but now Ibn Harith writes that he has raised the prices, and the buyers have agreed to the addition. But they decline to pay the money until I personally declare that I ratify the sale, and will demand no further addition, do nothing of that kind. You write to your deputy and tell him that I have made such a declaration, and that he is to give the people a sealed contract of sale.

I saw my opportunity to annoy Ibn Harith [by preventing him making any undeclared profit]. It would be necessary, I observed to the Caliph, to state the amount of the increase definitely in my letter.

Muqtadir turned a black look on Ali ibn Isa; and the latter, quaking, as I could well see, gave the figure. Insert that figure in your letter to your deputy, the Caliph told me. I invoked a blessing on him and took my leave; but as I was curious to hear the sequel, I walked away very slowly.

What could be more humiliating than that? I heard Muqtadir indignantly demanding of Ali ibn Isa. Why did you not mention the amount to me at the beginning, instead of reducing me to asking for further information? He kept repeating: What could be more humiliating? more improper? For it was a Sovereign's duty always to give all the essentials, in any matter of business; he should never leave anything out, so that the person he is addressing is driven to asking for elucidation. At the end of his tirade he went so far as to suggest that if I were to mention the incident in public it would injure not only himself but the very Caliphal office!

I could hear Ali ibn Isa reassuring him: I was his slave, the son of his slave, I was the recipient of his bounty, the nursling of his dynasty, there was not the slightest reason to apprehend that I would do anything of the kind. And so on.)

Ibn Qudayda (continues Ibn Abi Allan) had not the wherewithal to provide the large additional sum I had imposed on him. One night as I was sitting at home he came to my house and had himself announced.

What is the meaning of this, Abu Ja'far? said I, rising.

He began to remonstrate in a fawning tone.

What do you want? I asked.

You *must* reduce my rating, he replied; and give me some assistance from your own funds; for I solemnly declare to you that I have not the means to pay.

So I reduced his rating by a small amount, and lent him thirty thousand dirhams, in return for an I O U which I wrote and had attested by every qualified Witness in the neighborhood. I kept the paper at home, and put the money out of mind for some years; but I continued to devise other vexations, fines, and annoyances for the man, under which he melted and waned from day to day.

At last I knew that he was down and out; and then I demanded the debt. He concealed himself in his house. So I asked the Judge, your father, my sister's son, to help me; and he wrote a demand for assistance on my behalf to the Prefect of Police. Ibn Qudayda thereupon fled from home; and the Judge had him summoned to appear, by proclamation at the door of his house. This having no effect, I requested Baridi to have his agents force Ibn Qudayda out of hiding. Baridi managed to catch him unawares, and compelled him to appear along with me before the Judge. Having put in evidence of the debt, I asked the Judge to imprison him.

Actual imprisonment, he replied, is unnecessary: men of rank are not imprisoned in the common prison with the lower classes. But I give you permission to keep him in custody, either personally, yourself, or through some person you trust, as you please. So I lodged Ibn Qudayda in a Mosque close by the Judge's gate. Then I went to Baridi and told him that since my adversary was enjoying the Judge's protection, I begged his, Baridi's, for myself. For it is quite possible, said I, that Ibn Qudayda may suborn some of his laborers, or a gang of soldiers, to get him out of my custody and help him to reach Baghdad; and once there he will evade paying what he owes me, and will set afoot very dangerous intrigues. Accordingly, Baridi spoke to the Judge. It was arranged that I should hire a house near the Judge's prison, at my own expense; and there I installed Ibn Qudayda. Friends of mine kept an eye on him, and he was guarded by infantrymen whom I paid specially.

There he lay for more than a year, his debt unpaid, and his spirit exercised in devising imaginary schemes of vengeance against me. I did not care how long the payment was delayed, so long as he was my prisoner. But presently he fell gravely ill; and his mother, who was a relation of mine, came and begged me, weeping, to let him go. I declined, until they told me that he seemed to be dying; and then at last I yielded to his mother's entreaties, and let her take him away (not, however, without making her go bail for him).

Three days after his release he died. I took over some land which belonged to him in payment of the debt he had owed me.

How did you come to repent of being in Government service, Abu Qasim? I once asked Ibn Abi Allan. What was the cause?

This was the cause, said my great-uncle. Abu Ali Jubbai (the great Rationalist theologian) used to stay with me when he came to Ahwaz. I was Clerk to the Ahwaz municipality as well as deputy Finance Minister, so that all business used to pass through my hands. I really ran the whole place. Once a year, when the Land Tax collections began, Abu Ali Jubbai used to come to Ahwaz to arrange to have the taxes due from certain persons, who over the years had come to regard themselves as his dependents, added to the Land Tax on his own private estate at Jubba. Everybody treated him with the highest honor and respect whenever he came to town. As a rule he would only stay with me; and I used to settle his business with the Governor. The Governor, of course, was not always a friend of mine, nor was he always a man who realized Abu Ali's position, or else the amount at which his assessment was fixed would have been even lower than it was. But he would always remit at least half or a third of the tax due from him.

Returning to Jubba, Abu Ali never kept for himself any of the money which in an ordinary case would have been taken in taxes from an estate like his. He used to deduct from the gross amount the sum he was to pay to Government, and then distribute the remainder among the members of his religious following, stipulating in return that each of them should entertain for a whole year one of the poor students who attended his lectures; the actual expense these students put them to was small, not a fifth of the amount due which Abu Ali's high standing had sufficed to get remitted. Then he would go to his own house, and there take out of the revenues of his estate a full tithe, which he used to give in alms among the poor people of his village, Pool, where he maintained his disciples. And he did all this every year.

On one occasion, he was staying with me at the usual season, I had done what he wanted in the matter of his Land Tax, and we were sitting talking in the evening.

Abu Ali, I said to him, are you afraid of the consequences to me in the Hereafter of the profession I am following?

How could I but be anxious, Abu Qasim? he replied. For be sure of this: if you should die employed as you now are, you will never breathe the fragrance of the Garden.

Why not? I asked. How am I guilty? I am only an accountant — I act merely as a copyist, an employee of the Treasury. It may be that somebody will come to me with a grievance, some man whose Land Tax has been unduly raised; and if I reduce it for him and set matters straight, he is only too glad to give me a present. At times perhaps I may appropriate something which really belongs to the Sovereign; but it only represents a share in the booty of the Muslims, to which I have a right.

Abu Qasim, he rejoined, *GOD IS NOT DECEIVED.* Tell me this: is it not you who appoints the land surveyors and sends them out to make their surveys, which are supposed to be accurate? And don't they go out into the country, and raise the acreage figures by ten or twenty per cent, with pen on paper, and then hand in these falsifications of theirs, and do you not make up your assessment registers on the basis of these same falsifications? And then hand over these registers to the Collector's officer, and tell him that unless he produces so much money at the Collector's Office within so many days his hands will be nailed to his feet?

Yes, I admitted.

And then the officer sets out with his escort of soldiers, horse and foot, his despatch riders and speed-up men, and flogs and cuffs and fetters? and all the time he is acting on your instructions. For if you bid him let a man off, or give him time, he does that; whereas if you give no such permission he is merciless until the man pays up.

Yes, said I.

And then the money is deposited at the Collector's Office, and the receipt forms are issued to him from your office, with your mark on them?

Yes, said I.

Then what part of the whole business, asked Abu Ali, is

not of your undertaking? What part are you not answerable for? Beware of God, or you are lost. Give up your Government job. Provide for your future.

From such exhortations, from such grave warnings he would not desist until at last I burst into tears.

You are not more highly favored, he then said, nor more highly placed than Ja'far ibn Harb was: he held high office at court, his privileges and rank were almost those of a Vizier; and he was also an orthodox Believer, and a famous scholar, the author of more than one book which is still read. And yet Ja'far, when he was in office, and riding one day in a superb cavalcade, on the very crest of pomp and circumstance, suddenly heard a man reading the verse: *IS NOT THE HOUR YET COME WHEN ALL WHO TRULY BELIEVE MUST BE BROKEN AND CONTRITE OF HEART AT THE VERY MENTION OF GOD AND OF TRUTH REVEALED?* Ay, the hour is come! Ja'far exclaimed. Over and over again he said it, weeping. And he dismounted, and stripped off his dress, and waded into Tigris until the water came up to his neck. Nor did he come out again until he had given away everything he owned to atone for wrongs he had done, in reparations, pious foundations, and alms, doing everything that his system of Belief demanded, or that he thought his duty. Some passer-by, who saw him standing in the water and was told his story, gave him a shirt and a pair of breeches to cover his coming out; and he put them on. He gave himself to study and devotion from then until his death.

After a moment, Abu Ali said to me: Go, and do thou likewise, Abu Qasim. But if you cannot bring yourself to go the whole way, at least repent of being an official.

What Jubbai said made a great impression on me. I resolved that I would repent, that I would give up my job. For some time I conducted my affairs with this in view; and when I saw an opportunity of getting out of Government service, I repented, my mind made up that I would never take public office again.

THE PASSING OF
THE AGE OF REASON

The Rationalist craving is for totality of knowledge.

Marvellous! that man, who does not know how the hair of his own body grows black or white, should think himself capable of understanding the Creator of all. As to Him Who is Unchanging, Eternal, Uncreate, Who thus is like nothing else, only He can know in what manner He exists. That human minds are incapable of any certain description of Him is proved — by their failure to describe conclusively the nature of the tiniest creature.

Reflect upon God's creation, but do not reflect upon God, as Ibn Abbas said.

The intelligence of the intelligent is confounded in His Kingdom.

The Rationalists used to carry their heads pretty high. Then God sent Ash'ari; and their reign was over.

God's good; God's evil: His sweet; His bitter.

$\mathcal{A}$CTION ORIGINATES IN MAN, Abu Ali Jubbai used to maintain: a man's moral goodness or badness, his piety or impiety, are to be ascribed to his own sovereign will. Free Will is a prerequisite to action; it is a determining faculty along with those which comprise physical efficiency.

On this question of Free Will the Rationalist view is that the Traditional term Predestination refers only to creaturely trial and deliverance — to adversity and prosperity, sickness and health, to death and life and other acts of God. They do not admit that Predestination has reference to moral good and evil, virtue and vice; for they regard man himself as responsible for these. There is a Tradition that the Prophet said: *It is your own doing which will lead you to Paradise or to Hell as if you had been destined thereto;* and another that he said: *Every human being has two inclinations, one prompting him to good, the other prompting him to evil; but the help of God is nigh at hand, and he who asketh help of Him to fight the evil prompting of his heart shall have it.*

What God forbids is not of Him, as Hasan of Basra said. Violence and tyranny are not of God's decreeing. He does not command abominations. The guidance is from God; the error is man's own. Rationalists believe that God appoints Faith as a good and Unbelief as an evil. God, they say, creates the Unbeliever as a man but not as an Unbeliever. Then that man afterward turns to Unbelief. Abbad even denies that God appoints Unbelief in any sense at all.

DIALECTIC

One may (says Ash'ari) put this to a Rationalist: If you believe that Unbelief and wickedness are subject, like *ALL THINGS,* as God has said, to God's Power, and nevertheless hold that He does not will such things, then it follows necessarily from your position that most of what God wishes to exist does not exist, and that most of what God does not wish does exist. For there is more Unbelief in the world, not wished by God (as you maintain), than Faith conformable to His wishing. So that the larger part of what He wishes to be, is not.

This denies a certitude established by consensus of all True Believers, namely, that what God wishes to be, is; and what He does not wish to be, is not.

The argument makes it clear that God creates Unbelief and wickedness. And since God must be the Creator of those things, He must be the Willer of them, because He cannot create what He does not will.

When Rationalists and Humanists assert that human beings create evil, they thereby approximate the view of the Magian Dualists who maintain that there are two Creators. Humanists think that God creates good and Satan creates evil, that what God does not will may yet be. And they think that they are the sole authors of their own actions.

You Rationalists go even further than the Magian position: you think, as they do, that Satan has power over evil; but you also think that God has no power over it.

Now, God has told us of the Koran that *AS FOR THOSE WHO BELIEVE NOT, IT IS A BLINDNESS FOR THEM.* The Koran cannot be a guidance for a man to whom God has told us that it is a blindness. God Himself tells us that He creates most of His creatures for Hell. God commanded Abu Lahab to Believe; yet He must have known that he would not Believe. Nobody has power to Believe, in the teeth of God's Knowledge that he will not Believe. God therefore enjoins on

Abu Lahab a thing he cannot possibly do: He commands him to
Believe, and yet He knows that he will not Believe.

We, Followers of the True Way, hold that we ought not to
relegate any monotheist either to Paradise or to Hell, except in
the case of a man in whose favor God's Apostle himself has
borne witness that he should have Paradise (as he did for Abu
Bakr, for Abdallah ibn Salam, for Abd al-Rahman, Awf's son,
for Abu Ubayda, and for Sa'id, Zayd's son). We must hope that
sinners will attain to Paradise; we must fear that they will be punished in Hell.

OF THE TORMENTING OF INFANT CHILDREN

Most Rationalists think that God makes children suffer
for the sake of admonishment to their elders; and that He com-
pensates them for it in the Hereafter, since if He did not do so
His torturing of children would be an injustice.

One may say to such Rationalists: It is a fact, is it not?
that God tortures infant children in this world — with leprosy,
for instance, so that they lose hands or feet, and with other
torments too. Is that fair and proper?

If they answer yes, one may reply: If such things are justly
done in this world, you have no ground for denying that He may
well torture them in the Hereafter also, and that it will be just
for Him to do so there.

If on the other hand they answer: God's Purpose in torturing children in this world is that their parents may take warning from that sight; then one may reply: So if He does that, and
if that is just on His part, why should He not torture the little
children of Unbelievers in Eternity, to increase the sufferings of
their fathers by the sight of their sufferings? Why would not that
too be just?

But yet . . . We have heard that the Prophet of God said:
*A Fire will be kindled for all children on the Day the Dead shall
Rise; and they will be commanded: Leap into that Fire! And*

every child who leaps into that Fire will I bring into Paradise. But every child who will not I shall cause to enter Hell.

There is a Tradition that men questioned the Prophet concerning children who died early.

God knoweth what they would have done in after time, the Prophet said.

Ash'ari proposed to his teacher, the great Rationalist Abu Ali Jubbai, the case of three brothers, one of whom was a True Believer, virtuous and pious, the second an Unbeliever, profligate and impious, the third a baby. Suppose them all dead, said Ash'ari: what becomes of them?

The virtuous brother, Abu Ali answered, is set high in Paradise; the Unbeliever is in the deeps of Hell; the child will be among those who obtain salvation.

Suppose now, said Ash'ari, that the child wishes to ascend to the high station of his virtuous brother. Would he be allowed to do so?

No, said Jubbai. It would be said to him: Your brother obtained that place through his numerous works of obedience to God; and you have no such works to show.

Suppose then, said Ash'ari, that the child say: That is no fault of mine; Thou didst not let me live long enough, nor grant me any means of showing my obedience.

In that case, answered Jubbai, the Almighty would say: I knew that if I let you live you would have been disobedient, and incurred the dire punishment of Hell-fire; so I acted for your advantage.

Well, said Ash'ari; but suppose the Unbelieving brother were to say: O Lord of the Worlds, since Thou didst know what lay in his future, Thou knewest also, surely, what lay in mine: why didst Thou act for his good and not for mine?

Jubbai had not a word to offer in reply.

The Rationalist view of God is that *HE IS ONE,* and that *NOUGHT IS LIKE UNTO HIM.* Though *HE IS HEARER, SEER,* He is not a substance, object, or body, not a form, or flesh or blood, no person, neither essential nor accidental. He has neither length nor breadth nor depth. He is neither unifiable nor separable. He neither moves nor rests, nor is He divided. He has no parts, neither atoms nor members nor sides, nor any right or left or front or back or above or below, not being subject to the limitations of space or time. Nothing creaturely which is proof of creaturely contingency may be predicated of Him.

His Decrees comprehend Him not, nor do His Veils obscure Him. The senses cannot attain Him; and anything defined by mind or formed in thought is without resemblance to Him. He is the Eternal First, Prior to all created things. Eyes will never see Him nor the hearing hear Him. He is a Thing unlike things.

Rationalists deny that God has a Face, notwithstanding His own words *THE FACE OF THY LORD.* They deny that He has two Hands, notwithstanding His own words *I HAVE CREATED WITH MY TWO HANDS.* They deny that He has Eyes, notwithstanding His own words *UNDER OUR EYES IT FLOATED ON.*

The Jahmite God-strippers also deny that God has Face, Hearing, Sight, Eye, agreeing in that with the Christians, who do not believe that God is *HEARER, SEER,* except in the sense that He is Knowing. One eminent Jahmite thinks that God's Knowledge *is* God, and that God is simply Knowledge. Such a man should really pray thus: O Knowledge, forgive me and have mercy on me. God be exalted far above that!

If we are asked: Do you really think God has two Hands? we must reply: We do believe it, for His words *I HAVE CREATED WITH MY TWO HANDS* prove it.

An argument has been advanced to the effect that the

Hands are to be taken as Powers, and that the expression *MY TWO HANDS* really means: My twofold Power. The rule of the Word of God is this: It is to be interpreted literally. A word is not to be transferred from its literal meaning to a metaphorical one except under compulsion of proof.

Certain Rationalists have maintained that God's words *THE MERCIFUL IS SEATED ON THE THRONE* mean merely that He has dominion, reigns, exercises power. God, they say, is everywhere; and this denies that He is on the Throne. They hold that His being Seated is merely an expression referring to His Power. If they were right, the distinction between the Throne and the earth would be lost, for the Power of God extends over the earth and all worldly things, including privies; so that He would be seated on the Throne, and on earth, and on heaven, and on privies, and on everything. But since no True Believer regards it as right to say that God is seated on the privy, it necessarily follows from this consensus of Believers that being *SEATED* in this passage has a meaning particular to the Throne and does not refer to everything else. Be God exalted above their thought!

CONCERNING THE UNCREATEDNESS OF THE KORAN

God has said that the Koran is His Word. Among other proofs to be found in the Book that His Word is Uncreate is the passage *OUR WORD TO A THING WHEN WE WILL IT IS BUT TO SAY BE! AND IT IS.* Now, if the Koran were a created thing, *BE!* would have had to be said to It, whereupon It would be. That is: if God said to His Word: *BE!* there would have to be a Word creative to the Word.

This makes one of two alternatives necessary. Either, first, it leads to the conclusion that God's Word is Uncreate. Or else, second, one concludes that every Word is dependent on another and prior Word, and so by regression to infinity. Which is impossible. Since the second conclusion is impossible, it is certain that God has an Uncreate Word.

THE METAPHYSICS OF MURDER

Among Rationalists there is some disagreement on the question of a man's *appointed term* of life. Most of them say: The appointed term is the hour at which God knows that a man will die or be murdered; if he is murdered, he is murdered at his appointed term. But some followers of that school of thought maintain, with unique stupidity, that a man's appointed term is the time until which God *knows* that he will survive *if* he is not murdered!

One may say to such: If the murderer has, as you think, the power to choose that he will not murder his victim, in which case of course the latter will go on living, then he has the power either to cut short his appointed term or conversely to put it off. But it is impossible that an hour to which a man does not survive should be his appointed term: for such a notion does not tally with God's own words: *WHEN THEIR TERM COMETH THEY MAY NOT PUT IT OFF BY A SINGLE HOUR.*

THE METAPHYSICS OF THEFT

Rationalists, while admitting that sustenance is of God's providing, go on to say that a man who steals and consumes another man's goods or food is consuming what God provided for another, and not for him. They believe that God only provides sustenance for those to whom He commits the rightful ownership of things, so that it is not He who provides it for persons who steal those things.

To people who think thus one may say: Tell us now, in the case of a man who steals food and eats it, forbidden though that is, is it God who provides him with that forbidden thing by way of sustenance?

If they say yes, they abandon their notion of man's power over his own destiny, and agree.

But if they say no, they may be thus answered: Then in the

case of a man, a robber, who eats such forbidden things all his life, God is not providing him with the wherewithal to nourish his body. His flesh subsists and his bones are fortified by some other than God. That is dire Unbelief. It is question indeed whether such persons should even be tolerated.

The Creator is not necessarily foolish because He wills the folly of men. A man who leaves free access between his manservants and his maidservants, who then commit fornication with one another, when that man is well able to keep them apart, is a fool, is he not? Yet the Lord of the Worlds leaves free access between His servants and His handmaids, who commit fornication one with another, although He has the Power to keep them apart. Yet He is not a Fool.

Thus a man who wills folly is a fool. But the Lord of the Worlds wills folly and yet is not a Fool. A foolish man is under the Law of One above him; he is a fool to do what is forbidden him. But the Lord of the Worlds is not under a Law. There is not One above Him to prescribe His Acts, One Revealing, Inaccessible, Commanding, Correcting.

And yet, though evil, like good, be of God's creating, we should not speak of God as the Author of Evil. Evil proceeds from God as creature; but in His Agency it is just.

ASH'ARI'S CREED

The substance of that on which the Followers of the True Way take their stand is the confession of GOD, His Angels, His Scripts, His Apostles, the Revelation of God and the Tradition of the trustworthy related on the authority of God's Apostle; not one of these do they reject.

God is One, Single, Eternal. There is no other god.

Muhammad is His Servant and Apostle.

Paradise is Fact; and Hell is Fact. There is no doubt of the Coming Hour; and God will raise the Dead from their graves.

God's Place is upon His Throne, as He has said.

God has two Hands, as He has said — we do not question: In what sense? God has two Eyes, as He has said — we do not question: In what sense? God has a Face, as He has said.

It is not to be said that God's Names or Attributes are anything other than Himself. The Followers of the True Way confess that God has Knowledge, as He has said. They assert the existence of His Hearing and His Sight.

They believe that there is no good and no evil on earth except by the Will of God, and that all things are by the Will of God. They confess that there is no creator save God, and that God creates the works of men, and that men are incapable of creating anything.

God gives True Believers Grace to be obedient to Him; He forsakes Unbelievers. He is well able to act for the salvation of Unbelievers; nevertheless He wills not so to act, nor so to grace them that they Believe. He rather wills them to be Unbelievers in accordance with His Knowledge, forsaking and misguiding them, and sealing up their hearts.

Good and evil depend on the general and particular Decrees of God. The Followers of the True Way believe in His Decrees both general and particular, in His good and His evil, His sweet and His bitter.

They believe that they are not their own masters for weal or for woe, save as God wills, for He has said so. Committing their affairs to God, they declare their dependence on Him in all circumstances, their need of Him at all times.

They believe that the Koran is God's Uncreate Eternal Word.

They believe that God will be seen with sight on the Day of the Rising of the Dead: as the moon is seen on the night of her full shall the Believers see Him; but Unbelievers shall not see Him because they will be veiled from God.

They do not brand any Muslim an Unbeliever for any grave sin he may commit, for fornication or theft or any such grave sin;

but hold that such men are Believers inasmuch as they have Faith, grievous though their sins may be. Islam is the testifying that there is no god but God and that Muhammad is God's Apostle, in accordance with Tradition; and Islam, they hold, is not the same thing as Faith.

They confess that God changes the hearts of men.

They confess the Intercession of God's Apostle, and believe that it is for the grave sinners of his people and against the Punishment of the Tomb. They confess that the Pool of the Hereafter is Fact, that the Bridge is Fact, that the Rising after death is Fact, that God's Reckoning with men is Fact, and that the Standing in the Presence of God is Fact.

They confess that Faith is both word and deed.

They discountenance argument and disputation concerning Islam. They do not inquire: In what sense? or: Why? because such inquiry is Innovation in Islam.

They believe that God does not command evil, but forbids it; that He commands good, and has no pleasure in evil, though He wills it.

They acknowledge the Elders elect of God to be Companions of His Apostle as Fact; they cherish their virtues and eschew discrimination amongst them, giving priority to Abu Bakr, then Omar, then Othman, then Ali, and believing that they are the rightly guiding and rightly guided Caliphs, the best of all men after the Prophet.

They approve the Feast and the Friday Congregation and all gatherings for Prayer under the leadership of any Imam, be he pious or be he wicked. They believe in the precept of Holy War against polytheists. They approve Prayer for the welfare of all Imams of the Muslims and agree that they ought not to rebel against them with the sword, nor fight in any civil commotion.

They believe in the Examining Angels Munkar and Nakir who shall visit the dead with the Punishment of the Tomb, and in the Ascension, and in visions of sleep; and they hold that Prayer for departed Muslims, and alms in their behalf, after their departing this world, avail for them.

They believe that there is witchcraft in the world, and that the wizard is an Unbeliever, as God says.

They approve Prayer for every Muslim departed, be he pious or be he wicked. They confess that Paradise and Hell are created; and that he who dies, dies at his appointed term; that he who is slain is slain at his appointed term; and that Satan whispers to men and makes them doubt, then spurns them underfoot. They confess that God knows what every man will do, and has written that these things shall be. They approve patience under what God has ordained. For God's Servants they believe in serving Him, in the giving of sincere counsel to brother Muslims, and the avoiding of all grave sins: of fornication, of perjury, of party spirit, of self-esteem, of condemning other men.

They approve the avoidance of every person who calls to Innovation; they approve diligence in the Reading of the Koran and the writing of Traditions from the Companions; they approve study of the Law, pursued with humility, restraint, and good manners. They approve devotion to the known, and the shunning of what impugns it; they approve the abandonment of all mystification, all evil speaking, and all excessive care after food and drink. Of God alone is our grace, and He is our Sufficiency. How excellent is His Emissary! In God we seek help; in Him we trust.

And to *him* is our Returning.

Knowledge is immense and life is short. It is not a duty to learn all sciences, Astronomy, Medicine, Mathematics, and the rest, but only so much of each as bears upon religious Law. Much may be done with very little knowledge; and knowledge should never be separated from action.

It is told of Ibrahim ibn Adham that he once saw a stone on which was written: *Turn me over and read.* He obeyed, and found this inscription: *Thou dost not practice what thou knowest already; so why seek to know more?*

THE LAST ACTUAL CALIPHS

So surely had their luck run out, so blind were they, so unconscious of the design of destiny, that they flattered themselves with hope!

The reader might well consider whether these princes were not themselves responsible for their defenseless position, a consequence of their carelessness, of letting themselves be seduced from business to pleasure, of neglecting their secret service and failing to investigate the characters of their Viziers and officers, and the morale of their troops, of trusting to what is essentially unreliable — luck.

They did not trouble to study the history of earlier princes, the means employed by men who succeeded in preserving power: piety, in the first place, which kept their followers in order and gave a certain tone to their thinking; good secret service agents, in the second place, men whose duty it was to pry into the doings of their ministers day in and day out, and in every variety of circumstance; and lastly, never, if they could help it, merely irritating their ministers, but coaxing if that was necessary and striking hard at irreconcilables. Wise princes have always spent huge sums on intelligence, and never thought them huge in comparison with the profit from it.

I N THE YEAR 315 news reached Baghdad that the Qarmatian chief Abu Tahir was on the march. The Caliph sent a despatch north to Ibn Abi Saj, giving him news of Abu Tahir's movements and ordering him to march with all speed to Kufa; and a note was sent to the authorities at Kufa ordering them to have supplies and forage in readiness for Ibn Abi Saj and his army.

Ibn Azraq, a State Clerk, used to recall: It was I who had to write the Imperial despatches from the ministry to Ibn Abi Saj, ordering him back to fight the Qarmatians.

His answer went to the Caliph direct, not to the ministry; but I heard the senior Clerks discussing it. It claimed that the frontier he guarded was more seriously menaced than the Byzantine frontier, that he faced something huger than Gog and Magog. If, he said, I leave it unguarded, something worse than any Qarmatian peril will issue therefrom, something which may well be the beginning of the total ruin of the Empire.

The Clerks were very merry at the expense of this missive. Frontier? What frontier is he stationed at? they cried. Whom does he face? Mere Daylamites! Nothing but some Daylamite peasants! He means to amuse himself by defying the Sovereign, apparently.

So more despatches were composed, giving him positive orders to leave whatever he was doing and come back; and he obeyed. And he marched against the Qarmatians, and was killed.

But he had only been dead a very little time when an Alid propagandist and his general, Makan the Daylamite, marched out of the Caspian country into Rayy and wrested that province from the Sovereign's grasp. Then the Daylamite Asfar took the Caspian country from *them,* the Alid was killed, and Asfar marched into Rayy. Then Asfar's man Mardawij killed *him,* took over his army and lands, including Rayy, and began to conquer the neighboring provinces; for the regions Ibn Abi Saj had ruled had now been distributed among a set of Governors who did not care about governing.

From then on, the power of the Daylamite tribesmen grew and grew; and the power of the Sovereign dwindled and dwindled. Fresh encroachments were constantly breaking into it; there was nothing but revolt after revolt until Muqtadir was killed and Mardawij the Daylamite reached Isfahan, on his way to Baghdad itself, and another chieftain reached and captured Ahwaz.

The Daylamite Ali son of Buwayh (whom we call Prince Imad al-Dawla nowadays) was only Mardawij's lieutenant in Karaj in those days. But he seduced his men from their allegiance to Mardawij, captured Arrajan for himself, and then, at the head of only seven hundred Daylamite clansmen, he assailed the Imperial officer Yaqut, at the head of his vast force of regulars. And Ali made Fars and all the treasure accumulated there his own. It was not till he had got this head start that Mardawij bethought himself and sent a force to capture him. But then Mardawij was assassinated; and his retainers rallied to Ali son of Buwayh. For the man was now master of Fars: he had driven Yaqut out altogether, and was grown into a powerful sovereign.

It was only a few years later that Ali sent his brother, the Buwayhid who is now Prince Mu'izz al-Dawla, to Ahwaz. And the Buwayhid's power went on from strength to strength, until at last he became master of Baghdad itself. So the prophecy of Ibn Abi Saj was fulfilled. And the Daylamites became the rulers of the world.

Yet their name had been a proverbial expression of contempt. What kind of behavior is this? offended people used to say. Is it mere Daylamites we have to do with?

* * *

To return to the Qarmatian raid: when the rebel chief drew near to Kufa, the Imperial authorities took to their heels, so that he was able to seize all the supplies and fodder which had been got ready for Ibn Abi Saj. That general arrived outside the city to find himself a day late and the Qarmatians in possession.

The battle began on a Saturday, outside the gate of the town, the Qarmatians being only fifteen hundred strong. It is said that when Ibn Abi Saj saw the Qarmatian force he exclaimed, in utter contempt: What dogs are these? I give them one hour — in an hour the whole lot will be my prisoners. And before ordering the advance he gave instructions for the despatch announcing his victory to be drafted.

By the end of the day, Ibn Abi Saj was a prisoner. A large part of his force lay dead on the field; the rest were fugitives.

The news spread fast at the capital. High and low were in agonies of fear; and the whole population thought of migrating to Wasit, and thence to Ahwaz. Then came tidings that the Qarmatians had crossed Euphrates to Anbar and slaughtered the Imperial officers there. At this, Nasr the Chamberlain himself took the field, with the Hujari Guards, the Masaffi infantry, and every military Prince still in Baghdad. The Imperial Standard was borne in the van. It is a banner of ordinary shape, but black in color, bearing the legend in white: *Muhammad is the Apostle of God.* Munis the Victor was already outside Anbar, and the two joined forces; the two armies amounted to over forty thousand men. The meeting took place near the bridge over the Zubara canal, some two leagues from Baghdad. Nasr was advised to cut the bridge and gave orders that this should be done.

The Qarmatian chief advanced towards the canal, and having come within a league of the Imperial camp, spent the night where he was. Early next morning he started towards the bridge.

A negro foot-soldier, who came on in front of the Qarmatians, was an easy mark for the Imperial archers; but although he soon looked like a porcupine with the arrows which stuck in him, he advanced undismayed, and did not turn back till he had mounted the bridge far enough to find the span cut. For some time his comrades tried to cross the canal; but there were, they found, no fords. So, without turning their backs, they withdrew. The Imperial troops did not venture to follow them, or even to repair the bridge.

The counsel that it be cut proved to have been an inspiration heaven-sent; for had it remained standing, the Qarmatians would have crossed it undeterred by the numbers of the Imperial forces. Those forces would have run away; and the Qarmatians would have taken Baghdad. Indeed, most of the Caliph's troops fled in disorder back to the city as soon as they heard that the enemy had reached the canal, and before they had even set eyes on them.

The town of Hit was the next objective of the Qarmatians. But here the inhabitants turned artillery on them, many were killed, and they raised the siege. When this news reached Baghdad, the relief was universal. Muqtadir and the Queen-Mother gave a hundred thousand dirhams in charity.

The army now mutinied. There had already been a mutiny in Anbar by soldiers demanding higher pay; and the men stationed in Baghdad held out for the same demands. They clamored that they were sick of their misery: competition for the good things of this world was engrained in human nature — even if men were rich, men would still compete for them; and with how much the more reason they, being, as they were, so poor.

An extra dinar a head monthly was offered them; and the men accepted.

Ali ibn Isa, then Vizier, was well aware that supplies from the provinces were failing. He had reduced the pay-year for provincial officials to ten months, and that for Postmasters and Paymasters to eight. He had cut down the pay of the Household Troops, both infantry and cavalry, and the salaries of all Clerks and purveyors connected with them and all civilian officials. He had struck from the pay-rolls the salaries paid to infant children of stipendiary soldiers and other connections, and reduced the allowances of eunuchs, Attendants, courtiers, Table Companions, musicians, purveyors, and contact-men, and those of the retainers and dependents of Bureau chiefs. He had also cast a sharp eye over the salaries of deputy-chamberlains, servants, court-physicians, disbanded cavalry, astrologers, bedmakers, cooks, grooms, and other stipendiaries. And when he found that the additional pay conceded to the infantry since their return and mutiny amounted to two hundred and forty thousand dinars annually, his anxiety became despair. He knew that the soldiers would not *fight;* and he asked Muqtadir's permission to resign the Vizierate.

WIT'S END

A curious story is told by Ibn Furat's old Clerk Ibn Zanji of the manner in which Husayn ibn Qasim became Vizier.

Husayn ibn Qasim (he says), who used to be called Handsome, was a friend and confidant of mine. When he was in hiding, he used to invite me to his hideout and ask my advice; and he came to count on me as a devoted adherent. I tried all manner of schemes to get him appointed Vizier. My most effective operation was the one I am going to tell you about.

There was in Baghdad at that time a man known as the Danielite, who frequented my house and spent an occasional night there. This person divulged to me in confidence that it was his practice to concoct in an antiquated script the books which he ascribed to the Prophet Daniel; into these prophecies he introduced the names of various Imperial dignitaries, with the letters jumbled up, but perfectly intelligible when the letters were rearranged. He had made quite a reputation, and a good deal of money, out of these manufactures, had received large sums from Judge Abu Omar, his son, and other important personages, and was high in the good graces of Muflih the Negro since telling him that he had found from his books that he, Muflih, was a lineal descendant of Ja'far son of Abu Talib. This had gone down well with Muflih, who had given him a munificent reward for the discovery.

It occurred to me to suggest that the Danielite insert in his works a passage referring to my scheme. He was perfectly willing. So I gave him a description of Husayn, told him Husayn was unusually tall, and had a pock-marked face and a scar on his lip so that his moustache was very scant. The prophecy should declare that if such a man became Vizier to the eighteenth of the Abbasids, that Caliph would be fortunate in all his affairs, would triumph over his enemies, would conquer new lands and see the world flourish all his days.

I wrote these details down for him; and he promised to compose a pamphlet treating of divers matters and insert this paragraph in the middle of it. Thereafter I kept pressing him to produce the thing, until he informed me that it would require at least twenty days for the document to take on the right look, of venerable and indubitable antiquity: he would have to leave it in straw for several days, and then put it in his shoe and walk about on it for several days more to give it a yellowed antique tone.

Well, when the time he needed was past, he brought his work round for inspection. I turned to the section which interested me. Had I not known their origin, I could have sworn that these folios were beyond question ancient. So the Danielite went off with his handiwork to Muflih, and read him the passage, along with the rest.

Read that bit again! said Muflih.

He read it again. The negro went to tell Muqtadir about it. Let me see the book, said the Caliph; so Muflih fetched it.

Do we know anybody who answers to that description? Muqtadir asked.

I don't know anybody that could be, said Muflih. But the Caliph told him to think again, and seemed so anxious to find somebody the description could apply to that in the end Muflih answered: The only man I know whom that could apply to is Husayn ibn Qasim, the man they call Handsome.

Well, if any of his friends apply to you or want you to convey a message for him, let me know, said the Caliph; but keep this thing quiet, don't tell anybody. With these instructions Muflih took his departure.

Do you know anybody of this description? he demanded of the Danielite.

I only read what I find, answered he, in the Books of Daniel — beyond that I know nothing.

But he came to give me an account of what had happened; and I hurried with the news to Husayn. He was delighted, even ecstatic: triumph was in his face. Summoning his Clerk Abu Bishr the Christian, he handed him a letter, and instructed him to pay a call on Muflih at the earliest possible moment.

Next evening I went round again to see what had happened. Husayn called on Abu Bishr to tell the story in his own words.

Muflih had quite a number of callers with him when I arrived, said the Clerk. But he called me up above them all and made me sit at his side. Then, bidding me lean closer, he asked in a whisper what was the news with Husayn ibn Qasim. He listened to what I had to say, and replied: Give him my compliments, and assure him from me that I guarantee to manage his business for him. Muflih said more to the same effect: Husayn was to write to the Sovereign and he, Muflih, would deliver the letter and act as Husayn's intermediary with him. I came away perfectly confident, Abu Bishr ended, relying on God to see the matter through.

This Danielite scheme was one of the most effective causes of Husayn's appointment to the Vizierate, in the teeth of widespread disapproval and objection.

* * *

The Ibn Raiq brothers and some other persons had joined the intrigue to get Husayn the Vizierate. Now he was Vizier they wanted their money. The demands were exorbitant. Muhammad ibn Raiq and his brother even went so far as to lay hands on a vessel which had just docked from Ahwaz with all the State revenue from Ahwaz, Isfahan, and Fars aboard. When Husayn wrote, in terms of bitter complaint, to tell Muqtadir what had happened, the Caliph's only action was a mild remonstrance addressed to the sons of Raiq (who was a Freedman Client of his father's).

So the Vizier and the sons of Raiq came to a compromise: the latter kept half the money; the remaining half they released to the Government.

The financial crisis merely went from bad to worse. Husayn was forced to put State lands up for sale, from which he realized half a million dinars; and he anticipated half the revenue for the year 320 months before the collection of it could properly begin. But there was still no discoverable means of meeting the arrears of the fiscal year 319.

All this was known to the Caliph's cousin Harun; and Muqtadir himself was told. He decided to appoint Khasibi, who had been the Queen-Mother's Secretary and for a while Vizier; but when Khasibi was approached on the subject of assuming office again, he mentioned the facts of the financial situation and said that he was not prepared to misrepresent his powers to the Sovereign. So Harun suggested that Muqtadir personally appoint Khasibi President of the Bureaus of control, leaving the Bureaus of first estimate under Husayn, who was to draft the preliminary budget. In this appointment Husayn acquiesced; and Muqtadir, to silence rumor, conferred a Dress of Honor on him.

Husayn now proceeded to draw up his itemized estimates of revenue due from the provinces and of actual remittances expected; the heads of both the primary Bureaus and the Bureaus of control certified the figures. Total expenditure was estimated at a sum approximately equal to the revenue, in order to relieve the Sovereign's mind.

But Muqtadir handed the figures over to Khasibi, and told him to examine them in detail. Khasibi discovered that Husayn had disingenuously added to the sums which the provinces might reasonably be expected to yield, revenues from districts which had now passed out of the Sovereign's hands into the control of usurpers: Rayy and Isfahan, which were occupied by the Daylamites, Mosul and Diyarrabi'a, now in the hands of Munis and made over to him, Egypt and Syria, which had not transmitted any revenue at all for the past four years. All this came to an enormous amount. Further, the Vizier had not embodied in his estimate of expenditure increases which he himself had made in army pay and Attendants' allowances, and other items; nor had he deducted from expected receipts the revenues from the State lands he himself had sold.

Accordingly, Khasibi drew up a statement and laid it before Muqtadir; and a meeting of State Clerks was called.

When, at this hearing, the Clerks addressed questions to the Vizier, he began to scold them, and accused them of misrepresenting him. In what particular, he demanded, have I misled the Sovereign? Have we not the bonds of the revenue-farmers here?

God forbid that anyone should accuse the Vizier of misleading the Sovereign! was the answer. But nevertheless, the Vizier's budget was based on meeting liabilities for the year 319 out of revenue for the year 320. The revenue-farmers have sent in to the Bureaus of control statements of revenue for the year 'twenty already paid on account along with statements of the amounts they have undertaken to pay at harvest time. These statements are the occasion of our meeting here.

What are the amounts? Do you know? said Husayn.

I do, said Khasibi. And he produced a memorandum which he had drawn up himself. From this it appeared that the amount of revenue due for the year 'twenty from Agricultural Iraq, Ahwaz, and Fars already allocated, months before its collection could begin, was forty million dirhams; while the total still due from the revenue-farmers before the commencement of the fiscal year 321 was only twenty millions. The like of this budget, he ended by saying, has never been presented either in ancient or in modern times!

Husayn began to realize his situation. He was aghast, and tried to break up the meeting by shouting: You Clerks concoct such a budget as no Vizier ever perpetrated in his life, and then you hold me responsible for it.

There *is* certainly a misunderstanding somewhere, said one of the Clerks. No doubt it got in by oversight; but in any case it makes no difference to our real assets, one way or the other.

For this remark Husayn dealt him a blow.

We were called to this meeting, the Clerk retorted, for one purpose only: to look over the figures and to point out some facts to the Vizier.

Husayn made no attempt to argue, but turning on Khasibi, he assailed him with insults. The latter, now that the Vizier had been shown up for what he was, left the hearing. An accurate account of the whole was given to Muqtadir; Husayn was done for. After seven months of being a Vizier he found himself under arrest.

THE END OF MUQTADIR

Munis the Victor had begun to show signs of failing loyalty in the year 319. The occasion was this. Munis heard report of a meeting between the Vizier Husayn and a number of military officers, at which a plot against himself had been laid. He sent a message of complaint to the Caliph; but Muqtadir bade the messenger say anything he had to say to the Vizier. The man was arrested and scourged, and forced to give bond for three hundred thousand dinars.

When the Victor heard of this treatment, he quitted Baghdad, with all his officers and partisans, and made all speed up the river to Mosul. The Vizier sent a despatch to the Hamdanids who held that city ordering them to offer armed resistance to Munis' entry: Munis was a rebel. But although the Hamdanids had a force thirty thousand strong, and Munis no more than eight hundred, the former were routed, and Munis got possession of their goods and supplies. He occupied their lands, and became absolute master of the Mosul districts.

Officials now began to desert to him from Baghdad in parties, and in increasing numbers; and these refugees urged him to attack the capital. Nine months after he had taken Mosul, he set off downstream for this purpose.

As soon as the troops stationed in Baghdad heard that he was on his way, they mutinied. They wanted their arrears of pay, they said.

On the last day of October, Muqtadir himself rode out to the place of the expected battle, wearing the Cloak of the Prophet of God, the heirloom of the Caliphs, with the Prophet's Staff in his hand, and his son Abu Ali on the saddle before him. In procession rode members of the Helper families bearing copies of the Koran displayed, Readers chanting the Scripture aloud, troopers of the Hujari Guards in full armor surrounding him, and the Princes and Vizier riding behind. Loud were the prayers of the citizens for his victory as he passed through the streets.

When he reached the camp outside Baghdad, someone advised him to take his stand on a high place some little distance from the battleground, and he did so. The engagement was furious. Presently a message was sent to the Caliph begging him to show his face among his troops. Message after message came, but he would not budge, though those about him kept imploring him to go, assuring him that there could be no danger. At last he yielded, and rode off escorted by Muflih and some Attendants.

But before he reached the field his forces had been driven

off it in confusion; and the son of Munis' commanding officer met him as he rode through some open ground. The man recognized the Caliph, and sprang, all armed as he was, from his horse, crying: My lord the Prince of True Believers! He kissed the ground, and then the Caliph's knee.

At that moment up came some of Munis' Berber Guards. They closed round Muqtadir; and one of them felled him with a blow from behind.

I am the Caliph, damn you! Muqtadir cried out.

Then you're the one I'm out for! said the Berber, and forcing the Caliph down upon the ground, he cut his throat with a sword. The head was raised aloft upon a sword, and then upon a spear. Stripped of clothes, even of the drawers, the trunk was left lying stark naked until a laboring man, passing by, threw some hay over it, and digging a grave on the spot, buried it, and obliterated the traces.

When Muqtadir's head was brought before Munis, he burst into tears.

* * *

What Munis did emboldened those who were defying the State to a feat that such persons had not hitherto dreamed of: the capture of the capital. That day permanently weakened the Caliphate. It broke down Caliphal authority. The process continued at an increasing rate until things came to the condition we shall presently see.

The amount of revenue wasted by Muqtadir is worth noting, as a warning to any public administrator that he should not be fooled by the richness of his resources into forgetting to husband them. If he does neglect to husband them, however he tries, he will never catch up again. The situation is like the breach in a dyke: it starts no wider than a dirham. But it soon gets bigger, and then it is too far gone to be repaired. Muqtadir, besides what he spent on proper objects and in the right places, let more than seventy million dinars go in absolute waste. That is a larger amount than Rashid had accumulated for his successors, though of all the Abbasids no one hoarded more than he. Both Mu'tadid and Muktafi had managed to set aside a million dinars out of Provincial revenue each year of their Caliphate, after paying all ordinary and all extraordinary expenses.

And those who imagine that revenue can really be increased by extortionate taxation are mistaken. No, by *HIM WHO RAISED UP THE HEAVEN* and Who *GIVETH KINGSHIP TO WHOM HE WILL*. Nothing can make a country prosperous except good administration and sound policy: discipline of high and low, absolute authority in all dealings with the military and absolute justice in all dealings with the civil population.

A man who cannot manage his own town cannot manage a country. A man who cannot manage his own affairs cannot manage a town. A man who cannot rule soldiers is not fit to rule a civil population. And a man who cannot rule his servants is not fit to rule soldiers. And a man who cannot rule himself is not fit to rule servants.

FINANCE AS AN ADDICTION

My father (says Thabit) was on friendly terms with the middleman Ibn Qaraba. (This financier had persuaded Muqtadir that certain undeclared profits hitherto enjoyed by the Viziers might be diverted to the Caliph's pocket by having revenue for Caliphal expenses sent direct by the revenue-farmers to the Palace. He used to lend the Viziers money for current expenses from the accounts of the Baridis and other revenue-farmers, at a rate of nearly ten per cent.) Ibn Qaraba had been arrested, and tortured nearly to death; but Muqtadir's end came in time to save his life. So my father and I went to congratulate him on his escape.

Abu Sa'id, said Ibn Qaraba to my father, I regard you as a friend. What is more, you have prudence and good judgment. I want your advice as to what I had best do.

Tell me what about, said my father: I will give you a friend's advice.

You know, said Ibn Qaraba, that I was up to my neck in middleman's business; and as a result of my operations, advancing money at interest from the revenue-farmers' accounts, claims were brought against me, such claims as were never made on anybody before. I have had a fall. But my fine, which I have paid, was less than I had made; and I am at this moment the possessor of property producing twenty thousand dinars net income. There's not a man alive who owns as much land, in orchard and arable, or such furniture and household gear: crystal, cut glass, china, jewels, clothes; or more slaves and pretty page-boys, more retainers, more horses. And I have in hand three hundred thousand dinars cash for which I have no present use. Now, the Vizier, just appointed, is a firm friend of mine. When he comes up to the capital, do you advise me to confine myself to an occasional call, in order to keep up our relationship, without going back to my old activities? or should I take up the middleman's trade once more?

I never heard of such a preposterous consultation! cried my father. People usually ask advice when situations are difficult; when they are perfectly simple there is no need to ask advice. Think, God help you! If the consequences of your meddling were pleasant, by all means take it up again; but if they were unpleasant, if they exposed you to the loss of your life and your fortune both, don't! Why! men toil and sweat and get into trouble to make a mere fraction of what you now have. Praise God, and make the most of your fortune — you have reputation enough to keep it intact. Reap your harvest: security. And good health.

Ibn Qaraba listened to it all. I know well, said he, how sound your advice is: it is excellent advice. But I have an unlucky temperament, that will not sit down and take things easy. I simply have to go back to the old trade.

May God be good to you, said my father. We came away.

My boy, said my father to me, that man is the most complete fool I have ever seen. Men like that either get themselves murdered or die paupers.

It turned out as he prophesied: Ibn Qaraba ended his life in

the service of the Hamdanid Nasir al-Dawla, at one dinar a
month.

God preserve us from infatuation!

QAHIR, THEN RADI

As NEXT CALIPH Munis selected a son of Muktafi's; but the
prince declined the Caliphate. So the Victor made the proposal
to Mu'tadid's son Muhammad, who accepted. The nominee was
made to take an oath of fidelity to Munis, to his commander in
chief, and to the latter's Secretary. Having thus made sure of him
by oaths and covenants, they proceeded to do him homage; and
the new Caliph took the title Qahir Billah, the Conqueror
through God.

When Munis advised appointing Ali ibn Isa Vizier, his
commander objected. Times like these, he said, do not admit of
methods like Ali's. They need a man of larger ideas, not so
strict.

So Ibn Muqla was appointed Vizier.

Qahir's first act as Caliph was to have the Queen-Mother
scourged. He issued a proclamation making singing-girls, wines,
and liquors illegal. All males reputed to be singers or catamites
were arrested. Despite these measures, Qahir himself drank —
indeed he was rarely sober. He was passionately fond of music,
and took over such of the arrested singing-girls as he fancied.

A year or so after his accession, the Hujari and Saji Guards
(alarmed by reports circulated by Ibn Muqla) conspired to seize
the Palace and arrest the Caliph. They produced a son of
Muqtadir's, and set him on the throne. He took the title of Radi
Billah: the Content with God.

Radi sent for Ali ibn Isa; and the latter informed him that
he should, if he wished to comply with custom, tie himself a
banner. So he sent for one, tied it with his own hand, and
ordered it to be preserved. Next, Ali counselled him to secure
the Seal of Sovereignty; and this was delivered to him by the

functionary in charge of it. The original Seal is a silver ring with a bezel of Chinese iron, bearing the legend, cut in three lines:

Muhammad
Apostle
of God

Ali was told that Qahir steadfastly refused to abdicate. He frowned, and presently said: He must be deposed, and without hesitation: everyone knows what he deserves.

But it is not for us to establish dynasties, objected Judge Abu Husayn, who had been sent for and was present. King-making is a matter for the military. The only thing we are qualified for, or needed for, is attestation, and the legal taking of assurances.

Ali looked annoyed. But it was now time for Prayer; and all rose and took their leave.

Radi, without telling Ali ibn Isa, had Qahir blinded that night.

DAYLAMITES

The dream of the Daylamite chieftain Mardawij, ruler of Isfahan and the Mountain Province, was to take Baghdad, crown himself King, and restore the ancient Persian Empire.

He ordered a great crown made; it was studded with gems, and Abu Makhlad remembered seeing him, only a few days before the catastrophe of which we are to tell, seated on a golden throne in solitary state, leaning on a vast cushion of sovereignty; a silver throne spread with a carpet was set beneath him, and some large gilt chairs set below that. There were other arrange-

ments for seating his officers rank below rank. The common
crowd stood gaping at him from a distance, not venturing to
speak above a whisper, such awe and admiration did the grandeur
of it all inspire in them.

When the January Bonfire Night of 323 was approaching,
Mardawij ordered firewood collected from the mountains and
outlying districts, and assembled in the valley of the Isfahan
River and the marshes and thickets beside it. He then ordered
naphtha and naphtha-men, flame-throwers and other experts,
to be collected, and a great supply of tall candles laid in. There
was not a hill or brow of rising ground overlooking Isfahan
but had a stack of firewood and brambles on it; great towers of
tree trunks clenched with iron were erected and crammed with
firethorn and bamboo. Crows and kites were snared; and nut-
shells stuffed with cotton fluff and naphtha were attached to
their beaks and claws. In the Prince's private room statues and
huge obelisks of wax were set up. No one had ever seen such
things. On hills and heights, over the plain and in his private
chamber, in the very air, where the birds were to be freed, all
was to be one simultaneous blaze.

When the time came, a vast banquet was spread in the
fields adjacent to his quarters, thousands of sheep and oxen and
other cattle were butchered, and the place was decorated with
unprecedented splendor. All was at last ready; and the hour
approached for Mardawij to seat himself with his company, first
for the banquet, and then to drink. And he came forth to inspect
the banqueting-place and the devices for the conflagration.

The whole thing filled him with disgust. Even all this
was not enough.

The reason, as that Great Master among Clerks Ibn Amid
says, was the vastness of the plain of Isfahan; for when the eye
returns from roaming over any wide expanse of nature to light
on man-made things, they seem paltry, however big they are.

In a fury of mortified pride, without uttering a single
word, Mardawij went back into his great tent and lay down. He
turned his back to the door and muffled himself in his robes, as

a sign that no one should speak to him. An embarrassed attempt was made to assemble the guests; but most refused to come, and those who were already there went away again, saying: We doubt whether the Prince wants to see us.

Three days later, some Turkish·retainers of his broke in upon Mardawij as he took a bath, and beheaded him.

*   *   *

The real cause of the rise to power of the Daylamite Ali son of Buwayh was his natural generosity. To this noble quality he joined another nobler still: valor, at its greatest. And along with these personal characteristics should be counted some extraordinary strokes of pure luck, and a splendid horoscope.

To give an example of his generosity: when he found in the baggage of a defeated enemy quantities of fetters and other things which had been got ready for his own men when they should be captives, some of his officers suggested that they be used on their prisoners, and the latter paraded in the fetters they themselves had brought.

Nay, said Ali ibn Buwayh: let's rather pardon them. It's God Who delivered our enemies into our hands; let's thank Him for this Mercy. If we do, we are more likely to get more of His Grace. And we shall escape the sin of arrogance.

As an example of his luck, once, when he was without money to pay his troops, he was lying on his back trying to sleep and saw a serpent creep out of a hole in the ceiling above him. For safety's sake Ali ordered the ceiling pulled down; and in the space above were found coffers crammed with gold! He distributed the lot among his men.

On another occasion, he wanted something made for him and sent for a tailor: the man was deaf, and misheard what Ali said. From what he thought he heard he gathered that someone had betrayed a deposit lodged with him, and burst into protestations: It's nothing but twelve chests! but as God hears me I swear I have no idea what's inside them! So the twelve chests were sent for from the tailor's house: enormous sums of money were found in them.

Again, Ali was riding at the head of his troop, and suddenly his horse's forelegs sank into the ground. His men dug to see what the hollow was; and it proved to be a repository full of buried treasure.

When the Buwayhid had captured Shiraz, he opened negotiations with Baghdad, with a view to being officially invested with Fars as a fief, the investiture to be made by Radi himself. The Caliph agreed, and professed himself satisfied with Ali's offer of eight million dirhams annually, after payment of all regular or extraordinary provincial expenses.

The Vizier Ibn Muqla sent off the Robes and Banner, expressly ordering the envoy not to deliver them until he had got the stipulated sum of money. When the man was close to Shiraz, Ali rode out to meet him, and demanded the delivery of the insignia at the outskirts of the city. The envoy explained his instructions; but the Buwayhid so threatened and browbeat him that he handed the things over. Ali put them on, and rode into Shiraz clad in his Dress of Honor, with the standard borne before him. Although the envoy stayed on demanding the money, not one penny was ever paid him: all he got was promises and delays, until at last he fell ill and died there. He was brought back to Baghdad in his coffin the following year.

REVENUE-FARMERS

The financial situation at the capital deteriorated steadily. Ibn Raiq sent up no revenue from Wasit and Basra; the Baridis sent up nothing from Ahwaz; Ali ibn Buwayh had seized Fars, and Ibn Alyas, Kirman.

Abu Zakariyya of Susa describes hearing the following conversation between Abu Yusuf Baridi and his brother Abu Abdallah.

Brother, said Abu Abdallah Baridi (who thought of intriguing to get himself appointed Vizier), what I am afraid of is that when we go up to the capital the Hujari Guards will set on us — we shall be murdered. Even at this moment, with our brother Abu Husayn in Baghdad, I shouldn't be surprised to hear he had been killed.

We can write to Abu Husayn, his brother replied; he will look after himself. But as for what you say about the Hujaris, and your idea that we are ever going to set foot in Baghdad again, branded as we are with a fine of twenty million dirhams — never! Having got away with our lives once, out of the hands of Qahir and that damned Khasibi, why should we ever dream of going back? What's that you say? what about our Baghdad houses? they'll put them to pillage. Let them! Damn the houses! We are never going back to the capital. *We have no further use for the capital; the capital is going to ruin.* Give up that idea of yours entirely, Abu Abdallah: you cannot still be harboring a fancy like that. Think of the rottenness of the times. Think: the Empire is a thing of the past; the Caliph is a pauper. In the old days we used to be able to make money out of the Sovereign; but nowadays he is on all fours with us. Or rather, he could make money out of us: he would like a chance to ruin us — he could get our money. Unless we use these armies we have got together for our own protection, we shall have a fall; and it will be a long time before we see a day we can call our own again. Rest assured: I don't give you this advice without having provided the means for putting it into action.

I am saying all this in confidence, he concluded, but quite frankly; Abu Zakariyya here is someone we do not have to worry about.

THE END OF THE VIZIERAL SYSTEM

The Vizier Ibn Muqla suggested to Radi an expedition, to be led by himself, for the purpose of expelling Ibn Raiq from Wasit and Basra. Those provinces, he said, are virtually closed to you by Ibn Raiq's behavior; he refuses to transmit the revenue he farms. When other people see that a thing like that can be done, and is tolerated in Ibn Raiq's case, they will do the same. There will be no more remittances, and the Empire will cease to exist.

Radi ordered the Vizier to proceed with his preparations; and the Vizier's first move was the despatch of two envoys with an order that Ibn Raiq should send his Secretary up to the capital for examination.

Ibn Raiq not only declined to send his Secretary but bribed the two envoys to convey a secret message from himself to the Caliph, with the following offer: if he were called to the capital and entrusted with the administration, he undertook to defray all the Sovereign's necessary expenses, pay the army, and put the whole Government on an efficient basis; he would save the Prince of True Believers the trouble of worrying about any public business at all.

The Caliph, however, was not yet quite ready to betray his Vizier; so he did not take up the proposal.

Presently the Vizier found himself quite unable to keep things going; there was so little money that he begged permission to abandon the attempt and resign. So Radi arrested him and appointed Karkhi.

He too was unequal to the burden, and was soon completely at a loss. Demands were constant, and there were no supplies. After three and a half months of office he went into hiding. In his files were actually found uncashed cheques — a picture of business incapacity and apathy.

When Karkhi disappeared, Radi sent for Sulayman ibn Hasan; but he proved as helpless and resourceless as Karkhi. So necessity drove Radi at last to send to Muhammad ibn Raiq in Wasit, to remind him of his proposal and inquire whether he still stood by it.

Ibn Raiq received the messenger with favor and stated in his reply that he would stand by his offer. So Radi sent down an officer of the Saji Guards to inform him that he was appointed Prince and Commander in Chief of the Army; that the

Caliph created him by a new title *Prince of Princes* and vested in him the administration of Land Tax, Estates, and Public Security in all provinces whatsoever, and committed to him the management of the Empire. His name was to be mentioned in the Sermon; the Caliph was to address him by his honorific of Abu Bakr. Dresses of Honor and a Banner were despatched to him.

From that day the power of the Caliphal Viziers was at an end. The Vizier no longer controlled the provinces, the Bureaus, or the departments. He had merely the title of Vizier, and the right to appear in black, with sword and belt, when there was a Court. There he stood in silence.

Provincial revenue is transmitted nowadays to the Prince's Treasury; and the Princes expend it as they please, remitting as much as they see fit to the Sovereign for his personal expenses. The old Treasuries ceased to exist.

But the world was in the hands of usurpers, persons who had become provincial kings. Whoever got control of a region regarded himself as its owner, and kept the revenue from it. Wasit, Basra, and Ahwaz thus belonged to the Baridis; Fars to Ali the Buwayhid; Kirman to Ibn Alyas; Isfahan, Rayy, and the Mountain Province to Hasan the Buwayhid and his rival Washmagir; Mosul and the neighboring provinces to the Hamdanids; Egypt and Syria to the Ikhshid; the West and Africa to Abu Tamim; Spain to the Umayyad Prince; Khurasan to Nasr the Samanid; the southern provinces to Jannabi; the Caspian provinces to the Daylamite clansmen.

Nothing except Agricultural Iraq now remained in the hands of the Sovereign and the Prince of Princes.

THE END OF THE CALIPH'S HOUSEHOLD TROOPS

The Prince of Princes proposed to Radi a joint expedition downriver to deal with Baridi. The Caliph agreed, and the

march began. On arrival at Wasit, Ibn Raiq held an inspection
of the Hujari Guards. First he looked over the roll of deputy-
doorkeepers, of whom there were some five hundred, announced
that sixty would be kept, on reduced pay, and cashiered the rest.
Then he went right through the regiment, striking from the
pay-roll all persons irregularly appointed, all substitutes, all
women, all purveyors, and all fugitives from the Law. Alarmed
by this proceeding, the Hujaris at first refused to recognize its
validity; presently, however, they thought it best to give in.

At the next inspection, Ibn Raiq struck out many more.
The Guardsmen now mutinied and seized their arms; and the
Prince fought a furious engagement with them. It went against
the Hujaris: many were killed and many more taken prisoner; the
rest fled to Baghdad. But at the city the Prefect scattered them
with a charge of Mounted Police, and the soldiers went into hiding. Their houses were pillaged, and some of them burnt; and
all their property was confiscated.

Having thus dealt with the Hujaris, Ibn Raiq sent an order
that the Saji Guards, who had been placed in confinement,
should be executed; and except for Safi the Treasurer and Hasan
ibn Harun every man of them was put to death.

BACHKAM THE TURK

My father (says Thabit) told me of a conversation he had
with Bachkam, who used to be a retainer of Ibn Raiq's. Bachkam
told him the tale after he had become master of the capital and
had extinguished his former patron.

When a man who wields power is in an emergency, said
Bachkam to my father, he should hold mere money and property
cheaper than dirt. For if he can only keep *power,* he can replace
any money he has let go, many times over; whereas if he sets too
much store on possessions he may well lose the very thing he's
trying to save — his money — and his life as well. I remember
when Ibn Raiq commissioned me Governor of Ahwaz (to drive

out the Baridis and hold the place against them). He did it without consulting his Secretary Ibn Muqatil; and when Ibn Muqatil
heard about it he was furious, and went straight off to see Ibn
Raiq. What are you doing? he said. Is it true that you have decided to commission Bachkam to Ahwaz?

I have, said Ibn Raiq.

You are doing something very dangerous to yourself then,
said the Secretary. The Baridis, who are only Clerks, are more
than you can manage — since it is not in your power to get rid of
them — and here you are proposing to give a Government like
Ahwaz to a Turkish soldier, who has only been your man a short
time! This is what will happen: when he has got Ahwaz and
sees what an important place it is, and what a delightful place it
is, and what a rich place it is, he will want to rule the province for
himself. And the next thing will be that he will want to rule
more. He won't rest quiet till he has had a tussle for your government with you; he will have to, for the sake of keeping what
he's got. You're worrying now about getting Ahwaz away from
Baridi; but if you commission Bachkam Governor there, you may
as well stop worrying about Ahwaz and put it right out of your
mind; and direct your energies to keeping hold of other places.
And I hope you succeed. And you had better start worrying
about your own skin too — you're risking it.

These remarks made Ibn Raiq change his mind about me.
And I must say that the Secretary's advice was well meant, and
that it turned out true.

When this conversation was reported to me, I was in a
terrible state. For lack of better I consulted my interpreter Ibn
Yanal. But he had nothing to suggest: he merely tried to soothe
my feelings, telling me that after all I had every comfort, every
luxury, that I was as good as the Prince's brother.

You're a fool, said I. See that a boat is got ready and have
it waiting for me tonight. I had made up my mind to go and see
the Secretary myself.

Ibn Muqatil came of a family of small businessmen, I
knew, and had a petty mind; the effect of money on minds like

his is miraculous. So that night, when people were asleep, I took ten thousand dinars and got into the boat. When we reached the Secretary's gate, it was shut for the night. I knocked. The porter, without opening, told me that his master was asleep, and that the house was locked up for the night.

Go and knock on your master's door, said I. Wake him up. I'm come on important business.

The porter did as I told him, and I was shown in; I found the Secretary out of bed, and terrified by a visit from me at such an hour. What is it? he asked.

Something quite pleasant, said I: just a proposal I wanted to make to you, in private; so I waited till the passage was clear. And I have brought no one but my interpreter here. This is it: you know what the Prince had intended to do for me. But I am told now that he has changed his mind. I don't know why he should; and after all the publicity it is humiliating for me. You have been my patron, as well as he; I am your creature; and if I don't get ahead while you are with us, when shall I? Shall I ever be a man people respect? Now here are ten thousand dinars — a contribution from me to your exchequer. I know the Prince will take your advice; and I beg you to advise him to do as he originally planned.

The sight of the dinars was too much for Ibn Muqatil. Go away now, he said; and God keep you!

So I said good-bye to my money and went off. I knew I should get Ahwaz. Three days later, Ibn Muqatil went to call on the Prince.

That advice I gave you, he said, was given on the spur of the moment; I had not thought carefully about the matter. But I have been thinking it over since. I believe your original plan was right. If you leave Ahwaz to the Baridis, they will not stop there, rich as they now are; they can offer money enough to corrupt your army, and their next step will probably be to try for your place. Now, if you take the field against them yourself, that means war. And one never knows how war will go. If it goes against you, you will never get back on your feet again. And if you send any other man than Bachkam, he'll bungle it, and lose his campaign; and that will take the heart out of all your men. So it does seem better to send a commander like Bachkam, a man they dare not face. If he gets the place, he'll make an end of them. And you will still be master of the situation: you can if it suits you keep him on in that Government; or if you prefer you can always recall him before he becomes a real power. Ask the Blessing of God and proceed as you intended.

Ibn Raiq took this advice, and ratified my appointment. I don't think the Government of Ahwaz was dear at the price. The Secretary sold his soul, his master, and his future for ten thousand dinars. And in return for my money I got what I spent many many times over, and Ibn Raiq's Empire into the bargain.

THE LAST OF IBN MUQLA

When Ibn Raiq had taken Imperial affairs into his own hands, he had seized the estates of the ex-Vizier Ibn Muqla and his son. Ibn Muqla went to call on him and on various of his Clerks, fawning on them, to their great embarrassment, and begging for the restoration of the confiscated properties. Restoration was promised; but time went by, and nothing was done. So Ibn Muqla began to set intrigues against Ibn Raiq on foot, in every direction: he wrote to Bachkam, urging his chance of getting both the capital and Ibn Raiq's place; he wrote to the ruler of Rayy with similar suggestions; and he wrote to the Caliph Radi, advising the arrest of the Prince of Princes, and guaranteeing a million dinars from his estate.

Radi sent encouraging replies; and when Ibn Muqla had had time to feel sure of the Caliph, he received instructions to come secretly to the Palace by river, and stay there until the plot against Ibn Raiq had been safely carried out. So he took boat from his house, wearing an ordinary scholar's hood and low shoes.

But on his arrival at the Palace, no audience was given him.

By the Caliph's orders he was locked in a cell; and next day Radi sent a message to inform Ibn Raiq of the whole proceeding.

A fortnight later, Ibn Muqla was led from his cell and taken before Ibn Raiq's Chamberlain and other officers. His right hand was amputated. Then he was led back to prison, and the Chamberlain went to tell his master he had witnessed the amputation. . . .

In the evening of that day (says Thabit) I received a summons from Radi; the Caliph bade me go and treat Ibn Muqla's wound. I found the former Vizier in a locked cell. He was in a piteous condition; and tears sprang to his eyes at the sight of me. The forearm was dreadfully swollen, a rag of coarse blue cloth tied round it with a hempen cord. I undid the cord, and removing the rag, found underneath, on the place where the hand had been severed, a layer of horse-dung. I shook it off at once. A second cord, which had been tied tight round the arm, had sunk in by reason of the swelling; and the limb was beginning to blacken.

This cord will have to come off, I told him; and there ought to be camphor on the place, not horse-dung. This arm must be dressed with sandal and rose-water and camphor.

Go ahead, said Ibn Muqla.

Wait, interrupted the slave who had let me in: I'll have to get permission.

He went off to get leave, and presently returned with a box of camphor, saying: The Sovereign gives you leave to take what measures you think proper; he is to be well treated, and you are to give him priority of attendance until God restores him to health.

So, removing the cord, I applied the whole contents of the box to the wound, and anointed the arm. Ibn Muqla began to revive, and felt better; the throbbing calmed down. I did not leave until he had eaten some chicken, and declared that he could swallow no more. He took a drink of cold water, and seemed refreshed. So I left him.

On many subsequent days I visited him, until he was recov-

ered. As soon as I came in he always inquired after his son, and
was always cheered to hear that the young man was safe in hiding. But then he would sorrow and cry out for his lost hand:
I served the Caliphate with that hand — three times Vizier — to
three different Caliphs. And with that hand I twice copied the
Koran. And now — cut off like the hand of a common thief!

Next year Bachkam marched on the capital. Ibn Raiq fled,
and his forces scattered; and Bachkam, entering the city, had an
audience of Radi, who received him with high honor, bestowed
Dresses of Honor, tied a Banner for him, and appointed him
Prince of Princes in his old patron's place. Next day, the Caliph,
addressing him by his honorific, sent him a Table Companion's
Robes, along with the liquor, the perfumes, and the greetings
which completed his title.

At the time when Bachkam moved towards Baghdad, Ibn
Muqla was transferred from his first prison to a darker place.
For a while no more was heard of him; nor was I (says Thabit)
allowed to visit him any more.

Afterwards, his tongue was cut out; and still he lingered
on in prison. Then he was attacked by dysentery. Unattended,
untreated, he was obliged, I was told, to draw up his own water
from the well with his left hand and his teeth. In such agonies
he died. His remains were buried in the Palace, but after a while,
at the request of his family, exhumed and delivered to them.

Fools they are who go in at kings' gates.

THE DEATH OF THE LAST REAL CALIPH

Two and a half years later, on a Friday night in winter,
Radi died; there was a total eclipse of the moon at the time. The
cause of death was ascitical dropsy. His Secretary went into
hiding.

Thus ended the days of Radi, who was a scholar and a poet,
a master of elegant language, a man who loved learned company

and never lacked for friends, a man of liberal mind and generous temper. Among his verses this is found:

> *All pure things become corrupt;*
> *All things go to decay.*
> *The wayfaring of youth toward Death*
> *Is Death: Pain is the way.*
> *On every head only grey hairs should grow*
> *To warn us whither we must go.*
> *And thou who hopest still some good conclusion,*
> *Thou drowned man tossed in oceans of illusion,*
> *Tell me this: Where are they who hurried on*
> *Before us? Foot and footprint lost and gone!*
> *Mercy for all my many trespasses!*
> *Thou Best of all who know what Mercy is!*

RADI WAS THE LAST CALIPH

who at any time had troops and State Property under his personal direction, the last Caliph whose poems were made into a collected edition, the last to read the Sermon and pray in public regularly, the last who ever sat with Table Companions, and the last Sovereign whose expenses, charity, and bounties, retinue, stipend, and treasury, whose meats and drinks, feasts and household, whose affairs in general were conducted on the scale of the old Caliphate; and he too was the last Caliph who ever rode abroad in garments like those of the Caliphs of time gone by.

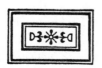

THE SOPHISTICATED

There's not a place in the world quite like Baghdad, not a place
in Baghdad quite like the Fief, not a place in the Fief quite like
Abu Khalif Street, and not a place in Abu Khalif Street quite
like mine!

> *I still think of Tigris bank*
> *When the dark closed and the moon sank,*
> *And a blue carpet was the river streaming,*
> *All embroidered with golden gleaming.*

> *And the waters babbled, from the trailing branches glanc-*
> *ing,*
> *Like girls round a player on a flute, singing and dancing.*

* * *

A man who believes that Abu Amr's is the correct style in
Reading, and Shafi'i's the correct view in Law, a man who owns
a drapery business and knows the poems of Ibn Mu'tazz by
heart, such a man may be called a perfect gentleman.

I N OUR BOOK OF MANNERS is included rare material such as:

What a gentleman should know about Wine; Types and Vintages;

Desserts and their arrangement; pyramidal compositions; formal compositions; with full instructions;

An outline of Cookery, indispensable for professional Diners Out, and desirable for every gentleman;

Modern Cookery; Aromatics, Spices;

Conversation: what subjects are suitable;

How to wash the hands in the presence of the Host; how to take leave;

How to circulate the Wine; royal and other anecdotes in this connection;

Intemperance and Temperance; conflicting views; suitable anecdotes;

How to beg and obtain bounties when dining out;

The Diner Out and his duties; his Patron's duties to him; the different functions of the Client and the Patron; the Guest and how he differs from the Host.

A gentleman does not care to eat giblets or gristle or the veins in meat. He does not care for kidneys or tripe, and always leaves the bits of meat and green herbs in soup uneaten in the dish. A gentleman never makes an audible sound when taking a sip of soup. He does not try to get the marrow out of a bone, nor do anything which would make his hands greasy. Taking much salt is a vulgar habit, and one should not dabble what one is a-bout to eat in the pickle-dish. A gentleman does not let the cake of bread which is laid before his place get greasy, nor does he reach for anything which is not set in front of him. He never licks his fingers, never crams his mouth with food, and never takes a large piece of some rich food which would make his mouth greasy. No gentleman takes two morsels of different things into his mouth at one time, or eats highly-seasoned *hors d' oeuvres,* which are a vulgar taste.

One should take only moderate mouthfuls, and masticate them thoroughly but in a leisurely way. Otherwise one will be infringing the Apostolic custom, and one will probably suffer from indigestion as well.

It is better never to wash the hands in the presence of prin-ces or of one's superiors. One should spare them the sight of what is distasteful even to oneself, and must be much more so to others. A host may beg his guests not to disturb themselves, and to wash at table; but only a fool would take him at his word. One should never pick one's teeth in company, of course.

A POPULAR DINER OUT, JAHZA THE BARMECIDE

At one single meal, Jahza told me, I once made five hun-dred dinars, five hundred dirhams, five splendid coats, and a gor-geous perfume-box.

How on earth? I asked.

Hasan Ibn Makhlad, you know, said Jahza, had this about him, that he was mean with his food and free with his money. He used to offer his guests food as well as wine, certainly; but if a man actually ate anything, it was the end of him. He loved people who were prepared to drink without eating. Well, one day when I was with him, he said to me: Abu Hasan, I am plan-

ning a breakfast party here tomorrow; why not spend the night
here and be one of us?

I could not do that, but I could come round as early as you
like in the morning, in plenty of time for the party, I told him.
What are you going to give us?

He mentioned various things which had been ordered, even
told me the instructions he had given his cook. So it was settled
that I should appear betimes in the morning; and I went home.
There I sent for my cook, and ordered precisely the same meal to
be got ready late that night. Then I went to bed.

Some time after midnight I got up. My meal was waiting;
I ate and washed, ordered my beast saddled, and was just on the
point of starting for Ibn Makhlad's when the people he had sent
to fetch me knocked at my gate. On my arrival he adjured me by
his life to tell him: had I eaten yet?

God forbid! said I; it was nearly sunset when I left, and it
is barely midnight now! Ask your servants what I was doing
when they arrived.

Yes, sir, he was just dressed, said they, and waiting for them
to finish saddling his mule so that he could start.

Ibn Makhlad seemed satisfied; and presently the meal was
served us. Appetite — I had not enough left to stand the smell of
the food. I could hardly even bring myself to toy with it. Our
host kept pressing me to eat. If I had obeyed, of course, he would
have crossed me off his list in his usual way; but I merely kept
assuring him: I *am* eating, sir: could anyone in the world eat
more than I am eating?

When the meal was removed, we sat over our wine, and I
began to drink by the pint, to my host's evident joy, for he supposed that I was drinking on an empty stomach, that is to say,
on the meal I had sat through in his company. By and by he
called for a song, and I began to sing. He listened, pleased, and,
as he listened, swallowed pint after pint, with higher and higher
pleasure, until, when I saw that the wine had got to his head, I
said: Sir, you are having a good time listening to my singing; but
when will good times begin for me?

Slave, my writing-case! cried Ibn Makhlad. When the case was brought, he wrote something and tossed it over to me: it was an order on his banker for five hundred dinars. I duly thanked him and began to sing again. Again he was delighted; again, and even more profusely, he expressed his appreciation. I thought I might ask him for something to wear....

A poet once asked the Sahib Ibn Abbad to give him something to wear, made of the same flowered silk which the Sahib's staff wore.

There is a story, said the Sahib, that a man once said to Ibn Zayda: Prince, give me some beast I can throw a leg over! whereupon the Prince ordered him a camel, a horse, a mule, and a donkey, and also a slave girl, saying: If I knew of any other kind of beast a man could throw a leg over, you should have one! And so now, we will order you a cloak, a shirt, a coat, trousers, turban, scarf, sash, robe and socks, all of our flowered silk. And if we could think of any other thing to wear which could be made of flowered silk, we should offer you that too. . .

Well, Jahza continued, Ibn Makhlad gave me five splendid coats. He then ordered that his guests should be perfumed, and a most magnificent perfume-box was produced, stored with quantities of incense, from which the slaves began to fumigate the company. When they had done, I said to my host: Sir, am I to be satisfied with mere vapors?

Why, what do you want? said he.

I should like my fair share of the box, I answered.

'Tsyours! cried he, and drinking off one final pint of wine, he keeled over backwards on to his cushion, as he always did when he passed out.

By now the sun was up and people were going to their businesses. I left with the others. Coming away I looked like a burglar emerging from premises where he has been plying his profession, with all the robes and the casket in a bundle on my slave's neck. I went home and had a nap, and then rode over to

Awn Street to see Ibn Makhlad's banker. I found him in his place of business and presented the order.

Are you the person named here? he inquired.

Yes.

You know, he said, that people like myself are not in business for the sake of our health?

I know that, said I.

The usual commission in cases like this, he went on, is ten per cent.

That will be all right, I answered.

The banker then said: My object in mentioning this was not to make a large profit out of you. Which do you prefer: to take your money on the usual terms I have mentioned? or to stay here till noon, when I shall have finished business, and then ride home with me, and spend the rest of the day and the night drinking with me? I may say I have heard of you, and have been wanting to hear you sing; and this is my chance to do so at a reduced rate! If you are agreeable, you shall have the full value of this order without deduction for commission.

I'll stay with you, said I.

So he put the order in his pocket, and went on with his business. When it was getting near Noonday Prayer, his slave brought round a fine mule; he mounted, and we rode away together, to a magnificent house — splendid furniture, expensive plate — only Greek slave girls in attendance, no boys. Leaving me in his saloon, he went off to the private apartments, and presently emerged fresh from the bath and dressed like a prince. Then, when he had perfumed himself and had personally fumigated me with a fine old ambergris mixture, we sat down to an elaborate meal.

The cuisine was exquisite. For our wine we adjourned to another sumptuous room where the dessert was arranged, with more valuable plate. We spent the whole night drinking: it was a much pleasanter evening than the previous one with Ibn Makhlad.

When morning broke, my host produced two purses, one

full of dinars, the other of dirhams, and weighed out five hundred dinars from the first. The dirhams in the other were newly minted, but these too he weighed out, five hundred, and said to me: Sir, those are in payment of the order, and these are a present from myself.

I pocketed the money and took my leave; but that banker became a friend of mine, and his house another home to me.

Jahza himself was stingy enough about food (says Ibn A'rabi the poet). I was once at a party he gave; we had eaten, and were sitting drinking, while our host sang, when a man came in late. Jahza offered him the covered wicker tray where the food of which we had eaten had been put aside. It seemed as if the new arrival had had nothing for a week: he ate the whole contents of the tray, and every dish was empty when he pushed it away.

Jahza watched this performance with a glare of rage, the rest of us with smiles. It was over at last.

Do you play backgammon? Jahza asked.

I do, said the guest.

So we set the board between them, and the game began. The play went steadily against Jahza; the dice seemed to know what numbers the other wanted and gave them. At last Jahza stalked to the opening of the tent where we were sitting, and raising his face heavenward addressed these words to God: I've got my deserts, for filling a man it had pleased Thee to starve!

A POPULAR DINER OUT NOT UNIVERSALLY POPULAR

No thanks of ours can e'er repay
What Jahza did for our distress:
He turned that face of his away
And let us see his horse's arse.

NOR AN ESTEEMED SINGER UNIVERSALLY ESTEEMED

One sultry summer's day I was at Isa's,
And Fahm was prevailed upon to sing.
It might have been midwinter's coldest night,
My teeth so chattered with my shuddering.

AN AUTHENTIC GENTLEMAN

One often sees a merchant worth four million dinars or
more who looks for all the world like one of his own employees,
as far as outward appearance goes.

But there is a Saying of the Prophet: *God dislikes it when*
people hide the fortune He hath graced them with.

It was my master's custom (says the old steward of Abu
Mundhir Nu'man ibn Abdallah), when winter came to an end,
to collect all the poplins, woollens, blankets, stoves, and other
winter furnishings he had used that season, and to put them up
to auction. Then he used to send to the Judge's Prison to inquire
what prisoners were lying there penniless who had been convicted on their own voluntary confession, and not on evidence for
the prosecution. Out of the price he had got for his goods Abu
Mundhir would pay their debts, or, if these were too heavy, compound for their release. He then looked to the petty tradesmen
of his neighborhood — confectioners, pedlars, and such people,
whose whole business capital might be from one to three dinars — and used to give them additional capital of ten dinars or a
hundred dirhams. He also felt for people who brought things
like kettles and pots and worn-out sheets to market, things that
would probably only be sold under pressure of extreme need,
and for old women who sold their spinning; he would pay such
folk many times what they asked for their wares and let them
keep the goods.

In the same way, when winter was coming on, he would
collect his brocades, his gold and silver tissues, his summer

matting and water-coolers and all his summer furniture, and devote them to like charities. When the next summer or winter came, he would lay in fresh supplies of whatever he needed.

At last I could stand these goings-on no longer.

Sir, said I one day, you are crippling yourself, and to no good purpose. Here you are buying these clothes and things at top prices just when the demand is greatest, and selling them at half price just when there's no market for them. It's throwing fortunes away. Under favor, let me do this: put up anything you want to auction, but when they're going to be knocked down let me buy them in for you, and keep them for next summer or winter; and then take from your funds an equal amount to the price, for these good purposes.

No, said Abu Mundhir, I don't want that done. These are things God has let me enjoy all my summer long, or all my winter; and He has brought me through to a time when I can do without them. How do I know I shall be alive next time such things are needed again? It may well be I have offended God either in the getting or the using of them. I would rather sell the things, and put the actual price to this purpose, by way of thanking God for preserving me till I no longer need them, and atoning for any offense I may have done in connection with them. Then, if God spare me to a time when I need such things again, they don't cost much. I can always get similar things afresh, and shall enjoy the novelty of them. And there's a further advantage in my selling them cheap and buying them dear: the small dealers I buy from and sell to make a profit out of me. What's good for them won't ruin me.

When any special delicacy or confection was served to Abu Mundhir (as the steward used to tell), he never cared to eat much of it, but would order it given out to the beggars almost untouched. Every day, whatever was taken away from his own table he used to order given out at the gate, along with the surplus from his slaves' meal in the kitchen. There was always a crowd of beggars clustered outside.

One day a friend of his, a gentleman of the Hashimite family, was dining with him. Dinner began with something very choice, but Abu Mundhir ordered it out to the beggars before much was gone. Then came a fatted kid; but before they had done justice to it he ordered that too removed and given away. Then came an almond dessert made up with pistachio nuts, one of his favorite things — it used to cost him fifty dirhams the dish.

They had only eaten a little of it when he said: Take it to the beggars now.

But the Hashimite gentleman took a firm grip of the glass it was in. My dear, said he, let's pretend *we* are the beggars, and enjoy our dinner. Why on earth pass everything you particularly like to beggars? What has a beggar to do with a dish like this? Beggars can do very well on beef and date-cake. So please, don't have this removed.

This is a custom of mine, said Abu Mundhir.

Then it is a very bad custom, said his guest; and we are not going to put up with it. If your beggars *must* have such a noble dessert, then order another dish of it for them, and let us enjoy this one. Or let us give them the cost of it in money.

Very well, said Abu Mundhir. I will countermand my order; and I will have another dish of this made for them. But as for money: no beggar would have the heart or spirit to make something like this, even if he were given the cost of it many times over. When a beggar gets coins, he spends them on things he needs more urgently; and he wouldn't in any case know how to cook such a dish. What I like to do is to share *my pleasures*.

* * *

If he has to choose between masculine conversation, and music, and being alone with a woman, a gentleman will always choose masculine conversation.

And let no speaker be interrupted; let him expatiate at ease, and travel by a path of his own choosing towards the end he has in mind, so that one thing may lead to another, as the proverb puts it: Talk's a branching tree.

A man who contents himself with what there is to know in his own locality cannot compare with one who spends his time in search of those strange but real facts which lie hidden in the mine of this world. The strangeness of a thing, it is obvious, consists only in the fact that we seldom happen to see it. But let a thing be strange *enough,* and it becomes an oddity or even a thing against nature — it seems incredible until one has actually seen it. Look at India: they have a number of customs there so different from ours here that they strike us as simply monstrous. One might almost think that the Hindus considered what was appropriate and then deliberately did the opposite.

They eat singly, for example, one by one, with dung for a tablecloth! They will sip cow's urine, but they will not eat beef! They generally ride without a saddle; but if they do use a saddle, they mount from what we consider the off side. Of two children in a family, they respect the younger more particularly, on the ground that the elder owes his existence to overpowering lust, while the younger was more considerately and calmly begotten. They don't ask leave to enter a house, but they do ask leave when they go away.

On these points of difference the Hindus regard themselves as our betters, just as we of course think of ourselves as the superiors. If we are going to criticize, we should not confine ourselves to Indian ways of doing things: plenty of Arab customs during the old Ignorance were both criminal and disgusting. Our forefathers used to sleep with menstruating or pregnant women; nay, several of them would make a compact to sleep with the same woman during the same menstrual period! In some of their worship the old Arabs used to whistle on their fingers and clap their hands. They used to eat unclean animals. It was Islam that put an end to that kind of thing among us, God be thanked for it!

To such a degree does Hindu usage differ from ours that they use us as bogies to frighten their children. They tell them we are the spawn of the Evil One. In their opinion there is no country but their own, no people like themselves, no rulers, no religion, no science to compare with theirs — a proud, infatuate, conceited, stupid people. In all justice, however, we must admit that looking down the nose at foreigners is by no means confined to the Hindus (and ourselves) but is the normal attitude of any one nation towards all others.

The real difference is between the thinking of the educated and the thinking of the uneducated in any nation. The former try to conceive those abstract and general principles which under-lie phenomena; the latter cannot get any further than what can be seen or heard. They are content with derived rules. For that reason a religious formulation meant for simple people cannot be too carefully worded. An example will show what I mean: some learned Hindu may refer to God as a *point,* meaning thereby that He cannot be described in terms of bodily extension. Along comes some uneducated fellow and reads the statement, and miss-ing the point of *point,* imagines God as small as a dot. This offensive comparison he cannot accept. God is surely bigger than that, he says: God must be at least twelve fingers long by ten broad!

The heathen Greeks before Christianity were really very like the Hindus: the educated classes thought in much the same way as educated Hindus, and the common people were as much given to idol-worship as the uneducated in India. It is amusing to compare the philosophic thought of the one nation with that of the other. All heathenism is essentially the same, of course — deviation from the truth, and only that. But the Greeks *did* have philosophers who discovered and worked out the elements of science as distinguished from vulgar superstition. To live by the findings of scientific thought is essentially aristocratic; the common crowd will always rush into muddled squabbling. Think of Socrates: he ventured to oppose the idol-worship of the herd, his fellow citizens, and at once eleven out of twelve Athen-ians, his judges, agreed that he must die. He died a martyr to truth.

There are never more than a few at any time or in any place who understand that world of abstract thought. The popular mind has a positive aversion to it. Only to pictorial representations of the abstract are common people accessible; and that is why so many religious leaders have sunk so low as to allow place to such imagery in their sacred books and places of worship. Jews and Christians, and above all Manicheans are offenders; but one can imagine an adequate illustration nearer home: suppose a portrait of the Prophet exhibited to some ignorant man or woman of us. Their rapture would make them kiss the picture, rub their faces on it, roll in the dust before it, as if it were the original and not an image they were seeing.

Here we have the beginning of what becomes idol-worship. Monuments are designed to keep alive the memory of venerated persons, prophets or sages, to make a lasting place of grateful respect for them in men's hearts when they die. But after long lapse of time, this origin of the monument is forgotten, and the veneration of it becomes a rule of life. The legislators of antiquity, trying to get at men on this weak side, made image-worship a duty.

Before talking about the ridiculous attitude of the Hindus in this matter of image-worship, one ought first to observe that it is the attitude only of the ignorant crowd. Those whose mental pilgrimage is towards freedom, those who study philosophy and theology are entirely free from worshipping anything but God. Such men would never dream of adoring an image purporting to represent Him. The main stream and essence of the Hindu world of thought is what the Brahmins think, for religion is their profession. On the subject of the nature of created things, the Hindus hold views close to those of the ancient Greeks, many of whom maintained that only the First Cause has real existence, since It alone is self-sufficing, and that what needs something else has only a dreamlike and unreal life. This, by the way, is the Sufi theory also. The Hindu Vasudeva says: The soul has knowledge inasmuch as it is freed from matter; so long as it is invested with matter it is not-knowing. That doctrine is actually identical with the Sufi view, for the Sufis teach that this world is a soul asleep, and the Other World a soul awake. The old Greeks also agreed with the Hindus; as Socrates said: Knowing is the soul's remembrance of what it learned before it entered the body.

But although intelligent Hindus abhor anthropomorphisms, the crowd and sectaries go beyond anything heard of before, speaking of wife and child, of copulation and other physical processes, all in connection with God, and in terms as silly as they are indecent. One of their famous idols used to be the Sun image at Multan, a wooden object covered with red leather, with two rubies set in its eyes. When the Muslims first conquered the place, and their commander found on inquiry that the immense treasure which had accumulated there was due to this idol and the offerings of pilgrims to it, he decided to leave the thing where it was. However, he humorously expressed his contempt by hanging a piece of beef round its neck! Later on, when the Qarmatians occupied Multan, they smashed the image to splinters and killed its priests.

Aristotle in one of his treatises says: You may raise the point that some Greeks attribute speech to idols and think of them as spiritual beings; it is a point on which, since we do not know, we cannot speak — a remark which puts Aristotle in a class far above that of fools and uneducated persons.

The first cause of idolatry, it is surely obvious, was the wish to commemorate the dead and console the living, though it has become a pernicious abuse at last. That is certainly what the Caliph Mu'awia thought, for when the Muslims who conquered Sicily in fifty-three sent him the crowned images of gold set with diamonds which they had captured, he ordered the things sent on to India, for sale to the local princes. These being objects of price, he thought it best to get the price; as to their being objects of abominable idolatry he felt not the slightest scruple. For him it was a question of policy, and not in any sense a religious matter.

It is the heart which is the true temple of idolatry. Judge Fadl Jumahi told me a story once. It had been told him by

Muhammad Jumahi, who heard it from the lips of Abu Hajjaj of
Thaqif.

I rode once, Abu Hajjaj said, as far as the Clan Amir
country, for no other purpose than to see the famous Majnun. I
found his father still alive in that country, a very old man, and
Majnun's brothers, now come to middle age. It seemed a happy
household; but when I spoke of Majnun, the old man cried out:
Ah, Majnun: my child I loved the best of all! He fell in love with
a girl of the Clan. She was a poor match for him; but still, when
their love was known, her father would not let my son have her;
he chose her another husband. We had to chain him up; but he
gnawed his lips and bit his tongue so that we were afraid for him,
and let him loose. He ran off into the waste hereabouts. They
take him food every day, and leave it in some open place: if it
catch his eye, he'll come and eat.

I asked if anyone would guide me to where he was, and
they told me I should ask a young clansman: He was Majnun's
friend in the old days, and he is the only one he still takes any
pleasure in. So I went to the youth and begged him to take me to
Majnun.

If 'tis his poetry you want, said he, I have them all by heart
myself, up to what he uttered yesterday. Tomorrow I go again:
if he speaks aught fresh, I'll bring it back for you.

It is himself I would see, said I.

If he see you, he'll only run away, the young man answered; and I am afraid he will be shy of me afterwards, and so
his poetry will be lost me.

But I begged and begged that he point out the way to me
at least, until in the end, Go and look, said he, in that quarter
of the waste yonder. If you get a sight of him, come up on him
very gently. He'll try to scare you off, and make as if to throw
at you anything he has in his hand. You should sit down as if
you paid no heed to him. But watch him out of the corner of
your eye, and if you see him quiet, try to recite something from
Qays, Dharih's son, the poet he loves best.

That very morning I went out to hunt Majnun. I discovered him after midday, sitting on a little hill, writing in the sand with his fingers. Without hesitating I walked towards him, but he sprang away like a wild beast startled, and ran to a stony place, and picked up a stone. I walked forward, and then sat down near him, and waited a while, for he still seemed mistrustful. When I had sat there a long time, he became more calm, and drew near, playing uneasily with his fingers. Then I looked towards him, and said: How beautiful they are, those lines of Qays, Dharih's son, when he says:

> *They say they'll ride away at dawn,*
> *Or the night that follows on.*
> *Then she who has been always here*
> *Will not be here, but gone.*

The madman fell into wild weeping. After a while he spoke: I am a better poet than that, he said; listen:

> *So did I love that when we touched*
> *I felt my hand would leaf,*
> *It swelled so moist. Therefore I call*
> *On Love for deadlier grief*
> *At every dark, till I am dead.*
> *And then, my Paradise,*
> *I wait for thee. We two will meet*
> *The Day the Dead shall Rise.*

As he was speaking, a gazelle passed in view; and away after her he scoured and was lost to sight. I left the place. But on the third day after, I went back to where I had seen him. I could not find him that day, and told his family so. They sent out the man who took him food to search, but he came back saying that the last meats were lying untouched where he had left them. At that his brothers and myself went out. All that day we hunted him, and all night; and at dawn we came upon him. He was lying in a dry and stony hollow, quite dead. His brothers carried him home; and I returned to my own country.

Everything comes to an end; and Love's end is death, if it is not ecstasy.

I myself (said Sanawbari) knew a man, a bookseller in Edessa called Sa'd. His shop was a great rendezvous for men of letters, and Sa'd, who was a clever, well-read man, wrote sentimental verse himself. Abu Mi'waj, myself, and various other Syrian and Egyptian poets were constantly at the shop.

There was a Christian merchant in the town who had a son called Isa, the most beautiful thing God ever made — a superb figure. The boy had a brilliant mind also, and was a brilliant talker; he used to sit with us and take down our poems, and although he was only a schoolboy at the time we were all very fond of him. With this boy Sa'd fell violently in love; and he wrote verse about him which made his passion common knowledge.

As the boy grew up, he felt an unmistakable vocation to the religious life. He spoke to his parents on the subject, and pleaded so hard that at last they yielded, and bought him a monk's cell by the usual arrangement with the Superior of the local Monastery. And there the boy went to spend the rest of his life. For the bookseller it was as if the sun had gone out. He closed his shop and saw none of his friends any more, and took to haunting the Monastery where the boy lived, writing more verses about him.

But the monks disapproved of a friendship of this kind; they forbade the boy on pain of expulsion to invite him to the Monastery again. When Sa'd saw that his friend was avoiding him, it broke his heart. He went in person to plead with the monks, but it was no use. It would be wrong, they said, and would give rise to scandal if they allowed his visits; and besides that, they were afraid of official displeasure. Next time Sa'd appeared before the Monastery, they shut the gate in his face and would not even allow the boy to speak to him.

This only made his lovesickness more violent; his passion now burst all bounds. He tore his clothes, went back home and set fire to everything in the house, and then took to living in the waste land hard by the Monastery, naked and insane, composing verse and weeping endlessly.

Once Abu Mi'waj and I, on our way home from a garden
where we had been to spend the night, saw him sitting in the
shadow of the Monastery wall; his hair was long and matted, and
his whole appearance altered. We greeted him, and tried to rally
the man.

Leave me alone, said he, with these whisperings of the
Devil! Do you see that bird? Ever since dawn I have been begging it to alight near Isa and give him a message from me.

And he turned away from us, and walked up to the
Monastery gate. It was immediately shut in his face.

Some time after this he was found lying near the Monastery, dead. Abbas ibn Kaygalag was Prince at the town in those
days; and when he and the townsfolk heard the news, they came
out in a mob to the Monastery, yelling: The monks have murdered him!

We'll have that boy's head! Ibn Kaygalag was saying;
we'll fire the place; we'll flog those monks! He proved so implacable that the Christians had to pay ten thousand dirhams to
redeem themselves and their Monastery. And whenever after this
the young man came back into town to see his parents, boys used
to yell after him in the streets: There he goes, the one who
murdered Sa'd the Bookseller! and pelt him with stones; so that
in the end he left our district, and settled in the Monastery of
Sam'an.

Ay, Love at the first is a dribble of dropping water,
But once risen over the soul a surging ocean.

According to Ptolemy, there are three types of love. The
first is that union of two souls which is properly termed Love.

There is no resisting this reciprocal force: it is the result of
two persons having their planets in Trine or Sextile aspect in the
horoscope. In such a case those two beings were created to love
one another, especially if in the nativity the planets are in Dignity, and not in Debility.

The second type, which Ptolemy calls the Adjuvant, occurs when two beings at birth have the Exaltation of a planet lying between their respective positions for the same planet, or Trine or Sextile to them. Such persons will be helpful to one another, and of this helpfulness will come friendship and affection.

The third type occurs when two people have the same planet in opposite degrees. If, further, the one has the body in its Exaltation, and the other has it in Fall, to the fascination which results from the general position is added the misfortune consequent on the further fact: their destinies will never be happily united.

That classic verse:

The ways of Love are three:
Heart in heart may lie,
Or lip and eye agree;
Or else a man can die!

is often quoted as evidence that the old poet adopted the same classification.

* * *

Abdallah ibn Omar told me (his father had told it him) that once when his father was in attendance on the Regent Muwaffaq, the Regent sent for two astrologers, the famous Abu Ma'shar and another. When they arrived, he said: I have something concealed about me: what is it?

Both astrologers took readings with their astrolabes and made calculations. Then the one declared that the concealed object was some fruit. Abu Ma'shar on the contrary said it was something animal.

You're right, said Muwaffaq to the first; and you, Abu Ma'shar, are wrong. And the Regent tossed forward an apple.

Abu Ma'shar stood dumbfounded. Then he studied his tables again for a while. Suddenly, rushing forward, he snatched the apple and broke it open.

GOD GREATER THAN ALL! he cried, holding it out to Muwaffaq. It was full of maggots!

I find that story rather hard to believe, said Judge Tanukhi. But I have seen things myself from time to time which have convinced me. One such thing was the time of my father's death. He cast his horoscope for that year himself. It would be a critical year for him, he told us; and he wrote to his son-in-law Judge Ibn Buhlul at Baghdad, stating that he would die that year and giving certain instructions.

He became slightly unwell. Before it appeared at all serious, I was with him when he got out his horoscope and studied it carefully; and I saw that he was weeping when he put it away again. He summoned his secretary, dictated his last will and testament, and had it attested that same day.

The astrologer Abu Qasim, who was called Saturn's Slave, came to visit my father in his sickness. He spoke comfortably to him, told him one could never be sure.

Abu Qasim, my father said, you are not a man to be mistaken about a matter of this kind, nor am I a suitable subject for that kind of consolation. Come and sit here.

And he showed him the sensitive point in the horoscope.

Why go on? Can either you or I, he said, doubt that the afternoon of Wednesday the seventh from the end of the month is astrologically the fatal time?

Abu Qasim made no reply. He could not bring himself to say Yes, for he was my father's old servant; so he said nothing. For a long time my father wept. Then he told a slave to bring a basin of water, washed out the horoscope and cut it into little pieces, and said good-bye to Abu Qasim, as a man does who knows that this is a parting for ever.

When the afternoon of that Wednesday came, my father died, exactly as he had predicted.

Even Abu Ali Jubbai, that great Rationalist, was an astrologer, and a very skillful one. Abu Hashim the Baker told me that the father of a child born in his neighborhood asked Abu Ali to cast a horoscope for it; and Abu Ali made a number of predictions, all of which came true afterward.

More than one common friend of mine and Abu Muhammad of Ramhurmuz, the metaphysician, has told me this as coming from Abu Muhammad himself:

When he decided to terminate his studies and return to his own city, he went to say good-bye to Abu Ali.

Don't start today, Abu Muhammad, his teacher said to him; there are astrological indications of death by drowning for travellers when such aspects as today's occur.

Why, Shaykh! I exclaimed (said Abu Muhammad). Can it be you I hear talking like this? you, who hold the views you do about astrologers' pretensions?

Abu Muhammad, said he, suppose that we were going by a certain road, and that someone told us the stretch ahead was haunted by a lion. In common prudence should we not avoid that road if we could take another, even though the man who warned us might be a liar?

I suppose so, said I.

Well then, Jubbai pursued, it is at any rate possible that God may have so ordered the chain of events that when the planets are in certain positions certain particular things happen. It is just as well to be on the safe side.

* * *

Don't trouble your head about Destiny, is what the Sufis say. What God, Who knows, chooses for His servant is better than what the servant, who does not know, will choose, for love is agreed to be the negation of the lover's choice by affirming the Beloved's.

But, for lofty sayings and minute indications concerning the real nature of love, Sumnun the Sufi was the man.

A thing can only be explained, he used to say, in terms of what is subtler than itself. But there is nothing subtler than love! In terms of what, therefore, shall love be explained?

On his way home from the Holy Cities once the people of
the town of Fayd requested him to give a lecture on his subject,
love. Accordingly he mounted the pulpit and began. During the
course of his address the whole audience disappeared.

Well, said Sumnun, turning to the lamp, I shall speak to
you. At this, the very lamp fell down and shattered into fragments which rolled away.

Durra the Sufi, who was a famous dancer, once told me:
If a man who has just come into money, an inheritance of two
hundred thousand or less, sends for us to entertain him, we call
him Short of Time.

What does that mean? I asked him.

Women call a boy Short of Time, the dancer said, if he
dies within a year or unweaned. And we call a man like that
Short of Time because we know that if he spends his money on
dancers his inheritance will last no longer than one of those
babies.

A dancer needs certain gifts of temperament and physique
in addition to his technical accomplishments. He should be born
with a spontaneous vivacity, an absolute sense of rhythm, and
that determined will to learn which enables a man to study and
in the end to master an art. Physically, he should be free
and long in the neck, clear down to the swell of the shoulders,
he should be graceful and finely made, supple in the loins, slender
in the waist, light in movement, and well-proportioned.

He must learn to time the floating and fall of the girdle-
ends, learn how to swell his skirts to any desired degree, how to
control his breathing, and how to stay absolutely motionless in
any position. He must have the strength to stand the long exercises, and must keep his feet and fingers under variable control,
so as to modify their movements in dances so different in mood
as for instance the Cameleer and the Dance of Aversion. A dancer must be unusually flexible, and be able to execute turns and

the swaying of the hips with great rapidity. His training includes a thorough knowledge of all the dances and their variations.

Dance rhythms fall into eight types: the Presto; the Four-beat Trill; the Scatter-Rhythm and its Allegro (two beats with a rest between); the First Andante (two heavy slow beats followed by a single accelerated beat) and its Allegro; the Second Andante (a single slow beat and two unequal beats running simultaneously) and its Allegro.

A good dancer can execute graceful turns without moving his feet from the axis, and has absolute evenness of movement in both right and left foot. There are two styles of movement in the lifting and placing of the feet: one on the beat, and the other retarded. The more skilled and refined a dancer is, the more voluptuous grace he can put into a movement strictly on the beat; and in retarded rhythm, the stricter his accuracy in the lift of the foot before he sets it down behind the beat.

* * *

Dancing and beating time are so engrained in the nature of the negro slaves who are so common in our slave markets that it is said: If one were falling from heaven to earth, he would still beat time on his way down!

They have the whitest teeth in the world, but their personal odor is unpleasant, and their skin coarse. Abyssinian women are very different — weak and flabby, and very often sufferers from tuberculosis. As singers and dancers they are useless, and they pine away in foreign countries. But one can trust them: their feeble physiques mask strong characters.

Turkish women are fair-skinned, graceful and lively; their little eyes are very enticing, though their figures are often squat. They always ride well, and are generous and clean, and clever cooks; but they are unreliable. A Greek woman generally has a red-and-white complexion, with smooth hair and blue eyes. She is obedient and adaptable, well-meaning and trustworthy. The men, whose orderliness and thrift make them useful stewards, are not infrequently experts at some craft or other.

Of all whites, the Armenian is the worst, as the dark negro is the worst of blacks. Although their figures are handsome, their feet are ugly. Chastity is something they have never heard of; and theft is just a habit. The only vice foreign to them is avarice. Leave an Armenian slave idle for an hour and he will get into mischief. His laziness is because he will not work, not because he cannot work. You have to take a stick and beat him to make him do as he is told.

Ay; starve a slave and he sleeps; feed him and he fornicates.

Even eunuchs. I once asked the eunuch Arib, whom I knew to be an educated and truthful man: Tell me something, Master, about castration: it is a subject on which the doctors disagree, for even Abu Hanifa refers to the marital capacity of eunuchs, and allows them at law to be the fathers of the children their wives bear.

Abu Hanifa is quite right, Arib told me: for during the process of castration, when the scrotum is opened and the glands removed, the patient is often the victim of shock, as a result of which one of the testicles disappears in the body; and the operator cannot always find it. Eventually, after the incision has healed, the gland reverts to its proper place. Abu Hanifa is consistent with the Word of God: *THE CHILD BELONGETH TO THE HUSBAND,* in those cases of marriage where a eunuch retains one of his glands.

I checked this with Abu Sa‘id at Nishapur, and he told me: It is certainly possible, for I have one myself.

One must be careful buying slaves. How many a swarthy girl with a dirty complexion has been sold as a golden blonde! How many a diseased girl as sound! How many a fat girl as slim!

The dealers can tint blue eyes black and yellow cheeks red, they know how to make a gaunt face buxom and a hairy cheek smooth. They can change spindle arms to plump ones, and can efface pockmarks as easily as pimples.

Never should a man buy a slave at the Festival Sales. How often at those Sales has a man bought a boy when he thought he was buying a girl! I have heard a slave dealer say: A quarter's worth of henna, and she's worth a hundred dirhams more. They make the hair look longer than it is by twining hair of similar color on to the ends, they remedy a foul breath with scents, and whiten the teeth with potash and sugar, or charcoal and salt. Then the girls are told to make themselves pleasant to old men and bashful men, but to be reserved and distant with young fellows, to inflame their desires and snare their fancies.

The perfect singing-girl is a Madina woman: she combines suavity and grace with coquetry and wit. She is never jealous, never in a temper, and never quarrelsome. And a girl from Mecca is a delicate creature, with her tiny ankles and wrists, and her languishing eyes. Abu Othman the Broker's opinion is that your ideal slave girl is your Berber girl, exported from her own country at nine years old, who spends three years at Madina and three years at Mecca, and then comes to Iraq at sixteen or so for a thorough training in elegant accomplishments. By the time she comes up for sale at twenty-five she will unite in her person the splendid racial qualities of the Berbers (and they are unrivalled as breeders), the coquetry of Madina, the delicacy of Mecca, and the culture of Iraq.

You speak of cultured slave girls. There is a story that one night al-Rashid was lying between two girls, one from Madina, the other from Kufa. The Kufa girl was massaging his hands, while the Madina girl massaged his feet, with such art that the Caliph's tool stood on end.

I see you have your eye on the property, said the girl from Kufa. Don't forget I want my lawful share.

The Tradition was related to me by Malik, said the other girl, on the authority of Hisham son of Urwa, who had it of his grandfather Zubayr ibn Awwam the Companion that the Apostle of God, God's Prayer and Peace on him! said: *If any man bring a dead ground to life, it belongeth to him.*

But the girl from Kufa caught her off her guard with a push, and grabbing the lot protested: Well, we have heard from A'mash on the authority of Haythama, who had it of Abdallah ibn Mas'ud that the Prophet, God's Prayer and Peace on him! once said: *The game is the man's who gets it, not his who puts it up.*

The game of a man with a woman is one of the games the angels like to watch, as the Prophet said.

We went into a garden one day, a company of friends (said Abu Suwayd), to buy some fruit; and we saw an old woman in one of the corners, bright-faced still, though her hair was white. She was combing her hair with an ivory comb.

We stopped in front of her; but she took no notice of us, not even drawing her veil across her face.

If you were to dye your hair black, old lady, said I, you would be prettier than any girl. Why don't you?

She raised her head, and looked at me with great eyes. Then she spoke — these verses:

> *What the years dyed, I dyed again.*
> *The color would not last.*
> *My deepest black was fugitive;*
> *The Dye of Time was fast.*
> *When I was what I am no more,*
> *I'd a haughty mind:*
> *I liked to have one man in front*
> *And one at work behind.*

Good enough, I cried, from an old woman! That yearning remembrance of sin — how sincere it is! and pretended remorse for vice — how false!

*An old man's groaning does not mean he's tired
Of life: he's merely tired of being feeble.*

As the proverb says, Having shows what Lacking hides. Raising his hand and touching the curtain behind which his slave girls were posted, our host called out: Sing something! And immediately they burst into music and song. One had a lute and one a pipe, another a harp and another castanets.

*Gild a cup with yellow wine, so pale's this silver day.
The world is veiled and pearled as if her bridal closed to-
     night.
You watch the snow. I count the petals trembling from
     their spray,
Roses not of the gaudy Spring, but of Winter's white.*

*We will have naught twixt cup and cup
But soon told tales;
Over us as we drink and sprawl
In lower case, beautiful tall
Cup-bearers shall stand up
Like stately capitals.*

*Pour tawny wine and reach to me, O white hand turning
     the blue bowl!
O Wine my Sun! O Bubble Moon! O Cup my Heaven! O
     Hand my Pole!*

*I pass my springs in Qutrabbul now, and flee the heats in
    quiet Karkh.*
*My mother Vine still suckles me, still stoops to me when
    noon is cruel;*
*Branches droop; a chinkless roof of spreading shade covers
    me over.*
*The doves that haunt there mourn and mourn like widow-
    ed women moaning their dirge;*
*And so their yearning sobs with mine, I think our trouble's
    the same old trouble.*

Like a child suddenly hungry, I rise and crawl to suck.
Like a dotard I make love to a tavern-keeper's daughter.
Long years, ay, generations have tried their teeth on her;
But safe in the thick of night I tear at the delicate veil
*Which Spider, that wild webster, wove her; I strike the
    crazy*
Tent and sagging ropes that Nobody once drew tight.
Right into her middle I thrust, I give her my awl;
And forth vivid as fire it springs — the wine! the wine!
Cups of silver gilt catch at it, sluice it round,
Cup and liquor so golden both that I fall to wondering
Which is the truer gold, and find this difference chief:
The goblet's gold is stagnant; the Liquor is the Living!

Some cups are sleek; but some bear Christian Crosses
And holy men babbling Gospel under a Heaven of bubbles,
Of stars that scatter and wink like pearls spilt from a string
Snapped by the giddy fingers of Virgins in wild play.

My immortal soul? I pawned the thing for liquor
*And a couple of mouths for kissing — a woman and a
    beaker.*
This I did because I know full well, and fear it:
Too soon they'll lie apart, this body and this spirit.

Have Faith, if Love's thy Faith. Let Envy scold,
Who hateth Love; and Slander say his say.
What hath Divine Compassion better made
Than beds where lovers body to body play?
When dying days discover living Love,
Let the world slip, if so the Love remain.
Thou One Compassionate! Us once before we die,
Even if only once, make One again!

Let me be impious and unlucky, Lord!
Only I ask that one hand all my life
Rest on my darling's thigh, and that the other
Finger the cup.

Fill up again! I know, as if I'd seen,
My place hereafter. Deep in Hell's Abyss!
Give me the stuff God's Holy Word forbids;
Pour full! the Christian priest and I in Hell
Can play it off upon the Fire as piss!

There amid casks and wine-vats, in a dress of gayest dye, the old man was, cup-bearers proud with beauty all about him, and glittering lights, myrtle and jasmine, the pipe and the lute. Go broach that cask! he cried. Let the lutes speak! he cried again, and turned from a snuffing of perfumes to a fondling of the fair.

Damned soul! no shame? I said to him.

He laughed aloud, and pleasantly answered me:
Love's sweetest single moment's just
When Lovesickness unmasks as Lust.

Is it not time, thou ancient thing, to leave off lechery? I cried. His mood turned sour; he growled; his face altered; and for a while he seemed to think. But when he spoke again, it was to say: Tonight's for good living, not for good words; this is a

night for drinking, and no night for dialectic. Whatever it may
be you have in mind to say will keep for our next meeting. Tomorrow.

I left him.

THE PRODIGAL

How many tales there are of prodigal heirs! I knew a
young man who was in a tremendous hurry to get through his inheritance. When he was down to his last five thousand dinars,
he told his friends he wanted to be rid of it as fast as possible, so
as to see what he would do when all was gone.

Some friend of his suggested that he invest all but five
hundred in cut glass of the most expensive quality, arrange it all
in front of the place where he usually sat when entertaining
guests, and give a party, using the last five hundred for singing-
women's fees, fruit, perfumes, wine, ice, and food. When the
wine was nearly finished, he should release two mice among his
glasses, and then let loose a cat to chase them.

The young heir liked this idea, and acted on it. At the
party he sat and drank himself drunk, and then shouted: Now!
His friend let the mice and the cat go; and crash! went the glass.
The host fell happily asleep.

His friend and the other guests got up and collected the
fragments. That broken glass would make a cup; that broken
goblet would make a pomade-jar with a little glue — so they
held an auction. The proceeds they divided up among themselves; and then they went away, leaving their host to his slum-
bers. He and his fortunes were no longer any concern of theirs.

A year passed by (says the author of the cat-and-mouse-in-
the-glass idea), and I suddenly thought: Why don't I go and see
what has become of that ill-fated young man? So I went to see.
He had sold his furniture and spent the proceeds. He had dis-
mantled his house and sold the materials — even the ceilings.

The only place with a roof still on it was the old porter's lodge; and there he was, lying on a bit of cotton sheet, wrapped against the cold in cotton-cardings and a secondhand quilt, looking rather like a quince in its cotton packing.

You poor fellow! said I. What's all this?

It's just what you see, said he.

Any regrets? said I.

Yes, I have one regret, he said.

What?

I long to see So-and-so again, the young man said. She was a singing-girl he'd loved, the one on whom he had spent the better part of his inheritance. He began to cry. I felt so sorry for him that I fetched him some clothes from my own house; and we went together to the place where the singer lodged.

She of course thought he must be in better circumstances again, and invited him in, asked us to sit down, and said to him, with a beaming smile: Well, how are things going?

He told her.

You had better go, said the girl at once.

Why?

If the madam comes and finds you here without any money, she'll be furious with me for letting you in. So go outside. I'll go upstairs, and we can have a talk through the window.

So he went out and sat down under the window in the street. As he was sitting there, the girl emptied a stewpan full of greasy water over him. Then she burst out laughing, for he certainly looked a sight.

He started weeping again, and presently said to me: So I'm come to that? Now I call God and you to witness this: I repent.

What's the use of repenting now? said I. I took him back to his house and stripped my clothes from him, and left him wrapped in his cotton as I had found him. I took my clothes home to be washed and gave him up for good.

For three years after that I heard nothing of him. Then one day, at Arch Gate, I noticed a slave clearing the way for some rider; and looking to see who it was, I recognized my old friend.

He was on a decent horse with a light silver-mounted saddle, well dressed and fragrant with scent. In the old days, of course, being of a Clerkly family, he had been used to ride superb thoroughbreds, and to sport the gorgeous harness and magnificent clothes that went with a family fortune like his. He saw me.

You fellow there! he called out.

I knew he must have come up in the world. Why, my lord Abu So-and-so! I cried, kissing his thigh.

Yes, said he.

What is all this? I asked.

God had Mercy, praise His Name! he said. But come along home! Home!

I followed him to his door. It was the old house, but put in repair. The place had been made into a single garden-court, and the buildings stuccoed, but not painted. Only one of the grand saloons was left; all the others had been cleared away and made part of the court. It made a good house, though it was not the lordly mansion of the old days.

He took me into the cabinet to which he had been used to retire for privacy in former times: it was restored to something of its former richness, and had some handsome furniture, though not quite like what I remembered. The establishment seemed to consist of four slaves; there was one old fellow I remembered, acting as porter, and a hired groom. My old acquaintance sat down, and the slaves served a meal: the plate clean but not very sumptuous, fair fruit and not too much of it, food presentable but not more than enough. We ate. Then I was served with some excellent date-wine, and he with date-jelly, the curtain was drawn, and we listened to some pleasant singing, with a censer of fresh aloes and ambergris mixture burning. I felt very curious to know how all this had come about.

Fellow, said he presently, do you remember old times?

I do, said I.

I am comfortably off nowadays, he continued; and I have gained something I think more valuable than all the wealth I ever owned — some knowledge of the world. Do you notice this furniture? It is not so grand as the old was; but middle-class people would call it luxury. The same for my plate. The same for my clothes. And he went over everything, saying after each item: It's not what the old was — the best — but it does.

Yes, he ended, all this does well enough instead. And that dreadful sense of strain is over. Do you remember that damned girl, and what she did to me? he resumed. And do you remember how you treated me yourself that day? Do you remember the kind of thing you used to suggest to me, day in, day out? And the day of the glass?

But that's all past now, said I, praise God, Who restored your losses. But tell me, how did you come by this fortune? Where did you get this girl who's singing for us now?

I gave a thousand dinars for her, he answered. That's the way I save singing-women's fees. I have everything well under control nowadays.

How did it come about?

On one and the same day an old servant of my father's and a cousin in Egypt died. Forty thousand dinars of legacy came to me when I was lying in cotton the way you saw me. And a sense of God's goodness came over me, and I made a resolution, never to waste money again, but to live within my means until I die. I spent a thousand dinars on repairs to this house. I spent seven thousand on the furniture and plate and clothing and stable and slaves that you see. I invested two thousand in trade. I buried ten thousand underground for emergencies; and for twenty thousand I bought an estate of land which gives me enough income to run this establishment without having to borrow before harvest.

That's how things go with me; and for a whole year I have been looking for you. I wanted you just once to see me prosperous, and with every likelihood of staying prosperous; and after that, you dirty rat, never to speak to you again. Slaves there! drag this fellow out by the foot!

And they *did* drag me out by the foot, right out of the house. I hadn't even time to finish my drink.

From that day on, if I met him riding in the street and he saw me, he would simply smile. But he would never have anything more to do with me or with any of his old friends.

THE SWORD AND THE PEN

PRINCES AND CLERKS

I was once standing in the presence of the Buwayhid Prince Mu'izz al-Dawla, when he said to his Vizier Saymari: I want half a million dinars — right now — it's a business that won't wait.

Surely you need more than that, Prince, answered Saymari; I need half a million myself.

You're my Vizier, aren't you? cried Mu'izz al-Dawla. Where else am I to get it?

But if, said Saymari, your revenue shows no such balance, where am I to get it?

The Prince flared up. By God! he roared, I'll have you locked in the privy till you produce it.

Lock me there! retorted Saymari. Do you imagine that even squatting there I shall produce ingots to that value?

The Buwayhid burst out laughing. All right, I let you off, he said.

To keep my life I killed, reaped money with a sword
For pleasure's sake.
I hate to think what comes — for ever with the Lord,
Or left to bake!

 BAGHDAD GANGSTER, who had successfully defied the Government, began to operate openly these days. His name was Ibn Hamdi. The Secretary to the Prince of Princes bestowed a Dress of Honor on him, put him on the stipendiary roll, and came to an arrangement with him, whereby Ibn Hamdi contracted to pay fifteen thousand dinars monthly out of the proceeds of robberies to be perpetrated by himself and his gang. The Secretary got him to sign the contract, and insisted on the terms being kept. Ibn Hamdi used to obtain the Collector's receipts for the payments he made regularly as they fell due.

One Friday, the deposed and blinded Qahir got out of the Tahirid Palace where he was kept, and began begging alms in the Congregational Mosque of the Old City of Mansur. There he was seen by a member of the Hashimite family, standing among the ranks of the congregation, saying: Spare me something — I am a man you used to know.

The Hashimite gentleman told him to stop it, gave him five hundred dirhams, and took him home.

In the year 332 the Caliph Muttaqi also had his eyes seared with a hot iron. When Qahir heard of it, he said: That makes two of us; all we want is a third.

And so it turned out, for the next Caliph, Mustakfi, was blinded too.

THE FALL OF BAGHDAD

News arrived that the Daylamite Prince Ahmad ibn Bu-wayh was marching on the capital. The Turkish and Daylamite troops in alarm moved their tents out to the Oratory. It was not long before the Buwayhid was reported at Bajisra; both the Prince of Princes Ibn Shirzad and the Caliph Mustakfi went into hiding, and the Turkish troops retreated to Mosul.

On a Saturday in January of the year 335 Prince Ahmad ibn Buwayh encamped at the Shammasia Gate of Baghdad; and soon Mustakfi emerged, to grant him an audience. At the meeting, the Buwayhid remained respectfully standing a long time, protesting his loyalty and letting himself be bound by solemn oaths. The Prince then put on the robes of office as Prince of Princes and was addressed by his honorific. He received the title Mu'izz al-Dawla (Strengthener of the Empire), his brother Ali was created Imad al-Dawla (Pillar of the Empire), and his brother Hasan created Rukn al-Dawla (Column of the Empire). Orders were given for the striking of their titles and honorifics on both dinars and dirhams.

The new Prince of Princes rode in his Robes to the old Palace of Munis; and his soldiery, Daylamites, Jilites, and Turks, proceeded to billet themselves on the citizens. It was a bitter annoyance; but it became regular practice, to which they have had to submit up to this day, fifty years later.

Twelve days after his investiture, the Prince Mu'izz al-Dawla decided that Mustakfi must be deposed. He went downstream to the Palace.

The Caliph was seated on his throne, with everybody standing according to his rank before him, when Mu'izz al-Dawla was announced. When he came in, the Buwayhid kissed the ground according to etiquette. Then, kissing Mustakfi's hand, he stood before him a little while in conversation before seating himself on a chair and giving permission for the introduction of an envoy from Khurasan, and another from Baridi.

This was the signal. Two Daylamites came forward,

stretching out their hands towards Mustakfi, and talking loudly
in Persian. The Caliph, supposing that they wanted to kiss his
hand, extended it to them; but they gave a tug and brought him
over, off his throne on to the ground. Then they threw a loop of
his turban-cloth round his neck and began to drag him towards
the door. Mu'izz al-Dawla rose from his chair at the same moment. It was a scene of confusion and outcry. Everyone scram-
bled for the door opening on the portico, and there was a fierce
crush. Many people started looting at once.

The Caliph was dragged along on foot to Mu'izz al-Dawla's
palace; and the Caliphal Palace was looted till there was not a
thing left.

Thus ended the days of Mustakfi's Caliphate. The Prince
sent for a son of Muqtadir's, and he became Caliph, taking the
title of Muti Lillah (The Obedient to God).

FAMINE

It was not long before war broke out between Mu'izz al-
Dawla and the Hamdanid Princes who ruled the northwestern
provinces. Prices at Baghdad rose so high that people had literally no bread at all; they ate dead bodies and grass — any creature, whatever it died of, even carrion. Knots of people could be
seen collected round a horse dropping dung, searching the dung
for barleycorns to pick out and eat. Cottonseed, moistened and
spread on a griddle, would be parched over the fire and eaten;
but this produced intestinal tumors of which most of the eaters
died. Those not yet dead had death written in their faces. Men,
women, children stood dying in the roads, begging with cries of:
I'm hungry! I'm hungry! till they fell and perished. If any man
got his hands on a scrap of bread, he hid it under his clothes,
otherwise it would soon be snatched from him. Burials fell behind the deaths, and the dogs devoured corpses.

The poor migrated in vast numbers; and endless processions lined the roads as far as Basra, where they hoped to find

dates to eat. But most of them fell by the way and died; and those who arrived died soon after.

A Hashimite lady was caught having kidnapped a child and baked him in an oven. The boy's body was partly eaten; and she was caught in the act of devouring the remainder. Her punishment was death. Houses and estates were sold for loaves, a bit of the loaf being assigned to the broker as commission.

Then a second woman was caught killing and eating children; and soon the deed became common, though many women were executed for it.

At last, however, the war was over, new crops began to come in, and prices fell.

ADMINISTRATIVE COLLAPSE

In this same year there was a fierce mutiny: the Daylamites assailed Mu'izz al-Dawla with violent abuse and threats. He was obliged to promise their arrears of pay by a stated date, and this promise obliged him to extort money from ordinary citizens by oppressive means.

It also drove him to wholly improper sources of supply. He assigned as fiefs to his officers, attendants, and Turkish Guardsmen the Sovereign's Estates, the estates of people in hiding, and Treasury liens on the estates of other civilians, with the result that the larger part of Agricultural Iraq was locked (a technical term meaning immune from Land Tax), and became inaccessible to revenue officers. Only a little land remained liable to taxation and was farmed for revenue, so that most of the Bureaus were left with practically nothing to do.

When administration is based on unsound principles, the fact, though it may be concealed for a while, will always manifest itself in course of time. The Government is like a man diverging from the highroad; at first his divergence is so slight that it goes unnoticed. But let him hold on, and he is lost: the farther he goes, the farther astray he is, and he realizes his error when it is too late to repair it.

Precisely such an error was Mu'izz al-Dawla's assigning most of the Agricultural Iraq districts in fief when they were out of cultivation (as a result of disturbances) and run down, so that the values were abnormally low. Further, the officials were lax with the assignees and took bribes, either directly or covertly; so that the fiefs were from the first assigned at inconsistent rates. As the years passed, and land began to be cultivated again, in some cases (where the basis was a quota of produce) the dues rose owing to increased yield. In other cases (where the basis was acreage, and the dues determined by current prices) dues were reduced, for when these lands were assigned to the soldiers prices had been abnormally high on account of the famine.

Those who profited by the change kept the fiefs they had got, of course; and the form of assessment made it impossible to exact the proper payment. Those who lost by the change turned their fiefs in, and got new ones to the value of their claims and losses. And the evil took a more malignant form: it became common practice for the soldiers to ruin their fiefs and take new ones of their own choosing in exchange. The turned-in fiefs were reassigned to persons whose only concern was to take off the land everything that was on it and render account of a mere fraction of their takings; they did not interest themselves in the slightest in cultivation. Then, taking a group of similar ruined fiefs which had been lumped together, they would have these reassigned to themselves on the basis of their current value, that value being now reduced to the lowest imaginable figure.

As years went by, the original deeds rotted away, the old assessments were forgotten, the irrigation canals went to ruin, the sluices got out of order, and the poor peasants were reduced to extreme misery. Some of them left their lands and went off to other countries, others patiently endured what could not be cured, and others were glad enough to make over all their old rights in the lands they worked to the assignees if by so doing they could obtain security against personal violence.

Agriculture slowed to a standstill. The Government offices were closed. The skills of the Finance Clerk and the revenue-farmer disappeared as those who had possessed them died and a generation which knew nothing of either rose. All that the modern assignees did was to commit their domains to the supervision of slaves and bailiffs, who kept no accounts and did not trouble themselves to improve the land or the methods of working it. They merely embezzled their masters' property in various indirect ways. Their lords recouped themselves by fining their agents and by brutal dealing with anyone they had business with.

The Irrigation officers departed; for the lands no longer belonged to the Sovereign, and there was nothing left to do beyond drawing up paper estimates for irrigation requirements and apportioning the sums among assignees who never paid their shares. Even if anyone paid, the money was embezzled instead of being expended on the objects for which it was levied. Drink the clear and leave the muddy, says the proverb; and on this principle the Inspectors shut their eyes to catastrophe and preferred to apply for Government pensions as they turned in the fiefs which had gone to ruin under their inspection.

In each district the administration fell into the hands of some powerful Daylamite favorite, who made it his seat and domain, and who as Governor was surrounded by crooked officials pursuing no policy beyond procrastination and keeping things going from one year to the next. What lands still remained outside the fiefs were assigned for revenue-farming purposes to two classes of men: the first consisting of military Princes and other officers, the second of members of the Clerkly and business classes. Withholding money, lodging appeals, and demanding abatements were the prime aims of these soldiers. Any insistence on payment of taxes due made enemies of them; they liked fighting, and had ample means for it. The disintegration of the Empire was due to them, for they furnished the personnel of rebellion. Lenient treatment only made their greed the fiercer.

The civilian Governors, on the other hand, milked the Government with greater finesse. They operated in combines,

and used financial inducements as a means of fortifying extra-
legal power and privilege. During the course of time these
local rulers became virtually independent in their provinces, and
subject to no interference in their dealings with mankind. The
weaker of their subjects could be fined, have their taxes raised or
their rights and pensions reduced at pleasure, for their rank and
means allowed it; the taxes of others, who had the power to defend themselves, might be abated, though for this service the
local dignitary generally got money on the quiet. People of the
more influential class might be useful to him in an emergency,
should he fall under Government scrutiny; but there was no
point in being soft with people who did not count.

It ceased to be customary to send in any form of balance
sheet to the Bureaus, or to issue any form of instruction to
provincial finance officers, or to pay any attention to complaints
or suggestions made by any Clerk. At the Revenue Audit, the
accountants confined themselves to mentioning the original terms
of the farming contract, the amount realized, and the amount in
arrears. There was no inquiry into the treatment of the population; the old regulations against letting land go out of cultivation
or measures for restoring waste lands were not mentioned; no
notice was taken of increased assessments for which there was no
warrant in the register, of improper collections or iniquitous
fines, or of the appearance in the expenditure column of sums
which had not in reality been spent. Should a Clerk dare to raise
any such question, he would, if he were a man of importance, be
guaranteed, degraded, fleeced, and killed — sold cheap by the
Sovereign. If he were poor and needy, he would be pacified
with a trifling sum and so go over to the enemy. You cannot
blame him. The Sovereign neither protected his life nor encouraged his zeal.

That, in brief, is the history of the revenue. On the other
side, expenditure went up and up. In the matter of liberality to
his retainers Mu'izz al-Dawla did whatever came into his head,
lavishing fiefs and increases of pay. His expenses continually
went up, and his revenues went steadily down; he allowed the

deficit to accumulate at an appalling rate. After the lapse of some years therefore the pay of the Daylamite troops had to be stopped. They cast a jealous eye on the luckier Turkish Guards, so that he had perforce to bind the Turks more closely to himself with higher and higher promotions, in the hope of counting on their aid against Daylamite disaffection. But the demoralization was not confined to one party; for the Turks were as frantic with greed as the Daylamites were with poverty.

Mu'izz al-Dawla made Muhallabi his Secretary or Vizier. The reason he chose him in preference to the more highly trained Clerks who were then still available in the capital was that he saw in Muhallabi all that was essential to the ruling of men, which was more than he saw in others who possessed more specialized skill in Clerkly work. Muhallabi spoke well and inspired respect, he had ideas about ways of raising money, he had some notion of the manner in which the ancient Vizierate had been conducted. And he was besides liberal and courageous, a man of letters, and a master of Persian.

The new Vizier reintroduced forms of professional etiquette which had become obsolete among Clerks, he brought waste lands back into cultivation and re-established sound methods of raising revenue.

In Basra, for instance, the oppression of the Baridis and their agents had reduced the area of land actually cultivated year after year; and each year the Baridis raised the amount due on every acre. Another of their characteristic malpractices was to begin getting in the Land Tax in March, which ruined the farmers and drove them to abandoning their farms. They also started to exact poll tax again, which ruined the members of the tolerated cults. They made a practice of rousing the feelings of the poor against the rich; yet they put a tax of seventy dirhams the *kurr* on wheat, as well as taxing all goods sold by measure, including oil! Basra people in consequence had begun to get out; but this only added to the burden on those who stayed.

Muhallabi went down to Basra. He arranged for a return to the ancient plan whereby the tithe was taken in kind, without any official figure based on either acreage or current prices being fixed. Then, roughly calculating the difference between what they would have to pay on this system and what they were currently paying, he recommended the taxpayers to purchase the difference between fair treatment and oppression by a down payment which would look good to Mu'izz al-Dawla. The Prince would be consoled for the reduced estimate by getting some ready money; also, he was not inaccessible to ideas of the fructifying effects of justice. He would think of the popularity the measure must inspire, and would consider the prospect of ultimately getting more money than before.

To this the taxpayers consented. The down payment was agreed upon — two million, two hundred thousand dirhams; and a contract was drawn up. After consideration, Muhallabi reduced the figure by two hundred thousand dirhams, the poorer taxpayers to be the exclusive beneficiaries by the reduction. He wrote to Mu'izz al-Dawla; the Prince approved the measure; and at a general meeting of the Basra citizenry the contract was sealed. People now began to put land into cultivation. The revenue went up. The old multiplied harbor-dues of the port of Basra were abolished, whereupon the actual amount from the simplified dues on ships went up till it reached an average annual yield of two million dirhams.

The case of Basra is merely one example of the good which Muhallabi did.

THE PROPHET'S SUNKEN DESCENDANTS

There had been a gang fight in Baghdad which led to serious rioting: the occasion which touched it off was a drunken brawl between an Abbasid and an Alid, in which the Alid was killed. His people cried for vengeance; in the ensuing tumult the mob took sides, and things became so serious that even the posting of Daylamite Guards in the various quarters did not allay the disturbance.

Thereupon, the Vizier Muhallabi arrested most of the Alids and Abbasids: notables, decent citizens, gangsters, criminals — all descendants of the Prophetic House. There were a number of Hashimite Judges, members of the Witness class, and holy men among the rest.

On a certain day Muhallabi held a sitting to examine them. He ordered a list made of all those members of the family known to be gangsters, all those of military age, all those who carried daggers. These persons, he announced, would be kept under arrest; the others were to be set at liberty.

One of the Hashimite Judges present ventured to deprecate this proceeding. He spoke in a very moderate tone, with a view to mollifying the Vizier, whom he addressed with great respect, when one of the Alids, Muhammad ibn Hasan, broke impatiently in, using coarse and violent language.

Muhallabi rounded on him: What, stupid as ever, you filth? for all those white threads on your head? As though I did not know what you have been and what you are, you fool and son of a fool. You are guilty of contempt for the Vizier's court, though you never let an opportunity slip of putting in: As the Vizier said to me ... and: As I was saying to the Vizier.... You seem to think Muqtadir is still on the throne, and that I am a Vizier of his. You do not seem to realize that it is Prince Mu'izz al-Dawla who sits on the throne today, a man who would regard your blood as a savory offering to God, a man who respects you as he would respect a dog. Slaves there! take him by the leg!

And before us all Muhammad was dragged out by the leg. The tall hat he had been wearing was left lying on the floor.

Muhallabi ordered him put in a covered boat and transported to Oman; and he was actually being put aboard a vessel bound downstream, with people crowding to kiss his hand, when the Caliph Muti sent to supplicate the Vizier in his favor. After some interchange of messages Muhallabi pardoned the man, but confined him to his house and took a bond from his family. He then put a selection of young Hashimites and other participants in the recent fray, with various convicts and troublemakers, in covered boats, under hatches nailed down, and sent them to prisons in the Ahwaz district, where they remained. Many died; and it was not till some years after Muhallabi's death that the few who still survived were set at liberty.

This measure effectually settled the tumult.

He was one of the very last of the munificent. I myself (says Judge Tanukhi) witnessed a scene which might have been a performance of the Barmecides. His Clerk of the Bureau for Agricultural Iraq had fallen from an open upper room in Muhallabi's palace overlooking the Tigris, and died of the effects eight days later. The Vizier was deeply grieved, and on the day after the funeral he payed a visit to the family. I went with him.

He spoke in the most beautiful way, comforting them and reassuring them. In him who is now gone to the Mercy of God you have lost the personality of Abu Husayn, he said, but you still have a father in me. And turning to the eldest son, he went on: I appoint you to your father's post. And I have an appointment also for your brother (at that time a lad of ten or so), with a stipend of (he named some generous amount, I have forgotten how much). I hope that he and my own boy will be friends: their ages are the same; they can finish their studies and grow up together, and your brother must always have a claim on my son.

Then, speaking to the Deputy Vizier, who had come with him, he said: Write the deed of appointment. And send for the people from whom the late Abu Husayn held leases, and tell them they are to renew them; for he had put most of his fortune into rights of entry, leases, and farms, which are all cancelled by his death. If there is any demur, offer higher rents, at my expense; insist on renewal, whatever the terms must be.

He then turned to the dead man's brother-in-law. Our friend, he said, had many dependents. I know how generous he was to his sisters and their children, and to other relatives, to whom his death would mean destitution. Pray go to the daughter of Abu Muhammad Madharai (the widow) and offer her my sympathy, and get from her a list of the ladies to whom the late Abu Husayn made allowances, and of the members of his household who are in reduced circumstances. When you have the list, he added to his Deputy, let them have a month's allowance at once, and give orders for the money to be paid regularly.

There was not a dry eye in the room. I saw even the Alid propagandist Muhammad ibn Hasan, who happened to be there at the same time, sitting with his eyes streaming tears, and loud in praise. He was a man never very eloquent except in his own behalf, and he disliked Muhallabi; but this noble behavior was too much for him, and the bad terms they were on did not prevent him acknowledging the truth.

I myself said: If death could ever be welcome, it must be so to a man cumbered with many responsibilities in these days of our lord the Vizier. What we have seen this day lets us think that the tales of proverbial generosity in the days of old may well be true.

At Muhallabi's once (says Chief Justice Ibn Ma'ruf) we were discussing luck and ill-luck; and Muhallabi said this:

Luck is never anything other than a combination of energy with humility, and ill-luck never anything other than a combination of laziness with egoism.

FEUDALISM INCREASING

As a result of various things Mu'izz al-Dawla did, his Turkish retainers began to mix threats with their demands for money. They seized estates by force, and pestered the ministers. The Prince gave an order that their pay was to be made a charge on the Wasit, Basra, and Ahwaz districts, and sent to those places representatives of the various ranks, to obtain from the finance offices there the full amount of the pay due to themselves and to those who remained on duty. It was arranged that every man so sent should have a daily allowance of ten dirhams, or twenty if a sergeant, until all the arrears due them had been collected. This allowance was meant to be temporary, not permanent. But the Prince had let loose mischief which cost him far more than paying from his own pocket would have done.

For the men were only too glad to let payment of the arrears be delayed, so long as they could stay on where they were and use their allowances as trading capital. And the civil officials were only too glad to go on paying these allowances rather than have the trouble of finding the whole amount due. Many of the retainers stayed on trading like this for two or three years, and acquired a taste for business, especially since they enjoyed exemption from post and excise duties on their goods.

Their next step was to offer what they called Protection (against tax collections) to small cultivators. In this way they got a hold on the land. The Finance officers who tried to collect taxes from the land they treated with contempt. They were willing to extend their Protection to businessmen or anyone else who applied to them. So the Government officials lost their hold; and the retainers made the population their serfs.

It was a process which has not only continued but grown worse, up to the time of this writing (about 1000 A.D.).

The transmission of revenue from Wasit, Ahwaz and Basra stopped altogether in the year 348. The Finance officials held a meeting and tore up the originals of the revenue-contracts. They wrote demanding redress of their grievances; but the disease was beyond cure now.

*   *   *

News came that the Byzantines had invaded the Muslim lands, burning, killing, and taking captive. People from upriver came down to Baghdad calling all True Believers to arms. They cried in Mosque and street; and a crowd fell in with them. All together marched to the Caliphal Palace and tried to break in through the windows, the doors having been closed to keep them out. They forced their way in, and reached the Presence. The Caliph, they shouted insolently, was unfit for the duties God had enjoined upon Imams of the Muslims.

The Buwayhid Prince was in Kufa at the time, ostensibly on pilgrimage to the Tomb of Ali, but really on a hunting trip. When he heard the news, he demanded money from the Caliph, to be expended on Holy War, which, he said, was the Sovereign's responsibility.

Holy War, the Caliph's reply ran, *would be my responsibility if I were managing things, and if I had money and soldiers at my command. But as things are, when all I have is a pittance insufficient for my personal needs, and it is you and the provincial rulers who manage everything, neither Holy War nor Pilgrimage nor any other of the Sovereign's responsibilities is any concern of mine. All you can claim of me is the title which is pronounced in the official sermon from your pulpits, as a help in keeping your subjects in order. If you wish me to renounce that last distinction, I shall be delighted to do so, and to leave everything to you.*

REVIVAL IN THE OUTLANDS

A GREAT PROVINCIAL ADMINISTRATOR

IMAD AL-DAWLA DIED; and his brother Rukn al-Dawla hurried to Fars to settle affairs. But his first action when he reached Shiraz was to visit his brother's grave by the Istakhr Gate, walking barefoot and bareheaded. For three days he stayed at the graveside, mourning continuously, till a deputation of notables appealed to him to come back into the city. He sent a share of the old Prince's personal estate to their brother Mu'izz al-Dawla: it consisted of one hundred and seventy retainers and a hundred loads of armor, with the uniforms and arms appertaining.

Then that great master Clerk Ibn Amid, Rukn al-Dawla's Vizier, came to Fars to teach his lord's son Fannakhusraw the art of being a king. The young man's title was Adud al-Dawla.

Our master, Adud al-Dawla often said, was Abu Fadl ibn Amid.

He was the only person I ever knew (says his Secretary) whose presence went beyond report of him. For one thing, he was the greatest Clerk of his age. No one else possessed so many professional accomplishments: command of Arabic with all its rare expressions, knowledge of Grammar and Prosody, felicity in wording and imagery, and the retention in memory of whole collections of poetry, both pre-Islamic and Islamic. During the time I was associated with him (and for seven years I was in attendance day and night), I may say that I never heard a poem recited to him but he knew its author's collected works by heart. I have heard him recite whole collections of odes by obscure poets, authors whom it astonished me that he should take the trouble of committing to memory.

I once asked him about it: Master, how can you waste your time memorizing the verse of such a writer?

You seem to imagine, he replied, that it costs me trouble. But I only need to hear it once to have it impressed on my memory.

He was speaking the truth. For occasionally I would recite to him a poem of my own, thirty or forty verses; and he used, as a sign of his approval, to repeat them to me. Sometimes he would ask for them afterwards, and request me to recite; but I could never get out three successive lines without his prompting. On several occasions he told me that in his youth he used to bet his fellow students that he would memorize a thousand lines a day. As he was far too serious and dignified a man ever to exaggerate, I asked him how he managed it.

I made it a condition that the lines must be written out, he answered. I would memorize twenty or thirty lines at a time and so be done with them.

What do you mean by being done with them? I inquired.

I never needed to go over them again, he answered: I would go over each batch once or twice and then put that page down and take up another.

As for his own compositions, his published collections of despatches give an idea of them. Every specialist in despatch-writing knows the admirable quality of his work. The same for his verse, both light and serious. In Koranic exegesis, knowledge of cruces and ambiguities, and acquaintance with the variant views current in the capital schools, he was a first-rate scholar. And as for Logic and Philosophy in its various branches, above all in Metaphysics, none of his contemporaries ventured to represent himself as a specialist in these fields before Ibn Amid unless he came to learn. I remember seeing Amiri at his court, on his way home to Khurasan, a man who, having grown old in Aristotelian commentary, deemed himself a competent philosopher. When this man came to realize the Great Master's attainments, his breadth and acumen, he humbled himself to being a student again, and read many difficult treatises with him.

The Great Master was by no means loquacious, and rarely talked unless questioned, and by someone capable of appreciating his response. Then indeed he came to life, and things would be heard from him such as none else could yield: eloquence, distinction of phrasing, subtlety of sentiment, and all fluent and easy. He was so well-bred, so kindly and simple, that when any specialist appeared he always listened quietly and appreciatively, as if he knew only enough of the subject to enable him to understand what was being said. It was only after long association, months or even years, if some such person made an inquiry, or

the Master was desired to amplify some theme which had been
brought up, that his tide would swell and his genius begin to
luxuriate, confounding the self-supposed specialist.

Such was his eminence in regular sciences. But when he
turned from these to Mechanics and Mathematics, he was unap-
proached. He was sole master of the secrets of certain obscurer
sciences such as Mechanics, which require the most abstruse
knowledge of geometry and physics, and the science of abnormal
motions, the traction of immense weights, calculation of centers
of gravity and so forth, enabling the performance of operations
beyond the power of antiquity: marvellous siege-engines, wonderful weapons such as projectiles which would produce extraordinary effects at an immense distance, and long-range burning-
mirrors.

His own manual dexterity and artistic talent were unheard-
of. I have seen him, in the room where he used to receive his
intimate friends, take up an apple or something of the sort, and
after amusing himself with it for a while send it spinning away,
with a face on it, carved with his fingernail more delicately than
any other man could have done it with all the proper tools, and
days to do it in.

On the battlefield, or on campaign, he was a lion for
courage. He was steadfast, resourceful, and skilled in the seizing of opportunities, prudent in command, and in strategy astute.
Many a time did he tell the story of the fight at Khan Lanjan,
God have Mercy on him! The Daylamite chieftain Ibn Makan
was in pursuit of his master Rukn al-Dawla's son and womenfolk, and had already caught up with his baggage and captured
his stores when the Great Master fell in with him.

At the first encounter, he used to say, my fellows took
to their heels; and Ibn Makan's men fell to plundering our
baggage. I myself stood where I was, but only out of pride. I
hadn't any hope of winning now, but simply stood my ground
like a man resigned to death or captivity. For as my situation
flashed over my mind, I said to myself: Supposing I did get away

with my life, and come before my lord again, what sort of face should I show him? Or what sort of tongue would it be, that could elaborate excuses to his face when I had deserted his nearest and dearest ones, his very hope of dynasty? To my way of thinking, death where I was would be pleasanter then the situation I imagined. So I made up my mind to die game.

I happened to be standing behind a rolled-up tent, one of my big double-poled ones. I could see them already cutting the ropes of it and snatching for the goods inside. If anyone noticed me, he never dreamed that I had any intention of resistance, in such a position and in such a plight.

But as I stood there, Ibn Makan's men being far too busy with the loot to attend to me, my retainer Ruwayn returned to me, then some others, and then a handful of my Arabs. I gave the order for a counterattack; my men raised a yell of Charge! and we proceeded to slaughter and take captives. Hardly a man got away; and an hour after sunset there was not an eye that winked in all Ibn Makan's force, except for our prisoners.

Of the Great Master's capacity as an administrator, his well-known Letter to Ibn Hindu gives some notion, with its detailed account of the disorder in which he found Fars, of the mismanagement of his predecessors, and of the measures necessary to be taken. From that Epistle a man may learn the whole duty of a Vizier. Only one thing stood in the way of his inaugurating the reign of Justice in the dominions he administered: that was the fact that his master Rukn al-Dawla, superior as he was to the other Daylamite chieftains of his time, still had the mentality of a freebooter, always in a hurry to get at the loot.

Rukn al-Dawla never saw reason to calculate the long-term effects of his actions, or to take precaution for the future of his subjects. In order to please his warriors, he would let them do what no one else could prevent them doing. Indeed, he had no choice, not being of old royal blood, and not having any monarchic authority among the Daylamites. He was only their chieftain by virtue of his freehandedness; and once an army gets used to this treatment, there is no weaning it.

Like Imad al-Dawla his elder, Rukn al-Dawla had lavished fiefs upon them, and donatives so liberal as to leave no hold for demand; but this notwithstanding, they were arrogant and greedy, wanting more than there was to be had. The utmost any Vizier could do was to find some provision for the Prince's expense from day to day by fining the humble or borrowing from the great. The ministers never got a chance, so constant were the importunities of Turk or Daylamite soldiers, to think out ways and means systematically. In order to dodge petitioners, they used to appoint secret rendezvous by night, sometimes riding out into the countryside, where they would hold council on horseback, with their legs crossed over their horses' necks, while they tried to devise some means of finding enough money for the following day. Any promising scheme, even of this limited scope, made a red-letter day of the occasion; it was regarded as a professional master stroke, and threw them all into transports.

But when that Great Master Ibn Amid accepted office as Vizier to Rukn al-Dawla, there was such a reformation that we have seen him ride back from the Sultan's Palace to his office and find no one but his head Clerks waiting for him. Or he would have an audience, and there would be nothing to discuss beyond such unforeseen petty emergencies as no prince nor minister can ever avoid. Such order and system did Ibn Amid introduce into the public service that he was able to devote most of his day to learning and the learned. And such was the respect he won himself from soldiers and civilians alike, that he had only to glance at a man in disapproval for the man's flanks to quiver, his limbs tremble, and his joints relax, as I have myself seen many a time.

Ah, if only his master had not been so unwilling to husband his realm! Rukn al-Dawla was never disturbed by a complaint that some caravan had been waylaid, or some flock lifted.

Well, he used to say, even Kurds have to live!

If that was the Prince's theory of retributive justice, if such were his views of agricultural economy, what could his minister do?

But when Ibn Amid went to Fars to teach his master's son Adud al-Dawla Fannakhusraw sound methods of administration, and the way to keep a kingdom, and the whole art of kingcraft, that craft of crafts, he found in Adud al-Dawla an apt pupil. That Prince never spoke of him but as the Great Master, or The Master. To him he used to attribute the success of all his policies and schemes, the preservation of his dominions, the keeping of his frontiers and suppression of his foes, his care for cultivation and his severity with disturbers of the peace, and his whole success in bringing the Empire back to something of what it had been in time past.

Some reader of these words, who did not actually see what Ibn Amid did in the course of his career, may imagine that I have been exaggerating. I swear by Him Who commanded us to speak truth, Who forbade us to utter a word otherwise, *I have exaggerated nothing.*

On the night of the second Thursday of December in the year 360, the Great Master died, at Hamadan; and with him eminence, in the fullest sense of that word, disappeared, for qualities which had been united in no other man in all Islam then passed away.

* * *

Night, and horse
Should know me again,
And weapon, and waste,
And paper and pen.

* * *

Wayfaring talk, as we rode from Tidingfall to the town,
Made me remember the times of youth, and the freshness of
*   things;*
And I said: After fifty years, thought-worn, and weak as a
*   nestling,*
I remember Venge, and Godfleet, youth, and the freshness of
*   things,*
Driving our camels to pasture over the hill, down the dale,
And how I made fire for the others, and rubbed the kindling-
*   sticks.*

*   *   *

A voice at the Broken Grounds said: Under my shadowy boughs
Many met loves have found rich place; the light of my storms
Has flashed with the flashing of laughter. Today my thunder-
*   fire*
Glares on the glaring stones only.
*   I looked and saw*
Those quarter-lands, wherethrough the four winds sweep at
*   night,*
And cried: Did any wind from them tell where they halted?
Ay, said the voice, they lighted to rest in the Mothersands;
And white gleam there the tents which cover tomorrow's suns.

DESPAIR

I keep aloof, having sufficient reason
In self-hate bitterer than my hate for you.
You say: Be comforted — life's a mere sleep,
And when it's done, what haunts the night is gone.
If life were quiet sleep, life would be sweet.
But life's a ghastly sleep, dreadful the dreams!

I once saw Time: churlish, a hairy face
Between cropped ears, the forehead of an ape,
A shrivelled nose, a beard which he averted
Insolently. And I remembered all
The noble, the magnificent who passed
And vanished. Time that I were gone! I said.

IT SO HAPPENED THAT IN THE YEAR 'SIXTY-ONE
(971 A. D.), after an absence of years, I revisited certain salons in
Baghdad. They were empty of those who had once thronged
them, whose conversation had once filled these rooms with life
and brilliance. I met only a few survivors from the ranks of
those old gentlemen; and when we fell into talk, it was soon
apparent that stories I loved to remember were old-fashioned
now, and hardly ever recalled.

At the house of Judge Muhammad the Hashimite that
year we were talking about how vast Baghdad had been in Muqtadir's day, and what a huge population there used to be here.
I mentioned a book I had seen at Muhallabi's, a description of the
city of Baghdad written in Muqtadir's time: a list of the public
baths gave ten thousand, as I recalled; there were also estimates
of the city population, of the shipping, and of the transient mari-
time population, and figures for the amounts of barley, wheat,

and so forth which the city had to import. As an example of the scale of things in the old days, the ice-dealers used to pay the watermen thirty or forty thousand dirhams every day for ice delivery alone.

That seems an incredible sum nowadays, said the Judge. But he went on to say that he had been informed by more than one of the older generation in the city that the population of Baghdad in the year 'forty-five was, by exact computation of both buildings and persons, just one tenth of what it had been in Muqtadir's time (some thirty years before).

We were talking about how tight things are nowadays, and how restless people are, how mean they have become, though they call it Thinking for Security, or Being Practical, how unwilling to take a risk modern businessmen are, and how reluctant folk are to give assistance to anyone in distress.

We were accounting for the change by the fact that they have less money.

If some scholar came up to the capital in the old days, said Abu Hasan ibn Yusuf, people we knew would send him a thousand dirhams or so without his having to beg of anyone. Yet we didn't know very many people. But now — it's only a few days since a gentleman of a great family came to me, telling a tale of poverty I could hardly bear. All he needed for a fresh start was thirty or forty dirhams, he said. And I could not think of a single person I could approach with any confidence that he would grant that sum. And this very year, a friend recommended by Abu Hashim Jubbai himself came to stay with us. We applied to a number of people, and tried hard to get him some financial assistance, without any result whatsoever.

In the street where I live, he went on, Mahrawayhi Street, there used to be various ex-Governors and Clerks living, and landowners and businessmen; and I used to calculate that their fortunes together amounted to four million dinars. Today there is not one person in the street who is worth as much as four thousand dirhams, with the lone exception of Abu Urban.

* * *

I talked once with Abu Hasan the Clerk of Ahwaz, a man wise and good, generous, eminent in his profession. He had governed Ahwaz for Abu Abdallah Baridi, then for Mu'izz al-Dawla, and had governed Basra for Abu Qasim Baridi, then for Muhallabi. He was one who had milked all the breasts of time, who knew affairs and their vicissitudes from experience.

We were discoursing of life's ups and downs, and of the coldness of a man's friends when he is out of luck; and I quoted the remark said to have been made by Ibn Furat: God bless the people I don't know, the people who don't know me either. That other saying also: I made a list of all the disasters I ever had, and someone I had done a kindness to was at the bottom of every single one, without exception.

That is true enough of our times, said Abu Hasan. But it is only lately that it has come to be true. Friends in the old days used to be faithful friends. And one curious result of this deterioration in human nature, this fading of the ideal of friendship, is that people have taken to trusting everybody they don't know, and thinking of them as inoffensive, while at the same time they think of the people they do know, the ones they call their friends, as likely to do them harm!

The reason is that they expect of others what they would not do for others themselves. If someone does a kindness to a man, that man acquires a taste for receiving kindnesses; but at the same time a slight resentment grows up in him. If he is perpetually acknowledging such kindnesses, he becomes servile. On the other hand, if he tries to give as much as he gets, that is really a kind of open war, and trouble won't be far behind — if not actual malice, then imaginary suspicions and misunderstandings which can't be set right. If you are intimate, then the confidence is itself a risk; for any trouble can only come from the combination of ill-will with knowing about you. You have less to fear from people you don't know. Even the man who robs in the street is less of a risk: he is quite impersonal — he does not care whether it's your money or somebody else's. It's the robber who knows you who is the greatest danger even in that regard.

So my advice to a sensible man in modern times is this: the fewer people you know, the better for you — you have fewer enemies to fear. Ibn Alwa put it very neatly in those verses of his:

> *Know nobody: your friend*
> *Will be your enemy.*
> *At dinners you eat poison*
> *Of which you well may die!*

Human nature has become meaner, I once heard Hasan the Astrologer, Governor of Ahwaz, say, even in the style of its envy. In the old days, envy of wealth took the form of trying to get rich too; envy of education took the form of trying to educate oneself; envy of munificence took the form of liberality. But in these days, when men are poor creatures incapable of emulation, they prefer to depreciate excellence. If a man's rich, they try to make him poor. If a man's educated, they accuse him of being wrongheaded. If a man's munificent, they insist that his generosity is really good business, and the conclusive evidence of his meanness.

If any survivor from the elder generation tells a story of the old times in the hearing of our present-day rulers and leading men (particularly if it deal with munificence or good nature, high fortune, heroism, tolerance, luxury, or lofty morality), they simply don't believe it, or at least call it exaggerated, being themselves persons incapable of realizing the like.

The reason for all this is a corruption in this age, a degeneration from the age now passed away. Instincts are altered for the worse. The old ways are outworn.

No man aspires to great things any more. The masses are too absorbed in making a living to care for such things; and our big men are content if they can satisfy their brutal appetites. We have reached that stage foretold in the Tradition declaring that times will get worse and worse, and mankind into greater and greater straits, till the Day of Judgment breaks on the dregs of the race. As the poet Mutanabbi once quoted in my hearing:

They entered Time
Still at prime,
And were well pleased.
We find Time
Foully diseased.

The age we live in is such that if any of us marries a daughter to the tomb, he really gets the most satisfactory son-in-law possible.

THE PEOPLE

It is of the very nature of the mass of men to let the unlordly lord it over them, to honor the dishonorable and declare the wisdom of the unwise. A crowd follows whoever gets in front of it; it cannot tell competence from incompetence, or truth from falsehood.

If anyone cares to weigh this opinion, let him first observe a group of educated men: a select few show signs of judgment, of culture, of intelligence. Then afterwards let him observe the crowd — wherever it flocks, wherever it gathers: he will never see a crowd assembled but round some bear-warden or entertainer who can make monkeys dance by beating a drum. It will go wherever pleasure and frivolity draw it. It may get excited about some false mystic, some miracle-working charlatan; or it may listen to the romancer's lies; or it may press to see some poor wretch beaten or hung.

Threaten it, and it obeys; fear it, and its license is infinite. Evil leaves it unmoved by indignation; good leaves it unmoved by gratitude. It does not discriminate: it cannot tell a good man from a bad.

There is a Saying of God's Apostle which confirms this: *There are,* he said, *two sorts of men: those who know and those who would learn; the rest are no better than a herd of brutes, and God cares nothing for them.*

Yes, I know God, says the common man.

The select few, pleased with themselves merely because they feel a longing for an Other World, call that longing Vision, or Ardent Love, of God. Everyone has pretensions; but no one achieves the real thing. Religious novices nowadays neglect their ascetic exercises and spend their time daydreaming, which they call Contemplation! Even Sufism, which was once a reality without a name, is today a name without any reality.

Someone asked a dervish why he wore blue, the mourning color.

God's Apostle, said he, left three legacies behind him: poverty, knowledge, and the sword.

Men of power took the sword and put it to bad use.

Scholars took the knowledge; all they did with it was to make teaching a profession.

Dervishes took the poverty and made it into a way of getting an idle living.

I wear my blue in mourning for the fate of these three kinds of men.

Muslims are sinners; Christians are perverse;
Jews are confused; and Magians are worse.
We are all sorted into two great kinds:
Clever godless and stupid godly minds!

BELIEF: STRUGGLE OR ACCIDENT

Wake up, you fools, wake up! Your religions are only ancestral frauds! Religious doctrines are nothing but the means which men of power use to make other men their slaves. All religions are equally erroneous. They are myths, invented by the cunning of people now dead.

You may find a man a master of his own trade, apparently perfectly intelligent and rational, yet, when it comes to religion, stupidly obstinate. Religiousness is part of human nature; and men think of their religion as a safe refuge. What a growing child hears from his elders is something that stays with him all his life. Monks in their cloisters, devotees in the Mosques — all alike swallow their creeds as a romancer's tale is swallowed, without thought of whether it is so or not. If one of these monks or devoted Muslims had been born in a Magian family, he would have been a professed Magian.

PESSIMISM

No man who thinks can see, and not be sad,
Religion made the tool of human greed.
All men are bad; and I distinguish not
This sort or that sort: I condemn the lot.
Trust none. Yet you're the thing you most should fear;
So when you are alone, beware, beware.

When you have set yourself at lowest, be sure you have set yourself where you belong, and have joined branch to trunk again. You were made of dirt; you will go back to dirt.

ABU ALA OF MA'ARRA

When I passed through Ma'arra, Abu Ala was regarded as ruler of the town. Although he is very rich, and has many slaves and servants, and all the townsfolk submit to him as subjects, he having renounced the world wears garments of hair cloth, never goes outside his house, and eats nothing but half a *mann* of barley bread a day. His gate is never shut; but his officers and disciples who administer the town only consult him on matters of real importance. He never refuses any money offered him. He fasts all

day, keeps awake all night, and will have nothing to do with
what goes on in the world.

The Prophets are no better than the Preachers:
They pray and slay and die
And still the miseries of human creatures
Go on and multiply.

Paradise, Hell: the sweet, the lurid Light
Both feed on Darkness; so we flit from state
To state like marsh-fire through the one long Night.

The wailing funeral was not long gone
Before a wedding pomp followed upon.
The Wheel groaned. Both went on into the dark:
The sob, the shouting sounded soon as one.

I laugh and drink; but in the cup
Drop orbs of scorn and pain:
I too was such a glass — I broke,
And shan't be whole again.

The creeping worm who preached on Flesh has shown
How I was once her bed. Now dust; once stone.

How comes it, Lord, the potter said,
That such a thing as I,
Thy slave, can make a bowl with which
None quarrel, if I try?

Some verses, said Abu Ala, are attributed to Rawandi:
The sharing of earth's goods mankind between
Was done by One Who was both drunk and mean!
If that couplet stood erect, it would tower in sin above the Pyramids in height. What refuge should a wise man seek from misery? It is ordained.

I am supposed to be a learned man. But I have neither knowledge nor intelligence. I am also supposed to be religious. But if I were unmasked, those who have criticized me would not think mere abuse enough: they would want me poisoned.

Aloud I utter lies improbable.
I whisper truths, they're scarcely audible.

It's better to spare a flea than to give alms.

I am Occasion's child.

This day is Today; and there is no difference between this day and another. How can you call one day a yesterday, and another a tomorrow? Past and future are always present for a man who thinks always of God. God's true servant has neither yesterday nor tomorrow.

When the time of Prayer comes, I perform the due washing copiously, and go to the place where I purpose to pray, and sit there a while, until my limbs are rested.

Then I stand up. There before me I see the Holy House; under my feet I feel the Bridge of Dread; there on my right lies Paradise; and Hell on the left; and the Angel of Death stands at my back. And to my mind this Prayer is my last.

But whether God deigns to accept of my praying or not I never know, when the praying's done.

LONGING

O God Who art Lord of the Greater Light, Lord of the

Lofty Throne and Keeper of the Swollen Sea, Lord of the Shadow and the Burning Sun, Sender of the Book and Master of the Nether Angels, Lord of all Prophets and Apostles, O Thou Who wert the Living One before all other life and shalt be the Living One after all other life when lives shall be no more, O Lord Thou Giver of life to the dead Who dost decree death to all living creatures, O Thou Living God, Who hast none besides Thee!

If only death, O God, stand between me and the Imam, that death Thou hast decreed for all Thy servants, then deliver me from my grave, though I be arrayed in my shrouding only, yet with my sword drawn and my naked spear in my hand, ready to answer my Captain's call and execute his bidding in all things near and far.

Show me his blessed face, O God! Prepare his way for him, that his staff may guide me therein. Through him rebuild thy cities. Through him revive Thy servants as Thou hast promised; and Thy Promise is sure. Make him manifest unto us, O God, who stands with us for Thee, who is born of the daughter of Thy Prophet and bears Thine Apostle's name, so that he may put an end to all things vain and worthless in this world, and establish the true and real in the sight of such as merit that. Appoint him to be the refuge of Thy oppressed servants, and a helping friend to all who have now no friend but Thee, that he may hasten the accomplishment of all which has been neglected of those things Thy Word requires of us.

Guard him, O God, safe in Thine own Stronghold from the evil of his enemies; but yet have Mercy, Lord, upon us helpless; remove the grief and sorrow of this people and grant his Coming. And may his Coming be soon. So be it by Thy Mercy, O Thou Most Merciful of all who know what mercy is! ◄§

* * *

People expect an Imam to come, said Abu Ala. What vanity! What folly! As if there could be any Imam but the mind of man.

My uncle took me to visit Abu Ala once. He was sitting on a worn hair matting, very old: an emaciated face deeply scarred with the smallpox which attacked him in his boyhood. He bade me come near him, and blessed me, putting his hands on my head. I was only a child then; but I can see him before me now. I stared at his eyes — one of them protruded horribly, and the other was so sunk in its socket that I could hardly make out where it was.

> *I am in a triple prison:*
> *Blindness, a narrow house, and a vile body.*

> *I wish this body was as dull*
> *As sod or stone, insensible.*
> *Flesh with spirit mixed and quick*
> *Is torment, for the two are sick.*
> *Wind, Wind, if Wind you are, expire!*
> *Fire, Fire, die out, if you are Fire!*

Leave me to my own pain. You too are Adam's get, all of you. And if the first of the bottle was dregs, what should the last of it be?

> *Curse us not, Lord. We come from Wicked Gate.*
> *You built it; but even angels look away*
> *When we go in and out at that dark place.*

> *In that hour when my father got a son*
> *The crime was done.*
> *I never did so criminal a thing*
> *To anyone.*

COMEDIES

The subtle suffer, even in happy fortune;
The simple, even in misery, are happy.

DISPOSING OF THE BODY

NCE UPON A TIME, in the city of Basra, there lived a tailor, a thriving tailor who liked his comfort and liked his fun. He and his wife used to make excursions to common places of entertainment; and once as they were on their way home from an afternoon's pleasure, they came upon a hunchback, a sight to set wrath giggling, a face and figure to end a man's worries and comfort sorrow. They felt they must see more of him; so they invited him to go home with them that evening for a little party.

The hunchback accepted the invitation, and fell in with them. By the time they got home, evening was drawing in; the tailor went out to the market, bought some fried fish, fresh bread, and lemons, with a dish of rose-conserve for dessert, and hurried back. The fish was served, and they began to eat.

Presently the tailor's wife took a large gobbet of fish, crammed it into the hunchback's mouth, and clapped her hand over his face.

Now, as God hears, swallow that at one gulp! she said, for I won't give you time to chew!

The hunchback accordingly bolted the morsel. However, in the middle of that same, there was a sharp bone, which stuck in his gullet. His hour, it seemed, was come; for he died on the spot.

No Strength nor Power there is but in God the High, the Great! the tailor cried. Poor creature! to die like this! and all on account of us!

Stop that and do something! said his wife.

Do what? said he.

Get up! she said. Take him up in your arms. Now muffle him in this silk shawl. I'll go in front; you come along after me, carrying him. Yes, now! tonight! Tell people as you go by: It's the boy — me and the mother are taking him to the doctor — he's got to have treatment.

So the tailor got up and took the hunchback in his arms. His wife walked in front, crying out: O child! child! O preserve thee! Where has it struck, this smallpox? Where does it hurt?

Child's got smallpox! said anyone who noticed. On they went, asking where they could find a doctor as they passed along, until people pointed them to a doctor's house. This doctor was a Jew. They knocked at the gate; and a colored maid came down to open the door. Seeing what she took to be a man carrying a child, and its mother in attendance, she asked: What business, please?

We've got a child here, answered the tailor's wife; we want the doctor to look at him. Give the master this quarter dinar for him to come down and look at my little boy — he's sick.

As soon as the girl went upstairs to tell her master, the tailor's wife slipped into the entry. Put him up there, and let's get out! she said. So the tailor carried the hunchback up the stairs, propped him against the staircase-wall, and off they went, he and his wife.

Meanwhile, the girl had gone into the Jew's room. There's a patient here, she said, downstairs at the door, with a man and a woman. They gave me this quarter dinar for you so you could give him something.

The Jew, in a rapture of joy at sight of the gold quarter, jumped to his feet and started off downstairs; but on his way in the dark he kicked against the body of the hunchback. Over it went and bumped to the bottom of the steps.

Hurry up, bring a light! he yelled to the girl; and when she brought it, down the stairs he stepped to examine the hunchback. He discovered that he was dead.

O Ezra and Moses! he moaned. O Heavens, O the Ten Commandments! O Aaron and Joshua son of Nun! I've knocked against the patient and he's fallen down the stairs and killed himself! However am I going to get this body out of the house? O Ezra's Ass! And lifting the body, he carried it to the inner room and told his wife what had happened.

What are you sitting there doing nothing for? cried she. If it stays like this till daybreak we shall both of us lose our lives. We must carry him up to the roof, and throw him into the True Believer's house next door.

Now their next-door neighbor was Comptroller of the Royal Kitchen. He used to bring home as perquisites huge quantities of fats and left-over foods. Unfortunately the cats and the mice got at these, the dogs would jump down off the roofs to worry any fat sheep-tail they scented, and so he used to lose a great deal of what he brought home.

Well, the Jew and his wife carried the hunchback up to the roof, and lowered him down the ventilator-shaft into the Comptroller's house, so that the body stood leaning against the wall. Then they went back down again.

It was not long that the hunchback's corpse had been posted there before the Comptroller, who had been spending the evening with some friends hearing a Reading of the Koran, came home and opened his door. As he was going upstairs with a lighted candle in his hand, he saw a human figure standing in the corner by the kitchen.

What's that? he exclaimed. By God! the thief that's been taking my property's nothing but a human. So it's you, he muttered towards the corpse, who snatch your findings, the lean and the fat, when I try to keep it away from cats and dogs! Here I've been killing every cat and dog in the quarter, committing mayhem on poor brute beasts, and it's you all the time coming down that shaft. I'll take it out on you myself!

And he grabbed for a great cudgel and creeping up near the figure dealt it a blow on the chest. Down it went.

The Comptroller took a look at him. Dead! He let out a yell of horror: No Power nor any Virtue but in God alone, the Supreme, the Omnipotent! he cried. Fear for his own skin took hold of him. Damn that fat! thought he. And damn those sheep-tails! They've made a murderer of me!

He took another look, and saw that it was a hunchback.

A hunchback! Wasn't that enough of a thing to be? he demanded. Did you have to be a burglar too, and prowl after meat and fat? O Thou Who protectest all, cover me with Thy saving Grace!

Well, he hoisted the body on to his shoulders and carried him down the steps and away from the house. The night was drawing to an end, so without stopping to rest he went hastily on till he'd got him as far as the beginning of the market-street; there he propped him up, standing on his feet against a shop wall in the entry to a dark alley; and leaving the thing there the Comptroller stole away.

After a while a figure appeared. It was a Christian, the Sovereign's broker, quite drunk: he had sallied out to go to the public bath, muzzily thinking it must be nearly time for matins. On he came, staggering, till he reached the place where the hunchback stood, at which point he squatted down to piss just round the corner before the shop. Presently glancing up, he saw somebody standing over him.

Now on the previous evening, a sneak-thief had snatched the broker's turban; and at the sight of the hunchback standing there in the gloom, he thought in a flash this fellow meant to do the same again. He sprang to his feet and doubled his fist and gave him a punch in the throat.

Over went the hunchback once more. The Christian gave a shout to summon the Market Watchman, then threw himself on the body, pummelling in drunken fury with one hand while he squeezed hard at his throat with the other. He was still at it when the Watchman came up. At the sight of a Christian kneeling on a True Believer and punching away, the Watchman shouted: Hey! what's all this?

He was after my turban! answered the broker.

Get up off him! Leave him alone!

So the broker stood up, and the Watchman, stooping over the hunchback, made the discovery that he was dead.

What's all this? he cried. Christians murdering True Believers? And seizing the broker he tied his hands behind his back and hustled him off to the house of the Police Magistrate, the broker muttering: Jesus! Messiah! Holy Virgin! how could I have killed him? he must have been in an awful hurry to die of a punch! — Intoxication was gone, and reflection come.

As soon as it was day, the Magistrate appeared. He sentenced the broker to instant execution, and ordered the sentence proclaimed through the city. The gallows was set up, the Christian was told where to stand underneath, and the hangman, having fitted the noose round his neck, was just about to hoist him up, when the Comptroller of the Royal Kitchen pushed into the crowd, crying to the hangman: Don't! Don't! I killed the man.

How did *you* come to kill him? said the Magistrate.

When I got in last night, he replied, I came upon that hunchback — he'd come down the windshaft to steal my goods. So I hit him with a stick, on the chest. And he died of it. I took him away and stuck him up in an entry. Surely 'tis enough for me to kill a Believer, and not be the death of a Christian as well. Let me be hanged!

Very well, let the broker go, and hang this other man as convicted on his own confession, said the Magistrate to the hangman. So the latter took off the rope from the Christian's neck and tightened it round the Comptroller's; he stood him in the proper place under the beam and was just going to haul away when the Jew doctor came scrambling through the crowd, yelling to the hangman: Stop! It was me! Only me! It just happened —

he came to my house for a treatment and I stumbled on him in the dark and he fell right down the stairs and died. Don't kill the Comptroller! Please! Just kill me!

All right, let the Comptroller go, and hang the Jew! said the Magistrate. So the hangman loosed the rope from the Comptroller's neck and made it fast round the Jew's. And lo and behold! the tailor appeared, forcing his way among the assembled people.

Enough! said he; 'twas me and none other; and thus: I went on excursion yesterday, and on my way home in the evening I ran into this hunchback. He was drunk, and singing away to a tambourine, so I stopped to enjoy the sight of him, and even invited him home. At supper my wife stuffed some fish in his mouth, and he choked on it, and died on the spot. We took him to the Jew's house and propped him up on the stairs, and came away. When the Jew kicked him over, he only thought he'd killed him.

Could that be how it was? said the Magistrate to the Jew. It could, said he.

Let the Jew go, said the tailor to the Magistrate; and if you must, hang me.

This must certainly be put on record, said the Magistrate, and he ordered the hangman: Let the Jew go; hang the tailor.

So the hangman, muttering: Take this — leave that — are we never going to get anybody hanged today? led the tailor forward and tied the noose on his neck.

Now this hunchback happened to be the Sovereign's favorite buffoon: he could not bear him to be out of his sight. When the drunken hunchback failed to return all night and next morning, the Sovereign made inquiry of his Attendants.

My lord! the Police Magistrate found him dead, and ordered the murderer to execution, they said. But a second murderer appeared, then a third, then a fourth, one and all claiming to be the one and only, and every man able to explain how it happened.

Chamberlain! cried the Sovereign, go down to the Magistrate's and bring the whole company here to me.

So the Chamberlain went down to the place of execution, where he found the hangman in the very act of discharging his office on the tailor.

Hold! he cried, and gave the royal order to the Magistrate. He took him and the tailor and the doctor and the Comptroller and the broker all together with the remains of the hunchback to the Sovereign Presence, where the Magistrate, kissing the ground, gave an account of the whole proceeding. Much astonished was the Sovereign, and much moved to mirth.

See that it's all written down, he commanded; and let it be done in letters of gold!

*   *   *

IN THE BAG

OME YEARS AGO I left Baghdad, the city where I was born, to go upon a journey, taking no companion except a lad to carry a light bag for me. And at a certain town we came to, I was buying and selling when suddenly a thieving scoundrel of a Kurd laid hands on me and grabbed my bag.

That's my bag! he shouted, and my goods inside it!

Hey! Believers! Rescue! I cried. Help! Criminal assault!

But the bystanders only said: Come on, both of you, to the Judge, and do as he decides.

I consented; and we appeared before the Judge.

What brings you here? said he. What happened?

We have had a disagreement, said I, and appeal to you: by your decision we consent to abide.

Which is the plaintiff? demanded the Judge.

The Kurd stepped forward. God prosper our lord the Judge! he cried; but this bag is mine, and all that's in it is mine. I missed it, and then I saw it in this fellow's possession.

When did you lose it? the Judge inquired.

Only yesterday, said he. And all last night I couldn't sleep for thinking of the loss of it.

Well, if the bag is yours, tell us what it contains, said the Judge.

In my bag when I lost it, said the Kurd, there were two silver pins, some eye-powders, and a handkerchief; and I left two gilt cups and two candlesticks in it besides. Yes, and there were some other things too: two tents, and a couple of dishes, and two hooks and a cushion and two leather mats, a pair of ewers and a brass tray and two basins and a kettle and ladle and a sacking-needle and a cat and some tweezers and a wooden trencher and a pair of saddlebags and two saddles and a coat and two fur overcoats, and one cow with two calves, a goat and two rams and a ewe and two lambs, and two green shelters, and a camel, and two she-camels, a buffalo and two bulls, a lioness, two lions, and a bear, and two foxes, one mattress, two beds, an upper room, two saloons, one porch, two anterooms, a kitchen, two gates, and some Kurds too. Those Kurds will all testify that the bag's mine!

The Judge turned to me. You, he said. What do you say is in the bag?

The Kurd's speech had made my head swim; I stepped forward and said: God prosper our lord the Justice! I had nothing in this bag of mine beyond a small tumble-down cabin, and another house that lacked a door (it had a dog-kennel, though), and a boys' school, and some young men shooting the bones, and a few tents with their poles, and the cities of Basra and Baghdad and the Palace of Shaddad ibn Ad and a forge and a fishnet and clubs and stakes and girls and boys, and also one thousand pimps prepared to give their solemn word that that bag belongs to me.

At that the Kurd began to weep and wail aloud. O my lord! he howled, everybody knows my bag — the things in my bag are famous — it has castles in it, and citadels, and cranes, and men playing chess and men playing checkers. And other things besides were in my bag: a brood mare and two colts and a stallion and two runners and two spears — very long ones — and a lion and a couple of hares and a city and two villages and a whore and a couple of pimps who cheated and a catamite and two gallows-birds and one blind man with two dogs and a cripple with two hobbledehoys and a priest and two deacons and a patriarch and two monks and a Judge and two Assessors. The Judge and the Assessors will tell you it's my bag!

Anything more to say? the Judge asked me.

God keep Your Honor! said I, in this bag of mine I had a hauberk and a sword and whole armories, and a thousand fighting rams, and a sheepfold with a thousand dogs — all barking — and gardens and vines and flowers and herbs and figs and apples and pictures and statues and flagons and cups and most beautiful slave girls and singing-women and marriage-feasts and a lot of confusion and a good deal of noise and vast estates and burglars and Beduin raids complete with swords and spears and bows and arrows, and true friends and true loves and old cronies and some of the boys and house-prisoners and Table Companions and a drum and pipes and flags and banners and sons and daughters and brides in all their finery and some more singing-girls and five Abyssinian women and three Indian women and four Medina women and about twenty Greek girls and some fifty Turkish girls, perhaps seventy Persian girls, eighty Kurdish girls, ninety Georgian girls, and the river Tigris, and the Euphrates too of course, and a fowling-net and a flint and steel and the Many-Columned Garden of Iram and a thousand scoundrels and procurers and a few racecourses and stables and Mosques and baths and a builder and a carpenter and a plank and one nail and a black slave with a pair of recorders and a captain and a caravan leader and towns and cities and a hundred thousand dinars and Kufa and Anbar and a score of chests full of choice stuffs and a score of grain-warehouses and Gaza and Ascalon and the lands from Damietta to Assuan and the Palace of Anushirwan and the Kingdom of King Solomon and all the country from Arabia to Khurasan and Balkh and Isfahan and all that lies from India to Sudan. And in that bag besides (God prolong Your Honor's life!) are some barbers' aprons and barbers' cloths and one thousand newly-sharpened razors for shaving Your Honor's chin unless Your Honor, anticipating my just resentment, decides that the bag is mine.

By God! cried the confounded Judge. Is this bag a bottomless Sea? Or is this bag the Day of Resurrection, which is to gather into one place the just and the unjust? Open the bag!

So I opened it. And behold! there inside was my bit of bread and lemon, and some cheese and a few olives.

I hurled it on the ground before that Kurd, and left the court.

ORNAMENT

THE TONGUE OF ABU ZAYD

Some of our scholars pronounce a feeble poem good because its author lived a long time ago. The same people call a genuinely good poem bad though its only fault is that it was composed in their own time, or that they have actually seen the author. But God has never restricted knowledge, poetry, or rhetoric to any particular age, nor made them the property of any particular class of men. He has always distributed these gifts among all kinds of His Servants. God caused every old thing to be new in its own day, and every classic to make its bow as an upstart.

AYS HARITH SON OF HAMMAM: When I climbed to the camel-back of exile, being driven by misery from my own folk, the shocks of Time tossed me to San'a in Yaman,

Which town I entered with empty wallets, beggared: I had not a meal; I found in my sack not so much as a mouthful.

There fell I to walking the streets like a wild man, roaming the crannies of the town as roams a thirsting bird,

My hunting glance, my wandering way bent ever, morning and evening,

To the chance of some generous man, before whom I might unravel the web of my brow, and frankly confess my need,

Or even some gentleman merely, whose manner at least might comfort me, whose conversation relieve my craving for refreshment,

Until full circle brought me round, and the opening of a gentler fate guided me, to a wide square, where a throng and a wailing were.

Into the thicket of that crowd I plunged, wondering what drew those tears,

And I saw in the middle of the ring a man of slender make,

With a pilgrim's gear upon him. And his was the sorrowing voice.

In periods rich with jewelry of words he assailed all ears
with rebuke of serious exhortation;

And the motley crowd had ringed him round as the halo
rings the moon, or the rind the fruit.

I crept nearer to catch something of that profitable discourse and gather up some of the pearls that fell;

He was in full career; and I heard from the throat of fluent
invention this:

O reckless insolent, who trailest the skirt of conceit!

O Hellbent on vanities, turning to stray after every trifling
tale!

How long wilt thou hold thy mad course, and relish the
pasture that poisons thee?

Provoking with thy frowardness Him who hath thy fore-
lock in His Hand,

Sallying forth in all the filth of thy life to brave Him Who
knoweth thy secret?

Why trouble to hide from thy neighbor? thou art in full
view of One Who watches thee. Why trouble to deceive thy
slave? Thy Master knows.

Dost think thy state will avail thee when it is time to go?
or thy money save when thy deeds damn thee? or late repentance
stay thee up when thou art already down?

Art thou not under sentence of death? then art thou ready?
Did grey hairs not warn thee? then what excuse? Is not the place
appointed for thy sleeping the niche of the grave? or hast aught
to say? Thy way runs straight to God; will any defend thee from
Him?

How oft hath Time awakened thee, and thou hast turned
to sleep again! How oft hath warning plucked thy sleeve, and
thou hast pulled away! the writing been on the wall and thou
hast shut thine eyes! Thou hast known truth and denied it.
Death has said Remember! and thou hast tried to forget. How
oft hath it been in thy power to bestow good, and thou hast bestowed nothing!

Preferring the hoarding of good things to the thinking of

good thoughts, and insistence on large dowry to continuance in charity,

Demanding honesty, yet defiling the very sanctuary of it, condemning deceit and practicing it, thou fearest man. Yet God is more truly terrible.

Woe, Woe to the seeker of this world! Were worldlings wiser one drop of the world were enough!

Then, laying his dust and letting his spittle subside, he took his pilgrim's bottle on his arm, and his staff under his armpit. And when the assembly saw that he rose and made ready to leave them now, every man put his hand in his pocket and filled him a pail from his own stream, saying: Use this for thine expense or share it with thy comrades.

He accepted with half-closed eyes and turned away, taking leave of any who would go with him, preferring his road to be unknown. But I, says Harith, went after the man, tracking and lurking out of his sight, till suddenly he, coming to a cave, slipped aside into it.

I gave him time to put off his sandals and wash his feet (for the performance of his piety), then ran in on him. And there I found him sitting opposite one who waited on him, discussing fine white bread and a roasted kid, with a bottle of strong liquor to his hand.

Fellow! I cried, was that all words and is this the reality?

Puffing a fiery puff as he would burst with wrath, he glared till I thought he would spring at me. But presently that fire died down; and he said:

I don these weeds to hunt my dinner!

If Luck were Justice, the mean would not be the mighty. Come eat; or if thou wilt, go tell!

I turned to his attendant and said: By Him we pray to spare us harm! I conjure thee to tell me, who is this?

This, said he, is that Light of all Outlanders, that Crown of all Scholars, Abu Zayd of Saruj!

The Damietta Meeting

NCE, IN A YEAR OF MUCH coming and going, I journeyed to Damietta.

In those days I trained the broidered robes of wealth and looked into the face of joy, travelling among comrades who, having broken the staff of strife, were suckled on the flowing milk of concord.

And it chanced that on a night fresh as the blooming cheek of youth and dark as youth's raven locks, putting our camels to their mettle we fared till the night-season had put off its prime, and dawning had wiped away the dye of dark. Then wearying of our march, inclining to drowsiness, we came upon a ground of little hills dew-moistened and a faint east breeze, and chose it as a place of rest for our white beasts, and an abode for our night-halt. And when the caravan had knelt down in that place, and the groan and roar of the brutes were stilled, I heard some man of resonant voice address his gossip in the camp: What rule, tell me, doth guide thy dealing with thy fellow man?

Another voice replied: I do my duty by my neighbor though he do me wrong; I let the rough have fellowship; I pardon a partner who ruins my trade; I love a friend though he pour me no better to drink than warm water; I give all I may to my comrade, though he return but a tithe of what he might; if I speak to any, 'tis as to my prince, my intimate is as my chieftain; I soften my answer to hate, and make polite inquiry of disregard; I am pleased with the crumbs of my due, and content with a scrap of my desert; injury tempts me not to complaint, nor the viper's bite to revenge.

Alas, my boy! replied the former voice. One should only hold to a man who holds, and value a man who pays. As for me, only to him who will requite I give. I will not honor the offish, nor plant for a plunderer, nor pray for a pinchpenny. For who has adjudged that I should be lavish and thou a miser? that I

*should be soft and thou harsh? that I should melt and thou freeze
fast? that I should blaze and thou smoulder? No, by God, weigh
word against word as coin; match deed with deed as a pair of
shoes. Whenever did love rise up and follow malice? What man
of honor is gladly low?*

*When the beams of the sun came forth, says Harith, and
dressed the sky in light, I sallied out before the camels had
risen, earlier than the early crow, and walked in the direction of
those voices of the night, peering into every face with a searching
eye, until I recognized Abu Zayd and his son, where they sat talking together. Threadbare were the cloaks upon them. I knew
that these were my two talkers of the night.*

*Fascinated by their culture, pitying their shabby estate,
I drew near and greeted them, and bade them come lodge with
me and spend my pound and my penny as their own. And to
those who travelled in our caravan I spoke of their merit, and
shook the fruited branches for them till they were covered with
gifts, the guests and friends of all.*

*Farther upon our way, we lay encamped one night in a
place whence we descried far off the walls and roofs of villages,
and spied the fires of hospitality. Here Abu Zayd, finding purse
full and poverty past, said to me: My body's dirty, my filth is
caked; wilt thou permit me to visit the bath in one of the villages
yonder?*

At thy pleasure, said I; but be not long.

*Quicker than eye can twinkle I'll be with thee again,
said he; and away he galloped like a race-horse down the track;
and Hurry! he said to his son.*

*We waited and watched for him that day as men watch
for the New Moon of a feast, and then sent to scout and spy after
him, until the aging sunlight failed and the wasted bank of day
had well-nigh crumbled in. Then, when our waiting drew beyond its term, and the sun's vesture faded, I said to my companions: We have lingered to the bitter end, and our time has been
lost: 'tis plain that he was lying. Therefore make ready for the
remove.*

And I rose to harness my camel, and lade her for departure, and we set forth, nor did we ever know what company he took in exchange for ours.

Dirty Work in the Divorce Court

NCE WHEN IT WAS *my intention to leave Tabriz, and I was foraging after company for the road, I encountered Abu Zayd of Saruj, huddled in his cloak, with a bevy of women about him.*

When I asked what he was doing, and where he was taking his party, he answered, pointing to one of the women; a most fair creature, in a most foul temper, it seemed: *There's the woman I married, hoping she would help me forget an exile's lot and cleanse me of the squalor of a bachelor's life; but all I got of her was sweat, perpetual as the sweat of a water-bag — now she kept me out of my conjugal right and now she plied me far beyond my strength, so that all along of her the poor old horse is clean foundered; and Cark and Care my partners are. So here we are on our way to the Judge. If he patch things up between us, then I say: Peace. If not, divorce — divorce.*

I felt inclined to see who would win, and how the case would end; so tucking my own affairs behind my ear I went idly along with the pair of them.

When he came before the Judge (a man who, believing in thrift, would put back in the larder the shreds he picked from his teeth), Abu Zayd crouched on his knees, and thus addressed him: Behold, this filly of mine refuses the bridle and is an incurable bolter, though I am more compliant with her than her finger-tips, ay, fonder than her own heart.

Out on you! said the Judge to her: don't you know that stubbornness is sin against your lord and master? and calls for the whip?

But look, said she, he's the kind of man who'll prowl round the back-door of me, and loves not only his neighbor but that neighbor's neighbor.

Fie! Fie! exclaimed the Judge to Abu Zayd. Do you sow your seed in the salt-marsh? and go looking for chicks where chick never hatched? May your cock never crow again!

By Him WHO SENDETH DOWN THE WINDS! cried Abu Zayd, she's a liar worse than Musaylima's wife.

No! by Him Who ringed the dove's neck and feathered the ostrich! she retorted, he's a liar falser than Musaylima's self!

At this Abu Zayd hissed like a flaring fire and blazed with a roaring rage and cried: A murrain on you! Slut and whore! Husband's bane and neighbor's bane! Will you plague me at home and give me the lie abroad? You know how it was when I wedded you and came to behold my own, and gazed at what was uglier than a monkey and drier than a strip of hide, tougher than palm-fiber and smellier than carrion, colder than a winter's night and wider than Tigris river! Yet I covered these faults! But now, though Shirin should give you her beauty, Zubayda her wealth, Sheba her throne, Buran her bed, Rabi'a her goodness, never hereafter would I stoop to such a saddle for my sitting, such a mare for a stallion of mine!

Whereat the woman bristled like a tigress; she rolled up her sleeves and tucked up her skirt and shouted at him: You! meaner than the man who shit in the well! more hopeless than a year of drought! and flightier than Hopper Hopperson the Flea! Throw your own shame on me? stick your blade in my reputation? when you know you're no more use than nail-parings, no more decent than a fart in company! Be Hasan of Basra for preaching! and be Jarir for love songs! Do you think I would ever take you as Imam at my prayer-niche or sword for my scabbard? No, by God! I'll have no such porter stand in my gate!

I see, said the Judge. You two are no better than the dirty old bag and the dirty old lining. You, fellow, stop your wrangling, and go in by the True Way; you, woman, stop your scolding, and be at home when he calls at the front door.

*By God! said the woman, I shan't keep my tongue off him
till he puts some clothes on me, nor hoist my sail for him till he
victuals me.*

*But Abu Zayd swore by three binding oaths that he owned
not a thing beyond the tatters upon him.*

*Now the Judge cast a sharp eye over their account. He
turned on the two of them a face constrained to grimness. Is it
not enough, said he, to befoul one another in a court of justice,
and to the degree of contempt of court, but you must proceed
from the shame of mutual insult to the wickedness of mutual
fraud? But both your bottoms, by God! have missed the privy.
For the Prince of True Believers appointed me to judge between
litigants, not to pay up for debtors; and by the thanks I owe his
grace for setting me in this seat and giving me power to bind and
to loose, unless you tell me the truth I will proclaim you in every
city and make you an example for all who have eyes to see.*

*As looks the serpent on the ground, Abu Zayd cast down
his eyes. Then, Give ear, said he. And he began to improvise:*

> *I'm he of Saruj; this woman's my wife;*
> *For the Moon has no peer but the Sun.*
> *The pair of us never really uncouple:*
> *Her cell and my monk are as one.*
> *And I really only water my garden.*
> *But now for five days, morning and night,*
> *In sordid hunger we've clean forgotten*
> *The taste of a sip and the feel of a bite.*
> *When even our patience came to an end,*
> *We were forced by want, whose touch is pain,*
> *To this trick, whate'er might come of it,*
> *Hoping some trifle of coin to gain.*
> *Hard times make even a gentleman*
> *Deviate somewhat from strict fact;*
> *So mend my luck; or send me to jail —*
> *My weal, my woe are Your Honor's act.*

Why, cheer up! said the Judge. Be easy; a man like you has a claim on our pardon, and on our large bounty.

The wife now sprang to her feet and drew herself to her full height; then, extending her arm to the public present, she too began to recite:

> *Ye men of Tabriz, your appointed Judge*
> *Is a peerless Judge. O blest appointment!*
> *Cramp when he put his hand in his pocket*
> *'s the one and only fly in the ointment.*
> *To send the old gentleman off rejoicing*
> *And leave me flat on my knees!*
> *Doesn't he know it was I who taught him*
> *To versify with ease?*
> *And I could, if I cared to, make His Honor*
> *The best joke in Tabriz?*

The Judge perceived that they were as impudent as eloquent. To give to one and turn the other off unmollified would, he saw, be no better than borrowing to pay a debt. He scowled and frowned and fussed and fumed and hemmed and hawed and shifted and twisted in sorrow and grief and cursed the office of Judge and damned all candidates for it and groaning as groan the raped, he said: Here's a staggering thing! Am I to be hit in the same place with two shots? and find for both parties? Where's all the money to come from? that's what I ask, where is it all to come from?

And turning to the officer of the court, he said: Today's no day for judgment or sentence; today's an unlucky day, a day a man gets into trouble, a critical day, a fatal day, a suitable day for robbery but not a day for justice. Get rid of these gas-bags for me, and shut them up with two gold coins. Then clear the court and shut the door; and give public notice that this is an inauspicious day, and the Judge is in mourning accordingly; I will not hear another case.

Amen! said the officer to the Judge's prayer, and shed a sympathetic tear. And he paid two shiners over to Abu Zayd and

his wife, and said: In the kingdom of men and devils I think
there's not a cleverer pair than you. But from now on show re-
spect for a court of justice: stint your smut — for it isn't every
Judge that's like His Honor of Tabriz.

THE CEMETERY

 *FELT MY HEART GROWING*
HARD within me once — 'twas while
I tarried at Sava. And the Tradition
came into my mind: that hardness of
heart is cured by visiting the tombs.
And when I came to the mansion of
the dead, the great storehouse of mould-
ering remains, I saw a cluster of people
standing over a fresh-dug grave, and a shrouded thing being
interred.

So I turned aside and drew near, thinking of man's end,
and remembering those of my own people who were gone.

And when the dead was sepulchred, and the crying of
Alas! was over, behold! there above I saw an old man standing
on a mound, propped on his staff, his mantle muffling his face,
who spoke and said:

LET THOSE WHO WORK, WORK FOR AN END
LIKE THIS.

How is it that the burying of one who was like you does
not pierce you to the heart, nor the pouring-in of the mould on
him appal you?

Will a man leave the friend he loved alone with the worms,
and retire to a privacy of pipes and lutes?

Little ye care for him who lies rotting there.

Hark! Who calls your name? Is that not Death? You hear
nothing?

You have forgotten how dark a place the grave is, and
what happens there.

But I, I seem to see you now, down you go into the vault, down, down, as your kin commit you to that narrow place.

There lies your body spread for the feasting of the worms, and shall lie till the coffin-wood is riddled and the bones crumble to nothing.

And after that — the examination of souls. NO ESCAPE!

The Last Meeting

FTER LONG LAPSE OF TIME, I fell in with certain travellers returning from a journey.

Any marvellous news? said I.

More marvellous than the Phoenix, they answered; and they told me they had spent a night at Saruj, and had seen the great Abu Zayd there, and he had put on the Sufi frock and was leading the rows at prayers, and was become a famous holy man.

At once I felt the pull of longing. A ready start, a strenuous journey, and there I was, alighting before the Mosque he worshipped in. And there he was, his company dismissed, standing upright in his prayer-niche, wearing a cloak pinned with a toothpick and a patched cloth. I stood awe-struck, as still as if I had broken in on lions unawares. When he had told his rosary, he raised his forefinger to me by way of greeting, without further word or asking of tidings, then went on with his Reading of the Book, and left me to wonder at his piety, and envy those among His servants whom God guides aright. Nor did he cease from worship and humility, Bow and Prostration, self-abasement and penitence, till the five Prayers were passed and today had become yesterday.

Then he took me to his lodging, and gave me a share of his loaf and olive-oil, and straightway rose to go into his oratory, and there remained alone in converse with his Lord.

When the morn shot up her darts of light, and that wakeful worshipper's reward was well earned, he closed his vigil with
a litany of praise, and then, and then only, lay down as if to rest.
But even as he lay he began to chant in tones that went to the
heart:

> Depart, my soul, from what thou still rememberest —
> The desert spring, the tenting and the trysting,
> The kissing in the night before remove —
> Farewell to that, for ever and for ever.
> 'Tis time to weep for days that flowed away
> In waste, for all fresh pages merely blotted,
> Find sorrow for nights rioted in such
> Sinning as never any dared, lust, lust
> Indulged to the uttermost on voluptuous
> Pillows in quiet rooms.
> How often did repentance, slowly vowed,
> Swiftly forgot, break in such sport, how often
> God's dread behest was kicked like a slipper aside.
> Yet man, as grey hairs come and mingle with
> The rest, has warning: Death is not far now!
> Tomorrow you'll be home, and home's the lonely
> Bottom of a grave. And O that horrible
> House, that lodging waste and comfortless
> So many pilgrims came to in time past,
> So many beyond count must come to yet,
> And there alighting enter out of freedom
> And lie down in a grim and gripping bed
> And stir no more until the Summoning.
> O Thou I hang my trust on! how my fears
> Grow on me every day! Forgive Thy slave!
> Thy erring, weeping slave, Most Merciful
> And Best! to Whom all human prayers go up.

So, in low voice, much mixed with sobbing, and with sighs, until for the weeping of those eyes I wept with him, as I had wept
for him in time past.

Pure now from his night-vigil, he went forth to his Mosque. I followed, and prayed among those who prayed behind him; and when the congregation dispersed and went their several ways, he fell again to muttered Reading of the Word, weeping the while as not Jacob wept.

I knew now he was entered into the company of the seven saints, and made up my mind to go away and leave him so alone. It seemed he read my purpose, for he sighed, as sorrowing, then said: IF THOU FRAME THY MIND TO A PURPOSE, THEN TRUST IN GOD. And I knew for certain that even in our dispensation there are men inspired. So I went near to him, and putting my hand in his, said: Give me a keepsake, Servant of God, true of counsel.

Keep Death full before thine eye, said he; and this now is the parting between me and thee.

That was his farewell. The tears ran from my eyes; I sighed as from my very entrails; for this was the last time we should ever meet.

THE MAN WHO NEVER
LAUGHED AGAIN

PON A TIME, a certain man of great estate, wealthy in gold and goods and servitors and slaves, departed this world to the Mercy of God, leaving one young son. When this son came to manly age, he gave himself to feasting and revelry, and the hearing of musical instruments and songs, and to generosity and the giving of gifts, and spent of the riches his father had left him till all the cash was gone. So he had recourse to selling his slaves and women, and his lands and houses, and so spent all he had had of his father, till in the end he came to beggary, and must needs labor for his living now with common laborers.

In this estate he lived on for a space of years, until one day as he sat beneath a wall waiting for someone to hire him, up to him came a handsome man, well-dressed, who gave him Good-day. Were you some friend of mine in the old days, uncle? said the young man.

I was never a friend of yours, my son, he answered; but I see that you have sometime been a gentleman, whatever you may be now.

Uncle, returned the youth, what's fated and foredestined will come to pass. But have you any work, fair uncle, to hire me for?

Yes, said he, I wish to hire you; the work will not be hard. What is it, uncle? asked the youth.

I have ten old gentlemen living in the same house with me, and we have no one to look after us, the other answered. If you will take service with us, you shall have what eating and clothing you need and a share in our luxuries and money to spend. And it may happen too that God through us will restore your fortune to you.

Hear and obey, said the youth.

But I make one condition, said the other.

What's your condition?

My son, he said, the only condition is that you respect our secret, whatever you see us do; and if you see us weep, that you never ask us why we weep.

Very well, uncle.

Then follow me, with God's blessing, said the man.

So the young man followed the elder to the public bath. His companion led him in and spoke for him, and had the crusted dirt cleansed from his body; then sending for a fine suit of linen, he clothed him in it, and took him to his house, and his associates. It was, he saw as he went in, a stately mansion, high-cornered and spacious, with open vaults facing one another across the court and sitting-rooms beside, in each a water-fountain. It was full of the song of birds, and he saw windows looking into an interior garden. The elder led the way to one of the rooms, a chamber gaily inlaid, its ceiling rich with precious blue and twinkling gold, its floor spread with silken carpets; and in this chamber were ten old gentlemen all clad in mourning, sitting opposite to one another, in tears, and wailing.

Wondering to see them thus, he was on the point of questioning the elder when he remembered the condition of his service, and therefore held his peace, while the old man committed to him a chest containing thirty thousand dinars, with the words: My son, take from this chest for our expenses and your own, whatever is proper; be faithful; and remember your trust.

Hear and obey, he answered. And day and night he was their servant, till after a time one of the company died. His fellows took and washed him, and shrouded him, and buried him in the garden behind their mansion. But Death withheld not his hand, taking away one after another, until at last only the one who had first hired the youth was left. The two of them lived on in the house with no third but God, year after year.

And then that old man too fell sick. When the youth saw

there was no hope of his life, he spoke gently to him, telling him how sorry he was, and said: Uncle, I have been your servant twelve years now, not failing your service a single hour. I have been faithful and served to the utmost of my power and strength.

Yes, my son, you served us. And my comrades are gone to the Mercy of God. And now we too must die.

Master, said the young man, you are in peril of death. One thing I wish that you would tell me: what was the cause of your weeping, of the everlasting wailing and mourning and sorrow of you all?

That, my son, concerns you not, he said. Do not require me to do what I must not do; I vowed to God never to tell creature of His the cause, lest he too suffer what we suffered. And if you would escape what we fell into, see that you never open the door yonder (and he pointed with his hand, and made a warning gesture). Only if you have a mind that what overtook us should overtake you also, then open it; and you will know why we did what you saw us do. And when you know, you will repent, when repentance will be vain.

Then his sickness grew on him, and he accomplished his span and departed into the presence of his Lord. The young man washed and shrouded him and buried him by his companions.

Seals were affixed upon the doors and contents of the house. But the young man stayed on there. He was alone now, and ill at ease; for remembrance of the life of those old men disturbed him. At last one day, as he sat pondering the words of his dead master, it occurred to him that he might at least go and see where the thing was. So he betook himself to that part of the mansion the dead had pointed to, and searched until, in a dark corner where he never went, he found a little closely-fitted door, over which the spider had woven her webs. It was fastened with four locks of steel; and at the sight of it, the old man's warning echoed in his mind, and he turned away.

For all that, his soul would have him open it. Seven days he mastered it; but on the eighth his soul mastered him.

I must, said he, I must open that door, I must see what

will befall in consequence. Nothing can avert a thing decreed and foreordained of God, and nothing will happen unless He has willed it.

So he rose, and broke the locks, and opened the door. When it stood open, there before him was a narrow passage. He followed it; for three hours he went on, until suddenly lo! he came out on the shore of a vast stream. So, marvelling, he fared on along the beach, gazing to right and left, when all at once he was aware of a mighty eagle, which had stooped from the sky, and had him in its talons, and was flying with him between heaven and earth. It flew till they came to an island in the midst of the sea, and there it let him fall, and left him.

Dazed he was, confounded by his plight, and knew not where he might go from that place. But one day as he sat idle there, lo! far off upon the sea, like one star in the sky, appeared the sail of a ship. The young man's very heart hung on that ship, in which it might be his deliverance should come to pass. He gazed and gazed, and she came on, and came on nearer still, until he could make her out to be a galley built of ivory and ebony, her oars of sandal and aloes-wood, and all inlaid with brilliant gold. Her crew were ten high-breasted maidens, fair as moons, who looked at him and came ashore to him, and kissing his hands said: Hail, King and Bridegroom!

Then there advanced towards him a lady radiant as the sun in a clear sky, carrying a bundle wrapped in a silk cloth. There enfolded was a kingly robe, and a gold crown set with precious stones. On his shoulders she threw the robe, and set the crown on his head; and the other girls, taking him in their arms, carried him to the galley. The vessel was spread with many-colored silken carpets. When all were aboard, they spread the sails and bore away over the abysses of the sea.

As they sailed on, he thought surely this was a dream. He had no notion whither he was taken; but presently they sighted land. The shore, he saw, was thronged with troops, splendid in complete steel, beyond count of all but God. And when the galley was made fast, there were led up five blood horses, with gilt saddles pearled and jewelled, for his choosing. He chose and mounted one; and the other four were led before him. Then, as he settled in his saddle, the banners and the standards were heaved up over his head, the kettledrums rolled and the cymbals clashed, the troops fell in to right and left, and the array moved forward.

The young man's mind still doubted whether he slept or waked; he could not credit all that pomp, but took it all to be the phantasmagoria of dreams.

On they rode, till they came to a plain of green meadow-land, with palaces and gardens in it, and trees and streams and flowers, and birds trilling the perfection of God. And from among those palaces and gardens at their approach another army poured, wide-tossing as a torrent in flood, and overspread the plain, and at a little distance halted. Then appeared riding forward from their center a King, with high officers walking before him. He rode straight to the young man and dismounted.

The youth, seeing him alight so courteously, dismounted too, and they gave one another gentle salutation. Then the King got to his saddle again. Come with us, guest, he said. The youth fell in beside him, and talking as they rode, with a procession of state before them, they came to a royal palace and alighted there. The King, taking the young man's hand in his, led in with his whole train, and seating his guest upon a throne of gold, sat down beside him, and threw back the scarf of his kerchief from the lower part of his face.

The King was a girl! Dazzling as sun in cloudless sky she was, full of beauty and filling him with desire, a high-bred, perfect face, but arch and full of coquetry.

King! she said to the youth, who was a-stare in the face of such riches and splendor, and foolish before her beauty; know that I am the Sovereign Lady of this country. All those troops you saw, both horse and foot, are women; there is not a man amongst them; for the men in this land of ours till the fields and sow and reap and busy themselves with our agriculture, and the building and repair of our cities, and the following of crafts and trades. It is the women govern here, fill offices of state, bear arms.

As they were talking, and he marvelling, a tall grey-haired old lady entered.

Vizieress, summon Judge and Witnesses! said the Queen; and when the old lady was gone, she turned again to the young man, and spoke affectionately to him, saying all she might to wile away his shyness, in speech more gentle than the breeze which comes with dawn. Are you content, she asked at last, to take me for your wife?

He would have kissed the ground before her; but this she would not allow.

My lady, he said, I am far humbler than these servants you command.

These servants? she inquired. These troops? these riches? Yes, what of them?

These all are yours, to do with as you will, said she, to order and give and grant as you see good. All things are to do with as you will, she said again, all except one thing: that door yonder (and she pointed towards a closed door): that door you must never open, for if you open it you will repent, when repentance will be vain.

She was still speaking when the Vizieress came before them with the Judge and Witnesses, old ladies of a reverend dignity, their hair long over their shoulders, whom the Queen commanded to draw up a marriage-contract between herself and this young man. So the ceremony was performed, the Queen ordered feasting and mustered her soldiery; and after the banqueting and the drinking he went in to his Bride, and found her a clean maiden, and did away her maidenhead.

Seven years he lived with her in all delight and comfort, in all the pleasant and the sweet of life, until one day he found that he was thinking of the door he must not open. She would not have forbidden me to open it, he thought, were it not that there behind lie things more precious than any I have seen yet. And he rose, and threw it open.

And lo! behind that door was the very Bird which had brought him to the island.

Ill met, said the Bird, O face that shall never laugh again!

At the sight of that Bird and the sound of those words, he turned to flee. But it was already upon him — it seized him and bore him far away, and flew with him between heaven and earth for an hour's space, till it let him fall in the same place from which it had first rapt him. Then it was gone.

Long he lay there bereaved of thought; but slowly then the power of thought came back. All the riches and glory and honor he had seen came back into his mind, the riding of the troops before him, the commanding, the forbidding; and he wept and wailed aloud. There on the shore of that great river where the Bird had left him he tarried for two months, hoping somehow he might find a way back to his Bride again. But one night as he lay wakeful, sadly musing, he heard one speak (and though he heard the voice, he saw no person), calling aloud:

H*ow great were those delights!*
Far, far from thee is the coming again of what is now gone by.
And for that how many shall be the sighs!

He heard; and knew despair. Never again should he meet his Queen, or recover that happy estate in which he once had lived. So he returned, weary and broken-hearted, to the house where he had dwelt with the old men. They too had suffered the like of what had befallen him, he knew: that was the cause of their lamenting and dejection; and they had, he saw, great cause. Bitter grief grew on him; he took to his chamber, and could do nothing now but weep, wailing and moaning of a pain without relief, caring no more for food and drink and pleasant scents and laughter till he died, and was laid in grave beside the elder graves.

* * *

THE MYSTIC PATH:
A DERVISH AUTOBIOGRAPHY

All religious Hope is the product of Despair.

The penitence of ordinary men is remorse for sin.
The penitence of saints is remorse for forgetting.
The penitence of Prophets is remorse for seeing the reach of others as beyond their own.

Make Me content with thine eye,
*   I will make thee content with thy heart.*
Make Me content with thy feet,
*   I will make thee content with thy hands.*
Make Me content with thy falling-asleep,
*   I will make thee content with thy waking.*
Make Me content with thy wishing,
*   I will make thee content with thy wanting.*

The Rationalists tried to purify the idea of God by the intellect's means of knowledge, and failed; the Sufis tried to purify it by the heart's means of knowledge. They succeeded.

If a man would be at peace

IN THE BODY, he must turn his back on this world; and if he would be at peace in the heart, he must clear his heart of any other-wordly desire also.

Passionate desire is of two kinds: the desire for pleasure, or lust; and the desire for reputation and leadership. The mere pleasure-seeker may be seen haunting taverns; he harms no one but himself. But the seeker for reputation and leadership can be found even in religious communities, not only corrupt but corrupting others.

Lust should not be thought of in too narrow a sense: it is dispersed throughout the body, and is served by all the senses; there is a story told of Abu Ali Siyah of Merv illustrating this:

I had gone to the public bath (says he), and in accordance with the Prophet's usage was shaving about my private parts when the thought came into my mind: Why not cut off this member which is the source of all lusts and so afflicts me? But then a voice whispered in my heart: Abu Ali, wilt thou meddle in My realm? Am I not the swayer of all thy members alike? Perform thy thought, and I swear by My Glory I will sow lust and passion a hundredfold in every hair that grows in that place.

* * *

When a novice approaches a Sufi Shaykh with the purpose of renouncing this world, the Shaykh according to rule will impose on him a three-years' spiritual discipline, the requirements of which if he fulfill, well and good; if not, he is told that he cannot be admitted to the Path. The first year he is everybody's servant; the second year he is God's servant; the third year he watches his own heart.

He can only really be everybody's servant by regarding himself as a member of the menial class, and all others as members of the master class, which means that he must see all alike, without the slightest discrimination, as his betters, and think it only right that he should work for them. He must not think of himself as condescending to serve, which stultifies his whole effort, and is dishonest.

He can only serve God when he has cut away all personal interest in this world *or the next*. Whoever worships God for the sake of anything is worshipping himself, not God.

And he can only watch his heart when his thoughts are collected, and all concern for his own future dismissed.

If he succeeds in this triple qualification, the novice may put on the patched frock. That patched frock is most properly compared to a winding-sheet. A pious man in the Hands of God is like a corpse in the hands of the washer of the dead.

My own teacher, whose disciple in Sufism I am, was Khuttali, a man who spent sixty years inwardly as well as outwardly withdrawn from the world, for the most part in the mountains of the Anti-Taurus range. He had many of the marks of a saint, but never affected the characteristic dress or external fashion of a Sufi, for he was hard against formalists. I never met anyone who inspired in me a greater sense of awe.

Once in early days I was pouring water on his hands, for his purification before prayer, and the thought came into my mind: Is everything predestination? why should people, unless they have to, make themselves slaves to spiritual directors, on the mere chance of being granted sight of a miracle?

My son, I know what you are thinking, said my Shaykh.

But be sure of this — there is a cause for everything God decrees.
When God purposes to give a member of an Army family like
you a royal crown, a kingdom, He grants him *Penitence,* and
employs him in the service of one of His friends, that through
the service he may receive some Grace.

He died in a village at the head of the mountain pass
going over to the River of Damascus. As he lay dying, with his
head resting on my breast (at that moment I was laboring
under a sense of hurt, as people often do, owing to the behavior
of a friend of mine), he said to me: My son, I will tell you an
article of Faith which will preserve you from all troubles if you
hold fast to it — whatever of good or evil God creates, never, in
any place or in any circumstance whatsoever, quarrel with His
act, or allow yourself to feel aggrieved.

That was my Shaykh's last injunction to me before he
yielded up his soul.

The perfection of saintship consists in seeing everything
as it really is. As soon as you have really renounced your self,
you will see that all mankind are necessary for the fulfillment of
God's Will. And as soon as you really turn to God, you will see
that you too are necessary for the accomplishment of what He
has decreed.

If you must delight in anything but God, at least delight
in another person; for that delight looks towards unification,
whereas delight in your self is turning your back on the Creator.
That is why the elder Saliba used to say that it is better for
novices to be under the authority of a cat than under their own.

In my early days, I went to visit Abu Qasim of Gurgan,
who possessed a marvellous power of explaining and developing
the inward experiences of a novice. One day I was sitting in the
Shaykh's presence telling him my experiences and visions for
his testing and corroboration — his skill in this was unrivalled —
and he was listening kindly to all I said. In the vanity and
enthusiasm of youth I was eager to tell all; and I began to think

that probably the Shaykh himself, in his novitiate, had never enjoyed such experiences as mine, or his attitude to me would not be so humble, and he would not be inquiring so earnestly into my spiritual state.

The Shaykh must have known exactly what I was thinking, for he soon said: My dear, you should know that my humility is not directed towards yourself or your experiences, but towards God, Who causes such experiences to occur. They are not peculiar to you: all seekers after God know such things.

I was utterly abashed by this rebuke. When he saw my mortification, he continued: Man has only two relationships to the mystic Path: as soon as he enters It, he imagines he has reached the End of It; and as soon as he is turned out of It, he puts what he formerly imagined into words. What he denies, what he affirms, his apparent release from self-existence and his existence are alike products of his imagination. Man's imagination is a prison from which he never escapes. What he has to do is simply to stand and wait, like a slave at a gate, allowing himself no other relationship than these two: his humanity, and obedience.

Formulation of the idea of reality is futile. If the idea exists already in the hearer's or reader's mind, it will not of course be destroyed by formulation; but if it does not exist, it cannot be created by such formulation, which only produces an unreal notion and may cause the student to take the formulation for the real thing — which is a deadly mistake.

MYSTICAL LISTENING:
THE USE OF THE BEAUTIFUL

We have five means of becoming aware of things: hearing, sight, taste, smell, and touch. As to Reality, God sent Apostles to speak their testimony of that; so that it is by listening that a man has to become aware of Him. For this reason, the people of the True Way regard hearing as a higher sense than sight.

The most beneficial listening is listening to God's Word. There is a Tradition to the effect that the Prophet asked Ibn Mas'ud to recite to him from the Koran, and when the latter exclaimed: What! I recite It to thee, to whom It was sent down by God? the Prophet answered: *I would like to hear It from another man.* The ancedote also indicates that listening is a higher condition than reciting; for the Reader may recite either with true feeling or without it. But the hearer's condition is more secure — for while speech is a sort of pride, listening is a sort of humility.

It is permissible to listen to poetry, since the Prophet used to do so. Some, considering *all* poetry permissible, spend their time listening to love songs, to celebrations of their darling's face or tresses or beauty-spot. But if one man says: It is God only that I hear, God only that I long for, in eye and cheek, in beauty-spot and ringlet; then it might follow that another man might feast his eye on cheek and beauty-spot, insisting that he likewise sees and seeks only God there. A third might then say that in the tactile experience of someone whose beauty may allowably be heard described, or beheld, he too is only seeking God, if no one sense is better adapted than any other for apprehending Reality. At this point the Law obviously ceases to apply, and the Apostolic saying: *every eye is an adulterer,* is without force.

Some shallow would-be mystics, seeing adepts in ecstasy during music, have fancied that these were transports of sensual emotion, and thought: It must be all right, or they wouldn't do it. And imitating the external behavior of those who were better than themselves, but neglecting the spirit, they have yielded to emotional ecstasies until they damned themselves, and led others to damnation. This indeed is one of the great evils of our time.

Harmony thrills the bodily temperament with delight; both physicians and philosophers have examined the subject at length. The results today are plain enough in the various modern musical instruments which have been developed for the stirring of lust and purveying of mere pleasure, in full accord with the Fiend.

There is a theory that the physiological temperament is actually composed of blended and harmonized sounds. Even camels and donkeys, as we often see, are pleasurably affected when their drivers sing. In both Khurasan and Iraq hunters who go after deer at night beat a brass gong, in order to come up on their game as they stand still, fascinated by the sound. And the same effect can be seen in infants, who stop crying when a tune is sung to them. Children affected in this way, the doctors say, are always intelligent, and make able men.

Theologians agree that listening to instrumental music is permissible so long as it is not merely for amusement, and does not induce sinful thought. But the merely permissible is proper for a beast alone. A man ought to seek spiritual good in everything he does.

Right listening consists in hearing everything as it is. Men are seduced, and their passions stimulated, by instrumental music because they hear unreally. Music is a presentment of Reality, which rouses the heart to long for God; those who listen with what is real in themselves participate in Reality; those who listen in selfish soulfulness participate in Hell. And Shibli describes music as an outward temptation and an inward premonition: if you know the password you will safely hear the premonition, but if you do not, by inviting temptation you are courting disaster. Another Shaykh puts it thus: Music makes the heart aware of what keeps it in exile, so that its effect is the heart's turning home to God.

My own spiritual director Khuttali used to say: Music's the poor traveller's provision; a man at journey's end has no more use for it.

The rules for the mystical hearing of music and poetry prescribe that it should not be practiced prematurely, that you should not make a habit of it, but should listen at long intervals,

so that familiarity may not degrade musical experience. A
spiritual director should always be present during the performance, the room should be cleared of outsiders, and the singer
should be of good character. Decorum should be maintained
until the music exerts its power; and you must be able to tell the
difference between a strong stimulation of ordinary human
emotion and the glow of religious ecstasy.

The listener should possess enough sensibility to render
him receptive to the Divine influence in music, and capable of
doing it justice; when its power over his heart begins to manifest
itself, he must not try to fight it off, nor, as its force wanes,
should he try to hold on to it.

No listener should ever disturb another engaged in listening, nor wonder what the music or poetry means to him. He
must never compliment the singer on his voice, nor, if he sing
out of tune, tell him so or be annoyed with him. He should really
be unconscious of the singer's presence, committing him to God,
Who hears all in tune. If a listener remains unmoved by what is
moving to others, it is a mistake to look with a sober eye on
their intoxication: he should remain quietly absorbed in his own
occasion.

I personally think that novices should never be allowed
to attend recitals. They are dangerous and seductive: women on
the neighboring roofs or elsewhere are apt to come and watch the
dervishes at their music. Occasionally, too, some debauched
young man is one of the party, since certain ignorant Sufis have
made a religious practice of this vice. Contemplation of the
beauty of boys and homosexual association with them are actually forbidden practices; anyone who maintains that they are
allowable is an Unbeliever. The Traditions invented to justify
them are wild. I have met people who regarded this as a
characteristic Sufi vice, and regarded Sufis with abhorrence for
that reason. But all the Shaykhs without exception have recognized its wickedness. It is the Incarnationists — God curse
them! — who have left the blot, to the scandal of God's saints.
For my own sins in this kind in time past I implore the Forgive-

ness of God; I beseech Him for His Help to keep me from contamination, outward and inward.

They once told Shaykh Rudbari that a certain Sufi enjoyed even frivolous music, having now attained the stage when he was no longer affected by fluctuations in his communion with God.

He has certainly attained something, said Rudbari: — Hell.

All mystics have their own degrees as listeners. What a Penitent hears increases his contrition; what the Lovesick hears intensifies his longing for the beatific Vision; what those who have Faith hear confirms their certitude; what a novice hears verifies some answer he has been granted; what a Lover of God hears helps him sever himself from this world; what is heard by the poor in spirit provides a firm foundation for their despair.

Music indeed is like the sun, which shines alike on all things, to various effect — burning, illumining, melting, nourishing.

Novices are agitated, adepts tranquil in their listening. One of Junayd's disciples used to evince such disturbance as to disturb his fellow dervishes; and the others complained of it to Junayd. The Shaykh told the man that if he continued so uncontrolled he could no longer be admitted to Junayd's circle at all.

I kept my eye on that dervish at the next recital, Jurayri said; his lips were tightly compressed, and he maintained quiet till the sweat started from every pore of his body. Then he fainted; and he remained unconscious the rest of that day. I hardly knew which to admire the more — his response to the music or his reverence for his spiritual director.

And Shaykh Faris told me that someone once laid a restraining hand on the head of a dervish who was in the transports of response, and told him to sit down. The man sat down, and died then and there.

I myself once saw with my own eyes, in the mountains of Azarbayjan, a dervish walking in meditation. He was singing rapidly to himself, weeping and moaning bitterly, these verses:

Never sun rose nor set but on one dream —
Thee.
Never sat I and talked but on one theme —
Thee.
Never, in joy or pain, spoke I of Thee
But love mixed with my breath went up.
Never stooped I to water in my thirst
But I saw Thee within the cup.
If the world held a road that might lead home to Thee,
Though I crawled on my face, I would have come to Thee.

As the last notes fell, his face altered. He sat down, and so stayed a while, leaning back against a crag. And then he gave up his soul.

One very hot day I came into the presence of the great Shaykh Muzaffar; my dress was travel-stained and my hair dishevelled.

Tell me what you would most enjoy at this moment, said he.

I should love to hear some music, said I.

The Shaykh at once sent for a singer and some instrumentalists. As the music played, I, young and enthusiastic, imbued with all the ardor of a novice, was deeply moved. After a while, my transports subsiding, the Shaykh asked me how I enjoyed it.

Immensely! I replied.

A time will come, he said, when music like this will mean no more to you than the croak of a raven. The influence of art lasts only so long as real contemplation is unattained; when contemplation comes, the reign of art is over. Take care not to become addicted to music, lest it grow into your nature and hold you back from what is higher than it.

THE TWO MODES OF SUFI LIFE

A dervish may be a Resident or a Traveller.

Residents are bound to observe the following discipline. Any Traveller who arrives at their house they must treat as an honored guest, not asking whence he comes, nor where he goes, nor what his name is; but thinking of him only as one who comes from God and goes to God and is called God's servant.

If their guest prefers to be alone, they must give him an empty room; if he prefers company, they must keep him friendly company, with no ceremony. When he composes himself to sleep, the Resident should offer to wash his feet, but not, if he declines, insist. Next day, he must propose a visit to the bath, and take the Traveller to the cleanest bathhouse available, keep his clothes when he visits the bathhouse latrine, and himself wait upon him, scrubbing his back and massaging his knees, feet, and hands, rather than hand him over to a strange attendant. If the Resident happens to have the means he should provide a new garment for his guest; if not, he should not worry, but just brush or wash his clothes for him to put on when he leaves the bath.

Should the Traveller stay two or three days, he should be invited, but not compelled, to visit any spiritual director or Imam who may be in the town. It is absolutely wrong to take a Traveller to call upon men of the world, or to attend their parties, or their funerals. Of all the tribulations I suffered when I was a Traveller the worst was to be carried off, time after time, and led about from the house of Khwaja So-and-so to the house of Squire Such-and-such. I kept a pleasant face; but I hated it. And I vowed that if ever I became a Resident I would never treat Travellers so outrageously. The great benefit one reaps from the company of the ill-bred is this determination: to tolerate their behavior in them and never to tolerate such behavior in oneself.

If a Traveller, feeling himself very much at home, makes some material request, the Resident is bound to grant it unquestioningly; except that if the travelling dervish is a mere low im-

postor the Resident is not obliged to do an actually base thing
in order to comply. If a dervish wants material things, what
business has he with devotees? Let him go into trade, and buy
and sell. Or let him be a soldier at court. I once set out from
Damascus with two brother dervishes to visit Ibn Mu'alla, who
was living in the country near Ramla. As we went along, we
agreed each to keep his mind concentrated on some desire which
he doubted whether to indulge or not, to see if that venerable
Superior would divine our thoughts without our expressing
them, and settle our doubts for us.

My thought was: I wish he would give me the Intimate
Supplications of Hallaj. One of my companions made up his
mind to ask Ibn Mu'alla to pray for him, that his disease of the
spleen might get better; and the other thought: I wish he would
give us some Color Candy.

Ibn Mu'alla knew. As soon as we arrived he ordered a
manuscript of Hallaj's Supplications brought me as a present.
Then he laid his hand on the sick man's belly; and the man did
feel relief. But turning to our companion, he said: Color Candy
is the kind of thing Army people eat. You wear a saintly dress;
but a saint's dress doesn't go with a soldier's appetite. Make up
your mind — one thing or the other.

So long as a dervish is devoted to his own interests, it is
quite wrong to help him gratify his selfishness, for in the Way
dervishes act as guides to one another, not as highwaymen. This
is perhaps a safe rule: so long as anyone perseveres in a selfish
demand, his friend should resist it; but as soon as he renounces
it his friend should satisfy it. When I was a Resident in Iraq,
at one time I wore myself out raising and giving money, and had
got terribly into debt. Anyone who wanted anything turned to
me; and I did not know where to turn for means to satisfy them.
Then I received a letter, from an eminent man, which contained
this: *Beware of distracting your own mind from God by trying
to satisfy people whose minds are occupied with vainer things.
When you meet a man of nobler mind than your own, then you
may safely distract your mind to satisfy his. But otherwise, never*

distract yourself; GOD IS ENOUGH FOR ALL HIS SER-VANTS. That piece of advice settled my problem for ever.

Almsgiving is a normal religious obligation, a man who has two hundred dirhams being required to give five, and so proportionally. It is really thanksgiving in kind for a benefit received.

Sufis think little of this ordinary almsgiving; for a man must be exceedingly avaricious to hold on to two hundred dirhams for a year and then give away only five. Some of the Shaykhs have accepted alms, others have declined them. Those forced by Divine compulsion to accept the povertarian life accept alms, not for their own wants so much as to relieve a brother Believer of his religious obligations. I once knew a dervish, for instance, to whom some Prince sent three hundred drachms weight of pure gold; the dervish went straight to a bathhouse, gave the whole sum to the superintendent, and went away.

A distinction has been made between liberality and generosity. The merely generous gives with discrimination, so that his act is not free of egoistic motivation. Generosity is the rudimentary stage of liberality; the really liberal man does not discriminate, so that his action is clear of self. The best working rule is the maxim that liberality acts on first thoughts. When second thoughts prevail, avarice is there.

An answer of Shaykh Abu Sa'id's illuminates this. A certain Nishapur merchant, who was a regular attendant at his meetings, was on one occasion asked to give by a dervish. He pulled out a couple of coins: one a gold piece, the other a small coin, and a clipped one at that; his first thought was to give the gold piece. But on second thought he gave the other. When the Shaykh's discourse was over, the merchant had a question to ask: Is it ever right for a man to argue with God?

You argued with God, said the Shaykh. It was God who told you to give a gold coin, but you gave the clipping.

A Sufi's blood may be shed and his property taken un-resentedly, as Shaykh Tustari said. Rudbari went to the house of one of his disciples in the man's absence and ordered all his household effects to be taken to the bazaar and given away. When the disciple returned, though he felt happy that his director had acted so freely, he made no comment. His wife, however, tearing off her dress and throwing it on the ground, cried: This is part of our property too!

That is unnecessary, and self-willed, said her husband. If we let the Shaykh be liberal with our goods, that is true liberality in us; but offering things is too deliberate.

I once, says Shaykh Farisi, set out for the Holy Places, with various others; and near Hulwan a band of Kurds fell on us, and stripped us even of our patched frocks. We offered no resistance, except for one of us, who got very excited. One of the Kurds simply drew his scimitar and killed the man, though we begged him to show mercy.

He's no Sufi! said the Kurd. That fellow was a traitor among the saints, and a man like that is better out of the way.

How so? we asked.

The very first step in Sufism, said the brigand, is liberality, and this fellow was so frantically attached to his rags that he quarrelled with his own friends. What kind of a Sufi is that? Ay, his own friends: for this long while we've been doing as you do yourselves — stripping you of worldly encumbrances.

If a dervish elects to be a Traveller, his Rule is that his wandering must be for God's sake, not for the pleasure of it. As he moves on bodily, so inwardly he should flee his sensuality. He must be ritually pure at all times, and must not neglect Prayer. His object must be either Pilgrimage or Holy War or the visiting of a holy site or search for religious instruction, to see a venerable person or Shaykh, or to go to a saint's tomb. His travelling will be defective otherwise. His necessaries are a patched frock to cover his nakedness, a rug to pray on, a bucket with a rope for ablution, shoes, and a staff for protection and other uses on his road.

When a Traveller comes to Residents' houses, he must be no trouble to them, he must never refer to any hardships he may have suffered on his journeys, never discourse on theology, tell anecdotes, or relate Traditions, all of which things savor of conceit. He must suffer fools gladly, for God's sake, and never speak ill of any.

In the matter of hospitality, the best rule is never to refuse the invitation of a dervish and never to accept the invitation of a moneyed man. Never should one frequent the houses of the moneyed, or ask a favor of one such. It is demoralizing for Sufis, since there can be no real congeniality between a worldling and a dervish.

It is not, however, the quantity of money that makes the moneyed man. No one who recognizes poverty as better than money is a moneyed man, though he be a king; and a man who does not believe in poverty is a moneyed man, however poor he is.

There are three allowable motives for begging, as more than one Shaykh has said: first, for the sake of mental liberty, since no anxiety is so engrossing as worry about getting something to eat; second, for the soul's discipline: Sufis beg because it is so humiliating and helps them to realize how little they are worth in other men's opinion, so that they escape self-esteem; third, to beg from men out of reverence for God, regarding all men as His agents — a servant who petitions an agent is humbler than one who makes petition to God Himself.

The begging Rule is this: if you beg and get nothing to be more cheerful than if you get something; never to beg of women or people who hang about the bazaar; as far as possible to beg in a selfless spirit, never using what you get for self-adornment or housekeeping, or buying property with it. You should live in the present; never let a thought of tomorrow enter your mind, or you are lost. A final rule is never to let your piety be seen in the expectation of more liberal alms on that account.

I once saw a venerable old Sufi who had lost his way in the

desert and came starving into the market place at Kufa with a sparrow perched on his hand, crying: Give me something, for this sparrow's sake!

Why do you say that? people asked.

I can't say: For God's sake, he replied; one must let an insignificant creature plead for worldly things.

Once, being at Tus, I asked Shaykh Gurgani the question: What is the minimum of acquirement a dervish should have in order to be worthy of the povertarian life?

He needs at least three acquirements, the Grand Shaykh replied. He must know the right way to sew a patch; the right way to listen; and the right way to take a step.

There were various dervishes present as well as myself when he uttered this saying; and when we came out, we were hardly clear of the door before every man began to apply it to himself personally, the ignorant with particular avidity. There's a real definition of povertarianism for you! they exclaimed; and most of them lost no time in sewing beautiful neat patches on their frocks and cultivating a formal walk — as for the listening, every man fancied he knew how to do that already.

Now I was devoted to the Shaykh, and I hated to see his words wasted. So I said: Come on, let us each produce a saying on this subject.

Everybody accordingly gave his own interpretation. When my turn came, I said: A right patch is a patch that's stitched because one's poor, and not for show: if it is stitched for poverty it is stitched right, though it be stitched badly. And a right word listened to is a word that falls on one's disposition, not on one's will, and is applied in earnest, not in play, and is apprehended by one's life, not one's mind. A right step is a step taken in true self-forgetfulness, and neither capriciously nor correctly.

Something of what I said was repeated to the Sayyid afterwards. He spoke well, and may God reward him for it! was his comment.

SOUL AND SPIRIT: THE DIFFERENCE

ETYMOLOGICALLY, SOUL MEANS THE ESSENCE and reality of any thing; in common parlance it has many and incongruous meanings: spirit, virility, body, blood, and so on.

All mystics regard the soul as the source and principle of evil, both of sinful acts and of bad qualities such as pride, envy, avarice, anger, hatred. Both soul and spirit are subtle things, existing in the body; but the spirit is the seat of good, the soul the seat of evil.

All Sufi Shaykhs and most orthodox Muslims consider that the spirit is a substantial, subtle thing coming and going by God's Decree, deposited in a man's body, but capable of quitting it while it is still alive, as in sleep.

On this point we are at variance with those heretics who maintain that the spirit is eternal, and worship it, regarding it as the all-active and all-ruling, terming it the Uncreated Spirit of God, and believing that it passes from one body to another. No popular error has ever been more widely accepted than this doctrine: it is held by the Christians, although expressed by them in apparently conflicting terms, and held by the whole body of Hindus, Buddhists, and Chinese. It is also supported by the consensus of the Shi'ite Sectaries, the Qarmatians, and the Esoterics, as well as by two false sects of self-styled Sufis.

God, said the Prophet, created spirits two thousand years before bodies. Spirits are therefore one kind of His creatures, which God joins to another kind of His creatures. It is in joining them that He produces *life*, in conformity with His predestination. The spirit in the body, says one of the Shaykhs, is like the fire in a pile of firewood — the fire is part of Creation, the pile was put together.

Whoever is ignorant of his own nature will be yet more ignorant of external nature. Intelligence is the attribute of the spirit of man, passion that of his soul, and sensation that of his body. Man is a microcosm, his spirit corresponding to Paradise, his soul to Hell, and his body to the place of Resurrection. Paradise is that of which Divine Content is the ground, Hell that of which Divine Anger is the ground; and similarly the Believer's spirit reflects the peace of Knowledge of God, his soul the error which veils him from God. Just as at the Resurrection the Believer must be released from Hell before he may come to Paradise, to real vision and pure love, so in this body a man must free himself from his soul before he can come to actual discipleship, of which the spirit is the principle.

When the Prophet was asked: What means it — the Greater War? he answered: *The struggle against one's soul.* He therefore adjudged the mortification of the soul superior to Holy War against Unbelievers. And this practice, mortification, is a means common to all religions.

Some maintain that salvation depends on predestined Grace, and not on mortification of the soul. It is not the case, they say, that the greatest struggler is the nearest to salvation, but that he who has most of Grace is nearest God. A monk worshipping in his cell may be far from God; a sinner in the tavern may be near Him. And this world shows us nothing nobler than the faith of a child, though a child is not yet subject to the Law, and belongs, in respect of that, to the same category as a madman.

The difference is really one of expression. Man is only guided to mortification by some flash of the Divine Beauty, and inasmuch as that flash was the cause of his mortification, Divine Guidance, or Grace, was its predestined antecedent.

Misguided mortification is a self-chosen human work; it gives rise to trouble and anxiety, and anxiety is always the mark of something wrong. There is a story told of Shaykh Siyah: I once saw my soul, he said. It was shaped like myself, but someone, seizing it by the hair, had given it into my hands. I bound it to a tree, and was on the point of destroying it when it cried out: Do not waste your efforts — I am God's army, and you cannot make me into nothing.

At the time I was a novice, says an eminent companion of Junayd, and had come to know how corrupt the soul was, and to know where it lurked in wait for me, I felt in my heart a continual sense of loathing for it. One day, a thing like a young fox seemed to come out of my throat, and God caused me to recognize that thing as my soul. I trampled it fiercely underfoot; but at every kick I gave it the thing grew bigger.

Other things are killed by blows; how is it that you swell? I cried.

Because I was created perverse, said the thing: I like what hurts other things; their liking is my hurt.

COMPANIONSHIP

Good breeding, said the Apostle of God, *is a part of Faith.* The beauty and propriety of all affairs, religious as well as temporal, depends on a certain discipline of breeding. Humanly, it consists in noble-mindedness; religiously, in observing the True Apostolic Way; in Love, good breeding is reverence. A person who neglects this discipline cannot ever possibly be a saint, for the Prophet said: *Good breeding is a mark of those God loveth.*

Towards God, one must keep oneself from disrespect in one's private as well as one's public behavior. We have it from a sound Tradition that once, when God's Apostle was sitting with his legs akimbo, Gabriel appeared and said: Muhammad, sit as servants sit before a master. For forty years Muhasibi never sat, but always knelt. I am ashamed, he replied when questioned, to sit otherwise than as a servant while I think of God.

Towards oneself, one must avoid what would be improper with a fellow creature or with God. For instance, a man must not lie, representing himself to himself as what he is not. And self-inspection should be modest: Ali is said never to have looked upon his own naked body.

In social intercourse the best rule is to act nobly and observe the Apostolic Way. Human companionship must be for God's sake, not for the soul's sake, nor for interest. He is a bad companion, said Razi, to whom you have to say: Remember me in your prayers. And he is a bad companion with whom you must flatter or apologize.

To novices in the Way solitude is fatal. Satan is with the solitary, as the Apostle said. The Sufi Rule is to treat all according to degree: elders respectfully, as fathers; one's own sort pleasantly and intimately, as brothers; younger people affectionately, as sons. It is not permissible to speak ill of the absent, nor to cast off a companion for anything he says or does, since a companionship begun for God's sake should not be severed by human words or actions. True mystics, regarding any act, see only agency in it: inasmuch as every human being belongs to God and is His creature, to quarrel with a human act is to quarrel with the Divine Agent.

OF MARRIAGE AND CELIBACY

God said: *WOMEN ARE A GARMENT FOR YE, AND YE FOR THEM.*

Marriage is permissible to all, both men and women. It is obligatory on all who otherwise cannot abstain from sin. And Satan, who is with the solitary, adorns lust and presents it beautified to the mind.

No human Companionship compares with marriage in quality of reverence and saving power where husband and wife are well suited. But no pain or care is a worse evil than an uncongenial wife. Therefore the dervish must consider well what he is about, weighing in his imagination the evils of marriage against the evils of celibacy, so that he may choose that state whose evils he personally can more easily master. Neither marriage nor celibacy are disastrous in themselves: the mischief lies in self-assertion, and in surrender to desires. The root of the matter is the difference between Retirement and Companionship as modes of life. Those who choose Companionship are right to marry; but to those who would retire from human affairs celibacy is an ornament.

I asked Gurgani what obligations were involved in human Companionship. Simply this, he answered: never pursuing your own interest — all the evil results that may arise from Companionship arise from selfishness. A selfish man is better off alone. The way to win at the game is to neglect your own interests, and to look after those of your fellow.

If a dervish, choosing the way of Companionship, marries, he should always be kind, he should provide his wife with food and lawful expenses, though he must never pay court to a ruling man for the sake of bounty. He should not indulge in sexual pleasure so long as any obligation to God remains unfulfilled. But as he prays before bed, let him say, as whispering to God: *Lord God, Thou hast mingled lust with Adam's clay for the peopling of Thy world, and in Thy Foreknowledge Thou hast willed this intercourse to me. Cause it to be for two things' sake: firstly as a lawful precaution against what is unlawful; and secondly grant me a child, saintly and acceptable, and one who may never divert my thought from Thee.*

Nowadays it is so impossible for a man to find a wife who is not demanding beyond all reason that many have embraced celibacy. The Sufi Shaykhs are unanimous that the best mystics are celibates. *In the latter days,* the Prophet said, *the light of load shall be best off.* And it was woman who brought on the primal calamity — Adam's. God preserved me from the perils of marriage for eleven years. And then it was my destiny to fall in love — and by description, with a woman I had never seen! Yet for a whole year my passion was so absorbing as almost to ruin my religious life, till God in His Lovingkindness at last took my miserable heart into His Keeping, and delivered me in His Mercy.

There is no lust so fiery hot but heroic effort can quench it; and for this reason: whatever vice proceeds from yourself, you yourself possess also the means that will remove it. You need nothing beyond yourself.

I travelled to a certain village, says Ibrahim Khawwas, to visit a revered man who lived there. His house, when I went in, seemed radiantly pure, like a saint's oratory, with two prayer-niches in different corners. In one sat the old man; in the other an old woman, clean and bright; both frail through much devotion. They gave me a very joyful welcome, and I stayed three days. Just before I left, I asked the old man: What relation to you is this chaste lady?

My cousin, and my wife, he answered.

But you have treated one another like strangers these three days! I said.

Yes, and for five and sixty years, was his reply.

How so?

We fell in love as children, said he; but her father, who knew it, would not give her to me. I was unhappy for a long while; but when he died, my father, as her uncle, gave me her hand. On our wedding night, she said to me: What happiness God has given us — bringing us together! We are afraid of nothing now. Let us refrain tonight from passion of the body, and worship God in thanksgiving. Very well, said I.

Next night she asked me to do the same; and on the third night I said: Two nights now we have given thanks for this happiness at your asking; and tonight let us worship God again, at mine. That was sixty-five years ago. We have never touched one another. And we spend our whole lives in thanksgiving for such happiness as ours.

Lust may disappear in two ways: one involves self-constraint, it is a *fast;* but the other lies quite outside the sphere of human action, even of mortification. It is a kind of fearful tenderness, it is true *love,* something which wells up as a result of the dispersion of one's thought, a love which gradually extends its dominion over all the different parts of the body (not merely the sexual), and takes away from the senses their sensual quality.

PRAYER AND ITS COROLLARIES: LOVE

ETYMOLOGICALLY, THE WORD PRAYER means remembrance and submissiveness; legally it means the five canonical Prayers at the five hours, and involves certain preliminary conditions — purification, a clean coat and an undefiled shirt, an uncontaminated place, turning towards the Direction, and the rest.

As far as a novice is concerned, the whole of the road to God, and any Station which may be his, will be included in the term Prayer.* For a novice, the purification must represent Penitence, the ascertaining of the Direction represent his dependence on his spiritual director, the Bow represent humility, the Stand mortification, the Prostration self-knowledge, the Creed intimacy with God, and the closing Salutation his detachment from the world. Shaykhs will order their disciples to perform four hundred Bows of Prayer in a day and night, to habituate their bodies to devotion.

The four necessities, says one of the Shaykhs, are these: a soul annihilate, faculties lost, a heart made pure, contemplation perfected. Abu Khayr Aqta, who suffered from a gangrened foot, was told by physicians that it must be amputated. He refused to allow the operation. His disciples suggested that it might be cut off while he was praying. He's really unconscious then, they said. The physicians acted on this advice; and Abu Khayr finished his Prayers to find that his foot had been amputated!

All Shaykhs have observed the Canon without reservation. I wandered the earth for forty years, says one, without ever missing public worship, but contriving to be in some town where there was a Mosque every Friday.

All the corollaries of Prayer are included in the Stations of love.

The word Love is said to be derived from a word meaning the seeds that fall on desert ground, the derivation being taken because love is the source of life, as the seed of the plant. And as these seeds, being scattered on the wilderness, settle into the earth, and though rain falls and sun shines and heat and cold pass

* Note. For the Prayer, see pp. 51-53

over them, yet they are not corrupted by changing weathers: they grow and bloom and yield; so love, once settling in the heart, is not corrupted by presence or absence, or by pleasure or pain, or by Separation from God or Unification with Him.

Some theologians maintain that the Divine Love mentioned in Revelation is one of those Traditional Attributes, like God's Face, His Hands, His being seated on the Throne, whose existence would seem rationally impossible had they not been declared Divine Attributes in the Koran and the Tradition of the True Way. We are therefore to affirm and believe them without questioning in what sense we do so. Such theologians would deny that the Love of God has any such meaning as we give it.

But God's Love of man, in truth, is His Goodwill and Mercifulness towards him. Love is one of the terms applicable to His Will, like Content, Wrath, and Mercy; and Will is His eternal Attribute. His Love is His Favor to man, and the reward given a man here and Hereafter, the preservation from sin, and the diversion of a man's thought from all that is other than God. And when God so distinguishes a man, that specialization of His Will is called Love.

Man's love towards God manifests itself in the heart of a devout Believer as reverence, the striving to please his Beloved, and the restless longing for vision of Him. For such a man, repose becomes a sin.

Man's love of God can have nothing common with creaturely love, for the former is an intellectual and volitional desire, the latter a thing of the body. The love of like for like is a lust, an instigation of the soul's, which would get at the essence of what it loves by sexual intercourse! But the love of one unlike What he loves looks towards intimacy with some Attribute, the hearing longs for Something which will never be spoken, the eye longs for Something it can never see. The truest lovers are those who are willing to die of His Nearness, and are not concerned to know what He is like, those who long to be overpowered, and die this death by approach, since for a phenomenal being the only way to the Eternal lies through Omnipotence. And of the two ways of loving God, that of being led by regard of His gifts to love of the Giver and that of being led by regard of the Giver to consciousness of His gifts, the latter is the higher way.

Among mystics, Sumnun asserts that love is the foundation of the whole Way, that all the Conditions and Stations of It are stages of love, that all resting-places may pass away except the resting-place of love, which shall never pass so long as the Way itself remains in existence.

Other Shaykhs, though they agree, yet since love is a current familiar word and they wish the doctrine of religious love to remain a doctrine for initiates, call it not love, but purity, or poverty.

Concerning Lovesickness there is much controversy. Some mystics hold that lovesickness for God may be, mankind being debarred from God as a man may be debarred from his beloved. God not being debarred from man, the term, they say, cannot be applied to God. But others have thought that the term Lovesickness may be applied to Him, on the ground that neither God nor Lovesickness has any opposite.

CONTEMPT

In the Path there is no taint or Veil more difficult to remove than self-esteem. And popularity does more than any other one thing to deter human nature from seeking to come to God.

The Contemptuary, or votary of Contempt, is careful never to resent whatever is said of him; and for the sake of his own salvation he must commit some act which is legally neither a deadly nor a trivial sin, but which will ensure his being generally disapproved.

I once saw enough of a certain Transoxiana Contemptuary to feel at home with him. Brother, I asked him on one occasion, why do you personally do these perverse things?

To make other people's opinion unreal to me, he answered.

Others follow the discipline of Contempt from an ascetic motive: they wish to be generally despised for the sake of mortification of the self. To find themselves wretchedly humiliated is their intensest joy.

Once finding that I was unable to master a certain difficulty in myself, and having in vain performed many devotional exercises in the hope of dispelling it, I repaired — as I had done with success on a former occasion — to the tomb of Bayazid at Bistam in northern Persia. For three months I stayed at the shrine, performing three ablutions and thirty purifications every day in the hope that the trouble would clear up. But it did not; so, deciding to leave, I took the road for Khurasan.

The Sufi Shaykhs of Khurasan in our time are too numerous to mention. I myself have in that province alone met three hundred so gifted as mystics that any one of them would have sufficed the world. The only explanation is to say that love's Sun, and the Way's Part of Fortune must be on the rising degree of the horoscope of that region nowadays.

One night I came to a village in that country where there was a religious house, with a number of aspirants to Sufism in residence. It is part of the Travellers' Rule to regard Residents as their superiors, since they themselves wander for the sake of their own salvation, while the Residents have settled in God's service; their own life is that of seekers, the other life a token of having found. Resident dervishes likewise are bound by their Rule to regard Travellers as their betters, as being detached from the world while they themselves are encumbered with it still. But ignorant Sufis are the vilest things God has made, just as wise Sufis are the noblest. The wise have Truth and no conceit; the ignorant have conceit and no Truth.

I was wearing an ordinary dark-blue frock, but none of the distinctive paraphernalia of a Sufi beyond a staff and a traveller's leather bottle; and these Sufis, not recognizing me, regarded me with a contemptuous eye.

He's not one of us as far as I can see, I heard one say to another.

They were quite right — I was *not* one of them. Still, I had nowhere else to pass the night. A dervish's food is whatever he happens to find, his clothing is whatever happens to cover him, and his home is wherever he happens to be.

They lodged me on a roof, themselves using an upper roof above it. Dry bread, green with mould, was set before me, while I inhaled the savory odor of their own feast. They kept up a running fire of jokes at my expense from their own roof, and after supper began to pelt me with the rinds of the melons they had eaten, by way of emphasizing their complacency with themselves and their low opinion of me.

O Lord God! I kept saying in my heart, over and over again; O Lord God! they wear the livery of Thy friends!

Had it not been for that, I could not have borne this treatment. But actually, the more they scoffed at me, the greater became my inward happiness, even to the point at which bearing this tribulation proved the means of delivering me from the difficulty which I mentioned. I saw then why the elders have always suffered fools.

CONTENT, OR DELIGHT IN FATE

Conceit can only be driven out of a man's head by vision of the Majesty or the Beauty of God, for in that manifestation a man perceives himself no longer.

Human Content, or Delight in Fate, is equanimity towards Fate whether Fate withholds or bestows. It is spiritual steadfastness in the contemplation of events whether they manifest the Divine Beauty or the Divine Majesty, so that whether a man burn in the fire of Wrath or shine in the light of Mercy it is all one. Both Wrath and Mercy are evidences of God. Whatever proceeds from Him is good.

Content comes only by love: it is the lover who is content with whatever the Beloved does. The fruit of this acquiescent Delight in God is a pure knowledge of Him.

This knowledge of God requires abandonment of forethought. Persistent forethought can only arise from ignorance of Predestination. The asserter of Unification with God must believe in Predestination, though he will always act as though he apparently believed in Free Will.

As the intellectual evidences of our religion are to be found among divines, so its visible evidences are to be found among the saints. The word Saint means Friend (of God). The active sense of the root indicates One who desires God; the passive sense One who is the object of God's Desire.

Bayazid defined a saint as one absolutely passive to Divine command and prohibition, since as a man's love for God increases, his heart feels greater enthusiasm for what He commands, and his body grows more remote from what He forbids.

A saint, said Junayd, is absolutely without fear. Fear is the expectation of some evil in the future, or of the future loss of some object of desire; but the saint is entirely the child of his present moment. He has no future. So he has nothing to fear. And likewise he has no hope. Nor does a saint know pain; for pain arises from some present harshness, and how should a saint, glowing with delight in the ordained, feel any harshness?

Miracles may be vouchsafed a saint, as a token of his veracity. A miracle is an act contradicting the customary; and miracles are a distinct species of those things foreordained by God. The miracle of the saint consists in some answer to prayer, the perfecting of some Condition, the empowering of some act, or the supply of necessary and due means of subsistence in some abnormal manner; whereas the miracles Prophets are granted to work consist either in producing something out of nothing or in changing the essential nature of some object.

Prophetic miracles are essentially public, saintly miracles private. For it is the function of the former to have an effect on others, while the latter concern only the person who works them. Further, the worker of prophetic miracles never has any doubt about the supernatural character of what he has wrought, whereas the worker of saintly miracles is never quite sure whether he has really wrought a miracle or has been unconsciously deceived. Even if, as Sari puts it, a man were to go into a garden full of trees, and every tree full of birds, and every bird cried out to him: Peace to thee, thou saint of God! and even if he had no inkling of trickery — even so, it might well be that he was being tricked.

The worker of prophetic miracles has authority over the Law. But the saint is bound to resignation, and obedience under Law. Saints are not preserved from sin: sinlessness is for Prophets only. Nor will a miracle be manifested to a saint unless he is in a Condition of Absence (from himself), a Condition of bewilderment in God. So long as saints are themselves, they remain veiled. It is only when the Veil is gone in the circle of Nearness (to God) that a miracle may occur. In that Condition, worthless stones are seen to be as precious as gold.

Once at Sarakhs I heard Khwaja Khazaini tell this curious story: One day when I was a boy (said he), I was sent out to a special place to fetch mulberry-leaves for the silkworms. When it drew on to the noonday heat, I climbed up into a tree and began to shake the branches; and as I was shaking away, Shaykh Abu Fadl passed by below. He didn't notice me; and I was sure he wasn't quite himself: he looked as if his heart was with God. Suddenly, raising his face, he shouted out boldly, as if to an intimate friend: It's more than a year, Lord, since You gave me a silver bit for a haircut — is that the way to treat Your friends?

No sooner were these words out of his mouth than I seemed to see all the trees around, leaves, boughs, roots, and all, turn into gold.

That's queer! said Abu Fadl in a startled voice. The least hint I utter — a backsliding. A man can't say a word to You, even just to relieve his mind.

One of the experiences of my own life which admits of no natural explanation was this:

I set out to make my way to Tus, intending to ask the Grand Shaykh Gurgani the answer to a question which was at that time disturbing me. When I reached the city, I found him sitting alone in his room in the Mosque, expounding precisely my difficulty to one of the pillars! So that I had my answer without asking my question!

Who are you talking to, Shaykh? I cried.

A moment ago, my son, he answered, God caused this pillar to speak, and it asked me a question, to which I am replying.

But anyone who spends all his time looking for true sages and mystics is wasting it. He will never find what he seeks. *Let him consider himself,* and he will see that the actuality of learning is universal. Let him turn from himself to God, and he will see that the actuality of Gnosis is universal. Let him seek learning and Gnosis of himself, let him demand actual practice from himself.

At bottom there are only two kinds of men: the man whose object of knowledge is himself — and his business is discipline; and the man whose object of knowledge is God — and his business is service and worship.

Retirement consists in choosing a solitary retreat, renouncing the company of one's fellow creatures, and quiet contemplation of the faults one commits; in trying to free the self from human contact and safeguarding other people from one's own bad actions.

GNOSIS

GNOSIS, OR KNOWLEDGE OF GOD, is of two kinds: cognitional (a matter of intellect) and Conditional (a matter of the heart).

Theologians and others give the term to right cognition; but the mystic Shaykhs call right Condition by that name. The Rationalist assertion that it is necessarily intellectual is disproved by the fact that within Islam madmen are deemed capable of Gnosis. Reason and the use of evidences are properly only a means to it, not the cause of it, which is solely God's Will and Grace, without which mind is blind.

God creating the body lodged its life in the spirit; creating the heart, He lodged its life in Himself. Knowledge of Him is supernatural, and is attainable only through continuous bewilderment of the reason; His Favor is a miraculous revelation to the human heart, the miracle being that a saint is led by Reality to deny the reality of his own existence. If God so wills, He makes some Act of His a guide; but willing otherwise, He makes that same Act an obstacle. Thus, Jesus was for some a guide to Gnosis, and for others a hindrance from it — the guided saying: Behold God's Servant! the hindered saying: Behold God's Son! Some likewise have been led to God by idols, and by sun or moon, while others have been led astray by those same things. Such guides are means to Gnosis, but not its cause; and no one means is better than any other in relation to Him Who is Author of them all alike.

Beware of pretending to Knowledge of God, said that Egyptian elder who is called the Man with the Fish. The knower grows more lowly every day. So *never* claim that you possess Gnosis, lest you perish in the pretension.

When a man feels desire or passion, he turns to his heart, willing it to lead him down to the soul, the seat of falsehood. And when he finds the evidence of Gnosis he also turns to the heart, willing it to guide him to the spirit, whence truth comes. But there is still a great difference between turning to one's heart and turning to God. When the Apostle was borne into God's Presence, he said: *I know not how to utter Thy Praise.*

Speak not, and I will speak, it was answered him. *Deem thyself unworthy to praise Me and I will make the universe thy spokesman. Every atom in it shall praise Me for thee.*

FAITH

Faith is belief in God, His Angels, His Books, said the Apostle. Etymologically the word means verification; but its principles are matter of controversy, some maintaining that Faith includes verbal profession, verification, and practice, others that it only includes the former two. The difference is devoid of substance: all the orthodox agree that it has a root and a branch, the root being inward verification and the branch observance of Divine command.

Those who have knowledge of God, though sinners, shall not remain in Hell for ever. But those who have only good works without knowledge of God will not enter Paradise, for the Apostle said: *None of ye shall be saved by his works.*

Whoever knows God, knows Him through some Attribute; and his noblest Attributes are of three kinds: those connected with His Beauty, His dreadful Majesty, and His Perfection respectively. His Perfection lying beyond the scope of all still imperfect things, there remain for men Beauty and Majesty. Men for whose knowledge of God His Beauty is the evidence are in a state of perpetual longing for vision of Him. Those whose evidence is the Majesty are in a state of perpetual abhorrence from their own attributes. Now not only is that perpetual longing an effect of love, but so is the abhorrence of human attributes the same; for the removal of the Veil of attributes is very and essential love. So that both Faith and Knowledge *are* love. And obedience is the token of love. To deny this, to neglect His Imperative, is to *know nothing* of Him.

Faith may be shortly described as absorption in the search for God. Where it exists, agnosticism disappears. *KINGS, WHEN THEY ENTER A CITY, LAY IT IN RUINS.*

Faith is the heart's belief in that Knowledge which issues from the unseen, said Ibn Khafif. For Faith is always faith in something not seen; it can only be attained if God strengthens certitude, and that by a gift of Knowledge from Himself.

PURIFICATION

After Faith, the first necessity is Purification. It is double — outward and inward, Prayer requiring a purified body and Gnosis a purified heart. They must go together: when a man washes his hands, he must wash his heart clean of worldliness; rinsing his mouth, he must purify it of the mention of any other thing than God; washing his face, he must turn it away from all familiar things towards God; wiping his head, he must resign his affairs to Him. The method of spiritual purification is a meditation on the evil of this world, realizing how false and fleeting the world is, and so emptying the heart of it: a result attainable only through mortification, of which the chief is to observe the external rules of discipline always.

Shibli one day purified himself to go to the Mosque; but as he went he heard a voice cry: Clean outside! but what's pure within? He turned back and gave away his whole property. Thereafter he was assiduous in purification. I never neglected any rule of purification, he said, but some vain conceit arose in my heart. When he was dying, and too weak to perform the rite, he made a sign to one of his disciples to purify him. The disciple, obeying, yet forgot to let the water flow through his beard; and Shibli, who could no longer speak, seized his hand and pointed to the beard, so that all was duly done.

As he who would serve God must purify himself outwardly with water, so he who would come near to God must purify himself inwardly, by Penitence.

Penitence, you must know, is the pilgrim's first Station on the Way to Reality. The word means Return; and this return has within it its own three Stations: Remorse, the return from great sin to duty; Contrition, the return from minor sins to love; and Homecoming, the return from selfhood to God.

As to its nature and property, the mystic Shaykhs think variously. Tustari and others believe that it consists in never forgetting your sins, but perpetually thinking of them with Remorse, so that you may not take pleasure in yourself because of any good you may have done, Remorse for an evil act being higher than good works. Junayd and others think the opposite, namely that Penitence consists in oblivion of sin, remembrance of which in contemplation is a Veil between God and man.

I learned more from this verse of an old poet, said Junayd, than from anything else in all the many books I read:

But what's my fault? I say. She answers: Dolt!
That you are there at all is your great fault.

When the memory of a sin stirs no more delight, Penitence is come, says Bushanji. And the recollection of sin must always be accompanied either by Remorse or desire. One who remembers sin and feels desire is a sinner still. The act of sin is less evil than the desire for it; for the act done is gone; desire goes on.

FASTING

Gabriel told me that God said: FASTING IS FOR ME, AND I REWARD IT. So runs the Tradition.

The religious practice of Fasting is a mystery. It does not look to a practical end. As Junayd put it: Fasting is half the Way.

One month's abstinence from sunrise to sunset without intermission is incumbent on every adult Believer of sound mind; the fast begins on the appearance of the moon of Ramadan and continues till the appearance of the Shawwal moon. The obligations involved include keeping the belly from food and drink, the eye from looking with lust, the ear from listening to slander, the tongue from vain or foul language, and the body from worldly pursuit and disobedience. And yet: *Many a one,* said the Prophet, *has no good of his Fasting except the hunger and thirst of it.* Merely to abstain from food and drink is child's play.

Hunger sharpens understanding. Involuntary hunger is not actual, for one who desires to eat, even though God may have decreed that he shall not, is virtually eating; the good results from hunger are for him who abstains, not for him who is debarred, from eating. Obedience or disobedience in me, said Qassab, depend on two cakes of bread: when I eat I discover in myself the stuff of every sin; but when I abstain I discover in myself the foundation of all religious action.

Simple people are satisfied that continuance in Fasting is possible, though medical men insist that the belief is absolutely without foundation. But I myself knew an old man who twice a year kept forty-day fasts in the desert. And I was present at the deathbed of Danishmand Banghari; he had tasted no food for eighty days, yet he had not missed public Prayer once. The explanation must be that continuance in Fasting is miraculous, and by Grace. It is well known that Shaykh Sarraj, called the Peacock of the Poor, coming to Baghdad for Ramadan, was given a private room in the Shunizia Mosque, and appointed to preside over the meetings of devotees until the Feast. During the course of the Ramadan Night Prayers he recited the whole Koran five times. One of the Mosque servants, who had brought him a loaf of bread to his room every night, discovered, after he left on the day of the Feast, all the thirty loaves untouched.

The fruit of voluntary hunger is Contemplation, to which the mortification is preliminary. The forty-day fasts of modern saints derive from that of Moses. When thirty days are done, the faster massages his teeth; then he fasts ten days more, and God speaks to his heart. The real hearing of a Word from God is not compatible with the subsistence of the natural temperament; the four humors must therefore be deprived of nourishment for forty days, in order that they may be utterly subdued, and that the subtlety of spirit may hold absolute sway over all.

SOME TECHNICAL TERMS THE MYSTICS USE

All craftsmen talking of the mysteries of their craft use certain words whose meaning is only understood by those who follow the trade. These technical terms serve a double purpose: to facilitate understanding by the apprentice, and secondly to keep the mysteries of the craft from unfit persons, the uninitiated. Sufi mystics have their own terms.

Station and *Condition:* A Station is a man's standing in the Way. It denotes his perseverance in fulfilling what is at that period of his life obligatory on him. He may not pass on from that Station without accomplishing all he is bound to do there. The first Station, for instance, is Penitence, the next Conversion, then Renunciation, then Trust, and so on. A man may not pretend to Conversion without complete Penitence, nor to Trust without complete Renunciation.

Condition, on the other hand, is Something that comes down from God into a man's heart quite independently of that man's power. One can neither keep away a Condition by one's own effort, nor keep it when it passes away. It is a Grace, and unconnected with mortification. Some Shaykhs have thought and others have denied that a Condition may last. Junayd says: Conditions are like flashes of lightning — the notion that they are lasting is a suggestion from the soul. But all agree that no man is a fit guide for others until he is *Confirmed,* and has escaped from the wheel of the Conditions.

Station is not the same as Confirmation. Everyone who longs for God has some particular Station, which is his clue at the beginning of his quest. Whatever good he derives from other Stations through which he may pass, he will finally rest in one, since one Station and its own quest include and call for complex combination and design, not merely conduct and practice.

Adam's Station, for instance, was Penitence, Noah's was Renunciation, and Abraham's Resignation. Contrition was Moses' Station, and Sorrow David's. The Station of Jesus was Hope, that of John the Baptist Fear. Our Prophet's was Praise. Whatever these men drew from other wells by which they dwelt a while, each man returned at last to his original Station.

But Confirmation is the final resting-place of the spiritually perfected. It is a higher level. Those who are at a Station of the Way may pass on from that Station; but beyond Confirmation it is impossible to pass. The Stations are stages along one's path; Confirmation is quiet within the shrine where the path ends. *Love at the first is quest; love at the last is rest. Water in the river-bed flows on; but when it reaches the Sea it flows no more; its taste is changed. Men whose craving is for water will turn from the water of the Sea. But men whose craving is for pearls will offer themselves to death, fasten the plummet of search to their feet, and plunge, determined either to win the pearl that's hidden there or lose dear life itself.*

What mystics call *Occasion* is a peculiar event as a result of which one loses all sense of past and future. It is as if an influence from God shoots down into the soul, and composes or collects the heart into a single moment, so that one retains no memory of what is gone, no thought of what is not yet come. People in general are incapable of this: they are merely ignorant of past or future.

There are two sorts of Occasion: one in Loss, the other in Gain, the former subjecting a man to Discrimination, the latter to Union. But in both kinds of Occasion one is *enforced,* for that Union or Discrimination is effected by God, independently of one's own will. When power of volition is thus shorn, whatever one does or experiences is the result of the Occasion itself.

Nobody can achieve Occasion — the reality of it — by exerting choice; it cannot be humanly acquired by any effort, or bought though a man offer his life for it. The will can neither draw it down nor fight it off.

Occasion is a sword that cuts, say the Shaykhs. It cuts off future and past by the roots. But a sword is a dangerous companion: it may make its owner a king, but it may also be the death of him. A man may worship his sword, may carry it on his shoulder a thousand years — yet when it comes to cut and thrust the sword cares nothing whose is the neck it severs, its master's neck as well as another's. Force is characteristic of it, and the man who has Occasion cannot wish the Force away from it.

But a Condition may descend upon Occasion to beautify it, as the spirit beautifies the body. When a man visited by Occasion is also possessed of Condition, he is as it were stabilized in the Condition, without which the Occasion may pass and be lost to him as if it had never been. So possessed, he ceases to be unrecollected. One may not talk of a Condition; what one does will be the evidence of its reality. That is why the Shaykhs say: To inquire about a Condition is absurd. It annihilates descriptive faculty. It banishes personal feeling, either joy or sorrow. In the pleasure of Occasion one is still with oneself; in the bliss of Condition one is with God. And ah! how far apart are these two degrees.

Once in the desert, Junayd records, I came upon a dervish, sitting under a mimosa tree in a flinty comfortless place, and asked him for what cause he sat there so still.

In this place I was visited by Occasion, said he; and here I lost it, so that now I sit here and mourn.

How long have you been here? I inquired.

Twelve years, he answered. Will the Shaykh be good enough to offer a Prayer for me, so that perhaps I may find my Occasion again?

I went on my way, performed the Pilgrimage, and prayed for him. My Prayer was granted, as I discovered on my way back; but he still sat in the same place.

Why don't you leave, now that your wish has come true? I asked him.

Shaykh, he replied, I settled in this desolate place where I lost my all; and would it be right to leave the place where I found my all again, and where I rejoice, knowing that God is here with me? Let the Shaykh go in peace; for I will mix my dust with the dust of this spot, that I may rise at Resurrection from this same dust where my delight has been.

SAY: GOD IS ONE runs the Word. The term *Unification* is used in three senses: one, Divine, that is, God's Knowledge of His own Unity; two, creative, that is, Decree creating Unification in a man's heart; three, human, that is, man's knowledge of God's Unity. Real Unification implies the knowledge as well as the assertion of a thing's unity. There is a saying of Junayd's that Unification is the parting of the eternal from what has originated in time. If the eternal is believed to descend into phenomena, or phenomena to participate in the eternal, no distinction of Divine Eternity and universal origination in time remains; the result is materialism. And the materialist knows no essential distinction between man and beast. Evil to him is simply what stands in the way of his desires; and everything with him turns on the question of pleasure and pain.

Unification disproves what human knowledge affirms about things. Ignorance merely contradicts knowledge; and ignorance is *not* Unification, which can only be attained by realizing the falsity of that appropriation of ideas to oneself in which both knowledge and ignorance alike consist. Unification is this, says Junayd again: that one should merely be a *persona* wielded by God, over which His Decrees pass, dead to both the appeal of mankind and one's answer to it, lost to sense and action alike by God's fulfilling in oneself what He has willed, namely that one's last state shall become one's first state, and that a man shall be what he was before he existed.

Bayazid said that even lovers are Veiled from God by their love. And there is this defect in love, that it must have a desirer and a desired — two. God may be the Desirer and man the desired, or man may be the desirer and God the Desired. In the former case, man's being is fixed in God's Desire. If man is the desirer and God the Desired, the searching creature can find no way to come to his Desire. In either case the canker of being remains in the lover.

It has been said that Gnosis is in the first instance an acquisition, but that it becomes finally an intuition. Man, however, with all his attributes, is quite other than God. If any human attributes are accounted Divine, then man himself must be accounted so; in which case the asserter of Unification, the Unifying act, and the One become three realities united in a causal relationship; and this is precisely a Trinity, on the Christian model.

The whole question cannot be understood without reference to the analogy of Composition and Discrimination. I myself am persuaded that Unification is simply a mystery, a Revelation, and that it does not admit of any human expression in words, least of all in elaborate phrases. During the course of a lecture by Husri, says a certain Shaykh, I fell asleep, and saw in a dream two angels, who came down from above and listened for some time to the discourse. Then one said to the other: It is the theory of Unification he speaks of — it is not the essence of It.

When I woke up, Husri was actually engaged in explaining Unification. He fixed me with his eye, and said: It is impossible to speak of actual Unification, So-and-so, one can only speak of the theory of it.

Composition is a mystery: the co-existence of the Divine Knowledge with the Divine Will. *GOD CALLS TO THE ABODE OF PEACE: AND GUIDES THITHER WHOM HE WILLETH*. He calls all; then He keeps some away. In Composition, God bade Satan worship Adam and willed the contrary, that he should not. *Discrimination* is the realm of the manifest, where the forbidden and the bidden are clear. Mystics use the latter term for such human acts as mortification; but Divine gifts such as the contemplative vision of God are ascribed to Composition. God's Love may be so absolute over His servant's heart that the man loses all control over his own actions, and his state is one of Composition, as Bayazid's was in the hour when he cried those words (normally forbidden): Glory to Me! How great is My Majesty!

Some shallow mystics, falling into an error not far removed from Unbelief, assert that results do not depend on our own exertions; and that since our devotions and mortification in the Discriminate state are imperfect they might as well be left undone. But even if Discrimination is recognized as an imperfect state, its authority should never be let go. It has been said that though Composition is privileged and Discrimination servile, they cannot be separated, for one of the works of privileged condition is to fulfill servile duties. A man cannot be released from self-mortification and religious duty without good excuse recognized by Law.

Composition in man is the compounding of *thought* with an object of *desire*. Majnun the mad lover so concentrated his thought on Layla that he saw only her in the whole world, and in his eyes other creatures assumed Layla's form. The mystic principle is the same. God has divided the single substance of His Love; and He bestows a particle of love as a peculiar gift upon each one of His friends, in proportion to their enravishment with Him. Then upon that particle He lets down the shrouds of humanity, nature, temperament, spirit, in order that by the powerful working of that ferment of love it may transmute to its own quality all other particles attached to it, until even the lover's clay is wholly converted into love, and every act and every glance of his is no more than the indispensable circumstantial condition of love.

Intoxication is a mystic term denoting ecstatic love for God; *Sobriety* proposes the attainment of some end. Bayazid and his disciples, who think Intoxication the higher way, maintain that Sobriety stabilizes human attributes which are the greatest of all Veils between God and man. But my own Shaykh, following Junayd, used to say that Intoxication is a playground for children, and Sobriety a mortal battlefield for men.

A mere blinding can never really free one from the bondage of phenomena. It is simply error of vision which keeps people sunk in the phenomenal world; it is by vision that one escapes the bondage. And there are two ways of seeing truly: one may see either with the eye of one's own subsistence (in God's Will) or with the eye of one's own annihilation. Seen through the eye of subsistence, the whole universe is less real than oneself: the self-subsistence of phenomena *cannot be seen.* Seen through the eye of annihilation, the whole creation is seen as unreal, so real is the subsistence of God. Either way leads free of phenomena.

Maghribi in the earlier part of his life passed twenty years withdrawn, living in deserts where he never heard the sound of a human voice, till his frame was wasted away, and his eyes shrunken to the size of the eye of a sacking-needle.

At the end of that term, he felt commanded to return to the companionship of men, and decided to go to those who live around the Holy House, for greater blessing. Hearing that he was coming, the Shaykhs of Mecca went out to meet him; and beholding a man so altered as hardly to seem a human creature, they asked: Tell us, Abu Othman, why did you go away? what did you see? and what did you gain?

What did I go for? he replied. Intoxication. And what did I see? The evil of Intoxication. And what did I gain? Despair.

GOD STRAITENETH AND ENLARGETH. Straitness and *Enlargement* are involuntary Conditions, the former denoting the contraction of the heart in the state of being Veiled, the latter the heart's expansion in the illuminated state. My own Shaykh used to tell me that both are the result of the same spiritual effusion from God upon man, which either stimulates the heart and depresses the soul, causing Enlargement, or depresses the heart and stimulates the soul, in Straitness. There is no love without jealousy; and the Straitened heart is evidence of God's Jealousy. And lovers always have to reproach one another; the heart Enlarged marks that mutual upbraiding.

John was in Straitness, Jesus in Enlargement; for John, according to a well-known Tradition, wept from the day he was born, and Jesus from the day he was born smiled. When they met, John used to say: *Jesus, hast thou no fear thou wilt be cut off from God?*

John, hast thou no hope of Mercy? Jesus would reply. *Neither thy tears nor my smiling will change Decree.*

Intimacy and *Awe* are two Conditions which all pilgrims in the Way to God know. Where the Majesty predominates in a manifestation to the heart, one feels Awe; where the Beauty of God predominates, then Intimacy. Awe is pain; Intimacy a joy.

Some Shaykhs have said that Intimacy is the novice's degree, and Awe the Gnostic's. If Intimacy is possible at all in later stages, it can only be Intimacy with His Praise. Perhaps (and this is my own view) the power of Awe is exerted upon the soul, towards the annihilation of the human nature in us, while the power of Intimacy, working in the heart, is towards Gnosis. By *Force* is meant that energy God gives a man to keep the soul from its desire. By *Grace* is meant the Divine energy lent towards the heart's subsistence. Followers of Grace say that it is the attainment of a desire; followers of Force say that it is this: God through His Will keeps man from his will. If a thirsty man plunged into a river, and that river immediately ran dry, that would be Force.

What we choose for ourselves is harmful for us. I desire only that God do my desiring for me, thereby preserving me from the evil of desire. If He keep me in Force, I do not wish for Grace. If He keep me in Grace, I do not wish for Force.

Knowledge inseparable from practice and Condition, so that the knower invariably expresses what he is, the Shaykhs call Gnosis, and such a knower they call a *Gnostic*. One who knows verbal formulations in such a manner that they are part of his memory system but not fact of his spirit, they call *Learned*. They use Learned as a term of disparagement.

By *Reality* Sufis mean simply God. By *Justice* they mean the relegation of everything to its proper place. Some of their terms are hard to put in other words, but they may be shortly indicated:

Excess: Something in the heart like an excess of light.

Fastness: the heart's special confidence that it will attain its end.

Proposal: the heart's affirmation of the object of its longing, in face of the actual negation of that object.

King: one whose actions do not allow of interference.

Notion: by this Sufis mean something occurring involuntarily to the mind, quickly succeeded by another thought. Those who are subject to Notions follow their first thoughts in religious matters. An incident of Khayr's discipleship illustrates this: The Notion came into his mind that Junayd, his Shaykh, was standing outside his door waiting. He dismissed the Notion;

but it returned a second time, then a third. So he went out to see;
and there was Junayd.

If you had acted on your first thought, said Junayd, I
would not have had to stand here all this time.

The question has been asked: How did Junayd come to be
aware of the Notion which had occurred to Khayr? All one can
say is that it was Junayd's function to know what his disciple
experienced.

Trial is the probation of a saint's heart by Fear, Straitness,
and so forth.

Affliction is the probation of a saint's body by sickness
and other troubles. Affliction is a blessing: there is Divine
recompense for supporting pain when the mystery of it is incom-
prehensible. The troubles which befall irreligious people are not
Affliction, but mere misery unrelieved.

Deception: appearance being contrary to truth. The term
is only used of Divine Deception, as when God shows a Believer
in the disguise of an Unbeliever until it is time for His Decree to
be revealed. There is one other use: of a mystic who conceals
good qualities under a wicked mask it may be said: He practices
Deception. This is the only exception: Sufis would not apply the
term to ostentation (though strictly speaking that is deceptive),
since they reserve it for Divine Action.

Drink, in Sufi parlance, is the sweetness of piety, the de-
lightfulness of Grace, the pleasantness of Intimacy. As water
is the body's drink, this pleasant sweetness is the heart's drink.

My Shaykh used to say that a novice without Drink is an
outsider, but a Gnostic who still has it is also an outsider. The
novice has to have it. But the Gnostic ought not to feel it, lest he
be transported with the feeling, instead of with God. If he
returns to his soul, he will never come to rest.

SUBSISTENCE AND ANNIHILATION

The best of the Sufi mystics do not use the expressions

Subsistence and Annihilation with reference to knowledge or Condition, but only to degrees of saintly perfection, applying them to those saints freed from the imprisoning Stations and the wavering Conditions, whose search has ended in finding, and who have discovered all the secrets of the heart. Such saints, recognizing how imperfect is even that discovery, have turned away from all things and purposely become annihilate in the Object of desire, losing all personal desires in the Essence of Desire. When a man thus becomes annihilate from his attributes, he reaches perfect Subsistence. He is neither Near nor Far from God, neither Sober nor Intoxicated. He has neither name nor sign nor brand nor mark.

Many shallow mystics have cried that Annihilation may be total. But Annihilation of substance is impossible. Whoever is Annihilate from his own will still subsists in the Will of God; for God's Will is everlasting.

Annihilation comes to a man through vision of the Majesty of God, through revelation of Omnipotence to his heart. Then, in that overwhelming sense of Majesty, both worlds are obliterate, Conditions and Stations appear as far away below that soaring vision, even anything he may have been shown of Grace vanishes into nothing; he becomes dead to reason, dead to passion, dead even to his own Annihilation; and in that Annihilation of Annihilation his tongue can only say: God! all mind and body being humbled and thrown down below.

The Divine mysteries come and go over the dervish, in such a manner at first that he still thinks of his affairs as his own, attributes his actions to himself, connects his ideas with himself. But once his concerns are freed from this tie of appropriation, his acts are no longer his own. Then he is merely a place over which Something passes, no longer a passer-by; he is the Way, and is a wayfarer no more.

When the dervish Makki lay dying, he spoke to me: If you see that I am saved, then, when they bear my body to the grave, strew almonds on it, and sugar, and say: There's for the wise.

But how shall I know? I asked him.

When my last moment comes, said he, put your hand in mine. If I press it, you will know that God has saved me; but if I let it go, you will know that my end has not been happy.

So I sat by him. In the moment of death he firmly clasped my hand. And when his bier was borne along, I scattered the almonds and the sugar on it, and said as he bade me: There, that's for the wise.

THE ABYSS

Commit your name to Me, so that in what you are known as I may meet you. Discard even all names, attributes, and portions of knowledge I may show you as part of the Majesty of the Vision of Me.

There is evil magic in all things, and names are witchcraft of letters. Free yourself from the names, you will free yourself from what they denote.

he MADE THE SEA MY STATION: I beheld ships sinking, and planks floating away. Then the planks too sank; and the Voice said: Nothing that floats escapes drowning.

Who, not taking ship to float, throws himself in, risks drowning.

Who takes ship to float and will not risk drowning, drowns.

In risk is a portion of safety: the Waves come, heaving up what is within them, and fall upon the Shore.

The surface of the Sea is Light, the end of the Light not to be come to, into such distance the path of the Light stretches. The Sea-bottom is Darkness beyond sounding; and between go the Monsters from which no one is safe.

Do not sail over the Sea, lest I Veil you from Myself by the vessel. Do not throw yourself in, lest I Veil you by the Sea itself. Within the Sea are wards and bounds; but what Sea-bound will stay you up? If you give yourself to the Sea and drown in it, you will be even as one of the Sea-creatures.

I should betray you if I pointed you towards anything but Myself. If you die into any other thing than Me, there you will remain even where and as you died.

This world is for him I have turned from it, and from whom I have turned it. The Other is for him to whom I have made It and Myself near things.

he MADE THE IMPERATIVE MY STATION. Do as I bid you! said the Voice. Do not wait for understanding: to wait to understand My Imperative is to disobey the Imperative and obey your understanding.

Do you know what it is which slows you from performing the Imperative? and tells you to wait till you understand? It is your soul, which craves to know, that she may stand higher than My Decrees, and walk at will in the paths of intellect. Intellectual apprehension has its various trends, the trends their channels, the channels their various outlets and mains, the mains their various windings.

Perform the Imperative in the instant I make it Imperative and trouble yourself not to understand. So Those of My Presence, the Angels of the Decrees, perform what They are commanded. Execute without question, and you will be of Me, and I of you. This is not jealousy; intellectual apprehension is another appointed Station, for I have made it an instrument of judgment. But when I reveal to you some understanding I shall command you imperatively to use that instrument for judgment then.

If I bid, and intellect intervenes, banish intellect. If your heart intervenes, dismiss your heart. Go alone, and you will go forward. If anything else is with you, it will stop you short of that advance; for intellect will bid you wait to understand. Only when it knows will intellect choose. And if the heart knows, the heart will follow its own desire.

LIGHTS AND DARK

he SAID: WHO ARE YOU? Who am I? Then I saw Sun and Moon and Stars and all Lights.

There is no other Light, said the Voice, in all the streams of the Sea of Me than these which you have seen. Then all things, until there was nothing, came to me and kissed me between the eyes and bid me Peace and stood aside in shadow.

This is your knowledge of Me, said the Voice; but My Knowledge of you is not yet. I saw my garments as it were attached to the entirety of Him, but not myself.

Look! worship of Me! said the Voice. And my garment bowed down; yet I remained standing, and did not bow down.

And now the Voice said: What am I? Sun and Moon went dark, all the Stars fell and went out, the Lights were quenched, and Shadow grew over all except Himself — my eyes saw nothing, my ears heard nothing, feeling departed; and then everything shouted: God Greater than All! and everything came at me with a drawn sword.

Now escape! said the Voice.

Where?

Fall in the Darkness!

I fell through darkness; and there in the dark I saw myself as a person, and heard: Never see any man but yourself; never try to come out of the Darkness until I take you out. When I take you out, it will be to show you Myself; and then you will see Me; and when you see Me there will never be anything beyond That.

he MADE TRAVEL MY STATION. I saw all the Roads: they were all underground.

There are no Roads aboveground, said the Voice. But I saw all men and women going aboveground, and those Roads empty; then I saw people turning their faces up to the sky, and they all stayed where they were on the ground. But others bent their looks upon the ground; they all went down underground and began to walk along the Roads.

Those who do not walk those Roads will never find Me, said the Voice; but now that you know where I am, never tell. Then I saw Him, Veiling all things, and connecting all things.

Keep to the Veiling, let the connections alone! said the Voice. Come in to Me without asking leave; if you ask leave, I will put a Veil between us. When you come, go without asking leave; if you ask leave, I will put you in prison. At each of these Words I saw the showing of a needle and the hiding of a thread.

Sit in the needle's eye, said the Voice; never leave it: when the thread enters, never grasp the thread; when it slips through, never hold it back. And rejoice: I love all who rejoice. Tell the others: It was only me He admitted, He turned you all away. For if they come with you, I will admit them and turn you away. And if they do not come, I will excuse them and blame you for their not coming.

So I saw that all persons must do as they will.

You are My friend, said the Voice: and if ever you cannot find Me, look for Me in the fiercest rebel against Me, and when you find Me there do not yourself rebel against him. If you cannot find Me there, take a sword and strike, but not to kill; you are responsible for him to Me. Between you and Me let all be clear to you. Between others and Me let nothing be clear to you; as to that, let it be open war between you and Me, and you on their part against Me.

Further, if I give you anything you want, sacrifice it, burn it, and go among the needy and stand in the shadow of some needy man and bid him ask it of Me. Never ask for yourself, lest I give to you and deprive another, which will put you in the opposite party to Me, forsaken of Me.

At that I saw the throwing away of all as the victory.

The Voice said: If you throw all away you will have nothing; and I love only the rich, and hate only the poor. I do not say that you are either rich or poor, for I do not give things names.

he MADE A STATION OF UNDERSTANDING MY STATION. The wider the Vision extends, said the Voice, the narrower grows Prayer: when I have concentrated your quality and heart in Vision of Me, What have you to do with supplication any more? Will you pray Me to remove the Veil? I have removed it. Will you pray Me to Veil Myself? If I do that, who is left for you to communicate with?

When you have seen Me once, there are only two things left to pray for: when I am absent for you, you may pray Me to keep you in My Sight; when you see Me, you may pray Me to enable you to say to a thing: Be! and that it shall be.

Yet I give you leave to pray in Absence. If you can calculate these things, subtract the degree of Vision from the degree of Absence and let whichever is the greater be the greater in what you pray for. But if when you eat I am not absent, I shall relieve you of the distraction of laboring for food. If when you go to sleep I am not absent, I shall not be absent when you wake.

Any resolve of yours to keep silence when you have Vision is a Veil; how much more any resolve to speak! Such a resolve can only come of Absence. I cannot appear to any eye but I annihilate that eye, nor to any heart but I annihilate that heart.

Ignorance is a Veil to Vision; but knowledge too is a Veil to Vision. I am all the unveiled Without; I am all the unrevealed Within.

Who knows the Veil is near the Revelation: the Veil is always one and the same Veil, though the occasions and materials are many — the specific Veils.

he MADE ANOTHER STATION OF UNDERSTANDING MY STATION. Eternity praises Me, said the Voice, being one among My Attributes; and out of the chanting of that praise I have made Night and Day, to be Veils over the eyes and fancies of men, and over their hearts and minds. Night and Day are the two Veils which cover all I have created; but since I chose you for Myself I lifted them, for you to see Me behind.

And now you have seen Me, stand fast in your Station, wait in the Vision. Otherwise you will be snatched by every thing that exists.

I lifted the Veil for this alone: that you should see Me. This is to make you strong enough to bear another Sight: the heavens splitting, and What then descends, and the manner of Its descent; and that you may see how That too comes from My

Presence, even as harmless Night and Day and every thing I show you comes.

*h*e MADE THE STATION OF UNDERSTANDING THE DUST MY STATION. Everything that is on the dust is of the dust, said the Voice. Therefore now consider the dust well, and you will eliminate what is of it, and will see in the dust that Power which transforms it from one visible individual to another, and then the individuals will no longer be distraction.

Take aids of ascetic practice against the wandering of your gaze; if your gaze no longer wanders at all, you will need the aids no more. But this dispensing with aids will not be until time has ceased to be for you; and there will be no time only when individuals have ceased to be for you; and there will be no individuals only when you cannot see them for seeing Me.

*h*e MADE THE STATION OF UNDERSTANDING HIS CLOSENESS MY STATION. No thing is any farther from Me than any other thing, said the Voice, except as I establish its closeness or its distance.

By experience of My Closeness you are enabled to know My Distance. My Closeness is immediately known to you, as by sensation; the first simple knowledge of it begins with your so perceiving the trace of Vision of Me in everything that this trace affects you more than what you know of the thing. But Closeness as you know it compared with Closeness as I know it is like your knowledge compared with My Knowledge.

I am Close. Yet not as one thing is near another. I am Distant. Yet not as one thing is far from another. Your own closeness and distance are not properties of yourself: it is I Who am both the Close and the Distant, My Closeness stretching into Distance and My Distance lying absolutely close. You measure your closeness and distance by space; Mine are not spatial. I am

closer to the tongue than its utterance in the very moment of
utterance.

Whoso witnesses Me formulates nothing. Whoso formulates Me witnesses nothing. A man who witnesses and then
formulates is Veiled by the formulation: what he witnesses is
no longer Real.

I make Myself known to you; yet you do not know Me —
that is Distance. Your heart has Vision of Me; yet it does not
see Me — that is Distance. You describe Me; yet your description has no correspondence with Me — that is Distance.

My Voice comes to you from your heart; yet the Voice is
really from Me — that is Distance. You see yourself; yet I am
Closer to you than your sight is — that is Distance.

he BROUGHT ME TO THE FURTHEST STATION OF UNDER-
STANDING. Never go out of your house except to enter Me, said
the Voice. But I am GOD; neither can you enter My Presence
bodily nor can you partake of My Knowledge imaginatively.

Whenever you see any thing with your heart and your eye
at once, whether an outward thing or an inward thing matters
not so long as I make you a spectator of its immediate subordi-
nation to Me, yet of its infinitesimal littleness with Me in the
terrible Majesty of My Omnipotence, I have appointed this
portion of Knowledge for you. You will know as a spectator
only; you will not be able to utter it; but in this I open a passage
beyond that knowledge, so that you may pass away from other
cognizances of the Infinite and the tongues which uttered them.

There I open My Gates to you.

Those Gates are only entered by one whose knowledge is
mighty enough to sustain knowledge of the Gates, so that you by
your knowledge hold up the Gates, and not They you. For mark:
I have caused you to have some comprehension of the Gates; but I
have not let you come within Their comprehension.

And so you come to the skirts of the Presence, where the
coming of one or another is made known. In this moment re-

flect: who you are, and out of what you came in; what you know which gave you the strength to enter, and why you listened, and learned enough to bear the weight of the Gates.

In the hour when I make you spectator of all existences at once in a single Vision, then at that Station I have certain forms, which if you find you know, call on Me by the forms. But if you do not know the forms, then in your agony invoke Me by the pain of that Vision.

The Vision will be thus: you will be given sight of the whole Height and Depth, the whole Length and Breadth, and the All within, and all those modes in which that Totality exists, as a thing manifest, eternal, entirely ordered, and convulsed in endless struggle. You will observe the existence of each thing; you will see its gaze bent in upon itself, since each particular of that Totality may only move on towards phases of itself; but you will observe whole regions of Totality visible to the eye, and in each an existence establishing its own holy song, each directed towards Me in worship, in its own Praising, staring at Me in a Glorification which distracts it from anything other than its continuance in its own devotion.

Then, when you see all existences with their faces so turned, say: Thou Who by manifestation of Thy Sovereignty art Conqueror of all things, making them Thine Own by the tyranny of Thy Strength, Thou alone art the Powerful. There is no resisting; there is no describing.

And when you behold the Staring (which is their only mode of glorifying), then say: O Merciful, O Compassionate! I pray to Thee now by Thy Mercy. By Mercy Thou hast established Thy creatures' minds in Thy Knowledge. By Mercy hast Thou given them their strength, and lifted them up to the mention of Thee, and stirred them unto yearning love for Thee. I pray to Thee now by Thy Mercy. By Mercy Thou hast made nobler before Thee the Station of that one of all Thy creatures whom it pleased Thee.

Knowledge you feel; realization of knowledge is something you may only see as a spectator. It was from the direction of your heart that I sent portions of knowledge to you. Was not that to withdraw you from the general to the special? What is it but Revelation that I made you privileged, making Myself known to you? So that you may now leave your heart behind, and abandon all the knowledge which once so filled your seeing. Does not Revelation mean that you are to dismiss everything, dismiss the knowing of everything, and be only a spectator of Me in what I make you see?

Let no fear alarm you at such a time as will come; and let no companion comfort you in the hour when I shall make you My spectator, and cause Myself to be known to you, though it may be but once in your lifetime. For I will tell you in that hour, and you will know, that you are My lover, inasmuch as you will deny all things for the sake of what I have made you see, so that I shall become your Sovereign Disposer; and you will come to where I am on one side and all things on the other side. You will be attached to Me; all things else shall attach to you, and not to Me.

Such is My lover. And know this: you are to be My lover. And all your knowledge then will be knowledge of My Love.

. . . no resisting . . . no describing . . .

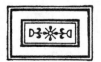

THE PUBLIC ROAD

Ordinary people prefer what they can understand.

The Definition of Orthodoxy

 LL MEN NEED TO KNOW that there is only one God. As First, He has always been. As Last, He will never cease to be. He is not enclosed in space: he is Eternal and Incomprehensible. He is the Hearer, Who hears all, and the Seer, Who sees all; of all His Attributes these are the only two men can apprehend, nor can any creature of His attain them all.

Man should also know that His Word is Uncreate, spoken through Gabriel and revealed to His Prophet.

Man should also know that Faith is of speech and act and thought. Faith may become greater and less — greater by obedience, less by resentfulness. Self-mastery is a part of Faith; and humble patience is to Faith what the head is to the body.

Man cannot know what is recorded with God upon the chapter of Faith, and exists sealed with Him; and precisely for this reason we may only say: That man is, please God, a Believer; or: I trust that I am a Believer. For there is no other resource — only hope. Man should conform to all laws and directions, for these are parts of Faith. So too are works of supererogation; and Faith can never be perfect, since works of supererogation can never reach an end.

One must love all Companions of the Prophet, for after the Prophet they are the best of human creatures. The best and noblest of them all after the Prophet is Abu Bakr the Truthful, next after him Omar son of Khattab, next after Omar is Othman son of Affan, and next after Othman is Ali, Abu Talib's son. May God bless them and have them near Him in Paradise, may He have Compassion on the souls of all the Companions. He who slanders Aisha has no part or lot in Islam. And of Mu'awia we should only say good things, nor should we ever be drawn into controversy about him, but we should invoke God's Mercy upon all.

Nor should we ever call a man an Unbeliever for neglecting any of the directions of the Law except only for neglect of Prayer: he who neglects to pray, without due cause, is an Unbeliever, for the Apostle of God has told us that.

These are the doctrines of the True Way, and of the community of Islam. God make us champions of religiousness of life.

And may He forgive us.

May He forgive all Believers.

THE PLEA

AND now, at the end of this book, I will ask you — and God direct your thinking upon this! — one general and decisive question:

Imagine a man coming to these countries from India or China, a man coming with the intention of studying the various religions found here.

Some of the inhabitants of these lands, he will be told, belong to a religion called Magianism. They worship stars and fires; and hold that God is the Creator of good and light, Satan the Creator of darkness and evil; that God and Satan wage endless war, but since neither can prevail, both remain perpetually frustrated and bewildered. These Magians also insist that it is

God's will and pleasure that a man lie with his mother or daughters, that a man purify himself with the foul urine of cows, and indulge in immoral conversation and dancing; they claim that the spirits of their dead ancestors revisit them once a year, and eat and drink of what is laid out for them, and take back food and drink with them to the world of the dead when they go; and they have other vicious occult customs and disgusting habits, unmistakably marking them as vessels of God's Vengeance. Furthermore, ancient prophecies directed against them may be found in the Books of the Prophets.

Others of the inhabitants are what are called Freethinkers. Our visitor will see that they are worse than the Magians in point of error, vice, filthiness, impurity, and stupidity.

Others again follow a religion called Christianity, one sect of whom maintain that God, seeing Satan's power growing formidable to Himself, and the Prophets incapable of effective resistance, suddenly discovered a Son, though the Son had been in Eternity and would be everlastingly; the Son entered the womb of a woman and was born of her, then grew up and struggled against Satan; but Satan, by agency of some of his followers, seized, killed, and crucified this Son. Another sect assume that what was killed was only the temple and habitation of the Son, a vehicle with whom the Son was so closely united that the Eternal Son ate what the creature ate, went to the privy when the creature did, and suffered at the time of his death.

Other inhabitants of these lands he will find professing a religion called Judaism which has a Scripture of so-called Prophetic Books. These Books show how their Prophets have cursed this people and declare that God has forsaken them, and scattered them in every country of the earth, and darkened their light, and sworn He will pity them no more.

But some of the inhabitants belong to a religion called Islam, Submission, pure and lofty. These maintain that God is One, Eternal, Peerless, Invincible since he is Omnipotent, and shall be Everlasting. He has no child, and no father. He is the Compassionate One, the Merciful, the First and the Last. The

Prophet of these people has prescribed for them on God's behalf piety to parents, fasting, prayer, purity, cleanliness. He has made good things legal and evil things illegal, has promised Paradise and warned against Hell-fire.

Now, to which of these creeds would that Indian or Chinese incline, assuming him to be a man of broad mind and sound judgment, simply an inquirer after truth?

And what could be God's objection to any one of His servants who could say to Him, Just and Compassionate as He is: I heard a Preacher call upon Thy Unity; I heard him speak of Thee as What is Greater than all things, and praise and glorify Thee. And I responded. I heard this Preacher telling us we must believe in Thy Prophet and Thine Elect, telling us we must pray, and fast, and give to the poor:

Clear the heart of heedlessness; clear the soul of sensual seeking. Tame hot lust with thought of the death that comes on fast; and fear that Day when every sin shall be seen in you by the scars it has left in you.

Think now of him who high above cries out of Heaven, making bones to stir and gathering mankind to a place where all illusions end, and pain and penitence endure. Yea for sure, a Crier to whom the crumbled bones must hearken, drawing together bodies long gone, down from the vultures' eyries, out of the bellies of beasts, up from the sea-bottom and from the mountain's ribs, till every limb finds its own socket and every bodily member grows again.

Fearful ordeal then, ye men, shall be your meed, your faces mottled with dust from the staggering of Earth, and blenched with horror, and you shall stand stark naked then and barefoot even as you were born. And the Crier shall cry: Attend ye! And through and through you all his look shall thrill, and ye dripping sweat and dark with grime. And the Earth with all its burden then shall shake, and the mountains totter and crash down and be swept far away by the rising storm.

Wide is every eye;
Not any eye may close
In that Standing-ground thronged with the people of
    Heaven and Earth.
And whilst all creatures stand to see What was foretold
    now real,
With ranks of Angels compassing them about,
Even in that instant Hell's darkness whelms them,
And the flame that smokes not laps them;
They hear it aroar, and sucking,
Uttering anger, raging.

Those who stand sink to their knees. And then shall the
guilty receive their doom for certain, and even the pure shall fear
and shrink, and the Prophets shall cringe in terror from the
Lord.

And in that hour they shall hear an Asking: Where is the
servant of God? Where the son of His handmaid? Where he who
was faithful to his own folly only? Where is he Death ravished
away unready?

All shall be discovered. All shall be called up to a Reckon-
ing for the use they made of their lives, pleading, prevaricating,
standing in terror in the Presence of Him Who Knoweth thought
the most secret. Then like a thunderbolt will come the Thunder
of God, and a Ruling with a rod of iron; and all the pleading
falter into nothing before a Book carefully kept, the accurate
Inventory of all their iniquities; and too truly then at last shall
the soul see its own plight, having no companion then, nor any
friend, but a Judge only, Impartial, but Inflexible utterly. AND
THE GUILTY SHALL BEHOLD HELL-FIRE, FORE-
KNOWING THEN AT LAST THAT THEY WILL FALL
THEREIN, AND FINDING THEN TOO LATE THAT
WAY OF ESCAPE FROM THE FIRE IS NONE.

But may God guide you and me into another Way, of His
Salvation, and lift from you and me the load of dark, and illu-
mine us with pure faith in His Unity through the gloom of

Doomsday. Of all the wells of wisdom sweetest and fullest is the Word of the Creator; of all gleams in this our darkness that is the most radiant light.

I obeyed the Preacher, hoping for reward with Thee as being meek to Thy Command. I was told I must be a Pilgrim to a far-away country; and I made this Pilgrimage without hesitating. Then I heard the Preacher exhort us to Holy War against Thine enemies who do not Believe in Thee nor pray to Thee:

How long, ye men, will ye hear warning and heed not?

And how long will ye abide the whipping and stir not?

Your ears shake off the Preacher's words. Or are your hearts too haughty to hear? The Fiend has roused up those others to fight for his lies, and they rise up and follow,

While the Omnipotent summons you to His Truth, and you ignore His Call.

Beasts fight for mate and cub; birds will die for their nests; yet Prophet and Revelation have they none. But you, who understand, and have the Law and wisdom, scatter away like startled camels before your foes.

God claims your faith and steadfastness; God promises His Help and Victory again.

Do you not really trust Him?

Do you doubt His Justice or His Goodness?

Give your soul, man, wholly up to Him unto Whom it doth belong. Put no trust in prudence: your prudence will not put off your appointed term to die.

War! War! ye men of heart!

Victory! Sure Victory! ye resolute!

Paradise! Paradise for you who march on!

And Hell! Hell for you who fly!

Victory's reward in this world, and the martyr's in the Next; and of these two how much the sweeter is the last!

Then stand by God; for HIM WHO HELPETH GOD WILL GOD MOST SURELY HELP.

So I prayed to Thee, and fought in Holy War, manfully as I might, wishing to please Thee in all things.

I had seen those unseemly and mysterious religions all round me; I left them aside, and held to what I thought the best way to please Thee. If, O my God, I was mistaken, and chose wrong, Thou hast great cause to pity Thy servant who did his utmost to discover what is really of Thee, and yet mistook the way to come to Thee.

My cousins, a plea like that would be accepted, and not despised, even by God's imperfect and exacting servants. How much more so then by Him Who is Most Merciful of all who know what mercy is: that Judge most Just, Who doth not ask of any soul more than that soul could do.

GOD_S

WAYS

Are Numberless As The Souls Of Men

Appendix

Muslim Science: The Body and the
Doctor

Sources

Chronology by Caliphates

Index of Principal Persons

Index of Selected Topics

Index of Poems

Index of Selected Anecdotes

THE BODY AND THE DOCTOR

Philosophy was laid in grave;
And this man raised her from the dead.
The dust had hidden Physic's track;
He found it, and showed where it led.

L IFE, OR ANY COMPLETENESS OR GOOD to which a creature may be destined, derives wholly and solely from the Primal and Supreme Reality which is the source of all good, and from the Strong Desire which continually proceeds therefrom.

What is to receive, however, requires specific capacity for the reception of destined good; a creature cannot receive indiscriminately. Wool, for example, cannot have the Form of wool and also the characteristics of a sword, nor water be water and also receive the Form of human nature.

The four Constituents, the principles or Elements, are physical entities, non-living and of negligible bulk. Even the simplest living thing is wholly unlike the Elements; and so also are the celestial bodies, created as they are to receive a mysterious corporeal vitality of their own. For the Elements are absolutely incapable of receiving life. It is their intermixture in compound bodies which accounts for the ability of such bodies to receive life. The Elements are *simple* entities, the primary components not only of the human body throughout all its parts but of all other bodies, whatever their Forms.

Natural philosophy distinguishes four primal Elements only; and this the physician must accept. Two are relatively light, two relatively heavy, the lighter being the fiery Element, Igneity, or more shortly Fire, and the aerial Element or Air; the heavier are the terrene, or Earth, and the aqueous or fluid, Water.

The common word air does not refer to what is signified

by Air: it means the atmosphere around us. If the atmosphere were absolutely pure, air might be called Air; but the Elements, for instance, cannot putresce; an Element can only change into another Element (for example, the Elemental Water of water may become Air by boiling). Atmospheric air is a composite substance with spatial relations, composed of true Air and the other Elements — aqueous particles, terrene particles, and fiery particles — all together. In the same way, when we speak of sea or lake as water, we do not mean elemental Water, but a composite in which Water, though predominant, is mixed with Air, Earth, and Fire.

Elemental Earth is to be thought of as normally central to existence. Its property is rest; and all other things naturally tend towards it from any distance, however great, inasmuch as they contain weight, or gross terrene particles. The natural properties of Earth are coldness (the opposite of heat) and dryness (the opposite of fluidity or moisture); and this Element is what holds bodily parts together in compact form.

Elemental Water is naturally situated by its relative density as exterior to Earth and interior to Air. Its nature is cold and fluid or moist, as water appears to our senses so long as there are no counteracting factors. Its purpose in creation is this: it lends itself readily to dispersion, and consequently can assume any shape without permanency. In the structure of things it thus provides the possibility of their altering shape, being spread, and being attempered. Shapes in moisture are readily fashioned and as easily lost; whereas dryness allows the assumption of form only with difficulty, and dry forms are resolved with similar difficulty. When dryness and moisture are both present in a thing, and the thing is more moist than it is dry, it is susceptible of shaping; if it is more dry than moist, this predominance renders its shape-character constant. Moisture counteracts the friability of dryness; and dryness counteracts the tendency to dispersion in moisture.

The aerial Constituent, or Air, is by its relative lightness naturally above Water and beneath Fire. Its nature is hot and moist in the sense spoken of above. Its use in the created world is to rarefy things, to make them finer, lighter, subtler, and softer, and consequently to facilitate upward movement.

The natural situation of Igneity, or Elemental Fire, is higher than the other three, occupying the inner periphery of the sublunary sphere and extending to the heavens. All things return to Fire at last because of this absolute lightness. Its natural properties are heat and dryness, and its use in structures is to mature, rarefy, refine, and above all to penetrate. Its penetrative power enables it to traverse aerial substance, to qualify the absolute coldness of the two heavy elements, and thus to bring all the Elemental properties into a harmony.

There is comparatively more of the two heavy Elements in the structures of the human bodily members, contributing to their repose or comparative fixity of state. The two lighter elements enter more largely into the formation of Vital Spirits, and contribute both to movement and change in them and to the movement of the members. *But it must always be remembered that it is the Form, the pattern or soul, of the creature, which is the actual motor, and not the Vital Spirit.*

Temperament is that composite quality which results from the mutual interaction of the prime qualities (heat, cold, moisture, dryness) in the Elements. So minutely intermingled are the Elements in a thing that a state of equilibrium, uniform throughout, is finally reached, and it is this outcome in quality which we term the Temperament of that thing.

THE DYNAMICS OF LIFE

God made the left side of the heart hollow to serve both as reservoir for the Vital Spirit and as its producing source. He created Vital Spirit to convey the faculties of the soul or Form to the appropriate bodily members. The Vital Spirit therefore serves both as ground for the unification of the soul's faculties and secondly as vehicle of emanation into the various material members and tissues.

This Vital Spirit God produces by combining the subtler particles of the bodily humors with Elemental Fire; at the same time producing the body-tissues from the coarser and more Earthy particles of the same humors. The relation of the Vital Spirit to the subtler particles is precisely like the relation of the body to the grosser. Just as the mingling of the humors results in a temperamental pattern which permits the visible physical formation, inconceivable without this mixture, so the mingling of subtler particles in a temperamental compound enables the Vital Spirit to receive the powers of the soul, which it could not do were the humors not so mixed.

Initially, Vital Spirit is to be conceived as a Divine emanation from potentiality to actuality proceeding without intermission or stint until the pattern is complete. Each bodily member, though substantially derived from the same set of humors, has nevertheless its own particular temperament, since both the proportions and the mode of the humoral commixture are peculiar to each member. Similarly three aspects or branches of the Vital Spirit are differently developed: the vegetative or Natural (that is, as considered with regard to vegetative process in the body, the Vital Spirit as located in the liver and associated with venous blood), the Animal or sensitive (as associated with nerve-fibers), and the Vital properly speaking (as located in the heart and associated with arterial blood). Each of these three has its own peculiar temperament, determined by the mode and proportions of the commixture of the subtler particles.

The body consists of many members. As to which is the original one there is no agreement; but the fact remains that one must have come into existence before others could develop from it. Similarly a prime Vital Spirit must be regarded as necessarily precedent to the others; and this, according to the most authoritative philosophers, is the Spirit located in the heart. Thence passing into the main physical centers, Spirit is located in them sufficiently to be modified by their respective temperamental characters. Its location in the cerebrum tempers it for receiving the Animal faculties of sensation and movement, location in the liver for receiving the Vegetative faculties of nutrition and growth, location in the generative glands for the Reproductive faculty.

Aqueity or moisture is the material cause of growth. But moisture does not develop or construct itself; it is not a self-creating being, but only undergoes change in virtue of a formative power acting upon it. This formative power or Form — the soul in the living creature — has its existence in Divine Decree. And the Form requires, in order to work, an instrument: this instrument is the Innate Heat.

A person at the period of life when growth has reached its limit approaches as near as may be to equability of temperament so far as co-equation of his members goes, the contra-action of hot members such as the heart with cold ones such as the brain, of moist ones such as the liver with dry ones such as the bones. But as regards the Vital Spirit and main organs, temperament can never approximate to ideal equability: the temperament of Vital Spirit and vital organs is always predominantly hot and moist. Heart and Vital Spirit, which are the root of life, are both extremely hot. For life itself depends on the Innate Heat referred to above, and growth depends on Innate Moisture. The Innate Heat both penetrates and feeds upon the Innate Moisture.

The Innate Heat of young creatures is derived from the sperm of their generation, which is very hot in nature. This initial heat is steadily used up. But the quantitative loss is made up, and more than made up, by the heat added as a result of progressive growth. On the other hand, the *proportional* or relative amount of Innate Moisture (on which the Innate Heat feeds) progressively diminishes, this being the mechanism by which Innate Heat remains at a constant level up to senescence. In the end, the moisture is inadequate in proportional quantity even to keep the Innate Heat constant. At life's outset, it had been adequate both to the feeding of the heat and to growth. But there comes a time when either one or the other or both must fail. It is clear that growth has to stop, for the Innate Heat cannot be the one to be sacrificed.

But at last the Innate Heat dies out. This is the death of the nature or Form to which every creature is destined, its *APPOINTED TERM*. The diversity of temperaments is what accounts for the different durations of creaturely lives, the differences in their natural terms. There are also, of course, what are called premature deaths; but these other causes exist also (like the Form) in the realm of Divine Decree.

PHYSIOLOGY

A body-fluid or *Humor* is that fluid moist physical substance into which our aliment is transformed.

That part of the aliment which has the capacity to be transformed into body-substance, either by itself or in combination with something else, is the healthy or *good* humor. It is what replaces the loss which the body-substance undergoes. The residue from the aliment, the *superfluity,* is *bad* humor, and is properly expelled.

Of the fluids, some are primary, some are secondary. The primary body-fluids are: the sanguineous humor, the serous humor, the bilious humor, and the atrabilious humor. The secondary body-fluids are either non-excrementitious, such as those located at the orifices of even the minutest channels and near the tissues, those permeating the tissues and capable of transformation into nourishment, a special almost congealed fluid, a fluid found among tissues from birth; or excrementitious.

The *Sanguineous Humor* (predominant in blood) is hot and moist. It is normally red, without offensive odor, and very sweet to the taste.

The *Serous Humor,* cold and moist in nature, occurs in normal and abnormal form. Normal serous humor is capable of transformation into blood by Innate Heat, and is in fact imperfectly matured blood. It is a kind of sweet fluid, not too cold compared with the body as a whole. It has no special locus or receptacle in the body, and is like blood in that it is equally necessary to all the tissues, which receive it along with the blood. Its essential function is twofold: first, to be near tissues in case of inadequate supply of their habitual nutriment — healthy blood — and, second, to qualify sanguineous humor before the latter reaches and nourishes tissues of lymphatic temperament. Its accessory function is to lubricate joints and all tissues and organs concerned in movement.

The abnormal forms of serous humor are:

one, the *salty,* warmer, dryer, and lighter than the other forms, made salty by the mixture of oxidized earthy matters of dry temperament and bitter taste with the normal moisture of the humor;

two, the *attenuated,* insipid or slightly salty as a result of the admixture of oxidized bile, which is dry and bitter; the resultant heating fluid is called the bilious serous humor;

three, the *bitter,* due either to admixture of atrabilious humor or to over-infrigidation;

four, the *sour,* found in two forms, one sour because the humor has fermented and then gone sour, the other sour through the admixture of acrid atrabilious humor;

five, the *vitreous,* dense and glassy, the original aqueity yielding to a vitreous appearance after condensation and increase in coldness.

The *Bilious Humor,* hot and dry in nature, is in its normal form the foam of blood, bright red, light, and pungent. Formed in the liver, it either circulates with the blood or passes to the gall-bladder. That which passes into the bloodstream subserves two purposes: it enables the blood to nourish such tissues or organs as need a certain amount of dispersed bilious humor (the lung, for instance); and mechanically it attenuates the blood, enabling it to traverse the very minutest channels of the body. The part which passes to the gall-bladder also serves two purposes: first the removal of some of the effete matter of the body and nourishment of the walls of the gall-bladder, and second, a dual function of cleansing food-residues and viscous serous humor from the bowel walls and stimulating the intestinal and anal muscles for defecation.

Besides the normal clear bilious humor in the liver and blood there are seven abnormal types, of which the first four are so by admixture of alien substance:

one, *citron-yellow* bile in the liver, due to admixture of attenuated serous humor, less hot than normal bile;

two, *vitelline-yellow* bile, the color of egg-yolk, in the liver, due to admixture of coagulated serous humor, still less hot;

three, *ruddy-yellow oxidized* bile, an opaque fluid in liver and blood due to simple admixture of atrabilious humor, and somewhat deleterious;

four, *oxidized* bile of another type, in the gall-bladder, due to spontaneous oxidation resulting in an attenuated fluid plus an ash which does not separate out; more deleterious than the last.

The three abnormal biles which result from internal change of substance are:

five, *hepatic* bile, in the liver, due to oxidation of the attenuated part of the blood, so that its denser part separates out as atrabilious humor; a moderately toxic bile;

six, *gastric leek-green* bile in the stomach, due to oxidation of vitelline bile; less toxic than the last; and

seven, *mildew-* or *verdigris-green* bile in the stomach, due to intense oxidation of vitelline bile and loss of all its moisture; very hot, and extremely toxic.

Of these the seventh is possibly derived from the sixth through increased oxidation resulting in total desiccation, which would account for its whitish hue. For we know that heating a moist body first blackens it, and further heating whitens it, the whiteness becoming evident when the degree of moisture is less than half-and-half. Wood, for example, first is charred black, and finally becomes white ash.

The *Atrabilious Humor,* cold and dry in nature, is in its normal form the *faex* or sediment of good blood, an effete matter, in taste between sweet and bitter. After its production in the liver it divides into two portions, of which one enters the blood and the other the spleen. The former, first, contributes to the nourishment of such members as require a trace of atrabilious humor in their temperament, as for example the bones; and, second, gives the blood its stamina, strength, density, and consistence. The latter portion, passing to the spleen, and no longer necessary to the blood, is primarily useful in clearing the body of effete matter, the spleen being the one organ to whose nourishment it contributes. Its secondary use is that, travelling to the mouth of the stomach by a kind of milking movement, one, it tones up, tightens, and thickens it; and, two, its bitterness, irritating the mouth of the stomach, stimulates the sense of hunger.

Similarly, that portion of bilious humor which passes to the gall-bladder is unnecessary to the blood, and what emerges from the gall-bladder is no longer needed by the organ. And just as the bilious humor passing to the intestine arouses peristalsis and so helps to withdraw food from the stomach, so the atrabilious humor after leaving the spleen arouses appetite and leads to the drawing-in of food to the stomach.

Wherefore thanks be to God the Best Artificer of all things, and unending His Praise.

Water is not counted one of the body-fluids because it is not a nutrient. By the word nutrient we mean something assimilable into the form of the human body; and such substances are always complex, never simple.

Galen regards the sanguineous as the only normal body-fluid, all others being excrementitious. But if sanguineous humor were the only nourisher of the various organs, it would be because the organs were all alike in temperament and nature. Actually, bone would not be harder than flesh were it not for the dryness of the atrabilious humor present in blood, nor would the brain be softer were it not for the presence in blood of the soft serous humor which nourishes it. We must conclude that in the blood are other humors than the sanguineous.

Moreover, when blood is withdrawn into a vessel, we see how it shrinks and how its various components visibly separate out: a foam (bilious), a turbid *faex* (atrabilious), an albuminous portion (serous), and a watery part such as passes in urine.

Some think that physical strength is due to abundance of blood, and weakness to its paucity. But it is not so. It is rather this: that the state of the body determines whether a nutriment will benefit it or not.

DIGESTION AND NUTRITION

Food undergoes a certain amount of digestion during the act of mastication. Since the mouth-lining is continuous with that of the stomach, there is as it were one continuous digestive surface; and as soon as what is chewed comes into contact with it a certain change takes place through the action of the saliva, which is digestive in virtue of the Innate Heat it contains. It is in this way that masticated wheat can be used as a poultice for the maturation of boils and abscesses, for which wheat merely brayed or even heated in water will not serve.

Once the food or aliment has entered the stomach, true digestion begins, not so much as a result of the stomach's heat as by heat from the surrounding members — the liver on the right, the spleen on the left (warm in virtue not of its substance but of its blood supply), the omentum in front, whose fat stores and reflects heat, and the heart above, which warms the diaphragm and so the stomach.

The first stage of digestion yields *chyle*, of the consistence of a broth, or sodden barley. This is drawn into the intestines, and its attenuated portion caused to enter into the roots of the mesenteric vessels which are found all along the intestinal tract. These vessels are slender and firm. Having entered these channels, the nutriment passes into the portal vein, enters the gateway of the liver, and thence travels through the liver along finer and ever finer divisions until it comes to the very fine hairlike channels which are the ultimate source of the *vena cava* emerging from the convexity of the liver. Were it not for the admixture of water consumed in excess of the strict requirements of the body, this passage could not take place. But thus distributed, the chyle is exposed to the digestive function of the whole of the liver, a function accomplished with great vigor, energy, and speed. The change of nutriment into blood is now complete. When the blood leaves the liver, the excess of water is removed, for it goes to the renal vessels and so furnishes the kidneys with the quantity and quality of blood best suited for their nutrition. It is the *fat* of the blood which is thus used, superfluous wateriness and a certain amount of sanguineous material passing down to the bladder and so away from the body.

The good blood meanwhile ascends into the superior *vena cava;* and its subsequent course is into smaller and smaller vessels, and at last into the finest hairlike channels. Having reached these, it as it were *sweats out* through their orifices and bathes the tissues of the body in accord with the Decree of God.

Bodily members are derived from the combination of the humors, as the humors are derived from the combination of aliments, and the aliments composed of the commingled Elemental Constituents. Members may be simple (of homogeneous structure throughout) or compound (such as the hand). Simple members are bones, cartilage, nerves both sensory and motor, tendons, ligaments, arteries, veins, the membranes (which are composed of extremely minute interwoven filaments and serve in some cases as organs of sensation to members in themselves insensitive), and last the flesh, in which muscle, fasciae, tendons, ligaments, connective tissues and other things are however included.

In every member there is a natural faculty, the Vegetative faculty, which subserves that member's own nutrition, a power securing attraction, retention, assimilation and unification of nutriment, and expulsion of effete matter. In addition, certain members possess a further faculty by which they act upon some other member.

The inability to decide between conflicting views upon the give and take among members is no hindrance in practice. One must realize, for instance, that whether or not the heart be the source of the sensory and motor powers in the brain, or the liver be the only source of the nutritive faculty as such, does not matter. Nor is it of any significance whether the brain contains within itself the source of the soul's powers, or whether such powers come only by way of the heart. Whatever be the truth, all that it concerns us to say is that there is a relation.

Again, one must realize that whether the Vegetative faculty of any member, bone for example, is intrinsic in virtue of that member's temperament, or whether it originates in the liver, or whether neither of these views is correct, does not matter. The thing to bear in mind is that there would be no operation of such faculty if there were no liver, and that if there were an absolute obstruction between the liver and the bone, the latter would cease to receive its necessary nutriment and its functioning would end, exactly as holds in the case of movement when some nerve-connection with the brain is severed.

The whole difficulty is best solved by regarding some members, heart, brain, and liver for example, as principal or vital, and others like veins, nerves, and generative organs as auxiliary to life.

FACULTY

The natural faculties are either dominant or subservient. Of the former, those which preserve the individual life are the nutritive and the augmentative, and those which preserve the race are the generative and the plastic.

In the process of nutrition, which replaces the loss incidental to life-process, three functions appear: one, *apposition* of the altered food as humor, faulty working of which function results in atrophy; two, *agglutination* of the nutriment to the tissues, faulty working of which results for example in fleshy dropsy; and three, true *assimilation,* which fails in such diseases as leprosy.

The generative faculty is double: in the first place there is what causes the formation of male and female sperm, the reproductive units; in the second place we have both the male creative power which specializes and rearranges the various energies in the sperm so that each member and tissue receives an appropriate temperament, and the female or plastic energy properly speaking, whereby, subject to Divine Decree, the members receive *configuration* — cavities, foramina, relations and so forth — all being held in control until they reach their appointed limits.

The vegetative faculties of attraction, retention, alteration, and expulsion are subserved by heat, cold, dryness, and moisture, though strictly speaking heat is the essential in all. For all the faculties act in virtue of movement, which is shown not only in attraction and repulsion of aliment, but even in its alteration, for the alteration of food consists in the separation of gross and aggregated particles, and the condensation of subtler and dispersed particles. Even in retention movement occurs, in the play of transverse fibers in the members. *And heat is necessary to movement as such.*

Disease

In medical writing, the word *cause* means that which initiates or tends to perpetuate a given state of the human body. *Disease* is an abnormal state of the body resulting in damage to it. It is the injurious effects which are commonly called the beginning of the disease; the abnormal state itself is either a *distemper,* which is the disturbance of some temperament, or an abnormal composition of morbid states emerging in a single disease. Inflammatory swellings are an example of composite states, since four things go to make them up: one, a distemper, associated with the formation of matter; two, local perversion of the Form; three, morbid configuration (change of size, or displacement); four, loss of continuity between properly continuous tissues, accompanying the discharge of superfluities into the tissue-spaces.

A *symptom* is a phenomenon consequent on this unnatural state. The following will serve as examples:

Cause: putrescence. *Disease:* fever. *Symptom:* thirst, headache.

Cause: fullness of lacrymal sacs from developmental error. *Disease:* obstruction of uvea. *Symptom:* loss of vision.

Cause: acrid flux. *Disease:* ulceration of lung. *Symptom:* flushed cheeks, curved nails.

One disease may originate a second, as colic may produce syncope, paralysis, or convulsions. And such origination may turn into a vicious circle: for example, disorder of the brain may affect the activity of the stomach and impair digestion; consequently the stomach will supply morbid vapors and imperfectly digested aliment to the brain, so increasing its disorder.

Some diseases, however, in giving rise to new ones, may themselves disappear. Thus quartan malaria often cures epilepsy, also podagra, varices, and arthralgias. A spasmodic disease may be cured by scabies, pruritus, and furunculosis. A certain type of diarrhoea is cured by inflammation of the eyes. Lienteria cures pleurisy. Bleeding piles removes atrabilious disorders, including sciatica, renal and uterine pain.

Possible relationships which the physician has to consider include: one, natural connection (as between stomach and brain through nerves, or uterus and breast through blood-vessels); two, channel (as from groin to leg) in which relation the less vigorous will take up excrementitious matter from the more vigorous (as the axillary region from the heart); three, simple contiguity (as neck and brain); four, initiation of function (as the diaphragm is concerned in drawing air into the lungs); five, subservience (as of nerves to brain); six, relationship through some third member (as brain, kidney, liver).

Diseases may be transmitted from one person to another; one, by infection of a house from a neighboring house, as lepra, scabies, variola, pestilential fever, septic inflammatory swellings, and ulcers are transmitted; by infection of a house which is in the wind-track of another; by infection of intent gaze (as eye-disease); by infection of imagination; by direct infection in the manner of phthisis, impetigo, and leprosy; or, two, transmitted by heredity (as vitiligo alba, premature baldness, gout, phthisis, lepra); three, racially transmitted; four, endemically transmitted (as elephantiasis in Alexandria, endemic goitre, and many other diseases).

The causes of disease may be simple and extra-corporeal (as trauma, heat, cold), antecedent and intra-corporeal (as repletion, or starvation), or conjoint (as sepsis may end with septic fever). Among extra-corporeal causes must be included the mind, which in causal relation is to be considered as distinct from the body: mental states of anger, fear, and the like must enter into consideration as causes of disease.

What are termed in medicine essential causes are things like pepper, which warms, or opium, which cools. Accidental causes are things like cold water, which warms inasmuch as it closes the pores of the skin and thus leads to retention of heat; hot water, which cools by opening the pores and thus liberating heat; scammony, which cools by expulsion of heating humor, and so forth.

When the body is exposed to extra-corporeal heat, the temperamental equilibrium is endangered. For resisting this danger, the body's Innate Heat is all-important. We depend on our Innate Heat for the neutralization of hot poisons, their expulsion and desubstantiation. The Innate Heat is the instrument of the body's nature for combating extraneous heat, the means by which the Vital Spirit expels or disperses such heat and oxidizes its material basis. It is of course also Innate Heat which combats extraneous cold.

Cold has no such positive power. It is not cold, but Innate Heat which protects the natural humors from the ruling of extraneous heating agents. If Innate Heat is feeble, then the means by which the natural faculties work on the humors is enfeebled, stagnation sets in, and extraneous heat now finds the humors defenseless against its own action; it conquers them, puts them as it were to its own use, and imparts alien movement to them. The result is what physicians call *putrefaction*.

SOME OBSERVATIONS ON THE EVIDENCES OF DISEASE

Certain signs indicate the disease directly, as rapid pulse indicates fever. Others indicate its position, as hard pulse indicates diaphragmatic pleurisy or undulant pulse inflammation in the lung-substance. Other signs indicate its cause, such as the various signs of plethora.

Plethora of the body-channels is excess in quantity of humors or Vital Spirit. The objective signs are: red face, full veins, tight skin, sluggish gestures, full pulse, high-colored or dense urine, scant appetite. Subjective signs are: sense of weight in the limbs, weak vision, dreams of weight or of difficulty in moving or of aphasia.

Plethora of faculty is unhealthiness in the *quality* of the humors, and risk of putrefactive disorder. Signs are: lassitude, loss of appetite, with less distention than in the plethora described above, dreams of itching, stinging, or burning, and fetid odor.

Ordinary obstruction to the flow of the humors is to be recognized by signs indicating accumulation of matters and by the patient's sensation of general fullness without his manifesting the signs of general plethora.

The states of the body are revealed by its movements and immobilities. Among other ways, movements vary in the degree of associated mental anxiety. Dry hiccough, for instance, indicates more deep-seated mental stress than coughing, although the latter is more vigorous.

The physician must know the essential structure, normal form, site, relations and functions of all members. Symptoms to be considered should include interference with function, discharges (which are not primary, but indicate maturation), pain, swelling, altered position, and special symptoms. Interference with function is usually secondary to disease of a subservient organ if any. Inflammations may signify essentially (as erysipelatous inflammation suggests the bilious humor, and scirrhus the atrabilious), or by position (as the right the liver, the left the spleen), or by shape (as a moon-shaped swelling in the right hypochondrion points to the liver, and an elongated one to the over-lying muscles, the rectus and adnexa).

Errors may arise because a painless primary disease escapes observation until the secondary disease has appeared. One is very apt to regard secondary diseases as primary and to overlook the real causes. The physician must diligently question the patient for signs indicating affections of neighboring or related organs. The easiest plan is to go over in one's mind all the various points connected with any interference with function. If any interference with function *prior in time* is discovered, then the malady of which the patient complains should be considered a secondary one. Some affections are usually secondary to others: for example, affection of the head secondary to some morbid state of the stomach is common, and the converse rare.

The patient's temperament is discernible from feel (the state of the nails, and so on), the condition of muscles, flesh, and fat, hair, body-color (especially changes in the color of eyes and tongue), conformation, responsiveness to heat and cold, sleepiness or wakefulness, and state of the functions and discharges.

PULSE

Pulse is a movement in heart and arteries (the receptacles of Vital Spirit) whereby the Vital Spirit undergoes influence from the air inspired. Every beat comprises: expansion; pause, contraction; pause.

In our opinion the observable features in pulse which enable the physician to discern bodily states are ten; they are:

one, quantity of diastole, to be estimated in terms of length and breadth and thickness;

two, quality of the impact transmitted to the observer's finger;

three, duration of each movement;

four, consistency of the artery;

five, emptiness or fullness of the vessel between beats;

six, feel — hot or cold;

seven, duration of the pauses;

eight, equality of force in successive beats;

nine, regularity or its opposite; intermissions;

ten, what may be termed the musical character — meter, rhythm, harmony, measure, accent.

A pulse increased in length, depth, and breadth is termed *large;* one increased in breadth and depth only is termed *thick,* its opposite *slender.*

The musical character of the pulse must always be considered. In music, sounds are juxtaposed in orderly relations of loudness, softness, interval and repetition; rates of utterance vary; attack may be abrupt or gentle, sharp or dull. Notes may be clear or indefinite, strong or weak. Volume may be full or thin, rhythmic sequence regular or irregular, the irregularities themselves orderly or disorderly. It astonishes me how many such relations in pulse are perceptible to touch; but I know that the perceptions can be got by practice.

Irregular pulses are of intermitting types (one component separated from the rest by a short interval, with a pause interposed elsewhere), of recurrent types (where a pulse increased in some component diminishes sharply in that and gradually enlarges again), or of continuous types (in which the alternation from slowness to swiftness and back, or from equality to inequality and back, and so on, is gradual and continuous).

Certain varieties of irregular pulse have received distinctive names:

gazelle pulse (modern jerking pulse): expansion interrupted, occupying longer time than usual, remaining at a certain height and then swiftly increasing to full height;

undulant pulse (modern bounding pulse);

vermicular pulse (modern creeping pulse);

formicant pulse, differing from vermicular in the great ease with which the rise, the anteposition or postposition of the pulse are perceived, with no perceptible irregularity of breadth;

serrate pulse (modern harsh pulse);

mousetail pulse (progressive inequality of volume, slowness, or weakness);

recurrent pulse (modern flickering pulse);

dicrotic pulse;

fading pulse;

spasmodic, thrilling, and twisted pulse;

cordlike pulse.

All the above are simple irregular pulses, the varieties of compound pulse are almost innumerable.

Irregularity, if vital power is unimpaired, is due to overweight of aliment or of some humor. If the vital power is impaired, irregularity shows a contest between some causative agent and the tissues. Other causes may be overfullness of the vessels (to be remedied by venesection), or viscidity of the blood. In the latter case the Vital Spirit becomes choked in the vessels; it is likely when Vital Spirit is pent in the cardiac region by overfullness of the stomach, or anxiety, or pain. Harsh pulse indicates diffusion of the products of decomposition or maturation through the vessel-wall, and also inflammatory deposits in fibro-muscular organs. Dicrotic pulse signifies approaching crisis, mousetail pulse weakening of the vital power . . . (the indications continue, and descriptions of the effects on the pulse of age, sex, temperament, season, locality, diet, wine, sleep, the act of waking up, athletic exercise, bathing, pregnancy, pain, inflammation, and various emotional states follow).

In a case of lovesickness one may arrive by the pulse at the identity of the loved person, if the lovesick patient will not otherwise reveal it. Such information opens up a means of treatment. The method is to go over many names repeatedly, keeping the finger on the pulse; and when it becomes very irregular or almost seems to stop at a name, repeat the series. By this method, I have discovered the beloved object's name. Then, in the same manner, go over names of streets, houses, professions, trades, families, even countries, mentioning each name in conjunction with that of the beloved object, and feeling the pulse all the time. Whenever it repeatedly alters at the mention of any particular, you may infer details of the beloved object's name, situation, appearance, or occupation. We have ourselves obtained most valuable information by this plan.

If thereafter you find no cure except to unite the two in lawful matrimony, you must do this. We have seen cases where health and strength were completely restored, and flesh regained after extreme attenuation, and after suffering from severe chronic diseases and protracted fevers as a result of excessive love; we have seen this recovery take place in a very short time when the patient was united with the beloved object. These results are astonishing; they make us realize how subordinate our nature is to the workings of the mind.

TWO EXCERPTS FROM THE URINOLOGY

Dark urine denotes: one, extreme oxidation; two, great coldness; three, extinction of Innate Heat and the approach of death; four, crisis; or, five, evacuation of effete atrabilious substance.

The first can be recognized by its causing scalding, and by the precedence of yellowness or redness. Sediment will be discrete and not homogeneous, discontinuous, and tending to yellow or brown. If the sediment tends to lemon yellow, it strongly suggests jaundice.

The second is recognized by previous green or livid tint. Sediment here is slightly coherent, dry-looking, and blackish. If the urine smells foul, the temperament will be hot; if it be odorless, the temperament will be cold.

The third will be recognized by general dispersion of the vital power.

As to the fourth, if at critical periods the urine does not darken, it is an ominous sign, especially in acute diseases. It is even more ominous if at the same time the quantity be small (evidence that the humor is already destroyed by oxidation), or secondly if the sediment be coarse.

Dark urine may be evidence of renal calculus. Its occurrence in aged persons is a bad sign, since in them it can only denote great destruction of tissue. In puerperal women its appearance is premonitory of convulsions. Finally, its appearance is serious at the onset of fevers as well as at their close if there is at the same time neither crisis nor abatement of symptoms.

Abnormal sediments in the urine are: one, flaky or squamous; two, fleshy; three, fatty; four, mucoid or slimy; five, purulent or ichorous; six, hairlike; seven, yeasty; eight, gritty; nine, ashy; or, ten, hirundiniform.

Squamous sediment is composed of large red or large white particles. If white, they come from the bladder (ulceration, desquamation, erosions); if red or fleshy, from the kidney. If brown or dark, or like fish-scales, they are a very bad sign, worse than the foregoing, and suggest the shedding of mucous linings. Particles from the bladder or kidneys may not signify much; in fact, if vesical they are a sign of recovery. Some have found cantharides producing white flakes like egg-membrane, which dissolve when the specimen is shaken, and give it a reddish tint. That too would be a sign of recovery.

Another squamous form resembles scrapings from intestines, the particles being less broad and less dense. If reddish, such sediment is termed orobeal, otherwise furfuraceous. Orobeal sediment indicates the presence of oxidized particles derived from the liver or the kidney or the blood. From the kidney, particles are more continuous and fleshy; in the other cases they are more friable.

Another, and more truly scaly sediment consists of small bodies like the husks of grain. Such denote either bladder trouble or grave colliquative disorder of the system as a whole. We diagnose bladder-trouble if (one) there is itching at the root of the penis, and (two) the urine is fetid; and especially if (three) pus is passed first. Such a condition is even more strongly indicated if (four) there are other evidences of maturation in the urine and (five) the veins over the bladder are healthy and there is no macula there. On the other hand we diagnose humoral liquefaction if there is fever, weakness, difficulty of micturition, and a brownish color to the sediment.

Squamous sediments other than those of vesical or renal and ureteral origin have a grave significance if occurring in acute diseases.

THERAPEUTICS

Treatment comprises three capitals: regimen and diet; the use of medicines; and manual or operative interference.

With regard to diet, the physician must remember that all eating taxes the digestive faculties; but he will only reduce or forbid food if he intends that the digestive faculties throughout the body shall be left free to complete the maturation or concoction of the humors. He should watch two dangers: the natural powers may be too much enfeebled; or the illness may become too severe. Diet may be reduced either in quantity or in quality; for a food may be bulky but poor in nutriment like potherbs and fruits, or slight in bulk and highly nutritious like eggs and the testicles of fowls. One should diminish the nutriment and increase the bulk taken in cases where appetite is excessive and crude humors have got into the blood. We lull the appetite by filling the stomach, and yet see to it that little nutritive matter gets into the blood, thereby enabling the crude digestive products already there to be matured.

Diminished quantity is the usual diet for acute illnesses. In chronic maladies the greater need is the maintenance of bodily strength, for crisis may be long delayed. So also in the earlier stages of an illness. But as symptoms become more severe, quantity is to be diminished, thus helping the digestive powers in the hour of crisis. And unless there are contra-indications, the regimen should be attenuant during the height of the disease.

Two other factors than nutritive value enter into the choice of aliment for a patient: one, slow (as in meat) or rapid (as in wine) rate of penetration and absorption; and two, compactness (pork, for example) or attenuation (figs, for example) of the substance of its digestive products in the blood. We need rapid penetration when we wish to remedy a loss of vital power. But we select slow-digesting nutritious foods when we wish to build up the patient's strength and fit him for strenuous exercise.

THE USE OF MEDICINES

Medicines are selected after considering: one, their quality — hot, cold, moist, or dry; two, quantity or dose, estimated both by weight and by degree of heat, cold, and so forth; and three, the appropriate time for administration.

As regards the first, once one knows the quality of the malady (a cold moist malady, for example), the appropriate medicine is one of opposite quality (a hot dry medicine in that case). As regards quantity, one has to consider both the nature of the member (its temperament, construction, position and relations, and its vigor) and the degree of illness. It is important to know the anatomical relations of the organ: if, for instance, there is morbid matter in the blood-channels of the liver, one will evacuate it by way of the kidney; but if it be in the bile-ducts, one will evacuate by way of the intestine. The physician must also know what substances to mix with his medicines in order to bring them rapidly to the affected organ. For instance, one must mix diuretics with a medicine intended for the urinary tract, and saffron with medicines intended for the heart.

When you wish to draw morbid matter from one member to another, first allay the pain. And take care that any transference of morbid matter is not by way of a vital organ. If it is necessary to evacuate matter from both brain and liver, moreover, never attempt both at the same stage of the disease. The order of importance of the vital organs is this: heart, brain, liver. To administer in full strength remedies which have a relaxing action either on vital organs or on organs closely related to them is simply to imperil life.

If there is no fear of danger to the vital power, we may

proceed in orderly fashion, using a mild remedy at first, and only proceeding to a stronger one if the first proves insufficient. Never be beguiled into forsaking this straight rule by mere tardiness of response.

When the malady is accompanied by pain, whether the pain be cause or effect, the first thing to do is to allay the pain. For remember that the help afforded by anything which stimulates the sensitive and vital faculties, such as joyfulness, is of great advantage. The physician tries if possible to make his patient happy, and always at least to make him calm.

When you do not know the quality of a malady, leave it to Nature. Never try to hurry things. Either Nature will cure it, or it will at last show more clearly as what it is. And remember too that not every plethora must be purged, nor every distemper reduced to its contrary. A good liberal regimen will often suffice in practice to remedy either plethora or distemper.

A distemper is either chronic and longstanding, in which case the treatment is strictly by *contrary;* or it appears at the terminal phase of an illness, in which case treatment is by *anticipation.* Administering theriac (Venice treacle) against the putrefactive processes usual with quartan fever is an example of treatment by contrary, as is the use of cold water against tertian fever. But evacuation, by hellebore in the case of quartan, or by scammony in the case of tertian, is an instance of treatment by anticipation: the hellebore acts on the atrabilious humor, the scammony on the bilious. And the object of administering them is to prevent or forestall morbid changes in their composition.

If in any given illness you are in doubt as to whether heat or coldness is responsible, and wish to find out by experiment, be careful not to overdo the experiment, and not to be misled by secondary symptoms it may give rise to. The appropriate moment for the test will be the same in either case; but one must be more apprehensive in using infrigidation. For heat is the friend of nature.

Moistening treatment and desiccation need equal caution; but the former may be more safely prolonged.

In procuring evacuation (by bloodletting, wet-cupping, purging, enemas, the use of leeches, and so forth) there are five points to consider:

one, removal of what is to be evacuated, followed by rest for the parts evacuated;

two, choice of organ and method: nausea, for instance, is removed by emesis, abdominal pain by purging;

three, choice of the right member of egress for the organ to be evacuated (thus, for maladies of the liver one must bleed the right basilic vein, not the right cephalic). Error here may be dangerous. The member chosen for egress must be less noble than that which is to be evacuated. And the channel of exit should also be the natural one: for the blood-vessels of the liver the urinary tract, but for the ducts of the liver the intestinal tract, as an example;

four, choice of the proper moment for evacuation. In chronic maladies, as Galen rightly says, one does not wait for maturation. But in acute maladies it is best to wait until the maturation stage has been reached, especially if the humors continue stagnant. Once they seem to be on the move, one must lose no time in getting rid of them. For the danger from their movement is greater than the danger from evacuating immatured humors;

five, the amount to be evacuated. Excessive evacuant treatment always brings about febrile conditions. When the patient is robust, and the humoral matter plentiful and depraved, the evacuation has to be gradual. Again, if the morbid material is either extremely viscid or widely diffused or admixed with much blood, it cannot be emptied at one sitting. This applies to cases of sciatica, longstanding arthritis, cancer, chronic skin-diseases, and obstinate furuncles.

If both bloodletting and purging are necessary, do the bloodletting first. This precept, from Hippocrates' Endemics, is generally sound; but there is an exception: if the plethora be of atrabilious and sanguineous humors so admixed as to be viscid and cold, one would begin with purging, because bloodletting would only increase the coarseness and viscidity.

Bloodletting is a method of general evacuation, removing excessive quantities of humors present in the blood-vessels. It is indicated, first, when the blood is so superabundant that disease is to be anticipated, and, second, when disease is already evident. Cases under the first category include: incipient sciatica or podagra or arthritis due to abnormal blood-state; persons on the verge of epilepsy, apoplectic seizure, melancholia with superabundant blood, pharyngotonsillitis, internal inflammatory masses, hot eye-disease, piles which generally bleed but have stopped bleeding, women who fail to menstruate, hot distemper of interior organs, and other cases.

Always remember that bloodletting is safer when the anticipated maladies are not yet evident. It should be avoided in the initial stages of evident disease; for it might fail to remove all that it was desired to remove, and would then have to be repeated, which would be enfeebling. Once maturation is passed, bloodletting is to be done unless there is some contra-indication. It is also useful for persons in whom repletion results in profuse sweating.

Purgatives act in virtue of specific resolvent property (as turbith), expressive power (as myrobalan), lenitive property (as manna), lubricant quality (as mucilage of fleawort or prunes), or a certain poisonous character (in the case of the violent purges) which works by direct aggressive action against the natural assimilative faculty. Purging is better than emesis in fevers. So long as a given drug merely expels superfluities, it will cause no restlessness. If it *does* cause restlessness, the physician knows that something more than the superfluity is being discharged.

The object of emesis is to empty the stomach without emptying the intestines. It is also used in treating the following chronic maladies: dropsy, epilepsy, melancholy, leprosy, gout, sciatica. Emesis clears heaviness of the head, clears the vision, removes nauseative dyspepsia. It benefits persons in whom bile is apt to pass into the stomach and decompose the food. It is also beneficial for flabbiness of body and for abscesses of the kidneys and bladder. It has a powerful effect in leprosy, in gastric epilepsy, jaundice, asthma, tremor, hemiplegia; and it is of great help to persons of predominantly bilious temperament and lean habit, for whom it should be procured once or twice a month, after a full meal. The bilious is the humor which most readily responds to emesis; the atrabilious humor is resistant to it.

The following is a list of foods and drugs which facilitate emesis: almonds dipped in honey; barley-water taken with its *faex* and honey; fresh pennyroyal; confection of bruised beans; decoction of radishes; decoction of narcissus-bulb; herb rocket; cucumber root boiled in honey; green marjoram; leeks; meat fat swallowed in lumps; oil of privet; old pickles; tepid chamomile tea; water with butter; radish soup; and a special dish made of unleavened bread, oil, melon, cucumber (either seeds or roots), well brayed and infused in sweetened water. The patient may prefer to use wine; but it will not do unless a large quantity be drunk. Ale may also act as an emetic if it be combined with honey and taken after a bath; but it will prove purgative as well. Strong emetics such as hellebore should be taken fasting unless there is some special contra-indication.

THE TREATMENT OF INFLAMMATORY SWELLINGS

Swellings may be hot, cold and soft, or cold and hard. Their causes may be immediate (blows, falls, bites) or indirect (plethora).

If a particular vital organ affected has no emunctory organ (that is, an organ which conveys waste matter away from it) the whole body must be treated, with a view to working on the affected part by recoil. This is what is called a *repercussive* treatment. It draws the inflammatory material to some different organ. An astringent influence is also to be introduced. For acute inflammatory swellings, astringent repercussives must be simply cold in temperament. But if the swelling is itself cold, the remedy must be combined with a calefacient astringent such as bog rush and the medicament derived from a certain species of oyster.

The inflamed organ may be itself the emunctory of a vital organ, as for instance the glands of the neck (related to the brain), the glands of the axilla (related to the heart), the glands of the groin (related to the liver). In such cases repercussives should on no account be employed. This is not because they would be an ineffective treatment for the inflammation there — it is not an ineffective treatment — but because in such cases *we want to leave the inflammation where it is.* Our object is to do everything possible to enlarge the swelling, and convey as much morbid matter to it from the vital organ as possible. We can do no good as long as there is disease in the vital organ, and our efforts must be directed to relieving that. Were we to employ repercussives, we should risk driving the morbid matter back to the vital organ, and make its state so bad at last that we cannot possibly amend it. That is why we try to draw morbid matter down always to an ignoble member, and actually encourage inflammatory process there, even going so far as to apply cupping or calefacient plasters to it, if by so doing we relieve the vital organ of which it is the emunctory.

The inflammatory mass thus made fluid may burst of its own accord, especially if it be in an emunctory. Promoting maturation will help; sometimes both that and incision are necessary. Maturation is favored by use of an agent which both obstructs and agglutinates, thus maintaining the heat of the affected part. The physician must watch meanwhile to see when the Innate Heat becomes feeble or the tissues begin to break down. That is the moment for removing the agglutinative agent, and for applying an aperitive medicament. A deep incision is now made, followed by dissolvent and desiccative applications.

The morbid matter of internal inflammatory swellings has to be removed by bloodletting and purging. Bathing, wine, exercise and avoidable emotions, such as anger, must be prohibited. Use repercussives in the early stages.

In the abdomen, swellings are not usually in the omentum, but in the intestine itself (the appendix, for instance); and in such cases it is dangerous to give aperients.

ANAESTHETICS

If it is desired to get the patient unconscious quickly and harmlessly, add sweet-moss or lignum aloes to wine. For deep unconsciousness, when great pain has to be borne, add darnel-water to wine. Or administer fumitory, opium, hyoscyamus (half a drachm of each); and nutmeg and crude aloes (four grains of each). These should be added to wine, and as much as necessary taken. Or boil black hyoscyamus with mandragora bark in water till it turns red, and add to wine.

REGIMEN

The art of maintaining health is not the art of averting death. Nor does it aim at securing the utmost possible longevity. It has two objects, and only two: one, the prevention of putrefactive breakdown; and, two, the maintenance of Innate Moisture at strength sufficient to safeguard the temperament peculiar to the person. Every person has his own appointed term of life, during which the desiccation inevitable to his given temperament may be withstood.

Regimen consists essentially in the regulation of exercise, food, and sleep. Exercise may be defined as voluntary movement entailing deep and accelerated respiration. As Hippocrates says, Medicine both purges and ages. And it is exercise which most surely prevents the accumulation of superfluities and prevents plethora.

As regards diet, care should be taken that the basis of a meal do not consist of medicinal foods such as pot-herbs, fruits, and the like. For tenuous things overoxidize the blood, as dense things render it phlegmatic. The meal should include meat (kid, veal, and yearling lamb are excellent), wheat, sweets of appropriate temperament, and fragrant wine of good quality. All other kinds of food should be regarded as medicinal or preservative. The more nutritious fruits are figs, grapes, and dates from regions to which they are indigenous.

An overindulgence in some medicinal food is to be corrected by contrary. If the aliment was cold (as cucumber or gourd), temper it with some opposite like onions or leeks.

No meal should be bulky enough to completely satisfy the appetite. A short sleep after a meal is useful; one should lie first on the right side, then on the left, and finally turn back again on to the right. Covering with wraps will aid digestion. The limbs should slope downwards, not upwards.

Water is the handmaid of nutrition. The quickest way of assessing the quality of water is by its weight: light water is healthier in all respects.

Fresh fruit is only good for those who do hard labor or take much exercise, or for persons of bilious temperament, or during the heats of summer. It renders the blood watery and apt to ferment; and unless seasonably taken paves the way for putrefactive processes.

When meat is roasted and taken with onions and eggs, it is very nutritious, but slow in passing through the intestines. Syrian white soup with rice and honey is particularly nourishing, and with the addition of onion dispels flatulencies. The flesh of partridge is dry and constipating; that of chicken moist, and relaxing to the bowels. Roast fowl is better if cooked in the belly of a kid or lamb, which will preserve its moisture. Chicken-broth tempers the humors more powerfully than fowl-broth, though the latter is more nutritious. Kid's flesh is better cold than warm, lamb's flesh better hot. Meat boiled in Persian style with water and vinegar is best served hot, and without saffron. If served cold, saffron should be added. Undigested bread is worse than undigested meat.

THE DOCTOR TO HIS PATIENT

I AND YOU AND THE DISEASE are three competing factors. If you will side with me, and do not neglect what I tell you to do, and do not eat what I forbid you, then we shall be two to one; and the two of us will beat the disease.

PAGES FROM A DOCTOR'S CASE-BOOK

Abdallah ibn Sawada had been suffering from attacks of mixed fever which came on sometimes at six-day intervals, sometimes as tertian, quartan, or quotidian. They were preceded by a slight rigor; and micturition was very frequent.

I gave it as my opinion that either these accesses of fever would turn into regular quartan, or that there was an abscess of the kidneys.

Shortly afterwards the patient passed pus in his urine. I told him these feverish attacks would not recur; and so it turned out.

The only thing which prevented me from definitely diagnosing abscess of the kidneys was his previous history: he had suffered from tertian and other fevers before, and this strongly suggested that his mixed fever might be due to inflammatory processes, which would tend to become quartan. Also, he did not complain of feeling in his loins as if a weight hung from him when he was standing; and I had neglected to ask him this question. Yet the frequent micturition should certainly have strengthened my suspicion that there might be abscess of the kidneys; the only thing was that I was unaware that his father had suffered from bladder weakness and renal abscess; nor did I know that he himself even when otherwise apparently healthy had suffered from weakness of the bladder. All this goes to prove that we cannot be too careful to make our inquiries complete, if God so please.

When he passed the pus in his urine, I administered diuretics until the urine became cleared of pus. After that, I prescribed terra sigillata, incense, and dragon's-blood. The malady left him; complete recovery was about two months later. That the abscess was a small one was indicated by his original failure to complain of weight in the loins. When afterwards, on his passing pus, I asked him whether he had noticed this symptom, he told me that he had. If the abscess had been extensive, he would certainly have mentioned this symptom; the rapid evacuation also showed how small it was.

He had called in other physicians; but not one of them offered a correct diagnosis even after the appearance of pus in the urine.

* * *

The son of Abd al-Mumin the goldsmith; lacrymal fistula. I prescribed an eyewash which I had prepared myself, to be rubbed in, being introduced by drops in the inner corner of the eye. He followed instructions and was cured.

This is not a real cure, however, I know: it simply shrinks and desiccates the fistula. But at least it does not clog up. I have known several cases. Galen says the same: it was from him I got the idea for compounding the eyewash I used.

* * *

A cotton-merchant, advanced age, suffering from chronic pain in the stomach. His doctors administered undiluted strong liquor; after drinking this, the whole pain descended into his navel region, and even with a full bladder he suffered from obstruction of his urine.

One of the regular diuretics procured him urination; he continued to use it regularly and to excess. I was not told. Its final effect upon the bladder was a condition in which the urine exuded involuntarily, containing a white crude admixture which looked to me like a catarrh (downflow of mucous discharge) from the upper parts, which had set in while some other matter was obstructing the urine. After that, he was attacked by paralysis of both legs at once.

I was now called in. When I visited him, I found the other

doctors anointing both legs with warm oil. I thought there must be bladder-disease, influence from which had affected the nerves running to the legs by contiguity. There was certainly inflammatory swelling in the region of the origin of those nerves. I therefore opened a vein in the sacral region and let him blood. In a few days he was able to move both legs; and his improvement continues up to present writing.

* * *

Case of Ibn Amrawayh: He was a man liable to meningitis, and had already suffered from it before I was called in, but had been cured by the escape of the superfluity (discharge) into the ear, with formation of fistulae there after bloodletting. Subsequently, however, suppuration in the ear became chronic, owing to poor medical treatment. When it became deep-rooted in the aural cavity, it gave rise to a . . . (part of the manuscript missing) . . . as we generally do by bloodletting, in order to make the abscess break out in the interior of the ear in case of chronic ulceration. The abscess did actually burst in the interior of the ear, and was cured by treatment.

However, there remained some residue of ill-natured humors in the patient. The cause was the neglect of energetic evacuation in treatment of the first attack; and the matter had turned into the ear. He proceeded to eat sheep's-head and grapes, and to excess. After this, he fell into continuous fever, became restless, and fiery and dry in temperament. When he took fruit juice and mild purgatives, he vomited them.

Three days later I went to see him, and found him suffering from violent headache, photophobia, excessive lacrymation and redness of the eyes. I let him blood; but owing to the presence of members of the family I hesitated to draw away a large quantity. It had been my intention to purge his nature on the following day, but meanwhile most of the symptoms subsided.

Then came from the ear-cavity symptoms of meningitis, and I was now afraid that he would be attacked by that disease. The strong purge which should have relieved him I failed to administer, through indecision, and for no other reason. What I did prescribe, purging cassia and the like, did him no good. So I ordered enemas to be administered on three successive days.

When after this period I went to see him again, I found him in a most critical condition: his mind wandering, his urine deep red, his face puffy. I thought of making him bleed at the nose; but there was such a crowd of people about, and no other reliable physician had seen him but myself; so I hesitated again. The one thing that I had with me was barley-water; and this I gave him, in hope of procuring him some relief. I also prescribed a draught: juice of vegetable marrow and mucilage of fleawort. But he neglected all now. On the fourth day after this, his condition became extremely critical, and the fatal symptoms appeared: one of his eyes became small, his tongue turned blackish and swollen. On the same day, at the very hour I expected him to die, he died.

His other doctors were ignoramuses. They had diagnosed facial paralysis due to excessive moisture of temperament.

MUSINGS AT THE LIMIT OF AVAILABLE KNOWLEDGE

THE SPECIFIC *Form* OF THE SUBSTANCE of a thing is really a kind of *action* distinct from its primary qualities of heat, moisture, and so forth. This action is not even a consequence of these qualities, but rather a consequence of the matter itself, or something it does in virtue of its substance when the substance is so arranged as to admit the superimposition of a specific pattern. A certain Form is in that case superadded over and above what is describable in terms of the primary qualities. This Form is that *perfection* of order which the arrangement of the matter takes on in accord with some capacity of its own. The magnetic power in the magnet is an example; so is what we call the nature inherent in the various species of plants and animals. It is no mere temperament of qualities. Really speaking it is something much more like a color or an odor, or even *intellect* or soul, or some other entity of the formal realm imperceptible to the senses.

From any such physical Form, in which the constituents are so to speak *fused,* there emerges a power which could not have appeared in the several constituents when separate.

As an illustration, the attractive power of iron in a magnet does not reside in any powers of its components, but arises itself out of the Divine Emanation which pervades all things and makes latent energies kinetic. If we go on to ask such questions as: What is specific property? What is that Form or nature? if we ask for instance: Why does a magnet have the specific property of attracting iron? it can only be said: It has this attractive power by nature. The application of terminology does not impart knowledge about the matter; nor will knowing terminology remove the real lack of knowledge about an obscure phenomenon.

People are not usually satisfied with an answer like this. They want to think that every property of a thing can be explained in terms of the qualities whose actual dependence on physical composition is well understood. Then when they find that a thing behaves in a way which cannot be explained in these familiar terms, they may rush to the conclusion that causality is wholly inscrutable, which is not true.

We may pass over as false various theories of magnetic force — that it is due to, one, heat, two, cold, three, some spirit who lives in the magnet, four, the emission of hook-shaped bodies, five, identity of nature in magnet and iron, or six, a vacuum in the iron. What is unsatisfactory about such ideas can readily be seen if we reflect on the manner in which a green twig derives from *its* constitution the nutritive faculty — the relation between magnetic property and a certain constitution in iron is the same sort of thing as the relation between vegetative property and a certain constitution in green wood. Why magnetic power is so much greater in iron than in another thing we simply do not understand; but our ignorance on this point is really no more complete than our ignorance on others. We do not know why any given body should take on color, odor, mental power, or any other property.

Of course, we can say that all such phenomena arise from the active principles originally blessed by God. And we can allow that the basis of any disposition emerging from some particular material constitution lies in some particular rearrangement of matter. But though we may guess that it is the proportion of various ingredients which accounts for the existence of a temperamental character, it is quite another thing to be definite about the real composition of a compound. Of that we shall remain ignorant as long as we live in this world.

> *And now, for all his art and remedies,*
> *The Doctor's called away; and so he dies.*
> *What ails the Doctor that he comes to die*
> *Of what he used to cure in time gone by?*
> *He who prescribed the drug passed on;*
> *He too who swallowed it is gone,*
> *Like him who brought it from so far away*
> *And him who bought it. So now all are clay.*

CHIEF SOURCES

ARABIC Books generally are full of quotation from earlier works (themselves often lost), so that material close to or contemporary with events is often preserved only in books written centuries later. In the opening chapter, for instance, all the poets and tale-tellers represented survive in anthologies made by Mufaddal Dabbi and by Hammad called the Transmitter in the eighth century, by Abu Tammam of Clan Taiy in the ninth, and Abu Faraj of Isfahan, whose *Book of Songs* is virtually the only source of anecdote about the fifth and sixth century heathen, in the tenth. Known names of poets are given here for honor's sake; but hereafter in general only main authors are named, whether they write originally or citing. Titles of works are generally given at the first mention of an author; thereafter most reference is by name for brevity. Bibliographies for nearly all authors named may be found in R. A. Nicholson, *A Literary History of the Arabs,* Cambridge University Press, 1941; or in the *Encyclopedia of Islam,* Luzac, 1913 - 1938.

THE DESERT
Description of north Arabian country from C. M. Doughty, *Arabia Deserta;* the *Gold-writ Ode* of Imrulqais, nicknamed The Much-erring King; verse by Thabit, Jabir's son of Clan Fahm, nicknamed The Man with a Mischief (his sword) under his Arm; by Khansa lamenting her brother Sakhr; by Abd al-Malik of Dayyan; by Amr son of Qami'a; by Malik, Harim's son; by Hittan of Clan Taiy; by Ishaq, Khalif's son; by Ibrahim of Nabhan; by Urwa, Ward's son, famous for generosity; by Durayd the Adder's son; Labid's lament for his clan, Amir; and a sister's lament for Thabit, Jabir's son; anecdote from the *Book of Songs,* by Abu Faraj.

818   *MUHAMMAD'S PEOPLE*

THE APOSTLE OF GOD AND THE BOOK

Capitalized passages are from the Koran; the rest mostly from Muhammad Tabari's ninth century *Chronicle of Prophets and Kings;* Ibn Hisham's ninth century recension of an earlier Biography of the Prophet; from Traditions, sayings or deeds of the Prophet handed down by "Chains" of authorities from his Companions, and put in books much later, particularly the book called *The Authentic,* composed by Muhammad Bukhari in the ninth century.

THE FIGHT FOR LIFE

The same sources; also Hujwiri's *Discovery of the Veiled,* a treatise on Sufism; Ali Tabari's theological *Book of Religion and Empire;* Ibn Khaldun's historical *Book of Examples;* Abu Faraj; a letter translated by Margoliouth; Suyuti's *History of the Caliphs.*

THE FIRST CALIPH

Tradition; Mas'udi's early tenth century chronicle *The Golden Meadows;* Muhammad Tabari; Suyuti; Abu Faraj; the tenth century *Fihrist* or *Index* of Muhammad Nadim of Baghdad; Baladhuri's ninth century *Book of Victories* and *Book* of *Lineages.*

THE CALIPHATE OF CONQUEST

Tabari; Suyuti; Bar Hebraeus' *Chronography;* Ibn Asakir's twelfth century *History of Damascus;* Baladhuri; Ibn Tiqtaqa's thirteenth century historical treatise called the *Fakhri* or *Book of Honor;* Tha'labi's (born 961) *Discovery of Koranic Exegesis;* Ibn Athir's thirteenth century *Lions of the Forest* (biographies of Companions); Ibn Hisham; Firdawsi's Persian epic *Book of Kings;* Ya'qubi's ninth century *Compendium of Universal History;* Maqrizi's fourteenth century *Mention of Writings and Annals;* Ibn Khalliqan's thirteenth century *Obituaries of Eminent Men.*

MISRULE

Tradition; Suyuti; Mas'udi; Tabari.

CIVIL WAR

Suyuti; Tabari; Ibn Hazm, an eleventh century Spanish Muslim; Nawbakhti's tenth century *Sectarian Differences;* Ibn Taymiya, a thirteenth century theologian; Mas'udi; Shahrastani's twelfth century *Treatise on Sects.*

THE WORLD AND THE FLESH

Tradition; Mas'udi; Ibn Tiqtaqa; Suyuti; Tabari; Ya'qubi; Ibshayhi's fourteenth century treatise on *Good Breeding;* Ibn Hazm; Abu Faraj; Baladhuri; Ibn Athir's *Consummation of Chronicles* or *Kamil;* the sixteenth century Egyptian mystic Sha'rani's *Fecundations of Lights; The 1001 Nights;* Qushayri's eleventh century *Tract to the Congregation of Sufis;* the Persian mystics Attar (thirteenth) and Jami (fifteenth century); Ibn Jawzi's twelfth century *History of the World;* Ibn Hisham; Shahrastani; Dinawari's ninth century *Book of Exhaustive Accounts;* Ibn Isfandiyar's thirteenth century *History of Tabaristan.*

THE FIRST ABBASID CALIPHS
AND THE BUILDING OF BAGHDAD

Ibn Tiqtaqa; Tha'alibi; Suyuti; Mas'udi; Tabari; Ibn Khaldun; Hujwiri; Ibn Muqaffa's version of the *Kalila and Dimna* Fables; Mubarrad's ninth century *Complete Breeding;* Abu Faraj; Ash'ari's tenth century *Islamic Discourses; The 1001 Nights;* Shahrastani; Ibn Abi Tahir's ninth century *History of Baghdad;* Biruni's eleventh century *Chronology of Ancient Nations;* Ibn Khalliqan; Qushayri; Attar. Shi'ite dogmatics from Ibn Babuya (? reference lost), tenth century.

HARUN AL-RASHID

Suyuti; Ash'ari; Ibn Khaldun; Mas'udi; Judge Muhassin Tanukhi's tenth century *Resurrections of Loquacity* or *Table-talk;* the *Divan* or Collected Poems of Abu Nuwas (born 747); Abu Faraj; *The 1001 Nights;* Hujwiri; *Divan* of Abu Atahiya; and unidentified sources translated by Palmer in his *Biography* and d'Herbelot in his *Bibliothèque Orientale.*

THE BROTHERS' WAR

Mas'udi; Suyuti; Tabari; an inscribed textile now in the Arab Museum, Cairo; the poet Blind Ali is quoted by Mas'udi.

INTELLIGENCE

Suyuti; Ibn Khaldun; Nadim; Ibn Khalliqan; Mas'udi; the ninth century philosopher Kindi; Qushayri; Shahrastani; Ash'ari; Ya'qubi; Abu Atahiya.

RESTLESSNESS

The ninth century poet Di'bil; Mas'udi; Nadim; Ibn Khalliqan; Tabari; Abu Tammam; Hujwiri; *The 1001 Nights;* Ma'ruf of Karkh and other early Sufis quoted by later writers; Ash'ari; Suyuti; Abu Atahiya; Jahiz' ninth century *Book of Animals;* the mystic Hallaj (see chapter A SAINT AND HIS FATE); Ibn Taymiya; Tradition; Hujwiri.

VIOLENCE AND QUIETISM

Di'bil; Mas'udi; Suyuti; Abu Fida's fourteenth century *Epitome of Informative Chronicles;* Tanukhi; Yaqut's twelth century *Discrimination of Countries;* Ibn Abi Tahir; Ibn Hazm; Maqrizi; Tha'alibi; Jawzi; Qushayri; Ibn Khaldun, Hujwiri; *The 1001 Nights; Divan* of Ibn Rumi, ninth century.

MONEY, MONEY, MONEY: THE LIFE AND DEATH OF A VIZIER

Hilal Sabi's eleventh century *Book of Viziers; The Experiences of The Nations,* by Ibn Miskawayh, secretary to the viziers Muhallabi and Ibn Amid; Suyuti; Mas'udi; Tanukhi; verse from Ibn Rumi and from an ode by Sharif Riza, tenth century, recited at the Caliph's reception of Khurasan Pilgrims.

A SAINT AND HIS FATE

Hujwiri; Tanukhi; Istakhri's tenth century *Provincial Roads;* Ibn Miskawayh; and Hallajian texts collected by Massignon in *Martyre et Passion d'al-Hallaj,* and in *Journal Asiatique,* vol. 218.

A GOVERNMENT JOB

Verse from *The 1001 Nights;* the rest from Tanukhi.

THE PASSING OF THE AGE OF REASON

Ash'ari's tenth century *Elucidation of Islam's Foundation* and *Islamic Discourses;* Shahrastani; Hujwiri.

THE LAST ACTUAL CALIPHS

Ibn Miskawayh, and Hilal's continuation of his *Experiences;* Tanukhi; Suyuti.

THE SOPHISTICATED

Tradition; verse of the learned merchant Diligh and of Ibn Mushahid quoted by a fourteenth century Egyptian, Subki; Tanukhi; Prince Mu'izz al-Dawla Buwayhi; Mas'udi; Hujwiri; Kushajim's *Good Breeding for Table-Companions;* Yaqut; Ibn Rumi; Istakhri; Sanawbari, Ibn Hajjaj, Khalidi, and other poets quoted in Tha'alibi's *Choice Jewel of the Age;*

Ibn Mu'tazz; Muqaddasi's tenth century *Elegancies of Geography;* Jahiz; *The 1001 Nights;* Istakhri; Ibn Qutayba; Makki; Ibn Abi Tahir; the thirteenth century philologist Ibn Sa'id; the twelfth century geographer Idrisi; Ibn Hazm; the twelfth century physician Ibn Butlan's *Almanac of Health;* the famous tenth century poet Mutanabbi; Ibn Hajjaj; Hariri (see Chapter ORNAMENT); Biruni.

THE SWORD AND THE PEN: PRINCES AND CLERKS

Tanukhi; Ibn Miskawayh; Ibn Mu'tazz; Suyuti; Ibn Hawqal; Mutanabbi; Ibn Arabi.

DESPAIR

Sharif Riza; Abu Ala of Ma'arra's eleventh century *Epistle of Forgiveness* and *Supererogatory Necessities;* Abu Bakr of Khwarizm; Mas'udi; Hujwiri; the philosopher Ghazzali's autobiography (about 1100); Nasir-i-Khusraw's eleventh century *Travels;* the ninth century ascetic Hatim the Deaf; Shi'ite prayer; and dogmatics from Ibn Babuya (?).

COMEDIES

Two tales from *The 1001 Nights.*

ORNAMENT

Quotation from Ibn Qutayba; and selections from the *Assemblies* called *Of San'a, Of Damietta, Of Tabriz, Of Sava,* and *Of Basra,* out of Hariri's *Assemblies* (about 1100), considered to be after the Koran the choicest monument of the Arabic language.

THE MAN WHO NEVER LAUGHED AGAIN

From *The 1001 Nights.*

THE MYSTIC PATH

From Hujwiri's mid-eleventh century *Discovery of the Veiled to the Lords of Hearts;* with quotations from other mystics, Niffari, Dhu'l-Nun Kalabadi; Rudbari; Ibn Jawzi; Jahiz.

THE ABYSS

The tenth century Iraq mystic Muhammad Niffari.

THE PUBLIC ROAD
The Caliph Qadir's Proclamation of Orthodoxy; Ali Tabari; tenth century sermons by Ibn Nubata; a Sufi saying.

THE BODY AND THE DOCTOR
From Sari's elegy on the physician Thabit ibn Qurra; Avicenna's *Canon of Medicine* (about 1000); Awfi's *Collection of Tales;* the thirteenth century Syrian physician Ibn Abi Usaybi'a; *Clinical Observations* by Razi (about 900); and from an elegy on the physician Ibn Masawayh (died 857).

CHRONOLOGY BY CALIPHATES

	Anno Domini	Page
MUHAMMAD	570-632	23-144

Caliphs

	Anno Domini	Page
ABU BAKR	632-34	145 ff.
OMAR	634-44	165 ff.
OTHMAN	644-56	181 ff.
ALI	656-61	193 ff.
HASAN	661	200 ff.
MU'AWIA	661-80	203 ff.
YAZID IBN MU'AWIA	680-83	212 ff.
ABD AL-MALIK	685-705	214 ff.
WALID IBN ABD AL-MALIK	705-15	226 ff.
SULAYMAN	715-17	231
OMAR IBN ABD AL-AZIZ	717-20	234 ff.
HISHAM	724-43	247 ff.
WALID THE PROFLIGATE	743-44	252 ff.
YAZID THE RETRENCHER	744	254 ff.
MARWAN THE ASS	744-50	255 ff.
ABU ABBAS THE SPILLER	750-54	263 ff.
MANSUR	754-75	266 ff.
MAHDI	775-85	281 ff.
HADI	785-86	293 ff.
HARUN AL-RASHID	786-809	295 ff.
AMIN	809-13	342 ff.

Chronology by Caliphates (continued)

Caliphs	Anno Domini	Page
MAMUN	813-33	358 ff.
MU'TASIM	833-42	381 ff.
WATHIQ	842-47	395 ff.
MUTAWAKKIL	847-61	397 ff.
MUNTASIR	861-62	410 ff.
MUSTA'IN	862-66	416 f.
MU'TAZZ	866-69	417 f.
MUHTADI	869-70	418 ff.
MU'TAMID	870-92	420 ff.
MU'TADID	892-902	435 ff.
MUKTAFI	902-8	444
MUQTADIR	908-32	445 ff.
QAHIR	932-34	596
RADI	934-40	596 ff.
MUTTAQI	940-44	646
MUSTAKFI	944-46	646 ff.

Under Buwayhid Rule

MUTI	946-74	648 ff.
QADIR	991-1031	770 f.

Buwayhid rule ended when the Saljuq Turks entered Baghdad in 1055 A.D.

INDEX OF PRINCIPAL PERSONS

MUHAMMAD, THE PROPHET
23-144 and 235 ff.; birth, 24;
marriages, 25, 74, 86, 106, 116,
137; description of Revelation,
26, 35, 38 ff., 64, 111; the
Flight, 65-74; wars, 80 ff., 83
ff., 91 ff., 99, 106 ff., 115, 124;
captures Mecca, 120 ff.; death,
136 ff.; person and manners,
141 ff., 235 ff.; burial, 149;
sayings, 156 f, and 210-746
passim

Clerks
Abu Mundhir Nu'man, 559 ff.,
618 ff.
Baridi family, 496, 561 ff., 594,
600 ff., 603 ff., 653 f., 670
Ibn Abi Allan, 555-568
Ibn Amid, 598, 659 ff.
Ibn Qudayda, 556-562, 564-566
Ibn Zanji family, 544, 548, 554,
586
Khasibi, Queen-Mother's Secre-
tary, 556 ff., 560, 589 ff.
Madharai family, 474 ff., 492 f.,
499 f., 657
Muhassin ibn Furat, 473-520 *pas-
sim*
See also Viziers

Companions (of the Prophet), 186,
191, 252, 579, 771
Abd Al-Rahman ibn Awf, 28, 180,
182 f., 243, 572
Amr ibn As, Conqueror of Egypt,
152, 177 f., 186, 196 ff., 209 f.
Khalid ibn Walid, 95, 117 f., 121,
123, 132, 152 ff., 160 ff., 166 f.

Companions (cont.)
Sa'd ibn Abi Waqqas, Conqueror
of Persia, 28, 50, 80, 96 f., 169
ff., 184, 190, 210, 213, 283
Talha, 28, 180, 182, 187, 190, 191
f., 195 f.
Zubayr, 28, 146, 180, 182 f., 187,
190, 191, 195 f.

Imams, Shi'ite
Ali the Younger, 421
Ali Naqi, 399 ff.
Ali Riza, 360 ff.
Hasan Askari, 420
Muhammad the Mahdi, 422 ff.
See also Ali, Hasan, Husayn

Judges, 293, 368 f., 373 ff., 377 ff.,
389 ff., 450, 490, 528, 542, 597
Abu Omar, 450, 468 ff., 542, 548
f., 587
Abu Yusuf, 302 ff., 310 ff.
Ibn Abi Duwad, 364, 368, 382,
389 ff., 399
Ibn Buhlul family, 542, 549, 560
ff., 630
Yahya ibn Aktham, 366-370

Lawyers, 227, 269 ff., 302 ff., 310
ff., 319, 541 f.
Abu Hanifa, 269 f., 302 f., 374,
634
Ibn Dawud, 541
Ibn Hanbal, 375 ff., 394, 537
Malik, 269 f.
Shafi'i, 269, 313
See also Trials and Hearings

Mystics, 713-758 *passim*
Bayazid, 428 f., 738, 751 ff.

Mystics (cont.)
Gurgani, 716 f., 728, 733, 742
Hallaj, 521-554
Ibrahim ibn Adham, 290 ff., 580
Junayd, 427, 430 ff., 522 ff., 721,
746, 748, 750 f., 753, 755 f.
Khayr, 431 f., 755 f.
Makki, 522, 525, 758
Nuri, 430, 434 f.
Rabi'a, 233 ff., 698
Shibli, 432 f., 521, 552 f., 745
Sufyan Thawri, 292 f., 374
Sumnun, 434, 631 f., 737

Soldiers
Abdallah ibn Jahsh, 81
Afshin, 385 ff.
Bachkam, 604 f., 607, 609
Baghir, the Turk, 406 ff., 410, 416
Bugha, 393, 406 ff.
The Guardsman and the Tailor,
437 ff.
Munis, 448, 451, 455, 466, 470,
483, 503 ff., 584, 591 ff., 596
The Nudes, 348
Rustam, 170 ff.
Tahir and Harthama, 346 ff.
Usama ibn Zayd, 136, 151 f.
See also Companions: Amr, Kha-
lid, Sa'd, Zubayr

Viziers
Abu Salama, 265
Barmecide family, 300 ff. (see
Barmecides)
Fadl ibn Rabi, 345 f.
Fath ibn Khaqan, 408 ff.
Qasim ibn Ubaydallah, 444
Abbas ibn Hasan, 444, 446 ff.
Ibn Furat, 446 f., 449-520 passim,
541, 670
Abu Ali Khaqani, 453 ff., 459 ff.
Ali ibn Isa, 446-520 passim, 543,
563 f., 586, 596 f.
Hamid, 471 ff., 542 ff.

Viziers (cont.)
Khaqani the Younger, 454, 460,
508-518
Sulayman ibn Hasan, 561, 563,
602
Husayn ibn Qasim, 586 ff.
Ibn Muqla, 451 f., 467, 561, 596,
600 ff., 607 ff.
Karkhi, 602
Saymari, (Prince's Vizier), 645
Muhallabi (Prince's Vizier), 653
ff.

Miscellaneous
Abbas, uncle of the Prophet, 86 f.,
97, 119 ff., 139
Abbasids, descendants of Abbas
137 ff., 149, 199, 203, 249 ff.,
263 ff., 361, 654 ff.
Abbasa, 325 f., 330 f.
Abdallah, father of the Prophet,
24
Abu Ala, pessimist, 674 ff.
Abu Bakr, Companion (see Caliphates), 27, 70, 77, 85, 90,
132, 137 ff., 423, 572, 579, 771
Abu Jahl, 29, 46, 48, 50, 70, 83, 85
Abu Lahab, uncle and enemy of
the Prophet, 30 f., 65, 571 f.
Abu Muslim, Abbasid propagandist, 255 ff., 266 f.
Abu Sufyan, Meccan noble and
enemy of the Prophet, 83 f.,
92, 119 ff., 125
Abu Talib, uncle and guardian
of the Prophet, father of Ali,
25, 30, 50, 61
Abu Zayd, anecdotes, 691-704
Aisha, wife of the Prophet, 74 f.,
137 ff., 164, 177, 180, 195,
202, 241, 771
Ali ibn Abi Talib, cousin and
son-in-law of the Prophet (see
Caliphates), 58, 61, 70, 80,

Miscellaneous
Ali ibn Abi Talib (cont.)
    94 ff., 110, 115, 121, 138 ff.,
    146, 149, 163, 180, 182 f., 187,
    221 f., 771
    In Shi'ite doctrine, 286, 412,
    414 f.
    In Sunnite doctrine, 221 f., 423
    ff., 579
Amin (*see* Caliphates), 322 ff.,
    340 ff.
Ash'ari, theologian, 569, 571, 573,
    578
Asma'i, man of letters, 299, 320,
    334
Alids, claimants of Caliphate (*see*
    Husayn), 247 ff., 264, 360 ff.,
    403, 494, 583, 654 ff., 657
Babak, Persian rebel, 383 ff., 394
Barmecides
    Yahya, 293 ff., 300 f., 321 ff.,
    330, 339
    Fadl, 301, 308 f., 335
    Ja'far, 309 ff., 320 f., 324 ff.,
    358 f.
    Jahza, 613 ff., 656
Boy Longlocks, or Rabia, Arab
    knight, 7 ff.
Buwayhids, Daylamite chiefs
    645-665 *passim*
    Ali, Imad al-Dawla, 583, 599 f.,
    603, 647, 659
    Ahmad, Mu'izz al-Dawla, 583,
    645, 647-658, 660
    Hasan, Rukn al-Dawla, 603,
    647, 659, 663 f.
    Fannakhusraw, Adud al-Dawla,
    660, 665
Danielite, The, charlatan, 586 ff.
Durayd the Adder's Son, Arab
    knight, 15 ff., 124
Fatima, daughter of the Prophet
    and wife of Ali, 80, 146, 163,
    202, 423 f.
Gabriel ibn Bakhtishu, physician
    306 ff., 316, 339 ff.

Hajjaj, Governor of Iraq, 217 ff.,
    227 ff.
Hamza, uncle of the Prophet, 46,
    96 f., 155
Harith, Arab lord, 10 ff.
Hasan ibn Ali, grandson of the
    Prophet, (*see* Caliphates),
    144 f., 163, 177, 200 ff., 265,
    412
Hasan of Basra, ascetic, 232 ff.,
    548, 570, 698
Hatim Taiy, model of generosity,
    127 ff.
Husayn ibn Ali, grandson of the
    Prophet, 142, 144, 177, 201 f.,
    212 ff., 265, 402, 412
Ibn Abbas, 180, 199, 203, 221,
    249, 569
Ibn Abi Saj, Governor of the
    Northwest Provinces, 450,
    466 f., 472, 483, 503, 582 ff.
Ibn Hawari, courtier, 466 f., 473
    f., 476 f., 479, 485, 499, 515
Ibn Muqaffa, man of letters, 270,
    276 ff.
Ibn Mu'tazz, Prince and poet, 466
    ff., 611
Ibn Qaraba the middleman, finan-
    cier, 479, 594 ff.
Ibn Raiq, Prince of Princes, 589,
    600 ff., 609
Ibrahim of Mosul, singer, 295, 329
Ibrahim ibn Mahdi, Prince and
    musician, 346 f., 361 ff., 384,
    388
Ishaq ibn Ibrahim, poet and civil
    official, 296, 308, 319 f., 329
    f., 364, 389 ff., 399, 402 ff.
Ja'far ibn Abu Talib, cousin of the
    Prophet, 58 f., 114, 118
Jubbai, theologian, 566 ff., 570,
    573, 630 f.
Khadija, wife of the Prophet, 25
    ff., 61, 75, 79, 106, 202
Mamun (*see* Caliphates), 324,
    340, 343 ff., 349, 353 ff.

Principal Persons (cont.)

Majnun, lover, 624 ff., 753

Marwan, Umayyad noble, 183, 189 f., 192, 202

Masrur, Chief Eunuch, 323, 333 ff., 340 ff.

Mu'awia ibn Abi Sufyan, Umayyad kinsman of the Prophet (see Caliphates), 125, 185 ff., 194, 196 ff., 201, 423 f., 624, 771

Muflih the Negro, Caliphal retainer, 507, 587 f., 592

Muntasir (see Caliphates), 405 ff., 410

Musaylima the Liar, 136, 155, 698

Mu'tazz (see Caliphates), 405 f., 417

Nasr the Chamberlain, 466-515 passim, 542, 545, 584 f.

Nazuk, Commandant of Police, 469, 482, 497, 505, 508, 512, 517 ff., 550, 553

Omar ibn Khattab, brother-in-law of the Prophet (see Caliphates), 46, 77, 94, 110, 119, 122, 140, 146 ff., 153 ff., 159, 423, 579, 771

Othman ibn Affan, son-in-law and cousin of the Prophet (see Caliphates), 28, 95, 125, 163, 221 f., 579, 771

Queen-Mother, the (of Muqtadir), 444, 448, 456, 463, 482, 549, 556 ff., 560, 589, 596

Sawda, wife of the Prophet, 79, 86 f., 106

Shafi Lului, Postmaster of Baghdad, 467, 475, 477 f., 483, 485, 489, 498 f., 510 ff.

Umm Musa, Stewardess of the Palace, 453, 463 f., 485

Yazdagird, Persian King, 169 ff.

Zubayda, wife of Harun al-Rashid, 295, 323, 330, 344 f., 348, 698

INDEX OF SELECTED TOPICS

THE KORAN

Warning
26 ff.

Doomsday and the Judgment of
Evil, 28-35 *passim*

Unbelief
31 ff., 35, 37 ff., 42 ff., 123

Prayer
33, 40, 52 ff., 77 ff.

Paradise
36 ff., 41 ff. (Yasin)

Prophecy
37 ff., 117, 141

Ad
45

Creation
49 ff.

Satan and Man
54 ff.

Noah
57

Jesus
59 ff., 112

Genii
64

Abraham and Lot
66 ff.

War
82 ff., 91, 98 ff., 115

Israel
87 ff., 99, 127

Law
100 ff., 131, 134 ff.

Light
111

Ablution
51, 100 f., 292, 735, 738, 745

Administration
91, 126, 132 ff., 150, 159, 163,
166, 168, 175 ff., 183, 205 ff.,
208, 220, 245, 247, 265, 301, 317,
327 ff., 365, 450-504 *passim*,
555-568 *passim*, 593 ff., 603, 649
ff., 658, 664

Analogy, one of the Four Roots of
Law, 158, 269

Army
80-99, 104, 107, 115, 117, 119 ff.,
152, 159, 167, 177 f., 185, 196,
206, 217 ff., 229, 247, 249, 259
ff., 338 ff., 346 ff., 355, 357, 361,
367, 382, 405 ff., 416 ff., 428,
437 ff., 455, 460, 462, 472, 482,
503 ff., 507, 518, 584 ff., 590,
592, 594, 596, 608 ff., 647, 649
ff., 657 ff., 663 ff.

Asceticism
25, 232 ff., 244, 279, 287, 290 ff.,
400, 524 ff., 527, 568, 674 ff.,
702 ff.
See also Sufis, 713-758 *passim*

Astrology
278, 294, 359, 628 ff., 671

Battles
Day of the Sandhills, 15 f.
Badr, 83 ff.
Uhud, 93 ff.
Muta, 117 ff.
Hunayn, 124 (*also* 16 ff.)
Yarmuk, 167
Qadisia, 172
The Zab, 259 ff.

Battles (cont.)
  Baghdad, 346 ff.
  Zubara Bridge, 584 f.
  Khan Lanjan, 662 f.

Begging
  133, 317, 432, 646, 673, 694, 725, 727 f.

Bureaucracy
  402 ff., 446-520 *passim*, 555-568 *passim*

Caliphate
  Origin, 137, 139, 146 ff., 150, 164, 166 f.
  Theory, 248 ff., 281, 283 ff., 304, 365 ff.

Ceremonial and Etiquette
  Primitive, 10 ff., 25, 27, 78, 130, 170 f.
  Apostolic, 51 ff., 100 ff., 109, 116 f., 120 ff., 129, 139, 142, 236 ff.
  Caliphal, 205 ff., 214 f., 231, 253, 258, 264, 293, 296, 303, 316, 325, 345, 387, 420, 470, 474, 584, 592, 596, 647
  Official, 267, 403, 446, 463, 468, 479, 483, 506, 560 ff., 563 f., 600, 603, 609

Christians
  xviii, 58, 87, 112 f., 127, 133, 168 f., 588, 627 f., 673 f., 683 ff., 729, 772

Classes, social
  104, 131, 135, 176 f., 191, 206, 317, 361 ff., 373, 423 ff., 432, 454 f., 482, 565, 611, 618 ff., 622 ff., 642 ff., 651 ff., 655, 658, 669, 671 ff., 715, 727

Clerks (civilian aristocracy)
  402 ff., 446-520 *passim*, 555-568

Clerks (cont.)
  passim, 582, 590, 642, 651 ff., 656

Consensus (of Believers), one of the Four Roots of Law, 158, 201, 269, 304, 571, 575

Dancing
  632 f.

Daylamites, Persian clansmen
  582 ff., 597, 647 ff., 651

Discussions
  The Pleasures of Old Age, 210
  Rare Words, 223 ff.
  Love, 321 f., 624 ff.
  The Koran, created or not, 373 ff.
  Generosity, 430
  The Ethics of Officialdom, 567
  Predestination, 573
  Foreign Oddity, 621 ff.
  Luck, 657
  Meanness, 668 ff.
  Humility and Proper Pride, 695 ff.

Divorce
  12, 87, 114, 200, 277, 310 ff.

Dress
  93, 130, 154, 174, 209, 231, 239, 253, 329, 345, 352, 382, 386, 409, 469, 557, 615, 618 f., 632, 715, 723, 728, 735

Drinking
  10, 53, 184, 212, 253 ff., 306, 310 f., 316, 400, 596, 612 ff., 637 ff.

Eunuchs, marriage of
  634

Fables
  The Cave, 78 f.

Fables (cont.)
The Jackal, 270 ff.
The Members, 287 ff.
The Man Who Never Laughed
Again, 705 ff.

Fasting
25, 59, 236, 419, 746 f.

Food
13, 207, 229, 231, 237 f., 298 f.,
302, 306 ff., 465, 509, 598, 612
ff., 619 f., 642, 648 f., 680, 724,
739, 747, 802, 807, 809 f., 813

Helpers (Madina converts)
93, 106, 120, 125 f., 146 ff., 191
Descendants as nobility, 362, 420,
592

Homosexuality
67, 345 f., 369 f., 596, 627, 720

Humor, 680-690 *passim*
142 ff., 208, 226, 252, 277, 297
f., 305 f., 309 f., 365, 423 ff., 435
f., 615, 617 f., 631 f., 635 ff.,
639, 645

Imam
As religious head of the Muslim
community, 191, 249 ff., 283 ff.,
462
As leader of Prayer, 234, 579, 723
In Shi'ite doctrine, 248, 284 ff.,
412 ff., 420 ff., 676 f.

India
621 f., 729

Jews
xviii, 65 ff., 87 ff., 115, 133, 187,
479, 681 f., 772

Koran
Revelation, 26, 35, 38 ff.

Koran (cont.)
Collection, 47, 155
As First of the Four Roots of
Law, 158, 269, 305, 373 ff., 514,
528
Question of its eternity, 297, 356,
372 f., 395 f., 575

Law
59, 100 ff., 133 ff., 151, 158 f.,
221, 269 f., 302 ff., 310 ff., 368,
373 ff., 393, 395, 475, 514, 611

Love
Romantic, 3, 6, 321, 624 ff., 732
ff., 753
Religious, 735 ff., 749, 751, 753

Magians
270, 276, 322, 389 ff., 571, 673
f., 771

Mahdi, the
246, 280, 420 ff., 492, 676 ff.

Medicine
239 f., 306 ff., 339, 340 f., 359,
608 f., 719, 735, 781-816

Miracles
242 ff., 715, 740 ff.

Music
212, 253 ff., 316, 329, 362 ff.,
614 f., 633, 637, 643, 717 ff.

Occultation (of the Imam)
421 ff.

Persia and Persians (Fars, Azarbayjan, Rayy, Khurasan, Mountain
Province, etc.), 106, 160 f., 169
ff., 175 ff., 178, 220, 223, 249,
251 f., 255 ff., 300 f., 340 ff.,
345, 354 f., 361, 384 ff., 428,
450, 466, 483, 522, 528, 534, 554,

Persia and Persians (cont.)
647 f., 659 f., 722, 738, 741 f.

Persianism
220, 238, 264, 389 ff., 597, 653

Pilgrimage
50, 65, 101, 109 ff., 116, 131 f.,
134, 230, 253, 317, 504 f., 548,
750

Poetry
23, 42, 92, 116, 128, 130, 222 f.,
299, 301, 319 ff., 334, 359 f.,
369, 610 f., 625 f., 627, 660 f.,
691, 718 ff.

Police
183, 206, 257, 336, 440, 505, 508,
565, 581

Prayer
Canonical, 30, 50 ff., 77, 100 ff.,
124, 143, 180, 184, 205 ff., 236,
298, 676, 735
Extempore, 199, 537 ff., 547, 550
f., 552 f.
Shi'ite, 412 ff., 676 f.

Predestination
98, 570 ff., 580

Prince of Princes, Prime Minister
replacing Vizier, 603, 647

Prodigality
253, 281, 296, 298 f., 305, 320,
370, 398, 404, 441, 640 ff.

Propaganda
249 ff., 255 ff., 422 f.

Qarmatians
491 f., 495, 504 ff., 582, 584 f.

Relics of the Prophet
260 f., 344, 355, 357, 592, 597

Religion, comparative
58 ff., 87, 89, 112 f., 621 ff.,
673 f., 771 ff.

Saints
426 f., 523, 713, 716, 740 ff.

Satan
54 ff., 291, 427, 528, 531 ff.,
580, 732

Seceders (sect)
199 f., 215 ff., 223

Sects (*see* Seceders, Shi'ites)
248 ff., 283 ff.

Sermons
Prophetic, 50, 62, 116, 134 ff., 138
Caliphal, 148 f., 166, 234, 258 f.,
299
Seceder, 216
Hajjaj's, 218 f., 222
Ordinary, 232, 603, 693 f., 770 f.,
773 ff.

Shi'a, Shi'ites, the sect of Ali
201, 212, 215, 247 ff., 360, 399
ff., 410 ff.

Slavery
13, 82, 101 f., 106, 135, 167, 173,
179 f., 244, 264, 278 f., 308, 310
ff., 315, 344, 352 ff., 383, 562,
633 ff.

Sufis or Dervishes, 713-758 *passim*
290 ff., 317 ff., 361, 365 ff., 425
ff., 523 ff., 631 ff., 673
Mystical Listening, 717 ff.
Two Modes of Life, 723 ff.
Love and Spirit, 728

Sufis (cont.)
  Difference between Soul and Spirit, 729 ff.
  Companionship, 731 f.
  Prayer and its Corollaries, 734 ff.
  Gnosis, 742 f.
  Technical Terms, 747 ff.

Sunnites ("Followers in the True Way of the Prophet"), 283, 290, 372

Supernatural, reports of the
  64, 395 f., 443, 519, 535, 544 ff., 557, 741 f., 752

Taxation
  115, 127, 131 ff., 151 f., 163, 178, 450, 456 ff., 566, 649 ff., 653 f., 658

Theology, 569-580 passim
  371 ff., 574

Torture
  278, 387 f., 442 f., 513, 608 f.

Tradition (the classical education in Islam)
  As social amenity, 156 f., 280 ff., 296, 368, 636
  As one of the Four Roots of Law, 158, 269, 304 f., 373 ff., 514

Tradition (cont.)
  As pietism, 235 f.
  As a career, 242, 269, 424, 502

Trials and Hearings
  Recusant jurists, 377 ff., 395
  Afshin, 389 ff.
  Musa and Ishaq, 403 f.
  Ibn Furat, 474 ff., 513 ff.
  Hamid, 486 ff.
  Ali ibn Isa, 492 ff.
  Hallaj, 548 ff.
  The Bag Case, 687 ff.
  Matrimonial Complaints, 697 ff.

Turks
  382, 397, 416 ff., 438 ff., 603 ff., 633, 649, 653 f., 657 f.

Vizierate (see Barmecides, Viziers)
  265, 300, 322, 328, 445-520 passim, 601 ff.

Women (see Khadija, Aisha, Rabi'a, Zubayda, Queen-Mother, Umm Musa), 3, 10 ff., 75, 86 f., 95, 102 ff., 114 f., 135, 153, 200, 223 f., 228 f., 240 f., 250, 305, 323, 325 ff., 330, 429, 434, 449, 453, 456, 511 f., 543, 633 ff., 641, 649, 680 ff., 697 ff., 710 ff., 720, 727, 732 ff.

INDEX OF POEMS

RELIGIOUS AND MYSTICAL
If only when we died, 416
Gold wherever we go, 432
When in my thirst, 525
My heart became an eye, 526
Ah! Was that me? or Thee, 526
Make me one, my Only One, 526
Into the Light flutters the moth,
526
The recall, then the silence, 527
There is a selfhood in my
nothingness, 530
I am my Love, 530
Who, hungering for God, 531
Have you no time to recognize
me, 535
Prophecy is the Lamp, 539
Have no truck with Us, 539
When the giving of Love is en-
tire, 540
Ay, go. Tell them I sailed, 540
I have renounced the Faith of
God, 541
For souls whose witness now de-
parts, 551
My Host, with His own ruthless
courtesy, 552
God threw a man into the Sea, 554
Make me content with thine eye,
713
Never sun rose nor set, 722

DESERT CLASSICISM
Here halt, and weep, 3
In the cleft of the rocks below
Sala, 9
A tent flapping in the desert air,
209
O empty walls! speak to my pain,
253

Desert Classicism (cont.)
Old homes of all we loved, 359
They say they'll ride away, 626
Night and horse, 665
Wayfaring talk, as we rode, 665
A voice at the Broken Grounds,
666

LOVE
If she lets thee love her, 6
We are the Daystar's daughters,
95
Rawda! thy lover's restless, 230
If Layla of Akhyal should come,
233
I saw Heaven's Maids too soon,
253
I shall not try to say, 426
There is a wild fawn, 442
I strain her in my arms, 442
She runs away, 442
Her eyes are all seduction, 449
So did I love that when we touch-
ed, 626
Ay, Love at the first is a dribble,
628
The ways of Love are three, 629
Have Faith, if Love's thy Faith,
639
Let me be impious and unlucky,
639
Love's sweetest single moment, 639
But what's my fault, 746

WINE
I lack no longer song-girls and
wine, 185
Pour, and let me hear the chuckle,
254
In song and wine, 281

Wine (cont.)
Four sweets, 315
Let's drain a cup, 329
Gild a cup with yellow wine, 637
We will have naught twixt cup and cup, 637
Pour tawny wine and reach to me, 637
I pass my springs in Qutrabbul, 638
My immortal soul? I pawned the thing, 638
Fill up again, 639

TIME
We are of Malik's stock, 8
Yet envy not even him, 14
Time has taught me something, 14
Endure, 15
All that delighted me, 225
Musalla's dreary now, 337
Get sons — for Death, 342
The blame is God's, 381
The loss of youth, 444
Season for folly — gone, 449
All pure things become corrupt, 610
What the years dyed, I dyed again, 636
An old man's groaning, 637
I once saw Time, 667
They entered Time, 672

ELEGY
Bind the binding on me fast, 8
The rising sun reminds me, 9
Umayma's gone, 15
Clan Amir's broken, 19
Beautiful he was, 19
Whoever endeavors in earnest, 164
Outside the abbey wall, 247
Why should I weep you, 356
And now, for all his art, 816

HUMOR AND SATIRE
Surpassing sorrow, 205

Humor and Satire (cont.)
He tried the targe, 225
How many a visitor, 226
Good old Pilgrimage, 230
I hear a weeping from Rusafa, 252
I knew you of old, 279
Concubines' sons, 279
O to have Umayyad tyranny, 279
My hand to sin, 316
The Caliph's goings-on are queer, 346
Tell the Vicar of God, 347
Come and see the wonder, 370
Our Caliph now is in a cage, 416
Tell the official Lords, 435
The moneyed man, 435
My noble and exalted friend, 436
I brought my poem, 436
We bow and scrape, 436
His Highness' mother, 436
The Vizier in gaol, 436
When people felt pinched, 482
No thanks of ours can e'er repay, 617
One sultry summer's day, 618
To keep my life I killed, 645
I'm he of Saruj, 699
Ye men of Tabriz, 700

PRAISE
Behold a man, 6
A man like sun in winter, 7
Never shaykh of us, 10
Lo the Prophet, 23
Out of the way, ye Unbelievers, 116
A famous man am I, 218
No true poet can be poor, 319
I feared thee once, 320
Come as I am, 342
God's Blessing on the union, 370
Prince of the True Believers, 388

MORTALITY
They revelled out the night, 400
The wailing funeral, 675

Index of Poems (cont.)

Mortality (cont.)
  Depart, my soul, 703

MISCELLANEOUS
  No grief for thy brother, 16
  There's no true life, 106
  I see coals glowing, 256
  We lie where thou hast thrown us, 257
  The traveller threw away his staff, 267
  You hide with a Hell-raising tongue, 298
  I said daily, 301
  Transgress His Law, 306
  Men most deceive themselves, 325
  Go to the trusted Slave of God, 327
  Had Ja'far feared death, 334
  Out of the World we went, 335
  What the high would not defend, 349
  I spoke to one who lay deadly wounded, 349
  My pulse settled down, 394
  A Caliph dies, 397
  The Turk as Sovereign Lord, 397

  The Umayyads foully murdered him, 402
  A star is gone, 449
  Where go they now, the litters, 505
  Be cruel to none, 555
  I still think of Tigris bank, 611
  And the waters babbled, 611
  I keep aloof, 667
  Know nobody, 671
  Muslims are sinners, 673
  No man who thinks, 674
  The Prophets are no better, 675
  Paradise, Hell, 675
  I laugh and drink, 675
  The creeping worm, 675
  How comes it, Lord, the potter said, 675
  The sharing of earth's goods, 676
  Aloud I utter lies, 676
  I am in a triple prison, 678
  I wish this body was as dull, 678
  Curse us not, Lord, 678
  In that hour when my father got a son, 678
  The subtle suffer, 679
  Philosophy was laid in grave, 781

INDEX OF SELECTED ANECDOTES

The Cleansing of Muhammad's Heart, 24

The Conversion of Hamza, 46

The Conversion of Omar, 46 f.

Ja'far and the Christian King, 58 ff.

The Grandee Converted, 69 f.

The Prophet and Aisha's Dolls, 75

A Kiss for Revenge, 84 f.

Death of Hamza, 95 ff.

The Reader's Shirt, 124

Muhammad and the Helpers, 125 f.

Generous Hatim, 127

The Drunken Camel, 143 f.

The Caliph Off to Market, 150

The Sanctimonious Thief, 158 f.

Hardened Hearts, 163

The Death of the Last Persian King, 174

The Path of Fasting, 179

The Drunken Governor at Prayer, 184 f.

The Dogs of Hawab, 195

Longing for the Desert, 209

The Fierce Sermon, 218 f.

The Ancient Persian's Advice, 221

An Ostrich in War, 229

The Buried Lover, 230 f.

Prayer for Rain, 243

Omar's Eating, 244

Murder of Abu Muslim, 266 f.

Falcon of Quraysh, 267 f.

The Strangling of the Lovers, 278

The Caliph's Gift Refused, 280

The Caliph Wishes He Were a Traditionist, 280

Mahdi and Pigeon Racing, 281 f.

A Mystic's Two Happy Times, 291 f.

The Sinful Stew, 298 f.

The Law Student's Supper, 302

Sharing a Lawyer's Fee, 305

The Dangerous Sauce, 306 f.

The Saint and Harun's Hand, 318

The Singer and the Devil, 329 f.

The Collarfish, 347

The Death of the Frightened Caliph, 353 ff.

Cursing the Head, 355

The Singing Prince and the Negro Barber, 362 ff.

Mamun and the Critical Boatman, 365

The Head That Turned and Spoke, 395 f.

The Yellow Feast, 404

Mutawakkil's Premonitions, 409

The Stunted Abu Bakr, 411

Dulaf: The Bastard and His Dream, 415 f.

The Preacher's Catch-all, 424 f.

The Saint and the Rouge, 429

You're My Slave, 431

The Tailor's Call to Prayer, 437 ff.

The Pre-emption Fee, 452

The Confused Survey, 458 f.

Sorting Orders and Forgeries, 459 f.

Ibn Furat and the Forger, 500 ff.

Hallaj and the Flute, 531

Hallaj and the Purse, 535

Hallaj's Advice to a Bride, 543

The Arm or the Napkin, 547 f.

The Inscribed Stone, 580

Prophecy Made to Order, 586 ff.

Finance or Retirement, 594 ff.

The Great Bonfire Failure, 598

Luck Finds Money, 599 f.

The Soldier Bribes the Secretary, 604 ff.

The Breakfast Without Food, 613 ff.

Jahza's Stinginess, 617

Selected Anecdotes (cont.)

Dessert for Beggars, 620
God Is Surely Bigger, 622
The Mad Lover, 624 ff.
The Bookseller, 627 f.
The Astrologers and the Apple, 629
The Effect of Sumnun's Sermon, 632
The Cultured Girls, 635 f.
The Cat and Mice and the Glass, 640
Three Blind Men, 646
Muhallabi's Visit of Condolence, 656 f.
The Hunchback, 680 ff.
The Earning of the Feast of Abu Zayd, 692 ff.
The Unbearable Music, 721
The Dervish Who Died Singing, 722

Ibn Mu'alla and the Three Dervishes, 724
The Alms-giver's Argument with God, 725
The Brigands and the Sufis, 726
For the Sparrow's Sake, 728
The Married Celibates, 733 ff.
The Amputation of a Foot, 735
Poor Lodging in a Monastery, 738 f.
The Tree Turned to Gold, 741
Gurgani and the Pillar, 742
Shibli's Cleaning, 745
The Peacock of the Poor and the Loaves, 747
The Dervish under the Mimosa Tree, 750
John and Jesus, 754

Among ERRATA

The story of Umayr and the dates (p. 85) belongs to the Day of Uhud and should be on p. 95.

A CATALOG OF SELECTED DOVER
BOOKS IN ALL FIELDS OF INTEREST

CONCERNING THE SPIRITUAL IN ART, Wassily Kandinsky. Pioneering work by father of abstract art. Thoughts on color theory, nature of art. Analysis of earlier masters. 12 illustrations. 80pp. of text. 5⅜ x 8½. 23411-8

ANIMALS: 1,419 Copyright-Free Illustrations of Mammals, Birds, Fish, Insects, etc., Jim Harter (ed.). Clear wood engravings present, in extremely lifelike poses, over 1,000 species of animals. One of the most extensive pictorial sourcebooks of its kind. Captions. Index. 284pp. 9 x 12. 23766-4

CELTIC ART: The Methods of Construction, George Bain. Simple geometric techniques for making Celtic interlacements, spirals, Kells-type initials, animals, humans, etc. Over 500 illustrations. 160pp. 9 x 12. (Available in U.S. only.) 22923-8

AN ATLAS OF ANATOMY FOR ARTISTS, Fritz Schider. Most thorough reference work on art anatomy in the world. Hundreds of illustrations, including selections from works by Vesalius, Leonardo, Goya, Ingres, Michelangelo, others. 593 illustrations. 192pp. 7⅛ x 10¼. 20241-0

CELTIC HAND STROKE-BY-STROKE (Irish Half-Uncial from "The Book of Kells"): An Arthur Baker Calligraphy Manual, Arthur Baker. Complete guide to creating each letter of the alphabet in distinctive Celtic manner. Covers hand position, strokes, pens, inks, paper, more. Illustrated. 48pp. 8¼ x 11. 24336-2

EASY ORIGAMI, John Montroll. Charming collection of 32 projects (hat, cup, pelican, piano, swan, many more) specially designed for the novice origami hobbyist. Clearly illustrated easy-to-follow instructions insure that even beginning papercrafters will achieve successful results. 48pp. 8¼ x 11. 27298-2

THE COMPLETE BOOK OF BIRDHOUSE CONSTRUCTION FOR WOOD-WORKERS, Scott D. Campbell. Detailed instructions, illustrations, tables. Also data on bird habitat and instinct patterns. Bibliography. 3 tables. 63 illustrations in 15 figures. 48pp. 5¼ x 8½. 24407-5

BLOOMINGDALE'S ILLUSTRATED 1886 CATALOG: Fashions, Dry Goods and Housewares, Bloomingdale Brothers. Famed merchants' extremely rare catalog depicting about 1,700 products: clothing, housewares, firearms, dry goods, jewelry, more. Invaluable for dating, identifying vintage items. Also, copyright-free graphics for artists, designers. Co-published with Henry Ford Museum & Greenfield Village. 160pp. 8¼ x 11. 25780-0

HISTORIC COSTUME IN PICTURES, Braun & Schneider. Over 1,450 costumed figures in clearly detailed engravings–from dawn of civilization to end of 19th century. Captions. Many folk costumes. 256pp. 8⅜ x 11¾. 23150-X

THE CLARINET AND CLARINET PLAYING, David Pino. Lively, comprehensive work features suggestions about technique, musicianship, and musical interpretation, as well as guidelines for teaching, making your own reeds, and preparing for public performance. Includes an intriguing look at clarinet history. "A godsend," *The Clarinet,* Journal of the International Clarinet Society. Appendixes. 7 illus. 320pp. 5⅜ x 8½. 40270-3

HOLLYWOOD GLAMOR PORTRAITS, John Kobal (ed.). 145 photos from 1926-49. Harlow, Gable, Bogart, Bacall; 94 stars in all. Full background on photographers, technical aspects. 160pp. 8⅜ x 11¼. 23352-9

THE ANNOTATED CASEY AT THE BAT: A Collection of Ballads about the Mighty Casey/Third, Revised Edition, Martin Gardner (ed.). Amusing sequels and parodies of one of America's best-loved poems: Casey's Revenge, Why Casey Whiffed, Casey's Sister at the Bat, others. 256pp. 5⅜ x 8½. 28598-7

THE RAVEN AND OTHER FAVORITE POEMS, Edgar Allan Poe. Over 40 of the author's most memorable poems: "The Bells," "Ulalume," "Israfel," "To Helen," "The Conqueror Worm," "Eldorado," "Annabel Lee," many more. Alphabetic lists of titles and first lines. 64pp. 5³⁄₁₆ x 8¼. 26685-0

PERSONAL MEMOIRS OF U. S. GRANT, Ulysses Simpson Grant. Intelligent, deeply moving firsthand account of Civil War campaigns, considered by many the finest military memoirs ever written. Includes letters, historic photographs, maps and more. 528pp. 6⅛ x 9¼. 28587-1

ANCIENT EGYPTIAN MATERIALS AND INDUSTRIES, A. Lucas and J. Harris. Fascinating, comprehensive, thoroughly documented text describes this ancient civilization's vast resources and the processes that incorporated them in daily life, including the use of animal products, building materials, cosmetics, perfumes and incense, fibers, glazed ware, glass and its manufacture, materials used in the mummification process, and much more. 544pp. 6⅛ x 9¼. (Available in U.S. only.) 40446-3

RUSSIAN STORIES/RUSSKIE RASSKAZY: A Dual-Language Book, edited by Gleb Struve. Twelve tales by such masters as Chekhov, Tolstoy, Dostoevsky, Pushkin, others. Excellent word-for-word English translations on facing pages, plus teaching and study aids, Russian/English vocabulary, biographical/critical introductions, more. 416pp. 5⅜ x 8½. 26244-8

PHILADELPHIA THEN AND NOW: 60 Sites Photographed in the Past and Present, Kenneth Finkel and Susan Oyama. Rare photographs of City Hall, Logan Square, Independence Hall, Betsy Ross House, other landmarks juxtaposed with contemporary views. Captures changing face of historic city. Introduction. Captions. 128pp. 8¼ x 11. 25790-8

AIA ARCHITECTURAL GUIDE TO NASSAU AND SUFFOLK COUNTIES, LONG ISLAND, The American Institute of Architects, Long Island Chapter, and the Society for the Preservation of Long Island Antiquities. Comprehensive, well-researched and generously illustrated volume brings to life over three centuries of Long Island's great architectural heritage. More than 240 photographs with authoritative, extensively detailed captions. 176pp. 8¼ x 11. 26946-9

NORTH AMERICAN INDIAN LIFE: Customs and Traditions of 23 Tribes, Elsie Clews Parsons (ed.). 27 fictionalized essays by noted anthropologists examine religion, customs, government, additional facets of life among the Winnebago, Crow, Zuni, Eskimo, other tribes. 480pp. 6⅛ x 9¼. 27377-6

PERSPECTIVE FOR ARTISTS, Rex Vicat Cole. Depth, perspective of sky and sea, shadows, much more, not usually covered. 391 diagrams, 81 reproductions of drawings and paintings. 279pp. 5⅜ x 8½. 22487-2

DRAWING THE LIVING FIGURE, Joseph Sheppard. Innovative approach to artistic anatomy focuses on specifics of surface anatomy, rather than muscles and bones. Over 170 drawings of live models in front, back and side views, and in widely varying poses. Accompanying diagrams. 177 illustrations. Introduction. Index. 144pp. 8⅜ x11¼. 26723-7

GOTHIC AND OLD ENGLISH ALPHABETS: 100 Complete Fonts, Dan X. Solo. Add power, elegance to posters, signs, other graphics with 100 stunning copyright-free alphabets: Blackstone, Dolbey, Germania, 97 more–including many lower-case, numerals, punctuation marks. 104pp. 8⅛ x 11. 24695-7

HOW TO DO BEADWORK, Mary White. Fundamental book on craft from simple projects to five-bead chains and woven works. 106 illustrations. 142pp. 5⅜ x 8. 20697-1

THE BOOK OF WOOD CARVING, Charles Marshall Sayers. Finest book for beginners discusses fundamentals and offers 34 designs. "Absolutely first rate . . . well thought out and well executed."–E. J. Tangerman. 118pp. 7¾ x 10⅝. 23654-4

ILLUSTRATED CATALOG OF CIVIL WAR MILITARY GOODS: Union Army Weapons, Insignia, Uniform Accessories, and Other Equipment, Schuyler, Hartley, and Graham. Rare, profusely illustrated 1846 catalog includes Union Army uniform and dress regulations, arms and ammunition, coats, insignia, flags, swords, rifles, etc. 226 illustrations. 160pp. 9 x 12. 24939-5

WOMEN'S FASHIONS OF THE EARLY 1900s: An Unabridged Republication of "New York Fashions, 1909," National Cloak & Suit Co. Rare catalog of mail-order fashions documents women's and children's clothing styles shortly after the turn of the century. Captions offer full descriptions, prices. Invaluable resource for fashion, costume historians. Approximately 725 illustrations. 128pp. 8⅜ x 11¼. 27276-1

THE 1912 AND 1915 GUSTAV STICKLEY FURNITURE CATALOGS, Gustav Stickley. With over 200 detailed illustrations and descriptions, these two catalogs are essential reading and reference materials and identification guides for Stickley furniture. Captions cite materials, dimensions and prices. 112pp. 6½ x 9¼. 26676-1

EARLY AMERICAN LOCOMOTIVES, John H. White, Jr. Finest locomotive engravings from early 19th century: historical (1804–74), main-line (after 1870), special, foreign, etc. 147 plates. 142pp. 11⅜ x 8¼. 22772-3

THE TALL SHIPS OF TODAY IN PHOTOGRAPHS, Frank O. Braynard. Lavishly illustrated tribute to nearly 100 majestic contemporary sailing vessels: Amerigo Vespucci, Clearwater, Constitution, Eagle, Mayflower, Sea Cloud, Victory, many more. Authoritative captions provide statistics, background on each ship. 190 black-and-white photographs and illustrations. Introduction. 128pp. 8⅞ x 11¾. 27163-3

CATALOG OF DOVER BOOKS

THE STORY OF THE TITANIC AS TOLD BY ITS SURVIVORS, Jack Winocour (ed.). What it was really like. Panic, despair, shocking inefficiency, and a little heroism. More thrilling than any fictional account. 26 illustrations. 320pp. 5⅜ x 8½. 20610-6

FAIRY AND FOLK TALES OF THE IRISH PEASANTRY, William Butler Yeats (ed.). Treasury of 64 tales from the twilight world of Celtic myth and legend: "The Soul Cages," "The Kildare Pooka," "King O'Toole and his Goose," many more. Introduction and Notes by W. B. Yeats. 352pp. 5⅜ x 8½. 26941-8

BUDDHIST MAHAYANA TEXTS, E. B. Cowell and others (eds.). Superb, accurate translations of basic documents in Mahayana Buddhism, highly important in history of religions. The Buddha-karita of Asvaghosha, Larger Sukhavativyuha, more. 448pp. 5⅜ x 8½. 25552-2

ONE TWO THREE . . . INFINITY: Facts and Speculations of Science, George Gamow. Great physicist's fascinating, readable overview of contemporary science: number theory, relativity, fourth dimension, entropy, genes, atomic structure, much more. 128 illustrations. Index. 352pp. 5⅜ x 8½. 25664-2

EXPERIMENTATION AND MEASUREMENT, W. J. Youden. Introductory manual explains laws of measurement in simple terms and offers tips for achieving accuracy and minimizing errors. Mathematics of measurement, use of instruments, experimenting with machines. 1994 edition. Foreword. Preface. Introduction. Epilogue. Selected Readings. Glossary. Index. Tables and figures. 128pp. 5⅜ x 8½. 40451-X

DALÍ ON MODERN ART: The Cuckolds of Antiquated Modern Art, Salvador Dalí. Influential painter skewers modern art and its practitioners. Outrageous evaluations of Picasso, Cézanne, Turner, more. 15 renderings of paintings discussed. 44 calligraphic decorations by Dalí. 96pp. 5⅜ x 8½. (Available in U.S. only.) 29220-7

ANTIQUE PLAYING CARDS: A Pictorial History, Henry René D'Allemagne. Over 900 elaborate, decorative images from rare playing cards (14th–20th centuries): Bacchus, death, dancing dogs, hunting scenes, royal coats of arms, players cheating, much more. 96pp. 9¼ x 12¼. 29265-7

MAKING FURNITURE MASTERPIECES: 30 Projects with Measured Drawings, Franklin H. Gottshall. Step-by-step instructions, illustrations for constructing handsome, useful pieces, among them a Sheraton desk, Chippendale chair, Spanish desk, Queen Anne table and a William and Mary dressing mirror. 224pp. 8⅛ x 11¼. 29338-6

THE FOSSIL BOOK: A Record of Prehistoric Life, Patricia V. Rich et al. Profusely illustrated definitive guide covers everything from single-celled organisms and dinosaurs to birds and mammals and the interplay between climate and man. Over 1,500 illustrations. 760pp. 7½ x 10⅝. 29371-8

Paperbound unless otherwise indicated. Available at your book dealer, online at **www.doverpublications.com**, or by writing to Dept. GI, Dover Publications, Inc., 31 East 2nd Street, Mineola, NY 11501. For current price information or for free catalogues (please indicate field of interest), write to Dover Publications or log on to **www.doverpublications.com** and see every Dover book in print. Dover publishes more than 500 books each year on science, elementary and advanced mathematics, biology, music, art, literary history, social sciences, and other areas.